THE NEW YORK PUBLIC LIBRARY®
PERFORMING ARTS DESK REFERENCE

A Stonesong Press Book

MACMILLAN • USA

MACMILLAN
A Prentice Hall Macmillan Company
15 Columbus Circle
New York, NY 10023

Library of Congress Cataloging-in-Publication data

The New York Public Library performing arts desk reference.
     p.   cm.
    "A Stonesong Press book."
    Includes bibliographical references and index.
    ISBN 0-671-79912-6 (hardcover)
    1. Performing arts—Encyclopedias.   I. New York Public Library.
PN1584.N49   1994   94-22673
791′.03—dc20   CIP

Designed by Irving Perkins Associates, Inc.

Manufactured in the United States of America

10 9 8 7 6 5 4 3 2 1

New York Public Library Project Sponsors

A Note from the Editors

Every attempt has been made to ensure that this publication is as accurate as possible and as comprehensive as space would allow. We are grateful to the New York Public Library for its suggestions. Our choice of what to include is based on our experience as researchers, writers and performing arts critics. The contents, however, remain subjective to some extent, because we could not possibly cover everything that one might want to know about the performing arts. If errors or omissions are discovered, we would appreciate hearing from you, the user, as we prepare for future editions.

We hope you find our work useful.

Contents

Introduction: How to Use This Book

The past several decades have seen an explosion in the popularity of the performing arts worldwide. Once the exclusive province of the wealthy, serious theater, music and dance are now accessible to everyone. Commercial and public television have brought the performing arts to a wider public than ever before possible, sparking popular interest in ballet, opera and drama. At the same time, rising awareness of folk-art forms has restored them to the public eye. These developments, in turn, have spurred the rise of regional theaters and performing arts centers in far-flung communities. Schools and colleges have broadened their performing arts curricula, libraries and museums have expanded their collections, and local newspapers have inaugurated daily arts coverage. And every year, performing arts festivals of all descriptions bring the arts to larger and larger audiences.

For the many people interested in learning about the performing arts, *The New York Public Library Performing Arts Desk Reference* provides accurate, introductory information. This single, easy-to-use volume is organized into three parts—Theater, Music and Dance—each of which is subdivided into specific topic headings. Within each part you will find abundant, basic data on the people, works, events, movements, dates, places and terminology of the performing arts. Illustrations and sidebars also help to bring the colorful history and personalities alive.

To find the information you need, simply refer to the table of contents or the index. Remember that the glossary and biographical listings in each part can provide additional facts about the people and ideas referred to in the rest of the text. The reference sources at the end of each part tell where you can find even more information about the topics that interest you. In addition, bear in mind that a single subject may appear in more than one section; 19th-century minstrel shows, for instance, are discussed in all three parts, from different perspectives. The index can help you locate such multiple mentions.

Part 1

THEATER

Glossary of Theater Terms

act: A unit of dramatic action composed of several scenes.

act curtain: The curtain that opens or closes to signify the beginning or end of an act.

action: The development of a play's story, or plot.

aesthetic values: Those elements of a production that are likely to appeal to an audience's sense of beauty, such as the style of the play, sets, costumes or lighting, etc.

antagonist: The counterhero or character who opposes the protagonist and sets up obstacles to the protagonist's objective.

apron: The area of the stage that extends beyond the proscenium arch.

arena: A type of theater in which the audience sits surrounding the stage.

aside: A speech addressed directly to the audience, or a comment a character makes to himself without the other characters hearing.

backing: A flat or double flat used to mask the area behind a door, window or other opening.

backstage: The entire area behind the stage, including the dressing rooms and green room.

barn door: A four-shutter device that fits into the color frame holder of a lighting instrument, shaping the beam and reducing scattered light.

batten: A long pipe or strip of wood from which scenery, lights or draperies are hung. It is attached to a set of lines hanging from the grid.

beat: The smallest unit of dramatic action, one of the building blocks of a scene, consisting of a moment that escalates conflict and leads to a climax.

blocking: Plan of the movement of performers on stage.

boards: An archaic term for the stage. An actor was said to have "trod the boards."

boom: A tall, vertical iron pipe with a heavy base, to which spotlights or floodlights are attached. Frequently masked by tormentors.

border (cloth): A narrow strip of canvas, muslin or velour hung above the stage to prevent the audience from seeing up into the flies.

border (light): A strip of medium-wattage lamps in a metal trough hung above the stage.

box office: The location, usually in the foyer of the theater, where seat tickets are reserved and sold.

box set: A standard interior set, showing three walls of a room, with the fourth wall removed so the audience can see the action.

C clamp: A clamp used to attach a lighting instrument to a pipe batten.

call board: A bulletin board near the stage entrance, on which information for the cast and crew is posted.

climax: In traditional dramatic structure, the most powerful moment in a play, after which the denouement occurs.

color frame: Frame used on lighting instruments to hold color gelatins.

conflict: In dramatic writing, the disturbance created by two opposing forces, either between characters or within a character, that causes them or him/her to behave in a certain manner.

counterweight: A sandbag or cast-iron weight used to counterbalance the weight of a piece of scenery hung from a set of lines. This system enables a single stagehand to raise or lower a heavy piece of scenery.

cue: The word or action at which an actor is expected to say a line, or at which a crew member is expected to perform some task, such as changing the lighting.

3

cue sheet: The sheet of paper on which the stage manager, lighting operator or sound operator has written his or her cues.

curtain call: The reappearance of the cast, after the final curtain, to receive the audience's applause.

curtain raiser: A performance, sometimes a one-act play, given just before the main presentation.

cyclorama or "cyc": A large, curved drop partly encircling the back of the stage and usually illuminated to simulate sky.

denouement (falling action): After the major climax of a play, the period of action during which events reach their final resolution and the protagonist's transformation is revealed.

dimmer: A device used to control the brightness of a lighting instrument.

downstage: The area of the stage closest to the audience.

dramatic values: The features of a play designed to evoke an audience's emotional response.

dramatist: A playwright.

drapes or draperies: Heavy cloth wings, borders and back curtains that enclose the stage, preventing the audience from seeing the back walls.

drop: A large piece of canvas or muslin hung from a batten and painted as scenery.

ellipsoidal spot: A spot with an ellipsoidal reflector, useful for illuminating the downstage areas from an overhead beam or from the front of the balcony.

exit line: The final line spoken by an actor before leaving the stage.

falling action: The denouement.

flat: A flat piece of scenery consisting of a wooden frame covered with canvas or muslin and painted.

floodlight: A lighting instrument that throws a wide, directional, though unfocused beam of light.

floor pocket: A recessed metal box in the stage floor that has several electrical outlets and is permanently connected to the switchboard.

fly: To suspend scenery or lighting instruments by lines from the gridiron above the stage.

fly gallery: A raised platform backstage, from which lines used to fly scenery are controlled.

fly loft, or flies: The area above the stage where flat scenery is flown and stored between performances.

follow spot: A high-wattage, variable-focus spotlight, usually located at the back of the theater or in a booth, that is used to illuminate performers as they move on stage.

foot iron: A piece of angled hardware that accommodates a stage screw and is used to secure scenery to the floor.

footlights, or foots: A metal trough housing a number of low-wattage lamps, located on the stage floor near the edge of the apron.

fourth wall: The imaginary wall that is removed from a realistic box set to permit the audience to view the action.

Fresnel: A graduated lens that throws a soft-edged beam of light.

gauze: A drop made of theatrical bobbinet (machine-made mesh netting), cheesecloth or another thin, loosely woven material; used to simulate glass in windows or other transparent features. See *scrim*.

gelatin, or gel: A thin sheet of colored plastic used in a color frame attached to a lighting instrument, to color the light from that source.

ghost light: A single work light left on at night when the theater is not in use. Theatrical superstition holds that it comforts the ghosts in the theater.

gobo: A metal cutout placed in the gate of an ellipsoidal spotlight to project a pattern or image.

green room: A room near the stage used by actors and crew, before or between acts.

grid, or gridiron: The steel framework above the stage, to which headblocks (blocks with three or more pulleys mounted on a single axle) and pulleys are attached, supporting the lines used to fly scenery or lighting equipment.

grip: A stagehand.

ground plan: The plan of a set, including the placement of furniture.

ground row: A long, low series of flats used to mask the base of a cyclorama and the strip lights with which it is illuminated.

house: The entire theater beyond the front of the stage. Also refers to the audience.

house lights: The lights that illuminate the auditorium.

house manager: The person responsible for activities taking place in the house and related to the audience.

improvisation: A situation in which performers make up dialogue and action on the spur of the moment.

inner, or false, proscenium: The two tormentors and the teaser, which together serve to reduce the proscenium opening.

leg drop: A drop with the center cut out, forming two wings and a border in one piece.

leko: A common term for an ellipsoidal spot.

light bridge: A narrow platform just behind the teaser, on which can be mounted lighting equipment.

light plot: A scale drawing with the type and location of each lighting instrument and the area it is intended to illuminate.

masking: Backings of flats, ground rows, draperies, etc., used to mask areas of the stage.

method: A style of acting that aims at extreme naturalism; the actor seeks to identify inwardly with the character and work from this inner identification to outward signs of character.

mugging: Playing obviously to the audience.

off book: The point during rehearsals when actors have memorized their lines and are no longer reading from a script.

offstage: All areas of the stage that are not part of the set.

oleo (roll curtain): A painted drop that rolls up or down, hung well downstage so that a scene can be played in front while a scenery change occurs in back; used extensively for vaudeville, melodrama and light musicals.

orchestra: In a modern theater, the main ground level of audience seating.

orchestra pit: A sunken area immediately in front of the stage, intended to accommodate an orchestra.

pace: The rate at which a scene or act is played.

pin connector: The two-pronged connector used to join cables and lighting instruments.

pin rail: The anchored rail or beam on one side of the stage, to which the lines of the grid are tied.

pipe batten: See *batten*.

places: The command to get into position, given to the actors by the stage manager when the performance is about to begin.

plot: The sequence of events that occur in a play.

practical: A term that refers to any prop, scenery or lighting (e.g., a lamp that an actor will turn on during a scene) that will be handled or used by actors.

prompt: To give actors their lines, or a key word in a line.

prompt book: The book kept by a stage manager or director in which all stage business and cues are noted.

props, or properties: Every physical article on the stage, except the scenery.

proscenium: The stage opening.

protagonist: The leading character of a play.

rake: To tilt or angle the stage floor so that it is no longer strictly horizontal.

repertory, or repertoire: The group of plays that a company is ready to perform. Companies that have an established repertoire are called repertory companies.

revolving stage: A large circular stage set into the permanent stage floor or on top of it, so that it can be rotated by hand or machinery. It holds a second stage set in back while the audience views the set in front. When the stage is turned, the second set becomes visible.

run a flat: To carry a flat.

sandbag: A canvas bag filled with sand and hung from a line behind the grid, used to counterweight scenery or to weight an empty line so that it can be lowered to the stage for scenery to be attached.

scene: A unit of dramatic action in which something occurs as a result of conflict.

scrim: A loosely woven material used on stage for window glass and special-effects drops. When light is shone behind the scrim, it becomes transparent. If the light source is in front of the scrim, it is opaque.

set, or setting: The arrangement of scenery to provide an environment in which the action of a play can develop.

set piece: A three-dimensional piece of scenery.

shutters: See *barn door.*

sight lines: The lines of sight from the extreme sides of the auditorium and from the rear of the balcony. They determine how much of the stage is visible to all parts of the audience.

soliloquy: A speech in which the audience hears what a character is thinking.

spatter: A scene-painting technique in which numerous small dots are applied by slapping a wet paintbrush against one hand.

spike: To mark in chalk or tape on the stage floor where furniture or scenery will be located.

spike marks: Marks put on the stage floor to give the exact position of furniture or set pieces.

spot, or spotlight: An instrument that throws a focused beam of light on a small area.

stage brace: An adjustable brace with a hook on one end and a foot iron on the other, used to brace scenery.

stage direction: Indications in a script of a character's movement, i.e., *He exits* or *He crosses to the table.*

stage left, stage right: The left and right side, respectively, of the stage from the point of view of an actor facing the audience.

stage manager: The person responsible for running the entire performance from opening curtain to final curtain call; he or she supervises all technical crews and is responsible for everything that occurs backstage.

stage screw: A large screw turned by hand, used to fasten a stage brace or foot iron to the stage floor.

strike: To take down a set and remove it from the stage.

strip light: Usually refers to low-wattage lamps set in a metal trough and used to illuminate backings or the base of a cyclorama or sky drop.

subplot: The secondary plot, or story line, in a play.

switchboard: The board that contains switches and dimmers used to control the lighting instruments.

teaser: The long, horizontal flat hung above the stage directly behind the curtain, which, combined with the vertical tormentors, creates an inner proscenium.

thrust stage: A stage that extends out into the auditorium so that the audience sits on three sides.

tormentors: The two vertical flats just behind the curtain that can be moved to adjust the width of the stage opening. In combination with the teaser, the tormentors form the inner, false proscenium.

trap: A door in the stage floor through which actors can enter or exit.

trim: As a noun, the draperies, curtains, pictures and other items included in a set for aesthetic reasons. As a verb, to adjust a drop or border so that it hangs at the correct height.

troupe: A company of actors.

upstage: As a noun, the area toward the rear of the stage. As a verb, to move while situated at the rear, forcing other actors to speak with their backs to the audience.

wardrobe: The stock of costumes kept by a theater company, usually in the care of a wardrobe chief.

wings: Flats or drapes located at the side of the stage and set parallel to the footlights to mask the offstage area. Also refers to the areas masked by the wings, as well as all areas to the sides of the stage.

work light: A single unshaded lamp, either on a stand or suspended from the flies, used to provide illumination for crews working onstage.

The Playwright's Work: Writing the Play

A traditional stage play portrays events acted out by characters and usually includes the transformation, by play's end, of a leading character. In order for a play to have a lasting effect on an audience, playwrights, also called dramatists, must communicate something of personal or social importance to their audience.

Dramatic works for the stage generally fall into one of three categories: full-length plays, one-act plays or musicals. A contemporary full-length play most often has a two-act format with an intermission between the acts, or occasionally consists of a single 90-minute act with no intermission; very few three-act plays are produced anymore. One-act plays are shorter, perhaps half an hour to an hour in length. Traditional musicals include songs and music as part of a story. Using a standard playwriting format, the average length on paper of a full-length play is eighty-five to one hundred pages; a one-act play runs about thirty to fifty pages. Because the expense of producing plays has risen steadily, plays requiring small casts and few sets are more likely to get produced than large-cast shows.

Topic, Theme and Setting

A play's theme is the message a playwright wants to communicate to an audience. Ideally, each scene amplifies, clarifies or reflects the theme. Plays often explore topics that are considered universal, affecting everyone. Playwrights may also choose to address, from a specific point of view, certain social and political issues in their work. Of course, many effective plays, such as Clifford Odets's *Awake and Sing* (1935), combine the two approaches, examining the personal predicament of the main character in the context of the larger world.

Ideally, the playwright creates a believable world in which to explore his or her theme. The setting—the place where the characters exist—must be clearly described and re-created. A dramatist usually includes these details in the script, providing the scene designer with a basis for creating the set. The description of the setting may include practical information about the historical period of the play and the social class, ethnicity and other important features of its characters. The location where the action occurs can also symbolize thematic elements in the play or the emotions of the characters. For example, in Jean-Paul Sartre's *No Exit* (1944), hell is represented by a room with no doors.

In contemporary drama, multiple settings are sometimes depicted by means of design elements: Lights, sound and multi-use set pieces may suggest a variety of locations. For example, stage platforms can be reconfigured, along with a change in stage lighting, to indicate scene changes. Unless a play is of epic scope, the playwright usually limits the setting to a few locations.

Characters

Through action and dialogue, the play's characters tell a story and illuminate the theme. Among the characters there is usually one, called the protagonist, who is considered most important. He or she generally undergoes some inner transformation by the end of the play. Because the protagonist is developed in great detail, playwrights sometimes compile a complete profile of their main character by the time they begin writing, perhaps deciding where their protagonist was born and now lives, what he or she looks like, does for fun, fears, dreams, even how he or she will die. In other words, playwrights create complete existences for their main characters so that they can write believable and consistent actions for them. Otherwise, an audience's attention to the play could be impeded by inconsistent qualities in its characters.

Character arrangement, or the company a protagonist keeps, further defines him or her and extends the possible range of a play's action. The main character's allies provide a support system, strongly or subtly underscoring the qualities of the protagonist. Antagonists, or villains, offer opposition to the protagonist. In addition to primary antagonists and allies, a number of secondary characters may also participate in the story. Secondary characters live on the periphery of the world inhabited by the protagonist and have a minor involvement in the story line. They may show up in either a subplot or the main plot.

Characters advance the plot of a play largely through the words they speak. One character may speak alone during a monologue; when two or more characters speak together, dialogue results. Soliloquies, such as those that appear in Shakespeare's plays, are monologues that represent a character's inner reflections. Dialogue offers dramatists a powerful tool: A character's personality and motives may be disclosed in only a few lines, and future events may be foreshadowed. Realistic stage dialogue usually employs informal language and may thus contain pauses, extra words, incomplete clauses, dangling modifiers, stuttering and other grammatically incorrect elements. The simplicity or sophistication of each character's language reflects the background and history assigned to that character. Playwrights further define characters through the melodic aspects of language—its inflections, rhythm, cadence and intonation. By listening to each character's language, the audience learns more about him or her.

Structure, Action and Conflict

Modern playwrights often experiment with dramatic structure while utilizing elements of traditional narrative structure to tell a story onstage. In its traditional form, a stage play starts at a time and place called an action point. This may not necessarily be the actual beginning of the story; much may have happened between the characters before the play's beginning. But the action point when and where the play begins serves to move the protagonist and the story forward.

The traditional play advances its story via the interplay of conflict and action. Conflict is any disturbance resulting from the collision of two emotional or social forces, whereas action is the activity produced in response to conflict. This relationship—between a conflict and the resulting action—lies at the heart of every dramatic scene. In a play, the pattern recurs and grows, building tension to a final climax that results in the protagonist's transformation. Rising action occurs in a play when the conflict/action progression generates new tensions and higher stakes as the story unfolds. When there is no shift in a play's energy, the story advances by means of static action. That is, characters argue but nothing new happens; something takes place on stage, but no obstacle is removed. The major moment of conflict at any play's core is referred to as the climax; this is the major event the protagonist experiences in trying to reach his or her goal. Afterward, falling action may resolve details of the plot or provide a brief aftermath.

Conflict and action

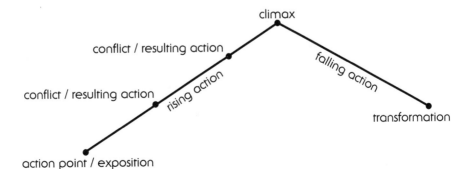

When a leading character attempts to achieve his or her objective, barriers to that objective create the conflicts that the protagonist must resolve by taking an action. Each action produces a reaction, usually introducing a new or changed obstacle. Either a physical or conceptual antagonist—a person or situation—presents an impediment, thwarting the protagonist. In traditional form, the playwright may build a direct protagonist/antagonist relationship by creating an antagonist who wants the same thing as the protagonist, or who desires to stop the protagonist. Tension between a protagonist and an antagonist holds an audience's interest because of the stress caused by the emotional stakes. If dramatists do their job well, the audience usually has an emotional investment in the story's outcome.

Conflict and action unfold in a series of scenes, the basic units of stage action. The action of a scene can be broken down into even smaller units, called beats. An act assembles a progression of scenes that offer increasing tension for the protagonist. In a standard full-length, two-act play, the central points of the dramatic story are usually stated twice. That is, the playwright creates an Act One climax as well as an Act Two climax. At the end of the first act, the playwright also includes a thread of unfinished action that serves as the action point of the second act. Whether one act or two, a play may employ flashbacks—jumps backward in time—to illuminate an aspect of a character or to explain the reasons for his or her actions. Because audiences sometimes find flashbacks distracting, most playwrights use the technique sparingly; poorly utilized, flashbacks can cause an audience to lose the thread of the story.

Written Format

A dramatist records the action of a play on the page in one of several written formats. One standard version places dialogue in single-spaced blocks below the name of the character speaking it, which is centered in capital letters. A line or two of space separates dialogue for different speakers. When the playwright needs to describe on- or offstage action, the stage directions are placed in parentheses. They may be indented, centered or positioned between the center of the page and the right-hand margin. The names of the characters mentioned in stage directions appear in capital letters.

HOW A PLAY LOOKS ON THE PAGE

SALLY: I don't know how to tell you this. We're almost out of money.

CAROL: (*Sarcastically*) I'm so glad I left you in charge of our finances.

SALLY: Well. I do the best I can. Sorry it's not good enough for you. (*Noise is heard offstage.*) What was that?

CAROL: The sound of wolves at our door. (*She crosses, hand outstretched.*)

SALLY: Yes?

CAROL: Hand it over.

SALLY: What?

CAROL: The rest of our money.

SALLY: (*Turning her back*) No. I can't. I won't.

CAROL: (*Crossing to door*) Have it your way.

Biographies of Major Playwrights

American

Albee, Edward (1928–——): Also producer, director. His best-known dramatic works combine realistic and absurdist elements, such as in *Who's Afraid of Virginia Woolf?* (1962). Other plays include *The Zoo Story* (1959), *A Delicate Balance* (1967 Pulitzer Prize) and *Seascape* (1975 Pulitzer Prize).

Anderson, (James) Maxwell (1888–1959): The majority of his work was originally produced in the 1930s: *Both Your Houses* (1933 Pulitzer Prize), *Winterset* (1935) and *High Tor* (1937). Anderson has been the only influential 20th-century dramatist to write successfully in blank verse. His other plays include *Anne of the Thousand Days* (1948) and *The Bad Seed* (1954).

Asch, Sholem (1880–1957): Also novelist. Written in Yiddish, this Polish-born dramatist's plays are mostly about issues within the Jewish community. His works include *Downstream* (1904), *The Messiah Period* (1906), *The*

God of Vengeance (1907), *Sabatai Zevi* (1908), *Wealthy Reb Shloime* (1913) and *Mottke the Thief* (1917).

Baraka, Amiri (1934–——): Also poet, essayist. Born Everett Leroi Jones, he became known during the 1960s for his plays concerning African-American issues, rights and liberation. His best-known plays include *Dutchman* (1964), *The Slave* (1964), *A Black Mass* (1966) and *Slave Ship* (1967).

Barry, Philip (1896–1949): He wrote witty comedies about the lives of the social elite. His works include *Holiday* (1928), *The Animal Kingdom* (1932) and *The Philadelphia Story* (1939).

Bullins, Ed (1934–——): The award-winning plays by this African-American playwright include *The Electronic Nigger* (1968), *In the Wine Time* (1968), *The Duplex* (1970), *In New England Winter* (1971), *The Fabulous Miss Marie* (1971) and *The Taking of Miss Janie* (1975).

Childress, Alice (1920–——): One of the first African-American women playwrights to have work produced on the New York stage, with *Gold through the Trees* (1952). Other plays include *Trouble in Mind* (1955), as well as *Wedding Band* (1966) and *Wine in the Wilderness* (1969).

Durang, Christopher (Ferdinand) (1949–——): A significant comic dramatist in modern American theater, he has written such plays as *The Marriage of Bette and Boo* (1973, revived 1985), *The Idiots Karamazov* (with Albert Innaurato, 1974), *A History of American Film* (1976), *Sister Mary Ignatius Explains It All for You* (1979) and *Beyond Therapy* (1983).

Fierstein, Harvey (1954–——): Also screenwriter, producer, actor. He writes about love, gay life and nontraditional family relationships. Plays include *Torch Song Trilogy* (1981), *La Cage Aux Folles* (musical, 1983), *Spookhouse* (1984) and *Legs Diamond* (musical with Charles Suppon, 1988).

Fuller, Charles (1939–——): He wrote *A Soldier's Play*, which won the Pulitzer Prize in 1982. Other works by this African-American dramatist include *In the Deepest Part of Sleep* (1974), *The Brownsville Raid* (1976) and *Zooman and the Sign* (1980).

Guare, John (1938–——): Also screenwriter. His plays often satirize aspects of American society, such as the American dream. Works include *The House of Blue Leaves* (1971), *Landscape of the Body* (1977), *Lydie Breeze* (1982) and *Six Degrees of Separation* (1991).

Hellman, Lillian (1905–84): Her plays examine the dark and often evil aspects of human nature and behavior. These dramas include *The Children's Hour* (1934), *The Little Foxes* (1939) and *Watch on the Rhine* (1941).

Henley, Beth (1952–——): Her dark, comedic plays contain elements of the Southern Gothic tradition. *Crimes of the Heart* won the Pulitzer Prize in 1981. Other plays include

The Wake of Jamey Foster (1982), *Am I Blue?* (1982) and *The Miss Firecracker Contest* (1984).

Inge, William (1913–73): His plays portray the life of small-town midwestern folk. Works include *Come Back, Little Sheba* (1950), *Picnic* (Pulitzer Prize 1953), *Bus Stop* (1955) and *The Dark at the Top of the Stairs* (1957).

Innaurato, Albert (1948–——): His plays and characters contain naturalistic and surrealistic qualities. Works include *The Transfiguration of Benno Blimpie* (1973), *Gemini* (1976) and *Gus and Al* (1989).

Mamet, David (1947–——): Also screenwriter, essayist. His writing style is noted for its dialogue, which makes use of American vernacular. Plays include *American Buffalo* (1977), *A Life in the Theatre* (1977), *Glengarry Glen Ross* (1984 Pulitzer Prize) and *Oleanna* (1992).

McNally, Terrence (1939–——): His plays include *The Lisbon Traviata* (1985), *Frankie and Johnny in the Clair de Lune* (1987), *The Ritz* (1975), *Bad Habits* (1973), the book for the musical *The Rink* (with John Kander and Fred Ebb, 1984), the book for the musical *Kiss of the Spider Woman* (Tony Award 1993) and *A Perfect Ganesh* (1993).

Miller, Arthur (1915–——): This eminent playwright's classic *Death of a Salesman*, about the awakening of Willy Loman, won the 1949 Pulitzer Prize. Other plays include *All My Sons* (1947), *The Crucible* (1953) and *A View from the Bridge* (1955).

Norman, Marsha (1947–——): Also screenwriter. Her realistic plays include *Getting Out* (1978), *'Night Mother* (1983 Pulitzer Prize) and *The Secret Garden* (musical, 1991).

Odets, Clifford (1906–63): An important social dramatist of the Depression era, he was associated with the Group Theatre. His plays include *Waiting for Lefty* (1935), *Awake and Sing* (1935), *Golden Boy* (1937), *The Big Knife* (1949) and *The Country Girl* (1950).

O'Neill, Eugene (1888–1953): Considered one of America's greatest playwrights, he wrote about troubled families and their psychological and spiritual dilemmas. Plays include *Beyond the Horizon* (1920 Pulitzer Prize), *Anna Christie* (1921, 1922 Pulitzer Prize), *Desire Under the Elms* (1924), *Strange Interlude* (1928 Pulitzer Prize), *Ah, Wilderness!* (1933), *The Iceman Cometh* (1946), *Long Day's Journey into Night* (1956, 1957 Pulitzer Prize) and *A Moon for the Misbegotten* (1957). O'Neill won the Nobel Prize for literature in 1936.

Rabe, David (1940–——): Among his subjects is the Vietnam War. Award-winning plays include *The Basic Training of Pavlo Hummel* and *Sticks and Bones* (both 1971). Other plays include *The Orphan* (1973), *Boom Boom Room* (1973) and *Streamers* (1976).

Saroyan, William (1908–81): Also novelist. He wrote about the triumph of innocence over the corrupt materialism of society. He won the 1940 Pulitzer Prize for *The Time of Your Life* (1939) but refused the award.

Shepard, Sam (1942–——): Also screenwriter, actor. His work explores human relationships, including complex emotional situations and their sometimes violent aspects. Plays include *Operation Sidewinder* (1970), *Buried Child* (1978, 1979 Pulitzer Prize), *Fool for Love* (1979) and *A Lie of the Mind* (1985).

Sherwood, Robert (1896–1955): Also biographer. His works include *The Petrified Forest* (1935), *Idiot's Delight* (1936 Pulitzer Prize), *Abe Lincoln in Illinois* (1938, 1939 Pulitzer Prize) and *There Shall Be No Night* (1940 Pulitzer Prize).

Simon, Neil (1927–——): Also screenwriter. He has had more Broadway comedy hits than any other playwright. His plays and musicals include *Come Blow Your Horn* (1961), *Little Me* (1962), *Barefoot in the Park* (1963), *The Odd Couple* (1965), *Sweet Charity* (1966), *The Star-Spangled Girl* (1966), *Plaza Suite* (1968), the book for the musical *Promises, Promises* (1968, with Burt Bacharach and Hal David), *Last of the Red Hot Lovers* (1969), *The Gingerbread Lady* (1970), *The Prisoner of Second Avenue* (1972), *The Sunshine Boys* (1972), *Chapter Two* (1977), the book for the musical *They're Playing Our Song* (1979), *Brighton Beach Memoirs* (1983), *Biloxi Blues* (1984), *Broadway Bound* (1986), *Lost in Yonkers* (1991 Pulitzer Prize and Tony award) and an adaptation of his movie *The Goodbye Girl* for a musical (1993).

Wasserstein, Wendy (1950–——): Also screenwriter. She is known for her comic dramas about women, including *Uncommon Women and Others* (1977), *Isn't It Romantic* (1981), *The Heidi Chronicles* (1988, 1989 Pulitzer Prize) and *The Sisters Rosensweig* (1992).

Wilder, Thornton (1897–1975): Also novelist and essayist. Works by this leading playwright include *Our Town* (1938 Pulitzer Prize), *The Skin of Our Teeth* (1942 Pulitzer Prize) and *The Matchmaker* (1954).

Williams, Tennessee (1911–83): Considered one of America's greatest dramatists, he wrote such plays as *The Glass Menagerie* (1945), *Summer and Smoke* (1947), *The Night of the Iguana* (1961), *A Streetcar Named Desire* (1947, 1948 Pulitzer Prize) and *Cat on a Hot Tin Roof* (1955 Pulitzer Prize).

Wilson, August (1945–——): He won the Pulitzer Prize for *Fences* in 1987, as well as in 1990 for *The Piano Lesson*. His plays, each set in a different decade of the 20th century, interpret the black experience in America. They include *Ma Rainey's Black Bottom* (1984), *Joe Turner's Come and Gone* (1986) and *Two Trains Running* (1992).

Wilson, Lanford (1937–——): His plays, first produced Off-Off Broadway, blend realism with nonrealistic techniques. Works include *The Madness of Lady Bright* (1964), *Balm in Gilead* (1965), *The Hot l Baltimore* (1973), *The Mound Builders* (1975), *Fifth of July* (1978), *Talley's Folly* (1979, 1980 Pulitzer Prize), *Angels Fall* (1982), *Burn This* (1987) and *Redwood Curtain* (1993).

British

Ayckbourn, Alan (1939–——): Also director. He writes comedies about middle-class morality, the best-known being *How the Other Half Loves* (1970), *Absurd Person Singular* (1973), *The Norman Conquests* (1974), *Bedroom Farce* (1977) and *A Small Family Business* (1987).

Barrie, J(ames) M(atthew) (1860–1937): His first successful play was *Walker, London* (1892). Other well-known works of this Scottish-born playwright include *Quality Street* (1902), *The Admirable Crichton* (1902), *What Every Woman Knows* (1908), *Dear Brutus* (1917) and his most famous play, *Peter Pan* (1904).

Beaumont, Francis (c. 1584–1616): This Jacobean dramatist was best known for his collaborations with John Fletcher. Their works include *Philaster* (c. 1610) and *The Maid's Tragedy* (c. 1611). Alone, Beaumont wrote *The Knight of the Burning Pestle* (c. 1607).

Behn, Aphra (1640–89): Generally deemed Britain's first professional female author, she wrote mostly comedies, including *The Rover* (1677), *Sir Patient Fancy* (1678), *The Roundheads* (1681) and *The Lucky Chance* (1686).

Churchill, Caryl (1938–——): Her work explores left-wing and feminist topics, such as gender roles. Her plays include *Owners* (1972), *Light Shining in Buckinghamshire* (1976), *Vinegar Tom* (1976), *Cloud Nine* (1979), *Top Girls* (1982), *Fen* (1982), *Serious Money* (1987) and *Mad Forest* (1991).

Coward, Noel (1899–1973): Also actor, composer, director. His best-known work as a playwright consists mainly of light comedies, including *Private Lives* (1930), *Design for Living* (1933) and *Blithe Spirit* (1941).

Dekker, Thomas (c. 1572–1632): Also pamphleteer. His plays about English life blend romance with realism. Works include *The Shoemaker's Holiday* (1599), *The Honest Whore* (with Thomas Middleton, 1604), *Westward, Ho!* (with John Webster, 1604), *The Roaring Girl* (with Middleton, 1607–08) and *The Witch of Edmonton* (with William Rowley and John Ford, 1621).

Eliot, T(homas) S(tearns) (1888–1965): Also poet and critic. His poetic dramas include *Murder in the Cathedral* (1935), *The Family Reunion* (1939) and *The Cocktail Party* (1949).

Fletcher, John (1579–1625): He collaborated with Francis Beaumont and other writers, including William Shakespeare on *The Two Noble Kinsmen* (1613) and *Henry VIII* (1613). His tragedies include *Valentinian* (1610–14) and *Bonduca* (1609–14); comedies include *Wit Without Money* (1614) and *Rule a Wife and Have a Wife* (1624).

Goldsmith, Oliver (1728–74): Also essayist, poet and novelist. This Irish-born author wrote works that attempted to make people laugh at their own foibles and foolishness. His best-known play is *She Stoops to Conquer* (1773).

Jonson, Ben (1572–1637): Also poet and literary critic. This Elizabethan's best-known works include *Volpone* (1605–06), *Epicoene: or, The Silent Woman* (1609), *The Alchemist* (1610) and *Bartholomew Fair* (1614).

Kyd, Thomas (1558–94): Author of *The Spanish Tragedy* (1589), he introduced the "tragedy of revenge," which became a popular form during the Elizabethan period.

Marlowe, Christopher (1564–93): Also poet. "Marlowe's mighty line" established blank verse as the standard writing style of Elizabethan playwrights. Plays include *Tamburlaine the Great: Part I* (c. 1586), *Tamburlaine the Great: Part II* (c. 1587), *The Tragical History of Doctor Faustus* (c. 1588), *The Jew of Malta* (c. 1589) and *Edward II* (1591).

Maugham, W(illiam) Somerset (1874–1965): Also novelist. His plays were so popular that in 1908 four ran simultaneously in London: *Lady Frederick, Mrs. Dot, Jack Straw* and *The Explorer*. Best-known plays include *Our Betters* (1917), *The Circle* (1921), *The Constant Wife* (1926) and *The Breadwinner* (1930).

Middleton, Thomas (c. 1580–1627): This Jacobean dramatist's dark plays examined the manners and mores of his time. Works include *A Trick to Catch the Old One* (c. 1604), *A Chaste Maid in Cheapside* (1611), *The Changeling* (with William Rowley, 1622) and *Women Beware Women* (c. 1625).

Osborne, John (1929–——): His works deal with the difficulties of life in contemporary Britain. His most famous play is *Look Back in Anger* (1956). Others include *The Entertainer* (1957), *Luther* (1961) and *Inadmissable Evidence* (1964).

Pinter, Harold (1930–——): Also director, actor. His absurdist plays include *The Birthday Party* (1958), *The Dumb Waiter* (1957), *The Caretaker* (1960), *The Homecoming* (1965) and *Betrayal* (1978).

Rowley, William (c. 1585–c. 1642): Also actor. He is best known for his collaborations with Thomas Middleton: *The Changeling* (1622) and *The Spanish Gypsy* (1623). His most famous individual work is *The Birth of Merlin* (c. 1608).

Shakespeare, William (1564–1616): (See also *The Life and Work of William Shakespeare*, page 71). The most influential writer in English drama, this Elizabethan is often called the most important and greatest dramatist of all time. His tragedies are *Titus Andronicus* (1594), *Romeo and Juliet* (c. 1595), *Julius Caesar* (1598), *Othello* (1602–03), *Hamlet, Prince of Denmark* (1600), *Timon of Athens* (1604–05), *Macbeth* (1605–06), *King Lear* (1605–06), *Antony and Cleopatra* (1606–07) and *Coriolanus* (1607–10). Comedies include *The Comedy of Errors* (1591–94), *The Taming of the Shrew* (1593–94), *The Two Gentlemen of Verona* (1594–95), *Love's Labour's Lost* (1593–95), *A Midsummer Night's Dream* (1595–96), *The Merchant of Venice* (1596–97), *Much Ado about Nothing* (1598–99), *The Merry Wives of Windsor* (1598–99), *As You Like It* (1599–1600), *Twelfth Night* (1599–1600), the "bitter" comedy *Troilus and Cressida* (1601–02), *All's Well that Ends Well* (1602–03), *Measure for Measure* (1603–04), *Pericles* (1606–08), *Cymbeline* (1609–10), *The Winter's Tale* (1610–11) and *The Tempest* (1611). The history plays are *Henry VI: Part I* (1589–91), *Henry VI: Part II* (1590–91), *Henry VI: Part III* (1590–91), *Richard III* (1593), *Richard II* (1595), *King John* (1596–97), *Henry IV: Part I* (1597–98), *Henry IV: Part II* (1597–98), *Henry V* (1598–99) and *Henry VII* (1612). (Note: The dates of much of his work can only be approximated.)

Shaw, George Bernard (1856–1950): Also journalist and critic. The intellectual, idea-infused and thought-provoking plays of this major Irish-born dramatist include *Arms and the Man* (1894), *Man and Superman* (1905), *Major Barbara* (1905), *Pygmalion* (1914), *Heartbreak House* (1920) and *Saint Joan* (1923).

Sheridan, Richard Brinsley (1751–1816): Also theater manager. This Irish-born dramatist's witty comedies include *The Rivals* (1775) and *The School for Scandal* (1777).

Stoppard, Tom (1937–——): Influenced by Samuel Beckett and the Theater of the Absurd, this Czech-born dramatist is best known for *Rosencrantz and Guildenstern are Dead* (1967), *The Real Inspector Hound* (1968), *Travesties* (1974) and *The Real Thing* (1982).

Tourneur, Cyril (1575–1626): His best-known tragedies of revenge, a popular Elizabethan form, are both based on Roman dramas by Seneca: *The Revenger's Tragedy* (1606–07; authorship of this play is in some dispute) and *The Atheist's Tragedy* (1607–11).

Webster, John (c. 1580–1634): This Jacobean dramatist is best known for two tragedies,

The White Devil (1609–12) and *The Duchess of Malfi* (1613–14).

Wilde, Oscar (1854–1900): Also novelist and poet. This Irish-born dramatist's satirical plays expose the contradictions of Victorian society. His best-known work is *The Importance of Being Earnest* (1895).

French

Anouilh, Jean (1910–87): Also screenwriter. His works deal with the loss of innocence in a corrupt society. His best-known plays are *Thieves' Carnival* (1938), *Antigone* (1944), *The Waltz of the Toreadors* (1952) and *The Lark* (1953).

Beckett, Samuel (1906–89): Also novelist. The major works of this influential Irish-born dramatist include the absurdist plays *Waiting for Godot* (1953) and *Endgame* (1957).

Corneille, Pierre (1606–84): This neoclassic dramatist's early masterpiece, *Le Cid* (1637), was criticized by French intellectuals because it diverged from the "classical unities" established by Aristotle in *The Poetics*. Other works include *Horace* (1640), *Cinna* (1641) and *Polyeucte* (1643).

Genet, Jean (1910–86): Novelist and a primary playwright of the Theater of the Absurd. His most famous plays include *The Maids* (1947), *The Balcony* (1956) and *The Blacks* (1959).

Giraudoux, Jean (1882–1944): Also novelist. Many of his plays are reinterpretations of Greek myth. Works include *Tiger at the Gates* (1935) and *The Madwoman of Chaillot* (1945).

Hugo, Victor Marie (1802–85): Also poet and novelist. Accepted as the leader of French romanticism, he wrote such plays as *Hernani* (1830), *The King Amuses Himself* (1832; the source for Verdi's opera *Rigoletto*), *Ruy Blas* (1838) and *The Burgraves* (1843).

Ionesco, Eugene (1912–1994): A leading exponent of the Theater of the Absurd, this Romanian-born dramatist created such works as *The Bald Soprano* (1950), *The Lesson* (1951) and *Rhinoceros* (1960).

Molière [Jean Baptiste Poquelin] (1622–73): Also actor, director and theater manager. His plays employed stylized characters from commedia dell'arte but gave them human qualities. Works include *The School for Wives* (1662), *Tartuffe* (1664), *The Misanthrope* (1666), *The Miser* (1668) and *The Bourgeois Gentleman* (1670).

Racine, Jean (1639–99): He was considered a master of the alexandrine line (a line of verse having 12 syllables and a set rhythm). Best-known works include *Andromaque* (1667), *Bérénice* (1670), *Phèdre* (1677) and *Athalie* (1691).

Rostand, Edmund (1868–1918): Also poet. Scholars consider his romantic work *Cyrano de Bergerac* (1897) to be a tour de force of dramatic poetry.

Sartre, Jean-Paul (1905–80): Also philosopher, novelist and essayist. This existentialist's plays are based on the idea that humanity exists in a universe without God and determines its own fate solely by its actions. Best-known works are *No Exit* (1944) and *Dirty Hands* (1948). Sartre won the Nobel Prize for literature in 1964.

German

Brecht, Bertolt (1898–1956): Also poet and director. His "Epic Theater" aimed to make the theater a tool of social change; its goal was to direct the audience away from empathy with the characters and toward intellectual understanding of the theme. Works include *In the*

Jungle of the Cities (1923), *The Threepenny Opera* (1928, with music by Kurt Weill), *Galileo* (1938–39), *Mother Courage and Her Children* (1941) and *The Good Woman of Setzuan* (1943).

Büchner, Georg (1813–37): His works include *Danton's Death* (1835) and *Woyzeck* (1836).

Goethe, Johann Wolfgang von (1749–1832): Also director, novelist and essayist. His best-known works for the theater include *Iphigenie on Tauris* (1787), *Torquato Tasso* (1790) and *Faust, Part 1* (1808) and *Part 2* (1832). He was codirector with Friedrich

Schiller at the Court Theater, where he helped develop a new approach to repertoire and innovative acting techniques that influenced German performance.

Schiller, Friedrich (1759–1805): Also historian. His plays include *The Robbers* (1781); *Love and Intrigue* (1782–83); *Don Carlos* (1787); a trilogy, *Wallenstein's Camp*, *The Piccolomini* and *Wallenstein's Death* (all 1799); *Maria Stuart* (1800); *The Bride of Messina* (1803) and *Wilhelm Tell* (1804). Closely associated with Johann Goethe, he is widely considered the national dramatist of Germany.

Greek

Aeschylus (525–456 B.C.): Known as "the father of Greek tragedy." Seven of his ninety plays survive complete; they deal with humans who come into conflict with the gods. Plays include *Prometheus Bound* (466 B.C.) and a trilogy, *The Oresteia* (458 B.C.).

Aristophanes (c. 448–380 B.C.): The main poet of Old Comedy, he satirized politics, philosophy and other playwrights. Eleven of his plays survive, including *The Clouds* (423 B.C.), *The Wasps* (422 B.C.), *Peace* (422 B.C.), *Lysistrata* (411 B.C.) and *The Frogs* (405 B.C.).

Euripides (480–406 B.C.): Last of the Greek tragedians. His plays explored human interaction and the idea that character, not the powers of the gods, shapes an individual's destiny. He was ridiculed by other dramatists for questioning war, traditional Greek values and society, and was banned from Athens. He

wrote ninety-two plays, of which nineteen survive, including *Alcestis* (438 B.C.), *Medea* (431 B.C.), *The Trojan Women* (415 B.C.), *Electra* (413 B.C.), *Orestes* (408 B.C.) and *The Bacchae* (405 B.C., produced posthumously).

Menander (c. 342–c. 292 B.C.): Major playwright of New Comedy, which depicted ordinary people in life situations. His subjects included family relationships, money and love problems. Only one of his plays survives, *Dyskolos* (*The Grouch*; 317 B.C.).

Sophocles (495–406 B.C.): The second of the Greek tragedians, he broke with the tradition of writing trilogies. His *Oedipus Rex* (430 B.C.) is one of the most often-produced plays. He wrote 132 plays, seven of which survive, including *Antigone* (441 B.C.), *Electra* (409 B.C.) and *Oedipus at Colonus* (404 B.C.).

Irish

Behan, Brendan (1923–64): A one-time member of the Irish Republican Army, he wrote plays that include *The Quare Fellow* (1954), *The Hostage* (1958) and *Borstal Boy* (1958).

Friel, Brian (1929–————): He first received recognition for *Philadelphia, Here I Come!* (1964). His body of work includes *Lovers* (1967), *Crystal and Fox* (1968), *The Freedom of the City*

(1973), *Aristocrats* (1979), *Faith Healer* (1979), *Translations* (1980), *The Communication Cord* (1982), an adaptation of Ivan Turgenev's novel *Fathers and Sons* (1987), *Dancing at Lughnasa* (Tony Award 1992) and *Wonderful Tennessee* (1993).

O'Casey, Sean (1880–1964): His works portray life in Dublin's slums. They include *The Shadow of a Gunman* (1923), *Juno and the Pay-* cock (1924) and *The Plough and the Stars* (1926).

Synge, John Millington (1871–1909): Also poet and cofounder of the Abbey Theatre with William Butler Yeats and Lady Gregory. He wrote about imaginative Irish peasant characters. Plays include *In the Shadow of the Glen* (1903), *Riders to the Sea* (1904) and *The Playboy of the Western World* (1907).

Italian

Pirandello, Luigi (1867–1936): Also novelist. He wrote about the conflict between illusion and reality. Best-known plays include *Right You Are—If You Think You Are* (1917) and *Six* *Characters in Search of an Author* (1921). Pirandello won the Nobel Prize for Literature in 1934.

Norwegian

Ibsen, Henrik (1828–1906): Called "the father of modern drama," he was the major playwright of the 19th-century realist movement. Plays include *Peer Gynt* (1867), *A Doll's House* (1879), *Ghosts* (1881), *An Enemy of the People* (1883), *The Wild Duck* (1884) and *Hedda Gabler* (1891).

Roman

Plautus (251–184 B.C.): His farcical plays were based on Greek comedies and performed in Greek dress. Among his surviving works are *Pseudolus* (191 B.C.) and *The Twin Menaechmi* (late 3d century B.C.).

Seneca (4 B.C.–A.D. 65): Also statesman. The structure of his plays followed the conventions of Greek tragedy, while his subject was the Roman Empire. Ninety plays survive, in- cluding *Agamemnon*, *Medea* and *Phaedre* (dates unknown).

Terence (184–159 B.C.): A writer of comedy whose surviving plays include *The Girl from Andros* (166 B.C.), *The Mother-in-Law* (165 B.C.), *The Self-Tormentor* (163 B.C.), *The Eunuch* (161 B.C.), *Phormio* (161 B.C.) and *The Brothers* (160 B.C.).

Russian

Chekhov, Anton Pavlovich (1860–1904): Also writer of short stories. He wrote about the aristocracy prior to the Russian Revolution. Productions of Chekhov's plays at the Moscow Art Theater were directed by Konstantin Stanislavski; they helped establish the influence of Russian theater worldwide. Works include *The Seagull* (1896), *Uncle Vanya* (1899), *The Three Sisters* (1901) and *The Cherry Orchard* (1904).

Gorky, Maxim [Alexei Maximovich Peshkovo] (1868–1936): Also novelist and writer of short stories. *The Lower Depths* (1902), a play about life in the slums, helped to establish him as a major dramatist.

South African

Fugard, Athol (1932–——): Also novelist. He writes about the South African political and social situation and the lives of working-class people of different races. Plays include *The Blood Knot* (1961), *Hello and Goodbye* (1965), *Boesman and Lena* (1969), *Sizwe Bansi is Dead* (1972), *Master Harold . . . and the Boys* (1982), *The Road to Mecca* (1984), *My Children! My Africa!* (1989) and *Playland* (1992).

Spanish

Calderón de la Barca, Pedro (1600–81): A dramatist of Spain's Golden Age, he wrote hundreds of plays. Works include *The Phantom Lady* (1629), *Life Is a Dream* (1635), *Devotion to the Cross* (1633), *Secret Vengeance for Secret Insult* (1635) and *The Mayor of Zalamea* (1640–44).

García Lorca, Federico (1898–1936): Also poet. His plays deal with the conflict between individuals and the conservative moralism of Spanish society. Plays include *Blood Wedding* (1933), *Yerma* (1934) and *The House of Bernarda Alba* (1936). Francisco Franco executed García Lorca at the start of the Spanish Civil War.

Tirso de Molina [Gabriel Téllez] (c. 1571–1648): A dramatist of Spain's Golden Age. His best-known play is *The Trickster of Seville and The Stone Guest* (1630), the first dramatic treatment of the Don Juan legend.

Vega Carpio, Lope de (1562–1635): A dramatist of Spain's Golden Age. Works include *Fuenteovejuna* (1612), *The Peasant in His Nook* (1611–15), *The King's the Best Magistrate* (1620–23) and *The Knight from Olmedo* (1620–25).

Swedish

Strindberg, Johan August (1849–1912): Also novelist. He is best known for his plays about the psychology of tortured male/female relationships. Most famous works include *The Father* (1887), *Miss Julie* (1889), *The Dance of Death Part I* (1900), *The Dance of Death Part II* (1900) and *A Dream Play* (1902).

Synopses of Major Plays

Greek

Agamemnon by Aeschylus (458 B.C.): Tragedy, first play of *The Oresteia* trilogy. Clytemnestra has committed adultery while her husband, King Agamemnon, has been away at war. Agamemnon returns with a captive, Cassandra, but Clytemnestra welcomes him home. In defiance of divine law, Agamemnon acts the boastful conqueror, setting off divine retribution. Clytemnestra stabs Agamemnon and Cassandra to death. Aegisthus, Clytemnestra's lover, arrives with armed men, and they both stand against the people, who protest their king's murder.

Antigone by Sophocles (441 B.C.): Tragedy. Polyneices has led a foreign army against Thebes, killing the king. When Polyneices is killed, Creon, the new king of Thebes, decrees that his body shall remain unburied. Antigone, Polyneices's sister and Creon's niece, openly attempts to bury her brother's body. Creon sentences her to be entombed alive, holding his ground even against the entreaties of his son, who is engaged to Antigone. When a prophet warns Creon of the consequences of his actions, he hurries to bury Polyneices and release Antigone. But Antigone has already committed suicide, and Creon watches as his son also kills himself. Creon returns home to discover that his wife has stabbed herself upon learning of her son's death.

Medea by Euripides (431 B.C.): Tragedy. While they were lovers, Medea had helped Jason steal the magical golden fleece from her father. Now, though Medea and Jason have been married for years, Jason plans to marry the daughter of Creon, King of Corinth, to gain political power. Jason exiles Medea, fearing that she will attempt revenge. But Medea sends her children to Jason's bride, bearing gifts of a poisoned robe and crown. When the children return, Medea kills them. Jason goes back to Medea, who will not let him bury the children.

Lysistrata by Aristophanes (411 B.C.): Comedy. Lysistrata proposes that the women of Greece withhold sex to force their men to stop the war they have been fighting. Agreeing reluctantly, the women go to the Acropolis and lock themselves in. Eventually, the men give in to the women and make peace.

Dyskolos by Menander (317 B.C.): The only entirely preserved example of Greek New Comedy. Living on a farm with his daughter and a servant is Cmenon, a misanthrope who abandoned his wife and stepson years before. When he refuses to give permission for his daughter to marry Sostratus, Sostratus seeks the assistance of Gorgias, Cmenon's stepson, to change the stubborn man's mind. Cmenon experiences an awakening after being rescued from a well by Gorgias. He reconciles with his wife, gives consent to Sostratus and his daughter and approves his stepson's marriage to Sostratus's sister.

Roman

The Twin Menaechmi by Plautus (late 3d century B.C.): Comedy. Searching for his twin brother, Menaechmus II of Syracuse comes to the city of Epidamnus. The actions and situations of the play stem from several cases of mistaken identity. The quack doctor, a much-used stock character of Roman comedy, first appears in this play.

The Mother-in-Law by Terence (160 B.C.): Comedy. Pamphilus unwillingly married Philumena, whom he has left without consummating their marriage. When he returns, he discovers that his wife is about to give birth. The play ends happily when it is discovered that Pamphilus and Philumena actually did consummate their marriage one night when Pamphilus was drunk.

Medieval

Everyman Anonymous (English, 15th century): Morality play. God orders Death to take Everyman. Anxious for someone to come with him, Everyman turns to Fellowship, Kindred, Cousin and Goods, but he is refused. Knowledge, Confession, Discretion, Strength, Beauty and Five-Wits all eventually desert him, too. Only Good-Deeds is prepared to go with Everyman. At the play's end a doctor interprets the moral for the audience.

The Second Shepherds' Play Anonymous (English, mid–15th century): Part of the Wakefield Cycle. Three shepherds commiserate about their lives as they guard their flocks. Mak steals a sheep while the others are sleeping. With his wife, Gyll, he hides it in their hut, in a cradle. The shepherds search unsuccessfully for the sheep. When they decide to give gifts to the baby in the cradle, they discover the stolen sheep. As punishment, they toss Mak in a blanket. Later, an angel appears to announce the birth of Christ. They visit the manger at play's end.

Elizabethan, Jacobean and 17th Century

The Tragical History of Doctor Faustus by Christopher Marlowe (English, 1588): Tragedy. Seduced by the promise of twenty-four years of earthly power and delight, Faustus promises his soul to the Devil. The play's fifteen scenes include parody and farce, concluding with a dramatic scene in which Faustus awaits his fate.

The Comedy of Errors by William Shakespeare (English, 1591): Comedy. Aegeon, an old merchant whose family had been separated many years earlier in a shipwreck, has received a death sentence through no fault of his own. Unbeknownst to each other, the members of his family are all in the city where Aegeon is to die. The presence of two sets of twins leads to humorous situations involving mistaken identity. After a series of chance occurrences and farcical incidents, Aegeon is saved, identities are revealed and the family is reunited.

Much Ado About Nothing by William Shakespeare (English, 1598): Comedy. Returning from battle, Claudio has fallen in love with Hero. But he believes that his friend, Don Pedro, is courting her, so Claudio defers. A comedic twist of fate forces Beatrice, Hero's cousin, and Benedick, a misogynist, into each other's arms. The courtship of Claudio and Hero is saved by Dogberry and his Watch, who expose trickery and wickedness along the way.

Julius Caesar by William Shakespeare (English, 1598): Tragedy. Caesar's ambition makes the aristocrats of Rome uneasy. Cassius, one of a group of conspirators, convinces Brutus to take part in the assassination of Caesar; Brutus stabs Caesar. Mark Antony, who has professed to be a conspirator, is actually in league with Octavius Caesar and Lepidus. When Octavius's army vanquishes the conspirators, Cassius and Brutus kill themselves.

As You Like It by William Shakespeare (English, 1599): Comedy. The lawful Duke has been displaced by his brother, Frederick, and has gone into hiding in the Forest of Arden. At Frederick's court, Orlando falls in love with Rosalind, the former Duke's daughter. When Frederick exiles Rosalind, she dresses as a boy and goes to find her father. She is joined by her cousin Celia (Frederick's daughter) and the jester Touchstone. Still disguised as a boy, Rosalind finds Orlando in the forest and offers to cure him of his passion. The play ends with a triple wedding and the announcement that Duke Frederick welcomes all back to court.

Hamlet, Prince of Denmark by William Shakespeare (English, 1600): Tragedy. Prince Hamlet's court has been corrupted. His mother, Gertrude, has married her late husband's brother, King Claudius, leaving Hamlet with the feeling that he can trust no one. Pretending to be insane, he attempts to reveal the scope of the conspiracy. He suspects Polonius, the lord chamberlain, and his daughter Ophelia, whom Hamlet had once wooed. After King Claudius reveals his own guilt, Hamlet cannot bring himself to kill him. Inadvertently Hamlet kills Polonius, an act which causes him to be exiled and Ophelia to go insane. Laertes, Ophelia's brother and Hamlet's former friend, challenges Hamlet to a duel. With the knowledge of the king and queen, Laertes poisons the tip of his rapier, while Claudius prepares a poisoned potion for Hamlet to drink. However, Gertrude dies of the poison prepared for Hamlet, who takes vengeance on the king. Laertes kills Hamlet with the poisoned rapier and is then killed with the same rapier.

King Lear by William Shakespeare (English, 1605): Tragedy. King Lear decides to divide his kingdom among his three daughters, with the largest share to be awarded to the one who loves him most. Unable to differentiate between insincere flattery and circumspect honesty, he banishes Cordelia, his trustworthy youngest daughter, and divides his kingdom between Goneril and Regan. These two daughters join forces to rob him of his possessions and his honor. Lear goes slowly insane but attains self-knowledge and recognizes his error in judgment. In a subplot, only after Gloucester is blinded and saved from suicide by his son Edgar does he perceive the evil nature of his illegitimate son Edmund.

Macbeth by William Shakespeare (English, 1606): Tragedy. Under the spell of three witches and incited by Lady Macbeth, Macbeth murders King Duncan, a guest in his castle. Although he now holds the crown, Macbeth is haunted by his act and grows obsessively paranoid. He murders Banquo, a fellow general in the Scottish army who suspects the truth. Upon seeing Banquo's ghost, Macbeth goes insane. Lady Macbeth commits suicide because of her guilt. Led by Macduff, a nobleman, and Duncan's son Malcolm, the Scottish army kills Macbeth and saves Scotland.

Volpone by Ben Jonson (English, 1605): Comedy. With Mosca's help, Volpone pretends to be gravely ill. He tricks Voltore, Corbaccio and Corvino into pledging him their fortunes by promising that they will inherit everything when he dies. Mosca and Volpone are delivered into the hands of justice. A subplot satirizes Sir Politic Would-Be and Lady Would-Be.

The Duchess of Malfi by John Webster (English, 1613): Tragedy. Motivated by greed and pride, the Cardinal and Duke of Calabria forbid their sister, the Duchess of Malfi, to remarry. But the Duchess and Antonio, master of the household, secretly marry and have a child. Bosola tells the Cardinal and Duke about the birth but cannot name the father. Avenging their honor several years later, the brothers kill the Duchess, her maid and two of the Duchess and Antonio's three children. A guilty conscience plagues Bosola; the Duke goes insane. The Cardinal plans to murder Bosola. In the final melee, the Cardinal, the Duke and Bosola receive fatal wounds.

Restoration and 18th Century

The Miser by Molière (French; 1669): Comedy. Harpagon is miserly in every way, which frustrates his children and clouds his judgment. Rather than agree to the mates chosen by their father, Harpagon's son and daughter choose their own. Cleante, the son, is his father's rival for Marianne. When Cleante forces him to choose between Marianne and a missing cash box, Harpagon picks the cash. Several other episodes satirize miserliness.

The Way of the World by William Congreve (English, 1700): Comedy. The plot of this play revolves around the wooing of Millamant by Mirabell. The dramatic climax is a scene in which the couple negotiate the terms under which both can tolerate their romantic partnership. Several romantic relationships complicate the plot.

She Stoops to Conquer by Oliver Goldsmith (English, 1773): Comedy. Though they have never met, Kate Hardcastle has been promised to Marlow in marriage. Marlow and his friend, Hastings, get directions to the Hardcastles' house from Tony Lumpkin, who tricks them into thinking it is an inn. The friends mistake Hardcastle for an innkeeper and Kate for a maid, but the confusion is finally resolved.

The Rivals by Richard Brinsley Sheridan (English, 1775): Comedy. Lydia Languish loves Captain Jack Absolute, alias Ensign Beverley. The captain's father, Sir Anthony Absolute, meets Mrs. Malaprop while trying to match his son with Lydia, Mrs. Malaprop's niece. Confusion of identities is the cause of much hilarity. Subplots involve the activities of other lovers and would-be lovers. The term *malapropism* was derived from the name of Mrs. Malaprop, who misuses words to comic effect throughout the play.

19th Century

A Doll's House by Henrik Ibsen (Norwegian, 1879): Drama. Married to an overprotective husband named Torvald, Nora Helmer is kept ignorant of the world. Several years before the start of the play's action, Torvald was ill and Nora needed money, so she signed her dying father's name to a note. Now, a servant threatens to reveal her secret unless she ensures that he will not be fired. In the mistaken belief that Torvald will think of the forgery as an act of love, Nora confesses. The servant tries to blackmail Torvald, claiming he will report the crime to the authorities. Enraged, Torvald berates Nora mercilessly until the servant finally agrees not to expose her. Nora realizes she must be free of her husband, who has always thought of her as mindless. She leaves Torvald and her children for a better life.

The Importance of Being Earnest by Oscar Wilde (English, 1895): Comedy. Two young men are pursuing two young ladies for marriage. However, one of the suitors is so lazy he may not have the vigor to fall in love; the other lacks social credentials. Their other problem is that the women they have chosen are only interested in men named Ernest. A baptism is planned to resolve this obstacle, while the others are resolved by the play's end.

Cyrano de Bergerac by Edmond Rostand (French, 1897): Romantic "heroic" comedy. Cyrano is so ashamed of his grotesque nose that he can't confess his love to his cousin, Roxane. In fact, when she falls in love with Christian, Cyrano offers to help the awkward young man by composing love letters and coaching him as he woos Roxane. Christian wins Roxane but dies in battle; Roxane becomes a nun. The truth finally comes out as Cyrano is dying.

Miss Julie by August Strindberg (Swedish, 1888): Tragedy. The daughter of a passive Swedish count and a dominating mother, Miss Julie has been taught the superiority of women and the lowliness of men. These beliefs conflict with her desire to have a romantic relationship. Julie is seduced by Jean, the count's valet, who only wants to use her to improve his social status. Julie exits to commit suicide when she realizes that she has lost her honor.

20th Century

Pygmalion by George Bernard Shaw (English, 1912): Comedy. Professor Higgins tutors a Cockney flower girl named Eliza in the arts of proper speech and manners, and she is accepted into upper-class society. Offended at being treated as an experiment, she leaves Higgins to find someone who will accept her for her true self.

Blood Wedding by Federico García Lorca (Spanish, 1932–33): Tragedy. Two families are feuding. The last living male of one family courts a girl who is believed to have had an affair with Leonardo, the only male of the rival family who is not in jail. The groom's mother grants permission for the marriage, but the bride-to-be takes up with Leonardo again on the night before her marriage. On the day of the wedding, the two lovers run away. They are found in the forest and the groom and Leonardo fight to the death.

The Children's Hour by Lillian Hellman (American, 1934): Tragedy. Karen Wright and Martha Dobie operate a boarding school from which one of their students runs away. To avoid being sent back to school, the girl tells her grandmother that the two teachers are having a sexual relationship with each other. The story is exposed as a lie, but it does permanent damage. Karen and Martha lose their libel suit when Martha's aunt fails to show up as a witness. Karen breaks her engagement and Martha, accusing herself of repressed lesbian feelings for Karen, commits suicide.

Awake and Sing by Clifford Odets (American, 1935): Drama. The Bergers, a Jewish family in the Bronx, are struggling through the Great Depression. The son, Ralph, wants to marry the girl he loves, but his family pressures him not to. His grandfather urges him to do something to help alleviate all the suffering in the world, while his mother begs him to contribute to the family income. At the play's end, he gives in to his grandfather. Other characters in the play grapple with their own individual conflicts.

You Can't Take It With You by George S. Kaufman and Moss Hart (American, 1936): Comedy. The Vanderhof house is filled with all kinds of eccentrics: Grandpa collects stamps and snakes; his daughter Penny is a painter-turned-playwright; Paul, her husband, makes fireworks in the basement with the iceman, who came eight years ago to make a delivery and never left. When one of Penny and Paul's daughters wants to marry into a staid and proper socialite family, the two families meet.

Of Mice and Men by John Steinbeck (American, 1937): Tragedy. Two migrant farm workers, George and Lennie, dream of owning their own land. Lennie, a slow-minded giant who doesn't know his own strength, is totally dependent on George. They have left their previous job because Lennie, drawn to soft things, tried to touch a young girl's dress. A fellow worker at their new job offers them money to buy land on the condition that Lennie stays away from Curley, the boss's son, and his wife. Curley's wife seduces Lennie into touching her hair, but then panics and screams. Trying to calm her, Lennie accidentally breaks her neck. George kills Lennie so that he will not be lynched by Curley's mob.

Our Town by Thornton Wilder (American, 1938): Drama. The play is set in Grover's Corners, New Hampshire, and is told in a series of episodes narrated by a "stage manager." It is the story of the courtship of George Gibbs and Emily Webb, whose happiness is short-lived, ending when Emily dies in childbirth. The final scene is set in the town cemetery, where the deceased residents of the town discuss how the beauty of life can never be understood or appreciated by the living.

Mother Courage and Her Children by Bertolt Brecht (German, 1939): Tragedy. Mother Courage is a merchant who sells goods to both opposing armies during a war. She eventually loses a son to a firing squad, her daughter is shot, and another son is brought to shame for plundering. Peace is declared, but war, which is perpetual, soon resumes.

Long Day's Journey Into Night by Eugene O'Neill (American, 1940): Tragedy. The Tyrone family is deeply troubled. James Tyrone buys worthless land. His wife, Mary, who spent time in a sanitorium after losing a child and becoming mentally ill, is addicted to the drugs she was given during childbirth. Their sons, Jamie and Edmund, are plagued by their own problems and ill health. One night while Jamie and his father drink heavily, Jamie experiences some clarity. Mary, lost in a haze of drugs and the past, appears onstage carrying her wedding gown.

Oklahoma! with book and lyrics by Oscar Hammerstein II; music by Richard Rodgers (American, 1943): Musical based on the play *Green Grow the Lilacs* by Lynn Rigg. Laurey agrees to go to the box social with Jud Fry, a farmhand who works for her Aunt Eller. At the social, Curly, the cowboy Laurey is smitten with, outbids Jud for Laurey's box lunch. Jud threatens Curly. Later, the two men fight and Jud is killed. After Curly is acquitted, he and Laurey ride off on their honeymoon. A subplot involves Ado Annie, who "cain't say no" to any man but finally agrees to settle down and marry Will Parker.

No Exit by Jean-Paul Sartre (French, 1944): Drama. The three characters in this existentialist play are recently deceased and confined together in an apartment in hell. As they form a triangle, the play illustrates the existentialist belief that individuals follow predetermined actions. This realization is the characters' punishment.

The Glass Menagerie by Tennessee Williams (American, 1945): Memory play. Tom Wingfield serves as both narrator and participant in this story of his family. His mother longs for her early days as a southern belle, and his disabled sister Laura creates her own reality with her collection of glass animals. Tom brings home a friend from work as a possible "gentleman caller" for Laura. In the end,

Tom abandons his mother and sister but is haunted by their memory.

Death of a Salesman by Arthur Miller (American, 1949): Tragedy. Willy Loman, a 63-year-old traveling salesman, has reached the end of the road. He is weary from travel and realizes that being a good guy has gotten him very little. His relationship with his sons is troubled, and one son convinces him that they are both failures. After losing his job, Willy goes to the garage to commit suicide so that he might leave his wife some insurance money; his wife is powerless to prevent it.

Rhinoceros by Eugene Ionesco (French, 1960): Satire. In a small French town, a person who has been transformed into a rhinoceros suddenly appears. Each resident of the town is transformed until only one individual stands against the mass hysteria.

Who's Afraid of Virginia Woolf? by Edward Albee (American, 1962): Drama. Abusive Martha and passive George, a college professor, are married. They invite Nick and Honey, a young couple who are new to the college, for cocktails. A long, drunken, sadomasochistic evening eventually destroys Martha's fantasy that she and George have a son.

Fiddler on the Roof with book by Joseph Stein; lyrics by Sheldon Harnick; music by Jerry Bock (American, 1964): Musical based on Sholom Aleichem's book of short stories, *Tevye's Daughters*. The dairyman Tevye and his wife, Golde, live in the poverty-stricken Jewish shtetl of Anatevka. They hire a matchmaker to find husbands for their daughters, but their daughters rebel. Escalating anti-Semitism forces Tevye and his neighbors to leave their country.

The House of Blue Leaves by John Guare (American, 1971): Black comedy. The play takes place on a day the Pope comes to New York. Artie, a zookeeper who dreams of becoming a famous lyricist, has a crazy wife named Bananas. Ronnie, their son, is AWOL from the army and wants to blow up the Pope. Ronnie and other characters are killed when his bomb goes off prematurely. Artie's mistress runs off with his old friend, a Hollywood producer who he hoped would give him a break. Finally Artie strangles Bananas, putting her out of her misery.

A Chorus Line with book by James Kirkwood and Nicholas Dante; lyrics by Edward Kleban; music by Marvin Hamlisch (American, 1975): Musical. During auditions for an upcoming musical, Zach, the director-choreographer, asks the dancers to tell a little about themselves. They do so through song. Dancers are eliminated until the chosen remain, executing the finale in top hat and tails.

Buried Child by Sam Shepard (American, 1978): Drama. Vince comes home to his grandparents' Illinois farm with his girlfriend Shelley. His grandmother, who tries to pass herself off as morally upright, is carrying on with the local priest. His drunken, dying grandfather has a dark secret. His father and uncle are crazed and abusive. Vince struggles to resolve his pain and conflict and to create a life for himself.

Talley's Folly by Lanford Wilson (American, 1980): Drama. Matt Friedman courts Salley Talley after being away for a year. Her family disapproves because he is Jewish, and has even threatened him with violence. Sally confesses the family secret to Matt: She is sterile. He loves her, though, and she agrees to elope with him.

A Soldier's Play by Charles Fuller (American, 1981): Drama. A black officer, Captain Richard Davenport, is sent to a Louisiana army base to investigate the death of a black sergeant, Vernon C. Waters. Davenport discovers not only that the Ku Klux Klan had motives for the murder, but that the black troops resented Waters's high-handed treatment. White officers are warned that someday there will be black officers who outrank them.

Crimes of the Heart by Beth Henley (American, 1981): Black comedy. The play depicts a day in the lives of three eccentric Mississippi sisters. Babe shot her husband because she didn't like his looks; Meg has been in and out of mental institutions; Lenny is generally frustrated and unhappy with life. During the play, their bizarre family history is revealed.

Torch Song Trilogy by Harvey Fierstein (American, 1981): Three one-act plays. In *The International Stud,* Arnold, a female impersonator, thinks he has met his true love, Ed, in a gay bar. *Fugue in a Nursery* shows Arnold and his new lover, Alan, visiting Ed's farm, where they meet his fiancée, Laurel. In *Widows and Children First,* Ed's marriage is not working out and he wants to reconcile with Arnold, who wants to adopt a boy named David. When Arnold's mother visits, Arnold declares his pain and affirms his hopes and desires for love and family.

'Night Mother by Marsha Norman (American, 1983): Drama. A widow, Thelma Cates, lives in a small rural house with Jessie, her troubled, divorced, middle-aged daughter. One night Jessie tells Thelma that she is going to kill herself. Her mother, at first disbelieving, engages her daughter in a discussion about Jessie's unhappiness and their mother-daughter relationship in an attempt to dissuade her. She fails.

Glengarry Glen Ross by David Mamet (American, 1984): Drama. In a real-estate office, salesman Richard Roma is in the lead for the monthly sales award, a Cadillac. Shelley Levene, a former top salesman, is not doing well. John Williamson, their boss, plays all the salesmen against each other to increase business. Their office is burglarized and a list of business leads is stolen. In the end, Williamson tricks Roma out of his car and the thief is exposed.

LONGEST BROADWAY RUNS

Play	Number of Performances*	Play	Number of Performances*
1. *A Chorus Line* (1975–90)	6,137	14. *Oklahoma!* (1943–48)	2,572
2. *Oh, Calcutta* (1976–89)	5,959	15. *Les Miserables* (1987–——)	2,116
3. *Cats* (1982–——)	4,485	16. *Pippin* (1972–77)	1,944
4. *42nd Street* (1980–89)	3,486	17. *South Pacific* (1949–54)	1,925
5. *Grease* (1972–80)	3,388	18. *Magic Show* (1974–78)	1,920
6. *Fiddler on the Roof* (1964–72)	3,242	19. *Phantom of the Opera* (1988–——)	2,271
7. *Life with Father* (1939–47)	3,224	20. *Deathtrap* (1978–82)	1,793
8. *Tobacco Road* (1933–41)	3,182	21. *Gemini* (1977–81)	1,788
9. *Hello, Dolly!* (1964–70)	2,844	22. *Harvey* (1944–49)	1,775
10. *My Fair Lady* (1956–62)	2,717	23. *Dancin'* (1978–82)	1,774
11. *Annie* (1977–83)	2,377	24. *La Cage aux Folles* (1983–87)	1,761
12. *Man of La Mancha* (1965–71)	2,328	25. *Hair* (1968–72)	1,750
13. *Abie's Irish Rose* (1922–27)	2,327		

* 1993 totals

Layout of the modern theater

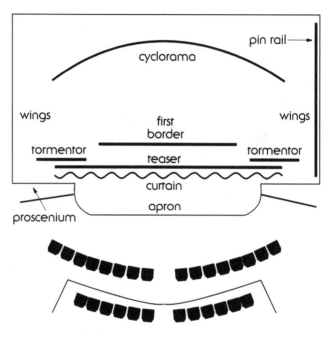

Inside the Theater: Producing a Play

Mounting a theatrical production requires much hard work by people who specialize in many different tasks. Once a theater company choses a script and, if necessary, secures the rights to produce it, the company's creative and technical staff begins the long process of bringing the play to life. A large, professional theater company has a correspondingly large staff; an amateur company is significantly smaller. (See the sidebar, *Job Descriptions for the Staff of a Theater Company*, page 34.)

Based on a personal interpretation of the play and after consulting with designers and technical staff, the director refines his or her directorial concept. He or she then devises a production plan that takes into consideration the technical facilities available, the type of stage, the production budget and other requirements. Before rehearsals begin the director, often with the set designer, devises a rough ground plan that represents the arrangement of all scenery, furniture and other set props as they will appear when the set is installed on stage. The ground plan allows the director to work with the actors during rehearsals in blocking the movement and business of each scene.

Set Design

Because the set serves as the audience's introduction to the play, the first requirement is that it reflect the appropriate location, style and period. Into the 19th century, stage settings were often no more than painted drops or formal architectural designs. It was not unusual for a production to have one historically accurate set while the rest of the scenes were played in front of stock scenery. However, during the 1860s in Germany, George II, Duke of Saxe-Meiningen, imposed a consistent visual style on his productions based on historical and cultural research. Sometimes considered the first modern director, Saxe-Meiningen toured Europe with his company during the 1870s, strongly influencing the European theater with his concept of unification of design elements. Thereafter, scenery evolved into a carefully planned and constructed stage environment. When directors and designers plan stage sets today, they try to create environments that enhance the themes and impact of plays.

The design approach for a production is usually determined by the director in cooperation with the design team. Together, they consider several factors as they decide on the "look" of a production: the director's concept for the play; the style and period of the work; the stage and theater space in which it will be performed; the abilities of the director, design team and technical staff; and the budget. A successful design approach will result in a stage set that fulfills three distinct functions: It provides a suitable background for the play's action; it conveys certain information to the audience in order to support their understanding and appreciation of the play; and it facilitates the flow of the action from scene to scene, act to act.

To achieve these goals, a set designer must evoke an entire environment with a few details. He or she must suggest rather than state and make a fragment represent the whole. In particular, arena-type and thrust stages drastically reduce the amount of scenery that can be used. Because of the sight lines for an audience completely surrounding an arena stage, the designer often relies only on furniture to suggest location and period. With an audience surrounding three-quarters of a thrust stage, the designer has the option of using some backing.

Traditionally, the style and period of scenery conforms to that of the entire production, suggesting either the period or style in which the play was written, or the period or style in which the director has chosen to stage the production. If the director has chosen to set *Hamlet* in modern times, for example, the set designer will most likely not design a traditional Elizabethan set. The hope is that the set reflects the mood or spirit of the production and is interesting to the audience. For instance, Maxim Gorky's *The Lower Depths* (1902) takes place amid squalor and poverty, but a designer can create a set that is aesthetically pleasing to the audience and enhances their appreciation of the play.

In their work, set designers obey the concepts governing line, mass, form and color in visual design. These elements produce different emotional responses; for example, straight lines can create a feeling of order and formality, whereas angular shapes evoke feelings of instability and unpredictability. Likewise, dark colors have a very different effect on mood than bright colors. The set designer has the task of utilizing these elements while maintaining balance in the set. He or she usually avoids creating a single strong focal point in the set so as not to disturb the balance of the stage picture as it is viewed by the audience.

The flat is the basic scenic unit. It consists of a wooden frame that is covered with canvas or muslin and then painted. Additional scenic units, such as stairways, doors and platforms, can be attached to flats. In place of flats, or behind flats with windows in them, a designer may employ a cyclorama—a backdrop onto which light is projected—to enclose the entire back and both sides of the stage. Often, designers use a cyclorama in conjunction with lighting effects to simulate sky; colored lights can create sunrise or sunset effects, or a blue sky. A cyc can do much to communicate mood or information (time of day, weather, etc.) to an audience.

To make sure the set facilitates the flow of the play's action, the designer considers the limitations of the stage space and the dramatic necessities of the script. Often the designer and director collaborate closely on a ground plan, which includes all details, from doors, windows, arches and fireplaces to stairs, platforms and the location of major pieces of furniture. Another important factor is the axis of the stage—whether the set is aligned parallel to the footlights or set at an angle (raked). Generally speaking, a parallel set is more formal and is used for classical plays. A raked set lends itself to modern comedy or fantasy, but of course there are notable exceptions to these generalizations.

When working out a ground plan, the designer must also consider sight lines. A set must allow as many members of the audience as possible to view fully the action on stage, while preventing them from seeing what happens offstage. In a proscenium set, the horizontal sight lines of greatest concern are those of audience members sitting in the seats farthest to the right and farthest to the left. By drawing an imaginary line from the seat on the far right to the proscenium opening on that side and extending it to the rear of the stage, the designer determines how much of the stage is visible from that seat. To determine visibility from the far left seat, the designer follows the same procedure from the opposite side. The onstage area between these two invisible lines is where most of the play's action should take place. Otherwise, certain members of the audience will have their view obstructed.

The vertical sight lines of most concern are those of audience members sitting in the front and back rows of the orchestra and in the back row of the balcony. By sitting in these seats, the designer can determine which areas are visible to all, or most, audience members. In order to keep the audience from seeing the backstage and offstage areas of a proscenium set, the designer masks any areas not intended to be part of the performance. Backings of flats, as well as leg drops and other draperies, mask offstage or wing areas. Draperies and borders mask fly space and lighting equipment above.

After creating a ground plan, the designer makes a sketch that shows in elevation what the completed set should look like from the audience. If necessary, he or she will then build a scale model (maquette) that shows a miniature version of the completed set in three dimensions, so that set carpenters and the director can know what the set will look like from all angles. Based on the model, the elevations and the ground plan, the designer produces working drawings that convey precise instructions to the set builders.

Stage Lighting

The techniques of stage lighting have evolved greatly since the days of Elizabethan theater, when no artificial lighting at all was used. Limelight, or calcium light, replaced candles and oil lamps during the early 19th century, making possible not only the illumination of the stage but of individual actors as well. Now, many theaters have computer-controlled lighting. Until the 20th century, theatrical design teams did not include lighting designers. Instead, the stage manager hung and focused lighting instruments. Generally accepted as the first lighting designer in theater history, and one of the greatest, was Jean Rosenthal, an American. In the 1930s she pioneered the concept of stage lighting as an art integral to the overall value of the production.

The chief function of stage lighting is to make the actors visible, but visibility is not the only consideration. Lighting contributes to the total stage effect in many ways. By using different colors in the lighting instruments and varying the intensity with which the set is lit, the designer can not only affect the mood of the play but also convey information to the audience, such as time of day, weather, even the season of the year. In addition, by increasing or decreasing the intensity of light, a lighting designer can give more or less emphasis to an object or individual. While lighting must not distract the audience from the action onstage, it may enhance design qualities and complement the set. Likewise, lighting alone can be used to identify or accent dramatic values that the director wishes to underscore. For example, a character standing alone in a spotlight makes a dramatic impression.

To help ensure that the lighting will accomplish what it is designed to do, the lighting designer draws what is known as a light plot. The plot indicates the locations of each of the required lighting instruments, along with the stage areas it is intended to light. To guide his or her work during a performance, the lighting board operator writes out a set of cue sheets, which include both warning and execute cues for each lighting change. Using the sheets, the stage manager signals the lighting board operator when to execute each cue during a performance. At the appropriate cues, board operators adjust the dimmer readings of lighting instruments to the levels agreed upon by the designer and director during rehearsals. They may adjust the levels of several instruments or just a few, depending on the degree of change required onstage.

Almost all stage lighting is incandescent and comes from lamps housed in metal instruments that direct or focus the rays in one direction. Most are equipped with color frames or other devices that control the color of the light. Cables connect lighting instruments to a central switchboard that turns instruments on or off and controls their brightness by means of dimmer switches. Various types of lighting instruments serve a variety of needs. These include several types of spotlights: plano-convex, Fresnel, ellipsoidal and follow. Other types of lighting devices include floodlights, beam projectors, strip lights, footlights and border lights.

Effects, Props and Costumes

Within the environment created by the set and lighting designers, sound effects, visual effects, props and costumes enhance the illusion of a play. The sound designer, in charge of recorded music as well as sound effects, can greatly affect the overall cohesion of the production. He or she may utilize sound-effects recordings or create effects manually. Common sound cues include doorbells and ringing telephones. To enhance realism, sound effects are commonly played through backstage speakers instead of speakers in the auditorium.

Other crew members operate visual effects, adding excitement and reality to a production. Visual effects may include flashes of fire and smoke, usually generated by a flashpot rented from a theatrical supply house. Special fog machines produce dry ice fog or smoke; it is blown onto the set through a hose by an electric fan inside the machine. Chemical fog machines generate smoke from a special oil-based liquid. The lighting operator, meanwhile, can simulate lightning by "bumping" up and down the dimmer of a lighting instrument, which creates a flashing effect.

All movable objects in a play—except lighting equipment, scenery and costumes—are classified as props. Play scripts often include prepared prop lists, but because there frequently are changes and substitutions, stage managers make their own lists as well. If a play is especially prop-heavy, a properties master or coordinator takes charge of locating, building and maintaining props. By the time the company approaches dress rehearsals, the stage manager has compiled a complete list of set or scene props. It might list large items of set dressing like furniture, rugs and three-dimensional set pieces; smaller decorative items such as curtains, lamps and vases; hand props, which are small items like pipes, books and letters handled by actors; and rehearsal props, which substitute for real props during early rehearsals.

The stage manager also prepares prop plots for each scene, indicating the position of all set props, as well as where they are located on offstage prop tables. Because stagehands must quickly and accurately rearrange the stage between scenes, the locations of all sets, furniture and many props are spiked, that is, marked with tape, chalk or paint on the stage floor. The stage crew often handles both scenery and props, but sometimes companies include a separate prop crew. If the company has a prop master or coordinator, he or she is responsible for acquiring and maintaining the production's props.

Similarly, the costume or wardrobe crew handles the costumes worn by the actors onstage. When planning the costumes for a production, the costume designer must create clothing that is consistent with the dominant mood of the play, while giving some clue as to the basic identities of the characters. Costumes indicate certain information about the characters, such as their age or social position. In designing period costumes, the designer usually tries to give an impression of the period, rather than re-creating flawlessly accurate historical costumes.

Actors usually apply their own makeup and understand the basic principles governing its use and application. They use makeup to give the audience an impression of their character's age, health and personality. In addition, actors with light-toned skin use makeup to counterbalance the bleaching effects of bright stage lighting. Makeup also accentuates expressive features, such as the eyes and mouth. Actors currently use two types of makeup: greasepaint and pancake (or cake). Greasepaint is oil-based and pancake is water-soluble, so the methods of applying them differ. Whichever kind of makeup an actor chooses, a mirror with lights on three sides—the top, right and left—eliminates the problem of shadows on the face during application, which can lead to distortion.

Rehearsals

During the rehearsal process, which generally lasts several weeks, all the elements of a production come together to form a unified whole. The director's concept of the play, all of the different designers' concepts of the physical production, and each actor's concept of his or her own role merge during rehearsals, ideally realizing the playwright's intentions. The exact number of rehearsals a company needs is determined by the difficulty of the play, the size of the cast and the physical complexity of the production.

During the preliminary stage of rehearsals, the director or stage manager starts preparing a prompt book, which includes notes on the movement and business of each scene; prop notes; all light, sound and curtain cues; and other information vital to the performance. The prompt book usually consists of a copy of the script in a looseleaf binder, with space in the margins for the necessary notes. Although it may be begun by the director, the prompt book is usually completed by the stage manager, who is in charge of everything backstage. The prompt book is the stage manager's essential tool and serves as a valuable record of the production.

The first rehearsal is devoted to a reading of the entire play. As rehearsals proceed, the actors memorize their lines and movement until they can rehearse without holding their scripts. The director gives notes to actors to help improve their performance, as needed. The crew holds technical rehearsals to run

JOB DESCRIPTIONS FOR THE STAFF OF A THEATER COMPANY

ACTOR: Performs the role of a character in the play.

ASSISTANT STAGE MANAGER: Assists the production stage manager in his or her duties and can replace him or her, if necessary. There may be one or more assistant stage managers on a production; an a.s.m. sometimes serves as the prop master or coordinator.

BOX OFFICE MANAGER: Is responsible for selling tickets and keeping accurate records of the box office's financial transactions.

CHOREOGRAPHER: Creates and supervises dance in the play.

COMPANY MANAGER: The general manager's representative at the theater and on tour.

COMPOSER: Composes original music, working closely with the playwright and lyricist on the overall concept. Supervises all original music.

CONDUCTOR: Conducts the orchestra during the performance. Often selects musicians. Rehearses singers.

COSTUME OR WARDROBE CREW: Includes the costumer and at least one crew member. Responsibilities include making, renting or borrowing all costumes and wigs; cleaning and repairing costumes; and helping actors into or out of costumes before, during and after a performance.

CREW: Does most of the physical work on a production, such as executing scenery shifts, running props, etc. Includes lighting and sound operators, prop crew and stagehands.

DESIGNERS: Design all settings, costumes, lighting and properties, subject to the approval of the producer, director and playwright.

DIRECTOR: Coordinates implementation of dramatic elements to communicate the playwright's intention. This includes guiding actors in their creation of characters, working out the staging and collaborating with designers on their concepts.

GENERAL MANAGER: The producer's right hand. Handles financial details such as contracts, expenditures, budgets, etc.

HOUSE CREW: Normally consists of a house manager, box office attendants, ticket takers, ushers and maintenance staff.

LIGHTING CREW: Consists of a chief electrician and assistants, including the lighting board operator. Responsible for hanging and focusing all instruments according to the lighting designer's plan and operating lights during performances.

LYRICIST: Writes lyrics to songs in the play.

MAKEUP CREW: Often combined with the costume crew. Responsibilities include procuring all makeup supplies, applying makeup to cast members who need assistance and supervising the makeup of others.

PLAYWRIGHT: Writes the play. If the playwright is involved in the production, he or she often works with the director on casting and furnishes and approves all changes to the script.

PRODUCER: Responsible for the entire financial side of a production.

PROP CREW: Includes a property master and, if necessary, assistants. The crew is responsible for procuring, building and handling all props used during the production, except for large set props.

PUBLICITY DIRECTOR: Is responsible for writing and placing newspaper stories, securing photographs of the production, preparing and distributing posters and flyers, and arranging special events to publicize the production.

SET CREW: Includes a chief carpenter, who supervises the construction of all scenery. The crew usually paints all scenery and set props (unless scene painters are used) before and after the set has been assembled on stage.

SOUND CREW: Consists of one person whenever most sound effects are on tape. Where electronic sounds are blended with live sounds, a bigger crew may be required.

STAGE CREW: Includes the stage carpenter and stage hands (also called "deck hands"). Duties include setting up and striking scenery before and after the performance, operating the lines for flying scenery, and opening and closing the curtain.

STAGE MANAGER: Supervises the cast and production crews during rehearsals and performances. Functions as liaison between cast and director. Sees that all technical aspects of a production are functioning properly. In the director's absence, the s.m. is responsible for seeing that the director's concept for the production continues to be carried out and that the quality is maintained.

TECHNICAL DIRECTOR: Supervises the technical facilities of a theater and the overall technical aspects of a production—lighting, sound, etc.—and troubleshoots when there are problems during a production.

through scenery shifts and lighting cues. When the actual performance dates approach, the entire company runs through one or more dress rehearsals designed to integrate the acting with the use of scenery, props, costumes, makeup and lighting. The director makes final adjustments to the staging and acting, while designers have the opportunity to smooth out any technical problems. Following dress rehearsals, the company should be ready to present their production to an audience.

Major Theaters and Companies

Abbey Theatre: Dublin's National Theatre Society Ltd. is commonly called the Abbey Theatre. Founded 1899–1903, it combined the Irish Literary Theatre with the Irish National Dramatic Company. Important productions of its early years were plays by J. M. Synge and W. B. Yeats. Its primary purpose was, and continues to be, to encourage new playwrights to pursue work of a quintessentially Irish nature.

Actors Theatre of Louisville: Located in Louisville, Kentucky, it is a leading American regional theater noted for encouraging young playwrights, producing new scripts and presenting the annual Humana Festival of New American Plays. It received a special Antoinette Perry (Tony) Award in 1980.

American Conservatory Theater (ACT): A well-known regional repertory company in San Francisco that combines performance with training.

American Place Theatre: A New York–based producing organization dedicated to the presentation of new American plays.

American Repertory Theatre (ART): Founded in 1979 by Robert Brustein, ART is an independent, not-for-profit producing organization located at the Loeb Drama Center at Harvard University in Boston. They present eclectic theatrical fare which includes new American plays, innovative productions of classical plays and experimental productions, such as *The King Stag* (1984), directed by Andrei Serban, and portions of Robert Wilson's epic, *CIVIL warS* (1985).

Arena Stage: Founded in 1950, this Washington, D.C., theater presents classics, new American and European plays, and musicals. Its complex includes a 500-seat modified thrust stage called The Kreeger, an 800-seat main stage (Arena Stage) and a cabaret, the Old Vat.

Berliner Ensemble: This influential German theater company was founded in 1949, dedicating itself to the epic theater of Bertolt Brecht. It has made its home at the Theater am Schiffbauerdamm since 1954 and conducts extensive international tours.

Birmingham Repertory Theatre: One of the most significant theaters in Britain during the first half of the 20th century. It opened in 1913, and the company is known for producing high-quality productions of noncommercial drama and for launching the careers of many well-known actors.

Bread and Puppet Theatre: A loosely attached group of New York performers founded by Peter Schumann in 1961, this company utilizes larger-than-life puppets in nonnarrative theatrical presentations. Addressing contemporary political and social issues, the group often offers its services for free, reflecting its founder's maxim that "Theatre is like bread, more like a necessity."

Circle in the Square: Founded in 1950 by José Quintero, Theodore Mann and others, this company was among the first to use an arena-style stage in its Greenwich Village, New York, theater. The company has presented important revivals, including Tennessee Williams's *Summer and Smoke* (1952), which helped to establish their reputation, as well as several stagings of Eugene O'Neill's works.

Circle Repertory Company: Founded in 1969 by Tanya Berezin, Marshall W. Mason, Robert Thirkield and Lanford Wilson, New York-based Circle Rep provides workshop support for plays-in-progress and presents new plays by American dramatists.

Citizens' Theatre: This Glasgow, Scotland, theater was founded in 1943 with the aim of producing the best British and European drama and the work of new Scottish playwrights. Since 1969, the innovative design of its productions has enhanced the theater's reputation as one of Scotland's foremost companies.

Covent Garden, Theatre Royal: Three theaters have occupied the London site of the present structure. The first, a 3,000-seat building, opened in 1732. It was destroyed by fire in 1808 and a second 3,000-seat theater opened in 1809. An increase in the price of seats caused the Old Price Riots, which eventually forced theater management to reinstate the old prices. In 1817, Covent Garden was one of the first theaters in England to install gaslight. The second theater closed in 1842 and reopened in 1847 as the Royal Italian Opera House. This theater burned in 1856, and a 2,100-seat theater opened on the site in 1858. Since its opening, the third theater has been associated with opera productions.

Deutsches Theater: Founded in 1883 as an ensemble repertory company, this German the-ater was taken over in 1904 by director Max Reinhardt, who made it into one of the most celebrated theaters in Europe prior to World War II. It continues to be an influential theater company in the eastern section of Berlin.

Drury Lane, Theatre Royal: The first Theatre Royal opened in 1663 and was destroyed by fire in 1672. A second theater opened in 1674. Under the long management of David Garrick (1747–76), the Drury Lane became known as one of London's greatest theaters. Among Garrick's accomplishments were innovations in scenic design and stage lighting, in association with Philip De Loutherbourg. The playwright Richard Brinsley Sheridan succeeded Garrick as manager and had the poorly maintained theater demolished in 1791 in order to build a new one. The third Drury Lane opened in 1794 but was destroyed by fire in 1809. The fourth building opened in 1812 and was equipped with gas lighting in 1817. Under the management of Alfred Butt (1924–31) the Drury Lane became home to the English musical and then, following World War II, to the American musical as well. The theaters on Drury Lane and vicinity house London's leading companies.

Empire Theatre: Built in 1893 by Charles Frohman, the Empire was for many years a favorite theater of New York audiences, presenting stars in hit shows. *Peter Pan* opened there in 1905; its boards were trod by such stars as Maude Adams, Ethel Barrymore, John Drew, Katharine Cornell and others. Until Frohman's death, the Empire served as his flagship theater and saw productions of American plays as well as important British and French imports. It had several owners before being demolished in 1953.

Federal Theatre Project: Established in 1935 under an act of Congress (the Works Progress Administration), the Federal Theatre Project provided work to theater professionals during the Great Depression and provided "free, adult, uncensored theater." Vocal opposition grew among conservative politicians when its productions were perceived as left-wing propaganda. Congress abolished the project in 1939.

Ford's Theatre: This Washington, D.C., theater is the site of President Abraham Lincoln's assassination by actor John Wilkes Booth on April 14, 1865. After the killing, the theater was converted into a storage building that later collapsed, allegedly during the 1893 funeral of John's actor brother, Edwin Booth. It reopened in 1968 after restoration by the government and now houses the Lincoln Museum.

Forrest Theatre: New York's Eugene O'Neill Theatre opened as the Forrest, named for actor Edwin Forrest (1806–72) in 1925. *Tobacco Road* played there from 1934 to 1941. In 1945 the theater closed, reopening after alterations as the Coronet. It received its current name in 1959.

Globe Theatre: Constructed in London of the timbers from James Burbage's Theatre, the Globe was built in 1599. Polygonal in shape, it featured an open yard encircled by a three-tiered gallery. It also had a tower or penthouse, from which a flag was flown when the theater was open. Attempts to reconstruct the Globe have been based mainly on drawings of the Swan Theatre, another 16th-century London theater, which many scholars theorize it resembled. Several William Shakespeare plays premiered at the Globe, performed by a company led by Richard Burbage, from 1599 to 1608. After having been destroyed by fire in 1613, the Globe was rebuilt with a tiled roof that replaced the thatched roof that was believed to have been the source of the fire. The second Globe reopened in 1614, closed permanently in 1642 and was demolished in 1644.

Goodman Theater: One of the oldest regional theaters in the United States, Chicago's Goodman presents main-stage repertory as well as experimental works on its smaller, second stage. Its theater school is affiliated with DePaul University.

Group Theatre, The: The Group Theatre was founded in 1931 by Harold Clurman, Cheryl Crawford and Lee Strasberg, who had previously been associated with the Theatre Guild. They believed theater should provide a forum for politically oriented plays. Among their notable New York productions were the first plays of Clifford Odets and Sidney Kingsley, among others. The Group Theatre disbanded in 1941. Harold Clurman's book, *The Fervent Years* (1945), recounts its history.

Guthrie Theatre: Founded by Oliver Rea, Peter Zeisler and Tyrone Guthrie, who wanted to establish a permanent repertory company away from New York, it opened in 1963 adjacent to the Walker Art Center in Minneapolis. Tyrone Guthrie and designer Tanya Moiseiwitsch created a 1,437-seat auditorium that surrounds a thrust stage; Guthrie's directorial work at the theater helped to popularize the use of the thrust stage. The Guthrie features classics and contemporary American and European plays and has a second stage for experimental work.

Habimah: Originally founded in Moscow in 1918, Habimah is perhaps the most important Hebrew-speaking professional theater of the 20th century. The company's early work was acclaimed by innovators around the world, including director Konstantin Stanislavski and playwright Maxim Gorky. Habimah became affiliated with the Moscow Art Theatre and then in 1931 settled in Palestine. In 1958 it was officially declared Israel's national theater.

Haymarket, Theatre Royal: This London theater opened in 1720 and became known for its political satires. Between 1776 and 1817, Haymarket provided a home for all the most popular plays and actors during the summers, when the Drury Lane and Covent Garden were closed. The crowd was so large for the first Royal Command Performance in 1794 that fifteen people were trampled and killed. The present structure was built in 1820, though its interior has been renovated many times. Gas lighting was finally installed during the late 1830s, making the Haymarket the last theater in London to use candlelight. A primary playhouse of London by the mid–19th century, it continues to be an important theater.

John F. Kennedy Center for the Performing Arts: The process of creating this national cultural center began during Dwight D. Eisenhower's presidency. It opened in 1971 as a tribute to the late President Kennedy. Located on the banks of the Potomac River in Washington, D.C., it houses three theaters, including the 1,142-seat Eisenhower, the 2,750-seat Concert Hall and the 2,318-seat Opera House. There are also three smaller houses, including the 512-seat Terrace Theatre and a 120-seat Theater Lab.

Living Theatre, The: An experimental ensemble group formed in 1947 by Julian Beck and his wife, Judith Malina, that helped to establish the Off-Off Broadway movement in New York. Presenting controversial avant-garde plays, the company performed for long periods outside the United States. After dissolving in 1963 it was revived in 1984; Judith Malina continues to run the group with Hanon Reznikov. Beck died in 1985.

Mabou Mines: The New York company was formed in 1970 after years of informal collaboration among its founders, JoAnne Akalaitis, Lee Breuer, Ruth Maleczech and others. Its experimental productions combine acting, narrative, video, film, music and other media.

Manhattan Theatre Club: Founded in 1970 by A. E. Jeffcoat and others, it presents full productions, workshops and readings of noncommercial works, as well as new plays.

Several of its productions have transferred to Broadway.

Mercury Theatre, The: Lasting only two years, the Mercury Theatre was founded in 1937 by Orson Welles and John Houseman as a repertory company to present innovative productions of classical plays. These included a modern-dress version of *Julius Caesar*. The group withdrew from the Federal Theatre Project in order to produce Marc Blitzstein's controversial leftist musical, *The Cradle Will Rock* (1937).

Mickery-Theater: Founded in 1965 in Amsterdam, the Netherlands, this company presents experimental productions by European and American companies, as well as its own work.

Morosco Theatre: Designed for the Shuberts by the architect Herbert J. Krapp, it served as a New York showcase for the productions of West Coast producer Oliver Morosco. Its stage saw original productions of plays by Thornton Wilder, Tennessee Williams, Arthur Miller, Robert Anderson and Arthur Kopit. The theater changed hands several times before it was torn down in 1982 and replaced with a hotel.

National Theatre: The National opened in Washington, D.C., in 1835 and was destroyed by fire in 1845, after which five Nationals have been located at approximately the same site. Throughout their individual histories, these Nationals have served as major venues for American theater.

Negro Ensemble Company: A renowned black theater company located in New York City, it was established by Douglas Turner Ward and others in 1967. Their aim was to secure a place where black theatrical talent could be "continuously presented, without regard to the whims of commercial theater." The group presents workshops and staged readings in addition to its main productions. It tours nationally and internationally and has garnered many awards and grants.

Neighborhood Playhouse, The: Located on New York's Lower East Side, this repertory theater was founded in 1915 as an educational and charitable organization. It featured plays by contemporary dramatists, as well as a series of popular revues called *The Grand Street Follies*. The company disbanded in 1927, but the Neighborhood Playhouse School of the Theatre continues to offer programs.

New Amsterdam Theatre: This ornate Times Square, New York, theater, which mainly housed musicals, was built in 1903 and served as a flagship of the Klau and Erlanger Organization. Most of the *Ziegfeld Follies* and other musical hits played there. For many years cabaret was performed in the enclosed roof garden.

New York Shakespeare Festival/Joseph Papp Public Theater: The festival was founded in 1954 by Joseph Papp "to encourage and cultivate interest in poetic drama with emphasis on the works of William Shakespeare and his Elizabethan contemporaries." Each year a summer Shakespeare Festival is held in the Delacorte Theatre in New York City's Central Park. Originally chartered by the State of New York Educational Department, the organization also has an Off-Broadway theater center at the Joseph Papp Public Theater. Until his death in 1991, Papp guided the organization and established its influence with many successful productions; one of the most well-known of which was *A Chorus Line* (1975). When Papp died in 1991, JoAnne Akalaitis was named his successor. In 1993, she was dismissed and George C. Wolfe became artistic director, with Kevin Kline as artistic associate.

Odeon: This Paris theater was built in 1782 to house the Comédie-Française, Europe's oldest operating theater company. In addition, the Odeon has been the home of other important French companies. It also served as a showcase for the best productions of the decentralization movement, which began in the early decades of the 20th century, launched by French theaters located outside the perimeter of the city of Paris. It is still used as a theatrical venue for foreign as well as French companies.

Old Vic Theatre: Constructed on the South Bank of London's Thames River, the Old Vic opened in 1818 to present melodrama. In 1833 the theater, which was originally named the Coburg, was renamed the Royal Victoria. It was nicknamed the Old Vic and gradually sank to the level of a "blood-tub," the lowest type of "gaff," or melodrama theater in the poorer section of London. The building was subsequently closed and sold, reopening in December 1880. In 1914, under the visionary management of Lilian Baylis, the theater presented its first Shakespeare season. It was damaged during World War II and repaired, reopening in 1950. From 1953 to 1958, the thirty-six plays in Shakespeare's First Folio were presented; from 1963 to 1976 the building became home to England's National Theatre. The Prospect Theatre Company used it for a few years, but then it stood empty until 1983, when it was bought by a Canadian businessman.

Open Theatre: Founded in 1963 by Joseph Chaikin, who had previously been a member of the Living Theatre, the Open Theatre became a respected Off-Off Broadway avant-garde group in New York. Among the group's best-known productions were *Viet Rock* (1966), *The Serpent* (1969) and *Terminal* (1970). The group disbanded in 1973.

Palace Theatre: A Broadway house built in 1913 by Martin Beck, it became a flagship of the Keith circuit and a popular vaudeville house. A common ambition for vaudevillians was the desire "to play the Palace." It became a movie theater in the 1930s and home to

Broadway musicals following its 1965 renovation. The most recent was *The Will Rogers Follies* (1991).

Playwrights Horizons: Founded in 1971 by Robert Moss, this New York City theater develops and produces new scripts, and presents readings, workshops and complete productions in its two theaters. Several of its productions, such as *Sunday in the Park with George* (1982), moved to Broadway, where they were given full-scale productions and enjoyed successful runs.

Provincetown Players: Susan Glaspell and her husband, George Cram Cook, founded the group in 1915 in Provincetown, Massachusetts. After their highly successful second season—due mainly to productions of *Bound East for Cardiff* and *Thirst*, both by Eugene O'Neill—they moved to New York's Greenwich Village. O'Neill became one of three in charge of the Provincetown Players in 1923 (the others were Robert Edmond Jones and Kenneth Macgowan); they presented several O'Neill plays, as well as work by other developing playwrights. The group folded in 1929.

Ridiculous Theatrical Company: Founded by Charles Ludlam in New York in 1967, this Off-Off Broadway theater was managed by him until his death in 1987, when Everett Quinton took over. Their witty productions often feature cross-dressing and other gender play.

Rose Theatre: One of London's oldest theaters, the Rose was unearthed during excavations in 1989. Originally built in 1587, it was most likely a fourteen-sided polygonal structure, with a stage about eighteen feet deep (smaller than the Globe's) that tapered toward the audience. Experts assume it featured an open yard encircled by a three-tiered gallery, and a thatched roof. Shakespeare's *Henry IV* was presented there in 1592. The Rose housed several companies, including Strange's Men,

the Admiral's Men and the Worcester's Men. It was demolished between 1605 and 1606.

Royal Court Theatre: This London theater opened in 1888 and was extensively renovated after bomb damage in 1940. Its early seasons featured works by George Bernard Shaw and others of the European avant-garde. After twenty years as a movie house, it reopened as a stage theater in 1952 and, beginning in 1956, mounted many important productions of the English Stage Company.

Royal Shakespeare Company: After the appointment of Peter Hall as director in 1961, Stratford's Shakespeare Memorial Company captured the attention of audiences and critics. It was Hall who changed the name of this English company to the Royal Shakespeare Company. In 1968 Trevor Nunn became artistic director, a position he held until 1986, when co-director Terry Hands took over. The RSC is divided into several groups: The Stratford-based Shakespearean company; the London-based company, which presents modern and experimental plays and classics at the Barbican Centre; and the touring company.

Swan Theatre: A sketch of this theater's interior, dating from 1596, was published in 1888. Its discovery caused scholars to revise their theories about Elizabethan theater. It is believed that a controversial production presented at the Swan in 1597 is likely to have prompted a prohibition on play performances in London. The Royal Shakespeare Company opened a new Swan Theatre at Stratford-upon-Avon in 1986.

Theatre Guild: The Theatre Guild of New York City was formed in 1919 as a successor to the defunct Washington Square Players. During the 1920s it mounted the works of Shaw, O'Neill, Maxwell Anderson, Robert E. Sherwood and others. Because of financial and artistic conflicts during the 1930s, some members of the Theatre Guild broke away and formed two other theater groups, the Playwrights' Company and the Group Theatre.

Walnut Street Theatre: Opened in 1809 in Philadelphia, the Walnut Street Theatre is the oldest active playhouse in America. For the better part of the 19th century it housed an important stock company.

Washington Square Players: New York's Washington Square Players (1914–18) are remembered for their productions of several foreign plays, as well as for being the group from which emerged the founders of the Theatre Guild.

Winter Garden Theatre: Opened in 1911, the Winter Garden served as a flagship for the Shuberts in New York. William A. Swasey was the original architect, but it was remodeled in the 1920s by Herbert Krapp. Its seating capacity is greater than that of most Broadway houses due to a very wide auditorium. It was home to many Al Jolson musicals in the 1910s and 1920s; in the 1930s it housed musical revues. For two periods, 1928–31 and 1945–48, it was a movie house. The musical *Cats* has had a long run at the Winter Garden.

Women's Project and Productions: This New York City group was established in 1978, originally as a program of the American Place Theatre. Its mission is to develop female talent and to rectify the underrepresentation of women artists in the American theater. It offers main-stage productions, workshops and readings.

Ziegfeld Theatre: Opened in 1927, this ornate New York theater was financed by William Randolph Hearst and designed by Joseph Urban and Thomas Lamb. Urban's murals covered the ceiling. After Florenz Ziegfeld's death in 1932, the theater became a movie house but reverted to live theater in 1944. It was torn down in 1966 and replaced by a skyscraper.

The Work of the Director

Perhaps the most important job of a play's director is to create an illusion of reality on stage and ensure its continuity throughout the production, in order that the audience may willingly suspend its disbelief and participate in the theatrical experience. The director leads an interpretive team whose job it is to transform a play script into a satisfying audience experience. Directors serve three basic functions as the leaders of this team. They first determine exactly what the playwright is trying to achieve with the play. Based on this interpretation, they next refine their directorial concept and devise a production plan that will produce the desired effect on the audience. Finally, they put their plan into action, using the script, the stage and the actors to create and sustain the illusion of reality necessary to the audience's full appreciation of the play.

In order to understand a play, the director studies its emotional and intellectual content, as well as its aesthetic qualities. He or she then determines the basic concept and style of the production. As part of the overall concept, the director considers the ideas, actions, character traits or relationships likely to arouse emotional or intellectual responses in an audience. These dramatic values might include, for example, the theme in Henrik Ibsen's *Ghosts* (1881) that the sins of the father will be visited on the sons, or the steamy sexuality of Tennessee Williams's *A Streetcar Named Desire* (1947). The director also evaluates a play's aesthetic values, which might appeal to the audience's sense of beauty. For example, the style of dialogue in a George Bernard Shaw play may delight the ear.

Actors are the director's medium. Beyond the mechanics of blocking out stage movement and composing the stage picture, the director encourages actors to reach into their imaginations and bring characters to life. The successful director shows actors how to achieve their common goal of communicating the play to the audience. Establishing guidelines to follow as they work toward that goal, the director helps actors understand those limitations while remaining free to develop their characters.

The director "blocks" the actors, instructing them on how to move about the stage. Actors might make entrances and exits, cross the stage, climb and descend stairs, run, dance or perform any number of other actions. A director also determines the "business" carried out by actors on stage—their gestures, expressions, postures and handling of stage properties.

The director coordinates actors' dialogue with movement and other stage business. In a play, dialogue consists of carefully selected and condensed speech that is organized into scenes by the playwright in order to reveal character and advance the action of the play. The director must establish a tempo, rhythm and pattern for the dialogue that both expresses the mood and atmosphere of the play and is comfortable for the actors.

Using blocking of the actors on the stage, the director sets out to create stage pictures that help communicate the playwright's meaning to the audience. The stage picture is what the audience sees at any particular moment during a performance. *Composition* is the term used to describe the design of the stage picture. When a scene encompasses the whole stage or a large part of it, the stage picture must have one or more points of emphasis. In fact, emphasis is the most important factor in the composition of the stage picture; without it, the audience has no visual clues to help them understand where to focus their attention. Emphasis also serves an aesthetic function by keeping the audience interested in watching the stage. Directors know that the human eye automatically searches for order; a stage picture has order when its composition has been organized around one or more points of emphasis.

To achieve emphasis in the stage picture, the director uses a number of techniques. He or she considers the body position of an onstage actor from the points of view of the audience and of the other actors in the scene. Body positions emphasize relationships within a scene or play. The director also uses different areas of the stage to generate emphasis, varying the location of action. On the stage, increased height always lends more emphasis to an actor, as does a large block of space surrounding him or her. Repetition, one of the most subtle means of emphasis, may involve placing an actor in a doorway or arch to repeat the visual line of his or her standing body.

Thus, directors present a three-dimensional, constantly changing picture on stage. To help them do their work, they divide the stage into six areas, called *down right, down center, down left, up left, up center* and *up right*. In theater parlance, *down* means closest to the audience and *up* means farthest away. Right and left are always determined from the perspective of an actor standing on the stage and facing the audience. Noting his or her decisions in these terms, the director chooses where to stage various scenes and how the stage should be arranged to provide the necessary playing areas. The arrangement of furniture, set pieces or architectural features should help make the actors' movements practical and natural.

Biographies of Major Directors and Producers

Abbott, George (1887–——): American director, playwright and actor. As coauthor and director, Abbott staged quintessentially American works. These include *On Your Toes* (1936), *The Pajama Game* (1954), *Damn Yankees* (1955) and *Fiorello!* (1959). In 1983 at the age of ninety-five, he staged a revival of *On Your Toes*.

Akalaitis, JoAnne (1937–——): American director and founding member of the theater company Mabou Mines. Her experimental works have been presented at theaters throughout the U.S. and Europe. In 1991, she was named artistic director of the New York Shakespeare Festival, succeeding Joseph Papp, a position she held briefly.

Anderson, Lindsay (1923–——): British director. He achieved success initially as a director while affiliated with George Devine's English Stage Company at the Royal Court Theatre during the 1950s. He directed at England's National Theatre and on Broadway, as well as in films.

Antoine, André (1858–1943): French director and actor. Founder of the Theatre Libre, a small experimental theater company, Antoine strove to present plays that dealt with contemporary issues in a naturalistic style, moving away from the melodramatic tendencies of the time. He introduced the plays of Henrik Ibsen and August Strindberg to the French as director of the Theatre Antoine and the Odeon.

Artaud, Antonin (1896–1949): French director and theoretician. His influence on theater comes largely from his book of essays, *The Theatre and its Double* (1938), in which he theorizes that Western society is out of touch with everyday reality. His "Theatre of Cruelty" attempted to create an emotional crisis in the audience, prompting it into social and individual awareness. Later directors, including Peter Brook and Jerzy Grotowski, were influenced by his ideas.

Bennett, Michael (1943–87): American director and choreographer. A former Broadway dancer, Bennett had his first directorial successes with *Promises, Promises* (1968) and *Coco* (1969). He collaborated with Harold Prince and Stephen Sondheim on *Company* (1970) and *Follies* (1971), for both of which he was both choreographer and codirector. Subsequently he directed *Seesaw* (1973), *Ballroom* (1978) and *Dreamgirls* (1981). His best-known work was his choreography and direction of *A Chorus Line* (1975), a musical about Broadway dancers that won several Tony Awards.

Brook, Peter (Stephen Paul) (1925–——): British director. Brook first gained success with the Royal Shakespeare Company. His productions for the RSC included *King Lear* (1962), *Marat/Sade* (1964), *US* (1966), which criticized U.S. intervention in Vietnam, and a production of *A Midsummer Night's Dream* (1970) set in a children's playground. His volume of essays, *The Empty Space* (1968), influenced other directors. In 1970 he assembled an eclectic creative team and established the International Centre of Theatre Research near Paris. The Centre encourages a collaborative approach to theater that transcends national and cultural boundaries. Their productions include *The Cherry Orchard* (1981), *The Tragedy of Carmen* (1985) and *The Mahabharata* (1985), a nine-hour epic that was originally performed in a quarry in France.

Chaikin, Joseph (1935–——): American director, actor and producer. Chaikin joined The Living Theatre in 1959. He formed The Open Theatre in 1963 as an experimental company to create and perform new works, such as *Terminal* (1970) and *The Serpent* (1970). He has since directed for numerous resident companies and has garnered five Obie awards. He published *The Presence of the Actor* (1972).

Clurman, Harold (1901–1980): American director, critic and author. One of his most important contributions to theater was as cofounder of the Group Theatre, where he directed five Clifford Odets plays; he wrote the book *The Fervent Years* (1945), which traced the history of the Group. He subsequently directed *The Member of the Wedding* (1950) and *Bus Stop* (1955), among other plays. Clurman served as theater critic for a number of publications, published more books and won several awards, including four honorary doctorates.

Foreman, Richard (1937–——): American director and playwright. In 1968 he founded the avant-garde Ontological-Hysteric Theatre in New York, and it continues to present only his work. His productions often utilize disturbing lighting and sound effects to disrupt the audience's thought processes. Works include *Total Recall* (1970), *Pandering to the Masses* (1975), *Le Livre de Splendeurs* (Paris, 1976), *Penguin Touquet* (1981) and *Egyptology* (1983).

Gregory, Andre (1934–——): American director and producer. Associated with the avant-garde movement of the 1960s, he founded The Manhattan Project, which adapted theater to unusual performance spaces. Their productions include *Alice in Wonderland* (1970), *Endgame* (1973), *The Seagull* (1975) and *Jinx Bridge* (1976).

Grosbard, Ulu (1929–——): Belgian-born American director. He made his New York debut with *The Days and Nights of Beebe Fenstermaker* (1962). Notable productions include *The Subject Was Roses* (1964), *A View from the Bridge* (1965), *The Investigation* (1966), *The Price* (1968), *American Buffalo* (1977), *The Wake of Jamie Foster* (1982) and *Weekends Like Other People* (1982). He has also worked in film and television.

Grotowski, Jerzy (1933–——): Polish director and theoretician. In 1965, Grotowski founded the Laboratory Theatre in Poland. His productions and theories, including his concept of a "poor theatre," have influenced world theater. His collection of writing, *Towards a Poor Theatre*, was published in 1968. He has lived in the United States since 1982.

Guthrie, Tyrone (1900–71): Anglo-Irish director. Guthrie was a popular international director of numerous Shakespeare productions and was director of the Stratford (Ontario) Festival from 1953 to 1957. His successful use of the thrust stage, which he developed at Stratford with designer Tanya Moiseiwitsch, led to public acceptance of alternative stage forms. He was a founder of Minneapolis's Guthrie Theatre, which was named after him.

Hall, Sir Peter (Reginald Frederick) (1930–——): British director and theater manager.

He was a force behind the establishment of the Royal Shakespeare Company and England's National Theatre. Director of the RSC until 1968, he succeeded Laurence Olivier as director of the National Theatre in 1971. There, he directed productions of *Tamburlane* (1976), *Bedroom Farce* (1977) and *Amadeus* (1979), which he also directed on Broadway. He was knighted in 1977 in recognition of his contributions to British culture.

Houseman, John [Jacques Haussman] (1902–88): American director, producer and author. During his career, he was affiliated with the Federal Theatre Project, the Mercury Theatre (which he cofounded in 1937 with Orson Welles) and the American Shakespeare Festival, among other companies. In 1972, Houseman founded the Acting Company, where he also directed. He published three books: *Run-Through* (1972), *Front and Center* (1981) and *Final Dress* (1983).

Kazan, Elia (1909–––––): American director. Kazan was a Group Theatre member as well as one of the founders of the Actors Studio. He is best known for directing such stage productions as *A Streetcar Named Desire* (1947), *Death of a Salesman* (1949), *Cat on a Hot Tin Roof* (1955) and *Sweet Bird of Youth* (1959). He retired as codirector of Lincoln Center's Vivian Beaumont Theater in 1964; since then, his directing appearances have been rare.

LeCompte, Elizabeth (1944–––––): American director and playwright. She has been the artistic director of the Wooster Group, New York's experimental theater collective, since 1979. In 1984, under director Peter Sellars, she was named associate director of the American National Theatre at the John F. Kennedy Center for the Performing Arts in Washington, D.C.

Logan, Joshua (1908–88): American director, producer and playwright. He was involved, in varying capacities, with many successful Broadway plays. As coauthor, director and producer he staged *South Pacific* (1949), for which he and Oscar Hammerstein received the Pulitzer Prize. He was director and coproducer of *Picnic* (1953) and director of *Mornings at Seven* (1939), *Charley's Aunt* (1940), *Annie Get Your Gun* (1946) and *Mister Roberts* (1948, coauthor). He also directed films and published two books: *Josh* (1976) and *Movie Stars, Real People and Me* (1978).

Mason, Marshall W. (1940–––––): American director. A cofounder of the Circle Repertory Company in New York (1969), he was its artistic director until 1987. He directed one of the first plays to deal with AIDS, *As Is* (1985) by William M. Hoffman. In 1983, Mason garnered an Obie Award for Sustained Achievement.

Meyerhold, Vsevolod Emilievich (1874–1940): Russian director. He began his career at the Moscow Art Theatre with Konstantin Stanislavski. Stanislavski, however, thought Meyerhold's staging of actors was "puppet-like" and asked him to leave the company. At the time, Meyerhold was developing his theories of the "actor-robot," a complex physical technique of acting. Embracing Bolshevism, he worked to incorporate political themes into his work but was eventually arrested by the Soviet government. It is believed that he was either executed or died in a prison camp. His status as a Soviet "nonperson" was revoked in 1955.

Mnouchkine, Ariane (1934–––––): French director. Her collaborative theater group, Theatre du Soleil, presents original work. The company's best-known productions under her leadership include *1789* (1970), *1793* (1972), *L'Age d'Or* (*The Golden Age*, 1975), *Mephisto* (1979), a Shakespeare cycle (1980s) and *Norodom Sihanouk* (1985), an epic about Cambodia.

Nichols, Mike [Michael Igor Peschkowsky] (1931–––––): American director, producer and actor. After establishing himself as an actor on Broadway in *An Evening with Mike Nichols and Elaine May* (1960), he made his Broadway directorial debut with *Barefoot in the Park* (1963). He subsequently directed several other Neil Simon plays, as well as *Streamers* (1976), *The Gin Game* (1977, also as producer), *The Real Thing* (1983) and *Hurlyburly* (1984). Winner of five Tony awards, he has also worked extensively in film.

Nunn, Trevor (Robert) (1940–——): British director. Nunn became the Royal Shakespeare Company's artistic director in 1968, succeeding Peter Hall. He has directed many classical productions, but his best-known work for the RSC is *The Life and Adventures of Nicholas Nickleby* (1980). He also directed *Cats* (1981) and *Starlight Express* (1984).

Papp, Joseph [Papirofsky] (1921–91): American director and producer. Papp founded the New York Shakespeare Festival in 1954, a company which has been instrumental in making theater accessible to the public in New York City. He directed several productions for the NYSF, including *Twelfth Night* (1958, 1963), *Hamlet* (1964, 1967, 1968 and 1983), *Boom Boom Room* (1973), *Buried Inside Extra* (1983) and *Measure for Measure* (1985). In 1958, he received the Tony Award for Distinguished Service to the Theatre.

Prince, Harold (1928–——): American producer and director. Prince has been involved in more than fifty successful musicals, plays and operas. As producer and coproducer he mounted *The Pajama Game* (1954), *Damn Yankees* (1955), *West Side Story* (1957), *Fiorello!* (1961) and *Fiddler on the Roof* (1964). As producer-director in collaboration with composer-lyricist Stephen Sondheim, he worked on *Company* (1970), *Follies* (1971), *A Little Night Music* (1973), *Pacific Overtures* (1976), *Sweeney Todd* (1979) and *Merrily We Roll Along* (1981). He directed *Phantom of the Opera* (London 1986; New York, 1988) and

Kiss of the Spider Woman (1993). His autobiography, *Contradictions,* was published in 1974.

Quintero, José (1924–——): Panamanian-born American director. He is a cofounder of New York's Circle in the Square Theater (1951) and a leading director of plays by Eugene O'Neill. These include *The Iceman Cometh* (1956, winner of the Vernon Rice Award), *Long Day's Journey Into Night* (1956, Tony award), *A Moon for the Misbegotten* (1958; 1973, Tony and Drama Desk awards), *Strange Interlude* (1963) and *A Touch of the Poet* (1977). He won the 1981 O'Neill Birthday Medal. His autobiography, *If You Don't Dance, They Beat You,* was published in 1974.

Rabb, Ellis (1930–——): American director, producer and actor. In 1960 he founded the Association of Producing Artists and served as its artistic director, winning an Obie and a Vernon Rice Award for his 1962–63 season. The APA joined the Phoenix Theatre in 1964; Rabb directed until the APA was disbanded in 1970. Noteworthy later productions have been *Twelfth Night* (1972), *The Royal Family* (1975), *Caesar and Cleopatra* (1977) and *Anatol* (1985). He received a Tony award for direction in 1976.

Reinhardt, Max (1873–1943): Austrian director. During the early years of the 20th century, he was one of the most successful stage directors in Europe. He incorporated new developments in acting, as well as those in stage design, into his productions. Reinhardt also directed a season of New York plays (1927–28) and Hollywood productions, including a film version of *A Midsummer Night's Dream* (1935).

Saks, Gene (1921–——): American director and actor. An actor who turned director in 1963, he is a leading director of comedy on Broadway. Some of his credits include *Mame* (1966), *Same Time, Next Year* (1975), *Brighton Beach Memoirs* (1983) and *Biloxi Blues* (1984, Tony award). He has also directed films.

Sellars, Peter (1958–——): American director. One of the youngest of America's major directors, he directed more than a hundred productions by age twenty-seven. From 1984 through 1986 he headed the American National Theatre Company at the John F. Kennedy Center for the Performing Arts in Washington, D.C. Among his productions are *Orlando* (1982), *The Visions of Simone Marchard* (1983), *Hang on to Me* (1984) and *The Count of Monte Cristo* (1985).

Serban, Andrei (1943–——): Romanian-born American director. He made his debut at La Mama, an experimental Off-Off Broadway theater, in 1970. His unconventional and often experimental works include a comic production of *The Cherry Orchard* (1977), *Agamemnon* (1977), *The Ghost Sonata* (1977), *The Marriage of Figaro* (1982), *Uncle Vanya* (1983) and *The King Stag* (1984). He has also directed several operas.

Stanislavski, Konstantin Sergeevich [Alekseev] (1863–1938): Russian director, actor and teacher. A cofounder of the Moscow Art Theatre (1898), he created the most important and widely used system of acting in the West. This regularized technique, known as the "Method," allowed actors to gain control of their bodies and emotions in order to present accurate representations of characters and plays.

Strasberg, Lee (1901–82): American director and teacher. In 1931, he cofounded the Group Theatre, which subscribed to the "Method" work of Konstantin Stanislavski. In 1950 he became director of The Actors Studio, which used the Method in its approach to productions and training. Strasberg is often remembered as a leading acting teacher and theorist.

Tune, Tommy (1939–——): Director, actor and choreographer. In 1973 he won a Tony award for his performance in *Seesaw*. He was choreographer and codirector for *The Best Little Whorehouse in Texas* (1978),

choreographer-director of *A Day in Hollywood/A Night in the Ukraine* (1981 Tony award, choreography), codirector of *Nine* (1982), and costar/codirector/cochoreographer of *My One and Only* (1983). In addition, he staged *Stepping Out* (1987) and *Grand Hotel* (1989). For the latter, he won Tony awards (1990) for direction and choreography. He codirected (with Peter Masterson) and also choreographed *The Best Little Whorehouse Goes Public* (1994) on Broadway.

Valdez, Luis (1940–——): Chicano-American director and playwright. After helping labor activist Caesar Chavez organize a strike of migrant workers in California in 1965, Valdez created El Teatro Campesino (Farmworkers' Theater), which in turn spurred the creation of other Chicano arts groups. He directed several successful productions for the company, among them *Zoot Suit* (1978) and *Corridos* (1983).

Ward, Douglas Turner (1930–——): American director, actor and playwright. He is best known as artistic director of the Negro Ensemble Company, for which he directed and played leading roles in several productions, including *Ceremonies in Dark Old Men* (1969) and *The River Niger* (1972).

Wilson, Robert (1941–——): American director. His opera-scale productions abandon the conventions of plot and character and consist of complex visual and aural imagery. Works include the eight-hour-long *Deafman Glance* (1970), *A Letter to Queen Victoria* (1974), *Einstein on the Beach* (1976) and *CIVIL warS* (sic, 1983).

Wolfe, George C. (1934–——): Director, producer and playwright. The producer of the New York Shakespeare Festival/Joseph Papp Public Theater, he won a Tony award in 1993 for the direction of *Angels in America*. He wrote *The Colored Museum* (1986), wrote and directed *Jelly's Last Jam* (1992) on Broadway, and directed Anna Deavere Smith's *Twilight: Los Angeles, 1992* at the Public and on Broadway in 1994.

The Art and Work of the Actor

As interpretive artists, actors transform the written words of a play into a theatrical experience through the dialogue and action of characters in a given set of situations. Working with the emotions, actors strive to elicit a sense of involvement and empathy from their audience. They create, expand and develop their characters, all the while attempting to remain true to the playwright's intentions. The play must be an actor's sole frame of reference. Within it, and under the guidance of a director, actors relate to other actors playing other characters, *re*acting as much as acting.

Actors use their bodies as instruments, moving to fit the demands of different characters and plots. The first law of stage movement is that every movement requires motivation and purpose. Actors can enhance character development, indicate mood, create atmosphere or reveal emotions through effective movement. They must also be able to articulate clearly and project their voices so as to be heard by the audience. To communicate the full intellectual and emotional content of each line of dialogue, they must know how to speak it. The best actors possess what the French actor Talma referred to as an "excess of sensibility"—a vivid imagination, acute awareness, insight into their role and an understanding of what the play and character are about.

The Evolution of Modern Acting

Until modern times, actors learned their trade by observation and experience. They served as actor-apprentices and worked their way up from spear carriers to speaking parts, learning what they could from veteran actors. They might receive some pointers, but in general, novice actors were on their own.

During the latter half of the 19th century, a Frenchman named Delsarte devised an elaborate system of acting based on mechanical techniques. He divided the actor's body into a trinity consisting of the torso, which he called the "vital zone," the head, called the "intellectual zone," and the face, called the "moral zone." In turn, he split each zone and every part of the mechanism into trinities, each part of which produced its own specific expression. Delsarte's students learned to act by memorizing and utilizing the appropriate gestures, vocal qualities and inflections dictated by this division of their bodies. For example, in order to depict fear, the actor opened his mouth and raised his hands to his chest, taking quick, short breaths.

Soon another school of acting emerged that was based on the inner life of characters. This approach was much better suited to the new drama of realism and naturalism, as audiences discovered after the Comédie-Française, in 1882, produced Henri Becque's naturalistic play *The Vultures* (1877) in the traditional style of acting. Defeating the realism of Becque's play, the actors used exaggerated gestures and vocal techniques, and directed much of their dialogue to the audience. In 1887, however, the Theatre Libre mounted a very different production of *The Vultures*. Its director, André Antoine, coached his actors in a naturalistic style of acting that brought the play to life. Antoine and other members of his cast used then-unconventional stage behavior; they turned their backs on the audience, spoke in a conversational style, and used fragmentary gestures of real life. The new technique confined the acting zone to their faces, and some body expression was lost, but with this and other productions Antoine helped to establish naturalistic drama in France.

The Stanislavski Method

The new interest in artistic realism demanded the invention of new methods of acting. Most famous and important among the innovators was Konstantin Stanislavski, the Russian director who helped found the Moscow Art Theatre. He formulated his method of acting during the early 20th century, and taught, directed and wrote about his technique. (His three books on acting are *An Actor Prepares, Building the Character* and *Creating a Role*.)

Stanislavski invented a system of acting that offered basic principles by which actors could refine their art. He devised a regularized technique, known as the "Method," that allowed actors to gain control of their bodies and emotions in order to interpret their characters accurately. Much of his emphasis was on preparation by means of a conscious technique that conditioned the actor to receive inspiration.

The Method starts from a series of exercises that develop actors' physical freedom on stage so that they can control their muscles, be keenly conscious during their performance, and see and hear on stage as they do in real life. According to Stanislavski, this is the foundation for effective communication among actors; it allows them to accept the circumstances of the play completely.

Building on this base, the Method then focuses on the connection between a character's inner psychological reality and external physical actions. Every physical action arises from an internal action, these two components creating an organic union. By breaking each action down in this way during the rehearsal process, actors can reach a greater understanding of the play and characters.

The Method requires an actor to ask what he or she as a person would do in a similar situation, helping to define similarities and differences between the actor and the character. In the process, the actor learns how to make a character three-dimensional and comes to understand his or her actions. Genuine emotion can result from this combination of inner reality and external action. In this way, Stanislavski believed, the Method could bring actors closest to what he defined as "metamorphosis."

The Group Theatre adapted Stanislavski's method during the 1930s. One Group Theatre veteran, Lee Strasberg, adapted Stanislavski's Method to teach American actors at the Actors Studio in New York, which he founded in 1947.

Strasberg and others developed a strenuous actor-training program, which included dance, other forms of physical movement, voice and diction, and exercises to enhance concentration, observation, imagination, improvisation and the memory of emotions. Practitioners of the Method also place great importance on the in-depth analysis of plays and characters.

The Method contrasted greatly with the "bio-mechanics" or "bio-dynamics" theory of acting followed by Stanislavski's Russian contemporary, Vsevolod Emilievich Meyerhold. Unlike Stanislavski, he believed actors should approach a role from the outside, through body and voice control. German playwright Bertolt Brecht also had little use for Stanislavski's approach in the style of epic drama that he originated. Brecht sought to alienate the audience and prevent it from identifying with his characters and plays. By doing so, he hoped to produce an intellectual, rather than emotional, response in the viewer.

Most criticism of the Method focuses on what some consider to be its abuse by performers who have outbursts during performances, distracting the audience from the play itself. But the value of the Method, applied properly, is that it can help actors approach their art in a systematic, reasoned way.

Training and Working

Permanent, residential acting companies in major cities offer the aspiring actor a place in which to learn the trade. Many countries have national academies of dramatic art. In the United States, most beginning actors find their training in community theaters or in university theater programs where academic classwork is supplemented by play production. College theaters provide excellent facilities for instruction in dramatic production.

ACTORS ON ACTING

"When I'm building a role, I start with a series of mental pictures and feel." —HUME CRONYN

"What you try to do in the theatre is to give a universal picture, through your own eyes and feelings, of the person you play. You try to be, in your way, what the person would be. You have a feeling about the thing. If you don't feel strongly about a part, or if that doesn't appeal to you, it's a mistake to do it." —KATHARINE CORNELL

"Once you set things you do and make them mean certain things, you then respond to the stimuli you yourself set up. Then you *feel*." —MAUREEN STAPLETON

"Every actor has, as a gift from God, his own method. My particular method is to go first by the sense of taste—physical taste. I actually have a physical taste for every part. Then I go to the other senses—hearing, seeing, touching. Thinking comes much later." —VLADIMIR SOKOLOFF

Only a small percentage of American actors make a living in the "legitimate" theater. Even if they do make money at their craft, stage actors in the United States face fierce competition for roles and are often unemployed for long periods, or do other work to support themselves while they audition for plays. Faced with these conditions, many turn to the film or television industry. Performers who become professional stage actors in the United States usually join the Actors' Equity Association (established 1913), the professional guild for actors which is also the union for professional stage managers.

Biographies of major Performers

American

Adams [Kiskadden], Maude (1872–1953): Actress. She began her acting career as a child and at age sixteen moved to New York, where she appeared in melodrama. For Adams, J. M. Barrie rewrote the character of Lady Babbie in the stage adaptation of his own novel, *The Little Minister* (1897). This part established her as one of America's leading actresses. Other Barrie roles in which she appeared include *Quality Street* (1901), *Peter Pan* (1905), *What Every Woman Knows* (1908) and *A Kiss for Cinderella* (1916). Adams also played classic roles, including Shakespeare's Viola, Juliet and Rosalind, and was one of America's most popular actresses.

Adler, Jacob (1855–1926): Actor. In 1887, Adler emigrated to America from Russia via London and became prominent in Yiddish-American theater. He established the Independent Yiddish Art Company, which premiered with *The Yiddish King Lear* (1892) by Jacob Gordin. Adler appeared regularly in various productions of *The Yiddish King Lear* for the rest of his career. He and his company presented several other Gordin plays over the years, as well as a Yiddish translation of *The Merchant of Venice* (1901). He played Shylock on Broadway in 1903 and 1905, performing in Yiddish while the other actors spoke in English. Adler retired in 1920 after suffering a stroke.

Adler, Stella (1901–92): Actress and acting teacher. A member of a family well known in the Yiddish theater (she was Jacob Adler's daughter), Adler joined the Group Theatre in 1931 and married its founder, Harold Clurman. She won praise for her portrayal of depression-era women in the Group Theatre's productions of *Awake and Sing!* (1935) and *Paradise Lost* (1935). She made her final New York appearance in *He Who Gets Slapped* (1945). In 1949 she founded the Stella Adler Conservatory, an acting school.

Bankhead, Tallulah (1903–68): Actress. Her first Broadway appearance was in 1918, but it was her appearance in London in *The Dancers* (1923) that started her down the road to fame. She garnered critical praise as Regina in *The Little Foxes* (1939) and won a *Variety*–New York Drama Critics' Poll for best actress as Sabina in *The Skin of Our Teeth*. With a deep, sexy voice and a reputation for the outrageous, Bankhead also played the queen in *The Eagle has Two Heads* (1947), as well as Blanche in *A Streetcar Named Desire* (1956, revival). She published her memoirs under the title *Tallulah* (1952).

Barrymore, Ethel (1879–1959): Actress. Ethel was the first of the children of Maurice Barrymore and Georgiana Drew to achieve fame as an actor. She starred on Broadway in *Captain Jinks of the Horse Marines* (1901) following a period in England as apprentice to her actress-grandmother, Mrs. John Drew (nee Louisa Lane), and her actor-uncle John Drew. Under the management of Charles Frohman she became immensely popular in the United States and Europe. Because of her theatrical lineage and her achievement in such plays as *A Doll's House* (1905), *The Second Mrs. Tanqueray* (1924), *The Constant Wife* (1926), various Shakespeare works and others, she was considered by many to be the First Lady of American Theater. In 1928 the Shuberts opened the Ethel Barrymore Theatre on Broadway, with the actress starring in *The Kingdom of God*. One of her final stage roles, Miss Moffat in *The Corn is Green* (1940), was also one of her most popular. Following her stage career, Barrymore appeared in films.

Barrymore, John (1882–1942): Actor. In his early career, the youngest child of Maurice and Georgiana Drew Barrymore appeared in farces and light comedies. Subsequently, he earned critical acclaim for his tragic roles in *Justice* (1916) and *Redemption* (1918). These were followed by what some consider to be the high points of his career, playing the title roles in the Arthur Hopkins/Robert Edmond Jones productions of *Richard III* (1920) and *Hamlet* (1922). Barrymore was considered one of America's greatest actors. He left the theater to appear in films, though he returned to the stage in 1939 to play a parody of himself in *My Dear Children*.

Barrymore, Lionel (1878–1954): Actor. The older son of American actress Georgiana Drew and Maurice Barrymore began acting at age fifteen. He learned his craft under the professional guidance of his grandmother, Mrs. John Drew (nee Louisa Lane). He first gained significant notice for his characterization in a small role in *The Mummy and the Humming Bird* (1903), in which he appeared

with his uncle John Drew. His skill at characterization was apparent in subsequent roles, including the boxer Kid Garvey in *The Other Girl* (1904). His most notable stage appearances were in *The Copperhead* (1917), *The Claw* (1921) and *Laugh, Clown, Laugh!* (1923), as well as two plays in which he costarred with his brother John Barrymore: *Peter Ibbetson* (1917) and *The Jest* (1919). Said to have referred to acting as the family curse, he left the theater for Hollywood, where he appeared in many film roles.

Booth, Edwin Thomas (1833–93): Actor and theater manager. The son of Junius Brutus Booth, he made his stage debut in 1849 and appeared in his first notable New York role in 1857. From 1864 to 1874 he managed several New York theaters, including the Winter Garden and Booth Theatre; he lost the latter in 1873 due to financial mismanagement. However, under his auspices successful productions of *Hamlet, Julius Caesar, The Merchant of Venice, Othello* and *Richelieu* were mounted. He is considered by some scholars to be the most popular tragic actor of his age. In 1888, Booth helped to found The Players, a club for actors and other interested individuals. The last years of his career were spent touring the United States and Europe; he made his final stage appearance in the title role of *Hamlet* (1891) at the Brooklyn Academy of Music. His brother, Junius Brutus Booth, Jr., (1821–83) was a noted manager-producer; another brother was John Wilkes Booth, the assassin of U.S. President Abraham Lincoln.

Booth, John Wilkes (1839–65): Actor. The son of Junius Brutus Booth and a brother of Edwin Booth, he made his first professional acting appearance in Baltimore as Richmond in *Richard III* (1855). He played the title role in the play in New York in 1862, by which time he had already established himself as an actor by touring the United States. His final performance was in *The Apostate* (1865) at Ford's Theatre in Washington, D.C. In April 1865, Booth assassinated President Lincoln at the same theater during a performance of *Our American Cousin.*

Booth, Junius Brutus (1796–1852): Actor. Born in England and first famous in London, he spent most of his career in the United States. He made his American debut in the title role of *Richard III* (1821). Other important roles included Shakespeare's Hamlet, Iago and Cassius. An important American tragedian, he was often compared to the English actor Edmund Kean, who was considered a rival. Booth also gained notoriety in America for his drinking and eccentric behavior.

Brice, Fanny (1891–1951): Comedienne and singer. She was featured in many Broadway revues, including various Ziegfeld Follies beginning in 1910. A popular star noted for her comedic talents, she also had a way with comic songs and torch songs. She appeared in musical plays, including *Honeymoon Express* (1913), *Nobody Home* (1915), *The Music Box Revue 1924–25, Fioretta* (1929), *Sweet and Low* (1930) and *Billy Rose's Crazy Quilt* (1931).

Cohan, George M(ichael) (1878–1942): Musical performer, writer, songwriter and producer. His first stage appearances were as a child with his family, as a member of the vaudeville team The Four Cohans. His New York debut was in the full-length play *The Governor's Son* (1901), which he authored. He was producing partners with Sam H. Harris from 1904 until 1920 and opened the George M. Cohan Theatre in 1911. Cohan was an important figure of the American musical comedy stage; among his most noteworthy plays are *Little Johnny Jones* (1904, including the songs "Yankee Doodle Boy" and "Give My Regards to Broadway"), *Forty-five Minutes from Broadway* (1905), *The Talk of New York* (1907), *Get-Rich-Quick Wallingford* (1910), *Seven Keys to Baldpate* (1913), *The Tavern* (1921) and *The*

Song and Dance Man (1923). His song "Over There" (1917) won him a Congressional Medal of Honor.

Cornell, Katharine (1893–1974): Actress. Considered one of the leading American actresses of her time, Cornell first appeared with the Washington Square Players in 1916. She is remembered for her interpretation of roles in plays by George Bernard Shaw, William Shakespeare, Anton Chekhov and Somerset Maugham. She played the title role in Shaw's *Candida* for several different productions, beginning in 1924. Directed by her husband Guthrie McClintic, she gave an acclaimed performance as Elizabeth Barrett in *The Barretts of Wimpole Street* (1931). Her last appearance was as Mrs. Patrick Campbell in *Dear Liar* (1960). Her memoirs, *I Wanted to Be an Actress,* were published in 1939.

Cronyn, Hume (1911–——): Canadian-born actor, director, writer. He made his professional acting debut in 1931 and his Broadway debut in 1934 in *Hipper's Holiday*. In 1942 he married the actress Jessica Tandy. Cronyn and Tandy first performed together in *The Fourposter* (1951), prompting the comparison to the husband-wife acting team of Lunt-Fontanne. The plays in which they have co-starred include *The Physicists* (1964), *A Delicate Balance* (1966), *Noel Coward in Two Keys* (1974), *The Gin Game* (1977), *Foxfire* (1982) and *The Petition* (1986). They have also appeared together in many films.

Dewhurst, Colleen (1926–91): Actress. Early in her career, Dewhurst appeared mainly Off-Broadway. On Broadway she received Tony awards for Mary Follet in *All the Way Home* (1960) and Josie in a revival of *A Moon for the Misbegotten* (1973). She became known for her performances in O'Neill plays, though she performed successfully in classics as well. She appeared in 1988 revivals of *Ah! Wilderness* and *Long Day's Journey into Night*.

Drew, John (1827–62): Actor. Though his career was short-lived, he achieved success playing Irish characters. He also became known for his portrayal of eccentric characters, such as Meddle in *London Assurance*, William in *Black-Eyed Susan* and Sir Lucius O'Trigger in *The Rivals*. Beginning in 1853 he took over management, with his wife (nee Louisa Lane), of the Arch Street Theatre in Philadelphia. Shortly before her husband's death, Louisa became sole manager, a position she successfully held for thirty years.

Drew, John (1853–1927): Actor. A son of John and Louisa Drew, he trained under his mother at the Arch Street Theatre in Philadelphia before moving to New York. Drew garnered favorable reviews for his New York and London performances of Petruchio in *The Taming of the Shrew* during the 1880s. A star of the American stage for almost thirty-five years, he published his memoirs, *My Years on the Stage*, in 1922.

Drew, Mrs. John (Louisa Lane) (1820–97): American actress and theater manager. Originally a child star, Mrs. John Drew became an important presence in American theater. In addition to being the matriarch of the Drew-Barrymore family, she managed the Arch Street Theatre in Philadelphia, first with her husband and then single-handedly. From 1861 to 1892 it thrived as one of America's greatest stock companies. Drew toured frequently from 1880 to 1892 as Mrs. Malaprop in *The Rivals*, one of her best-known roles. Her actress daughter Georgiana (1856–93) married English actor Maurice Barrymore in 1876.

Evans, Maurice (1901–89): English-born American actor. He joined the Old Vic company in 1934, where he played leading Shakespearean roles. Coming to New York in 1935, he played Romeo to Katharine Cornell's Juliet, receiving critical acclaim. Evans was considered a master of Shakespearean roles. Other successes include a long Broadway run in *Dial M*

for Murder (1952). He was also coproducer of two Broadway hits, *The Teahouse of the August Moon* (1953) and *No Time for Sergeants* (1955) and appeared on television and occasionally in films.

Ferrer, José (1912–92): Actor, producer and director. As an actor, Ferrer achieved successes as Lord Fancourt Babberley in a revival of *Charley's Aunt* (1940), as Iago to Paul Robeson's Othello (1943) and in the title character in *Cyrano de Bergerac* (1946), for which he received a Tony award in 1947. In 1947 he became a director of the New York City Theatre Company at City Center, where he produced and appeared in several productions. One of these was an acclaimed performance as Jim Downs in *The Shrike* (1952), for which he received Tony awards as actor and director.

Fiske, Minnie Maddern [Marie Augusta Davey] (1864–1932): Actress and director. Born into a show-business family, she was considered one of America's best actresses. A successful child actress, she made her adult New York debut in *Fogg's Ferry* (1882). After marrying Harrison Grey Fiske, editor of the *New York Dramatic Mirror*, in 1890, she wrote several one-act plays and promoted realism and the work of Henrik Ibsen. In 1893 she appeared in *Hester Crewe*, a play by her husband. While remembered for her performances in plays such as *Tess of the D'Urbervilles* (1897), *Hedda Gabler* (1903) and *Ghosts* (1927), she is also known for her conflicts with the Trust (the Theatrical Syndicate), a group that controlled major American playhouses. Her final appearance on a New York stage was in *It's a Grand Life* (1930).

Fontanne, Lynn (1887–1983): English-born actress. She and her husband, actor-director Alfred Lunt, gained a reputation as the foremost acting couple in the American theater when they joined the Theatre Guild in the 1920s. Some of their most popular performances were in plays by George Bernard Shaw, Robert Sherwood, Noel Coward and Jean Giraudoux. In the 1930s their most memorable performances were in plays written specifically for them, including *Elizabeth the Queen* (1930) and *Reunion in Vienna* (1931). They appeared with Noel Coward in his *Design for Living* (1933). The couple performed throughout the 1940s and 1950s, and in 1958 appeared in *The Visit* at New York's former Globe Theatre, which was renamed the Lunt-Fontanne to coincide with the opening of the show.

Forrest, Edwin (1806–72): Actor. Considered one of the greatest tragic actors of the American stage, Forrest made his major debut as Norval in the play *Douglas* (1820) at the Walnut Street Theatre in Philadelphia. During the next few years he toured in roles for which he would become known, including Damon in *Damon and Pythias* and Tell in *William Tell*. His New York debut was in the title role of *Othello* (1826). He also performed the title roles in *King Lear, Hamlet, Macbeth* and *Metamora*. In 1849 his rivalry with the English actor William Macready caused the Astor Place Riots, when fans loyal to Forrest attacked the New York theater where Macready was performing, causing several deaths and injuries. Forrest's popularity decreased, though he continued to perform until shortly before his death.

Gordon [Jones], Ruth (1896–1985): Actress and screenwriter. Her acting debut was as Nibs in a revival of *Peter Pan* (1915). She subsequently gave successful performances in many plays, including *Saturday's Children* (1927) and *Ethan Frome* (1936). She made her London debut in *The Country Wife* (1936). One of her best-known later stage roles was as Dolly Levi in *The Matchmaker* (London, 1954; New York, 1955). She cowrote several screenplays with her husband, Garson Kanin, and appeared in several films.

Harrigan, Edward (1845–1911): Actor and playwright. He wrote the sketches and lyrics to the songs that made Harrigan and Hart (Tony Hart) a highly popular vaudeville attraction. Harrigan went on to write extended playlets that became so popular that he turned them into full-length musicals. These works, centering on the life of the Mulligan family, included *The Mulligan Guards' Ball* (1879), *The Mulligan Guards' Surprise* (1880), *The Mulligans' Silver Wedding* (1880) and *Cordelia's Aspirations* (1883). Harrigan and Hart separated when their New York playhouse, the Theatre Comique, burned down in 1884, though Harrigan enjoyed another important success with *Reilly and the Four Hundred* (1890).

Harris, Julie (1925–———): Actress. She made her Broadway debut in *It's a Gift* (1945), but it was not until her performance as Frankie Addams in *The Member of the Wedding* (1950) that she received noteworthy critical attention. Other successes include roles in *I Am a Camera* (1951), *Skyscraper* (1965), *Forty Carats* (1968), *In Praise of Love* (1974) and a tour of *The Belle of Amherst* (1976), a one-woman show about Emily Dickinson. In 1993 she appeared Off-Broadway in *The Fiery Furnace*. Harris has received five Tony awards. She has also appeared on television and in film and wrote *Julie Harris Talks to Young Actors* (1972).

Hart, Tony (1855–91): Actor. He is remembered almost soley for his partnership with Edward Harrigan, whom he met when he was sixteen, as half of the popular vaudeville team of Harrigan and Hart. Hart's boyishness and tenor voice complemented Harrigan's fatherly looks and baritone voice. His best-known role was one that recurred in the duo's series of plays about the Mulligan family: He performed in black face as the family's maid, Rebecca. (See *Harrigan, Edward*.)

Hayes [Brown], Helen (1900–93): Actress. Considered one of the finest actresses of the

American theater, Hayes began acting professionally as a child. A major adult success came with her role as Norma Besant in *Coquette* (1927). Two of her best-known stage roles included Mary Stuart in *Mary of Scotland* (1933) and Queen Victoria in *Victoria Regina* (1935); her London debut was as Amanda Wingfield in *The Glass Menagerie* (1948). She also appeared in *Happy Birthday* (1946), *The Wisteria Trees* (1950), *Mrs. McThing* (1952), *Time Remembered* (1957), *A Touch of the Poet* (1958), *The Show-Off* (1967) and *Harvey* (1970), as well as in films and on television. In 1955 the Fulton Theatre was renamed the Helen Hayes in her honor. It was torn down in 1982 to make way for a hotel, and the following year the Little Theatre was renamed the Helen Hayes.

Hirsch, Judd (1935–——): Actor. His New York stage credits include *Barefoot in the Park* (1966), *The Hot l Baltimore* (1973), *Knock Knock* (1976), *Chapter Two* (1977), *Talley's Folly* (1979), *The Seagull* (1983), *I'm Not Rappaport* (1985) and *Conversations with My Father* (1992, Tony award). Hirsch appears extensively on television and in films.

Jefferson, Joseph (III) (1829–1905): Actor. One of the most popular comedic actors of the 19th century, Jefferson came from a theatrical family and as a youth began to act in supporting roles. In 1857 he was hired by actress-manager Laura Keene to be a member of her company, with which he played successfully in *The Heir-at-Law* and *Our American Cousin*. He achieved fame as the title character in *Rip Van Winkle* (beginning 1865) in both the London and New York productions, a role he played for several years. He produced his own version of *The Rivals* (1880), and his performance as Bob Acres to Mrs. John Drew's Mrs. Malaprop was critically praised. He made his final stage appearance in 1904.

Lansbury, Angela [Brigid] (1925–——): London-born actress. After first appearing successfully in film, Lansbury came to Broadway, where her early roles were as the wife in *Hotel Paradiso* (1957) and as Helen in *A Taste of Honey* (1960). She is perhaps best known for her musical-theater roles, the first of which was Cora Hoover Hoople in Stephen Sondheim's *Anyone Can Whistle* (1964). She played the leads in the musicals *Mame* (1966), *Dear World* (1969), a revival of *Gypsy* (1974) and *Sweeney Todd* (1979), the last two garnering her Tony awards.

Le Gallienne, Eva (1899–1991): English-born actress and producer. Le Gallienne made her London debut in 1914. Her first American successes were as Julie in *Liliom* (1921) and Princess Alexandra in *The Swan* (1923). In 1926 she founded the Civic Repertory Theatre, which presented classics and new plays at affordable prices. She directed and acted in many productions with the company until it disbanded in 1933. A success in her later career was as Fanny Cavendish in a revival of *The Royal Family* (1975). She is author of *At 33* (1934) and *With a Quiet Heart* (1953).

Lunt, Alfred (1892–1977): Actor and director. With his wife, Lynn Fontanne, he was half of one of the most popular and successful husband/wife acting teams in American theater. Lunt had had a successful career before meeting Fontanne, but after their marriage in 1922 they performed only as a team for almost forty years. (See *Fontanne, Lynn*.)

Marlowe, Julia (1866–1950): English-born actress. She began her career as a child and made her adult New York debut in *Ingomar* (1887). During the next decade she appeared in *The Hunchback* and *The Rivals* (1896), gaining in popularity. Following her separation from her first husband, Richard Taber, with whom she had acted for several years in Shakespearean roles, she created the title role in *Barbara Frietchie* (1899) and appeared in

When Knighthood Was in Flower (1901). Later in her career Marlowe and her second husband, E. H. Sothern, became known for their successful acting partnership in Shakespeare's plays. She retired from the stage in 1924.

Martin, Mary (1913–90): Actress and singer. She made her Broadway debut in 1938 in the musical *Leave It to Me*. Her best-known stage roles were in productions of the Rodgers and Hammerstein musicals *South Pacific* (1949) and *The Sound of Music* (1959), as well as in the leading role of *Peter Pan* (1954).

Merman [Zimmerman], Ethel (1909–84): Actress and singer. One of America's leading musical comedy stars, Merman had roots in cabaret and vaudeville. She made her Broadway debut in *Girl Crazy* (1930). Her starring role in *Anything Goes* (1934) was the first in many Cole Porter musicals; others included *Red, Hot and Blue* (1936), *Du Barry Was a Lady* (1939), *Panama Hattie* (1940) and *Something for the Boys* (1943). Other well-known performances were in *Annie Get Your Gun* (1946) and *Gypsy* (1959). She also appeared in films.

Mostel, Zero [Samuel Joel] (1915–77): Actor. He made his Broadway debut in 1942 in the musical revue *Keep 'Em Laughing*. His best-known stage successes were as Leopold Bloom in *Ulysses in Nighttown* (1958; revived 1974), John in *Rhinoceros* (1961), Pseudolus in an adaptation of a Plautus play called *A Funny Thing Happened on the Way to the Forum* (1962), and as the original Tevye in *A Fiddler on the Roof* (1964; revived 1976). He also appeared in films.

Page, Geraldine (1924–87): Actress. Her first noteworthy performance was in the New York revival of *Summer and Smoke* (1952), for which she received critical acclaim. Her Broadway debut was as Lily in *Midsummer* (1953). Other performances included the plays *The Rainmaker* (1954), *Sweet Bird of Youth* (1959), *The Three Sisters* (1964), *Absurd*

Person Singular (1974) and *Agnes of God* (1982). She also appeared extensively in film.

Parsons, Estelle (1927–——): Actress. Known to film audiences for her Academy Award–winning performance in *Bonnie and Clyde* (1967), Parsons appeared on Broadway in *The Seven Descents of Myrtle* (1968), *And Miss Reardon Drinks A Little* (1971) and *The Pirates of Penzance* (1981). Off-Broadway she appeared in a one-woman show, *Miss Margarida's Way* (1977). She has also appeared most recently in *Extended Forecast* (1993). She now works in regional theater as well as in films.

Peters, Bernadette (1948–——): Actress, singer and dancer. She made her stage debut at age thirteen in the road company of *Gypsy*. A popular musical star since her success in the Off-Broadway musical *Dames at Sea* (1968), she has appeared on Broadway in *On the Town* (1971), *Mack and Mabel* (1972), *Sunday in the Park with George* (1984), *Song and Dance* (1985, 1986 Tony award), *Into the Woods* (1987) and *The Goodbye Girl* (1993).

Rivera, Chita [Dolores Conchita Figueroa Del Rivero] (1933–——): Actress and dancer. She was a chorus member in several musicals before receiving critical attention in *Shoestring Revue* (1955). Her early roles included performances in *Seventh Heaven* (1955) and *Mister Wonderful* (1956). She originated the role of Anita in *West Side Story* (1957) and starred in *Bye, Bye Birdie* (1960), *Bajour* (1964), *Chicago* (1975), *Merlin* (1983), *The Rink* (1984, Tony award), *Jerry's Girls* (1985) and *Kiss of the Spider Woman* (1993), for which she garnered a Tony.

Robeson, Paul (1898–1976): Actor and singer. After his stage debut in 1921, he appeared in noteworthy productions of *All God's Chillun Got Wings* (1924) and *The Emperor Jones* (1925). He performed the role of Joe in the London production of *Show Boat* (1928) and in the 1932 New York revival. One of his greatest successes was as Othello to José Ferrer's Iago in 1943; he had previously played the role in London in 1930. An African-American, Robeson was an outspoken critic of racism as well as a communist supporter. His autobiography was called *Here I Stand* (1958).

Sands, Diana (1934–73): Actress. One of the first African-American actresses to appear on the New York stage in leading roles. After several Off-Broadway plays, she acted on Broadway in *A Raisin in the Sun* (1959). She won critical acclaim for her performance in *Blues for Mister Charlie* (1964). The first play in which she crossed racial boundaries was *The Owl and the Pussycat* (1964).

Sothern, E. H. (1859–1933): Considered one of the great Shakespearean actors of his day, Sothern made his stage debut in New York in *Brother Sam* (1879). He was a member of Daniel Frohman's Lyceum Theatre company from 1885 to 1898, where he had one of his greatest successes playing a dual role in *The Prisoner of Zenda* (1895). His career peaked when he acted in Shakespearean roles opposite his second wife, Julia Marlowe, beginning in 1904.

Tandy, Jessica (1909–——): English-born actress. She made her Broadway debut in 1930 in *The Matriarch* and received critical acclaim for her performance as Blanche in *A Streetcar Named Desire* (1947, Tony award 1948). She acted with her husband, Hume Cronyn, in *The Fourposter* (1951), *The Physicists* (1964), *A Delicate Balance* (1966), *Noel Coward in Two Keys* (1974), *The Gin Game* (1977), *Foxfire* (1982, Tony award) and *The Petition* (1986). She has also appeared with and without Cronyn in films.

Welles, (George) Orson (1915–85): Actor and director. He made his first stage appearance in 1931 at the Gate Theatre in Dublin and gained some notice for his 1933–34 performances opposite Katharine Cornell in *Romeo and Juliet, Candida* and *The Barretts of Wimpole Street*. In 1936 he directed an all-black version of *Macbeth* for the Federal Theatre Project. He was cofounder, with John Houseman, of the Mercury Theatre, where he directed and played Brutus in a modern-dress version of *Julius Caesar* (1937). After adapting, directing and appearing in Jules Verne's *Around the World in 80 Days* (1946), he did not appear on the New York stage again until 1956, when he played Lear at New York's City Center. He also directed and appeared in films.

Worth, Irene (1916–——): Actress. She spent much of her career in London, where she appeared at the Old Vic in *Othello* (1951) and *The Merchant of Venice* (1953), and at other theaters. In New York she appeared in *The Cocktail Party* (1950), *Toys in the Attic* (1960) and *Tiny Alice* (1964, Tony award 1965). Other New York appearances included *Sweet Bird of Youth* (1975, Tony award), *The Cherry Orchard* (1977), *The Chalk Garden* (1982) and *Lost in Yonkers* (1991, Tony award).

Australian

Anderson, Dame Judith (1898–1992): Actress. She made her debut in Australia in 1915 and came to the United States in 1918. Her New York stage appearances included *Cobra* (1924), *As You Desire Me* (1931), Lavinia in *Mourning Becomes Electra* (1932) and Gertrude to John Gielgud's *Hamlet* (1936). She made her London debut in 1937, playing Lady Macbeth to Laurence Olivier's *Macbeth*. One of her greatest performances is considered to be the title role in *Medea* (1947); she also played the nurse in a 1982 revival of the play.

Caldwell, Zoe (1933–——): Actress and director. After several seasons spent acting in Australia, England and Canada, she debuted in the United States at the Guthrie Theatre and then in New York in *The Devils* (1965). She is best known for her roles in *The Prime of Miss Jean Brodie* (1968) and *Medea* (1982), for which she received Tony awards.

Austrian

Lenya, Lotte (1900–81): Singer and actress. A foremost interpreter of Bertolt Brecht's plays, she helped to popularize his work internationally. She was best known for her performances of Brechtian roles, such as Jenny Smith in *Little Mahagonny* (1927) and Pirate Jenny in *The Threepenny Opera* (1928). Appearances in other plays included the New York and London productions of *Brecht on Brecht* (1962). She was married to the composer Kurt Weill, who wrote the scores for many of Brecht's works.

British

Alleyn, Edward (1566–1626): Actor. One of the best-known figures in Elizabethan theater, he was the leading actor of the Admiral's Men theater company, for which Christopher Marlowe was the chief dramatist. Alleyn appeared in Marlowe's *The Tragical History of Doctor Faustus* (c. 1589), *The Jew of Malta* (c. 1590) and *Tamburlaine the Great* (c. 1587). He was considered a rival of the leading Shakespearean actor, Richard Burbage.

Ashcroft, Dame Peggy (1907–91): Actress. She made her stage debut in England in 1926 and her New York debut in 1937 in *High Tor*. A noted early performance was as Juliet in *Romeo and Juliet* (1935), opposite Laurence Olivier and John Gielgud, who alternated as Romeo in Gielgud's production. Among her many successful roles was Nina in *The Seagull* (1936), the dual role of a prostitute and her supposed male cousin in *The Good Woman of Setzuan* (1956) and the title role in *Hedda Gabler* (1954). In 1962, a theater named for her was opened in London.

Bates, Alan (1934–——): Actor. He studied at the Royal Academy of Dramatic Arts and first appeared in London in *The Mulberry Bush* (1956). He made his Broadway debut as Cliff in *Look Back in Anger* (1957). After garnering critical praise as Edmund Tyrone in *Long Day's Journey into Night* (1958), he created the role of Mick in *The Caretaker* (1960) and played the title role in *Butley* (1971). He then repeated his London roles in *The Caretaker* and *Butley* in New York. Most recently, he has appeared mainly in films, restricting his live performances to the London stage.

Burbage, Richard (c. 1567–1619): Actor. He was the son of James Burbage (c. 1530–97), who built the Theatre, the first permanent playhouse in London. The leading member of the Lord Chamberlain's Men for more than twenty years, he originated such Shakespearean roles as Richard III, Lear, Othello and Hamlet. The company resided at the Globe Theatre, which was constructed by his brother, Cuthbert Burbage (c. 1566–1636), of timbers from the Theatre.

Burton [Jenkins], Richard (1925–84): Actor. He made his British stage debut in 1944; his American debut was as Richard in *The Lady's Not for Burning* (1950). He subsequently worked with leading companies in England

and the United States, and was renowned for his Shakespearean roles. Burton is remembered mainly as a film actor.

Campbell, Mrs. Patrick (Beatrice Stella Tanner) (1865–1940): Actress. Her most memorable roles included Paula in *The Second Mrs. Tanqueray* (1893) and the title role in *Hedda Gabler* (1907). She created the role of Eliza Doolittle in George Bernard Shaw's *Pygmalion* (1914). She is frequently associated with Shaw, who was one of her admirers.

Evans, Dame Edith (1888–1976): Actress. Among her best-known roles were those of Millamant in *The Way of the World* (1924) and Lady Bracknell in *The Importance of Being Earnest* (1939), which she also played in the film. She is considered one of the finest actresses of her time, known for her performances in Restoration and Shakespearean plays, as well as for her interpretations of Shaw and Chekhov.

Finney, Albert (1936–——): Actor. He began his career in 1956, enjoying his first major success in the title role of *Billy Liar* (1960). He performs in comedic as well as tragic roles. Notable performances include the title role in *Luther* (1961) and the Scottish rebel in *Armstrong's Last Goodnight* (1965). He has also appeared in many films.

Garrick, David (1717–79): Actor, dramatist and theater manager. Considered a great English actor, he first gained notice with his debut as Shakespeare's Richard III in London (1741). His acting technique was simpler and more understated than that of most actors of his time. He played contemporary theater roles as well as such Shakespearean leads as Hamlet, Macbeth, Romeo and Lear. He was a popular comedic actor as well. As manager of the Drury Lane he introduced various reforms to English theater, such as prohibiting the audience from sitting on the stage, masking stage lighting and painting naturalistic backdrops.

Gielgud, Sir John (1904–——): Actor and director. The grandnephew of English actress Ellen Terry, he made his stage debut in 1921. The success that gained him public and critical notice was the title role of *Richard of Bordeaux* (1932). He appeared in modern plays, but he made his reputation playing Shakespearean roles, notably in *Hamlet* (London, 1934; New York, 1936). In 1935 he alternated with Laurence Olivier as Romeo and Mercutio in his own production of *Romeo and Juliet*. He wrote *Early Stages* (1938) and *Stage Directions* (1963).

Guinness, Sir Alec (1914–——): Actor. In 1938, he first attracted attention playing Aguecheek in *Twelfth Night* at the Old Vic, where he established himself playing the title role in *Hamlet* (1939). That year he also played the role of Bob Acres in *The Rivals*. He made his later career mainly in films, but continued to appear on stage as well until recently.

Harrison, Rex (1908–90): Actor. He began his career in England but achieved success in the United States with his performance in the New York production of *Sweet Aloes* (1936). His most notable success was as Professor Higgins in the musical *My Fair Lady* (1956), a part he played in the film version and with which he remains associated. He was also well known as a film actor.

Irving, Henry [John H. Brodribb] (1838–1905): Actor and manager. He toured as an actor in England for ten years before achieving success in the London productions of *The Belle's Strategem* (1866) and *Hunted Down* (1866). Irving was manager of several London playhouses, including the popular Lyceum Theatre, which he managed for twenty years. He played opposite Ellen Terry in several successful Shakespearean productions at the Lyceum. Irving is considered one of England's greatest actors.

Kean, Edmund (1789–1833): Actor. He is considered one of England's best actors of tragedy. In 1814 he received critical praise for his innovative portrayal of Shylock in *The Merchant of Venice,* whom he played as a homicidal maniac. Kean's most memorable Shakespearean roles included Richard III, Hamlet, Othello, Lear, Timon and King John. His son, Charles Kean, also became a popular actor.

Langtry, Lillie [Emilie Charlotte le Breton] (1853–1929): Actress. Daughter of the Dean of Jersey, she married the diplomat Edward Langtry and became prominent in London society, forming a close friendship with King Edward VII. In 1881, she became the first English society woman to appear on stage, where she became a popular actress, as much for her physical attributes and position in society as for acting talent. She organized her own company, which toured England and the United States.

Laughton, Charles (1899–1962): Actor and director. He made his stage debut in England in *The Inspector General* (1926). From 1933 to 1934 he appeared in several plays at the Old Vic, including *The Cherry Orchard* (1933), which won him some acclaim. After appearing mainly in films, Laughton appeared in the Los Angeles production of *Galileo,* which he had adapted with Bertolt Brecht. He also directed and appeared in *Don Juan in Hell* (1951), a production which achieved much critical success.

Lawrence, Gertrude (1898–1952): Actress. She appeared mainly in musical comedy after having achieved notable success in *Private Lives* (1930). She garnered a 1952 Tony award for *The King and I* (1951), and appeared in various Noel Coward plays and in several New York productions.

Macready, William Charles (1793–1873): Actor and theater manager. Considered one of England's best tragic actors, this rival of Edmund Kean made his debut in 1810. His best-remembered performance was in *King Lear*

(1834). Macready managed both the Covent Garden (1837–39) and the Drury Lane (1841–43), where he introduced several reforms, including the concept of full rehearsals. His rivalry with American actor Edwin Forrest led to the Astor Place Riots in 1849, in which Forrest's fans attacked the New York theater where Macready was performing, killing and injuring several people.

Oldfield, Anne (1683–1730): Actress. One of England's best-known actors, Oldfield had initial success in *The Careless Husband* (1703). As Sylvia in *The Recruiting Officer* (1706) and Mrs. Sullen in *The Beaux' Stratagem* (1707), both by George Farquhar, she won critical praise. One of her best-known roles in comedy was as Lady Townly in *The Provok'd Husband* (1728).

Olivier, Laurence Kerr, Lord (1907–89): Actor and director. Considered one of England's greatest actors, Olivier made his theatrical debut in 1922 in a schoolboys' performance of *The Taming of the Shrew*. In 1937 he joined the Old Vic, where he gained notice for his performance in a production of *Hamlet* (1937). His acclaimed performances include Shakespearean roles: Henry V, Coriolanus, Richard III, Macbeth, Othello, King Lear and both Romeo and Mercutio in *Romeo and Juliet*. He appeared in modern dramas, as well as in many films. In 1963 he was named director of England's first National Theatre at the Old Vic.

Plowright, Joan (1929–——): Actress. She became known for appearances in contemporary plays, such as *The Lesson* (1958) and *A Taste of Honey* (1960), but she also appeared in many successful productions of classics by Shakespeare, Ibsen, Chekov and others. She married Laurence Olivier in 1961.

Redgrave, Lynn (1943–——): Actress and writer. Daughter of actors Michael Redgrave and Rachel Kempson, she made her professional debut in a London production of *A*

Midsummer Night's Dream (1962). She then became one of the founding members of England's National Theatre. She made her Broadway debut in *Black Comedy* (1967). Other Broadway credits include roles in *My Fat Friend* (1974), *Knock Knock* (1976), *Mrs. Warren's Profession* (1976), *Sweet Sue* (1987) and the one-woman show *Shakespeare for My Father* (1993), which she wrote. She has also appeared extensively in regional theater, film and television.

Redgrave, Sir Michael (1908–85): Actor. He made his professional debut in 1934 and acted with many leading English companies. With Sir John Gielgud, Sir Laurence Olivier and Sir Ralph Richardson, he is considered one of the major English actors of the 20th century. His best-known roles include Rakitin in *A Month in the Country* (1943) and several Shakespearean roles, such as Richard II, Hamlet, Prospero, Shylock, Lear and Antony. He appeared successfully in films and wrote the books *The Actor's Ways and Means* (1953) and *Mask or Face* (1958); his autobiography, *In My Mind's Eye*, was published in 1983. His daughters, Vanessa Redgrave and Lynn Redgrave, and his son, Corin Redgrave, are also actors.

Redgrave, Vanessa (1937–——): Actress. Daughter of actors Michael Redgrave and Rachel Kempson, she debuted with her father in the London production of *A Touch of the Sun* (1958). Other well-known roles include Rosalind in *As You Like It* (1961), Nina in *The Seagull* (1964) and Jean in *The Prime of Miss Jean Brodie* (1966). She made her Broadway debut as Ellida in *The Lady from the Sea* (1976). She played Lady Torrance in *Orpheus Descending* in London (1988) and New York (1989). She has also appeared extensively in film.

Richardson, Sir Ralph (1902–83): Actor. His stage debut was in 1921, but it was not until after joining the Old Vic Theatre company in

1930 that he became one of Britain's leading actors. Throughout his career he played roles in plays by William Shakespeare, George Bernard Shaw and other classical and modern authors. His final stage performance was in David Storey's *Early Days* (1980).

Rutherford, Dame Margaret (1892–1972): Actress. She established her talent with her portrayal of Aunt Bijou Furze in Sir John Gielgud's production of *Spring Meeting* (1938). Other successful roles include Madame Arcati in *Blithe Spirit* (1941), Lady Bracknell in *The Importance of Being Earnest* (1947) and Lady Wishfort in *The Way of the World* (1953). She was particularly known for her skill in comedy and appeared in films as well.

Scofield, Paul (1922–——): Actor. He played a variety of classic and modern roles, his best known being Sir Thomas More in *A Man for All Seasons* (1960) and Lear in Peter Brook's production of *King Lear* (1962) with the Royal Shakespeare Company. He has appeared in many plays by contemporary authors such as John Osborne, Christopher Hampton and Athol Fugard.

Siddons, Sarah (1755–1831): Actress. One of the most respected English actresses of tragedy, she won acclaim as Isabella in *The Fatal Marriage* (1782) and Belvidera in *Venice Preserved* (1782), as well as in Shakespearean roles. Her best-known role was as Lady Macbeth, with which she made her farewell appearance in 1812.

Smith, Dame Maggie [Margaret Natalie] (1934–——): Actress. Among Smith's early performances were roles in *As You Like It* and *Richard III* (1959–60) with the Old Vic company. Also at the Old Vic, she appeared in *The Rehearsal* (1961), as well as in the double bill *The Private Ear* and *The Public Eye* (1962), for which she garnered critical praise. During the first season of England's National Theatre, she appeared in *The Recruiting Officer*, *Miss Julie* and *Hay Fever* (1963–64). Since the

1960s she has appeared extensively in film, but she has also spent many seasons with the Stratford Festival company in Ontario. She won a 1990 Tony award for her performance in *Lettice and Lovage*.

Terry, Dame Ellen Alice (1847–1928): Actress. She made her first stage appearance as a child. In 1878, she began a twenty-five-year collaboration with the actor-manager Henry Irving, during which she played opposite him in several Shakespearean roles, including Ophelia, Portia, Viola and Beatrice. George Bernard Shaw wrote for her the role of Lady Cecily Waynflete in *Captain Brassbound's Conversion* (1906). She also toured the United States and Australia, teaching Shakespeare. Actor Sir John Gielgud is her grandnephew.

Thorndike, Dame Sybil (1882–1976): Actress. She made her London debut in 1908 and acted at the Old Vic from 1914 to 1918, playing Shakespearean heroines and characters like Puck in *A Midsummer Night's Dream*. Her most distinguished performances after World War I include the title role in *Saint Joan* (1923). During World War II she toured; after the war she appeared in many contemporary plays, among them *The Linden Tree* (1947) and *Family Reunion* (1957).

Ustinov, Peter Alexander (1921–———): Actor, dramatist and director. He made his London debut in a 1939 sketch performed at the Players' Theatre, which was run in the style of a Victorian cabaret. He has acted in many of his own plays, including *The Indifferent Shepherd* (1948), *The Love of Four Colonels* (1951), *Romanoff and Juliet* (1956), *Photo Finish* (1962), *Halfway Up the Tree* (1967) and *The Unknown Soldier and His Wife* (Chichester, 1968; London, 1973). He has also written and acted in films.

Canadian

Lillie, Beatrice (Lady Robert Peel) (1898–1989): Actress and comedienne. In 1914, she made her revue debut in London in *Not Likely*. She then achieved great success with her New York debut in *Charlot's Revue of 1924*. She played in *Charlot's Revues* in London and New York until 1926. *An Evening with Beatrice Lillie* (1952), with which she toured the United States, England and Canada for four years, is generally considered the pinnacle of her career. Her last appearance was as Madame Arcati in *High Spirits* (1964), the musical version of *Blithe Spirit*.

Plummer, Christopher (1929–———): Actor. He started his career as a Shakespearean actor in the roles of Mark Antony, Henry V, Hamlet and Richard III, among others. He achieved recognition performing at the Stratford (Connecticut) Festival Theatre in 1955, at Stratford, Ontario, starting in 1956, and at Stratford-upon-Avon in 1961. He received a Tony award in 1973 for his portrayal of the title role in the musical *Cyrano* and has also been very active in films.

French

Bernhardt, Sarah [Henriette Rosine Bernard] (1844–1923): Actress. After making her stage debut at the Comédie-Française in 1862, she became an extremely popular international performer. In 1880 she played her best-known role, Marguerite in *La Dame aux Camelias*, which became a staple of her career. She was also famed for her roles in *Phèdre*, *L'Aiglon* and other plays; one of her most famous roles was as Hamlet.

Irish

Allgood, Sara (1883–1950): Actress. A principal player at Dublin's Abbey Theatre, she appeared in its first productions in 1904. Among her best-known roles were Widow Quin in *Playboy of the Western World* (1907), Juno Boyle in *Juno and the Paycock* (1924) and Bessie Burgess in *The Plough and the Stars* (1926). After 1940, she appeared in films.

O'Toole, Peter (1932–———): Actor. Beginning his career in 1955 at the Bristol Old Vic, he became a leading actor recognized by London critics. Notable roles include Hamlet (1963) and John Tanner in *Man and Superman* (1982). He is also a popular film actor.

Italian

Duse, Eleonora (1858–1924): Actress. Considered one of the finest tragic actors of theater, she had her first big success in *Thérèse Raquin* (1879). Duse won the praise of George Bernard Shaw in 1895, when she and Sarah Bernhardt both appeared as Magda in London productions of *Heimat*. She was also acclaimed for her roles in several of Henrik Ibsen's plays.

The Greek Theater

Modern Western drama originated with the ancient Greeks, who performed plays during festivals to honor their gods. During four artistic periods that spanned several hundred years, the first playwrights of tragedy and comedy mastered the art of poetic drama. Techniques for making and using costumes, masks and properties evolved at the same time, and theaters were built that housed audiences of thousands. The four periods in the development of ancient Greek theater overlapped and merged, but they remained distinct enough to be considered separately.

The **Dionysian, or Ritual, Period,** began with the rise of the cult of Dionysus and ended about 550 B.C. By that year, the professional actor had emerged and wooden theaters had been built, generally trapezoidal in shape. This period is considered to have ended with the establishment of the first playwriting contests.

The **Athenian, or Classical, Period** was the era of the great tragic poets Aeschylus (525–456 B.C.), Sophocles (c. 495–406 B.C.) and Euripides (480–406 B.C.), and of the comic poet Aristophanes (c. 448–c. 380 B.C.). During this period, Aristotle (384–322 B.C.) wrote *The Poetics,* analyzing the function and structure of tragedy and the unity of time and action in dramatic form.

During the **Hellenistic, or Colonial, Period,** which covered the years between 350 B.C. and 250 B.C., the shape of the performance area changed, and tragedy became less popular. Old Comedy evolved into New Comedy, as the subject of comic drama moved from politics and philosophy to the everyday life of humanity.

Starting about 250 B.C., the **Greco-Roman Period** lasted into the era of Roman dominance, which began in the 1st century A.D. The major playwrights of the age, Plautus (250–184 B.C.) and Terence (190–159 B.C.), wrote in Latin but from Greek models.

Dionysian Ritual and Contests

Before they developed formal theater, the ancient Greeks held festivals to honor Dionysus, the Greek god of wine and fertility. The center of the ceremonies was the dithyramb, a hymn sung by a chorus while mimes and dancers portrayed events in the life of Dionysius; it culminated in the sacrifice of a goat. Sometime during the 5th century B.C., the ritual began to incorporate true dramatic elements and was organized as a competition. Playwrights submitted their plays, written in verse, to state officials. Each submitted a trilogy of three tragedies, as well as a satyr play about the gods, goddesses and heroes of Greek legend. The comedic satyr play dealt with the same tragic theme or story contained in the trilogy.

The Greek theater structure originally consisted of a round playing area with altar, surrounded by bleachers, and was located near a temple. Over time the layout changed, but the classical Greek theater remained simple. The audience sat in the theatron—tiers of seats arranged in a horseshoe shape on a hillside and divided into wedges by aisles.

Because women were not allowed to act, all roles were played by men. The tragic actor's body was entirely covered so that he might become anonymous and portray both gods and heroes; he wore a large mask over his face to indicate the sex and main personality trait of the character he was portraying.

Of primary importance in Greek theater, the chorus narrated and reacted to onstage events. It also gave advice and opinion, established mood and predicted future action. Composed of as many as fifty performers, the chorus sang or chanted its lines in unison. As individual actors became more important over time, the role of the chorus gradually diminished. It shrank in size until it disappeared entirely.

Thespis, the winner in 534 B.C. of the first public contest for tragic poets, was the first actor to distinguish himself from the chorus. He did not simply narrate events but stepped away from the chorus, speaking lines and assuming a character. This created controversy and Thespis was warned by lawmakers about the dangers of his behavior. The term *thespian*—which as an adjective means "dramatic" and as a noun "actor"—is derived from his name.

Tragedy and Comedy

In *The Poetics,* his treatise on constructing plays, Aristotle gave ancient play-wrights guidelines for writing drama. He stated that a play requires unity of time and action; that is, only one action, or main story, can happen at a given time. (The neoclassical critics of the 18th and 19th centuries, especially in France, expanded this guideline to include the unity of place.) He also discussed the notion of catharsis, although he did not give an exact definition of the idea. Scholars, however, generally agree that catharsis is the essential process and function of tragedy: The play arouses pity and fear in the audience and then purges them of these feelings, leaving them somehow stronger. Seeking to trigger catharsis, Greek tragedians addressed humanity's fate in a world where the gods interfere in people's actions and lives.

The most noted writers of Greek tragedy were Aeschylus, Sophocles and Euripides. Altogether they wrote more than 150 plays based on Greek legends. Aeschylus is known as the father of Greek tragedy. His ninety plays, seven of which have survived to the present day, are the oldest in existence; they focus largely on people who come into conflict with the gods' laws. Aeschylus is probably best remembered for his trilogy, *The Oresteia* (458 B.C.).

Many scholars consider Sophocles's play, *Oedipus Rex* (430 B.C.), the apex of Greek tragedy. It tells the story of Oedipus, King of Thebes, who discovers he has killed his father and married his mother. The play continues to be performed frequently and is a testament to the poet's skill.

Contemporary opinions differed about Euripides, who questioned traditional values of Greek society. Abandoning the customary focus on the relationship between humankind and the gods, his plays explored interpersonal relationships and the concept that character shapes destiny. In *The Trojan Women* (415 B.C.), Euripides condemned war at a time when the Greeks were at war. He was ridiculed by other dramatists for attacking traditional beliefs and was eventually banished from Athens.

Comedic plays entered the festivals fifty years after tragedies. Aristophanes, the main poet of the Old Comedy style, satirized politics, philosophy and other playwrights. In his most famous play, *The Clouds* (423 B.C.), he satirized the philosopher Socrates. One hundred years after Aristophanes, Menander wrote the first New Comedy, setting the standard for dramatic comedy for the centuries that followed. The subject of Menander's more than a hundred plays was humanity's personal, daily life—family relationships, money, love problems and the like.

EGYPTIAN THEATER

Mystery surrounds the birth of theater. Some scholars believe that the components of Greek theater originated in ancient Egypt. However, very little is known about Egyptian drama. Hieroglyphic texts indicate the existence of theater, but there is no archaeological evidence of any actual theater structure.

In about 110 B.C., the engraved script of a play, *The Triumph of Horus,* complete with dialogue and stage directions, was discovered on the walls of the Temple of Edfu; by then the work was already 1,100 years old. The play tells of a ritual battle in which a hero-king harpoons and kills a hippopotamus-demon. It seems to have been performed at annual festivals that lasted for five days.

Another hieroglyphic discovery, known as the *Abydos* or *Osiris* passion play, dates from 2500 B.C. It may also be a dramatic text of some kind, though scholars have no evidence that it was ever performed.

The Evolution of Western Theater

Like much of Western culture, theater evolved from ancient Greek traditions. The Greeks created the essential dramatic forms, tragedy and comedy, and developed the basic structures of the play and the theater experience that survive to this day. Building on the foundations laid down by the Greeks, the ancient Romans ushered Western theater through the next stage of its history.

Roman Theater

The Romans conquered Greece and absorbed many elements of its culture. In 240 B.C., Livius Andronicus (c. 284–204 B.C.) became the first Roman playwright to adapt Greek comedies and tragedies, translating them into Latin for performance at annual festivals held to honor the gods.

Cities of the Roman Empire (27 B.C.–A.D. 476) built progressively larger, more elaborate permanent theaters, where audiences viewed both comedies and tragedies. The plays either featured Greek subjects and characters or were modified Greek plays that communicated Roman stories or ideas. Only fragments of Roman tragedies have survived. However, several comedies by Plautus (Titus Maccius Plautus, c. 251–184 B.C.) have endured. He adapted the Greek New Comedy of Menander and others, setting the action in Rome and using everyday details of Roman life. Terence (Publius Terentius Afer, c. 184–159 B.C.), whose work focused more on character development than plot, also left behind a number of comedies.

The Roman tragedies that have survived were written by Seneca (Lucius Annaeus Seneca, 4 B.C.–A.D. 65). Because they were never staged, they are known as "closet dramas." Playwrights during Elizabethan and Renaissance times borrowed many of Seneca's innovations, including, for example, the theme of revenge and the use of ghosts, witches and horror. Seneca wrote about the tyranny and violence of Roman emperors, as well as political intrigue in other countries.

Permanent Roman theaters differed from Greek theaters. They boasted a stage 100 to 300 feet long and a semicircular orchestra where important people were seated. It is believed that the orchestra was sometimes flooded for water ballets. The background for the stage action was the *scaenae frons,* a two- to three-story-high wall decorated with columns and statues. According to the philosopher and writer Cicero, in some theaters the scaenae frons was painted gold.

Audiences in the Roman Empire favored "spectacles," especially violent ones. To witness these events, they flocked to amphitheaters—round venues with raised seats. One such amphitheater was the Colosseum, which could seat 55,000. Amphitheaters contained giant elevators that lifted animals, humans and scenery from underground chambers to tunnels that led to the arena. On occasion, an amphitheater would be flooded to hold ships filled with slaves, who fought until none were left alive. Sometimes convicted criminals were substituted for actors and were killed as part of an afternoon's entertainment.

Christian leaders vehemently opposed the theater, especially the pantomime troupes who often made fun of Christian rituals. Priests were forbidden to attend the theater in Rome. After the fall of the Roman Empire, during the Dark Ages, Christian strictures against theater stalled the further development of formal theater and playwriting.

Drama in the Middle Ages

Although little evidence survives of any theater in Western Europe during the Dark Ages, various forms of religious drama appeared between the 10th and 15th centuries. By the 12th century, priests inserted tropes—short dialogues sung in Latin by the priest and choir—into the Mass. They further dramatized their subjects by assuming the roles of characters.

Gradually, priests began to use props in their tropes. Before long, the whole church was used as a theater and the congregation became more involved. Theater gradually moved outside of churches throughout Europe, at different rates in different places. Some of the earliest professional theater companies developed in England during the Middle Ages.

There are several forms of medieval drama. The **liturgical play** was a drama derived from a trope. A more complex form of medieval drama was the **mystery play,** which was based on stories from the Bible. This type of play was arranged in cycles, a format in which groups of one-act plays were presented in Biblical order. The **miracle play** told stories of religious miracles, some of which—the lives of the saints, for example—did not come from the Bible. The **morality play,** which dated from the 15th century, contained characters that represent virtues and vices, such as Good Deeds, Justice, Wisdom or Folly. These plays served as entertaining lessons in right and wrong.

Many of the plays of the Middle Ages survive; the best-known morality play, *Everyman* (Anonymous, 15th century), is still frequently produced. But by 1600, the popularity of religious drama had declined significantly in Europe. Each culture was well on the way to developing its own form of drama based on nonreligious subjects, performed more and more often by professional players.

Renaissance Theater

The European cultural flowering known as the Renaissance began in Italy during the 14th century. During this period, permanent theater buildings were constructed so that the aristocracy could view not only comedies and tragedies but also the **intermezzi** they had come to prefer—pastorals and opera based on mythological or biblical themes, presented between the acts of other plays.

Pastorals were set in an ideal countryside where life was happy and carefree. In this setting, satyrs and other exotic creatures complicated the love relationships between nymphs and shepherds. **Opera** appeared later in the Renaissance and included dialogue and choral passages chanted to musical accompaniment.

The comedies of early Renaissance Italian playwrights were based on those of the Roman dramatists Plautus and Terence. Later, the **commedia dell' arte** (comedy of professional artists) arose in Italy and thrived from 1550 to 1750. Professional actors performed in organized commedia troupes that traveled from town to town, performing on wooden stages in marketplaces and public squares. Without written scripts, the actors improvised highly stylized dialogue and action against sketchy plots or scenarios. Commedia plays usually revolved around lovers' attempts to marry in the face of various stumbling blocks, jealousies and misunderstandings.

Commedia employed stock characters such as the lover, the servant or the old man. These characters appeared in many plays, where they used the same name, costume, mask and character qualities. The *zanni,* the comic servants who appeared as mischief makers, acrobats and dancers, were especially popular stock characters. Many contemporary improvisation and theater companies continue to use commedia techniques in their work.

By the 16th century, Spanish playwrights came to be influenced by Italian writers. An important theme in the theater of Spain's Golden Age was the conflict between love and honor. Lope de Vega Carpio (1562–1635) wrote at least 1,500 plays in verse form; Pedro Calderón de la Barca (1600–81) followed Vega as one of Spain's great dramatic poets. Permanent theaters with proscenium arches and painted scenery were built in Madrid, Seville and Valencia.

The Renaissance reached its height in England under Elizabeth I during the late 16th century. Because the English embraced Protestantism instead of Roman Catholicism, the queen banned the religious plays and cycles that had reached their peak in the Middle Ages. Playwrights and performers turned their energies toward nonreligious subjects.

English writers studied and imitated the works of the ancient Greeks and Romans, yielding *Gorboduc* (1561), the first native English tragedy, and *Ralph Roister Doister* (c. 1534–52), the first native English comedy. Great playwrights of the period included Thomas Kyd (1558–94), John Lyly (1554–1606), Christopher Marlowe (1564–93) and William Shakespeare (1564–1616), who is generally considered to be the greatest English-language playwright in history.

The Elizabethan stages were the first buildings constructed in England specifically for the presentation of plays to the public; they provided permanent homes for theater companies. It is believed that most such stages consisted of a forestage that extended into the audience, a curtained inner stage, and an upper stage or balcony. The first English playhouse was named The Theatre; many of Shakespeare's plays were premiered at a famous venue called The Globe.

Theater remained popular throughout the early years of the 17th century, during the reigns of James I and Charles I. The kings preferred **masques,** lavish court entertainments designed to glorify the monarch in attendance. Ben Jonson, who wrote *Volpone* (1605–06) and *The Alchemist* (1610), was popular with the general public. After the Puritans defeated Charles I in a civil war in 1642, they closed or burned down all theaters and forbade acting.

Theater in the Modern Period

English theater revived soon after the restoration of the monarchy in 1660, although theater was no longer intended for the general public, as it had been under Queen Elizabeth. Charles II granted the right to produce plays to two companies that performed primarily for the Court. The deep Elizabethan stages were replaced by the picture-frame stage. During this period, the comedy of manners was the most important dramatic form to emerge in England. Witty, stylish and sophisticated, these plays portrayed the adventures of elegant upper-class men and women. Oliver Goldsmith and Richard Sheridan are two noteworthy writers of Restoration-era comedies of manners.

Between 1650 and 1750 during the reign of Louis XIV, French audiences flocked to see works by neoclassical writers, who closely followed ancient Greek and Roman traditions. The most popular French playwright during this period was Molière (1622–73), who satirized current trends and fashions, yet created characters with depth. The tragedies of French neoclassical dramatists Pierre Corneille (1606–84) and Jean Racine (1639–99), as well as the comedies of Molière, adhered to the strict rules of classical Greek and Roman drama: They consist of five acts of verse, take place in a single location, develop a single story, and span a time period no longer than that of the performance itself.

Toward the end of the 18th century, German theater emerged as a world force. Because of social upheavals, the beginning of this period was known in Germany as the *Sturm und Drang* ("storm and stress"). Johann Wolfgang von

Goethe (1749–1832), who wrote poetic dramas, and Johann Christoph Friedrich von Schiller (1759–1805), who wrote historical tragedies, are the best-known dramatists of this period. Since the late 18th century, theater has been an important element of German life and culture.

Throughout the 19th century, European theater experienced a trend toward naturalism. Serious playwrights, performers and audiences increasingly rejected melodrama in favor of realistic portrayals of characters and situations. By the end of the 19th century, this artistic movement came to be called realism. Realist playwrights wrote plays about everyday life and contemporary social problems. Norwegian playwright Henrik Ibsen led the realist movement in theater; Swedish playwright August Strindberg is another major realistic playwright of the period. In Russia, director Konstantin Stanislavski (whose Moscow Art Theatre introduced the realist plays of Anton Chekhov) revolutionized the art of acting by making it more naturalistic. The realist impulse remains a familiar and powerful force in contemporary theater.

The Life and Work of William Shakespeare

William Shakespeare was born in Stratford-upon-Avon, England, probably on April 23, 1564. His father was a wealthy glover and a town burgess. Except for his christening, historical records offer no information on Shakespeare's youth before his marriage to Ann Hathaway in 1582; he fathered three children, including a pair of fraternal twins. Likewise, virtually nothing is known of Shakespeare's life from 1585 to 1592. It may be that he left home and family to tour with a group of London players. By 1592, his name was sufficiently familiar in London theaters for Robert Greene, a scholar and rival playwright, to refer to him as an "upstart crow."

During his early playwriting years, Shakespeare collaborated with other writers. Some experts contend that he may not have been sole author of the major plays accredited to him, but it is generally accepted that by 1592 he worked alone. He was associated for many years with a successful theater company known as the Lord Chamberlain's Men, which built and occupied the most popular of the Elizabethan theaters, The Globe. Shakespeare not only acted with this company but eventually became a leading shareholder and its principal playwright. The company included some of the most famous actors of the day, including Richard Burbage, who, it is believed, originated the roles of Hamlet, Lear and Othello.

It was during his first ten years at the Globe (1599–1608) that Shakespeare wrote most of his greatest plays, including *Much Ado About Nothing, As You Like It, All's Well That Ends Well, Measure for Measure, Troilus and Cressida, Julius Caesar, Hamlet, Othello, King Lear, Macbeth, Antony and Cleopatra, Coriolanus* and *Timon of Athens.* He borrowed the subjects of his thirty-seven plays from

Greek tragedies, Roman comedies, poems, the Bible and world history. Shakespeare frequently combined one or more of these influences in a single play. *King Lear,* for example, combined history with an Elizabethan play and a novel. *The Comedy of Errors* had its origins in two plays by Plautus, a Roman playwright of New Comedy.

Shakespeare's plays diverged from the rules of classical Greek and Roman drama. They took place over extended time periods and in multiple locations, and depicted violence onstage. *Antony and Cleopatra,* for example, is set in Egypt and Rome over a twelve-year period. *Henry IV*, about events following Richard II's murder, blends tragic and comic elements and introduced the comic role of Falstaff.

Shakespeare wrote about an eclectic group of characters: the ardent Cleopatra, the tortured Hamlet, the evil Richard III and the jealous Othello. He also included commonfolk in his plays, such as drunkards, shepherds and thieves. Elizabethans appreciated violence, so he incorporated duels, beheadings and other brutality. His audiences believed in the hidden, magical world, so he incorporated witches, ghosts, fairies and other mystical entities.

The plots of Shakespeare's romantic comedies, such as *Twelfth Night, As You Like It* and *A Midsummer Night's Dream,* often revolve around love affairs frustrated by miscommunication, mistaken identity and other misunderstandings. With their happy endings, these plays follow in the joyful, celebratory traditions of ancient festival holy days and romantic medieval chivalry. For instance, the magical night of *A Midsummer Night's Dream* casts a spell on the characters, forcing the audience to accept the play's illusions. The tale of enchantment supersedes everyday rationality, so the audience is free to experience unfiltered emotions. In this way, the play functions much as ancient festivals did, allowing participants to set aside the mundane in favor of the unseen.

In his history plays, Shakespeare dramatized specific events or the lives of historical personalities. The three parts of *Henry VI* and *Richard III,* for example, deal with the War of the Roses, a period of history with which Elizabethan audiences were familiar. All Shakespeare's English history plays examine individuals involved in political turmoil and the ways in which their psychology intersected with the social order. This distinguishing characteristic set his work apart from other Elizabethan theater.

Shakespeare's tragedies, such as *Hamlet, King Lear* and *Macbeth,* also examine the inner lives of the characters. In all his tragedies, order is restored by a just universe.

Shakespeare's plays were well received at the Globe. James I, in fact, honored the Lord Chamberlain's Men with the title King's Men in recognition of their work. By that time, Shakespeare had moved to Southwark in order to be near the Globe, though he maintained business interests in Stratford. Some scholars believe that by 1613, when fire destroyed the Globe, Shakespeare's popularity was being challenged by younger playwrights, such as Francis Beaumont and John Fletcher. It is believed that Shakespeare spent his last years in Stratford and sold his shares in the Globe, which was being rebuilt.

When Shakespeare died in Stratford in 1616, no collected edition of his works existed. Some texts of his plays had appeared in individual editions during his lifetime, but these were published without his guidance, sometimes reproduced from his manuscripts or from theater prompt books. In 1623, John Heminges and Henry Condell, two members of the King's Men, published a collection of the plays they believed to be authentic; it is called the *First Folio*. In an opening poem, Ben Jonson, Shakespeare's rival and critic, asserts Shakespeare's superiority over not only other English playwrights but also the master Greek and Roman dramatists.

QUOTABLE SHAKESPEARE

"A horse! A horse! My kingdom for a horse!" —*RICHARD III*, V:4

"Life's but a walking shadow, a poor player,
That struts and frets his hour upon the stage
And then is heard no more. It is a tale
Told by an idiot, full of sound and fury,
Signifying nothing." —*MACBETH*, V:5

". . . We are such stuff
As dreams are made on, and our little life
Is rounded with a sleep." —*THE TEMPEST*, IV:1

"If music be the food of love, play on." —*TWELFTH NIGHT*, I:1

"Get thee to a nunnery." —*HAMLET*, III:1

"Though this be madness, yet there is method in't." —*HAMLET*, II:11

"To be, or not to be: that is the question." —*HAMLET*, III:1

"The quality of mercy is not strained." —*THE MERCHANT OF VENICE*, IV:1

"What's in a name? That which we call a rose,
By any other name would smell as sweet." —*ROMEO AND JULIET*, II:2

"How sharper than a serpent's tooth it is
To have a thankless child." —*KING LEAR*, I:4

Asian Theater

Theater in various forms has existed in Asia for more than a thousand years, but it is only within the past two hundred that much Asian theater has been seen by Westerners. Each Asian country, as well each region within each country, has its unique theatrical history. Indian, Japanese and Chinese theater prevails in Asia today.

India

Leaving few traces of its early history, Indian theater evolved from Sanskrit literature between the 1st and 10th centuries A.D. One piece of evidence provides a glimpse of ancient Indian theater: the *Natyastra,* a document that dates from between 200 B.C. and A.D. 200. In addition to telling the mythologized story of the origin of theater, it discusses acting, the organization of theatrical companies, and how makeup was used to indicate characters' nationalities and castes.

Based on myth and legend, Sanskrit theater was performed at religious festivals to honor the gods. Companies of actors traveled to temple festivals under the leadership of actor-managers, who probably also functioned as directors of the performances. It is believed that men and women traveled and acted in separate, as well as mixed, troupes.

The evolution of Hindu drama was disrupted when Muslims invaded India during the 16th century. The tenets of Islam prohibited theater, or at least discouraged it, so the form fell from official favor under the Mogul Empire (1526–1857). By contrast, Vaisnavism, a movement of Hinduism that developed in response to Muslim domination, encouraged theater until the 19th century. Vaisnavists used theater to demonstrate their faith directly to deities by depicting the acts of the gods. This differed from the practices of orthodox Hinduism, which relied heavily on religious ritual.

As the Mogul Empire declined and the British gained power on the subcontinent, Indian theater began another stage of development. Seeking an alternative to British theater, wealthy Bengalis in 19th-century Calcutta built private home theaters where they could watch Indian drama. They created their own plays, which incorporated Indian music and songs in a Western format. The best-known works of this period are *Red Oleanders (Raktakurabi)* and *The King of the Dark Chamber (Raja)*, both by Rabindranath Tagore, who won the Nobel Prize for literature in 1913.

By the late 19th century, Indian artists were managing their own public theater companies. Calcutta now has as many as three thousand amateur theater companies, which are professionally run but which maintain their amateur rank for tax reasons. Some theaters present shows in repertory for several years, so long as there are audiences to see them.

Japan

The three traditional Japanese theater forms are the **No,** the **Kabuki** and the **Bunraku.** Developed during Japan's medieval period (1185–1600), No is the oldest. Important Buddhist shrines and temples each housed their own No troupes by the mid-14th century. The powerful samurai class, which dominated Japan's imperial court, gave No performers samurai rank as a gesture of admiration. Throughout the 17th century, No performers held this rank, and only their sons were allowed to carry on the tradition.

In structure and technique, both No and Kyogen theater, No's comic form, follow Zen principles of restraint. Traditional No drama recounts episodes of Japanese history and might be said to resemble small-scale opera. No performers wear masks; during a performance's climax, they combine rhythmic dancing with song.

Kabuki theater, a provocative new form, emerged at the end of Japan's medieval period. Originating as a kind of dance, Kabuki was expanded into full-scale theater by a dancer and priestess named Okuni. Painted scrolls show Okuni in various roles, including one as a warrior engaged in a transaction with a prostitute. Indeed, early Kabuki performers were prostitutes who used the amusement to entice clients. Depicting life in Japanese cities, Kabuki theater evolved into an art form in the early 18th century. At that time, male casts began to perform multi-act plays that lasted a full day. They created specific Kabuki forms of acting, dance and music for different styles of plays.

Bunraku, an amalgam of narrative storytelling, puppetry and music, appeared in Japan's cities during the 16th century. Performances centered around Buddhist tales, feudal war epics and romances. In early Bunraku, a single narrator chanted, spoke or sang the story and any occasional dialogue. Puppeteers held small dolls over their heads to illustrate the story.

In contemporary Japan, professional No and Kyogen actors earn their livelihood primarily as teachers. The country has five No schools, each with its own theater. Contact with the West does not appear to have affected No theater's performance style; traditional Bunraku remains popular as well. By contrast, Kabuki has incorporated new western-influenced dramatic techniques. Contemporary Western-style theater has also evolved in Japan.

China

Classical Chinese theater combines techniques from mythological Bronze Age dances with the plot lines of imperial court dramas and the teachings of Confucius and Lao Tzu. Although these elements have been reshaped through the ages, Chinese theater still employs a traditional opening ceremony rooted in ancient forms. It presents the eight Buddhist immortals, beings who are featured in plays still popular in China.

Traditional Chinese theater is essentially musical and choreographic in nature. A stage without scenery or realistic properties emphasizes performers' movements while an orchestra evokes mood. Actors move to the front of the stage to describe certain facts to the audience, using specific gestures set to music. If an actor needs a chair, the audience ignores the prop person who comes onstage to position it. A chair might be placed on a table to represent a mountain, which an actor then climbs.

Puppet plays became popular during the T'Ang Dynasty, which began in A.D. 618 and lasted for more than six hundred years. There may have been a connection, dating from ancient times, between shadow puppetry and funerals. Other drama in the T'Ang, as well as the Sung Dynasty that followed, featured single dancing or singing performers on stage. During the Sung Dynasty, several-act plays appeared, but they still featured only one performer on stage at a time.

Drama in north and south China varied: Northern drama was melodic and southern was rhythmic. The aural aesthetics of the northern form relied on soothing music, while the more visual southern form featured costumes and movement to drums.

K'Un Chu developed in the early 16th century during the Ming Dynasty. Combining and refining northern and southern forms, it became the national drama of China for three hundred years. Though its foundations were musical, its most popular writers were poets.

Peking Opera, or *Ching Hsi,* became popular during the late 18th century. A mixture of words, dance, acrobatics, music and gesture, it continues to be a very popular form even today. The conventions of this theater are very strict, prohibiting any gesture or movement by an actor that does not have specific meaning. There are no sets; props are used to indicate the location of the story. Elaborate costumes communicate characters' age, social status, personality and other information to the audience. Specific rules for makeup also dictate the way in which specific character traits are portrayed.

Popular Chinese drama blends a rich national tradition with regional styles. Despite threats over the years from the communist government, mainland China appears to be preserving its traditional art forms. Peking Opera is also promoted by the Taiwanese government.

British Theater in the 20th Century

During the 20th century, British theater has made a significant contribution to the development of world theater. Early in the century, the works of Anglo-Irish playwright George Bernard Shaw dominated the London stage. His themes and his irreverent style greatly influenced the trends of native English drama. Other popular playwrights included J. M. Barrie, who wrote fantasy plays such as *Peter Pan* (1904), Noel Coward, who wrote witty social comedies, and Somerset Maugham.

At the turn of the century, experimentation in commercial theater was considered risky; there was already an established trend toward long runs and grand staging. One exception was the Royal Court, which from 1904 to 1907 offered seasons of repertory that introduced the works of Hauptmann, Maeterlinck and Schnitzler to London audiences. For the most part, the new "theater of ideas" was pioneered by small, semiprofessional theater companies that could afford to take risks. Many such groups emerged outside London, giving rise to quality theater in smaller cities.

The pioneers of British repertory theater believed in the role of theater as an effective social force. They viewed the dominance of the London commercial theater and its profit-making system of actor-managers, stars and long runs as obstacles to innovation. To encourage experimentation, regional theaters began to present several plays in repertory each season instead of one long-running play. The Gaiety Theatre in Manchester, which included actress Sybil Thorndike, risked the production of work by several local playwrights. Experimentation, however, did not produce large box-office draws, so regional theaters ultimately turned to less costly small plays with small casts. The heyday of civic and repertory theaters passed.

Another important innovation of the 20th-century theater in Britain (as in the United States) was the rise of the nonacting director. For many centuries, theater companies were run by actor-managers who not only guided the staging of the plays but acted in them as well. Early in the century, however, the theater community questioned the ability of actors to direct themselves. One of the most notable managers of the early 20th century was Lilian Baylis of the Old Vic, which staged all the plays in the Shakespeare *Folio* between 1915 and 1923. Under her leadership, the Old Vic gained a reputation as England's leading theater during the 1930s. It showcased the talents of actors Laurence Oliver, Michael Redgrave, John Gielgud and Charles Laughton, as well as director Tyrone Guthrie and others. Since World War II, the primacy of the nonacting director has increasingly been taken for granted.

For a while following World War II, English theater experienced a brief revival of poetic drama, exemplified by T. S. Eliot's later plays and by Christopher Fry's *The Lady's Not for Burning* (1948). But this poetic renewal was soon swept aside by growing interest in the works of Samuel Beckett, Bertolt Brecht and Eugene Ionesco. Soon British theater witnessed a revival of native English drama; many historians date this reawakening to a production of John Osborne's *Look Back in Anger* (1956) at the Royal Court.

Within a few years, the Royal Court was committed to staging works by new English playwrights. At the same time, the work of Joan Littlewood's Theatre Workshop captured public and critical attention. This working-class community theater's production of Robert Bolt's *A Man for All Seasons* (1960) showed the influence of Brecht on Littlewood, who wanted to make English audiences think. Brecht also had a noticeable effect on English playwrights who emerged after the Lord Chamberlain's powers of censorship were abolished in 1968. Popular playwrights like Harold Pinter and Tom Stoppard also credited Beckett and Ionesco as influences. In their plays, they dealt more with human behavior than with politics.

Even as British theater found its own modern voices, the works of William Shakespeare remained compelling. The prestige of Stratford's Shakespeare Company grew steadily; the company rose to prominence after the appointment of Peter Hall as director in 1960. Hall changed the company's name to the Royal Shakespeare Company in 1961 and continued to produce the Bard, as well as revivals and premieres of other playwrights' work. In 1986, the old museum at Stratford was converted into the open-stage Swan Theatre, giving the RSC a venue specifically designed for production of post-Shakespearean classics.

The vitality of British theater also led to the establishment of the National Theatre Company in 1962. The company debuted with a production of *Hamlet* at the Old Vic. Artistic director Laurence Olivier and literary manager Kenneth Tynan produced English and foreign classics, as well as new work by Stoppard, Peter Shaffer and Trevor Griffiths. In 1973 Olivier was replaced by Peter Hall. Three theaters—the Lyttleton, the Olivier and the Cottesloe (1976 and 1977)—have opened during Hall's tenure. They are located at the Royal National Theatre complex on London's South Bank.

Outside of the mainstream, the Fringe Theatre movement began in the 1960s, corresponding to Off-Off Broadway theater in the United States. The movement started with small theater groups who rented buildings on the "fringe" of the Edinburgh Festival, an international performance festival that originated in 1947 and continues today. From these groups emerged theater companies that attempted to gain a voice in theater and politics. Fringe companies included the Pip Simmons Group, the feminist Monstrous Collective, and the labor activist groups Belt and Braces, Red Ladder and North West Spanner. A company called Shared Experience focused on storytelling techniques, while Hull Truck used improvisation as a play-development technique, and Moving Being combined dance and drama. These groups, many of which no longer exist, helped launch the community theater movement that spread throughout England during the 1970s.

After the 1970s, alternative theater declined in England. Three trends characterized British theater in the final years of the 20th century: the popularity of musical theater, the appearance of a distinctive genre known as performance art, and the operation of theater companies as touring repertory groups rather than as permanent ensembles. As in the United States, rising theater production costs and the popularity of movies and television have had a negative effect on the popularity of English theater.

Ireland

A specifically Irish school of drama emerged in 1897, when poet William Butler Yeats and two patrons—Lady Augusta Gregory and Edward Martyn—

founded the Irish Literary Theatre with the goal of de-Anglicizing Irish theater. The centuries-long coexistence of the Celtic and English languages in Ireland had produced an authentic national speech, and the Irish Literary Theatre set out to establish a national literature in this language. In 1902, the Fay brothers' Irish National Dramatic Company staged Yeats's *Cathleen ni Houlihan*. The following year, the brothers joined forces with Yeats and Lady Gregory to form the Irish National Theatre Society.

The Society presented two plays by Yeats, as well as Padraic Colum's *Broken Soil* and John Millington Synge's *In the Shadow of the Glen,* in 1903. Colum and Synge wrote of small-town peasant life, abandoning the verse drama of Yeats in favor of prose. The emerging Irish style is evident in the stylized, poetic peasant speech of Synge's *The Playboy of the Western World* (1907).

Promoted by the Irish National Theatre Society, Irish drama flourished. The Society acquired a permanent building in 1904, commonly called the Abbey Theatre.

With few exceptions, Irish drama from the 1920s to the 1950s concerned contemporary social issues and was written in realistic prose. Though not unique to Ireland, the "sovereignty of words," as Yeats referred to it, became a primary feature of Irish drama. Important playwrights of the period include Yeats, Synge, Sean O'Casey, George Shiels and Denis Johnston. In Dublin, the Gate Theatre (founded in 1928) was a significant presence, while in Belfast the important companies formed during this period included the Group Theatre (1940–60), the Arts Theatre Studio (1950–77) and the Lyric Players Theatre (founded in 1951).

During the 1940s and 1950s Irish theater was somewhat dormant, with the notable exceptions of Brendan Behan's *The Quare Fellow* (1954), *The Hostage* (1958) and *Borstal Boy* (1958). The subject matter of much 20th-century Irish drama is political, and when Irish theater was revitalized during the mid-1960s, the work of new dramatists continued along these lines, presenting social ideas through the lives of individual characters. Brian Friel has written what many consider to be the most substantial and important body of work in contemporary Irish drama. His plays include *Philadelphia, Here I Come!* (1964), *Lovers* (1967), *The Freedom of the City* (1973), *Translations* (1980), *The Communication Cord* (1982), an adaptation of Ivan Turgenev's novel *Fathers and Sons* (1987), *Dancing at Lughnasa* (1990) and *Wonderful Tennessee* (1993). In 1980, Friel formed the Field Day Theatre Company in Derry, which produces his work and that of other writers. The Abbey Theatre continues as the Irish National Theatre, producing works by contemporary playwrights in addition to classics and revivals.

Theater in the United States

During the colonial period of American history, the southern British colonies were notably more hospitable to theater than those to the north. In Puritan New England, theater was denounced; between 1700 and 1716, several British colonies passed laws against theater. Despite this, *Ye Bare and Ye Cubb,* written by William Darby, was performed in 1665 at Cowles Tavern in Accomac County, Virginia. It was the first English-language play on record to be presented in the colonies.

Before the middle of the 18th century, colonial America witnessed sporadic theatrical activity. An amateur production of *Romeo and Juliet,* mounted in New York in 1730, was probably the first Shakespeare play to be presented in America. Then, starting about 1749, theater began to be produced consistently in Philadelphia, with New York following suit by 1800. The first professional theater company in the colonies was formed in October 1751. Originally based in Philadelphia, the company appeared briefly in New York, then opened a temporary, wooden playhouse in Williamsburg, Virginia, and became known as the Virginia Company of Comedians.

The London Company of Comedians, which was renamed the American Company of Comedians in 1763, was the best-known troupe of traveling professional actors in early American history. Philadelphia's Southwark Theatre, built in 1766, was the first permanent theater building erected in America; it stood until 1912. There, the American Company of Comedians became the first professional company to produce native drama, producing Thomas Godfrey's *The Prince of Parthia* (1767). On tour, the company introduced new British plays, even though many American religious leaders actively opposed theater.

Following the Revolution, playwrights wrote about the lives of American-born characters. Stock American characters of the first half of the 19th century included the Indian, the Yankee, the city boy and the brave frontiersman. Beginning in 1852, many theatrical versions of Harriet Beecher Stowe's novel *Uncle Tom's Cabin* were produced, marking the first time issues of race and slavery were dealt with onstage.

During the 19th century, the number of theaters increased and many technological and design innovations were made. Gaslighting was first used in the United States at Philadelphia's Chestnut Street Theatre in 1816. In New York, Steele MacKaye remodeled the old Fifth Avenue Theatre and renamed it the Madison Square Theatre in 1880. He installed the most elaborate equipment ever seen in an American theater, including overhead and indirect lighting and a moving stage that allowed for rapid scene changes.

By the mid-19th century, stock companies—ensembles attached to established theaters—began to offer new plays, as well as revivals of classics, and they remained strong. However, as individual stars grew in luster, becoming the magnet used to attract audiences, stock companies lost their prominence.

Vaudeville and the comic operettas of Gilbert and Sullivan became popular during the latter part of the century. The rise of realism, which offered a more honest portrayal of life, coincided with the decline of melodrama. Realist plays abandoned melodramatic conventions, including spine-tingling rescues and happily-ever-after endings. For inspiration, American playwrights looked to the work of Henrik Ibsen and the European realist movement.

As American theater became a more profit-oriented business, powerful producers, such as the Frohman brothers, emerged. Daniel Frohman took over Steele MacKaye's Lyceum Theatre in 1885, and his stock company performed there until 1902. His brother Charles's two theater companies helped to create such stars as Maude Adams and Ethel Barrymore. Charles Frohman became best known for organizing a theatrical trust in 1896, uniting himself, the Klau and Erlanger Company (a booking firm), and several theater owners. The Theatrical Syndicate or "Trust" monopolized American theater by controlling bookings, playhouses and actors.

Early 20th Century

In 1900, producers Jacob, Lee and Sam Shubert challenged the Syndicate and broke its monopoly. The Shuberts gained control of many theaters in New York and across the country, arranged bookings with independent managers, and produced their own shows. The Shubert Organization remains an important power in American theater today.

During the 1910s, amateur theater groups organized around the country. New York's Washington Square Players produced Ibsen, Shaw and Chekhov, plus new works by American playwrights, starting in 1914. In 1916, the Provincetown Players staged two Eugene O'Neill plays, *Bound East for Cardiff* and *Thirst*. And in 1919, members of the by-then-defunct Washington Square Players founded the Theatre Guild, which, beginning with Elmer Rice's *The Adding Machine* (1923), aggressively produced original American works.

Stagehands had already organized their own union by 1893. Then following World War I, the Actors' Equity Association (founded in December 1912) focused on improving actors' working conditions by unionizing their profession. The famous actors' strike of 1919 ended when producers finally agreed to minimum contract terms, better rehearsal and working conditions, and higher salaries.

Beyond the Horizon, O'Neill's first full-length play, was produced on Broadway in 1920 and won a Pulitzer Prize. Some scholars assert that this play's production marks the beginning of modern American drama. Within a few years, O'Neill's work dominated American theater.

All-black revues, such as Noble Sissle and Eubie Blake's *Shuffle Along* (1921) and *Blackbirds* (1928), were popular in the 1920s. On Broadway, musical comedies featured the work of George Gershwin, Cole Porter and Richard Rodgers. Jerome Kern and Oscar Hammerstein II's *Show Boat* (1928) was a popular hit of the decade. Operetta remained popular as well.

The 1920s were an important decade in the development of acting as an art form. In 1923, Konstantin Stanislavski's Moscow Art Theatre company visited New York. Two members of the MAT stayed in New York to teach at the American Laboratory Theatre. Many of their students, such as Harold Clurman and Lee Strasberg, formed their own companies. Eva Le Gallienne started her Civic Repertory Theatre at the Fourteenth Street Theatre in 1926.

George S. Kaufman earned a reputation as one of the most important comedic playwrights of the 1920s. Two other writers, Ben Hecht and Charles MacArthur, produced what is considered to be perhaps the best American farce of the 1920s, *The Front Page* (1928). Serious dramatists also wrote important original works during that decade: *What Price Glory* (1924), by Maxwell Anderson and Lawrence Stalling, presented an unromantic depiction of war; O'Neill's *Desire Under the Elms* (1924) dissected New England Puritanism. Other O'Neill plays of that decade include *The Fountain* (1925), *The Great God Brown* (1926) and *Strange Interlude* (1928), which won a Pulitzer Prize.

As the 1920s drew to a close and motion pictures and radio began to compete with theater for audiences, many theater buildings around the country converted from stage entertainment to the cinema. Soon the professional theater was centered almost exclusively in Manhattan. The Great Depression reduced the number of theaters even further. Some American drama of the 1930s, such as Clifford Odet's *Waiting for Lefty* (1935), examined the country's state of crisis.

Rising popular interest in African-American literature, sparked during the Harlem Renaissance of the 1920s, influenced American theater in the 1930s. Langston Hughes's *Mulatto* (1935) became the longest-running play by an African-American playwright of that decade, with 373 performances.

During the Depression, the Works Progress Administration funded the Federal Theater Project in order to create jobs. This was the first government-subsidized producing organization in United States history. Because many of the productions were left of the political center or perceived to be so, opposition to the project grew among conservatives. In 1939, the government abolished the WPA.

In 1931, several members of the Theatre Guild formed the politically conscious Group Theatre. Founders Harold Clurman, Cheryl Crawford and Lee Strasberg were joined by Clifford Odets, Sanford Meisner, Stella Adler and others. Under Strasberg's direction, the Group developed an acting technique based on Stanislavski's teachings, known as the Method, for the realistic plays they staged. Producing not only *Waiting for Lefty* (1935) but *Awake and Sing!* (1935), the Group Theatre introduced audiences to the work of Odets. The company lasted until 1941.

Seeking a way to survive in the depressed economy, five playwrights—Maxwell Anderson, Elmer Rice, Robert Sherwood, Sidney Howard and S. N. Behrman—banded together to form their own Broadway producing organization, the Playwrights' Company. Among the company's memorable productions were Sherwood's *Abe Lincoln in Illinois* (1938), Anderson's *Knickerbocker Holiday* (1938) and Behrman's *No Time for Comedy* (1939).

During the 1930s, producers also turned to profitable musicals, which drew audiences seeking relief from the stresses of the Depression. One of the most popular was George S. Kaufman and Howard Deitz's *The Band Wagon* (1931), with music by Arthur Schwartz and dancing by Fred and Adele Astaire. Another was *Of Thee I Sing* (1931), by George and Ira Gershwin, Kaufman, and Morrie Ryskind. *Porgy and Bess* (1935), by Dubose Heyward and George and Ira Gershwin, was also produced during this period.

Comedies provided another counterpoint to the anxieties of the decade. Popular comic plays written during the 1930s include O'Neill's *Ah! Wilderness* (1933), Claire Booth Luce's *The Women* (1936), George S. Kaufman and Moss Hart's *You Can't Take It with You* (1936) and *The Man Who Came to Dinner* (1939), William Saroyan's *The Time of Your Life* (1939), and Howard Lindsay and Russel Crouse's *Life With Father* (1939). Important realist drama continued with O'Neill's *Mourning Becomes Electra* (1931), Lillian Hellman's *The Children's Hour* (1934) and *The Little Foxes* (1939), John Steinbeck's *Of Mice and Men* (1937), and Thorton Wilder's *Our Town* (1938).

During the 1930s, the nation's favorite acting couple was Alfred Lunt and Lynn Fontanne. Many critics referred to Katharine Cornell and Helen Hayes as the First Ladies of American Theater; other popular actresses included Eva Le Gallienne and Ruth Gordon. These women had powerful box office draw.

Broadway musicals drew ever-larger audiences in the 1940s: Irving Berlin's *This Is the Army* (1942), Rodgers and Hammerstein's *Oklahoma!* (1943) and *Carousel* (1945), and Leonard Bernstein's *On the Town* (1944) were high points of the war years. After the war, the musical boom continued. Popular productions included Rodgers and Hammerstein's *South Pacific* (1949) and *The King and I* (1951), Irving Berlin's *Annie Get Your Gun* (1946), Lerner and Loewe's *Brigadoon* (1947), Cole Porter's *Kiss Me Kate* (1948), and Frank Loesser's *Guys and Dolls* (1950).

Thornton Wilder's *The Skin of Our Teeth* (1942) was one of the few comedies with a serious theme that was written during this time. In the immediate post-war period, established writers produced several notable works, including O'Neill's *The Iceman Cometh* (1946), Hellman's *Another Part of the Forest* (1946), and Anderson's *Anne of the Thousand Days* (1948). Popular plays, such as Joshua Logan's *Mr. Roberts* (1948), examined America's wartime idealism.

During the 1940s Tennessee Williams, Arthur Miller and William Inge emerged as major playwrights. Williams's *The Glass Menagerie* opened on Broadway in 1945 to wide critical praise; *A Streetcar Named Desire* (1947) won both the Pulitzer Prize and the New York Drama Critics' Circle Award. After Miller's *All My Sons* (1947) won the New York Drama Critics' Award, his *Death of a Salesman* (1949) won both that award and the Pulitzer Prize. Inge's *Come Back, Little Sheba* (1950) was the first of his several successful plays.

Late 20th Century

After World War II, Broadway had commercial success with comedies like John Patrick's *The Teahouse of the August Moon* (1953), Wilder's *The Matchmaker* (1955; it later served as the book for the 1964 musical *Hello, Dolly!*), Jerome Lawrence and Robert E. Lee's *Auntie Mame* (1956), and Paddy Chayevsky's *The Tenth Man* (1959).

Of extreme importance to American theater in the 1950s, however, were the Off-Broadway and regional theater movements spurred by Broadway's sky-rocketing production costs and the need for professional theater outside New York. One of the first major successes of Off-Broadway theater was José Quintero's revival of Williams's *Summer and Smoke* (1952) at Circle in the Square. Other important Off-Broadway theater groups formed: Judith Malina and Julian Beck founded The Living Theatre in 1947, and Joseph Papp created the New York Shakespeare Festival in 1954. Among the regional theaters that opened in the 1950s were Washington, D.C.'s, Arena Stage (founded in 1950), the Actors' Workshop in San Francisco (founded in 1952), the American Shakespeare Festival in Stratford, Connecticut (founded in 1955), and the Alley Theatre in Houston, which opened in 1947 and became fully professional in 1954.

In the 1950s and 1960s, theatrical collectives, such as the Living Theatre, Richard Schechner's Performance Group and Joseph Chaikin's Open Theatre, explored the sociological, political and aesthetic relevance of theater and experimented with the relationship between performer and audience.

Starting in the late 1950s, lofts, cafes and other spaces were converted into theaters in what is now known as the Off-Off Broadway movement. Caffe Cino, run by Joe Cino, presented new works by such playwrights as Lanford Wilson and Sam Shepard. Ellen Stewart's Cafe La Mama, founded in 1962, continues to produce new playwrights today. Other important groups included Judson Poets' Theatre (1961), the American Place Theatre (1964) and Theatre Genesis (1964). As the Off-Off Broadway movement grew, its members formed the Off-Off Broadway Alliance (OOBA) in 1972. The Alliance continues to function as the Alliance of Resident Theatres/New York (A.R.T./New York).

Resident nonprofit theater grew rapidly as well. Important regional companies established during this period include the Guthrie Theatre in Minneapolis (1963), Actors Theatre of Louisville, Kentucky (1964), Trinity Square Repertory Company of Providence, Rhode Island (1964), the Long Wharf in New Haven, Connecticut (1965), the Yale Repertory Theatre in New Haven (1966), and the American Conservatory Theatre in San Francisco (1966). Several performance complexes, such as Lincoln Center for the Performing Arts in New York and the John F. Kennedy Center in Washington, D.C., incorporate important theaters among their constituents. In New York, the Shakespeare Festival's Public Theatre, the Circle Repertory Company, the Manhattan The atre Club and the Acting Company provided noncommercial experimental spaces for theater artists.

Meanwhile on Broadway, one of the most successful playwrights of the 1960s was Neil Simon, who wrote *Barefoot in the Park* (1963), *The Odd Couple* (1965) and *The Last of the Red Hot Lovers* (1969), among other popular comedies. Following earlier successes with one-act plays like *The Zoo Story* (Berlin, 1959; New York, 1960) and *The American Dream* (1961), Edward Albee gained a reputation as a major dramatic playwright when *Who's Afraid of Virginia Woolf?* opened in 1962 (Tony award, 1963). He won the Pulitzer Prize in 1966 for *A Delicate Balance*. Traditional musical theater remained popular: *Camelot* (1960), *She Loves Me* (1963), *Fiddler on the Roof* (1964), *Funny Girl* (1964), *Hello, Dolly!* (1964), *Man of La Mancha* (1965), *Mame* (1966) and *Cabaret* (1966) enjoyed great success. Starting with *Hair* (1967), rock music began to change Broadway musical theater.

Rock, of course, was the music of a generation dedicated to civil rights, antiwar, and gay, lesbian and feminist causes. Young artists brought their concerns to the theater in the 1960s, forming a number of companies that embraced radical politics. African-American theater became a force, and black playwrights created a large body of excellent work: Lorraine Hansberry's *Raisin in the Sun* (1959), Ossie Davis's *Purlie Victorious* (1961), James Baldwin's *Blues for Mister Charlie* (1964), Amiri Baraka's four plays—*Dutchman* (1964), *The Toilet* (1964), *The Slave* (1964) and *Slave Ship* (1969)—and Ed Bullins's *The Electronic Nigger* (1968). African-American women, such as Adrienne Kennedy and Ntozake Shange, wrote plays of poetry and passion. Inspired by the revival of African-American culture, a number of black theater companies were formed. The New Lafayette and the Negro Ensemble Company, both founded in New York in 1967, premiered important plays by African-American dramatists.

Other minority causes spurred theatrical activity in the 1960s and 1970s. In 1965, Luis Valdez established El Teatro Campesino in California to support striking migrant farm workers. This company helped to launch the Chicano theater movement, which continued to grow in the ensuing decades and, in turn, sparked the development of Cuban-American and Puerto Rican-American theater. Similarly, Hanay Geiogamah's Native American Theater Ensemble emerged in the 1970s out of the American Indian Movement of the late 1960s.

As the nation struggled with the issues raised by the Vietnam War, antiwar plays emerged at the end of the 1960s, performed by the San Francisco Mime Troupe, the Bread and Puppet Theatre and other groups of varying size and structure. Plays included Megan Terry's *Viet Rock* (1966), Joseph Heller's *We Bombed in New Haven* (1968), and David Rabe's plays *The Basic Training of Pavlo Hummel* (1971), *Sticks and Bones* (1971) and *Streamers* (1976). In addition to the Broadway musical *Hair*, plays reflecting the counterculture that surrounded the antiwar movement included Michael Weller's *Moonchildren* (1972) and Robert Patrick's *Kennedy's Children* (1973).

Coinciding with the birth of the gay-rights movement during the late 1960s was the formation of gay and lesbian theater groups. While gay theater had long entertained gay people, it gained a broader commercial audience when Mart Crowley's *The Boys in the Band* (1968) ran for 1,001 performances Off-Broadway. The steady growth of gay and lesbian theater throughout the 1970s led to the formation of the Gay Theatre Alliance in 1978. Not until the 1980s, however, did straight audiences really accept gay subjects in theater. Harvey Fierstein's *Torch Song Trilogy* (1981) won the New York Drama Critics' Circle Award, as well as a Tony for best play.

As the women's movement gained momentum, feminist theater strove to provide a voice for women and their concerns. Groups that formed around the country during the 1960s and 1970s included the New Feminist Theater, which was founded in 1969, the Rhode Island Feminist Theater, the Women's Project at the American Place Theatre, At the Foot of the Mountain, Women's Interart Theater, and Spiderwoman Theater Workshop. These companies, many of which still survive, examined a variety of topics, such as abortion, rape, domestic violence, motherhood and gender identity. Successful feminist companies have matured with the women's movement, presenting sophisticated, in-depth treatments of many other issues relating to women. Playwrights with a strong feminist vision include Alice Childress, Megan Terry, Maria Irene Fornes, Ntozake Shange, Rosalyn Drexler and Marsha Norman.

During the 1970s and 1980s, such established avant-garde artists as Richard Foreman, Robert Wilson and Lee Breuer abandoned traditional theatrical structures to present personal visions. Foreman's Ontological-Hysteric Theatre bombards audiences with images; Breuer, JoAnne Akalaitis and Ruth Maleczech's Mabou Mines combine acting, narrative techniques and mixed media in their work. Other experimental artists working since the 1980s utilize mixed media as well, for instance the Wooster Group formed by Spalding Gray, Meredith Monk, Ping Chong, JoAnne Akalaitis, Martha Clarke and Elizabeth LeCompte.

In the 1970s and 1980s, Broadway increasingly marketed sure-fire successes. Among the shows produced were many musical revivals and productions transferred from Off-Broadway and regional theaters, as well as hits from London. Neil Simon dominated Broadway comedy with *The Prisoner of Second Avenue* (1971), *The Sunshine Boys* (1972), *California Suite* (1976), *Chapter Two* (1977), *Brighton Beach Memoirs* (1983), *Biloxi Blues* (1985), *Broadway Bound* (1986) and *Lost in Yonkers* (1991), which won the Pulitzer Prize. Edward Albee won the Pulitzer for *Seascape* in 1975, and important drama also came from Sam Shepard, Lanford Wilson and David Mamet. Shepard's plays include *The Curse of the Starving Class* (1978), *Buried Child* (1978), *True West* (1980), *Fool for Love* (1983) and *A Lie of the Mind* (1985). Wilson's *Hot l Baltimore* (1973) set an Off-Broadway record and *Talley's Folly* (1979) won a Pulitzer Prize. Mamet won the New York Drama Critics' Circle Award for *American Buffalo* (1976) and the Pulitzer Prize for *Glengarry Glen Ross* (1984).

Meanwhile, composer-lyricist Stephen Sondheim dominated American musical theater after the mid-1970s. His work includes *Company* (1970), *Follies*

(1971), *A Little Night Music* (1973), *Pacific Overtures* (1976), *Sweeney Todd* (1979) and *Sunday in the Park With George* (1984), which won a Pulitzer Prize. By the mid-1980s, the American musical was relying more on a concept or theme, rather than a book or story. As a result, choreographer-directors rose to new positions of importance. They included Bob Fosse, who staged *Pippin* (1972), *Chicago* (1975) and *Dancin'* (1978), and Michael Bennett, who created *A Chorus Line* (1975) and *Dreamgirls* (1981).

Among the musical hits that originated in London were *Cats* (1981), *Starlight Express* (1984), *Les Miserables* (1985) and *Phantom of the Opera* (1986).

Since the 1980s, contemporary American theater has depended on nonprofit resident companies, both inside and outside New York, more than at any time since the 19th century. Such theaters as the New York Shakespeare Festival, Playwrights Horizons, Steppenwolf Theatre Company and the Goodman Theatre in Chicago, American Repertory Theatre at Harvard, the Mark Taper Forum in Los Angeles, and the Actors Theatre of Louisville originate important new plays. High production costs make working in New York very risky, especially for high-budget musicals.

Production values of the American theater have remained very high since the 1980s. The Broadway musical has no equal in terms of production quality. However, American theater has suffered from a shortage of writers and composers who can attract the large audiences that make grand-scale productions cost-effective. This is due in part to the loss of a great many talented artists to AIDS. The theater also faces greater and greater competition from the television and film industries.

NO THEATER ALLOWED!

In 1750, the Court of Massachusetts enacted a law stating: " . . . no person or persons whatsoever may . . . let, or suffer to be used or improved, any house, room, or place whatsoever, for acting or carrying on any stage-plays, interludes, or other theatrical entertainments, on pain of forfeiting and paying for each and every day, or time, such house, room, or place, shall be let, used, or improved, contrary to this act, twenty pounds. And if . . . any person or persons shall be present as an actor in or spectator of, any stage-play, &tc. where a greater number of persons than twenty shall be assembled together, every such person shall forfeit for each time five pounds. One-half to his majesty, one-half to the informer."

A TABLE FOR TWO

In the days before integration, the proprietor of the Stork Club preferred not to admit blacks. Even so, comedian George Jessel escorted African-American singer Lena Horne to the posh show-business hangout. When they arrived, the maitre d' made a cursory check of the reservation book and announced he had no tables available.

"Mr. Jessel," he asked, "who made the reservation?"

"Abraham Lincoln," Jessel replied.

American Musical Theater

Some historians view the New York production of *The Black Crook* (1866) as the starting point of American musical theater. During the colonial era, theatrical musical entertainment had been limited to ballad operas presented by English touring companies. Comic operas were popular after the Revolutionary War, and burlesques reached the United States during the 1830s. However, *The Black Crook*—a melodrama with French female ballet dancers—differed from all previous American musical productions in the way in which it utilized music and dance.

The American premiere of Gilbert and Sullivan's *HMS Pinafore* (1879) popularized comic operetta in the United States. In the 1880s, the full-length comedic musical plays of Harrigan and Hart delighted audiences. Reginald De Koven's comic opera *Robin Hood* (1891) is considered another classic of this period.

Late in the 19th century the musical theater form known as revue appeared. This was a collection of songs, dances and comedy sketches loosely interwoven by a plot or theme. *The Passing Show* (1894) was the first American production to define itself as a "review." Around the same time, a musical written and performed by an African-American premiered: *Clorindy or The Origin of Cakewalk* (1898). For the first time, significant numbers of white theatergoers saw a show written and performed by blacks.

By the turn of the century, most shows on the American musical stage fell into the categories of comic opera, operetta or musical comedy. George M. Cohan created a series of patriotic musical comedies based on contemporary characters and settings. Victor Herbert, considered an important composer for the American stage, composed such works as the operetta *Babes in Toyland* (1903). *Follies of 1907,* the first of Florenz Ziegfeld's annual revues, featured elaborate scenery, chorus dancers and stars.

During World War I, musical theater in the United States became more distinctly American. Irving Berlin successfully brought ragtime to the stage in *Watch Your Step* (1914). Jerome Kern demonstrated that contemporary American characters, situations and musical styles could make good musical theater, revolutionizing the form: During the 1920s, he took a new direction with his

Show Boat (1927), a prototype for later musical plays. Some scholars consider Kern the father of American musical theater as it is known today.

Musical revues became extremely popular during the 1920s, a decade when African-American culture began to have an influence on the Broadway stage. Beginning with *Shuffle Along* (1921), a succession of African-American musicals and revues attracted large audiences. These shows introduced new dance styles and helped make jazz more popular. At the same time, a new generation of composers influenced by jazz made their mark: George and Ira Gershwin collaborated on *Lady, Be Good* (1924), *Oh, Kay* (1926), *Funny Face* (1927), *Strike Up the Band* (1930) and the Pulitzer Prize–winning *Of Thee I Sing* (1931), which was the first musical to win a Pulitzer. For their part, Richard Rodgers and Lorenz Hart created a series of revues, *The Garrick Gaieties* (1925, 1926, 1930), as well as *Dearest Enemy* (1925), *A Connecticut Yankee* (1927) and *Present Arms* (1928).

During the Great Depression, distinctly American musicals proliferated on the Broadway stage. Cole Porter emerged as a force with his trademark clever, witty productions, which included *Fifty Million Frenchmen* (1929), *The New Yorkers* (1930) and *Anything Goes* (1934). Some of the most enduring works of the American musical theater appeared during these years, including George and Ira Gershwin's *Porgy and Bess* (1935) and Rodgers and Hart's *On Your Toes* (1936). For a brief period, a few musicals revolved around political themes, including the Group Theatre's antiwar *Johnny Johnson* (1936), which reflected the pacifist feelings of the 1930s, and the Mercury Theatre's production of Mark Blitzstein's *The Cradle Will Rock* (1937), which dealt with the conflict between capitalism and socialism.

Although Rodgers and Hammerstein's immensely popular *Oklahoma!* (1943) shared many characteristics with operetta, it diverged from the form in many ways. Among its innovations were the depiction of a murder on stage and a choreographed dream-ballet sequence to augment the action. Subsequent Rodgers and Hammerstein collaborations, such as *Carousel* (1945), *South Pacific* (1949), *The King and I* (1951) and *The Sound of Music* (1959), continued the process of invention.

Musical comedy thrived in the 1940s and 1950s. In addition to the contributions of Rodgers and Hammerstein were such successes as *Annie Get Your Gun* (1946) with a score by Irving Berlin; *Guys and Dolls* (1950) with a score by Frank Loesser; and *The Pajama Game* (1954) and *Damn Yankees* (1955), both with scores by Richard Adler and Jerry Ross. In 1956 Lerner and Loewe changed American musical theater with their adaptation of George Bernard Shaw's *Pygmalion* into the musical *My Fair Lady*. Other adaptations of plays, films and novels became popular musical theater: *West Side Story* (1957) was based on *Romeo and Juliet*; *Man of La Mancha* (1965) was based on Miguel de Cervante's novel *Don Quixote*; and *Fiddler on the Roof* (1964) was based on Sholom Aleichem stories. Some creators of musical comedy continued to explore new subjects and settings: *Gypsy* (1959) told the story of burlesque stripper Gypsy Rose Lee, *Cabaret* (1966) was set in decadent 1930s Berlin, and *Hair* (1967) brought rock and roll and nudity to the Broadway musical stage.

An important new composer-lyricist, Stephen Sondheim, contributed to the American musical theater during the 1970s and 1980s. His innovative shows included *Company* (1970), *Follies* (1971), *A Little Night Music* (1973), *Pacific Overtures* (1976), *Sweeney Todd* (1979), *Merrily We Roll Along* (1981) and *Sunday in the Park with George* (1984). Sondheim is considered a major force in recent American musical theater.

Also influential during the 1970s and 1980s were the choreographer-directors. Dance-focused shows of the period included Bob Fosse's *Pippin* (1972), *Chicago* (1975) and *Dancin'* (1978) and Michael Bennett's *A Chorus Line* (1975) and *Dreamgirls* (1981), among others.

Rising production costs and restrictive ticket prices have made contemporary musical theater a risky business in recent years, decreasing the number of new productions to reach Broadway. Popular Broadway musicals of the early 1990s included a revival of Frank Loesser's *Guys and Dolls* (1992) and Marsha Norman's musical adaptation of the novel *The Secret Garden* (1991). Also successful have been the long-running British imports *Cats* (1982), *Les Misérables* (1987), *The Phantom of the Opera* (1988), and *Miss Saigon* (1991). The grand Broadway musical, unique in the world, survives with *The Will Rogers Follies* (1991) and *Jelly's Last Jam* (1992). In the future, however, American musical theater may look more like *Falsettos* (1992), the combination of two related one-act musicals that originally ran Off-Broadway during different seasons. The show features a small cast and deals with timely subject matter: a man who leaves his family for his male lover.

Theater for the Masses: Some Popular Forms in the West

Burlesque

American burlesque, a style of variety performance that emerged during the late 19th century, was inspired by a number of sources, including traditional burlesque, British variety entertainment, black minstrel shows, and "leg shows" like *The Black Crook* (1866), a musical play featuring female ballet dancers in flesh-colored tights. American burlesque shows consisted of three parts: In the first, song-and-dance acts by groups of female performers were contrasted with comedy routines by male comedians. Part two presented magic, acrobatics and other acts performed by men only. A grand musical finale comprised part three. Until 1925, audiences could attend either "clean" or "dirty" burlesque; after that, most clean shows went dirty to increase the return at the box office.

From the early 1900s to 1935, the Minsky Brothers were the leading producers of American burlesque; by the 1920s they owned more than a dozen houses. They introduced belly dancers, known as "cootchers," and the illuminated runway from Paris. Female performers never stripped down completely in burlesque, but the shows were loaded with sexual double entendres, as well as flirtation between performers and the audience. Among burlesque strippers, Gypsy Rose Lee was one of the most memorable. Phil Silvers, Abbott and Costello, Jackie Gleason and other famous comedians got their start in burlesque.

Inevitably, the sexual content of burlesque offended some religiously oriented Americans. New York courts banned the runway in 1934 and all burlesque in 1942.

Comedy

Defined by the Greek philosopher Aristotle as "the painlessly ugly," ancient dramatic comedy was infused with a festive spirit that offered audiences escape from the cares and concerns of everyday life. On late medieval stages, comedy amused audiences with techniques familiar to them, including slapstick, puns, satire and fantasy. Religious plays of the time, although not explicitly comic, often featured devils who were both humorous and evil. During and after the Renaissance, William Shakespeare, Molière, Lope de Vega Carpio and Ben Jonson all wrote comedy in a range of forms that crossed national boundaries. But for the following few centuries, drama critics—and many playwrights—tended to view comedy as inferior to tragedy.

During the 20th century, dramatic comedy in legitimate theater ran the gamut from George Bernard Shaw to Neil Simon. In addition, American commercial theater often featured other kinds of comic entertainment, including variety, revue, burlesque and vaudeville. Various comic subgenres—farce, parody and satire, for instance—survive as devices in dramatic theater.

In the second half of the 20th century, stand-up comedy gained an audience in the United States. Many popular actors of the time, including Woody Allen, Bill Cosby and Robin Williams, started their careers as stand-up comedians. Numerous critics consider Lenny Bruce, who worked in Greenwich Village nightclubs during the early 1960s, as the first important political stand-up comedian. He shocked audiences with profanity and challenged America's conscience and self-image. Political comedy has flourished since Bruce's death in 1966, as has stand-up in general. Especially since the mid-1980s, the United States has experienced a boom in the number and quality of stand-up comics. Inspired by the examples of Billy Crystal, Whoopi Goldberg, Roseanne Arnold and others, many young performers have come to view stand-up as a step on the road to broader success.

Stand-up comedy has become a serious money-maker across the United States. The comedy club boom, which was first viewed as a fad in the entertainment industry, is now taken more seriously. In addition, cabarets and theaters feature comedy troupes, improvisational comedy groups have their own theaters, and performance art spaces feature their own comedy shows. On the threshold of the 21st century, stand-up comedy represents a new area of promise in the performing arts.

Melodrama

Melodrama was a popular form of theater in the 19th century that was eventually dismissed by critics and equated with sensationalistic spectacle and overacting. Its many variants developed late in the 18th century in France. In 1800, Guilbert de Pixerecourt premiered *Coelina,* a play in which a villain schemes to separate young lovers. England soon premiered its own melodrama, *A Tale of Mystery,* which was an adaptation of *Coelina* by Thomas Holcroft, in London in 1802. In subsequent years, melodrama played in large theaters in London, Paris and Berlin. It featured exotic and spectacular settings, large casts and loud music that underscored blatant emotion. As the technical sophistication of theaters allowed for increasingly complex special effects, melodrama evolved toward more complicated plots and "sensation scenes" involving avalanches, explosions, speeding trains and the like.

During the 1860s, suspenseful melodrama became popular in the United States: In Agustin Daly's *Under the Gaslight* (1867), a man is tied to railroad tracks as a train approaches; his *A Flash of Lightning* (1868) places the hero on a burning steamship; and *The Red Scarf* (1868) features the rescue of a man tied to a log inching toward the blades of a sawmill. By the turn of the 20th century, realism began to replace melodrama. Melodrama did, however, have a major influence on the budding motion picture industry.

Revue

Revue consists of songs, comedy sketches, dance and music loosely organized around a plot or connected by a theme. The word *revue* can be traced to 18th-century France; it has been performed throughout Europe in various popular forms for at least two centuries. In the United States, revue developed during the late 19th century and caught on in the first three decades of the 20th century. It ranged from immensely popular productions like the *Ziegfeld Follies* (1907–57) to intimate shows for small audiences, such as the *Greenwich Village Follies* (1919–28). Revue diversified when film and television also adopted the form, as seen in such works as the films of director Busby Berkeley and the topical television revue. On stage, revues such as *Oh, Coward* (1972) or *Side by Side by Sondheim* (London 1976; New York, 1977) focused on the works of a single composer.

Variety and Vaudeville

Variety shows were a popular style of urban entertainment during the 19th and early 20th centuries. Performed in the music halls and pubs of Europe and

VAUDEVILLE SLANG

Cigarettes: "coffin nails"
Dancer: "hoofer"
Failure: "all wet," "all washed up," "a flop"
Total failure: "We died in . . . "
Exit: "shuffle off to Buffalo"

Loud laughter from the audience: "belly laughs"
Perform: "strut your stuff"
Small-town circuit: "death trail"
Success: "a wow," "a panic," "a riot"

America, variety consisted of a collection of attractions, known as turns or numbers, that were unrelated to any theme. During performances the audiences ate, drank and smoked. The music-hall show, which gradually came to be called variety as it gained legitimacy, was the common form in Great Britain. In America, variety was known as vaudeville.

Nearly anywhere in the United States, vaudeville performers could play one-night stands in small houses. When New York's Palace Theater opened in 1913, it became one of the country's largest and best-known vaudeville theaters; performers dreamed of "playing the Palace." Some houses featured continuous vaudeville, which allowed audiences to enter at any time between 9:30 A.M. and 10:30 P.M. and see a performance.

Vaudeville shows were standardized into two parts with an intermission. The show's opener included animals, acrobats or any act that would not be disrupted by the noise of an entering audience. Then came song-and-dance acts, comedy acts, jugglers, male and female impersonators, ventriloquists, etc. These acts usually ran ten to twenty minutes, although Al Jolson, among others, stayed up to an entire hour. Performers most desired the slot that came before the closing or headlining act. Popular headliners included Jolson, George Burns and Gracie Allen, Will Rogers, W. C. Fields and George M. Cohan.

Vaudeville grew increasingly sophisticated by the 1920s. Nevertheless, it declined in popularity due to several factors, including the development of the motion picture. Many vaudeville houses were turned into movie houses. Though it eventually died out, vaudeville enriched American entertainment, honing the talents of popular stars and performers who would later become familiar to audiences through movies, radio and television.

GYPSY ROSE LEE, THE BURLESQUE QUEEN

Gypsy Rose Lee, American burlesque performer, said, "I know men aren't attracted to me by my mind. They're attracted by what I don't mind."

Lee once cabled her insurance company after an expensive item of clothing had disappeared: "Gown lifted in Hotel Imperial." The company responded, "Your policy does not cover that."

Performance Art: Performers Become the Art

In Europe and the United States during the 1960s, many visual artists began to incorporate performance into their work. Instead of making art, they themselves became the art: English artists Gilbert and George, for example, made "living sculpture" out of their own bodies. During the 1970s, performance was accepted as a medium of artistic expression—comparable to painting, sculpture or printmaking—in its own right. Many artists chose this medium, and as a result, art spaces devoted to performance sprang up in major international art centers, museums sponsored performance art festivals, colleges introduced performance classes, and specialized publications appeared. The performance art of the 1970s, 1980s and 1990s defies easy definition, as it draws on painting, architecture, poetry, music, dance, video, film, slides and narrative, using them in various combinations.

In New York, artists such as Robert Wilson and Richard Foreman created performance art theater on a grand scale in the 1970s. Dominated by visual images, their work was termed "The Theatre of Images" by critic Bonnie Marranca. Wilson took the psychology of an autistic teenager as material for many of his productions. Often written in collaboration with a company, the texts of his plays retained misspellings and other errors as a means of disregarding the conventional use and meaning of words. Wilson's works include *A Letter for Queen Victoria* (1974) and *Einstein on the Beach* (with composer Philip Glass, 1976). Foreman's work in the 1970s included *Pandering to the Masses: A Misrepresentation* (1975), during the performance of which his taped voice spoke directly to the audience to ensure that they "correctly" interpreted each part of the piece while it was happening.

The downtown New York scene offered fertile ground for performance art. The Kitchen, the Limbo Lounge, 8BC, the WOW Cafe, P.S. 122 and other spaces opened in the late 1970s and early 1980s to house less grand—but no less interesting—presentations. Performance styles generally expressed the sensibility of younger artists. At the WOW (Women's One World) Cafe, for instance, artists such as Peggy Shaw, Lois Weaver, Deb Margolin and others developed a body of work that challenged gender and sexual identity with humor and pathos.

By the early 1980s, the avant-garde performance art movement was gaining legitimacy in the commercial world. Hailed as cultural messengers, performance artists became celebrities. Laurie Anderson, to name but one, presented *United States,* an opus of song, narrative and visuals, at the Brooklyn Academy of Music in 1982. While projecting hand-drawn pictures, blown-up photographs taken from TV, and truncated film onto huge backdrops, Anderson spoke and sang songs about life, as a vocalizer distorted her voice. Her show reached a broad audience, helping to popularize performance art more widely.

So, too, did Eric Bogosian, a trained actor who started out as a solo performer. Beginning in 1979 with the character Ricky Paul, a macho entertainer with a twisted, dirty sense of humor, Bogosian created a series of characters. By the mid-1980s, they comprised a range of American male types: angry, often violent or hopelessly passive. Bogosian's solo performances include *Men Inside* (1981), *Drinking in America* (1985) and *Banging Nails in the Floor With My Head* (1994). In just a few short years he successfully moved into the commercial arena while maintaining the title "performance artist."

Commercially successful performance artists began to face the dilemma of accepting celebrity while maintaining their artistic integrity in the search for new aesthetic expression. John Kelly created minidramatizations of conflict-ridden artist Egon Schiele's biography; Karen Finlay examined sexual excess and deprivation; Ethyl Eichelberger combined drag, romance and satire, impersonating Nefertiti, Clytemnestra, Elizabeth I and Catherine the Great.

Among notable artists, filmmaker and sculptor John Jesurun thrived in the performance club atmosphere. He presented *Chang in a Void Moon* (1982), a "living film serial," in weekly episodes at the Pyramid Club in New York's East Village. Using staging techniques adapted from movies—camera pans, flashbacks and jumpcuts—his work reflected the prevailing high-tech mentality of the 1980s. In *White Water* (1986), live actors and "talking heads" projected on twenty-four closed-circuit monitors engaged in a ninety-minute verbal battle over illusion and reality. *Deep Sleep,* performed at La Mama Cafe in 1986, portrayed a young boy imprisoned in film.

As it became more accessible to general audiences, new work was presented with greater attention to costumes, sets and lighting. This new theater borrowed from the broadcast and print media, used written scripts, and incorporated other elements of traditional theater. First presented at an experimental venue called the Performing Garage, works such as Spalding Gray and Elizabeth LeCompte's *Trilogy* (1973) and Gray's *Swimming to Cambodia* (1984) later showed up on the legitimate theater circuit. Theater performers around the world were influenced by the movement and change in New York's performance art community, adapting freer forms to their own creations.

By definition, performance art can be anything at all, as long as the artist works without rules or guidelines. But by the mid-1980s, the public's acceptance of performance art as fashionable and fun entertainment almost defeated the form's intentions. Still, many new performers, as well as veterans from the 1970s and 1980s, continue to develop material and perform at P.S. 122, La Mama, the WOW Cafe, Dixon Place and other spaces. As performance art evolves, it continues to defy easy definition.

The Role of the American Drama Critic

Theater has always had its critical observers, beginning with Aristotle in classical Greece. In modern theater, critics serve several functions. Most importantly, they assess a production's value from the point of view of their previous theatergoing experience and their concepts of the art form. This critical review offers feedback to the theater artist, provides insight to the theatergoer, and serves as a record for history.

The role of the American theater critic has evolved over time. Because theater was considered dangerous by outspoken religious leaders in the late 18th century, the function of the critic was to censor in order to protect the public from violations of social and moral laws. An 1832 book by William Dunlap, *History of American Theatre,* notes that in 1796 six anonymous men organized a "band of scalpers and tomahawkers" to review New York productions.

Generally regarded as the first American drama critic of importance, Washington Irving reviewed the New York stage in the early 19th century for the *Morning Chronicle* and *The Salamagundi.* Still, few daily newspapers routinely published theater reviews until the 1850s. Before then, reviews more often appeared in short-lived drama magazines. Because play reviewing was held in low regard, novice reporters were often sent to review the opening night of a play. As a rule, only productions that advertised in their paper received any attention.

Toward the end of the 19th century, theater critics gradually refined their approach, and popular criticism began to resemble what we see today. The country's first important theatrical weekly, the *New York Dramatic Mirror,* was launched in 1879. Its editor, Harrison Grey Fiske, used the newspaper to establish the Actors' Fund, a charity for needy performers. The paper also sought to fight the business practices of the Theatrical Syndicate (the "Trust"), a group of producers and managers who for a period monopolized virtually all American playhouses and dictated business practices.

The popular press increasingly demanded clever and witty reviews; critic Alan Dale, first of the *Evening World* and then of the *Journal* and the *American,* wrote caustic reviews that helped to sell newspapers during the late 19th and early 20th century. However, he alienated producers and theater owners, who tried to ban him from their theaters.

Some critics worked to improve American theater. James G. Huneker, at the New York *Sun,* promoted the performance of the new, realistic drama of Henrik Ibsen and George Bernard Shaw in America. At *Atlantic Monthly* during the 1880s, William Dean Howells explored the possibilities of realistic American drama. Edward Dithmar, with the *New York Times* from 1877 until his death in 1917, fostered the work of American dramatists and broke with tradition by judging plays by his immediate reaction instead of on moral grounds. Using sarcasm and satire, George Jean Nathan, one of the most admired drama critics of his day, wrote for *The Smart Set* (1909–23) and became coeditor with H. L. Mencken beginning in 1914. He admired European as well as American dramatists and published Eugene O'Neill's early work.

Writing on and off from 1914 to 1922, Alexander Woollcott helped to establish the *New York Times* as a premier source of drama criticism in the 20th century. John Mason Brown, a fellow critic who worked at several influential publications during the first half of the 20th century, called Woollcott "a sizzling mixture of arsenic and treacle." Taking over in 1925, Brooks Atkinson served as chief drama critic of the *Times* until 1960 (with a few years out during World War II to serve as a war correspondent). Atkinson enhanced the paper's prestige and influence in theater. Walter Kerr, drama critic at the *Herald Tribune* from 1951 to 1966, became the drama critic for the *New York Times* in 1966. He held the post briefly, then continued to write Sunday critiques for the paper, bringing a unique historical perspective to his work. Kerr earned a Pulitzer Prize for his several books on theater.

Between 1981 and 1993, Frank Rich served as the chief drama critic at the *Times,* thus qualifying as perhaps the most influential reviewer in the country. Many theater professionals and audience members alike are critical of the *Times*'s power to determine the success of a production and even to cause Broadway shows to close after a few performances due to unfavorable reviews.

Outside New York, the influence of individual newspaper critics has usually remained local or regional. Claudia Cassidy of the *Chicago Tribune* (1942–65) and Richard Coe of the Washington *Post* (1936–81), among others, had an impact on American theater through their writing.

As the number of American newspapers has declined, magazine reviews have become more influential. Important magazine critics have included Harold Clurman in the *New Republic* and the *Nation*; Eric Bentley and Robert Brustein in the *New Republic*; Robert Benchley, Wolcott Gibbs, Brendan Gill and Edith Oliver in *The New Yorker,* and John Simon in *New York* magazine. Members of the theater profession rely on *Billboard* and *Variety* for reviews, and the *Village Voice* keeps readers up-to-date on what is happening Off-Off Broadway, as well as in avant-garde performance.

TYPES OF CRITICS

NEWSPAPER CRITICS traditionally attend the opening night of a production and write reviews based on their immediate responses to the work, for publication the next day.

TELEVISION AND RADIO CRITICS often work under the same deadline pressure as newspaper reviewers; some head for the studio directly after the performance to air their material.

MAGAZINE CRITICS may take more time to prepare their work, writing in-depth analyses of the production.

SCHOLARS AND ACADEMICS analyze a script, or even an entire genre of drama, in great detail; they may write about a single playwright, a period of dramatic history or dramatic theory.

TOUCHÉ

Watching a certain Broadway opening, writer Robert Benchley became bored with the play. When a telephone rang on an empty stage, he muttered, "I think that's for me," and headed for the exit.

An interviewer once asked director Mel Brooks what he thought of critics. "They're very noisy at night," he replied. "You can't sleep in the country because of them." When the interviewer explained he was asking about critics, not crickets, Brooks responded, "Oh, *critics*. What good are they? They can't make music with their hind legs."

Critic George Jean Nathan observed: "The drama critic who is without prejudice is on the same plane as a general who does not believe in taking human life."

In 1934, critic Brooks Atkinson reviewed a bomb at the Fulton Theatre, writing: "When Mr. Wilbur calls his play *Halfway to Hell,* he underestimates the distance."

After one of his shows was panned by all the major New York critics, producer David Merrick searched telephone directories until he found seven people who had the same names as the newspaper critics. He paid the imposters to give enthusiastic quotes for his production, which he then published in full-page ads, using their names. The *Herald Tribune* was the first to discover the prank and kill the ad, but by that time the joke was on the critics, all over town.

From Stage to Screen: Film's Origins in Theater

New art forms do not simply appear; they have roots in the cultural and social context of their time. The phenomenon of the motion picture appears to have arisen directly from the romantic and realist movements in art, drama and literature that developed throughout the 19th century. In turn, those movements reflected broader social and cultural changes, notably the growing influence of science, the scientific method and objective reasoning. Simply put, theater audiences gradually became more visually and realistically oriented; the development of motion pictures was a response to this preference.

As manager at London's Drury Lane Theatre, David Garrick implemented new forms of scenery and design. Beginning in 1771, Philip de Loutherbourg worked with Garrick to improve theatrical lighting and scenic systems, achieving greater pictorial realism in staging. In 1773, de Loutherbourg began to design extravagant theater spectacles, concentrating on lighting effects, such as castles in sunlight and moonlight, as well as on landscape and perspective scenery. Theater effects continued to reflect the objective or scientific point of view over the next century.

During the 19th century, the novel and the play tended toward both realistic and romantic influences. Popular melodramas contained exaggerated and sometimes implausible plot elements, but scenic designers made an effort to underscore realistic values in the productions. As playwrights manufactured more extreme romances, scenic designers took the opposite route, creating more realistic sets and effects. Designers had to support the increasingly glamorous and farfetched ideas of the playwrights, but in doing so they strove to provide an elaborate, overarching pictorial realism. In the crafts of playwriting and staging, realism and romanticism converged.

The realist-romantic movement, with its increasing emphasis on pictorial values, coincided with the invention of the motion picture. Between 1824 and 1832, inventors developed a number of devices that used still photographs to create the illusion of motion. By 1860, posed photographs were successfully animated. A third surge of development began in 1870, when posed, still photographs were projected by a beam of light. Once the relationship between photography and projection was established, progress was rapid. Photography on celluloid was then patented. In 1879, Thomas Edison demonstrated a kinetoscope, a device in which a strip of film passed between a magnifying lens and a light source at the rate of up to forty frames per second.

Meanwhile, the graphic evolution of the theater continued. At London's Princess Theatre, manager Charles Kean presented classical plays with a meticulous eye for historical accuracy. Each of his productions was accompanied by a book-length volume documenting historical sources. For the set design of *Macbeth* (1852), Kean sought background on pre-Norman buildings from an architectural historian. Kean was also the first of his contemporaries to use focused limelight effectively.

Romanticists with a realistic bent also flourished in France and the United States, where scientific progress was on the upswing in other fields as well. The realist impulse spread to writers, including the novelists George Eliot, Henry James and Thomas Hardy, and even to such romanticists as Robert Louis Stevenson, Arthur Conan Doyle and Rudyard Kipling. In drama, Henrik Ibsen, Anton Chekhov and August Strindberg stood out in the realist movement. The Irish playwrights, meanwhile, were both romantics and realists. By the time the motion picture arrived, realism and romanticism in fiction and playwriting had reached a pinnacle; thereafter, greater pictorial realism would be fulfilled only by the new medium.

Theater artists continued to experiment on the stage, however. They produced such hybrid forms as Alexander Black's *Miss Jerry* (1894), which seemed to preordain the development of cinema. For this "picture-play," the script was read in a darkened hall while more than three hundred photographs taken from life were projected on a screen. Shown during several hours at the rate of about two per minute, the pictures imparted life and motion to the play.

In light of the production of *Miss Jerry,* the rapid development of experimental theater forms might have been expected to take place in the early 20th century. But it did not, and some scholars argue that it was the arrival of the motion picture that checked this potential movement. In the early 1900s, film and theater could hardly be differentiated; realism and romanticism—which probably would have declined by then—were given a new lease on life in film.

As the motion picture evolved, new filming techniques widened the gap between drama on stage and on film. Both forms, however, continued to require the emotional involvement and participation of audiences. Over the years, the basic similarity between them—the acting out of a story—allowed for the adaptation of a great many plays for the movies, some more successfully than others. Among the productions translated to the screen have been

Oklahoma!, Death of a Salesman, A Streetcar Named Desire, Mister Roberts, West Side Story, Hair, Driving Miss Daisy, Prelude to a Kiss and *Glengarry Glen Ross*.

Whether on stage or on screen, a dramatic performance is required. The writer of a script develops a protagonist who undergoes some change as a result of the series of conflicts that make up the plot. The movie screenplay shares some similarities with the play script, but there are key differences. (See *The Playwright's Work: Writing the Play,* page 7.)

A screenwriter tells a story in about twenty to thirty scenes, each averaging three to five pages in length. The entire script totals about 120 pages and has the continuous flow of a seamless story. There are many variations, but a standard screenplay breaks down into three "acts." The first thirty pages—six or seven scenes—correspond to a play's Act One, setting up the situation that propels the protagonist forward into the next act. The fifteen or so scenes of the next sixty pages make up Act Two, in which major obstacles and near defeat (around page seventy-five) lead to a big climax. The final pages are devoted to Act Three; in it the action winds down and the protagonist undergoes his or her transformation.

Theater Awards

Members of the theater community give and receive scores of awards each year. Annually, dozens of organizations honor actors, playwrights, producers, directors, designers and other theater professionals for their contributions to the field. Here are a few of the most significant.

The Antoinette Perry Memorial (Tony) Award

American Theatre Wing
250 West 57th Street
New York, NY 10019
(212) 765-0606

League of American Theatres and Producers
226 West 47th Street
New York, NY 10036
(212) 764-1122

One of American theater's most coveted prizes, the Tony is awarded annually by the League of American Theaters and Producers and the American Theater Wing, a service organization formed in 1939 to assist in war-relief efforts. First presented in 1947, the Tony was named for Antoinette Perry, one of the founders of the Wing. The Tonys are an industry award limited to productions presented in officially designated Broadway theaters. Awards are presented in multiple categories; winners since 1990 are listed here.

1993 Play: *Angels in America*, Tony Kushner
Musical: *Kiss of the Spider Woman*
Revival: *Anna Christie*
Actor (play): Ron Leibman, *Angels in America*
Actress (play): Madeline Kahn, *The Sisters Rosensweig*
Actor, featured (play): Stephen Spinella, *Angels in America*
Actress, featured (play): Debra Monk, *Redwood Curtain*
Actor (musical): Brent Carver, *Kiss of the Spider Woman*
Actress (musical): Chita Rivera, *Kiss of the Spider Woman*
Actor, featured (musical): Anthony Crivello, *Kiss of the Spider Woman*
Actress, featured (musical): Andrea Martin, *My Favorite Year*
Director (play): George C. Wolfe, *Angels in America*
Director (musical): Des McAnuff, *Tommy*
Best book of musical: Terence McNally, *Kiss of the Spider Woman*
Best original musical score: John Kander and Fred Ebb, *Kiss of the Spider Woman*; Pete Townshend, *Tommy*
Scenic design: John Arnone, *Tommy*
Costume deisgn: Florence Klotz, *Kiss of the Spider Woman*
Lighting design: Chris Parry, *Tommy*
Choreography: Wayne Cilento, *Tommy*
Special Award: *Oklahoma!*, in recognition of its 50th anniversary
Special Award, Outstanding Regional Theater: La Jolla Playhouse, California

1992 Play: *Dancing at Lughnasa*, Brian Friel
Musical: *Crazy for You*
Actor (play): Judd Hirsch, *Conversations with My Father*
Actress (play): Glenn Close, *Death and the Maiden*
Actor, featured (play): Larry Fishburne, *Two Trains Running*
Actress, featured (play): Brid Brennan, *Dancing at Lughnasa*
Actor (musical): Gregory Hines, *Jelly's Last Jam*
Actress (musical): Faith Prince, *Guys and Dolls*
Actor, featured (musical): Scott Waara, *The Most Happy Fella*
Actress, featured (musical): Tonya Pinkins, *Jelly's Last Jam*
Director (play): Patrick Mason, *Dancing at Lughnasa*
Director (musical): Jerry Zaks, *Guys and Dolls*
Best book of musical: William Finn and James Lapine, *Falsettos*
Best original musical score: William Finn, *Falsettos*
Scenic design: Tony Walton, *Guys and Dolls*
Costume design: William Ivey Long, *Crazy for You*
Lighting design: Jules Fisher, *Jelly's Last Jam*
Choreography: Susan Stroman, *Crazy for You*
Revival: *Guys and Dolls*

Special Award, Outstanding Regional theater: Goodman Theater of Chicago

Special Award: *The Fantasticks*, Off-Broadway's longest-running show

1991   Play: *Lost in Yonkers*, Neil Simon
Musical: *The Will Rogers Follies*
Actor (play): Nigel Hawthorne, *Shadowlands*
Actress (play): Mercedes Ruehl, *Lost in Yonkers*
Actor, featured (play): Kevin Spacey, *Lost in Yonkers*
Actress, featured (play): Irene Worth, *Lost in Yonkers*
Actor (musical): Jonathan Pryce, *Miss Saigon*
Actress (musical): Lea Salonga, *Miss Saigon*
Actor, featured (musical): Hinton Battle, *Miss Saigon*
Actress, featured (musical): Daisy Eagen, *The Secret Garden*
Director (play): Jerry Zaks, *Six Degrees of Separation*
Director (musical): Tommy Tune, *The Will Rogers Follies*
Best book of musical: Marsha Norman, *The Secret Garden*
Best original musical score: Cy Coleman, Betty Comden and Adolph Green, *The Will Rogers Follies*
Scenic design: Heidi Landesman, *The Secret Garden*
Costume design: Willa Kim, *The Will Rogers Follies*
Lighting design: Jules Fisher, *The Will Rogers Follies*
Choreography: Tommy Tune, *The Will Rogers Follies*
Revival: *Fiddler on the Roof*
Special Award, Outstanding Regional Theater: Yale Repertory Theatre

1990   Play: *The Grapes of Wrath*
Musical: *City of Angels*
Actor (play): Robert Morse, *Tru*
Actress (play): Maggie Smith, *Lettice and Lovage*
Actor, featured (play): Charles Durning, *Cat on a Hot Tin Roof*
Actress, featured (play): Margaret Tyzack, *Lettice and Lovage*
Actor (musical): James Naughton, *City of Angels*
Actress (musical): Tyne Daly, *Gypsy*
Actor, featured (musical): Michael Jeter, *Grand Hotel*
Actress, featured (musical): Randy Graff, *City of Angels*
Director (play): Frank Galati, *The Grapes of Wrath*
Director (musical): Tommy Tune, *Grand Hotel*
Best book of musical: Larry Gelbart, *City of Angels*
Best original musical score: Cy Coleman, David Zippel, *City of Angels*
Scenic design: Robin Wagner, *City of Angels*
Costume design: Santo Loquasto, *Grand Hotel*
Lighting design: Jules Fisher, *Grand Hotel*
Choreography: Tommy Tune, *Grand Hotel*
Revival: *Gypsy*

New York Drama Critics Circle Award

Founded in 1936, the **New York Drama Critics' Circle** consists of New York print-media critics. It gave its first award during the 1935–36 season and currently distributes up to three awards annually: Best Play (American and Foreign) and Best Musical of the season. Winners since 1968–69 are listed here.

1992–93   Foreign play: *Someone Who'll Watch Over Me*, Frank McGuiness
American play: *Angels in America: Millenium Approaches*, Tony Kushner
Musical: *Kiss of the Spider Woman*, John Kander, Fred Ebb and Terence McNally

1991–92   Foreign play: *Dancing at Lughnasa*, Brian Friel
American play: *Two Trains Running*, August Wilson
Musical: (no award)

1990–91   Foreign play: *Our Country's Good*, Timberlake Wertenbaker
American play: *Six Degrees of Separation*, John Guare
Special citation: Eileen Atkins for her performance in *A Room of One's Own*
Musical: *The Will Rogers Follies*, Cy Coleman, Peter Stone, Betty Comden and Adolph Green

1989–90   Foreign play: *Privates on Parade*, Peter Nichols
American play: *The Piano Lesson*, August Wilson
Musical: *City of Angels*, Larry Gelbart, Cy Coleman and David Zippel

1988–89   Foreign play: *Aristocrats*, Brian Friel
American play: *The Heidi Chronicles*, Wendy Wasserstein
Special citation: Bill Irwin for *Largely New York*
Musical: (no award)

1987–88   Foreign play: *The Road to Mecca*, Athol Fugard
American play: *Joe Turner's Come and Gone*, August Wilson
Musical: *Into the Woods*, Stephen Sondheim and James Lapine

1986–87   Foreign play: *Les Liaisons Dangereuses*, Christopher Hampton
American play: *Fences*, August Wilson
Musical: *Les Misérables*, Claude-Michel Schonberg and Alain Boublil

1985–86   Foreign play: *Benefactors*, Michael Frayn
American play: *Lie of the Mind*, Sam Shepard
Special citation: Lily Tomlin and Jane Wagner for *The Search for Signs of Intelligent Life in the Universe*
Musical: (no award)

1984–85   Foreign play: (no award)

American play: *Ma Rainey's Black Bottom*, August Wilson
Musical: (no award)

1983–84   Foreign play: *The Real Thing*, Tom Stoppard
American play: *Glengarry Glen Ross*, David Mamet
Musical: *Sunday in the Park with George*, Stephen Sondheim and James Lapine
Special Citation to Samuel Beckett for his body of work

1982–83   Foreign play: *Plenty*, David Hare
American play: *Brighton Beach Memoirs*, Neil Simon
Musical: *Little Shop of Horrors*, Alan Menken and Howard Ashman (based on a film by Roger Corman)
Special Citation to Young Playwrights Festival

1981–82   Foreign play: *The Life and Adventures of Nicholas Nickelby*, adapted by David Edgard
American play: *A Soldier's Play*, Charles Fuller
Musical: (no award)

1980–81   Foreign play: *A Lesson from Aloes*, Athol Fugard
American play: *Crimes of the Heart*, Beth Henley
Musical: (no award)
Special Citations to *Lena Horne: The Lady and her Music* and to the New York Shakespeare Festival production of *The Pirates of Penzance*

1979–80   Foreign play: *Betrayal*, Harold Pinter
American play: *Talley's Folly*, Lanford Wilson
Musical: *Evita*, Andrew Lloyd Webber and Tim Rice
Special Citation to Peter Brook's Le Centre International de Créations Théâtrales for its repertory

1978–79   Foreign play: *The Elephant Man*, Bernard Pomerance
American play: (no award)
Musical: *Sweeney Todd*, Hugh Wheeler and Stephen Sondheim

1977–78   Foreign play: *Da*, Hugh Leonard
American play: (no award)
Musical: *Ain't Misbehavin'*, conceived by Richard Maltby, Jr.

1976–77   Foreign play: *Otherwise Engaged*, Simon Gray
American play: *American Buffalo*, David Mamet
Musical: *Annie*, Thomas Meehan, Charles Strouse and Martin Charnin

1975–76   Foreign play: *Travesties*, Tom Stoppard
American play: *Streamers*, David Rabe
Musical: *Pacific Overtures*, Stephen Sondheim, John Weidman and Hugh Wheeler

1974–75   Foreign play: *Equus*, Peter Schaffer
American play: *The Taking of Miss Janie*, Ed Bullins
Musical: *A Chorus Line*, Michael Bennett, James Kirkwood, Nicholas Dante, Marvin Hamlisch and Edward Kleban

1973–74 Foreign play: *The Contractor*, David Storey
American play: *Short Eyes*, Miguel Pinero
Musical: *Candide*, Leonard Bernstein, Hugh Wheeler, Richard Wilbur, Stephen Sondheim and John Latouche

1972–73 Foreign play: *The Changing Room*, David Storey
American play: *The Hot l Baltimore*, Lanford Wilson
Musical: *A Little Night Music*, Hugh Wheeler and Stephen Sondheim

1971–72 Foreign play: *The Screens*, Jean Genet
American play: *That Championship Season*, Jason Miller
Musical: *Two Gentlemen of Verona*, adapted by John Guare, Mel Shapiro and Galt MacDermot
Special Citations to *Sticks and Bones* (David Rabe) and *Old Times* (Harold Pinter)

1970–71 Foreign play: *Home*, David Storey
American play: *The House of Blue Leaves*, John Guare
Musical: *Follies*, James Goldman and Stephen Sondheim

1969–70 Foreign play: *Borstal Boy*, Frank McMahon (based on Brendan Behan's autobiography)
American play: *The Effect of Gamma Rays on Man-in-the-Moon Marigolds*, Paul Zindel
Musical: *Company*, George Firth and Stephen Sondheim

1968–69 Foreign play: (no award)
American play: *The Great White Hope*, Howard Sackler
Musical: *1776*, Sherman Edwards and Peter Stone

The Pulitzer Prize

The Pulitzer Prize Office
702 Journalism
Columbia University
New York, NY 10027
(212) 854-3842

While not awarded by the entertainment industry or theater critics, the Pulitzer Prize is much sought-after by playwrights. Awarded almost every year since 1918 for various literary and journalistic achievements, the Pulitzer honors outstanding American plays, preferably those dealing with American life.

1993 Tony Kushner, *Angels in America: Millenium Approaches*
1992 Robert Schenkhan, *The Kentucky Cycle*
1991 Neil Simon, *Lost in Yonkers*
1990 August Wilson, *The Piano Lesson*
1989 Wendy Wasserstein, *The Heidi Chronicles*
1988 Alfred Uhry, *Driving Miss Daisy*
1987 August Wilson, *Fences*

1986	No award
1985	Stephen Sondheim, James Lapine, *Sunday in the Park with George*
1984	David Mamet, *Glengarry Glen Ross*
1983	Marsha Norman, *'Night Mother*
1982	Charles Fuller, *A Soldier's Play*
1981	Beth Henley, *Crimes of the Heart*
1980	Lanford Wilson, *Talley's Folly*
1979	Sam Shepard, *Buried Child*
1978	D. L. Coburn, *The Gin Game*
1977	Michael Christofer, *The Shadow Box*
1976	Michael Bennett, James Kirkwood, Nicholas Dante, Marvin Hamlisch and Edward Kleban, *A Chorus Line*
1975	Edward Albee, *Seascape*
1974	No award
1973	Jason Miller, *That Championship Season*
1972	No award
1971	Paul Zindel, *The Effect of Gamma Rays on Man-in-the-Moon Marigolds*
1970	Charles Godone, *No Place to Be Somebody*
1969	Howard Sackler, *The Great White Hope*
1968	No award
1967	Edward Albee, *A Delicate Balance*
1966	No award
1965	Frank D. Gilroy, *The Subject Was Roses*
1964	No award
1963	No award
1962	Frank Loesser, Abe Burrows, Willie Gilbert and Jack Weinstock, *How to Succeed in Business Without Really Trying*
1961	Tad Mosel, *All the Way Home*
1960	George Abbott, Jerome Weidman, Sheldon Harnick and Jerry Bock, *Fiorello*
1959	Archibald MacLeish, *J. B.*
1958	Ketti Frings, *Look Homeward, Angel*
1957	Eugene O'Neill, *Long Day's Journey Into Night*
1956	Frances Goodrich and Albert Hackett, *The Diary of Anne Frank*
1955	Tennessee Williams, *Cat on a Hot Tin Roof*
1954	John Patrick, *The Teahouse of the August Moon*
1953	William Inge, *Picnic*
1952	Joseph Kramm, *The Shrike*
1951	No award
1950	Richard Rodgers, Oscar Hammerstein II and Joshua Logan, *South Pacific*
1949	Arthur Miller, *Death of a Salesman*
1948	Tennessee Williams, *A Streetcar Named Desire*
1947	No award
1946	Russel Crouse and Howard Lindsay, *State of the Union*

1945   Mary Chase, *Harvey*
1944   No award
1943   Thorton Wilder, *The Skin of Our Teeth*
1942   No award
1941   Robert E. Sherwood, *There Shall Be No Night*
1940   William Saroyan, *The Time of Your Life*
1939   Robert E. Sherwood, *Abe Lincoln in Illinois*
1938   Thornton Wilder, *Our Town*
1937   George S. Kaufman and Moss Hart, *You Can't Take It With You*
1936   Robert E. Sherwood, *Idiot's Delight*
1935   Zoe Akins, *The Old Maid*
1934   Sidney Kingsley, *Men in White*
1933   Maxwell Anderson, *Both Your Houses*
1932   George S. Kaufman, Morrie Ryskind, and George and Ira Gershwin, *Of Thee I Sing*
1931   Susan Glaspell, *Alison's House*
1930   Marc Connelly, *The Green Pastures*
1929   Elmer Rice, *Street Scene*
1928   Eugene O'Neill, *Strange Interlude*
1927   Paul Green, *In Abraham's Bosom*
1926   George Kelly, *Craig's Wife*
1925   Sidney Howard, *They Knew What They Wanted*
1924   Hatcher Hughes, *Hell-Bent for Heaven*
1923   Owen Davis, *Icebound*
1922   Eugene O'Neill, *Anna Christie*
1921   Zona Gale, *Miss Lulu Bett*
1920   Eugene O'Neill, *Beyond the Horizon*
1919   No award
1918   Jesse Lynch Williams, *Why Marry?*
1917   No award

Other Awards

DISTINGUISHED BROADWAY PERFORMANCE AWARD
Drama League of New York
165 West 46th Street
New York, NY 10036
(212) 302-2100

The Drama League is an audience organization consisting primarily of interested theatergoers. It gave its first Distinguished Broadway Performance Award in 1935. Currently, it grants three awards each year to winners determined by a joint committee of board members and members of an advisory board.

DRAMA DESK AWARD
Drama Desk
1900 Broadway
New York, NY 10023
(212) 724-9400

The Drama Desk awards are voted on by critics, reporters and editors who regularly cover New York theater for print or broadcast media. The Drama Desk, which makes no distinction between Broadway and Off-Broadway shows when considering nominees in each category, absorbed the Vernon Rice Award, first given in 1955 to honor Off-Broadway productions.

OFF-BROADWAY (OBIE) AWARD
The Village Voice
50 Cooper Square
New York, NY 10003
(212) 475-3300

Obies, first given in 1956, are awarded by the reviewers of New York's *Village Voice* newspaper.

OUTER CRITICS CIRCLE AWARD
Outer Critics Circle
101 West 57th Street
New York, NY 10019
(212) 765-8557

The Outer Critics Circle consists of print and broadcast journalists who cover New York theater for out-of-town, national and international media. It gave its first award in 1950.

Theater Funding Sources

The following is a selected list of grants available to individual theater artists. Further information about grants, fellowships, prizes, writers' colonies and residencies available to individuals and theater companies may be obtained by contacting state arts agencies, as well as other sources. See *Additional Sources of Information on Theater* (pages 111–118) for publications on funding and for helpful membership and service organizations.

Grants and Fellowships: Playwrights

Actors Theatre of Louisville
316-320 West Main Street
Louisville, KY 40202
(502) 584-1265

The Great American Play Contest is a competition for one-act and full-length plays that have not had previous Actors Equity productions or Equity waivers. Winners receive a cash award and are considered for production by the Actors Theatre of Louisville.

American Academy and Institute for Arts and Letters
633 West 155th Street
New York, NY 10032
(212) 368-5900

The Award of Merit Medal is given in several categories, including playwriting. The Richard Rodgers Production Award subsidizes a production in New York of a musical play by authors and composers who are not already established in the field. Applications are not accepted; nomination is by members of the academy only.

American College Theatre Festival
Kennedy Center for the Performing Arts
Washington, DC 20566
(202) 416-8850

The ACTF offers several programs and awards to individuals: The David Library of the American Revolution Award goes to student writers and college theaters for full-length plays on the subject of American freedom. The ASCAP Musical Theatre Award recognizes outstanding achievement in the creation of a work for the musical theater by college and university students. The Jane Chambers Playwriting Award is for a new play in which the central character and the majority of principal roles are women. The Lorraine Hansberry Award goes to the best student-written play on the black experience in America. Each award includes a cash stipend.

Anisfield-Wold Award in Race Relations
321 Cherry Hill Road
Princeton, NJ 08540
(609) 924-3756

One award is given annually for a published work of creative fiction, including drama, that addresses racial issues. The winner receives a cash stipend.

Asian Cultural Council
1290 Avenue of the Americas
New York, NY 10019
(212) 373-4300

Supports residencies for playwrights, composers, librettists and lyricists in Japan for a variety of purposes, including creative activity, research and training.

Beverly Hills Theatre Guild, The
Box 148
Beverly Hills, CA 90213
(213) 273-3033

The Beverly Hills Theatre Guild—Julie Harris Playwright Award Competition awards cash to three American playwrights whose submitted works earn the vote of independent professional evaluators.

Colonial Players, Inc., The
Theater-in-the-Round
108 East Street
Annapolis, MD 21401
(301) 956-3397

The Biennial Promising Playwright Award provides a cash award and a showcase opportunity to a script appropriate for arena production by an aspiring playwright.

Forest A. Roberts Theatre
Northern Michigan University
Marquette, MI 49855-5364
(906) 227-2553

The Forest A. Roberts/Shiras Institute Playwriting Award offers a cash award and produces winning plays.

Jenny McKean Moore Fund for Writers
3306 Highland Place, NW
Washington, DC 20008
(202) 363-8628

Sponsored jointly by the Fund and George Washington University, the grant allows the winning writers to spend a year as visiting lecturers at the university, teaching two courses per year. Two grants are given annually, one each for creative writing and playwriting.

Jewish Community Center
3505 Mayfield Road
Cleveland Heights, OH 44118
(216) 382-4000

The Jewish Community Center of Cleveland Playwriting Award Competition offers a cash prize and a staged reading, by the center, for a new play that provides fresh and significant perspectives on the range of Jewish experience.

Mary Roberts Rinehart Fund, The
Department of English
George Mason University
4400 University Drive
Fairfax, VA 22030
(703) 323-2936

Grants in Aid for drama are given in odd-numbered years to help unpublished writers to complete their work. Work must be submitted by an established sponsoring writer or editor, though no written recommendations from the sponsor are necessary.

Money for Women/Barbara Deming Memorial Fund
Box 40-1043
Brooklyn, NY 11240-1043
Phone not available

The fund awards biennial grants to playwrights, composers, librettists and lyricists.

National Endowment for the Arts (NEA)
Theater Program
1100 Pennsylvania Avenue, NW
Washington, DC 20506
Phone not available

The NEA's Fellowship for Playwrights assists playwrights of exceptional talent, allowing them to set aside time for writing, research, travel or career advancement.

National Repertory Theatre Foundation
P.O. Box 71011
Los Angeles, CA 90071
(213) 629-3762

The National Play Award is a cash award that goes to a playwright and to a professional theater for a paid Actors Equity production.

New York State Council on the Arts
915 Broadway
New York, NY 10010
(212) 387-7061

NYSCA's Individual Artist Program includes funding for project support in the creation of new works in various fields, including theater.

San Francisco Foundation, The
685 Market Street
Suite 910
San Francisco, CA 94105
(415) 543-0223

The James D. Phelan Award is available to writers of drama. Applicants must be native-born Californians.

Sunset Cultural Center
P.O. Box 5066
Carmel, CA 93921
(408) 624-3996

The Festival of Firsts Playwriting Competition encourages and develops new plays for the theater. Plays must be full-length and never before produced.

University of Chicago
Court Theatre
5706 South University
Chicago, IL 60637
(312) 702-7005

Offered biennially, the Charles H. Sergel Drama Prize is awarded to encourage the writing of new American plays.

Wagner College
Department of Speech and Theatre
631 Howard Avenue
Staten Island, NY 10301
(212) 390-3256

The Stanley Drama Award is given to the best play or musical submitted to the competition. The script must be accompanied by a completed application and a written recommendation from a theater professional.

Grants: Performers

Affiliate Artists Inc.
37 West 65th Street
New York, NY 10023
(212) 580-2000

This organization gives Community Residencies for solo performing artists in dance, music performance and theater. It also runs an Affiliate Artists Residency

Program, sponsored by corporations, foundations and government agencies, for young professional actors and other artists in communities throughout the country.

American College Theatre Festival
Kennedy Center for the Performing Arts
Washington, DC 20566
(202) 416-8000

The Irene Ryan Acting Award gives cash awards to outstanding college and university student actors.

Art Matters
131 West 24th Street
New York, NY 10011
(212) 929-7190

The Awards to Individuals program funds individual artists in ongoing, unrestricted, project-specific visual arts work and performance work with a strong visual emphasis, including performance art.

National Endowment for the Arts (NEA): See *Grants: Other* listing below.

National Institute for Music Theater
Kennedy Center for the Performing Arts
Washington, DC 20566
Phone not available

The George London Grants for Singers give cash awards to young opera and musical theater singers. The Fellowships in Composition are for creators and their immediate collaborators, for example, stage and music directors, coaches and accompanists.

Grants: Other

American College Theatre Festival
Kennedy Center for the Performing Arts
Washington, DC 20566
(202) 416-8000

The American College Theatre Festival conducts twelve regional theater festivals with workshops for college and university students each year. As many as twenty of the most diverse regional college and university productions are invited to Washington, D.C., to participate in a two-week, noncompetitive national festival at the Kennedy Center, with all expenses paid.

National Endowment for the Arts (NEA)
Promotion of the Arts—Theatre
1100 Pennsylvania Avenue, NW
Washington, DC 20506
(202) 682-5425

The NEA has several programs for theater professionals, including: Director Fellows, which provides individual grants to stage directors in their early career development; Fellowships for Playwrights; Fellowships for Mimes and Solo Performance Artists; Distinguished Artist Fellowships in Theater; and Stage Designer Fellows.

Additional Sources of Information on Theater

Theater Reference Books

Banham, Martin, ed. *The Cambridge Guide to World Theatre*. Cambridge, England: Cambridge University Press, 1988.

Hartnoll, Phyllis, ed. *The Oxford Companion to the Theatre*, 4th edition. Oxford, England: Oxford University Press, 1983.

Books on Theater History

Brockett, Oscar G. *The Essential Theatre*, 4th edition. New York: Holt, Rinehart and Winston, Inc., 1988.

Hartnoll, Phyllis. *A Concise History of Theatre*. New York: Harry W. Abrams, 1968.

Hewitt, Barnard. *History of the Theatre from 1800 to the Present*. New York: Random House, 1970.

Kernodle, George R. *The Theatre in History*. Fayetteville: University of Arkansas Press, 1989.

Mitchley, Jack, and Peter Spaulding. *Five Thousand Years of the Theatre*. London: Batsford Academic and Educational Ltd., 1982.

Nicoll, Allardyce. *The Development of the Theatre*, 5th ed., rev. New York: Harcourt Brace, 1966.

Sitarz, Paula Gaj. *The Curtain Rises: A History of Theater from its Origins in Greece and Rome through the English Restoration*. White Hall, Virginia: Shoe Tree Press, 1991.

Books on Theater Theory

Dukore, Bernard F. *Dramatic Theory and Criticism: Greeks to Grotowski*. New York: Holt, Rinehart & Winston, Inc., 1974.

Schechner, Richard. *Public Domain*. Indianapolis: Bobbs-Merrill, 1969.

Selden, Samuel. *Man in His Theatre*. Chapel Hill: The University of North Carolina Press, 1957.

Shank, Theodore. *The Art of Dramatic Art*. Belmont, California: The Dicksenson Publishing Co., Inc., 1969.

Books of Play Synopses

Samuel French, Inc. *1994 Basic Catalogue of Plays*. New York: Samuel French, Inc., 1994.

Shank, Theodore. *500 Plays*. New York: Drama Book Publishers, 1991.

Script Anthology Books

Block, Haskell M., and Robert G. Shedd, eds. *Masters of Modern Drama*. New York: Random House, 1962.

Dukore, Bernard F., ed. *17 Plays: Sophocles to Baraka*. New York: Thomas Y. Crowell Co., 1976.

Gassner, John. *A Treasury of the Theatre*, various editions. New York: Simon and Schuster.

Books on Playwriting

Cassady, Marshall. *Characters in Action: A Guide to Playwriting*. Lanham, Maryland: University of America Press, 1984.

Egri, Lagos. *The Art of Dramatic Writing*. New York: Simon and Schuster, 1972.

Hull, Raymond. *How to Write a Play*. Cincinnati, Ohio: Writer's Digest Books, 1983.

Pike, Frank, and Thomas Dunn. *The Playwright's Handbook*. New York: New American Library, 1985.

Books on Acting

Chekhov, Michael. *To the Actor on the Technique of Acting*, rev. ed. New York: Harper Perennial, 1991.

Eaker, Sherry, ed. *The Back Stage Handbook for Performing Artists*. New York: Back Stage Books/Watson-Guptill, Inc., 1989.

Hagen, Uta, with Haskel Frankel. *Respect for Acting*. New York: Macmillan Publishing Co., Inc., 1973.

McGaw, Charles. *Acting is Believing: A Basic Method*, 5th ed. New York: Holt, Rinehart & Winston, 1987.

Stanislavski, Konstantin. *An Actor Prepares*. Translated by Elizabeth Hapgood. New York: Theatre Arts Books, 1936.

Books on Directing

Clurman, Harold. *On Directing*. New York: Macmillan Publishing Co., Inc., 1972.

Dean, Alexander, and Lawrence Carra. *Fundamentals of Play Directing*, 3rd ed. New York: Holt, Rinehart & Winston, 1974.

Hodge, Francis. *Play Directing: Analysis, Communication and Style*. Englewood Cliffs, New Jersey: Prentice-Hall, Inc., 1971.

Stanislavski, Konstantin. *My Life in Art*. Translated by J. J. Robbins. Boston: Little, Brown, 1924.

Books on Scene and Costume Design, Stage Lighting and Makeup

Buchman, Herman. *Stage Makeup*. New York: Watson Guptill Publications, 1971.

Corson, Richard. *Stage Makeup*, 5th ed. Englewood Cliffs, New Jersey: Prentice-Hall, Inc., 1975.

Mielziner, Jo. *Designing for the Theatre: A Memoir and a Portfolio*. New York: Bramhall House, 1965.

Parker, W. Oren, Harvey K. Smith, and R. Craig Wolf. *Scene Design and Stage Lighting*, 5th ed. New York: Holt, Rinehart & Winston, 1985.

Rosenthal, Jean, and Lael Wertenbaker. *The Magic of Light*. Boston: Little, Brown, 1972.

Books on Stage Management

Gruver, Bert. *The Stage Manager's Handbook*. Revised by Frank Hamilton. New York: Drama Book Specialists, 1972.

Books on Theater Training

Everett, Carol J. *The Performing Arts Major's College Guide*. New York: Prentice Hall, 1992.

Peterson's Guides to Graduate and Professional Programs: An Overview. Princeton: Peterson's Guides, updated yearly.

Books on Funding

Annual Register of Grant Support: A Directory of Funding
Sources, 1993, 26th edition. New Providence, New
Jersey: R.R. Bowker, 1992.

Green, Laura R., ed. *Money for Artists: A Guide to Grants
and Awards for Individual Artists*. New York: ACA
Books, 1987.

Lesko, Matthew. *Getting Yours: The Complete Guide to
Government Money*, 3rd ed. New York: Penguin
Books, 1987.

List of Grants and Awards Available to American Writers,
14th edition. New York: PEN American Center,
1987.

Marketing Guides for Playwrights

Dramatists Sourcebook. New York: Theatre Communications Group, published annually.

Writer's Market. Cincinnati: Writer's Digest Books, published annually.

Directories of Non-Profit Theaters

Theatre Directory. New York: Theatre Communications
Group, updated annually.

Magazines and Newspapers

American Theatre
Theatre Communications Group
355 Lexington Avenue
New York, NY 10017
(212) 697-5230

A monthly magazine, with scholarly tendencies, about American theater.

Back Stage
330 West 42nd Street
New York, NY 10036
(212) 947-0020

A service weekly for the communications
and entertainment industry.

Lighting Dimensions Magazine
135 Fifth Avenue
New York, NY 10010
(212) 677-5997

A magazine for lighting professionals.

Theatre Crafts International
135 Fifth Avenue
New York, NY 10010
(212) 677-5997

Covers the international theater, film and
television design and technology scene.

Theatre Week
28 West 25th Street
New York, NY 10010
(212) 627-2120

A weekly magazine with articles about
New York, national and international theater.

Variety
475 Park Avenue So.
New York, NY 10016
(212) 779-1100

The trade newspaper for theater, film and
television industry professionals.

Libraries and Museums

Bread & Puppet Museum
RD 2, Rte. 122
Glover, VT 05839
(802) 525-3031

Puppetry, theater, masks.

Center for Puppetry Arts
1404 Spring Street
Atlanta, GA 30309
(404) 873-3089

International puppets; toy and poster collection.

Hampden-Booth Theatre Library at the Players
16 Gramercy Park South
New York, NY 10003
(212) 228-7610

Collections pertaining to the American and English stage, manuscripts.

Hocking Valley Museum of Theatrical History, Inc.
34A Public Square
Nelsonville, OH 45764
Phone not available

Scenery, organs, chairs, dressing rooms.

Hot Springs Area Arts Center
303½ N. River
Hot Springs, SD 57747
(605) 745-6696

Rotating exhibits.

John and Mable Ringling Museum of Art
5401 Bay Shore Road
Sarasota, FL 34243
(813) 355-5101

18th-century Italian theater.

New York Public Library for the Performing Arts, The
40 Lincoln Center Plaza
New York, NY 10023
(212) 870-1670

Circulating and reference collection on dance, drama and music. Prints, letters, manuscripts, documents, photos, posters, films, videotapes, memorabilia, dance, music, recordings.

Tabor Opera House Museum
306-310 Harrison Avenue
Leadville, CO 80461
(719) 486-1147

Paintings, theater history.

Vent Haven Museum
33 W. Maple
Fort Mitchell, KY 41011
(606) 341-0461

Ventriloquial figures, rare books, manuscripts, films, records, playbills.

Membership and Service Organizations

The following is a selected list of professional theater associations across the country:

Alliance of Resident Theatres/New York (A.R.T./New York)
131 Varick Street, Room 904
New York, NY 10013
(212) 989-5257

Trade and service organization for New York City's nonprofit professional theater.

American Music Theater Festival
2005 Market Street
One Commerce Square, 18th floor
Philadelphia, PA 19103
(215) 851-6450

Fosters the development of music theater as an American art form.

American Theater Critics Association (ATCA)
1326 Madison Avenue
New York, NY 10128
Phone not available

Fosters communication between American theater critics.

ASSITEJ/USA (International Association of Theatre for Children and Young People)
270 West 89th Street
New York, NY 10024
(212) 769-4143

Advocates the development of professional theater for young audiences.

Black Theatre Network
Box 11502, Fisher Building Station
Detroit, MI 48211
(313) 577-7906 (publications)

A national network of professional artists, scholars and community groups; offers several publications.

Dramatists Guild, The
234 West 44th Street
New York, NY 10036
(212) 398-9366

Professional association of playwrights, composers and lyricists.

Foundation Center, The
79 Fifth Avenue
New York, NY 10003
(212) 620-4230

Nationwide service organization established and supported by foundations to provide a single authoritative source of in-formation about foundation giving; offers several publications.

Hispanic Organization of Latin Actors (HOLA)
250 West 65th Street
New York, NY 10023
(212) 595-8286

A service organization for Hispanic performers and related artists.

International Center for Women Playwrights
c/o Department of English
306 Clemens Hall
S.U.N.Y. at Buffalo
Buffalo, NY 14260
(716) 645-2578

Supports women playwrights around the world; publishes a newsletter.

International Theatre Institute of the United States (ITI/US)
220 West 42nd Street, Ste. 1710
New York, NY 10036
(212) 944-1490

An international theater organization and clearinghouse for information and services; maintains an international library covering 142 countries.

League of American Theatres and Producers
226 West 47th Street
New York, NY 10036
(212) 764-1122

Negotiates labor contracts and government relations; conducts and sponsors research on commercial theater.

League of Chicago Theatres/Chicago Theatre Foundation
67 East Madison, Ste. 2116-2117
Chicago, IL 60603-3013
(312) 977-1730

A trade and service organization for Chicago theater companies, theater personnel and freelance artists.

League of Historic American Theatres (LHAT)
1600 H Street, NW
Washington, DC 20006
(202) 783-6966

Concerned with restoration and maintenance of historic American theaters.

League of Off-Broadway Theaters and Producers (LOBTP)
130 West 42nd Street
New York, NY 10036
(212) 730-7130

Seeks to advance the Off-Broadway theater in New York.

League of Resident Theaters (LORT)
c/o Center Stage
700 N. Calvert Street
Baltimore, MD 21201
(410) 685-3200

Seeks to advance the regional professional theater in the United States.

National Foundation for Jewish Culture
330 Seventh Avenue
New York, NY 10001
(212) 629-0500

Provides a number of programs in the field of contemporary Jewish theater.

National Theatre Conference (NTC)
Art and Drama Center
Baldwin Wallace College
Berea, OH 44017
(216) 826-2239

Limited to 120 members that include noncommercial academic and nonacademic theaters; collaborates with other major organizations on matters of policy and action.

New Dramatists
424 West 44th Street
New York, NY 10036
(212) 757-6960

A service organization for member playwrights.

Non-Traditional Casting Project
355 Lexington Avenue
New York, NY 10017
(212) 682-5790

Addresses and seeks solutions to the problems of racism and exclusion in the theater and related media, particularly as they relate to creative personnel.

Playwrights' Center
2301 Franklin Avenue East
Minneapolis, MN 55406
(612) 332-7481

A service organization for playwrights.

Playwrights' Platform
43 Charles Street
Boston, MA 02114
(617) 720-3770

A developmental theater for new plays, for New England playwrights.

Theatre Bay Area
657 Mission Street, Ste. 402
San Francisco, CA 94105
(415) 957-1557

A resource center for San Francisco theater workers, including 3,200 individuals and 200 theater companies.

Theatre Communications Group (TCG)
355 Lexington Avenue
New York, NY 10017
(212) 697-5230

A service organization for nonprofit professional theaters and performers; fosters interaction between members; offers several publications.

Theatre Historical Society (THS)
6510 41st Avenue, N.
Hyattsville, MD 20782
Phone not available

Preserves and makes available the history of popular theater in the United States.

Theatre Library Association (TLA)
111 Amsterdam Avenue
New York, NY 10023
(212) 870-1644

Gathers, preserves and makes available records of theater in all its forms; membership includes curators, librarians and scholars.

United States Institute for Theatre Technology (USITT)
8 West 19th Street
New York, NY 10011
(212) 924-9088

Serves the interests of those interested in the advancement of theater techniques and technology.

Volunteer Lawyers for the Arts
1285 Avenue of the Americas
New York, NY 10019
(212) 977-9270

Arranges free legal representation and counseling to the arts community.

Women's Project and Productions, The
7 West 63rd Street
New York, NY 10023
(212) 873-3040

Assists the development of American women playwrights and directors.

Unions:

Actors Equity Association
165 West 46th Street
New York, NY 10036
(212) 869-8530

Association of Theatrical Press Agents and Managers (ATPAM)
165 West 46th Street
New York, NY 10036
(212) 719-3666

Dramatists Guild, The
234 West 44th Street
New York, NY 10036
(212) 398-9366

International Alliance of Theatrical and Stage Employees (IATSE)
1515 Broadway
New York, NY 10036
(212) 730-1770

Society of Stage Directors and Choreographers (SSDC)
1501 Broadway
New York, NY 10036
(212) 391-1070

United Scenic Artists (USA)
575 8th Avenue
New York, NY 10018
(212) 736-6260

Part II:
MUSIC

Glossary of Musical Terms

absolute music: Music that derives its form completely from itself, rather than from the formal schemes or story lines employed in program music or opera.

a cappella: Singing unaccompanied by instruments. The term comes from the diminutive of the Italian word for chapel, *cappella,* and translates literally as "in the church style."

accelerando: Gradually quickening the pace.

adagio: At a slow pace that is slower than andante but not as slow as lento.

addolorato: Sorrowful, pained.

affettuoso: With affection or feeling.

affrettando: Hastening.

agitato: Agitated.

air: A simple song or melody with or without words, for voice or instrument. The term is *ayre* in its original Old English spelling.

alla breve: With the breve, that is, in duple or quadruple meter. The half note is used as the unit of time, so each half note represents a beat, indicated by the sign ¢ for cut time. (c indicates common time or ¼.)

allargando: Gradually becoming slower, yet louder and more stately.

allegretto: Lively, but not to the extent of allegro.

allegro: Livelier than allegretto, but not as energetic as presto.

alto: The highest range of the falsetto male tenor voice and the lower range of women's and boys' voices.

andante: Moderately slow; literally, at "walking" speed.

animato: Animated, with spirit, and quickening the tempo.

answer: A response to a musical phrase or subject, most often occurring as part of a fugue.

anthem: A form of sacred vocal work of the Anglican church, sung with or without accompaniment. Anthems are generally austere compositions.

arabesque: Borrowed from Arabic or Moorish architectural parlance, the term describes decorative flourishes in a work. Arabesque is most often associated with the works of Robert Schumann and Claude Debussy.

aria: A complex and often lengthy vocal solo in an opera or oratorio.

arpeggio: Playing the tones of a chord separately in succession, as with a harp.

a tempo: An instruction to return to regular tempo.

atonal: Lacking a recognizable relationship between tones as they are established in the diatonic or chromatic scales.

augmentation: Repetition of a musical figure or phrase using notes of longer duration than the original; opposite of diminution.

augmented chord: A chord with a major third and a sharp fifth.

auxiliary tone: A grace note placed directly above or below a principal harmonic note.

bagatelle: A brief, light, often humorous piece of music. Beethoven composed three Bagatellen for piano.

ballad: A descriptive song that tells a story. Historically, the term was applied both to light, simple songs accompanied by dancing and to romantic or historical operatic poems set to music.

bar: A vertical line drawn perpendicularly across the musical staff to divide it into measures. Also, a measure of music.

baritone: The intermediate male voice, which is lower than tenor but higher than bass.

bass: The lowest, deepest male voice. Also, the lower part or staff of a musical composition, as indicated by the bass clef. Contrasts with treble.

bass clef: The clef placed on the fourth line of the staff, locating F below middle C.

beat: The basic time unit of music, sometimes marked by the hand movement of a conductor.

bel canto: Literally "beautiful singing," the term usually describes operatic singing in the traditional Italian manner, particularly characterized by works of the 17th through 18th centuries.

bis: An instruction to musicians to play a passage of a composition twice. Its literal meaning is "encore" or "twice."

blue note: A blues term describing the lowering of certain notes, particularly the third and seventh notes of the major scale.

bouche fermée: With "closed mouth," that is, like humming.

bowing: The use of a bow to play an instrument, such as the violin, or the signs that indicate the direction in which a bow is drawn.

break: The point at which the singing range shifts, differentiating tenors, sopranos and altos.

breve: A single note that is the time equivalent of two whole notes, or semibreves.

brio: Vigor, brilliance.

buffo, buffa: As an adjective, comic. As a noun, a male or female singer of comic parts.

cadence: A chord sequence that moves to a point of harmonic resolution.

cadenza: A vocal or instrumental performance, usually extemporaneous, that occurs toward the end of a piece.

calando: Becoming slower and fainter.

canon: A polyphonic composition or section of a composition in which one part is imitated by another voice or instrument. The echo starts before the original part has ended, producing an overlapping effect.

cantata: A short vocal work of either a sacred or a secular nature that originated in 17th-century Italy. It is usually sung by a chorus (but sometimes by a single voice) with instrumental accompaniment. Johann Sebastian Bach, Alessandro Scarlatti, George Frideric Handel and Benedetto Marcello were noteworthy cantata composers.

canto: The chief melody of a song.

capriccio: In the 17th and 18th centuries, a term used to describe a short instrumental piece in a fanciful style.

carol: In the broadest sense, a joyous song, generally associated with a season or religious event, sung by a group. Often linked with Christmas, carols are called *noëls* in France and *Weitinachtslieder* (Christmas Eve songs) in Germany. Carols were especially popular at Yuletide in England during the 19th century.

catch: A type of partsong, or round, popular in the 17th through the 19th centuries, in which overlapping singers' voices suggest humorous meanings.

chamber music: Traditionally dating from the 17th through 19th centuries, music meant to be played in an ordinary room or small concert hall. Compositions of this type are performed by small groups of from two to eight musicians, the string quartet being especially popular.

chanson: In the broadest sense, any French song with repeated verses. More specifically, a song sung solo or ensemble, popular in Renaissance Italy, that arose from the troubadour tradition.

chorale: A Protestant hymn adapted from plainsong.

chord: A combination of three or more tones played simultaneously.

chord of rest: See *tonic.*

chromatic: Containing tones outside the diatonic, or natural, scale. A chromatic scale encompasses the twelve pitches of an octave and progresses by semitones rather than by the whole tones of the diatonic scale. See also *tempered scale.*

clef: A sign placed in front of the key and time signatures at the beginning of a composition and repeated on each staff. Treble clef indicates the higher part of a composition; bass clef indicates the lower. Clef determines the placement of notes on the staff.

coda: A longer passage tagged onto the end of a piece of music to provide a conclusion. Also, a distinct section of a musical composition.

common time: Four quarter notes to the measure; written ¼ or indicated by a **c**. Compare *alla breve.*

composition: A musical piece.

consonance: The harmoniousness of two or more sounds.

continuo: An important component in baroque ensemble music, a bass part for a keyboard or stringed instrument that is played throughout a piece; also called thoroughbass. This is the same as basso continuo, where a bass instrument doubles the bass voice in the keyboard.

contralto: The lowest female voice; also called alto.

contrapuntal: Based on counterpoint.

counterpoint: The combination of two or more melodic parts so that they support one another yet remain independent. The word *point* was once used interchangeably with *note.*

countertenor: A male alto who can sing falsetto. The word is often used interchangeably with *alto.*

crescendo: Growing louder.

da capo: Repeat from the beginning and end at a designated point usually marked fin or finé.

decrescendo: Growing softer. Synonymous with diminuendo.

degree: A space or line of the musical staff; also a numbered and named position (i.e., I tonic, II supertonic) of a scale, indicating pitch.

diatonic: The whole tones of the natural scale; also a musical scale with five whole tones and two semitones. Contrasts with chromatic.

diminished chord: A chord with a minor third and flat fifth.

diminuendo: Gradually waning; decrescendo.

diminution: Repetition of a musical figure or phrase using notes of shorter duration than the original, the purpose of which is to ornament the work; opposite of augmentation.

dissonance: The discordance of two or more sounds.

divisi: Literally, "divided." Indicates that players who ordinarily play in unison are to separate and play two or more distinct parts.

dominant: The fifth tone of the diatonic scale, or V chord.

doppio movimento: Doubling the speed.

dot: A mark used several ways in musical notation: Placed above a note, it indicates staccato; placed after a note or rest, it directs musicians to increase the time value by half. A double dot extends the time value by an additional ¾ of the note's original time value.

downbeat: The first beat of a measure, indicated by the downward motion of a conductor's hand or baton.

duet: A composition for two voices or instruments, or the musicians who perform such a composition.

dynamics: Variations in the loudness or intensity (energy) of music.

eighth note: A note whose time value is ⅛ of a whole note.

enharmonic: Notes that are written differently but sound the same in the tempered scale. For instance, A-flat and G-sharp sound the same, as do C-sharp and D-flat.

ensemble: Literally, "together." Refers to a group of musicians who perform multipart compositions together.

expression marks: Words or signs accompanying music to help performers interpret how it is to be played.

falsetto: The top register of the male voice. Tenors often employ this technique to extend their range.

fantasia: An unconventional, usually instrumental, and often extemporaneous work that does not follow a standard style or structural form. Sixteenth-century lutenist Francesco Canova du Milano is credited with first developing such compositions.

fifth: A musical interval encompassing five tones on the diatonic scale.

figure: A repeated musical pattern.

flat: The symbol (♭) that indicates the lowering of a note by one semitone.

form: The overall structure of a musical work, based on length, variety and unity. Symphonies and sonatas are two musical forms.

forte: Loud and strong.

fortissimo: Very loud.

fourth: A musical interval encompassing three whole and one half steps on the diatonic scale.

fugue: A contrapuntal composition in which a theme or subject is developed by the successive entry of a number of voices (vocal or instrumental), all imitating one another. Though developed in the Middle Ages, the form reached full expression in the Baroque era (from the end of the 16th to the mid-18th centuries) with Bach. Mozart and Beethoven continued to develop the form.

fundamental note: The root note of a chord; the note on which a chord is built.

glee: A short composition, arranged in parts for three or more male voices, and usually sung a cappella.

glissando: Gliding quickly up and down the scale.

grace note: A nonessential note used to embellish a melody.

grave: Gravely and slowly; largo.

grazia: Gracefully and elegantly.

Gregorian chant: A type of plainsong thought to have originated with monks under Gregory I (Pope from 590 to 604) and recorded at the earliest in manuscripts of the 10th century.

half note: A note whose time value is half that of a whole note.

half step: A semitone.

harmonics: The study of musical sound, or the tones produced by touching a stringed instrument at nodal points (notes of a chord other than the fundamental).

harmony: The structure, combination and relation of chords in a composition; also, the simultaneous notes in a chord. Compare *melody*.

homophony: Having a single melody supported by an accompaniment, in contrast to polyphony.

improvisation: Creating music as it is being performed.

I chord: See *tonic*.

incidental music: Music played during a drama for mood and background; also, music played between other pieces.

intermezzo: Music played between acts of a drama or opera; also, a short work performed in concert.

interval: The distance in pitch between a group of tones, counted from the lowest tone to the highest and including the starting and finishing tones. There are several types: A perfect interval consists of the first (prime), fourth, fifth and octave tones. A major interval contains the second, third, sixth and seventh tones of the major key or mode. An augmented interval is half a tone larger than a major or perfect interval (the upper tone is sharpened or the lower tone is flattened). A minor interval is half a tone smaller than the corresponding major interval (the upper tone of the major interval is flattened or the lower tone is sharpened). A diminished interval is half a tone shorter than a perfect or minor interval.

intonation: Accuracy of pitch.

inversion: The transposition of the notes in a chord, interval, theme or part.

key: A series of tones considered in relation to the tonic. Musical works are often described as being in a particular key, based on the tonic note.

keynote: A tonic note, i.e., the first tone of a diatonic scale.

key signature: A cluster of sharps or flats that indicate the key of a musical composition, written at the beginning of each staff.

largo: Slowly and grandly; grave.

leading tone: The major seventh tone of any scale; a subtonic.

ledger line: A short line placed above or below the staff to hold notes that are too high or low to appear on the staff itself.

legato: Smoothly; opposite of staccato.

leitmotif: A recurring musical phrase tied to a character or situation in a drama, especially associated with Richard Wagner.

lento: Very slowly, but not to the extent of grave or largo.

libretto: The text of an opera, operetta, oratorio or other dramatic musical work.

lyrics: The words of a song.

madrigal: A contrapuntal composition for three or more voices, usually sung without accompaniment. Madrigal originated in medieval Italy.

maestoso: In a majestic manner.

major scale: A diatonic scale in which half steps fall between the third and fourth and between the seventh and eighth tones.

marcato: Accented.

martelatto: Strongly accented.

measure: A segment of a musical composition delimited by two bars; also called a bar.

mediant: The third degree of the diatonic scale.

melody: An arrangement of successive single tones. Compare *harmony*.

meter: The arrangement of rhythmic units in a musical composition.

mezzo: Literally, "half." The term is often used to describe the variety of singing voices. A mezzo-soprano, for example, has a range between a soprano and an alto.

middle C: On the piano, the note C located closest to the middle of the keyboard.

minor: A diatonic scale with a half step between the first and third tones.

modulation: The contrast between keys and the movement from one key to another.

molto: Very much. For example, molto vivace means very spirited.

monophony: Music consisting of a single melodic line without accompaniment.

mordent: A musical ornament created by switching rapidly between a principal note and one above or below it.

morendo: Gradually diminishing.

motion: The rise and fall of a melody.

movement: A distinct section of a long composition, usually with its own specifications for speed, key, character and the like.

natural: Not sharp or flat.

ninth: A nine-step tonal interval (i.e., an octave plus a second).

nocturne: A romantic composition, usually for piano, popular in the 19th and 20th centuries.

note: A sound of distinct tone and duration; synonymous with tone.

octave: A musical interval encompassing the fundamental and the 8th degree of the diatonic scale.

octet: A composition for eight voices or instruments; or, the ensemble of musicians who perform such a work.

opera: A dramatic performance set to music, in which most or all dialogue is sung.

opera buffa: A variety of comic opera with 18th-century origins.

opera comique: Literally "comic opera," but actually a type of opera characterized by the inclusion of spoken dialogue.

operetta: A light opera, usually of short duration, that might include spoken dialogue. Jacques Offenbach and Johann Baptist Strauss are among the better-known composers of operetta.

oratorio: A musical composition for voice and instruments that relates a sacred story but is performed without costumes, scenery or action.

orchestra: A large assemblage of musicians who play the diverse instruments and musical parts called for in ensemble music; a term usually used in relation to symphony music.

overture: An instrumental piece usually used as an introduction to a larger composition, such as an opera.

parallel motion: The simultaneous movement of two or more melodies in consistent intervals.

part: A chord-based composition in homophonic style. The melody resides in the uppermost notes of the chords.

partsong: A song for two or more voice parts, without accompaniment. Partsong is usually less polyphonous than a madrigal.

passing note: A note—usually a nonharmonic tone—played between chords as a means of melodic movement between them.

pasticcio: A work created by more than one composer; term for musical work that draws on diverse sources for inspiration. Also, a type of operatic melody first popularized in the 18th century.

pause: A sign indicating that a note or rest should be held longer than is normal.

pentatonic: A five-toned musical scale, omitting the fourth and seventh tones. The black keys on a piano are an example.

phrase: A group of notes that form a distinctive theme (or melody) in a composition.

piano: Softly.

pianissimo: Very softly.

pitch: The highness or lowness of a tone in relation to others. Determined by the frequency of a vibration, pitch is the standard by which instruments are tuned.

pizzicato: A term indicating that an instrument's strings should be plucked, not bowed.

plainsong: Religious music without defined meter (that is, rhythmically free), generally sung unaccompanied. Gregorian chant is a form of plainsong.

poco: Little. For example, poco a poco means little by little.

polyphony: Music with two or more simultaneous melodies. Opposite of homophony.

precipitato: Hurriedly, precipitately.

presto: In rapid tempo.

program music: Music that illustrates or interprets a story or visual work.

progression: An aural succession of tones or chords.

quarter note: A note whose time value is ¼ of a whole note.

quartet: A composition for four voices or instruments; also, the musicians who perform such a work. A piano quartet includes a piano, violin, viola and cello, while a string quartet consists of first and second violins, a viola and a cello.

quintet: A composition for five voices or instruments; also, the musicians who perform the piece. A piano quintet comprises a string quartet plus a piano.

recitative: A musical vocal style, common to opera, that imitates speech.

reed: A woodwind instrument, such as a clarinet or saxophone, played by placing the mouth on the reed (elastic strip) and causing it to vibrate with air.

refrain: A musical phrase that is repeated, usually after the verses of a song.

resolution: The progression from a dissonant tone or chord to a consonant one.

rest: A silence or pause in a musical composition or part that lasts a given number of beats or bars; also, the symbol used to indicate a rest (see page 137).

rhapsody: An instrumental work, usually for the piano, of the 19th or 20th century. Associated with such composers as Antonin Dvorak, Johannes Brahms and Franz Lizst.

rhythm: A pattern of beats formed by the duration and accentuation of notes.

riff: A short, repeated, rhythmic phrase usually associated with popular music or jazz.

rinforzando: An accent sometimes followed by a short but strong crescendo.

ritardando: Gradually becoming slower.

ritornello: An often-recurring instrumental passage in a vocal work, particularly as known in the 17th century; also, a tutti passage of a concerto, as practiced in the second half of the 17th century and the 18th century.

rondo: An instrumental composition with a refrain.

root: The fundamental note of a chord, upon which it is built.

round: A perpetual canon for three or more melodic voices, in which each singer enters at a different time; parts are repeated indefinitely, as opposed to having a finite ending.

scale: A set of ascending or descending notes that progress in the steps or half steps consistent with that scale (i.e., major/minor, etc.) and vary in pitch and interval.

second: On a diatonic scale, the interval between two adjacent notes.

semitone: Half of a whole tone, a half step.

septet: A composition for seven voices or instruments; also, the ensemble of musicians who perform the work.

sequence: Repetition of a melodic or harmonic pattern, each repetition starting on a different tone.

serenade: A musical performance that pays tribute to a person, generally a loved one. Most often associated with the outdoors, a serenade is an instrumental piece for a small ensemble.

seventh: A musical interval encompassing seven tones in the diatonic scale; also, leading tone.

sextet: A composition for six voices or instruments; also, the ensemble of musicians who perform such a work.

sharp: The symbol (♯) that indicates the elevation of a note's pitch by one semitone.

signature: A sign placed on the staff to indicate the key or tempo of a composition.

sixth: A musical interval encompassing the first and sixth tones in the diatonic scale.

slur: A curved line that joins two or more notes

and indicates that they should be performed legato.

solo: Literally, "alone." Refers to a performance by a single musician.

sonata: An instrumental composition of three or four independent yet related movements, prevalent from the 17th century onward. In the 18th century, sonatas for stringed instruments marked the beginnings of the classical style, typified by Domenico Scarlatti and Carl Philipp Emanuel Bach.

soprano: The highest female or boy's voice; or, the part in a composition written for the highest voice or instrument.

sostenuto: Sustained, prolonged.

sotto voce: Softly, in a low voice.

staccato: Disconnected, distinct, with separation; opposite of legato.

staff: The set of horizontal lines and spaces upon and around which musical notes are written. Also called a stave.

stretto: The overlapping entrances of voices in a fugue.

subdominant: The fourth tone of the diatonic scale, or IV chord.

subito: Suddenly.

subject: The principal group of notes that form the basis of a composition, especially the theme of a fugue.

submediant: The sixth tone of the diatonic scale.

subtonic: The scale degree just below the tonic; seventh tone of the diatonic scale (leading tone).

suite: An instrumental composition made up of a set of movements, often associated with or condensed from a larger dance or opera.

supertonic: The second tone of the diatonic scale.

symphonic poem: An orchestral work of a programmatic nature in one movement.

symphony: A large work for orchestra, comprised of four or more movements. The form came into its own in the 18th century with the Italian composer Giovanni Battista Sammartini.

syncopation: A shift in the rhythm of a composition that accents a normally weak beat.

tempered scale: A scale, such as our chromatic scale, in which the acoustical accuracy of the interval has been adjusted so that all notes of the scale are an equal distance from one another.

tempo: The speed at which a composition is played.

tenor: The highest naturally occurring adult male voice; also, an instrument of this range or a part written for such a voice.

tenuto: Elongated.

ternary: A musical passage made up of three sections. The first and third sections are exactly or nearly identical. The second part, although closely related to the other two, provides contrast in a different key. The direction *da capo* often initiates the third part.

tetrachord: Four notes that span a perfect fourth interval. Associated with ancient Greek music, it originally referred to four notes played on a lyre.

theme-and-variation: One of the earliest instrumental forms, it consists of a musical idea or theme (usually a melody) that is repeated in variations with differing structures. Variations must bear a recognizable relation to the original theme.

third: A musical interval encompassing three tones in the diatonic scale.

thoroughbass: See *continuo*.

time: The rhythm or speed of a composition; also, one measure of a composition.

tonality: The key of a musical composition (the arrangement of tones in relation to the tonic key).

tone: A sound of definite pitch and duration; a musical note; the character or emotion of a sound; a step.

tone poem: See *symphonic poem*.

tonic: Adjectival form of tone; as a noun, refers to the first tone of a diatonic scale, that is, the keynote.

tonic sol-fa: A system of musical notation that substitutes syllables for staff notation to represent the notes of the scale. "Do" is the tonic, followed by "re," "me," "fa," "sol," "la," "ti" (or "si").

transpose: To change the original key of a composition.

treble: The highest part, whether of voice or instrument, of a musical composition; also, soprano. The treble clef indicates the upper staff in sheet music. Contrasts with bass.

treble clef: The clef placed on the second line of the staff, locating G above middle C.

tremolo: A trembling effect produced by rapidly repeating a note.

triad: A chord consisting of three tones: the root, the third above the root and the fifth above the root.

trio: A composition for three voices or instruments; also, the musicians who perform such a work.

triplet: Three notes of equal duration played with a time value of one beat.

triple time: Three beats to a measure.

turn: Ornamental notes played in quick succession and connecting a principal note with others above and below it.

tutti: Literally, "all." Directs the entire instrumental or vocal section to join in.

twelve-tone: Associated with Arnold Schönberg, a musical piece in which the twelve chromatic tones determine the structure.

unison: The playing of separate musical parts in the same pitch and at the same time.

unito: Literally, "united." Directs orchestral players to perform together. Opposite of divisi.

upbeat: A weak beat within a bar, especially the last beat of a measure, indicated by the conductor's upward hand or baton motion.

vamp: A rhythmic, repeated accompaniment, over which instrumental or vocal solos are performed in popular music and jazz.

variation: The alteration of a theme by changes in rhythm, harmony, key and the like.

veloce: Rapidly.

vivace: In a lively, vivacious manner.

volume: The fullness of a vocal or instrumental tone.

whole note: In common time, a note with four beats.

whole tone: An interval of the major second, i.e., the interval between two notes on a diatonic scale.

The Elements and Theory of Music

Every kind of music, from the simplest traditional chant to the most elegant orchestral symphony to the loudest rock and roll, derives from the same basic elements. These raw materials—rhythm, melody, harmony and form— combine in an infinite variety of ways to create pleasing, ordered sound. At times one of the elements may stand alone, or some may intertwine without the others, but most modern music relies on all four. The fourth element, form, is covered in later sections ("Variation, Arrangement and Improvisation" and "A Brief History of Classical Music"). Harmony, the third element, produces the chords, scales and tonic keys that can give music astonishing depth and texture. As they discovered the subtleties and capabilities of the harmonic system, musicians formalized them in music theory. In addition, the demands of harmony, and the complexity of its relationship with rhythm and melody, required a precise system of written notation that evolved over several hundred years. An understanding of the essentials can greatly enhance the enjoyment of music.

Rhythm

Humans naturally hear the patterns in sounds. They pick up on a regular pulse, they detect strong and weak beats, and they respond to rhythm with physical movements. Rhythm is the controlled movement of sound in time. The duration of tones, the number of times they repeat and the pattern with which they sound determine the rhythm of a musical passage. As the rule behind the duration of each pitch, rhythm regulates all the musical relationships within a composition.

Musical time is usually organized by means of a basic unit of length known as a beat; some beats are stronger than others and receive more emphasis. Beats fall into groups known as bars or measures, each containing a fixed number of stressed and unstressed beats that are organized in a regularly recurring pattern. Meter, the organization of notes with respect to time, creates a regular pulse made up of beats. It is identified at the beginning of a composition, or at any point in the piece where it may change, by a time signature. Usually written as two numbers, one above the other as in ¼, a time signature is placed on the staff after the clef and key signature. The lower number indicates the unit of each measure that gets one beat and the upper indicates the number of units in each measure.

Duple meter contains two beats to a measure, accented generally on the first beat; triple meter has three, also accented on the first beat; quadruple meter, or common time, has four beats, with accents generally on the first and third beats. Compound meters contain five, six, seven or more beats to the measure, with accents marking the metrical pattern. According to the tempo, or pace, of the music, the beats in a measure occur slowly or rapidly. If the rhythm is syncopated, the accent falls on a weak beat of the measure instead of a strong beat, such as on the second beat in triple meter. Syncopation—the intentional upset of a normal accent—is a popular way to avoid a monotonous rhythmic pattern and create tension in music.

Melody and Harmony

Listeners most often remember the melody of a piece of music. In the most basic sense, a melody is a succession of tones perceived as a consciously arranged unit.

That is, listeners don't respond to tones separately, but in relation to each other within a pattern. A melody generally consists of a pair of two phrases. Separately, each phrase has specific meaning in the larger musical structure; together, two phrases form a musical passage that has even greater meaning.

Melody's partner, harmony, dictates the movement and relationship of tonic intervals and chords in a piece of music. An interval is the distance between two tones. In the familiar do-re-mi-fa-sol-la-ti-do scale, the interval do-re is called a second, do-mi a third, do-fa a fourth, do-sol a fifth, do-la a sixth, do-ti a seventh, and the interval between one do and the next an octave. The two tones of an interval sound either simultaneously or in close succession.

Three or more tones sounded together in a single unit of harmony make a chord. In a composition, melody is heard above the supporting harmony of chords. Because chords have meaning only in relation to other chords, harmony governs the progression and overall organization of a composition's tones. The most common chord in western music, the triad, combines the first, third and fifth members of the scale, that is, do-mi-sol. Similarly, other triads may start from any one of the other degrees of the scale (re-fa-la, mi-sol-ti, etc.). Nevertheless, the triad built on do plays a special role as the I chord or tonic, known as the chord of rest. The chord of rest serves as a sort of destination for the active chords, which seek resolution there. Music acquires its dynamic thrust, its movement and direction, from this ongoing search for resolution. Accomplishment of this resolution is known as a cadence.

Just as important to this movement is the chord built on sol, the fifth step of the scale. When sol-ti-re, the V chord or dominant, seeks resolution to the restful do triad, it fulfills the basic formula of harmonic activity. The dominant-to-tonic resolution is the most common final cadence in Western music. Less important but still significant is the triad built on the fourth step of the scale, fa. Known as the IV chord or the subdominant, fa-la-do also seeks resolution to the tonic. When it does, the progression IV-I creates a somewhat less powerful cadence than V-I, but the subdominant stands as one of the three triads at the foundation of the harmonic system.

Despite the word's soothing connotations, harmony encompasses more than pretty chord progressions. Clashing or unresolved intervals known as dissonance produce the tension in music. Dissonance corresponds to restlessness and activity, while consonance implies relaxation and fulfillment. As a result, the dissonant chord creates tension and the consonant chord resolves it. Each complements the other.

Keys and Scales

Melody and harmony derive part of their character from the key in which they are pitched. Key refers to a group of related tones with a common center, or tonic; those tones serve as the building blocks for a given composition. When a piece is composed in the key of D, for instance, it is based upon the family of tones that revolve around and gravitate to the tonic D. A composition's relation to a central tone is known as its tonality.

As indicated by the key, the tonic or key center serves as the starting place of the scale used in a given composition. A scale is a series of tones arranged in consecutive order, either ascending or descending. It covers an octave made up of eight notes running from do to do, which represent the tones of the key. In Western music, the octave is divided into twelve equal tonic intervals, each a half tone apart. An eight-note scale may start from any of the twelve semitones of the octave, which form what is known as a chromatic scale. Thus, the eight notes of the scale account for twelve semitones. Western music is based on two contrasting eight-note scales, the major and minor scales. The type of scale used in a composition determines how the eight notes of the octave cover the twelve semitones.

On a piano keyboard, the pattern of the keys clearly and exactly illustrates the arrangement of whole and half tones in the two types of scales. Each key, whether black or white, is separated from its nearest neighbor, either black or white, by a semitone. Depending on whether it is considered in relation to its upper or lower neighbor, each black key has two names; for example, the black key between F and G is both F-sharp and G-flat. Playing only the eight white keys on the piano from C to C yields the C major scale, which is the basis of the familiar do-re-me-fa-sol-la-ti-do pattern. Because it skips several half tones (represented by the black keys), it covers the twelve-semitone chromatic scale in eight notes: whole step, whole step, half step, whole, whole, whole, half, where each whole step represents two semitones and each half step represents one semitone. A major scale may start from any point without altering this sequence of whole and half steps.

What sets the minor scale apart from the major is that the third degree, or note, is lowered a half step (the C minor scale, for instance, contains an E-flat instead of an E) and the sixth and seventh degrees of the scale are altered as follows: In the natural minor scale, the sixth and seventh steps remain un-altered, so the C-natural minor scale would run C, D, E-flat, F, G, A-flat, B-flat, C. Another version of the minor scale, the harmonic, raises the seventh degree a

Piano keyboard

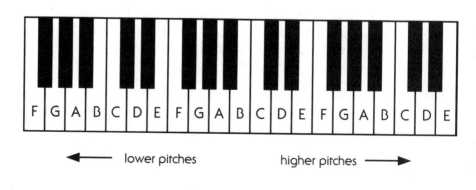

◀━━━━ lower pitches   higher pitches ━━━━▶

The standard minor scale

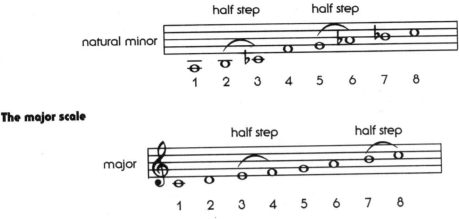

The major scale

half tone (e.g., B-flat to B), while the third type of minor scale, the melodic, raises both the sixth and the seventh degrees a half tone (e.g., A-flat to A, B-flat to B) on ascent, but naturalizes those notes on descent. Like the major scale, the minor scale may also begin on any of the twelve tones of the octave without changing the basic pattern of whole and half steps.

Transposition—the shift from one key to another, as from C major to D major, for example—changes the tonic and the level of pitch, but the melody line remains the same because the pattern of whole and half steps remains constant. The contrast between keys and the movement from one key to another is an essential element of musical structure known as modulation. With advance musical preparation a modulation can occur smoothly, or it can happen abruptly if the shift in tonal center is not properly prepared for. An important source of variety in music, modulation allows any chord to be interpreted in any key. The technique relies on the ambiguity of the single chord, which derives its meaning from the surrounding harmony.

To achieve a smooth modulation, the composer chooses a chord, known as a pivot chord, which occurs both in the original key of the composition and in the key to which the composer wishes to modulate. A simple modulation would use a pivot chord that leads naturally to the dominant chord of the new key. The modulation is established by a cadence in the new key. For example, in a modulation from the key of C to G major, the pivot chord is both the tonic chord in C and the subdominant in G. A common form of modulation is a movement from a major key to its relative minor, which lies down a minor third (one-and-a-half steps) on the scale. Such a modulation might be from C major to its relative minor, A minor. Another typical modulation flows from a major key to its parallel minor, from C major to C minor, for example. Theoretically, almost any chord could serve as a pivot chord; however, those less directly connected to the new tonality make the modulation more abrupt (sometimes a desired effect).

The major and minor keys comprise the standard harmonic system of

Western music. During the Classical and Romantic periods, composers explored the contrasts of color, mood and emotional intensity evoked by the major and minor keys and established the contrast between them as a crucial element of musical structure. In the 20th century, some musicians rebelled against major/minor tonality. Convinced that the musical possibilities of the old harmonic system had been fully developed, they clamored for something new. Some composers moved toward atonality—composition without a tonal center—while one, Arnold Schönberg, developed the 12-tone system, or serial technique. He designed his "tone row" to replace the traditional harmonic structure that had dominated music for centuries. In the 12-tone system, none of the twelve notes have any special importance; because all the notes are equally significant, harmony does not depend on any single tonal center. Composers throughout Europe and the Americas picked up Schönberg's serial technique and developed it even further in the decades after its introduction. Some composers have used it exclusively, while others have adapted parts of it. Even Schönberg went on to break some of his own rules.

How to Read Music

Reading music is like reading another language. Like any other language, musical notation evolved over centuries, originating in antiquity and adapting to new systems of musical thought as they appeared.

Musical notation charts the duration and pitch of the sounds in a composition. Each discrete sound is represented by a symbol called a note. Its position on the staff—a series of five parallel lines and four intervening spaces—indicates its pitch. On the staff, each line and space represent a different degree of pitch. Just like an English sentence, the series of notes on the staff reads from left to right.

To indicate the set of pitches to which that staff refers, a symbol known as a clef stands at the head of the staff. The treble clef delineates pitches within a relatively high range, such as that of the violin or flute. Also referred to as the G clef, this clef shows where the G above middle C falls. The bass or F clef, meanwhile, refers to a lower group of pitches, such as those of the cello or double bass. It indicates the location of the F below middle C. Similarly, the alto and tenor clefs, known as C clefs, mark the location of middle C. They accommodate middle-range pitches, such as those of the viola and the upper register of the cello.

Staff and Ledger lines

Clefs

bass

alto

treble

Pitches, commonly called notes, are named after the first seven letters of the alphabet, from A to G. The location of the pitches on the staff depends on which clef is in use. For pitches that fall above or below the staff, short lines called ledger lines are added to illustrate their location.

Pitches on the treble clef

Pitches on the bas clef

Pitches on the alto clef

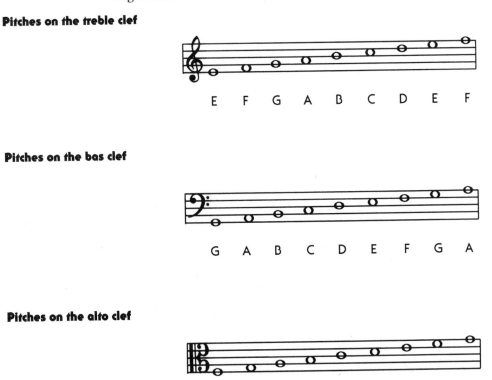

Some Key signatures

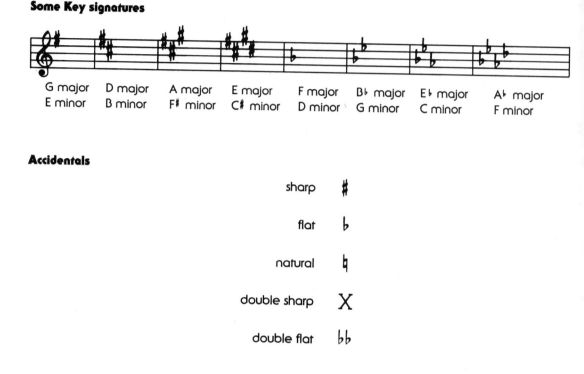

G major	D major	A major	E major	F major	B♭ major	E♭ major	A♭ major
E minor	B minor	F♯ minor	C♯ minor	D minor	G minor	C minor	F minor

Accidentals

sharp ♯

flat ♭

natural ♮

double sharp X

double flat ♭♭

The key signature at the head of the first staff of a piece of music establishes the key of the piece and denotes the number and location of sharps or flats in the scale. Additional signs, known as accidentals, can temporarily alter the pitch of a written note. Placed before the note at issue, a sharp sign raises the note one semitone, and a flat sign lowers the pitch one semitone. By contrast, a natural sign cancels an existing sharp or flat note. The double sharp and double flat, meanwhile, raise and lower the pitch of a note by a whole tone.

Notes of different visual types have different durations relative to the beat of the music. Standard musical notation includes whole notes, half notes, quarter notes, eighth notes, sixteenth notes, thirty-second notes and sixty-fourth notes, where each has a duration half as long as the next longer one. If a quarter note represents one beat, then a half note lasts for two beats and so on. When a group of three notes is to be played in the time normally utilized by two, they are indicated by a triplet that visually links them. Alternately, a tie links successive notes of the same pitch into one sustained sound with the combined duration of the linked tones. To extend the time value of a note by half, a composer places a dot after it. A dotted half note in ¼ time, for instance, lasts 3 beats, two for the half note and one for the dot. Finally, silences are indicated by symbols known as rests—whole rests, half rests, quarter rests, eighth rests and sixteenth rests—that correspond in time value to the notes.

When composers of serious music began to move beyond traditional musical concepts—with electronic music, for example—conventional notation could

Notes

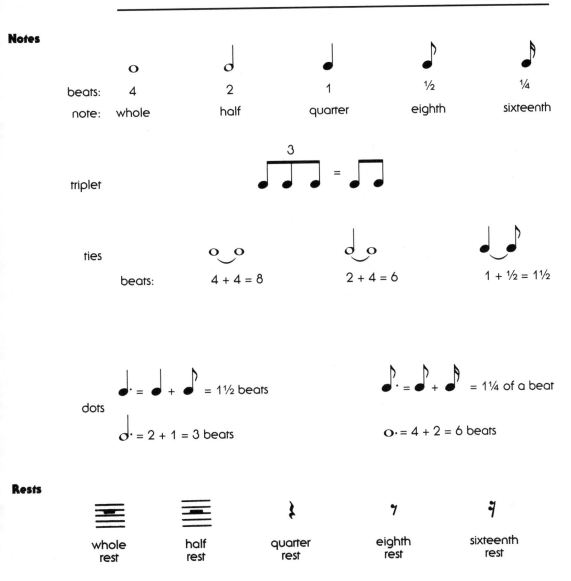

Rests

not adequately record their new musical techniques and philosophies. As experimentation and innovation spread, new notation devices proliferated. These modifications include the abandonment of key signatures, which have no validity in atonal music or music that avoids a tonal center, unusual time signatures, tampering with barlines, personalized dynamic markings, variations in standard techniques such as the *pizzicato* (plucked string) or *col legno* (with the wood of the bow), microtonal divisions (intervals smaller than a semitone), tone clusters, exploitation of units smaller than the standard whole-, half-, quarter-, eighth-, and sixteenth-notes, symbols for vocal effects such as a laughing voice, murmured tones, or notes half-spoken/half-sung, and verbal directives as part of the score. Editorial comments in a preface and throughout the score are often necessary to explain the individual composer's symbols to the performer.

Variation, Arrangement and Improvisation

In their search for new sounds, musicians in many cultures and historical periods have relied on similar techniques. These techniques allow them to explore the potential of previously composed pieces as well as to leave existing music behind and create something entirely fresh. Starting with a framework as complex as a symphony or as basic as a single phrase, the musical innovator may work by the processes of variation, arrangement or improvisation.

Variation and Arrangement

One of the oldest performing principles known to musicians, variation has retained a vital role in music from the earliest times to the present day. Simply put, it is a technique by which a musical theme is repeatedly stated, either in an altered form or in altered settings. As it repeats, the theme itself may vary, or be modified, in many ways, depending on the type of music to which it belongs, be it classical, jazz, blues, Turkish, West African, Balinese or any other. The kinds of instrumental or vocal performers involved also affect the variation process.

In general, variation focuses either on changing or on adding to the existing music, but it may also combine these two approaches. In order for a musical alteration to be a true variation, each version of the theme must contain certain consistent elements even as others change. Different compositional styles and techniques yield different relationships between the constant and variable elements in a piece. In each musical era, for instance, composers have used specific harmonic combinations that produce musical textures distinct to that era.

The term *arrangement,* meanwhile, describes one of two processes: It involves either the adaptation to another medium of a composition written for one medium, or the simplification or elaboration of a piece with or without a change of medium. For example, a popular song might be arranged for solo piano or for a full orchestra; the same song might be arranged to sound mournful or impassioned, whether played on solo piano or guitar. Arrangement differs from *transcription* (a term often used interchangeably with it) in that transcription implies a more literal transference between media, rather than the kind of creative recomposition or paraphrasing done by an arranger.

Practical arrangements requiring little artistic skill also fall into a separate category from true arrangements that display the arranger's musical imagination and expertise.

With varied motivations, musicians have practiced arrangement throughout history. Some arrangements seek to broaden the audience for a particular composition, others to challenge the technical abilities of music students at various levels, still others to allow a piece to be played using instruments for which it was not originally intended. More recently, commercial arrangers have adapted compositions for use in film, television and advertising. Copyrighting—the legal practice that grants a single person the exclusive right to reproduce, publish and sell a composition—places some restrictions on arrangers, but they are free to work with material whose copyright has expired or to license the right to arrange a copyrighted work.

Improvisation

Variation and arrangement are two tools of the improvisor, who in fact practices each technique while playing. Starting from a phrase or melody, the improvisor creates an impromptu performance that can move far beyond its starting point. When playing from a score, musicians exercise interpretive freedom within an established framework; but when they improvise, their imagination guides their playing in an unplanned way, allowing and sometimes demanding split-second innovation. In either situation, performers respond to the general mood of their audience as well as to their own feelings at the moment. That response shows up in any live performance, but during improvisation it may be more intense or obvious. Likewise, the audience's reaction may be more immediate and heightened than it is to music played from a score.

A musician cannot improvise successfully unless he or she has reached a certain level of technical competence. The greater the underlying skill, the more elaborate and elegant the improvisation can be. On the other hand, even the most sophisticated technician may not possess a talent for improvisation. Technical fortitude must go hand in hand with musical creativity. This combination is a gift that allows the improvisor to master the arts of composing and performing simultaneously.

Probably one of the most universally enjoyed musical activities, improvisation has a place in almost every period of musical history and in the music of almost every culture. However, improvisation has seldom been adequately acknowledged or completely understood, often misjudged as a phenomenon of the 20th century alone. Perhaps this reflects its elusive, changeable nature, which defies analysis and explicit description. By definition, improvisation cannot be reduced to theory, and although observers have attempted to transcribe it, standard musical notation cannot accommodate the quirks and subtleties of the technique. Rooted in irregularities, improvisation cannot be recorded using notation defined by uniformity and symmetry. Technical descriptions are simply inadequate.

Those who do not practice improvisation sometimes harbor misconceptions and find it difficult to appreciate and fully comprehend. The general confusion about improvisation arises in part from one of the essential problems of formal musical education in the West: Its great emphasis on historical comparison and on the acquisition of centuries of musical knowledge often discourages creativity. Classical music, by its very character, provides an unlikely setting for improvisation. The opposite is true of many other types of music, such as the classical music of India and the 20th-century American form, jazz.

But classical music owes much to improvisation, which was very important during the Baroque period (1685–1750). In those days, composers expected to perform their own compositions, and they customarily wrote down only a skeleton or bare outline of what was to be played. Vocal and instrumental improvisation not only served as a means of variation but also celebrated the act of music-making. In fact, 17th-century organ music relied on performers' spontaneity, and throughout the 17th and 18th centuries, certain types of chamber music were improvised over a figured bass (a system that economically notated a harmonic framework for the "working-out" or improvisation of the melody). Musicians and composers alike accepted the practice of ornamentation, by which the written melodic line was embellished improvisationally in performance (to be written down later by the composers). Compositions included standard embellishments, represented by signs, that performers interpreted with a certain freedom. In short, performing musicians were expected to decorate, to supplement, to vary, and to embellish—to "improve," as it was often called.

Eventually, classical composers decided that the unpredictability of improvisation was neither desirable nor practical. They began to confine improvisation to certain areas of their compositions, such as the cadenza, a virtuoso passage inserted before the close of a movement. Finally, they eliminated improvisation altogether. Western classical music came to be governed by a formalized, theoretical framework of rules and regulations. This shift made improvisation all but inaccessible to the majority of classical musicians, including those of the 20th century. Still, some written classical works—notably the fantasia and rhapsody—have an improvisatory quality, although the composer's ideas are fully notated.

A Brief History of Musical Instruments

Each culture has its own distinctive array of musical instruments. Despite the great variety found in sound-producing implements today, however, most of them descend from a relatively few prehistoric prototypes. Archaeological digs on several continents have revealed a surprising similarity among forms of ancient musical instruments. Simple bone flutes and rattles strung together from shells, teeth and hooves typified the Paleolithic period, about two million years ago. Excavations of Neolithic sites yield end-blown conch-shell trumpets (possibly used for masking or amplifying the voice), clay drums covered with animal skins, slit drums made of hollowed bamboo or tree trunks, and gourd-type xylophones. On such instruments many cultures based their first tribal and folk musical traditions.

Non-Western Traditions

Today, the musical instruments used by people outside the Western (i.e., European) tradition provide clues to the form of their ancient instruments, as many have changed very little over time. In Mexico, for instance, indigenous peoples use rattling vessels and slit drums similar to those of the ancient Mayas, who worshipped nature gods and often carved their instruments to resemble animals. Throughout South America, multicaned wood, clay, metal or stone panpipes (held vertically and played by blowing across the top) appeared as early as 200 B.C. and probably long before. These are still common instruments of the Andes.

In Africa, where drums have always been associated with ceremony, percussion still constitutes a complex language associated with births, weddings and deaths. Today, as in antiquity, open-ended drums, upright cone drums, and slit drums of myriad forms are essential to this vocabulary. Many communities consider drums such powerful and sacred objects that only the local leader can own them. African instruments are also used symbolically. For example, among the Shona of Zimbabwe, pieces performed on the *mbira*—an idiophonic or self-sounding instrument consisting of bamboo or metal tongues attached to a resonator—celebrate various stages of life. Horns of ivory or bark, one-stringed musical bows, shell trumpets, and an endless variety of xylophones are among the other African instruments that have been played for millennia.

In ancient Asia, the Sumerians left pictographs on cuneiform that depict flutes, harps, silver reed pipes, and gold horns and trumpets. Representations of enormous, six-foot-wide drums that required two players suggest contact with China, where such drums proliferated in antiquity. Pictographs and archaeological remains from China also indicate the early use of bronze bells and stone chimes. Later, during the Tang Dynasty (618–907), a period during which poetry and art flourished, a lutelike instrument called the *p'i-pa* developed and became a popular solo and ensemble instrument. During the Sung Period (960–1280), the *ch'in,* a type of zither, was associated with the gentleman scholars of Confucianism. Chinese musicians continue to use it to this day.

Western Traditions

The development of Western music is easier to trace. Its foundations were laid in ancient Greece, where music was essential to ceremony, particularly in the 7th to 5th centuries B.C. Members of the cult of Apollo sang poetic songs or recited epic poems accompanied by the *kithara,* a plucked string instrument, and the *lyra* (lyre), its smaller counterpart. Dionysian cultists favored the *aulos,* a wind instrument with either a single or double reed. The aulos later became essential to Greek drama, figuring heavily in performances of works by Euripides, Sophocles and Aeschylus. When Greece became a Roman province in 146 B.C., the musical traditions of the two cultures intermingled. The Romans adopted Hellenistic art music but preserved their own tradition of military music, which was played on brass instruments, particularly horns and trumpets.

Following the development of plainsong—especially associated with Gregory I (Pope from 590 to 604), medieval European music gradually grew more polyphonous. After the 11th century, multiple melodies and harmonies were employed instead of the simple tunes of old, and musicians developed instruments to suit the new styles. Characteristic instruments of this era include the harp, an ancient instrument that was further refined in the British Isles; the *vielle,* a bowed instrument favored by wandering minstrels, or *jongleurs,* which prefigured the Renaissance viol family; the psaltery, a member of the zither family that was played by plucking or striking the strings; and the lute, a contribution of the Moorish invaders in Spain. Among wind instruments, new developments included the recorder (a type of end-blown flute) and the shawm, a reed instrument that was the precursor of the oboe. Organs also appeared in medieval Europe. Enormous organs consisting of several thousand pipes were built for churches, but artisans also made positive (medium-size tabletop) and portative (portable) organs for outdoor dancing and festive ceremonies.

As with all the arts, music experienced a tremendous flowering in the Renaissance. Secular music gained unprecedented popularity and was increasingly played in the home. Technological advances produced more sophisticated instruments, leading to added nuance in instrumentation. With the addition of solo stops, the tonality of organs became increasingly subtle and varied. Large church organs were also enhanced by pedal keyboards, first used in the late Middle Ages in Germany.

Vocal polyphonic music was by now well established; instrumental styles followed suit. Viols—the fretted and bowed instruments from which the violin family of the 17th century would descend—began to appear. They were often played by musical groups called consorts, along with harps, kettledrums, recorders and flutes. Introduced in the Middle Ages, the lute now came into its own and was especially popular as a solo instrument to be enjoyed at home.

THE FEMALE ORCHESTRAS OF ANCIENT EGYPT

During the New Kingdom period (1559–1085 B.C.), Egypt experienced a golden age during which arts and culture, including music, flourished. The traditional Egyptian repertoire was enriched by an influx of new harps, lyres, drums and other instruments from Southwest Asia. At the same time, female musicians rose to prominence, performing at banquets and funerals and playing sacred music at ceremonies in honor of Egyptian deities.

Tomb paintings and papyri from Thebes, the royal city, depict all-female orchestras playing harps, lutes, double oboes, lyres, tambourines, clappers and sistrums in luxurious settings. The images show women adept at multiple musical skills, such as singing while playing the harp or dancing while making music on the lute or oboe. In some cases, women performed with male orchestras. Several tomb paintings dating from Queen Hatshepsut's reign portray a lone female lutenist at the center of a male orchestra, strumming her turtle-shell instrument like a guitar.

Many of the female musicians actually came to Egypt from Asia as slaves, bringing their instruments with them. Despite their lowly origins, some rose to positions of respect and even reverence. These women earned special titles, such as the "chantresses of the residence of Amen," who were sworn to celibacy. Another group, the Meret, were considered the keepers of song and ceremonial music and were entrusted with the task of beating time with clappers during cere-monial rites. Often, women of the Theban elite played oboes and other instruments to accompany religious rituals, usually to honor Mut, Lady of Heaven. A surviving oboe of the period is decorated with scenes of female oboists playing before this deity.

As in many cultures around the world, music was essential to the worship of Egyptian deities and an indispensable element of any ceremony, for it was believed to placate the gods. In fact, many of the deities worshiped at Egyptian festivals were goddesses associated with music. Hathor, goddess of joy and fertility, was also the supreme deity of music and dance, as well as the patron of rhythmic instruments such as sistrums, clappers, drums and rattling collars. Hand-shaped wood and ivory clappers were usually carved with images of Hathor. Often depicted on gold- and silver-encrusted harps, Maat was the goddess of divine justice and harmony, which were thought to result from the spiritually balancing effects of musical ritual.

Egyptian folk tales also allude to the link between women, goddesses and music. One classic papyrus story, "The Birth of Kings," tells of a woman who has trouble giving birth to quintuplets. She is assisted by the goddesses Isis, Nephthys, Meskhenet, Heket and Khnum, who transform themselves into musicians during the episode. They even bring along rattles, both to celebrate the births and to amuse the babies.

Aside from the familiar pear-shaped version, there was also a Spanish type of lute called the *vihuela,* similar in appearance to the guitar, its successor. The shawm also continued to enjoy a wide audience.

Like the shawm and recorder, the clavichord and harpsichord had been invented in the 14th century, but it was during the Renaissance that musicians recognized the potential of the keyboard. The clavichord was used most often as a solo instrument for home gatherings, while the harpsichord, with its slightly greater volume and more forceful tone, was used both alone and in ensembles. But more important was a development of the Baroque musical period (1685–1750): the piano. Invented in Italy, it was originally called the pianoforte, or "soft-loud," a reference to the quality of the sound produced by the hammer striking the strings. The piano increased in popularity during the late 18th century.

Also attributed to Italy, the violin family (violins, violas and violoncellos) swiftly gained popularity during the Baroque period. In particular, it was Bach, the composer of organ fugues and clavier music, who fostered the popularity of the violin family by writing works for solo violin and violoncello. Other characteristic Baroque instruments were the oboe, piccolo, bassoon and transverse flute. During this era, the guitar supplanted the vihuela.

The Classical period (1750–1820) saw the rise of Haydn, Mozart and Beethoven. All composed music for the string quartet, ensuring the continued popularity of the violin family. Beethoven, in particular, spurred the ascendancy of the piano, which assumed a leading role in chamber performances. During the Romantic period (1820–1900), the piano became more technologically refined, with an improved keyboard mechanism. As a result, pianists achieved previously unknown levels of virtuosity. Liszt, Clara Schumann and Chopin were among the great concert pianists of the era. Also during this period, valves were added to brass instruments, giving them greater versatility. The banjo—an adaptation of an instrument brought to the Americas by African slaves—became a popular instrument as well.

In the 20th century, many instruments—the guitar, the piano and even the flute and the violin—were electrified, enabling their sounds to be amplified and manipulated electronically. Electronic synthesizers, capable of producing and altering sounds electronically, were introduced in the 1950s. Additional advances in computer technology have continued to influence music, but a renewed interest in folk and acoustic instruments has reconfirmed the timeless appeal of the most ancient instrumental forms.

Illustrated List of Musical Instruments

Stringed Instruments, Plucked

Guitar Family: Successor to the vihuela, the guitar is a flat-bodied stringed instrument of Spanish origin. It has a long, fretted neck and usually six strings, which are plucked with the fingers or a plectrum, or pick. Members of the family include the banjo, a long-necked, fretted instrument with a circular body resembling a drum. Strung with at least four strings but usually five, the banjo is generally played with the fingers but sometimes with a plectrum. It is a descendant of African instru-

Guitar

ments brought to the Americas by slaves. Another member of the family, the four-stringed ukulele, originally came from Portugal but was popularized in Hawaii in the late Victorian era and on the United States mainland following World War I. See also *Electric Guitar,* page 155.

Harp: An ancient, universally known instrument with strings stretched across a triangular frame, the harp dates from at least the third millennium B.C. Originating in Mesopotamia and Egypt, the harp eventually appeared in medieval Europe and Britain, taking the forms of the double harp, with two rows of strings; the triple, or Welsh, harp, with three rows of strings; the single-action pedal harp; and the modern double-action type, whose strings can be raised two semitones by the pedal action.

Harpsichord Family: The harpsichord is usually a double keyboard instrument whose strings run at right angles to the keyboard and whose stops are plucked by quills or leather points. It was especially popular from the Renaissance until the beginning of the 19th century. The spinet, capable of less tone color and volume than the harpsichord, is a small, one-keyboard harpsichord with a trapezoidal or wing shape; its strings run at an oblique angle to the keyboard. (The name *spinet* was also later applied to a small piano.) The virginal differs from the spinet in that its strings run parallel to the keyboard and it has a rectangular or polygonal shape.

Lute Family: The lute is an ancient stringed instrument whose early forms include the long-necked *pandoura* of ancient Greece and Rome and the short-necked fretless *'ud* of the Middle East. It entered Europe during the Middle Ages, brought to Spain by Moorish invaders. Especially popular during the Renaissance, the lute is pear-shaped with a short neck, fretted finger board and a variable number of strings that can be played with a plectrum or the fingers. Types of lute include the chittarone, a bass lute with a greatly extended neck; the mandolin, which has a short neck with a flat or round back; and the sitar of India, with long neck, movable frets and a gourd resonator. The sitar's strings—seven principal and twenty sympathetic (vibrating in response to other strings)—are plucked with a plectrum.

Harp

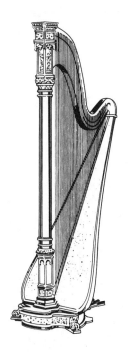

Lute

Lyre: In ancient Greece, where it originated, this instrument was referred to as the *lyra* and had a resonating body that usually consisted of a tortoise shell. Resembling a small harp, the lyre has strings that are stopped with the left hand and played with a plectrum.

Vihuela: This medieval and Renaissance Spanish instrument is strung like a lute but has a guitarlike body and is played with a plectrum or the fingers. It is sometimes considered a member of the guitar family.

Zither: This flat-backed instrument consists of a wooden box with a fretted board over which strings are stretched. It is played on a table or resting on the knees, although some early zithers were played upright. One of the most ancient forms is the aeolian harp, whose strings varied in thickness and were wind-activated. Later types of zithers include the psaltery, a medieval version that often had a trapezoidal or triangular shape. Another type of zither, the dulcimer, is struck with light hammers, rather than plucked. It, too, was developed in Europe during the Middle Ages but is thought to have been introduced there by way of Persia.

Stringed Instruments, Hammered

Clavichord: Popular from the Renaissance through the 18th century, the clavichord is a rectangular keyboard instrument set atop a table or resting on its own legs. While a key is held down, strings running along the long side of the instrument are pressed by metal tangents to produce a vibrato effect.

Piano: Originally called the pianoforte—a reference to the soft (*piano*) and loud (*forte*) sounds it can produce—the piano has a broad range of power, expression and rich sounds that allowed it to supplant the clavichord and harpsichord, neither of which could be made to rise and fall in sound level. This large keyboard instrument, whose strings are struck by hammers, was introduced around 1700 in Italy, but it did not achieve great popularity until the Classical period of Haydn, Mozart and Beethoven. In upright pianos, the strings are vertical; in wing-shaped grand pianos, they are horizontal.

Stringed Instruments, Bowed

Hurdy-gurdy: This viol-shaped instrument of the Middle Ages was also associated with traveling musicians of the 17th century. Usually having four strings, it is cranked to activate a wheel rubbed with resin, which serves as a bow. Two of the strings are acted on by keys, producing a tune. The other two vibrate to create a droning bass line.

Viol Family: Popular fretted instruments of the Renaissance, viols were preceded by the medieval *vielle* and later superseded by the violin family. Viols have a fretted finger-board, deep body, flat back, sloping shoulders and usually six strings. The bass viol is sometimes called a viola da gamba (or gamba), a name that refers to the upright position in which all viols are played (*gamba* is Italian for "leg"). Treble viols rest on the knees; tenor and bass viols between the legs. The fretless viola d'amore has sympathetic strings that vibrate when other strings are played directly.

Violin Family: These orchestral four-stringed instruments became popular around 1700, although they were developed in the 16th century. Unlike viols, they have a shallow body, right-angled shoulders and a fretless finger-board. The violin is the principal and highest-pitched member of the family. The viola, slightly larger than the violin, is the next-highest-pitched member of the violin family. The larger violoncello, popularly called the cello, is a rich-toned bass instrument. Largest and lowest-pitched of all the violins is the double bass, which sometimes has a fifth string or a mechanical device that brings its lowest pitch down to C.

Violin

Viola

Violincello

Double bass

Wind Instruments, Open Mouthpiece

Flute Family: Member of an ancient family of sideblown, reedless, woodwind instruments, today's standard transverse orchestral flute came into being in the 19th century. Variations include the smaller piccolo (pitched an octave higher), the larger alto flute and the bass flute.

Panpipes: Ancient and varied in form, these instruments are associated most closely with Peru, Africa and Melanesia. They are played by blowing across the openings of a set of vertical pipes, each with its own pitch.

Flute

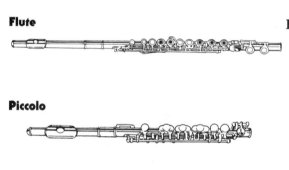

Piccolo

Pipe Organ: A keyboard controls the flow of air to this instrument's pipes, where sound is produced according to woodwind principles. Greco-Roman instruments prefigured the organ; by the 10th century simple organs were widely used in religious services throughout Europe. The Middle Ages saw the rise of the smaller portative (portable, used at outdoor functions) and positive (indoor tabletop) organs, as well as of early pedal keyboards. Solo stops (sets of individual pipes of graduated size) were introduced during the Renaissance. See also *Electronic Organ,* page 155, and *Reed Organ Family,* page 150.

Recorder Family: These reedless, woodwind instruments are distinguished from flutes in that they are endblown. The eight-holed recorder was popular from the Renaissance through the 18th century. Closely related, the six-holed flageolet was developed in 17th-century France. Double and triple flageolets were invented later.

Wind Instruments, Reed Type

Bagpipe Family: The bagpipe consists of a windbag that is inflated either by means of a mouth pipe, as in the Scottish Highlands, or by bellows, as with Northumbrian and Irish-type pipes. Melody is fingered on the chanter pipe; drone pipes emit a single pitch. Scottish bagpipes have three drones, two in unison, one an octave lower. The bagpipe is an ancient instrument, with Asian predecessors dating from the first millennium B.C.

Bassoon Family: This double-reed, conical-bore instrument is built in four joints: the wing, butt, long joint and bell. Dating from the Baroque musical period (1685–1750), only two types of bassoon survive today. The nor-

mal bassoon has a range two octaves lower than the oboe, while the contrabassoon sounds an octave further down. Bassoons are sometimes considered members of the double-reed family.

Clarinet Family: Developed in the late 17th century, the clarinets are single-reed, cylindrical instruments with a slightly flared bell, usually made of wood. They are transposing instruments; that is, their sounded pitch corresponds to, but differs from, the standard notated pitch. Common orchestral types have a variety of pitches, notably B-flat and A. The bass clarinet's tones are an octave lower than B-flat. The E-flat clarinet is the sopranino.

Bassoon

Contrabassoon

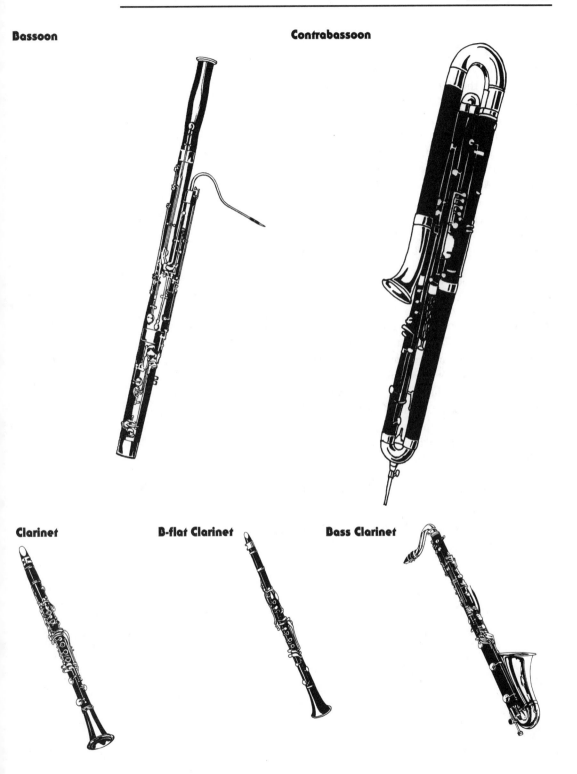

Clarinet

B-flat Clarinet

Bass Clarinet

Oboe Family: These double-reed orchestral instruments consist of a conical tube with various sound holes and keys. First appearing in Europe in the 17th century, oboes descended from Renaissance shawms, loud double-reed instruments appropriate for outdoor use. The modern oboe has a flared bell, while other family members, such as the English horn and oboe d'amore, have hollow ends shaped like bulbs. The oboe produces a nasal tone, while the oboe d'amore has a slightly lower pitch. Pitched to a distinctly melancholy sound, the baritone (bass) oboe is known as the English horn.

Oboe

Reed Organ Family: The reed organ differs from the pipe organ in that its sound is generated by a metal tongue that vibrates against a resonator. Related instruments include the harmonica, or mouth organ, a 19th-century invention. Associated with Confucian ritual, the ancient Asian mouth organs known as *sheng* are bowl-shaped with vertical bamboo pipes equipped with brass reeds. The similar Japanese *sho* is a staple of traditional court music. Also belonging to the family is the accordion, comprised of two reed organs operated by individual keyboards and joined by a pleated bellows.

Baritone/bass oboe

Saxophone Family: Dating from the mid-19th century, these single-reed metal instruments are named for inventor Antoine Adolphe Sax. There are two principal categories: the orchestral saxophone and band (military) saxophone. Of the former, which ranges in pitch from bass to soprano, only the melody (C tenor) saxophone is actively used today. Military saxophones are more commonly seen, particularly the alto and tenor types.

Saxophones

soprano

alto

tenor

baritone

Wind Instruments, Brass Type

Horn Family: Though the term *horn* can apply to any wind instrument descended from actual animal-horn models, today it commonly designates an orchestral valved instrument with a flared end, or bell. Common today is the French horn, a circular, flared-end brass instrument with a range of more than three octaves. Valved horns date from the 19th century, but their predecessors include signaling instruments of antiquity, Renaissance hunting horns, and horns with crooks of the 18th century.

Saxhorn Family: These valved brass instruments, ranging in pitch from soprano to contrabass, were invented by Antoine Adolphe Sax in the mid–19th century. Those in use today—notably the alto horns, baritones and euphoniums—are modified versions of Sax's originals.

Trombone Family: A tubular brass instrument, the trombone consists of two sections: a slide with mouthpiece and a conical section terminating in a flared bell. The slide alters the pitch of the instrument. Trombones range in size from soprano to contrabass, though tenor and bass trombones are the standard orchestral instruments. Valveless trombones were known as early as the 16th century; valves were added in the early 19th century.

Trumpet Family: The trumpet's curved form is thought to have been a Renaissance development. Persisting until the early 19th century, the valveless, or natural, trumpet then gained valves. Today's soprano version consists of a bent tube from which extends a flared bell on one end and a mouthpiece on the other, with three valves to vary the pitch. Several sizes exist. The favored orchestral type is C, while B-flat is used for popular music. Also included in the family is the cornet, similar but with a slightly wider bore. The bugle is slightly smaller and lacks valves.

Tuba Family: This largest-valved brass instrument has a bass pitch. There are several types, including the circular, marching-band tubas known as sousaphones. The most common orchestral types are double B-flat, double C, E-flat and F. Developed in its modern form in the 19th century, the tuba descends from such ancestors as the serpent, a serpentine brass or woodwind instrument popular from the 16th through 18th centuries that extended to about eight feet in length.

French horn

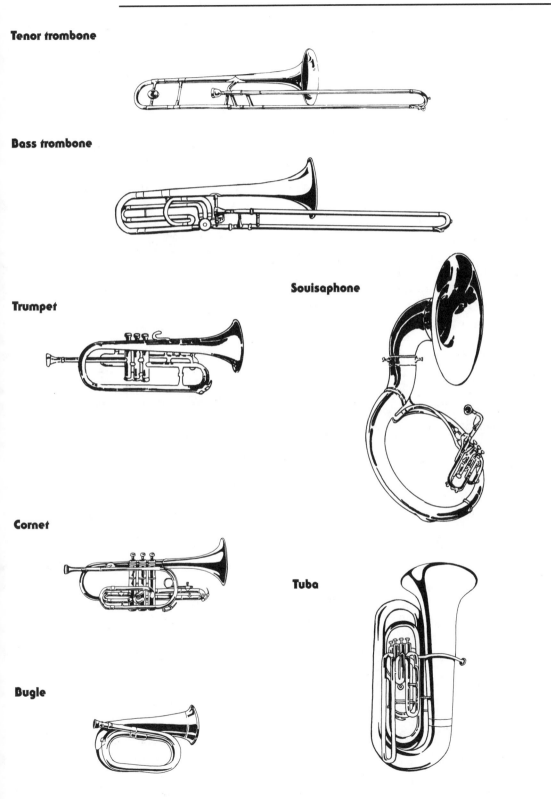

Tenor trombone

Bass trombone

Trumpet

Souisaphone

Cornet

Tuba

Bugle

Percussion Instruments, Definite Pitch

Glockenspiel: In the shape of a Greek lyre, the glockenspiel consists of metal bars of various lengths, arranged in two rows and played with small hammers to produce tinkling tones. It is an 18th-century invention.

Kettle Drum: A hemispherical copper, brass, metal or fiberglass frame over which is stretched a head of parchment, plastic or calf-skin. The drum is tuned by adjusting the tension of the head with screws or rods on the rim. An essential orchestral instrument, it is played with mallets and comes in several sizes, usually in groups of four. An Eastern instrument, it was introduced to Europe in the 15th century by Arabs, who used it as a cavalry instrument.

Tubular Bells: Hung vertically in a frame, a series of metal tubes of varying lengths are struck with mallets to produce bell-like tones. An 18th-century invention, tubular bells are standard orchestral instruments.

Xylophone Family: These ancient and varied instruments include the ten-key vertical types of Southeast Asia, as well as the many African types. Actively used today in Central and

Kettle drum

Latin America, the African-originated marimba generally has gourd resonators and is often played by more than one person simultaneously. Western orchestras use a type of xylophone consisting of bars of wood or other material, arranged in keyboard fashion in gradually increasing lengths. Equipped with tubular resonators below the bars, this instrument is played with mallets.

Percussion Instruments, Indefinite Pitch

Bass Drum: This large, shallow and cylindrical two-headed drum has a low, resonant pitch and lends itself to both marching bands and symphony orchestras. It is usually placed on a stand on its side or suspended and struck with felt-headed sticks. It was not used actively in Europe until the 18th century; its direct ancestors, the enormous bass drums of Japan and Southeast Asia, date from 3000 B.C.

Castanets: These concave, shell-shaped pieces of wood or ivory fit into the palm and are

clapped together. Connected into pairs by a cord, they are played by dancers; mounted to a surface and shaken, they are used in the orchestra.

Cymbals: Concave, circular metal plates that meet only at the edges when clashed together, cymbals are thought to be of Asian origin. Played in an orchestral setting, they are hand-held or are mounted and struck with a metal stick. Drum sets include specific types of cymbals: the ride cymbal, crash cymbals (called sizzle cymbals when studded with loosely vibrating rivets) and a pair of hi-hats, which are clashed together with a pedal.

Gong: Usually circular, this rimmed metal disk is suspended and struck with sticks or mallets to make a sonorous sound. A knob, called a boss, located at a gong's center lends it a definite pitch, while flat gongs (sometimes called tam-tams) lack specific pitch. Part of the Western orchestra, the gong is of Asian origin.

Side Drum or Snare Drum: Originally a medieval Swiss military instrument, this small metal or wooden cylinder has two heads. One or more parallel chords or wires, known as snares, stretch across the lower head to augment vibration. Striking the upper head with wire brushes or sticks produces reverberations in the lower head.

Tambourine: A drumhead stretched over a shallow frame fitted with jingling metal disks, the tambourine can be played in a variety of ways: by shaking, rubbing or striking with the hand or sticks. It was originally a Middle Eastern instrument.

Tenor Drum: Slightly deeper than the side drum and lacking snares, the tenor drum is a marching instrument usually played with felt-headed sticks. It is a 19th-century invention.

Triangle: Formed into a triangular shape that is left open at one angle, this metal rod is played with another metal rod to produce a tinkling sound.

Electronic Instruments

Electric Guitar: Guitars whose sounds are amplified by means of an electronic pickup convert string vibrations into electrical impulses. Introduced around the 1920s, the electroacoustic guitar has a conventional, hollow body. The solid-body, which became popular in the 1940s, replaces the sound box with a thick piece of wood or fiberglass. The advantages of the solid-body are that it does not produce feedback (sound resulting from placing the guitar in front of the amplifier) and it is capable of holding a tone longer than the electroacoustic.

Electronic Organ: Introduced in the 1930s, this instrument uses rotating tone wheels, vibrating reeds or, most recently, fixed-pitch oscillators to generate sound comparable to that of an acoustic organ.

Musical Instrument Digital Interface (MIDI): This industry-standard interface in its most basic form allows musicians to play multiple digital instruments from one trigger mechanism by transmitting information in a series of digital codes. It can also be used for more complex arrangements, such as connecting a variety of instruments—keyboards, synthesizers and drum machines, for example—to a master computer.

Signal Processor: A number of devices (e.g., limiters and compressors, delay-based processors, pitch transposers, equalizers) alter signal sounds transmitted from electrified instruments. They are capable of altering pitch, tone and other elements of the instrument, even making one instrument sound like another.

Synthesizer: Equipped with a keyboard, this machine employs solid-state circuitry to duplicate the sounds of various instruments. It can both generate and modify sounds. The earliest models appeared in the late 1920s and 1930s. One of the popular later types was the Moog, named after inventor Robert Moog.

AUTOMATIC INSTRUMENTS

In the age of the music-generating computer chip, automatic instruments might seem like a recent development, but they actually date back as far as the Middle Ages. These mechanical devices—the most familiar being the player piano—produced music when cranked or wound.

In medieval Europe, carillon bells marked the hour in many towns, played either by a trained *carillonneur* or mechanically, by a revolving pin- or peg-covered cylinder. This technology was applied to keyboards during the reign of Henry VIII, who had an automatic virginal (a type of harpsichord) in his instrument collection.

By the end of the 16th century barrel organs appeared. Operated via a hand crank, these organs contained a bellows that set pins in motion and caused the pipes to sound. Instruments of this type reached a high level of popularity, versatility and technical sophistication by the 18th century. Some offered a selection of up to ten tunes, written expressly for them by such composers as Michael Haydn and Emanuel and Friedmann Bach. Equipped with a miniature barrel organ, the "flute clock" inspired compositions by Handel. Evolving still further, a type of barrel organ called the serinette, sometimes referred to as the "bird organ," was used to teach birds to sing.

In the 19th century, Maelzel's panharmonicon attempted to simulate the sound of a full orchestra, complete with clarinets, flutes, violins, cellos, drums and triangle. Beethoven, a friend of Maelzel, wrote music for the instrument.

The late 19th century saw the introduction of the piano player, a device that turned an ordinary piano into an automatic instrument. Early in the next century, the piano player developed into the player piano, which incorporated built-in paper rolls that activated the instrument's hammers. The same technology was applied to other instruments, from violins to banjos and band organs designed to imitate a full orchestra.

Paper-roll technology reached its zenith with the advent of the reproducing player piano, which could record a piece played on it. Predating actual sound recording, the reproducing player piano could recreate the subtleties of an individual artist's performance. Most of the great artists of the early 20th century, including Rachmaninoff, Debussy and Gershwin, made piano rolls for various companies. Thanks to the virtuosity of automatic instruments, these recordings preserve the composers' ideas of how they wanted their works to be performed.

Biographies of Notable Musicians, Composers, and Promoters

Classical

Albéniz, Isaac (1860–1909): Composer and pianist. Born in Spain, Albéniz was a child prodigy who traveled to the southern United States, where he made a living through his playing. Back in Europe he toured, establishing himself as a virtuoso; he also began to write piano pieces. In London in 1892 he wrote the music to the opera *Pepita Jiménez,* but the most important and famous of his works is the piano suite *Iberia* (1906–09), which was inspired by original Spanish rhythms, melodies and folklore.

Anderson, Marian (1902–93): Contralto. Anderson first appeared as a soloist at New York's Lewisohn Stadium in 1925 and in 1929 gave a recital in Carnegie Hall. Her 1930 European tour brought her fame, especially for her renditions of Negro spirituals. Her 1955 operatic appearance at the Metropolitan Opera marked the first time an African-

American had sung there. She also sang at the inaugural balls for presidents Eisenhower (1957) and Kennedy (1961).

Angeles, Victoria de los [Victoria Gómez Cima] (1923–––––): Soprano. Born in Barcelona, Spain, Los Angeles was a great success as Marguerite in *Faust* in Paris in 1949 and as Mimi in *La Bohème* in London in 1950, the same year she debuted at Carnegie Hall. In 1951 she sang Marguerite at the Metropolitan Opera, where she performed until 1961. She sang brilliantly in her guest season at the Vienna State Opera (1957) and was also very successful at the Bayreuth Festival in 1961 and 1962.

Bach, Johann Sebastian (1685–1750): Composer. A giant in the world of music. Bach's works are the supreme example of German Baroque style. Born in Germany, he published his first work in 1708; a virtuoso organist, he spent most of his life as music director of various churches. A radical thinker, he perfected the division of the octave into twelve equal semitones, as demonstrated in the *Well-tempered Clavier* (1722–44). In fact, Bach's preoccupation with numerical balance and technical devices resulted in some of the most pleasing music ever composed. A prolific composer, he wrote much sublime music, including the *Brandenburg Concertos* (1721), the *St. Matthew Passion* (1729), the *Christmas Oratorio* (1733–34) and the cantata *Wachet auf, ruft uns die Stimme* (1731).

Barber, Samuel (1910–81): Composer. An American, Barber studied piano as a child. His early works, such as the popular *Adagio for Strings* (1938), resist modernism and, instead, employ lyrically romantic and eloquent harmonies and melodies. His later works, such as the orchestral suite *Medea* (1956), experiment with tonality, dissonance and theme. His first opera, *Vanessa* (1958), and his Piano Concerto (1962) each won Barber a Pulitzer Prize.

Bartók, Béla (1881–1945): Composer and pianist. Bartók, a native of Hungary, devoted his early years to conducting field research in order to distinguish an authentic Hungarian folk tradition; his book *Hungarian Folk Music* (1931) remains a classic in the field. His opera *Duke Bluebeard's Castle* premiered in 1918 and cemented his reputation. An exceptional pianist, Bartók toured the United States and Russia from 1927 to 1929, playing his own compositions, which employed a unique combination of folk elements within a modern dissonant context. His *Concerto for Orchestra* (1944) is one of his most popular works.

Battle, Kathleen (1948–––––): Coloratura soprano. An American, Battle is admired for the purity and brilliance of her tone. Her singing debut in 1972 at Italy's Spoleto festival began a career both on the operatic stage and as a soloist performing internationally with philharmonic orchestras. In 1977 she debuted at the Metropolitan Opera in Wagner's *Tannhäuser.*

Beethoven, Ludwig van (1770–1827): Composer. A central figure in the history of music. Beethoven, a German, appeared to have limitless inspiration and talent for composing his powerful and dramatic works. His early music was influenced by the formality of Haydn, while in his middle years he took on a more Romantic style, as typified by the *Moonlight Sonata* (1820). The last period of his music is marked by striking innovation, as demonstrated by Symphony No. 9 (1824). A few of his timeless works are the *Sonata pathétique* (1799), Symphony No. 3 ("Eroica," 1803–04) and the lovely bagatelle "Für Elise" (1810). It is an amazing fact that Beethoven wrote most of his works after he had gone deaf in 1802.

Berg, Alban (1885–1935): Composer. The Viennese-born Berg was a student of innovative composer Arnold Schönberg. After seeing Büchner's romantic play *Wozzeck* in 1914, Berg transformed it into an opera, which opened in Europe to extremely critical reviews in 1925. After being well received in America in 1931, it was eventually recognized worldwide as a masterpiece. Berg wrote the *Lyric Suite for String Quartet* (1927) and began composing music for Wedetrend's tragic play *Lulu,* but he died before completing it. Against the protests of his widow, his publishers commissioned Viennese composer Friedrich Cerba to finish the opera. Berg's work combines modern dissonant chords with classical symphonic sound.

Berio, Luciano (1925–——): Composer. The Italian-born Berio has challenged traditional notions of musical theory by incorporating "nonmusical" sounds, multimedia approaches and a wide variety of musical genres into his works. An early experimenter with electronic music, this avant-garde composer also put his early training in musical theater to use by writing a number of complex, multigenred stage presentations, such as *Laborintus II* (1963–65). His most famous work is *Sinfonia* (1968) for orchestra and chorus, in which he juxtaposes a wide array of disparate musical elements.

Berlioz, Hector (1803–69): Composer. Berlioz's style was the apex of French musical Romanticism. His most famous work is *Symphonie fantastique* (1830), while his symphony *Roméo et Juliette* (1839) is considered one of the most successful musical adaptations of Shakespeare's play. From 1842 to 1847 Berlioz toured Europe and Russia; he composed *La Damnation de Faust* in 1846. *Te Deum,* for three choirs, orchestra and organ, was a great success in 1855. From 1856 to 1858 Berlioz composed *Les Troyens.*

Bernstein, Leonard (1918–90): Conductor, composer and pianist. Enormously versatile and gifted, Bernstein held various conducting and teaching posts until 1958, when he became the

first American-born music director of the New York Philharmonic, a post he held until 1969. He also wrote the scores for a number of Broadway musicals and films. His best-known work, in collaboration with Stephen Sondheim, was the hit musical *West Side Story* (1957).

Bing, Sir Rudolf (1902–——): Opera impresario. Austrian-born Bing directed New York's Metropolitan Opera from 1950 to 1972. He also founded England's Glyndebourne Opera Festival in 1934 and served as the first director of the Edinburgh Festival (1947–49). He became a British subject in 1946 and was knighted in 1971.

Bizet, Georges (1838–75): Composer. Bizet, a Frenchman, is known for radiant orchestration and magnificent melodies and harmonies. Primarily a composer of operas, his masterpiece was *Carmen* (1875). Earlier operas included *Docteur Miracle* (1857), *Les pecheurs de perles* (1863), *La jolie fille de Perth* (1866), and an abandoned score found and produced after World War II as *Ivan the Terrible.*

Brahms, Johannes (1833–97): Composer. A classical German symphonist whose four symphonies rank among the finest ever written, Brahms began his career as a pianist. In 1853 he was befriended by Clara and Robert Schumann, who recognized his genius. Brahms first composed choral music and songs, such as the masterpiece *A German Requiem* (1854–1868), as well as piano and chamber music. But it is in his four symphonies, written from 1855 to 1885, that he truly excelled; their flawless structure is heightened by a mastery of variation and an overall effect of fluid sound.

Britten, (Edward) Benjamin (1913–76): Composer. Britten's early successes included *Phantasy in F Minor for String Quartet* (1932), *Simple Symphony* (1934) and various film scores. Born in England, in 1939 he visited the

United States, where he wrote the songs "Les Illuminations" (1939) and "Serenade" (1942). Back home, the composer premiered his first opera, *Peter Grimes,* in 1945. It proved astonishingly successful, and he followed it with *The Rape of Lucretia* (1946), *Billy Budd* (1951) and *The Turn of the Screw* (1954). His most intriguing work, *War Requiem* (1962), honors the dead of many wars.

Bruckner, Anton (1824–96): Composer and organist. Austrian-born Bruckner served as organist at Linz cathedral (1856–58), during which time he was enormously influenced by composer Richard Wagner. His *Mass in F Minor* (1867–68) is considered his best sacred work; he also wrote nine symphonies. He performed in London in 1871, and in 1875 was appointed lecturer at the University of Vienna. It was only toward the end of his life that Bruckner saw his markedly original and spiritual works attain the recognition they deserved.

Cage, John (1912–92): Composer. This foremost contemporary American composer started his career in 1938 with a piece for "prepared piano," in which objects are placed directly on the piano strings to create a variety of sounds. He became interested in Zen philosophy and created *4'33"* (1952), in which no sound is intentionally produced. In 1952 his first musical "happening" involved audience members in the creation of musical expression. Cage employed the Chinese oracle book *I Ching* when composing works such as *Music of Changes* (1951).

Callas, Maria [Maria Kalogeropoulos] (1923–77): Soprano. Born in New York City, Callas made her professional debut at sixteen with the Royal Opera in Athens, Greece, where she also had her first major success in 1942 as Tosca. She debuted in Italy in the title role of *La Gioconda* in Verona in 1947 and then performed at Milan's La Scala from 1951 through 1962. After a tremendous debut at the Metro-

politan Opera in the title role of *Norma* (1956), she sang there only sporadically until her retirement from opera in 1965.

Carter, Elliott (1908–——): Composer. Carter's early works are characterized as neo-Classical; he later adopted the twelve-tone compositional method of Schönberg. Technically, this important modern American composer's greatest accomplishment is metrical modulation, in which the value of the basic musical unit is lengthened or shortened in order to bring about another metronomic speed. This innovation is perfected in his *String Quartet No. 1* (1951). Carter won the 1950 Pulitzer Prize for his *Second String Quartet* (1959).

Caruso, Enrico (1873–1921): Tenor. An Italian possessed of one of the most beautiful tenor voices ever, Caruso had his first big success in 1898, when he sang as Loris at the world premier of *Fedora* in Milan. After performing in Europe, he sang the Duke in *Rigoletto* at the Metropolitan Opera in 1903, where he subsequently appeared in thirty-six other roles. He excelled in Italian operas, and his performances, especially in *Tosca* and *La Juive,* became the standard against which other singers judged their technique.

Casals, Pablo (1876–1973): Cellist. Born in Spain, Casals was a child prodigy who became a solo cellist at the Paris Opéra in 1895 and by 1903 had toured Europe and the Americas. In 1905 he formed a trio with pianist Alfred Cortot and violinist Jacques Thibaud; this renowned ensemble appeared together until 1937. In 1919 he founded and conducted the Orquesta Pau Casals in Barcelona, in 1950 he established the annual Padres Festival, and in 1956, the yearly Casals festival. Casals was also a talented composer.

Chopin, Frédéric (1810–49): Composer and pianist. Born in Poland, Chopin was an unsurpassed genius of the piano who, in life and art, embodied the Romantic ideal. Although a virtuoso, he had an introspective personality ill suited for a performing career; he made his living by teaching and composing. Chopin is credited with taking bold steps beyond traditional piano technique to give that instrument sublime expression. All of his works, from the winsome *ballades* to the emotional *études,* show a marked individuality and general excellence.

Cliburn, Van (1934–——): Pianist. Texas-born Cliburn debuted with the Houston Symphony Orchestra at age thirteen. He became world-famous in 1958 after triumphing at the International Tchaikovsky piano competition. In 1962, a piano competition was established in Texas and named in his honor.

Copland, Aaron (1900–90): Composer. The early works of this outstanding American composer, such as the Concerto for Piano and Orchestra (1926), show a jazz influence. Some of his later works rely on American folk themes, including the orchestral work *El Salón México* (1933–36) and the ballets *Billy the Kid* (1938), *Rodeo* (1942) and *Appalachian Spring* (1944). His famous *Lincoln Portrait* (1942) combines orchestral music with narrated excerpts from Lincoln's speeches and letters. A patriotic style enlivens Copland's most famous work, *Fanfare for the Common Man* (1942). He also composed film scores for eight movies, including *Of Mice and Men* (1939), *Our Town* (1940) and *The Red Pony* (1948).

Debussy, Claude (1862–1918): Composer. Modulating tone and delicate sonority made the French-born Debussy's works musical embodiments of Impressionism. A master of the piano, he composed works in various genres. His masterpiece is the instrumental *Prelude à l'après-midi d'un faune* (1894); other major works include his opera *Pelléas et Mélisande* (1902), and the orchestral works *La Mer* (1903–05) and three Nocturnes (1892–99).

Domingo, Plácido (1941–——): Tenor. One of the dominant opera singers today, Domingo was born in Madrid but moved to Mexico as a child. He debuted at the National Opera in Mexico City in 1959 and made appearances in Monterey and Dallas (both 1961). He performed with the New York City Opera (1965) and debuted at the Metropolitan Opera in *Adriana Lecouvreur* in 1968. Domingo has also tried his hand at conducting, starting with *La Traviata* at the New York City Opera in 1973, to favorable reviews. He published an autobiography in 1983 and was honored to sing Otello at the centennial celebration at La Scala in 1987. In 1993 he joined Luciano Pavarotti in a special performance at the Metropolitan Opera.

Donizetti, Gaetano (1797–1848): Composer. An Italian opera composer known for setting romantic stories to soaring melodies, Donizetti began his career in Venice with the production of *Enrico di Borgogna* (1818). In all, Donizetti composed more than seventy operas, including such masterpieces as *Lucrezia Borgia* (1833), *Lucia di Lammermoor* (1835), *The Daughter of the Regiment* (1840) and *Don Pasquale* (1843).

Dvořák, Antonin (1841–1904): Composer. Deeply influenced by his native Czech folk traditions, Dvořák had his earliest successes with *Moravian Duets* (1876), three *Slavonic Rhapsodies* (1878) for orchestra, and the popular *Slavonic Dances* (1878). *Stabat Mater* (1876–77) also helped establish his reputation, as did the much-respected *Carnival Overture* (1891). As director of the National Conservatory of Music in America, Dvořák wrote his most famous work, his Symphony in E-flat, *From the New World* (1893), which reflected his admiration for African-American and Native American music.

Falla, Manuel de (1876–1946): Composer. In 1905 Falla, a Spaniard, had his first success when he won a prize for his opera *La Vida Breve.* Influenced by Impressionism, he produced the ballet *El Amor brujo* (1915), which was derived from Andalusian-gypsy folklore and songs. His poetic piece for piano and orchestra *Noches en los Jardines de España* (1916) followed, as did *El Sombrero de Tres Picos* (1919), his most popular ballet. His epic cantata *Atlántida* remained unfinished at his death. Falla is remembered for his quintessential Spanish sound.

Ferrier, Kathleen (1912–53): Contralto. An outstanding English singer, Ferrier attracted much attention as a soloist in George Frideric Handel's *Messiah* at Westminster Abbey in 1943 and when she sang the title role in the premiere of Benjamin Britten's *Rape of Lucretia* (1946). She toured the United States in the late 1940s and early 1950s, but her last and most famous role was as Orfeo in Christoph von Gluck's *Orfeo et Euridice* at London's Covent Garden in 1953. Her career was cut short by cancer.

Fiedler, Arthur (1894–1979): Conductor. Fiedler reigned over the Boston Pops orchestra for more than forty years, beginning in 1930. He attracted enormous audiences by combining symphony repertory, semiclassics and popular music in his concerts. This American conductor began his music career as a violinist for the Boston Symphony Orchestra in 1915.

Flagstad, Kirsten (1895–1962): Soprano. Norwegian-born Flagstad had her first great success at the Bayreuth Festival in 1934 in the role of Sieglinde in Richard Wagner's *Die Walküre*. An engagement at the Metropolitan Opera the next year established her as the foremost Wagnerian soprano of the era. Beginning with guest engagements in London and Vienna in 1936, she toured the world until her retirement in 1954. She directed the Norwegian opera from 1958 to 1960.

Galway, James (1939–——): Flutist. The emotional performances and varied repertory of Irish-born Galway have earned him the following of a pop star. After playing in world-

class orchestras, such as the Berlin Philharmonic, he embarked on a career as a soloist in 1975 and continues to appear with orchestras and chamber groups.

Gilbert, William (1836–1911): Librettist. An English writer and the creator, with Arthur Sullivan, of the Gilbert and Sullivan comic operas, Gilbert first worked as a journalist. After meeting Sullivan in 1870, he teamed up with him to create their incredibly successful works. Gilbert was knighted in 1907. See also *Sullivan, Arthur,* page 171.

Glass, Philip (1937–——): Composer. A widely recognized contemporary American composer, Glass in 1968 formed the Philip Glass Ensemble to perform his aharmonious music, which meshes rhythmic passages to create a mesmerizing and sometimes dramatic effect. A collaborative effort with avant-garde director Robert Wilson led to the critically acclaimed opera *Einstein on the Beach* (1975). Glass's other operas include *Satyagraha* (1980), based on the life of Gandhi, and *Akhnaten* (1984), an Egyptian epic. He scored the movies *Koyaanisqatsi* (1981) and *Mishima* (1985).

Gluck, Christoph von (1714–87): Composer. This German opera innovator eschewed the Italian tradition of fantastical opera by advocating simpler stories, greater realism and music that advanced the action. His first work in the new style was *Orpheus and Euridice* (1762). Also notable among Gluck's more than forty-five operas are *Alceste* (1767), *Paris and Helen* (1770) and *Echo and Narcissus* (1779).

Gounod, Charles (1818–93): Composer. Gounod, who was born in Paris, composed mainly operas. His first work, *Sapho* (1851), brought little acclaim, but his next, *Faust* (1859), won renown. After *Faust,* Gounod composed nine more operas, including *Mireille* (1864) and *Romeo et Juliette* (1867). Gounod also wrote a variety of oratorios, cantatas, secular music and orchestral music.

Granados, Enrique (1867–1916): Composer and pianist. This remarkable Spaniard slowly established his reputation by giving recitals. His zarzuela (operetta) *Maria del Carmen* (1898) had more success than the operas he wrote thereafter, with one exception: his masterpiece *Goyescas,* with a libretto by Periquet, inspired by the etchings and paintings of Goya. Granados's orchestral intermezzo to the opera *Intermezzo* is a beautiful and popular work. He is also remembered for his excellent piano composition *Danzas españolas.*

Grieg, Edvard (Hagerup) (1843–1907): Composer. Grieg's work combines the passionate lyricism of Romanticism with the nationalistic influences of his homeland, Norway. By 1867 he had composed the first of ten sets of *Lyric Pieces for Piano,* which established his reputation. In 1869 he premiered his masterful Piano Concerto to much success, and in 1870 he traveled to Rome, where he was befriended by Franz Liszt. From 1874 to 1875 he wrote the music to Ibsen's *Peer Gynt* at the author's request; its resounding success put him much in demand throughout Europe.

Handel, George Frideric (1685–1759): Composer. This German organist had his first success with the opera *Almira* (1705). A visit to Italy, where he produced *Agrippina* (1710), had a profound musical influence on him; thereafter he became a master of Italian technique and style. Handel visited London in 1710 and remained there the rest of his life. His first opera in England, *Rinaldo* (1711), was a great success, as were the instrumental *Water Music* (1717) and the operas *Giulio Cesare* (1724) and *Rodelinda* (1725). He then turned his genius to oratorios, producing *Saul* (1739) and *Israel in Egypt* (1739), among others. Handel's masterpiece is the transcendent *Messiah* (1742).

Haydn, Franz Joseph (1732–1809): Composer. This Austrian master is credited with per-

fecting symphonic composition and with establishing four-part writing as an integral part of composition. Much of Haydn's work was composed solely for his patron, Prince Nikolaus Esterházy of Eisenstadt, although by the end of his life he achieved considerable fame. His most memorable symphonies include No. 49, in F minor, "La passione" (1768), No. 44, in E Minor, "Trauersinfonie" (1772), and No. 45, in F-sharp minor, "Farewell" (1772). Haydn also wrote concertos, dramatic works, sacred music and string quartets.

Heifetz, Jascha (1901–87): Violinist. This Lithuanian-born prodigy was regarded as one of history's greatest virtuosos, admired for his purity of tone. He earned higher fees, played in more places and sold more recordings than any violinist before him. He was a soloist with the Berlin Philharmonic at age eleven and debuted in Carnegie Hall the same year, launching his worldwide touring career.

Hindemith, Paul (1895–1963): Composer. A major figure of 20th-century music, German-born Hindemith pioneered *Gebrauchmusik* ("functional music") with an educational and social purpose. He rejected Romanticism's excesses for the simplicity of Bach and the classical composers, blending traditional counterpoint with dissonance. His major works include an opera, *Cardillac* (1925); a chamber work for strings, *Kammermusik* (1922–30); and *Symphonie Metamorphoses* (1945).

Horne, Marilyn (1934–——): Soprano and mezzo-soprano. Horne is an American operatic and concert singer known internationally for a wide-ranging repertoire, including coloratura roles. In 1954 she joined The Los Angeles Opera Guild, her first affiliation. Horne debuted at the Metropolitan Opera House sixteen years later as Adalgisa in *Norma.* She gave other memorable performances at the Metropolitan Opera in *Carmen, The Barber of Seville* and *The Italian Girl in Algiers.*

Horowitz, Vladimir (1903–89): Pianist. Russian-born Horowitz was a virtuoso in Europe before his 1928 debut with the New York Philharmonic Orchestra. He gave recitals regularly until 1953, when he took a twelve-year hiatus from the stage. He spent those years as a recording artist and private teacher, then returned to the stage in 1965 with a performance at Carnegie Hall. Another retirement followed from 1969 to 1974, during which he made several recordings. In 1978 at Carnegie Hall, Horowitz celebrated the fiftieth anniversary of his American debut and in 1982 made his first European appearance in thirty-one years at Royal Festival Hall in London. He toured Japan the following year and in 1986 ended his sixty-one-year absence from his homeland with a recital tour of Russia.

Humperdinck, Englebert (1854–1921): Composer. As a youth in Germany he assisted composer Richard Wagner with productions of Wagner's *Parsifal.* Humperdinck went on to create fairy-tale operas, and his masterwork, *Hansel and Gretel* (1893), brought him world fame. His only other popular success, *Die Königskinder* (1910), debuted at the Metropolitan Opera House.

Ives, Charles (1874–1954): Composer. Ives was an American insurance executive who advanced 20th-century music with complex polytonal and polyrhythmic structures. He composed complex and dissonant works for choruses, symphonies and chamber groups, incorporating American sacred and secular tunes into his writing. In 1947 he won a Pulitzer Prize for his Third Symphony, but his most popular works are the First Piano Sonata (1909) and Piano Sonata No. 2 ("Concord").

Lind, Jenny (1820–87): Soprano. Known as the "Swedish Nightingale," Lind made her operatic debut in Stockholm in 1838 and subsequently sang throughout Europe to astounding success. She appeared in such operas as *La Sonnambula, La fille du régiment* and Giuseppe Verdi's *I Masnadieri*, in which she created the role of Amalia. Lind retired from opera in 1849 but continued her concert and oratorio career, which included an 1850 tour of the United States sponsored by P. T. Barnum.

Liszt, Franz (1811–86): Pianist and composer. Gifted with great piano virtuosity, Hungarian-born Liszt embodied Romanticism. A child prodigy, he lived and performed in Paris from 1823 to 1835, where he met Frédéric Chopin, Hector Berlioz and Niccolo Paganini. After touring Europe with phenomenal success, he retired from the stage to compose and teach. The *Transcendental Études* (1854), the B-Minor Piano Sonata (1854), the *Faust* symphony (1853–61), and the piano concertos are among his major works. An innovator of the modern symphonic poem, Liszt was also an important influence on composer Richard Wagner, his son-in-law.

Lutoslawski, Witold (1913–94): Composer. He was the foremost contemporary Polish composer, whose early works were limited to the neo-Classical style by political restrictions. After the political atmosphere changed in 1956, Lutoslawski embraced modern Western music, employing aleatory and dodecaphonic techniques, having been influenced by Béla Bartók, to whom he dedicated *Musique funèbre* for string orchestra (1958), and John Cage. His major works include Symphonies No. 2 (1966–67) and No. 3 (1972–83).

Ma, Yo-Yo (1955–——): Cellist. The Chinese-born Ma is known for his unpretentious musicianship. He earned his reputation as a virtuoso after training at the Juilliard School and Harvard and now appears with all the world's major orchestras. Besides playing in a chamber music ensemble with Isaac Stern, he regularly appears with pianist Emanuel Ax. Ma has made numerous and well-received transcriptions for the cello. He received the Avery Fisher Prize in 1978 and a Grammy Award in 1984.

Mahler, Gustav (1860–1911): Conductor and composer. In 1897 this Austrian was given the position of music director of the Vienna Court Opera, serving simultaneously as the conductor of the Vienna Philharmonic (1898–1901). He was made principal conductor of the Metropolitan Opera in 1907, and in 1909 was also appointed conductor of the New York Philharmonic. He returned to Vienna in 1911. As a composer, Mahler was a symphonist in the grand Romantic style; some of his major works are *Das Lied von der Erde* (1911), nine complete symphonies, and *Des Knaben Wunderhorn* (1892–1901).

Massenet, Jules (1842–1912): Composer. Massenet was the foremost French opera composer of the late 19th century and winner of the coveted Prix de Rome (1863). He produced the first of his twenty-five operas, *Hérodiade,* in 1881, but found his greatest success with the lyrical operas *Manon* (1884), *Werther* (1892) and *Thaïs* (1894).

Masur, Kurt: (1927–——): Conductor. Born in Germany, Masur studied piano and cello at the Breslau Music School from 1942 to 1944. He began his professional conducting career in the early 1950s, leading orchestras at the Erfort City Theater from 1951 to 1953 and the Leipzig City Theater (1953–1955). In 1955 Masur served as conductor of the Dresden Philharmonic Orchestra for three years before assuming the duties of senior music director at the Komische Opera in East Berlin. In the early 1970s Masur began conducting in the West, making his American debut with the Cleveland Orchestra in 1974. In 1988 he became principal guest conductor with the London Philharmonic and in 1991 he took over the musical directorship of the New York Philharmonic, a position he still holds.

Mehta, Zubin (1936–——): Conductor. Born in India, Mehta won a conducting competition in Liverpool, England, in 1958. He was given his first full engagement to conduct the Vienna Symphony Orchestra in 1960, and was appointed music director of the Los Angeles Philharmonic Orchestra in 1962, simultaneously serving as director of the Montreal Symphony (1961–67). In 1977 he became musical director of the Israeli Philharmonic and a year later left his Los Angeles position to direct the New York Philharmonic, a post he held until 1991.

Melba, Dame Nellie (1861–1931): Coloratura soprano. Australian-born Melba was the greatest prima donna of her generation, reigning at the Metropolitan Opera during the 1890s. She debuted on stage as Gilda in a Belgian production of *Rigoletto* in 1887 and at the Metropolitan Opera in the title role of *Lucia di Lammermoor* in 1888.

Mendelssohn, Felix (1809–47): Pianist and composer. Mendelssohn, a German, was a virtuoso in the Romantic style. In 1829 he visited England for the first of ten times and composed *The Hebrides Overture* in Scotland. In 1835 he was appointed conductor of the Leipzig Gewandhaus Orchestra; it was in that city in 1843 that he opened his famous Conservatory of Music. Among Mendelssohn's outstanding works are the oratorio *Elijah* (1846), his Octet for Strings (1825), the Six Preludes and Fugues, Op.35 and *Songs without Words.*

Menotti, Gian Carlo (1911–——): Opera composer. Italian-born Menotti emigrated to the United States in 1927 to attend the Curtis Institute of Music in Philadelphia. He is most admired for his operas *The Medium* (1945), *The Telephone* (1947) and *The Consul* (1950), for which he won the Pulitzer Prize. *Amahl* *and the Night Visitors,* Menotti's holiday opera, premiered on television in 1951.

Menuhin, Yehudi (1916———): Violinist. An American virtuoso regarded as a master of Bach, Menuhin began a decades-long performing career as a soloist with the San Francisco Symphony at age eight. He debuted at the Metropolitan Opera in 1925 and in Paris in 1927, winning a large international following. Menuhin founded a school for talented young musicians in Surrey, England, in 1963. He continues to perform, record and write about violin playing.

Monteverde, Claudio (1567–1643): Composer. One of the earliest composers of opera, this Italian brought dramatic characters to life through music. Only a few works have survived, such as *L'Orfeo* (1607), regarded as the first opera, *The Return of Ulysses* (1641) and *The Coronation of Poppea* (1642). Monteverde also wrote nine books of madrigals.

Mozart, Wolfgang Amadeus (1756–91): Composer. The works of this musical giant whose works remain unrivaled in the richness of their lyricism and melody. During his lifetime, Austrian-born Mozart was hailed for his musical ability, although he was unable to earn a decent living through his skill. It is only in death that his genius has been fully appreciated. A few of Mozart's outstanding works are the operas *The Marriage of Figaro* (1786), *Don Giovanni* (1787), *Così fan tutte* (1790) and *The Magic Flute* (1791). His instrumental achievements include the Piano Concerto in D Major (the "Coronation" Concerto, 1788) and Symphony No. 41 ("Jupiter," 1788).

Mussorgsky, Modest (1839–81): Composer. One of the most influential Russian musicians of his day, he created operas, symphonies, piano works and song cycles. His most notable creations include the opera *Boris Godunov* (1874), the symphony *A Night on Bald Mountain* (1867), the piano suite *Pictures at an Exhibition* (1874), and the song cycle *Songs and Dances of Death* (1877).

Norman, Jessye (1945———): Dramatic soprano. Norman, an American, sings both in operas and on the concert stage. She began her early career in Europe, debuting professionally with the Deutsche Oper Berlin as Elisabeth in *Tannhäuser,* and appeared at Milan's La Scala in *Aïda* (1972). One year later, she made her New York debut as a concert soloist at Lincoln Center.

Offenbach, Jacques (1819–80): Composer. The most famous light operas by this Frenchman include *La Belle Hélène* (1864), *La Vie Parisienne* (1866), *The Grand Duchess of Gerolstein* (1867), *La Périchole* (1868) and *Les Brigands* (1869). His only full-length opera was *Tales of Hoffmann*, produced in 1881 after his death.

Ormandy, Eugene (1899–1985): Conductor. Born and trained in Hungary, Ormandy became a U.S. citizen in 1927. In 1929 he conducted the New York Philharmonic and in 1930 the Philadelphia Orchestra. He then went on to the musical directorship of the Minneapolis Symphony Orchestra from 1931 to 1936, whereupon he became the associate director of the Philadelphia Orchestra and then musical director in 1938, a position he held for forty years to much international acclaim.

Ozawa, Seiji (1935———): Conductor. Japanese-born Ozawa is popular for his vitality at the podium. He first gained renown as an assistant conductor for the New York Philharmonic (1951–52) under Leonard Bernstein. In 1964 he became the conductor of the Chicago Philharmonic and thereafter conducted in Toronto, London, Berlin, Tokyo and other major cities. Since 1973 he has served as musical director of the Boston Symphony Orchestra.

Paderewski, Ignacy (1860–1941): Pianist. This Polish statesman's poetic playing made him one of the most popular musicians of his era. His recital career began in Vienna in 1887. His only successful composition was the opera *Manru* (1901). An ardent Polish patriot, he served as prime minister in 1919 and represented Poland at the Versailles Peace Conference and in the League of Nations at the end of World War I. Paderewski fled Poland when Germany invaded in 1940 and declared himself president-in-exile. He died in New York City.

Paganini, Niccolo (1782–1840): Violinist and composer. This fabled Italian transformed the art and technique of the violin. He began touring Europe successfully in 1797 and crafted six violin concertos, twelve sonatas for violin and guitar, and twenty-four caprices for solo violin, all of which demanded virtuoso technique.

Partch, Harry (1901–74): Composer. This extremely innovative American was a self-taught musician who implemented a forty-three-tone scale, which he employed on the twenty musical instruments he invented. During the Great Depression, he wandered throughout the United States, observing folk life and gathering incongruous bits of text to use in future works. Partch's output includes the dance satire *Bewitched* (1955), an example of his goal of the integration of elements from a wide range of cultures and eras. He also wrote a number of film scores.

Pavarotti, Luciano (1935–——): Tenor. The foremost Italian tenor today, Pavarotti debuted as Rodolfo in *La Bohème* in Italy in 1961, a role he went on to sing in Vienna and London. He appeared as Alfredo in *La Traviata* in Milan and as Rodolfo at his debuts with the San Francisco Opera (1967) and New York's Metropolitan Opera (1968), where he also made his solo debut in 1978. His popularity has been furthered by frequent telecasts of his performances.

Penderecki, Krzysztof (1933–——): Composer. Although his output includes more traditional choral works of sacred music, such as *St. Luke Passion* (1966), the Polish-born composer is best known for pieces in his strikingly modern compositional style, in which he makes both traditional and nontraditional uses of instruments and all types of sounds. His technique yields works of ever-shifting patterns of rhythm and meter, which flirt with atonal and dissonant characteristics. His *Threnody in Memory of Victims of Hiroshima* (1959–60) is his most famous work.

Perlman, Itzhak (1945–——): Violinist. Considered the foremost violinist today, Perlman was born in Tel Aviv, Israel, and studied at the Juilliard School in New York. He won the Leventritt Competition in 1954, which garnered him an appearance with the New York Philharmonic and the support and friendship of Isaac Stern. Tours of the United States and Europe followed, and he acquired a reputation as a virtuoso who enjoys numerous genres and plays them with versatility.

Pons, Lily (1904–76): Coloratura soprano. A French-American famous for the flexibility of her voice, Pons debuted in 1920 in Delibes's opera *Lakmé*. In 1931 she made her first appearance at the Metropolitan Opera in *Lucia di Lammermoor,* a performance that led to thirty years as a principal soprano there. In addition to stage appearances, she sang on radio and television and in motion pictures.

Previn, André (1929–——): Conductor. A naturalized American who was born in Berlin, Previn began his career in Hollywood as an orchestrator and arranger for motion pictures. He won Academy Awards for *Gigi* (1958), *Porgy and Bess* (1959), *Irma la Douce* (1963) and *My Fair Lady* (1964). In 1963 Previn made his conducting debut with the St. Louis Symphony Orchestra; he has since been the principal conductor for symphony orchestras in Houston and London.

Price, Leontyne (1927———): Soprano. Price's subtle interpretations have won her great acclaim. After studying at the Juilliard School of Music, she broke color barriers by becoming the first African-American to establish a successful career with the Metropolitan Opera. She debuted there in 1961 as Leonora in *Il Trovatore*. In 1964 she received the Presidential Medal of Freedom.

Prokofiev, Sergei (1891–1953): Composer. In 1914, Russian-born Prokofiev composed his Piano Concerto No. 1, a piece filled with the dissonant harmonic combinations typical of his style; his famous Symphony No. 1 ("Classical," 1916–17) followed. During World War I, he traveled to Japan, the United States and Paris, where he composed the ballets *Chout* (1920), *Le pas d'acier* (1924), and *L'enfant prodigue* (1920). Back home he composed his most popular works, the ballet *Romeo and Juliet* (1935–36), the opera *War and Peace* (1941–52) and the children's favorite, *Peter and the Wolf* (1936).

Puccini, Giacomo (1858–1924): Composer. Born into a famous Italian musical family, he received formal training from an early age. His first opera, *Le Villi* (1884), was a success; it was followed by *Manon Lescaut* (1893). His next three operas, *La Bohème* (1896), *Tosca* (1900) and *Madama Butterfly* (1904), were masterpieces that propelled Puccini to operatic fame. *Turandot* was left unfinished at his death, but the final scene was completed by Franco Alfano.

Purcell, Henry (c. 1659–95): Composer. One of England's greatest Baroque composers, he served the royal court by creating hundreds of works of chamber music, sacred music, odes, welcome songs and stage music, including his full-length opera *Dido and Aeneas* (1689). In 1679 he became the organist at Westminster Abbey.

Rachmaninoff, Sergei (1873–1943): Composer and pianist. This Russian's Prelude in C-sharp minor (1892) brought him his first worldwide recognition. He then began a career as a virtuoso pianist, conductor and composer. He debuted his Concerto No. 2 for Piano and Orchestra in Moscow in 1901; it remains a classic of the 20th century. In 1917 Rachmaninoff left Russia and made yearly tours of Europe and the United States, where he settled in 1939. His Romantic-influenced style is evident in his famous Piano Concerto No. 3 (1909), Symphony No. 2 (1907) and the Rhapsody on a Theme of Paganini (1934).

Rampal, Jean-Pierre (1922———): Flutist. This prominent French musician with a specialty in 18th-century music played flute in the orchestra of the Vichy Opera (1946–50) and served as the first flutist of the Paris Opera (1956–62). He made his first solo tour in 1947 and became increasingly popular as a virtuoso technician, with many recordings and stage appearances to his credit.

Ravel, Maurice (1875–1937): Composer. Although often compared to Debussy, this French composer, known for his orchestrations, early demonstrated a highly personal style of classical structure, combined with a taste for bold experimentation. His many brilliant works include *Jeux d'Eau* for piano (1901), String Quartet in F (1902–03) and the song cycle *Shéhérezade* (1903). The ballet *Daphnis et Chloé* (1909–11) is perhaps Ravel's most important work, but it was his famous *Boléro* (1928) that brought him the worldwide recognition he deserved.

Rimsky-Korsakov, Nikolai (1844–1908): Composer. This Russian made his conducting debut in 1874, with his own Symphony No. 3. His remarkable orchestrations, exemplary of the idiomatic Russian school, include *Capriccio espagnol* (1887), *Scheherazade* (1888) and the *Russian Easter Overture* (1888). His best operas are *Mlada* (1889–90), *Christmas Eve* (1894–95) and *Sadko* (1894–96), although his most popular work is the revised version of Mussorgsky's opera *Boris Godunov*.

Rossini, Gioacchino (1799–1868): Composer. One of the greatest Italian opera composers of the early 19th century, he was equally adept at comedy and drama. His principal works include *Tancredi* (1813), *The Italian Girl in Algiers* (1813), *The Barber of Seville* (1816), *Otello* (1816) and *William Tell* (1829). Rossini's professional success made him one of the most influential and wealthy citizens of his day.

Rostropovich, Mstislav (1927–——): Cellist and conductor. Admired as an exceptional stylist and technician, this Russian debuted as a soloist with the Moscow Philharmonic and in the United States at Carnegie Hall in 1956. Composers honored him with original cello compositions, including Shostakovich's Concerto in E Flat for Cello and Britten's Suite for Cello. Rostropovich emigrated to the United States in 1977 to conduct the National Symphony Orchestra. He won the Presidential Medal of Freedom in 1987.

Rubinstein, Anton (1829–94): Pianist and composer. A child prodigy in Russia, he played piano before Frédéric Chopin and Franz Liszt at the age of ten. After musical training and touring, he wrote three operas, *Dmitri Donskoy* (1852), *The Siberian Hunters* (1853) and *Thomas the Fool* (1853); he also began touring again, an activity he undertook for the rest of his life. His most famous work is probably the *Ocean Symphony* (1851). Rubinstein was known as an outstanding interpreter, especially of Beethoven's sonatas; he also established the Imperial Conservatory in St. Petersburg (1862) and the Rubinstein Prize (1890).

Rubinstein, Artur (1887–1982): Pianist. This Polish-born child prodigy made his American debut in 1906 at Carnegie Hall. During World War I he performed with the London Symphony Orchestra, and from 1916 to 1917 he toured Spain and South America to great success. He toured the United States from 1919 to 1932; during World War II he lived in Hollywood and played on film soundtracks. In 1958 he made an emotional return to Poland, and retired in 1976. Rubinstein excelled in performing the Romantic composers.

Saint-Saëns, Camille (1835–1921): Composer. This prolific Frenchman emphasized clarity and order in his orchestral works and operas, abhorring modern influences. His love of theater inspired his most famous opera, *Samson and Delilah* (1877). Other notable works include the Third Symphony (1866), *Danse macabre* (1875), and his masterpiece, *The Carnival of Animals* (1922).

Salerno-Sonnenberg, Nadja (1961–——): Violinist. Italian-born Salerno-Sonnenberg has made a meteoric professional rise. Educated at the Curtis and Juilliard schools of music, she first debuted with the Philadelphia Orchestra in 1971. In 1981 she became the youngest person to win the prestigious Naumberg Violin Competition, leading to a recording contract and concert dates. She currently appears forty to fifty times a year on stage.

Satie, Erik (1866–1925): Composer. Satie, a Frenchman, broke with the extravagance of Romantic tradition to pursue subtle simplicity in his compositions. Known for his wit and eccentricity, he influenced the course of early 20th-century music with piano works, such as *Trois Gymnopédies* (1888), and the ballets *Parade* (1916), *Mercure* (1924) and *Relâche* (1924).

Scarlatti, Alessandro (1660–1725): Composer. He set the style for Italian opera in the 18th century, in part by establishing as a standard the *Da Capo* aria, in which singers repeat phrases or sections within an aria. Composer of hundreds of cantatas and more than a hundred operas, Scarlatti wrote such famous operatic works as *La Rosaura* (1690), *Il Tigrane* (1715) and *Trinfo dell'onore* (1718).

Schönberg, Arnold (1874–1951): Composer. Born in Austria, Schönberg moved to the United States when the Nazis came to power. In 1924 he perfected the technique of twelve-tone composition, ushering in a thoroughly modern chapter in musical theory. The first of his works to use this method integrally is the *Piano Suite,* Op. 25 (1924). His other outstanding works include *Verklärte Nacht* (1899), the choral work *Gurrelieder* (1911), the symphonic poem *Pelleas und Melisande* (1905) and Klavierstück, Op. 33a (1928–29).

Schubert, Franz (1797–1828): Composer. An Austrian of awesome productivity, Schubert was creator and master of the German Romantic lieder (art song). He wrote music for poems by Goethe and Schiller, among others. His most famous lieder are "Der Erlkönig" (1815), "Der Wanderer" (1819) and "Death and the Maiden" (1817); notable song cycles include *Die schöne Müllerin* (1823) and *Die Winterreise* (1827). He also wrote sacred, theatrical and orchestral works.

Schuman, William (1910–92): Composer. A master of the American idiom, Schuman was a versatile, cosmopolitan composer. Initially interested in popular music and jazz, he eventually turned to more classic forms. However, he still employed the modern innovations of complicated contrapuntal frameworks, dissonance without atonality, and strongly contrasting melodies. His *A Free Song* (1943) won Schuman the first of two Pulitzer prizes. Other major works include the opera *The Mighty Casey* (1953), the choreographic poem *Judith* (1950) and his ten symphonies. He was also president of the Julliard School of Music and first president of Lincoln Center for the Performing Arts.

Schumann, Robert (1810–56), and **Clara** (1819–96): Composer; pianist. Robert was a German writer and composer of Romantic sensibilities whose works expressed deeply felt emotions. His most famous works are the piano piece *Davidsbündlertänze* (1837), the *Etudes symphoniques* (1834–37) and the C major Symphony (1846). He married Clara in 1840 and remained devoted to her until his early death—Clara outlived her husband by forty years. After his death she toured Europe as an acclaimed pianist and earned a reputation as a fine teacher.

Scotto, Renata (1933–——): Soprano. Scotto is an Italian opera singer who began as a light soprano and graduated to more dramatic roles. She won praise from critics for her superb technical control in such productions as *La Wally,* her La Scala debut (1953); the Edinburgh Festival's *La Sonnambula* (1957); and her Metropolitan Opera debut as Cio-Cio-San in *Madama Butterfly* (1965).

Scriabin, Aleksandr (1872–1915): Composer. Scriabin, a Russian, created music based on philosophical and metaphysical concepts. He absorbed ideas from contemporary poets and artists, such as the painter Wassily Kandinsky. His first significant orchestral work, *The Divine Poem,* premiered in Paris in 1905. Also widely performed are *Prometheus* (1910) and *Poem of Ecstasy* (1908).

Segovia, Andrés (1893–1987): Classical guitarist. A master craftsman, this Spaniard made his official debut in Granada at age sixteen. In the following years he played in Madrid, Paris, Barcelona and South America; he had his first U.S. performance at New York City's Town Hall in 1928. Segovia helped revive the guitar as an important concert instrument and, to that end, transcribed many works by other composers, including Bach, for the guitar.

Serkin, Rudolf (1903–91): Pianist. Russian-born Serkin interpreted music with great sensitivity and intelligence. A pupil of Arnold Schönberg, he debuted in the United States in 1933 in Washington, D.C. In 1934 he played with the New York Philharmonic and launched a touring career in the United

States. From 1938 to 1968 he taught at the Curtis Institute of Music in Philadelphia, acting as the school's director from 1968 to 1970.

Shankar, Ravi (1920——): Sitarist. The most famous sitarist in the world, Indian-born Shankar first performed in America in 1956. His subsequent tours of the United States and Europe introduced a wide audience to this instrument. His popularity exploded when the Beatles' George Harrison studied sitar with him. A respected composer, Shankar wrote the film scores for *Gandhi* (1982) and the *Pather Panchali* trilogy, among others.

Shostakovich, Dmitri (1906–75): Composer. The foremost 20th-century Russian composer, he suffered in the oppressive political climate of the Soviet Union. His opera *Lady Macbeth of the District of Mtzensk* (1934) was deemed inappropriate by Soviet authorities, as was his ballet *The Limpid Brook* (1935). His Symphony No. 7 ("Leningrad," 1942), however, which depicted Soviet victory over the Nazis, won wide acclaim at home and abroad. Thoroughly modern in technique, he employed dissonant harmonies and complex contrapuntal structures.

Sibelius, Jean (1865–1957): Composer. Most famous for his symphonic works, Sibelius often expressed his love for his native Finland in such symphonic poems as *Finlandia* (1900), *The Swan of Tuonela* (1893) and *Tapiola* (1925). He wrote a total of seven symphonies (1899–1924), as well as the famous Violin Concerto in D Minor (1903–05). Sibelius stopped composing at the end of the 1920s, although he lived for three more decades.

Sills, Beverly (1929——): Coloratura soprano. Sills, an American, made her operatic debut at age seventeen in a Philadelphia company's production of *Carmen*. In 1955 Sills joined the New York City Opera and in the next decade won worldwide acclaim for her portrayal of Lucia in *Lucia di Lammermoor,* singing at La Scala and Covent Garden. In 1975 she made her debut at the Metropolitan Opera in *The Siege of Corinth,* receiving an eighteen-minute ovation. She was director of The New York City Opera from 1980 to 1989, when she became its president. In 1991 she joined the board of the Metropolitan Opera, and became chairman of Lincoln Center for the Performing Arts in 1994.

Stern, Isaac (1920——): Violinist. This Russian-born American was a child prodigy and in 1936 made his debut playing with the San Francisco Symphony Orchestra. It wasn't until his Carnegie Hall recital in 1943, however, that he became known as a virtuoso. First performing in Europe in 1948, he continues to tour the world. A vibrant and energetic performer, Stern has a significant recorded repertoire. He has been president of Carnegie Hall since 1960.

Stradivari, Antonio (1644–1737): Violin craftsman. From Cremona, Italy, Stradivari created more than a thousand string instruments in his lifetime but is remembered chiefly for his extraordinary violins. Prized for their tone, Stadivari's priceless violins are widely considered the most beautiful string instruments ever crafted, particularly the *Alard* model, made in 1715.

Strauss, Johann, Johann II, Josef, and Eduard: Composers. Johann Strauss (1804–49), head of this family of Austrian composers, is remembered as "The Father of the Waltz"; his most enduring work is probably the "Radetzky March." He had three musical sons: Johann II (1825–99), known as "The Waltz King," whose works include the famous waltz *An der schönen blauen Donau* ("On the Beautiful Blue Danube," 1867) and the operetta *Die Fledermaus* (1874); Josef (1827–70), a conductor and composer of 283 musical compositions; and Eduard (1835–1916), a conductor and composer who toured Europe and the United States and also composed approximately three hundred works.

Strauss, Richard (1864–1949): Composer. A leading figure in the birth of modern music, Strauss remained at heart a Romanticist despite the political upheaval in his native Germany before and during World War II. He established his reputation through the brilliant symphonic poems *Don Juan* (1899), *Tod und Verklärung* (1890) and *Macbeth* (1890), which incorporate composer Richard Wagner's motif method. Other successful works include the opera *Der Rosenkavalier* (1909–10) and, toward the end of his life, the emotionally laden *Four Last Songs* (1948).

Stravinsky, Igor (1882–1971): Composer. An immensely influential modern composer, Russian-born Stravinsky departed from previous musical methods and achieved a stunning originality. He is particularly remembered for his early masterpieces: the ballets *The Firebird* (1910), with its distinct Russian flavor; *Pétrouchka* (1911), with its bursting rhythms and striking harmonies; and especially *Le sacre du printemps* ("The Rite of Spring," 1913). The latter work astounded audiences with its dissonance, quickly changing meters and dynamic sound. Stravinsky later composed in a neo-Classical style; major works from this period include the opera-oratorio *Oedipus Rex* (1926–27) and a work for piano and orchestra, the Capriccio (1929).

Sullivan, Arthur (1842–1900): Composer. The son of an English musician, he established himself with the cantata *Kenilworth* (1864) and his *Irish Symphony* (1864). *Cox and Box* (1867) was the first comic opera for which Sullivan wrote the music; his first successful collaboration with humorist William Gilbert as librettist was *Trial by Jury* (1879). The team's most memorable ventures were *H.M.S. Pinafore* (1878), *The Pirates of Penzance* (1879) and *The Mikado* (1885). Sullivan composed in many genres—oratorios, ballets, cantatas, operas and even hymns; he wrote the music to the song "Onward, Christian Soldiers" (1871). See also *Gilbert, William,* page 161.

Sutherland, Dame Joan (1926–——): Coloratura soprano. Australian-born Sutherland is one of the leading sopranos of the 20th century and a specialist in *bel canto* repertory. Her first London appearance, in a 1952 production of Mozart's *The Magic Flute* at Covent Garden, led to the title role in *Lucia di Lammermoor* there in 1959. Thereafter, she sang internationally, leaving her stamp on leading roles in Bellini's *Norma,* Rossini's *Semiramide* and Verdi's *La Traviata.* In 1979 she received the title Dame of the British Empire.

Tchaikovsky, Peter (1840–93): Composer. He was a popular Russian composer with a particular gift for sentimental melody that gave his music enduring appeal. His first major success was the opera *Evgeny Onegin* (1878), but he is best remembered for his ballets *Swan Lake* (1876), *The Sleeping Beauty* (1889) and *The Nutcracker* (1891–92). The technically brilliant Symphony No. 6 ("Pathétique," 1893) reflected on Tchaikovsky's unhappy personal life.

Te Kanawa, Kiri (1946–——): Lyric soprano. This New Zealander was educated in London. She made her Covent Garden debut in *The Marriage of Figaro* (1971) and her Metropolitan Opera debut in *Otello* (1974). She has won acclaim for her beautiful legato singing in many operas, including the title role in Strauss's *Arabella,* Pamina in *The Magic Flute,* Mimi in *La Bohème* and Marguerite in *Faust.*

Telemann, George Philipp (1681–1767): Composer. A contemporary of Bach and Handel, this German was a prolific composer, mostly of church music. Greatly respected in his day, he wrote forty-four liturgical passions and scores of cantatas and psalms. He also composed forty operas, of which only one, *Pimpinone* (1725), is still performed.

Thomson, Virgil (1896–1989): Composer. This American wrote folk hymns and ballads into his scores. His notable works include the opera *Four Saints in Three Acts* (with libretto by Gertrude Stein, 1934); *Symphony on a Hymn Tune* (1928); Symphony No. 2; a ballet, *The Filling Station* (1937); and liturgical music, including *Missa Pro Defunctis* (1960). He also served as the music critic for the *New York Herald Tribune* from 1940 to 1955.

Tibbett, Lawrence (1896–1960): Baritone. An American, Tibbett performed at the Metropolitan Opera for twenty-five years (1925–50). He sang roles in French and Italian operas and the title role in Louis Gruenberg's *Emperor Jones* (1933), which was created especially for him. He also sang in an original production of Howard Hanson's *Merry Mount*.

Toscanini, Arturo (1867–1957): Conductor. Perhaps the foremost conductor in history, Italian-born Toscanini debuted in 1886. From 1887 to 1898 took his native land by storm, conducting in all its major cities. He was chief conductor at La Scala from 1898 to 1903 and again from 1906 to 1908, and then became principal conductor of New York's Metropolitan Opera in 1908. He served as artistic director of La Scala (1921–29) and as principal conductor of the New York Philharmonic (1928–36). In 1937 he formed and conducted the NBC Symphony Orchestra, with which he toured and recorded until his death.

Vaughn Williams, Ralph (1872–1958): Composer. An avid collector and admirer of the folk songs of his native England, Vaughn Williams displayed the influence of that genre in his earliest pieces, including *Three Norfolk Rhapsodies* (1906). A composer of awesome scope, he set poems by Walt Whitman to music in *A Sea Symphony* (1910). *A London Symphony* (1914) reflects scenes from everyday London in four movements, and *Pastoral Symphony* (1922) elicits the natu-

ral setting for which it is named. He composed nine symphonies, plus operas, stage works and sacred music in a style that is inexplicably yet quintessentially English.

Verdi, Giuseppe (1813–1901): Composer. A giant in the field of Italian opera, Verdi created works that remain the mainstays of opera companies worldwide. His first success was *Nabucco* (1842), followed by *Ernani* (1844). *I Masnadieri* and *Jérusalem* (1847) cemented Verdi's reputation, but it was *Rigoletto* (1850) that stamped him as a genius. The operas *La Traviata* (1853), *Aïda* (1871), and *Otello* (1887) are timeless works in the operatic repertoire; his last significant work, *Falstaff* (1893), is one of the greatest comic operas of all time.

Vivaldi, Antonio (1678–1741): Composer and violinist. An Italian Baroque master, Vivaldi took Holy Orders in 1703 and was appointed director of concerts at the Ospedale della Pietà, a home for foundlings, where he served, off and on, for most of his life. An excellent violinist, he is most remembered today for *The Four Seasons* and the many works he wrote for violin, including 230 concertos, which were widely studied by Johann Sebastian Bach. His body of work also includes ninety sonatas and thirty-eight operas.

Von Stade, Frederica (1945–——): Mezzo-soprano. This American specializes in works by Mozart and Rossini. She attended the Mannes School of Music and apprenticed at the Metropolitan Opera in secondary roles. After spending a year singing in Europe (1972), she returned to the Met in 1973 to sing the lead role of Rosina in *The Barber of Seville*. She continues to perform internationally.

Wagner, Richard (1813–83): Composer. A visionary giant in the field of stage music, Wagner changed the course of German opera and had untold influence on those who followed him. His most famous group of works is the timeless opera cycle *Der Ring des Nibelungen* (1876), whose heroic-mythic themes were symbolic of high philosophical ideas. Other inspired works include *Parsifal* (1882) and *Tristan und Isolde* (1859), whose prelude is a masterpiece of fluid harmonies. Wagner also introduced the idea of *leitmotif* to music.

Weber, Carl Maria von (1786–1826): Composer. Weber is recognized for bridging the gap between the Classical and Romantic styles in German music. A giant in the field of opera, Weber had success with *Silvana* (1810) before composing his masterpiece, *Der Freischütz* (1820), which was based on a German fairy tale and imbued with supernatural elements typical of later Romantic works. Weber also wrote the operas *Euryanthe* (1823) and *Oberon* (1826), as well as outstanding piano works and other instrumental compositions.

Weill, Kurt (1900–50): Composer. In collaboration with playwright Bertolt Brecht as librettist, he composed the ground-breaking *singspiel* (a modern reinterpretation of the "singspiel," a type of German opera with spoken dialogue) *The Rise and Fall of the City of Mahagonny* (1926). The team then produced *Die Dreigroschenoper* in 1928, which appeared in the United States as *The Three-Penny Opera*. Stylistically, this work realized his *Stück mit Musik* ("Drama with Music") form, which changed the modern musical stage. Weill emigrated from Germany to the United States during World War II and wrote Broadway musicals, including *Knickerbocker Holiday* (1938) and *Lost in the Stars* (1949).

Country and Western

Cash, Johnny (1932–——): A preeminent American country-music singer and songwriter, Cash scored in 1955 with the hit "Cry, Cry, Cry," followed by the classic "I Walk the Line" (1956), "Don't Take Your Guns to Town" (1959) and "Ring of Fire" (1963). His album *Blood, Sweat and Tears* (1960) championed the working class, and *Bitter Tears* (1964) protested the treatment of Native Americans. *At Folsom Prison* (1968) gained him international exposure, and in the 1980s he recorded with Willie Nelson, Bruce Springsteen and Paul McCartney, among others.

Cline, Patsy [Virginia Patterson Hensley] (1932–63): Born in Virginia, Cline started performing on the radio at age fourteen. Her first hit was "Walking After Midnight" (1957), followed by the quintessential "I Fall to Pieces" (1961), "Crazy" (1961) and "She's Got You" (1962). Her emotionally charged style appealed to both country and pop audiences; then, at the height of her career, she was killed in a plane crash. Cline was inducted into the Country Music Hall of Fame in 1985.

Ford, Tennessee Ernie [Ernest Jennings] (1919–91): Ford was an American country music singer and performer of great national popularity. He recorded with Capital Records (1949–76), cutting such hit singles as "Mister and Mississippi" (1951). His best-selling song "Sixteen Tons" (1955) sold more than four million copies. From 1955 to 1961 he appeared on his own television show and received continually high ratings.

Haggard, Merle (1937–——): This California-born singer, guitarist and songwriter portrayed the rough life of prisons and barrooms. His biggest hit was "Okie from Muskogee" (1969). His first nationwide hit, "Strangers" (1965), led to a contract with Capitol Records. The album *Just Between the Two of Us* (1966) was a top-selling LP. In 1983 he collaborated with singer Willie Nelson on the album *Pancho and Lefty*.

Harris, Emmylou (1947———): Harris is an American country singer whose clear, sweet voice has produced such albums as *Pieces of the Sky* (1975), *Roses in the Snow* (1980), *Evangeline* (1981) and *Brand New Dance* (1991). Between 1976 and 1987, she received six Grammy Awards. In 1980, the Country Music Association named her Female Vocalist of the Year.

Jones, George (1931———): This Texas-born country music singer and songwriter made his first recording, "Why Baby, Why," in 1955. His first hit record, "White Lightning" (1959), launched a successful career. He was named Country Singer of the Year by *Rolling Stone Magazine* in 1976 and received a Grammy Award for Country Vocal in 1980. From 1968 to 1975 he was married to country superstar Tammy Wynette.

Lynn, Loretta (1935———): Lynn is an American country singer whose first successful single was "Honky Tonk Girl" (1960). By 1970 she had recorded two dozen hits, including "Fist City" (1968), "Woman of the World" (1969) and "Coal Miner's Daughter" (1970)—the title she chose for her autobiography (1976). She was named Country Music Association Female Vocalist of the Year three times and was inducted into the Country Music Hall of Fame in 1988. In 1971 she won a Grammy Award.

Nelson, Willie (1933———): In 1961 this American country musician and songwriter wrote the Patsy Cline hit "Crazy," and the next year he recorded two other hits, "Touch Me" and "Willingly." His albums include *Here's Willie Nelson* (1963), *The Troublemaker* (1976), *Stardust* (1978) and *Born for Trouble* (1990). He has appeared in *Honeysuckle Rose* (1980) and other films and in 1989 won a Grammy Award for lifetime achievement.

Parton, Dolly (1946———): A multitalented American cross-over performer, Parton found fame in 1967 as a featured performer on the country-music TV show "Porter Wagoner." She composed and sang the country hits "In the Good Old Days" (1968), "My Blue Ridge Mountain Home" (1969), "Joshua" (1970), "A Coat of Many Colors" (1971) and "Jolene" (1974). Her pop hits include "9 to 5" (with Kenny Rogers, 1980). A hard-working performer, Parton has also had success as an actress in such films as *9 to 5* and *Steel Magnolias*.

Rogers, Kenny (1938———): This Texas-born entertainer and recording artist has a broad appeal that has spawned eleven platinum and eighteen gold albums. His hit singles include "Ruby, Don't Take Your Love to Town" (1969) and "The Gambler" (1978). In 1980 he recorded the album *Gideon* and in 1983 collaborated with singer Dolly Parton on the song "Islands in the Sun." He won Grammy Awards for best male country vocalist in 1977 and 1978.

Straight, George (1952———): This American country-music vocalist has two gold singles, "Fool Hearted Memory" (1982) and "Unwound" (1981). His albums include *I've Come to Expect It from You* (1990) and *If I Know Me* (1991). Straight was named Entertainer of the Year by the Country Music Association in 1985 and 1986. In 1991 the American Music Association named him Top Country Vocalist.

Williams, Hank (1923–53): Williams, an American country-western singer and composer, was most famous for the songs "Cold, Cold Heart" (1951) and "Your Cheatin' Heart" (1953). He dominated country music during his lifetime, producing six or more hits a year with his group, The Drifting Cowboys. Other Williams classics include "Hey, Good Lookin'," "Howlin' at the Moon," and "Baby We're Really in Love."

Wynette, Tammy (1942———): This Mississippi-born country singer has a throbbing voice that has told of women's suffering in love. Her first hit single, "I Don't Wanna Play House" (1968), was followed by "D-I-V-O-R-C-E" (1968), "Womanhood" (1970), "Stand By Your Man" (1970) and "Til I Can Make It on My Own" (1976), among others. She has sold more than eighteen million records and was named the Country Music Association's Female Vocalist of the Year in 1968.

Folk

Baez, Joan (1941———): She is an American folk singer and outspoken champion of liberal causes, whose passionate soprano voice is inimitable. Her hits include "Mary Hamilton" (1960), "There But for Fortune" (1965) and "Joe Hill" (1970), which she sang at Woodstock before releasing it on vinyl. In "Diamonds and Rust" (1975), she sang about her relationship with Bob Dylan. Baez was a committed protester of the Vietnam War and later turned her energies to human rights campaigns in Latin America.

Collins, Judy (1939———): An American with a beautiful, clear soprano voice, Collins began her career as a folk singer but has demonstrated her abilities in various musical genres. Her hits include "Both Sides Now" (1967), the spiritual "Amazing Grace" (1970) and "Send in the Clowns" (1975). She has also recorded songs by a wide variety of artists, including the Beatles' "In My Life" (1966), Jacques Brel's "La Colombe" (1966) and Kurt Weill's "Pirate Jenny" (1966).

Guthrie, Woody (1912–67): The songs of this American singer, songwriter and influential folk hero dealt with the Great Depression, the people of the Dust Bowl, the unemployed and the rest of society's bereft. A supporter of social reform, he played at protest marches and on picket lines. His best-known songs are "This Land Is Your Land," "So Long, It's Been Good to Know Ya," "Goin' Down the Road," and "Reuben James." His son, Arlo (1947———), also records folk music and scored his biggest hit with the song "Alice's Restaurant" (1967). The younger Guthrie starred in the movie based on the song two years later.

Leadbelly [Huddie Ledbetter] (1888–1949): This folk singer, composer and master of the twelve-string guitar was the first internationally known African-American musician from the Deep South. Folklorist John Lomax of the Library of Congress, discovered Leadbelly in a southern jail and brought him to New York, where he performed and recorded such classics as "Gray Goose," "Good Morning Blues," "Goodnight Irene," and "Rock Island Line."

Odetta [Odetta Holmes] (1930———): She performed spiritual and blues songs in the 1950s before leading the American folk movement of the early 1960s and influencing Bob Dylan and Joan Baez. Her standbys include "House of the Rising Sun" and "If I Had a Hammer." Odetta has sung at Carnegie Hall and has toured throughout the world, including the Soviet Union in 1974; she has also acted on stage and in films.

Seeger, Pete (1919———): A Harvard dropout who was influenced by Woody Guthrie and Leadbelly, Seeger forged the American folk-music revival, equipped with a banjo. He formed his group, the Weavers, in 1948, but his support of radical humanist causes got the group blacklisted. Seeger persevered and wrote such songs as "If I Had a Hammer" (1956), "Guantanamera" (1963) and "Where Have All the Flowers Gone?" (1960). He remains involved in ecological projects.

Jazz, Blues and Ragtime

Armstrong, Louis (c. 1898–1971): In the early 1930s, this enormously influential American jazz trumpeter made a series of famous recordings in which his improvisations revolutionized jazz. He toured the world in the 1930s and then led his own big band from 1935 to 1947; in 1947 he organized the first of his All-Stars jazz groups. Armstrong became a hugely successful entertainer, appeared in some sixty films and, with his distinctive, gravely voice, recorded many popular songs.

Basie, Count [William Basie] (1904–84): Basie was an American bandleader and pianist whose name was synonymous with the big-band style of swing music. From 1935 to 1950 he toured with the Count Basie Orchestra and became internationally famous with the song "One O'Clock Jump." Other popular Basie orchestra tunes included "Jumpin' at the Woodside" (1938), "Taxi War Dance" (1939) and "Oh, Lady Be Good" (1939).

Bechet, Sidney (1897–1959): This New Orleans-born clarinetist and soprano saxophonist was known primarily for classic jazz recordings. In 1919 he toured Europe with the Southern Syncopated Orchestra, playing blues solos; he also played with the Duke Ellington Orchestra. In 1923 Bechet opened his own swing jazz club in New York City. He returned to Europe in 1951 to live permanently in France.

Blake, Eubie [James Hubert Blake] (1883–1983): Blake was an American jazz pianist and composer of more than three hundred songs. After succeeding with the piano rag "Charleston Rag" (1899), he became partners with songwriter and singer Noble Sissle. Together they produced the Broadway smash *Shuffle Along* (1915) and created several more Broadway shows, including *Blackbirds of 1930*. In 1978 the show *Eubie,* showcasing his work, opened on Broadway. In 1981 he received the Presidential Medal of Freedom.

Coleman, Ornette (1930–   ): This American saxophonist and composer's experimental improvisations and compositions prefigured avant-garde jazz. A self-taught music theorist, he showcased his mastery of ensembles in *Free Jazz* (1960), a record that included a thirty-seven-minute improvization by his band. This work and others influenced the course of jazz throughout the 1960s. He continues to perform and record, releasing the album *Virgin Beauty* (1988) and the original soundtrack recording for the film *Naked Lunch* (1992). Coleman appears regularly with his band, Prime Time, and has played at Carnegie Hall, at the 1991 JVC Jazz Festival and as the opening act for The Grateful Dead at the Oakland Coliseum in 1993.

Coltrane, John (1926–67): One of the most influential American saxophonists in history and a brilliant improviser, Coltrane created such standards as "Giant Steps" (1959), "Naima" (1959), "Equinox" (1960) and "Impressions" (1961). From 1955 to 1957 he was a sideman in Miles Davis's quintet. In the next decade, his experimental improvising took jazz to a higher level, as illustrated in the albums *Coltrane's Sound* (1960), *Crescent* (1964) and *A Love Supreme* (1964).

Condon, Eddie (1905–73): An American banjo player and guitarist, Condon worked with such giants as Louis Armstrong, Fats Waller and Red Nichols. He recorded with The Rhythmakers (1938) and then promoted jazz concerts at the Town Hall concert hall in New York City (1942–46) and hosted a jazz program on television. In 1945 he opened his eponymous nightclub in New York City.

Corea, Chick (1941–   ): An American jazz pianist, Corea worked in Latin bands before joining Miles Davis's ensemble in 1968. He formed the groups The Circle (1970) and Return to Forever (1971–73), incorporating Latin rhythms into jazz with such popular tunes as "Windows," "Spain" and "Crystal Silence." In 1985 he established The Elektric Band, which performed and recorded.

Davis, Miles (1926–92): Davis was an American jazz trumpeter whose eminence among jazz musicians drew other great performers to his bands. He first led bands in 1948 and then played and recorded with Charlie Parker, Coleman Hawkins, Sonny Rollins and Art Blakey. A 1955 appearance at the Newport Jazz Festival brought wide recognition. His recordings include the albums *Miles Ahead* (1957), *Four and More* (1964), *On the Corner* (1972) and *Decoy* (1984).

Dorsey, Tommy (1905–56): This American trombonist and band leader was famous for his popular bands and smooth style of playing. His brother Jimmy Dorsey (1904–57) was a saxophonist and clarinet player. Together they led the popular Dorsey Brothers Orchestra in the early 1930s. Tommy's recording of "The Tea for Two Cha Cha" reached the pop charts in 1958.

Ellington, Duke [Edward Kennedy Ellington] (1899–1974): This American's Kentucky Club Orchestra began recording his early compositions, including "East St. Louis Toodle-oo" and "Black and Tan Fantasy," between 1923 and 1927. A five-year engagement at Harlem's legendary Cotton Club (1927–32) assured Ellington's national reputation and made famous his so-called "jungle style," as heard in "Rockin' in Rhythm" (1930), "It Don't Mean a Thing" (1932) and "Mood Indigo" (1930). In the 1930s Ellington began to compose such extended works as "Creole Rhapsody" (1931) and "Reminiscing in Tempo" (1935); the monumental *Black, Brown and Beige* appeared in 1943. By the late 1940s Ellington was composing film scores, music for theater productions and even liturgical music. Ellington continued composing, recording and performing until his death. All told, his legacy encompasses some two thousand jazz compositions.

Ferguson, Maynard (1928———): A Canadian trumpeter and band leader, Ferguson commands the trumpet's difficult top register with finesse. He leads thirteen-piece bands of outstanding quality throughout the United States and Europe, playing such pop tunes as "Gonna Fly Now" (1978), the theme of the motion picture *Rocky*.

Fitzgerald, Ella (1918———): A year after winning an amateur contest at Harlem's Apollo Theatre in 1934, this American signed on with Chick Webb's band, with whom she recorded the now-famous "A-Tisket, A-Tasket" (1938) and "Undecided" (1939). She later pursued a solo career to worldwide acclaim and recorded with the likes of Duke Ellington and Count Basie. Best known for her improvisational scat (nonsense-syllable) singing, Fitzgerald has had a wide influence on other jazz and popular singers.

Gillespie, Dizzy [John Birks] (1917–93): Trumpeter, composer and bandleader, Gillespie was one of the principal developers of bop in the early 1940s. He started out playing trumpet in the famous 1930s bands of Cab Calloway and Duke Ellington. In the 1950s he led big bands as well as smaller combos, playing a more classic jazz style in such trademark pieces as "A Night in Tunisia" (1946) and "Birks Works" (1951).

Goodman, Benny (1909–86): Goodman was the most famous clarinetist of the swing era. Performing professionally by the age of twelve, he went to New York in 1928 and played in various bands. In 1934 he formed his own band, which appeared on the popular radio program "Let's Dance." A versatile clarinetist, Goodman was also one of the first famous bandleaders to hire black jazz musicians. He is best known as a virtuoso jazz performer in the era of swing—hence his nickname "The King of Swing."

Henderson, Fletcher (1897–1952): Bandleader and pianist, Henderson created a call-and-response-style interplay between the brass and reed sections of his bands. His widely imitated band played at the Roseland Ballroom for ten years, starting in 1924. Notable recordings include "Copenhagen" (1924), "Sugar Foot Stomp" (1925) and "Shanghai Shuffle" (1924). In 1938 he became a full-time arranger for Benny Goodman's band.

Herman, Woody (1913–87): Herman was a bandleader and singer who played clarinet as well as alto and tenor saxophone. His expertise on instruments and his high standards produced bands of international renown, including Herman's Herd (mid-1940s), Second Herd (founded in 1947) and Swinging Herd (founded in 1962). Herman's recordings include "Lemon Drop" (1948), "Lady McGowan's Dream" (1946) and "Summer Sequence" (1946).

Holiday, Billie (1915–59): Widely regarded as one of the greatest female jazz vocalists ever, Holiday recorded regularly from 1935 to 1942. Her recordings are hallmarks in the annals of American jazz music. Her hits include "Strange Fruit" (an antilynching song, 1937), "Fine and Mellow" (1937), "Gloomy Sunday" (1941) and "Lover Man" (1944). Possessed of a light, rhythmic and sad voice, Holiday became an extremely popular performer, but drug abuse led to the deterioration of her health and her untimely death.

Jolson, Al [Asa Yoelson] (1886–1953): A popular Russian-born American singer and actor, Jolson performed in vaudeville, burlesque and minstrel shows and first appeared as his famous blackface character Gus in the 1912 silent film *Whirl of Society*. His performance in blackface of "My Mammy" in the 1927 film *The Jazz Singer* is an American classic. Other

famous songs include "California, Here I Come" (1921), "Swanee" (1919), "Toot, Toot, Tootsie!" (1921) and "Sonny Boy" (1928).

Jones, Quincy (1933–——): An American jazz musician, composer, arranger and conductor, Jones started as a piano player with Lionel Hampton in the 1950s and has since written music for fifty-two motion pictures. As a vice president at Mercury Records, he produced and arranged for recording artists. He has also recorded his own music, winning the Grammy Award for best album, *Back on the Block*, in 1991.

Joplin, Scott (1868–1917): This "King of Ragtime Writers" published his first piano rags, "Original Rags" and "Maple Leaf Rag," in 1899. The latter came to be the most famous piano rag ever and garnered Joplin a fair amount of financial success. Ever striving to elevate the genre, he wrote a rag ballet and two rag operas (*Treemonisha* and *A Guest of Honor*), but his artistic genius truly resides in his short piano rags, of which he wrote approximately fifty.

King, B. B. [Riley B. King] (1925–——): American blues guitarist and singer King is regarded as one of the most innovative blues artists of his era. His first hit was "Three O'Clock Blues" (1950). Within a decade he was widely recognized outside the blues world, touring Europe with his band beginning in 1968. He toured with the Rolling Stones in 1969, recording the popular songs "Just a Little Love" and "I Want You So Bad."

Krupa, Gene (1909–73): This American drummer and bandleader was the first major drum soloist of jazz. In 1934 he joined Benny Goodman's Orchestra, with which he played his famous solo on the recording "Sing, Sing, Sing" (1937). In 1938 he formed Gene Krupa and His Orchestra, one of the most successful bands of the 1940s. Krupa's artistry set the standard for jazz drumming.

Marsalis, Wynton (1961———): This New Orleans-born jazz trumpeter is adept at both jazz and classical music. He was a trumpet soloist with the New Orleans Philharmonic Orchestra (1975) and a student at the Juilliard School of Music from 1979 to 1981. In 1980 and 1981 he played with Art Blakey's Jazz Messengers before going solo. He was the first musician to win Grammy awards for both jazz and classical recordings (1984).

Miller, Glenn (1904–44): This popular American trombonist and bandleader is remembered for leading the most famous dance band of the swing era. After playing in other bands, he successfully established his own in 1939. Some of its hits were "Moonlight Serenade" (1939), "In the Mood" (1939), "Chattanooga Choo Choo" (1941) and "A String of Pearls" (1941). In 1942 Miller disbanded the group to go into military service and lost his life in an airplane crash two years later.

Monk, Thelonious (1917–82): This American composer and pianist helped pioneer bop music. Acclaimed and controversial, he often dispensed with conventional harmonies and styles of playing. His celebrated compositions include "Round Midnight" (1954), "Ruby, My Dear" (1947), "Blue Monk" (1954), "Off Minor" (1947) and "Epistrophy" (1941). In 1960 he was elected to the *Downbeat Magazine* Hall of Fame and in 1968 became one of a handful of jazz musicians ever to appear on the cover of *Time*.

Morton, Jelly Roll [Ferdinand Morton] (1885–1941): Louisiana-born composer and pianist Morton brought New Orleans–style jazz to its height. His creations represent the first important compositions of jazz. With the band Red Hot Peppers, he made classic jazz recordings in 1926 and 1927, including "Grandma's Spells," "Black Bottom Stomp" and "The Pearls." In the 1930s he managed and played in a jazz club in Washington, D.C.

Parker, Charlie (1920–55): An American jazz composer and alto saxaphonist, Parker forever changed jazz by introducing complex harmonies and innovative rhythms. His compositions include "Now's the Time" (1945), "Yardbird Suite" (1946) and "Relaxing at Camarillo" (1947). After playing bop with Earle Hine, Billy Eckstine and Dizzy Gillespie in the early 1940s, he formed his own quintet in 1947 and recorded some of jazz's most influential pieces.

Rich, Buddy [Bernard Rich] (1917–87): An American singer and drummer who played with lightning speed, Rich first led a band at age eleven and joined Joe Marsala's band in 1937. He played with Tommy Dorsey's Orchestra (1939–45) and in his own big band (1966–74). In the mid-1970s he opened a club, Buddy's Place, in New York City.

Rollins, Sonny [Theodore Rollins] (1930———): He is an American tenor saxophonist in the bop tradition and a genius at thematic improvisations, in which a soloist develops *leitmotifs* from the main theme. Among his recordings are the landmark "Valse Hot" (1956), "St. Thomas" (1956), "Blue 7" (1956) and the album *Way Out West* (1957). He wrote the score for the motion picture *Alfie* (1965) and continues to tour worldwide.

Shaw, Artie (1910———): An American clarinetist, bandleader and composer, Shaw was known for his excellent musical technique. He toured with bands for a decade before his first successful group made a hit rendition of "Begin the Beguine" (1937). Shaw formed the group Grammercy Five in 1940, gaining popularity with the songs "Fresni" (1940) and his own "Summit Ridge Drive" (1954).

Smith, Bessie (1894–1937): An American singer and the most successful black musician of her time, Smith was dubbed "Empress of the Blues." After starting out with Ma Rainey's Rabbit Foot Minstrels (1912), she made her first recording, "Down-hearted Blues" (1923), and gained immediate popularity. Her 150 other recordings on the Columbia label include "The St. Louis Blues" (1925), "Cake Walkin' Babies" (1925), "Baby Doll" (1926) and "Alexander's Ragtime Band" (1927).

Vaughn, Sarah (1924–90): An American contralto with a wide range, she performed with Billy Eckstine's orchestra (1944–45) and John Kirby's orchestra (1945–46) before going solo in 1946. Her classic recordings include the songs "Body and Soul" (1946), "It's Magic" (1947) and "Lullabye of Birdland" (1954), as well as the albums *After Hours* (1961) and *How Long Has This Been Going On* (1978). Vaughn won Grammy awards in 1983 and 1988.

Waller, Fats [Thomas Wright] (1904–43): This American pianist, singer and composer advanced the art of jazz piano. He made his recording debut with "Musical Shoals Blues" and "Birmingham Blues" in 1922 and published the compositions "Wild Cat Blues" and "Squeeze Me" the next year, establishing himself in jazz. Waller's most popular works were the songs "Ain't Misbehavin' " (1928) and "Honeysuckle Rose" (1929).

Waters, Muddy [McKinley Morganfield] (1915–83): This African-American blues legend was born in Rolling Fork, Mississippi, and in 1941 was recorded by archivist Alan Lomax for the Library of Congress. After moving to Chicago in 1943, he perfected his powerful bottleneck electric guitar playing and emotional vocal delivery. Waters recorded "I Can't Be Satisfied" (1948), "Rollin' Stone" (1950), "Honey Bee" (1951) and "I Just Wanna Make Love to You" (1954), as well as other blues classics. His overseas tours in the 1950s and 1960s brought Chicago-style blues international respect. He and his band continued to perform and record until his death; notable albums from his later period include *Hard Again* (1977) and *I'm Ready* (1978).

Young, Lester [Willis Young] (1909–59): A New Orleans–born tenor saxophonist, he had instinctive phrasing and a gift for melody. His first acclaimed recordings were solos on the 1936 records "Lady Be Good" and "Shoe Shine Boy." In 1939 he recorded the classic album *Lester Leaps In,* and in 1945 his original composition, "These Foolish Things," was hailed as a masterpiece. He played with Billie Holiday and, in later life, at the Newport Jazz Festival and European venues.

Rock, Pop and Reggae

♀ **[Prince Rogers Nelson]** (1958–——): Known for much of his career as Prince, this Minneapolis native sings provocative lyrics over a combination of rock, soul and funk. A self-taught composer and performer, he plays dozens of instruments with equal skill. In 1978 he recorded his debut LP, *Prince—For You*, on which he sang and played all 27 instrumental parts. He scored his first hit single, "I Wanna Be Your Lover," in 1979 and became known for his wild stage presence and scandalous attire. His platinum 1982 album, *1999*, contained such hits as "Little Red Corvette" and "Delirious" and was followed in 1984 by *Purple Rain*, the soundtrack for the hit movie of the same name, in which he starred. One of the biggest-selling albums in history, it contained classics such as "I Would Die 4 U," "Let's Go Crazy" and "When Doves Cry." Subsequent albums, recorded with his bands The Revolution and The New Power Generation, include *Sign o' the Times* (1987), *Lovesexy* (1988), *Graffiti Bridge* (1990) and ♀ (1993), from which he took his new name. Major singles include "Raspberry Beret" (1985), "Kiss" (1986), "U

Got the Look" (with Sheena Easton, 1987), "Thieves in the Temple" (1990) and "Cream" (1991). Under various names, he has also written for and produced other artists.

Ade, King Sunny [Sunday Adeniyi] (1946——): Born in Nigeria, Ade is largely responsible for introducing the musical style *juju* to the mainstream market. He released many albums on his own label and performed socially conscious songs with his twenty-three-piece band, the African Beats, which is extremely popular in Nigeria. The Beats gave a breakthrough concert in London in 1983; since then, their albums, such as *Synchro System* (1983) and *Aura* (1984), have had wide mainstream appeal.

Beatles, The (1962–70): George Harrison, John Lennon, Paul McCartney and Ringo Starr formed the Beatles in their hometown of Liverpool, England. They released their first single, "Love Me Do," in 1962; their first two albums, *Please Please Me* and *With the Beatles,* reached number one in England in 1963. By 1966 they had released five more albums, from which came eight number-one singles in the United States. The ground-breaking *Sgt. Pepper's Lonely Hearts Club Band* (1967) became a classic almost instantly. Their final three albums—*The White Album* (1968), *Abbey Road* (1969) and *Let It Be* (recorded before *Abbey Road,* but not released until 1970)—confirmed the Beatles' reputation as innovative popular musicians. The group officially dissolved in 1970, and all four pursued solo careers. In 1980 Lennon was shot and killed by a deranged fan in New York City.

Berry, Chuck (1926——): This American's blend of blues, R&B and rock 'n' roll guitar playing has had immeasurable influence on the world's rock musicians. His first single, "Maybelline," sold a million copies in 1955 and was followed by "Roll over Beethoven" (1956), "Rock and Roll Music" (1957), "Johnny B. Goode" (1958) and "Sweet Little Sixteen"

(1958). An enthusiastic performer, Berry perfected a legendary duck walk.

Bowie, David (1947——): The first hit single for this English rock composer and performer was *Space Oddity* (1969). In 1972, he released his first hit album, *The Rise and Fall of Ziggy Stardust and the Spiders from Mars,* playing the androgynous role of the sexy Ziggy. Other hit albums included *Diamond Dogs* (1974), *Young Americans* (1975), *Station to Station* (1976), *Heroes* (1978) and *Let's Dance* (1983).

Byrne, David (1952——): This Scottish rock composer is the principal musician in the American new-wave rock band The Talking Heads. Their first album was *Talking Heads '77* (1977). Other albums included *More Songs About Buildings and Food* (1978) and *Fear of Music* (1979). *Speaking in Tongues* (1983) hit the top-ten charts with its single "Burning Down the House." A popular film and album of the group in concert, *Stop Making Sense,* was released in 1984.

Clapton, Eric (1945——): Britain's premier blues guitarist in the 1960s, Clapton played with the groups The Yardbirds and Cream, introducing American blues to a large British audience. In 1970 he formed the group Derek and the Dominos and released his classic rock ballad "Layla" on the album *Layla and Other Assorted Love Songs,* a commercial failure in the United Kingdom, but a success in the United States. His hit albums include *461 Ocean Boulevard* (1974), *August* (1986), *Journeyman* (1989) and *Unplugged* (1992), which won a Grammy Award for best album.

Costello, Elvis [Declan Patrick McManus] (1954——): Born in England, Costello is the most enduring singer-songwriter to hail from the punk–new wave movement. His debut album, *My Aim is True* (1977), put Costello on the map. Backed by the Attractions, he made other albums, including *This Year's Model* (1978), *Armed Forces* (1979) and *King of*

America (1986). All display the tightly controlled, acid lyrics Costello is famous for, with the latter album demonstrating an R&B and Country influence.

Domino, Fats [Antoine Domino] (1928–——): He is a New Orleans native who pioneered a New Orleans–style rock 'n' roll. For a decade he minted hit singles for Imperial Records, starting with "The Fat Man" (1949), which sold one million copies. He followed with such famous singles as "I'm in Love Again" (1956), "Blueberry Hill" (1956), "Blue Monday" (1957) and "I'm Walking" (1957). By 1958 he had sold thirty million records.

Doors, The (1967–1973): Comprised of John Densmore, Robbie Krieger, Ray Manzarek and Jim Morrison, this Los Angeles–based psychedelic rock band released their eponymous first album in 1967. It featured the hits "The End," "Light My Fire" and "Break on Through." The Doors established an infamous reputation for eerie, distinctive music and erotic, apocalyptic lyrics. In 1968 "Hello, I Love You" reached number one, but Morrison's death of a heart attack in Paris three years later virtually finished the band.

Dylan, Bob [Robert Allan Zimmerman] (1941–——): This American's first three albums, *Bob Dylan* (1962), *The Freewheelin' Bob Dylan* (1963) and *The Times They Are a-Changin'* (1964), reflected the folk tradition of social protest. Songs such as "Blowin' in the Wind" established Dylan as a voice for his generation. It was with the albums *Bringing It All Back Home* and *Highway 61 Revisited* (both 1965) that he demonstrated a shift toward rock; the ambitious *Blonde on Blonde* was released in 1966. Other albums followed that were less well received, but by the mid-1970s Dylan again found his creative stride with *Blood on the Tracks* (1975), *Hard Rain* (1975) and *Street Legal* (1978). Throughout the 1980s Dylan toured with various groups and

formed The Traveling Wilburys, and recorded the commercially successful *Oh Mercy* (1989).

Graham, Bill (1931–91): This American theatrical producer and concert promoter was born in Berlin. He headed Wolfgang Records (1976–82) and produced nationwide tours for Bob Dylan; Crosby, Stills, Nash and Young; and George Harrison. He also owned the famous rock venues the Fillmore East and the Fillmore West. He produced the Rolling Stones World Tour in 1988. Graham also created benefit concerts, such as Save Our Cities (1976) and Live Aid (1988). In 1991 he served as executive producer for the motion picture *The Doors*.

Grateful Dead, The (1965–——): This San Francisco–based rock group is led by singer and guitarist Jerry Garcia. Their music epitomizes the spirit of the 1960s counterculture and has won a devoted following. In 1965 the Dead signed with Warner Brothers and released their first album, *The Grateful Dead,* but didn't make a hit album until *Workingman's Dead* (1970). Other hits followed: *Blues for Allah* (1976), *In the Dark* (1987) and *Built to Last* (1989).

Hammer [Stanley Kirk Burrell] (1962–——): After recording with small labels, this American rap singer signed with Capitol records in 1988 and released the album *Let's Get It Started,* topping the charts. Other albums included *Please Hammer Don't Hurt 'Em* (1989) and *To The Extreme,* made with fellow rapper Vanilla Ice (1990).

Hendrix, Jimi (1942–70): The first African-American musician to gain a huge following as a rock star, Hendrix formed the Jimi Hendrix Experience with Mitch Mitchell and Noel Redding. A wild stage performer, he was known to play guitar with his teeth and even to set the instrument on fire. His hits include "Hey Joe" (1966), "Purple Haze" (1967) and "All Along the Watchtower"

(1967). Since his drug-overdose death at twenty-seven, no one has been able to imitate his soaring, original guitar style.

Holly, Buddy [Charles Hardin] (1936–59): Holly was an American rock musician who sang a style he dubbed "Western bop," which spiced country-and-western songs with a rhythm-and-blues influence. He recorded the national hit "That'll Be the Day" (1957) with The Crickets and followed it with a second hit single that year, "Peggy Sue." In 1958 he recorded "Rave On" before dying in a plane crash while on tour.

Ice-T [Tracey Morrow] (c. 1950——): He is an American rap singer whose "gangsta rap" style portrays the violent streets of his native South-Central Los Angeles. His first single, "The Coldest Rap" (1982), came out on an independent label. He appeared in the movie *Breakin'* (1984) and released a debut album, *Rhyme Pays* (1987). It was followed by many hits, including *Power* (1988), *Iceberg/Freedom of Speech . . . Just Watch What You Say* (1989) and *O.G.-Original Gangster* (1991). For the film *New Jack City* (1991) he contributed the title song to the soundtrack and also played the part of an undercover policeman.

Iglesias, Julio (1943——): After winning a song festival in 1968 and subsequently landing a record contract, Iglesias became the most popular singer in his native Spain and in Latin America for two decades. In the 1980s he crossed over to English-speaking audiences with the albums *Julio* (1983) and *1100 Bel Air Place* (1984); he has sold more than one hundred million albums. His hits include "Begin the Beguine," "Quiereme Mucho" and "To All the Girls I've Loved Before," which he also recorded with Willie Nelson.

Jackson, Michael (1958——): At age six, this African-American was the lead singer for the Jackson Five, a teeny-bopper group made up of his brothers. He went solo when the group broke up, and his album *Off the Wall* (1979)

sold nearly ten million copies. Even greater success followed with *Thriller* (1982), which sold an astounding thirty million copies and whose accompanying music videos were wildly popular. The album *Bad* followed in 1987 to similar success. Jackson remains the best-known popular singer in the world.

John, Elton [Reginald Kenneth Dwight] (1947——): John is a prolific English rock singer, composer and piano player. His first popular success, "Your Song" (1970), was followed by a string of gold and platinum hits, including the albums *Elton John* (1970), *Honky Chateau* (1972) and *Goodbye Yellow Brick Road* (1973); the 1973 singles "Crocodile Rock," "Daniel" and "Benny and the Jets"; and the single "Don't Let the Sun Go Down on Me" (1974).

Joplin, Janis (1943–70): Born in Texas and influenced by blues singers, Joplin developed her own throaty, raw style that has been unmatched since her untimely death of a drug overdose. As lead singer of the San Francisco–based blues band Big Brother and the Holding Company, Joplin contributed memorable vocals on "Piece of My Heart" (1967) and "Ball and Chain" (1967). Her posthumous solo album, *Pearl* (1971), contained the classic "Me and Bobby McGee."

King, Carol [Carole Klein] (1942——): Born in Brooklyn, New York, King teamed up with Gerry Goffin in 1959 to write songs professionally. By 1967 they had written a string of hits for various performers, including "Up on the Roof," "Chains," "Will You Love Me Tomorrow?" and "Natural Woman." King's 1971 album, *Tapestry,* with its hits "You've Got a Friend," "So Far Away" and "It's Too Late," was enormously successful, selling more than fifteen million copies. She has also written film scores.

lang, k.d. [Katherine Dawn Lang] (1961——): A Canadian country-music singer and composer, lang recorded her early albums *A Truly Western Experience* (1984) and *Angel with a Lariat* (1986) with her group, The Reclines. Her 1988 tribute to singer Patsy Cline, *Shadowland,* brought widespread recognition that grew with *Absolute Torch and Twang* (1989), for which she received a Grammy Award for best female country singer. In 1992 she released the jazz-influenced *Ingenue.*

Led Zeppelin (1968–80): This English four-man heavy-metal band was best known for their rock anthem "Stairway to Heaven." They debuted at England's Surrey University in 1968, the year they backed the groups Vanilla Fudge and MC5 in a U.S. tour. They released their first album, *Led Zeppelin,* in 1969. Hit albums include *Led Zeppelin II* (1969), *Led Zeppelin III* (1970), *Houses of the Holy* (1973), *Physical Graffiti* (1975), *The Song Remains the Same* (1976) and *In Through the Out Door* (1979).

Little Richard [Richard Penniman] (1935–——): One of 12 children, he was thrown out of his parents' Macon, Georgia, house at age 13 and began performing blues in nightclubs. He recorded his first song at age 16 and in 1955 gained stardom with "Tutti Frutti," a crossover hit widely credited as one of the first examples of true rock and roll. In rapid succession Little Richard produced many other classics, such as "Long Tall Sally" (1956), "Rip It Up" (1956), "Send Me Some Lovin'" (1957) and "Good Golly, Miss Molly" (1958), and appeared in three films. At the height of his fame, he underwent a religious conversion and retired to sing gospel. Since 1964, his attempts to make a pop comeback have attracted more notice for his outrageous costumes and mannerisms than for his musical talent.

Madonna [Madonna Louise Ciccone] (1958–——): Born in Michigan, she moved to New York City and released her first album, *Madonna* (1983), which contained the runaway

dance hit "Holiday." With *Like a Virgin* (1984) and a national tour, Madonna's popularity exploded, especially among her teenage "wanna-be" fans. *True Blue* (1986) and *Like a Prayer* (1989) followed. Provocative music videos contributed to her success and image; in 1992 she released the explicit and controversial photography book *Sex,* along with the accompanying album *Erotica.* Madonna has also acted in numerous films.

Marley, Bob (1945–81): Marley, a Jamaican, formed his reggae group, the Wailers, with Peter Tosh and Bunny Livingston in Kingston in 1963. Their album *Burnin'* (1973) included "Get Up, Stand Up" and "I Shot the Sheriff"; *Natty Dread* (1974) contained "No Woman No Cry" and "No Jah Seh." *Rastaman Vibration* (1976), their most popular album, included the hit single "War." *Survival* (1979) and *Uprising* (1980) reflected Marley's political and Rastafarian views. Marley died of brain cancer.

Mitchell, Joni (1943–——): A Canadian singer and songwriter, she came to the forefront of the folk movement during the 1960s with the poetic song "Both Sides Now" (1968). Her sixteen albums trace the evolution of her music from folk to rock to jazz to a mingled pop style. Her albums include *Court and Spark* (1974), *The Hissing of Summer Lawns* (1975, a foray into avant-garde jazz), *Mingus* (1979, recorded with jazz legend Charles Mingus), *Dog Eat Dog* (1985), *Chalk Mark in the Rain Storm* (1988) and *Night Ride Home* (1991). In 1993 she was inducted into the Rock and Roll Hall of Fame.

Paul, Les (1915–——): The mechanical ability of this American harmonica, guitar and banjo player led to the modernization of recording studios and the development of an early model of electric guitar. A radio star in the 1930s, he formed the popular Les Paul Trio in 1936. In 1952 Gibson manufactured his electric guitar with great success. In 1988 Paul was inducted into the Rock 'n' Roll Hall of Fame.

Police, The. See *Sting,* below.

Presley, Elvis (1935–77): Influenced by rhythm-and-blues, this American rock 'n' roller made his earliest recordings at Memphis's Sun Studio in 1954. RCA put him under contract in 1956, and Presley quickly released "Blue Suede Shoes," "I Got a Woman" and "Tutti Frutti." "Heartbreak Hotel" (1956), his first number-one hit, reflected a shift toward a younger, white audience, as did "Hound Dog" (1956) and "Jailhouse Rock" (1957). Presley's controversial gyrating hips furthered his popularity, and his musical style changed again, to the romantic teen-idol sound already popular in America. "It's Now or Never" (1960), "Are You Lonesome Tonight?" (1960) and "Can't Help Falling in Love with You" (1961) reflect this shift. During the 1960s, his music was subsumed by his work in films, but he returned to the stage in 1969 and made yearly tours of the United States until 1975, after which he played only infrequently in Las Vegas. His death caused an incredible outcry of grief, and Graceland, his home in Memphis, remains a shrine for his many fans.

Reed, Lou (1942———): This American rock vocalist and guitarist is known as "the nihilist of rock." He first gained a reputation for avant-garde music that incorporated screeching, screaming and white noise. In 1965 he helped found The Velvet Underground, leaving it in 1970. His debut album, *Lou Reed* (1972), was followed by his only gold record, *Transformer* (1973). Other albums include *Berlin* (1973), *Sally Can't Dance* (1974), *Metal Music Machine* (1975), *Walk on the Wild Side* (1977) and *New York* (1979).

Rolling Stones, The (1964———): Comprised of Englishmen Mick Jagger, Brian Jones, Keith Richards, Mick Taylor, Charlie Watts, Ron Wood and Bill Wyman, they created early albums (*The Rolling Stones,* 1964; *Rolling Stones No. 2,* 1965; and *Out of Our Heads,* 1965) that demonstrated a rebellious rock 'n' roll image. 1965's "(I Can't Get No) Satisfaction" and "Get Off My Cloud" and 1966's "Paint It Black" and "Ruby Tuesday" were all hits. They released the critically acclaimed album *Beggar's Banquet* in 1968; *Let It Bleed* (1969) and *Sticky Fingers* (1971) followed. *It's Only Rock 'n' Roll* (1974), *Black and Blue* (1976) and *Some Girls* (1978) had mass appeal in the 1970s, but albums like *Tattoo You* (1981) showed a more musically mellow band. The Stones continue to record well into the 1990s.

Simon, Paul (1942———): Along with Art Garfunkel (1942———), with whom he began collaborating in high school, this American had his first major hit with "The Sounds of Silence" in 1966. The duo's 1968 soundtrack for the film *The Graduate* was highly influential, while the 1970 album *Bridge Over Troubled Water* sold millions. After their breakup, Simon recorded the critically acclaimed *Still Crazy After All These Years* (1975) and broke new ground with 1986's *Graceland,* which was heavily influenced by South African music and became an international bestseller. Simon followed this album with the Brazilian-influenced *Rhythm of the Saints* in 1990.

Simon and Garfunkel. See *Simon, Paul,* above.

Smith, Patti (1946———): This American poet, singer and musician was dubbed the "poetess of punk" for her artistic contributions to punk rock. Her debut album, *Horses* (1975), was followed by *Radio Ethiopia* (1976). Her biggest hit, *Easter* (1978), featured the popular single "Because the Night" and was followed by *Wave* (1979). Her band, The Patti Smith Group, accompanied her on recordings and in concert.

Spector, Phil (1940———): He is an American songwriter and producer who advanced pop music in the 1960s. His productions featured a trademark "wall of sound" that layered instrumentation behind the vocals. After writing the hit "To Know Him Is to Love Him" (1957), he launched his own label, Phillies, in 1962 and created more than twenty hit singles. He also produced popular groups such as The Crystals ("Da Doo Ron Ron") and the Ronettes ("Be My Baby"). Spector helped produce albums for The Beatles, The Righteous Brothers, The Ramones, and Ike and Tina Turner.

Springsteen, Bruce (1949———): He defined American Rock in the 1970s and 1980s with his E-Street band. They made their debut in 1973 with *Greetings from Asbury Park, NJ*. Other albums, including *Born to Run* (1975) and *The River* (1980), demonstrated Springsteen's understanding of American romanticism and rebellion. *Born in the U.S.A.* (1984) represented a return to rock 'n' roll after the acoustic sound of *Nebraska* (1982). Wildly popular and critically acclaimed, he disbanded the E-Street band in 1990 and continued to record and tour on his own.

Stewart, Rod (1945———): Formerly a member of the Jeff Beck Group and the New Faces, this Englishman launched a solo career with the 1971 R&B–influenced album *Every Picture Tells a Story*. It included the classics "Maggie May" and "Reason to Believe." No other album was as successful, but he continued a string of hit singles with "Tonight's the Night" (1976), "Do Ya Think I'm Sexy?" (1978) and "Have I Told You Lately That I Love You?" (1993).

Sting [Gordon Matthew Sumner] (1951———): Born in England, Sting formed The Police with Stewart Copeland and Andy Summers. The group released *Outlandos d'Amour* (1978), *Regatta de Blanc* (1979) and *Zenyatta Mondatta* (1981), for which Sting wrote all the hit songs. *Ghost in the Machine* (1981) and *Synchronicity* (1984) followed. After the group's breakup came Sting's first solo album, *Dream of the Blue Turtle* (1985), reflecting a heavy jazz influence. Other solo albums include *Nothing Like the Sun* (1987) and *Ten Summoner's Tales* (1993).

Talking Heads, The. See *Byrne, David,* page 181.

Taylor, James (1948———): A poetic and sweet-voiced American singer-songwriter, Taylor recorded the now-classic early album *Sweet Baby James* in 1970, which included the title hit and "Fire and Rain." Taylor continues to record steadily; other hits include "You've Got a Friend" (1972), "How Sweet It Is" (1975), "Handy Man" (1977), "Up on the Roof" (1979) and "That's Why I'm Here" (1985). His 1974 marriage to singer Carly Simon ended in divorce in 1982.

Tosh, Peter [Winston Hubert McIntosh] (1944–87): Born in Kingston, Jamaica, Tosh formed the reggae group The Wailers with Bob Marley in 1963, but left it in 1974 to pursue solo projects. A Rastafarian, he formed his own record label and released his first solo album, *Legalize It* (1976), which advocated the legalization of marijuana. A string of lackluster albums followed. Tosh was murdered in Jamaica in 1987.

U2 (1977———): This Irish rock group is composed of Bono (Paul Hewson), Adam Clayton, The Edge (David Evans) and Larry Mullen. The band shows continuing musical creativity and unchecked popularity. Early albums such as *War* (1983) and *The Unforgettable Fire* (1984) expressed concern with social and political situations, while *The Joshua Tree* (1987) and *Zoo Station* (1991) are more introverted. Their musical integrity and big-arena sound have gained U2 a huge worldwide audience.

Velvet Underground, The. See *Reed, Lou,* above.

Who, The, (1965–83): This English rock band was made up of Roger Daltrey, John Entwistle, Keith Moon and Pete Townshend.

The group began as mod rockers and released *My Generation* in 1965. Townshend penned the first rock opera, *Tommy* (1968), to critical success, and The Who became a 1970s supergroup with the releases of *Meaty, Beaty, Big and Bouncy* (1971), *Quadrophenia* (1974) and *Who Are You* (1978). Kenny Jones replaced Moon after his death of a drug overdose in 1978.

Young, Neil (1945———): A native of Canada, Young moved to Los Angeles in 1966 to play guitar with the group Buffalo Springfield. His most successful solo album, *Harvest* (1972), included the hits "Heart of Gold," "Old Man" and "Needle and the Damage Done." A member of Crosby, Stills and Nash from 1969 to 1970, Young brought his distinctive, melancholy style to "Helpless" and "Ohio."

Salsa

Blades, Reuben (1948———): This Panamanian-born American singer, songwriter and composer of salsa music was affiliated with Famia Records in New York City from 1974 to 1983. In 1984 he signed with Electra Records, producing such albums as *Nothing But the Truth* (1988). He was nominated for Grammy awards in 1983 and 1984 and has appeared in several motion pictures, including *The Milagro Beanfield War* (1988) and *The Super* (1991).

Colón, Willie (1950———): An American salsa musician and singer from the South Bronx, Colón incorporates rhythms from rock and African music into the traditional salsa beat. His album *Cosa Nuestra* (1972) was the first of several gold albums and included the hit single "Che Che Colé." In 1990 he released the album *American Color,* which contained the AIDS-related song "El Varon," a popular success in Latin America.

Cruz, Celia (c. 1924———): This Cuban-born singer, dubbed "The Queen of Salsa," has performed and recorded since the 1940s; she made more than fifty albums by 1993. After emigrating to the United States in 1960, she signed with Seeco Records in 1965, cutting more than twenty albums on that label. In 1982 her fans filled Madison Square Garden for a special tribute, and in 1987 she received the New York Music Award for Best Latin Artist.

Puente, Tito (1923———): Puente, an American orchestra leader and composer, is known for his lively arrangements of salsa and other Latin music. With the Tito Puente Orchestra he dominated Latin music in the 1950s. His ninety-five albums include *Dance Mania* (1958) and *Dance Mania II* (1963), both bestsellers. He received Grammy awards in 1975, 1983, 1985 and 1990.

Soul, Motown and Gospel

Brown, James (1928———): Known as "the Godfather of Soul," Brown combines soul singing with dance rhythms to form his own brand of funk. His early hits include "Night Train" (1962) and "Prisoner of Love" (1963); funk hits include "Sex Machine" (1970) and "Hot Pants" (1971). He reflects on the African-American experience in "Say It Loud—I'm Black and I'm Proud" (1968) and "Living in America" (1986). His live performances are marked by unflagging energy and screaming vocals.

Charles, Ray (1930———): This American rhythm-and-blues singer and instrumentalist is widely regarded as the father of modern soul music. In 1953 he joined Atlantic Records. His first hit song, "It Should Have Been Me" (1954), was followed by other hit singles: "Swanee River Rock" (1957), "What'd I Say" (1959), "Georgia on My Mind" (1960), "Hit the Road Jack" (1961) and "I Can't Stop Loving You" (1962).

Franklin, Aretha (1942———): The daughter of a famous Detroit preacher, Franklin sang gospel as a child and landed a recording contract by the age of eighteen. Her first huge hit, in 1967, was "I Never Loved a Man," followed by "Respect" (1967), "Chain of Fools" (1968), "Think" (1968) and "Natural Woman" (1968). Possessed of a tremendously powerful voice, Franklin plays to consistently sold-out audiences. Her popular 1985 album, *Who's Zoomin' Who,* shows that she remains the "Queen of Soul."

Gaye, Marvin (1939–84): The works of this African-American are the epitome of "Motown Sound." His enduring hits include "I Heard It Through the Grapevine" (1967), "Ain't No Mountain High Enough" (with Tammi Terrell, 1967) and "Ain't Nothing Like the Real Thing" (with Tammi Terrell, 1968). After Terrell's death, Gaye recorded the solo hits "What's Going On" (1970), "Mercy Mercy Me (The Ecology)" (1970) and "Sexual Healing" (1982). He was shot and killed by his father during an argument.

Gordy, Berry (1929———): This American is the founder of Motown Industries, which brought a distinctive style of rhythm-and-blues to American pop music. Motown Records forged its first release, "Bad Girl" by Smokey Robinson and the Miracles, in 1959. Motown's stable came to include Diana Ross and The Supremes, Gladys Knight and the Pips, The Jackson Five, Martha Reeves and The Vandellas, The Marvelettes, Marvin Gaye, and The Temptations.

Jackson, Mahalia (1911–72): The stirring renditions of this American singer and interpreter of gospel songs helped popularize gospel in the United States. She left her native New Orleans at age sixteen to perform in churches as part of a quartet, first recording gospel songs in 1934. During the next decades she proved a popular recording artist, especially after a successful concert at Carnegie Hall in 1951.

Robinson, Smokey [William Robinson] (1940———): The first recording artist at Motown Records, this American singer had his first pop hit, "Shop Around," with The Miracles in 1960. This led to other successes: "You've Really Got a Hold On Me" (1963), "Tracks of My Tears" (1965), "I Second That Emotion" (1967) and "The Tears of a Clown" (1970). He also wrote and produced hit songs for fellow Motown singers.

Ross, Diana (1944———): Detroit-born Ross was lead singer of the pop group The Supremes from 1958 to 1970. The group joined Motown Records in 1961 and rose to the top of the pop charts with "Baby Love" (1964), "Where Did Our Love Go" (1964) and "Stop! In the Name of Love" (1965). Ross turned solo in 1970 with the hit single "Reach Out and Touch." In 1972 she debuted in motion pictures with *Lady Sings the Blues,* a biography of Billie Holiday, in which she played the lead role.

Wonder, Stevie (1950———): This American singer and musician successfully blended rock elements into rhythm-and-blues. He made his first record with Motown at age twelve, hitting the charts four years later with "Uptight" (1966). Other hit songs included "For Once in My Life" (1968), "My Cherie Amour" (1969), "Signed, Sealed, Delivered I'm Yours" (1970), "Superstition" (1973), "You Are the Sunshine of My Life" (1973) and "Part Time Lover" (1985).

Tin Pan Alley and Other American Favorites

Berlin, Irving (1888–1989): This Russian-born composer became the voice of America when he published the song "Alexander's Ragtime Band" (1911). Another early work, "When I Lost You" (1911), sold a million copies of sheet music. Berlin wrote "God Bless America" in 1918; it later became the country's unofficial anthem. By 1929 he was writing songs for now-classic Hollywood musicals, including *Puttin' on the Ritz* (1929), *Top Hat* (1935), *Easter Parade* (1948) and *Annie Get Your Gun* (1950). His song "White Christmas" (1942) is one of the best-selling ever.

Cohan, George M. (1878–1942): Cohan introduced distinctly American musical comedy to mainstream theater. He wrote his first musical comedy, *Little Johnny Jones,* in 1904; it contained such popular songs as "Yankee Doodle Boy" and "Give My Regards to Broadway." He followed up that success with *George Washington Jr.* and *Forty-five Minutes from Broadway,* both in 1906. Although a talented actor, Cohan is best remembered for composing spirited songs, of which "Over There" (1917) is probably the most famous.

Cole, Nat King (1919–65): This American singer and pianist was known for his relaxed and elegant delivery. In 1939 he formed The Nat King Cole Trio, which had a national hit, "Straighten Up and Fly Right," in 1943. In 1948 he launched a solo career with such trademark songs as "Mona Lisa" (1950), "Too Young" (1951), "Answer Me My Love" (1953) and "A Blossom Fell" (1954). Cole also appeared in several motion pictures, including *The Nat King Cole Musical Story* (1955).

Foster, Stephen Collins (1826–64): Foster was the first professional American songwriter. He published his first song, "Open Thy Lattice, Love," in 1844; "Away Down South" (1848) and "Oh! Susanna" (1848) followed to much success. Many of his popular sentimental songs are still sung today, including "Old Folks at Home" (1851), "My Old Kentucky Home, Good Night" (1853), "Camptown Races" (1854), "Jeannie with the Light Brown Hair" (1854) and "Beautiful Dreamer" (1864). His unhappy personal life led to alcoholism, and he died in poverty.

Garland, Judy [Frances Gumm] (1922–69): This American singer and film star was under contract at MGM Studios from 1935 to 1950. Her most notable motion pictures were musicals, such as *The Wizard of Oz* (1938), *Meet Me in St. Louis* (1944) and *A Star Is Born* (1954). After leaving MGM she took many concert tours, making a legendary appearance at Carnegie Hall in 1961, where she sang her standards "Over the Rainbow" and "You Made Me Love You."

Gershwin, George (1898–1937): A brilliant American composer, Gershwin had his first success at age twenty-one when he released the song "Swanee" (1919), which sold more than a million copies of sheet music. It was followed by the wildly successful *Rhapsody in Blue* (1924) and *An American in Paris* (1928). Gershwin scored Broadway shows, including *Strike Up the Band* (1927) and *Funny Face* (1927), and films, including *Shall We Dance?* (1937) and *A Damsel in Distress* (1937). His most ambitious undertaking was the opera *Porgy and Bess* (1935); his early death left his potential unrealized.

Hammerstein, Oscar, II (1895–1960): With Otto Harbach, this librettist cowrote the books for such musicals as *Rose-Marie* (1924) and Gershwin's *Song of the Flame* (1925). In 1927 he wrote the libretto for Jerome Kern's *Show Boat,* which is considered his masterpiece. He then joined composer Richard Rodgers, and together they created some of the best-loved

American musicals of the 20th century: *Okla-homa!* (1943), *Carousel* (1945), *South Pacific* (1949), *The King and I* (1951) and *The Sound of Music* (1959). Hammerstein later wrote screenplays and lyrics for Hollywood films. See also *Rodgers, Richard,* below.

Hart, Lorenz (1895–1943): This American lyri-cist started his famous collaboration with composer Richard Rodgers in 1919. They had their first success with *Garrick Gaieties* (1925) and followed that with a string of Broadway triumphs, including *A Connecticut Yankee* (1927), *On Your Toes* (1936), *Babes in Arms* (1937), *The Boys from Syracuse* (1938) and *Pal Joey* (1940).

Lerner, Alan Jay (1918–86): Lerner was an American lyricist and playwright. His collab-orations with composer Frederick Loewe (1904–88) resulted in such celebrated Broad-way shows as *Brigadoon* (1947), *Paint Your Wagon* (1951), *My Fair Lady* (1956) and *Cam-elot* (1960), as well as the score for the movie *Gigi* (1958). Lerner also worked with com-posers Kurt Weil, André Previn and Burton Lane. See also *Loewe, Frederick,* below.

Liberace [Wladziu Valentino Liberace] (1919–87): Pianist and composer. This popular American entertainer played Milwaukee nightclubs in the early 1940s, appearing as a soloist with the Chicago Symphony Orches-tra when it toured the city. In 1952 he debuted on television at KLAC in Los Angeles with his medley of semiclassics; in 1954 he filled Madison Square Garden. His film appear-ances include *Sincerely Yours* (1955) and *The Loved One* (1965).

Loesser, Frank (1910–69): This American com-poser and lyricist is best known for the Broadway shows *Guys and Dolls* (1950), *The Most Happy Fella* (1956) and *How to Succeed in Business Without Really Trying* (1961). He also wrote many popular songs, including "I Don't Want to Walk Without You" (1942), "Baby, It's Cold Outside" (1949) and the World War II ditty "Praise the Lord and Pass the Ammunition" (1942).

Loewe, Frederick: (1904–88) The work of this American composer of scores for musical the-ater is renowned for its gorgeous melodies. His most famous compositions for the stage, all written in collaboration with lyricist Alan Jay Lerner, include *Brigadoon* (1947), *Paint Your Wagon* (1951), *My Fair Lady* (1966), *Gigi* (1958) and *Camelot* (1960). See also *Lerner, Alan Jay,* above.

Minnelli, Liza (1946–——): The daughter of Judy Garland, this American singer and ac-tress has been successful in film, theater and on the concert stage. She won two Tony awards for performances in *Flora the Red Menace* (1965) and *The Act* (1977), as well as an Oscar for the film *Cabaret* (1972). Other mem-orable motion pictures include *The Sterile Cuckoo* (1969) and *Tell Me If You Love Me Junie Moon* (1970). In 1988 she toured interna-tionally with singers Sammy Davis, Jr., and Frank Sinatra.

Porter, Cole (1891–1964): Yale-educated, Porter was an extremely successful American com-poser of melodic and witty songs that retained a classic elegance. These included "I Get a Kick Out of You" (1934), "Miss Otis Regrets" (1934), "Anything Goes" (1934) and "I've Got You under My Skin" (1936). Porter also wrote musicals, the most famous of which is *Kiss Me Kate* (1948), and film scores, the most success-ful of which was *High Society* (1956).

Rodgers, Richard (1902–79): He was a composer of highly popular Broadway musicals, many with librettos by Oscar Hammerstein II. His major successes include *Oklahoma!* (1943), *Car-ousel* (1945), *South Pacific* (1949), *The King and I* (1951), *Flower Drum Song* (1958) and *The Sound of Music* (1959). He launched his career work-ing with American lyricist Lorenz Hart (1895–1943) on such classic musicals as *Pal Joey* (1940) and *Babes in Arms* (1937). See also *Ham-merstein, Oscar, II,* above.

Sinatra, Frank (1915——): An idol for bobby-soxers in the 1940s, with hits that included "Dream" (1945) and "Full Moon and Empty Arms" (1946), this American crooner was in a slump by 1947. An excellent acting performance in the 1953 film *From Here to Eternity* reestablished his career; his 1954 hit "Young at Heart" went to number one. Sinatra remained popular throughout the 1950s and 1960s with various hits, including "It Was a Very Good Year" (1964) and "Strangers in the Night" (1966). The 1980 album *Trilogy* spanned his career. Sinatra still performs to sold-out houses.

Sondheim, Stephen (1930——): He is a gifted American composer who enjoyed his first big success writing the lyrics to Leonard Bernstein's *West Side Story* (1957). He won a Tony award as composer and lyricist for the musical *A Funny Thing Happened on the Way to the Forum* (1962) and a Grammy for the song "Send in the Clowns" from the musical *A Little Night Music* (1976). He also scored the popular musical *Sunday in the Park with George* (1982), among others.

Sousa, John Philip (1854–1932): He was the American composer of such marches as "Semper Fidelis" (1888), "The Washington Post" (1889) and "The High School Cadets" (1890), which brought him fame. Sousa conducted the U.S. Marine Band from 1880 until 1892, whereupon he formed his own band. Sousa was world-renowned for his marches, which include "Manhattan Beach" (1893), "El Capitan" (1896) and the famous "Stars and Stripes Forever!" (1896). Band music such as Sousa's had a direct influence on the birth of jazz.

Streisand, Barbra (1942——): This Brooklyn-born singer and actress reached stardom in the Broadway hit *Funny Girl* (1964). For the film version of the play (1968) she won an Academy Award. Other popular motion pictures include *The Way We Were* (1973). With the films *Yentl* (1983) and *The Prince of Tides* (1990), she served as director, producer and star. Her more than twenty gold albums have yielded many Grammy awards.

A Brief History of Classical Music

Music is intended to be heard and re-heard. When a people deems a body of indigenous music worthy of repeated performance over hundreds of years, that music acquires a permanent place in the culture. Eastern and Western societies alike refer to such enduring music as classical. In Europe, classical music features distinctive instrumentation that includes violins and other stringed instruments, flutes and other woodwinds, trumpets and other brass instruments, pianos and a variety of percussion. Through European migrants who claimed North America as their own, the United States and Canada inherited Europe's musical legacy and now help to develop and carry on the classical tradition. The Western classical tradition has roots in antiquity.

The Origins of Western Music

Because the people of ancient Greece and Rome had no regularized system for writing music, modern scholars base their understanding of ancient music on speculation and a great deal of educated guesswork. Nonetheless, they have little doubt that modern European music incorporates elements present in the music of antiquity. As written records show, the Greeks believed that music influenced a person's moral character; indeed, the philosopher Plato (c. 427–347 B.C.) considered music an important part of a citizen's education. The Romans felt likewise and probably adopted music from Greek culture as Rome overshadowed Greece. In turn, Roman musical notions spread throughout Europe as the Roman Empire expanded.

During the Dark or early Middle Ages (A.D. 476–1000), European art and music functioned largely as an adjunct to religion. Christianity replaced the old European religions, thereby perpetuating various Jewish traditions on which it was based. Among those traditions were certain musical styles, as well as the practice of daily prayer accompanied by the singing of psalms. As Christianity grew, it also absorbed and recombined European musical influences. The Church of Rome came to dominate the spiritual life of Europe and, temporarily, its musical life. One of its popes, Gregory I (reigned 590–604), made an early contribution to Western music when he required that specific chants—single lines of vocal music sung with a Latin text and no instruments—accompany certain parts of the religious service. Known today as Gregorian chants, these plainchants were preserved by oral tradition and later in written manuscripts.

As caretakers of the chants, the monasteries also served as some of the earliest European educational institutions. During the Gothic period or later Middle Ages (c. 1100–1400), universities were founded and great cathedrals built to carry on the continent's cultural and religious heritage. In music, vocal polyphony emerged from chant, allowing two or more voices (and, later, instruments) to perform complementary lines of melody simultaneously.

Three of the earliest forms of polyphony that evolved from the church chant were organum, clausula (cadence or close) and the motet. Organum is basically a type of harmonized singing featuring two or more voices: a tenor plainchant and a duplum (a second voice), triplum (third voice) and quadruplum (fourth voice). Between the 9th and 13th centuries, several distinct styles of organun developed. As polyphonic music developed, these voices moved with greater independence, in parallel and contrary motion. Clausula is a section of medieval organum in which textless contrapuntal parts (two-, three- or four-part settings) are set in strict rhythm in relation to the plainchant on which the organum is based. It denotes the conclusion of a passage. The motet is a vocal piece that combines phrases from melodies with more rhythmically complex clausala. In time, more freely composed melodies evolved from this clausala.

Although the Church preserved some of its music, much secular music was lost to history before the development of written notation. It was not until troubadours and minstrels began to flourish around the 10th century that composers (who for the most part were unknown) began to write down secular music. One of these composers, a Frenchman named Guillaume de Machaut (1300–77) was particularly significant for his contribution to the polyphonic style called *ars nova* (the "new art"). Many historians have labeled him the first of the great Western composers.

The Renaissance period in music (c. 1400–1600) began with the Burgundian school, led by French composer Guillaume Dufay (c. 1400–74). He is credited with the invention of a new style, known as *fauxbourdon* ("false base") (c. 1430). The fauxbourdon style was a three-part setting in which the lowest melodic line or *cantus firmus* ("fixed song") was altered, producing a "false" or derivative melody. It allowed composers to achieve clearer harmonic textures. Dufay was also a major influence in the standardization of four-part harmony. Together with the Flemish school that appeared later in the century, the Burgundian school was called the Netherlands school; it established the vocal style for sacred music that prevailed throughout the Renaissance. Other notable musical developments of the 15th century included the growing popularity of lute and keyboard music, the introduction of the madrigal, and the evolution of the medieval motet into larger polyphonic forms of sacred vocal music.

With the approach of the High Renaissance about 1450, such innovations as the printing press signified the end of the static, church-dominated society of the Middle Ages. Around this time, the most notable composers of the Netherlands school, Josquin Despres (c. 1440–1521) and Orlando de Lasso (c. 1532–94), created richly expressive harmony. Their style contrasted with the classical temperance of the Venetian and Roman schools, both outgrowths of the Flemish school. Among the prominent masters of the Venetian school was Giovanni Gabrieli (c. 1553–1612); the Roman school's Palestrina (c. 1525–94) also deserves mention. In England, the madrigal reached new heights in the hands of such composers as John Dowland (1563–1626), Thomas Morley (1557–1602), Thomas Weelkes (c. 1575–1623), John Wilbye (1574–1638), Orlando Gibbons (1583–1625) and William Byrd (c. 1543–1623). The many other worthy composers of the Renaissance are too numerous to mention here.

Renaissance music was not originally intended for the concert stage; because its intimacy and subtle nuances can sometimes be lost in the large concert halls of today, it is generally performed in smaller settings. In particular, the nature of *a cappella* music, that is, vocal work done without instrumental accompaniment, is better served in more intimate surroundings. A relatively small percentage of Renaissance music was written down and preserved.

The Baroque Period

By 1600, polyphony had reached the peak of its development and musicians became interested in exploring new possibilities. The modern musical age began in the Baroque period (c. 1600–1750) with the introduction of homophony, the reliance on a single melody supported by harmonic accompaniment. The power and popularity of homophony would pave the way for the standard classical repertoire known today. The period also saw a most significant transition from the use of medieval church modes to the major/minor system of tonality. Other important innovations of the Baroque period included the introduction of "figured bass" (a shorthand system to notate chords) under melodies, the development of equal temperament (the tuning system still used today), and the creation of such musical forms as the fugue, toccata, prelude, recitative and aria.

As the Renaissance taste for moderation and balance declined, artists in the Baroque period developed a fondness for extravagance and ornateness. They also cultivated a religious intensity and pursued an interest in a form of religious musical drama called oratorio. Recognized musicians worked within the patronage system, which had operated for some time but reached its pinnacle during the Baroque and subsequent Classical period. Under this system, composers were employed at royal courts and by wealthy aristocrats, churches and city councils. Working on commission according to the dictates of their employers, they created music for specific occasions and for immediate use. The focus was not on the significance of their work for posterity.

Some musicologists prefer to divide the Baroque period into three stages—early, middle and mature. The early stage was one of experimentation, by which the transition from Renaissance to Baroque styles proceeded gradually. Significant at this stage was a group of gifted Venetian composers. In Venice, serious musical activity centered around the Cathedral of San Marco. Giovanni Gabrieli (c. 1553–1612), one of the extraordinary composers associated with this famous basilica, found its architecture perfectly suited to performances by vocal and instrumental groups who answered one another from all sides (antiphonal music). Gabrieli also influenced emerging Baroque homophony by emphasizing chordal texture over polyphony. The developments in Venice spread across Europe via musicians who came from far and wide to study there. Among Gabrieli's students was German composer Heinrich Schutz, a significant predecessor of Bach. A key figure in the musical shift from Renaissance to Baroque styles, Shutz combined German and Italian influences in his music. His genius is only just beginning to receive the attention it deserves.

During the middle Baroque period, the innovative composer Claudio Monteverde, a master of the old Renaissance style, absorbed the new trends and bridged the gap between the contradictory values of Renaissance and Baroque music. He was also a major influence on the future of opera, one of the dramatic musical forms that emerged in the last decades of the 17th century. Although the most famous musician of his time, Monteverde was virtually forgotten fifty years after his death and much of his music was lost. Audiences of the time moved on to new music and composers, but scholars have fortunately reacquainted the world with some of Monteverde's music in recent years.

In its mature stage, Baroque music reached the form currently associated with the period, culminating with the works of Johann Sebastian Bach and

George Frideric Handel. Bach, the most celebrated Baroque composer, hailed from a family descended from many generations of musicians. He produced an enormous *oeuvre,* including masses, motets, passions, oratorios and hundreds of instrumental works. Handel was born the same year as Bach, but the two musical heroes never met. Handel composed about forty operas in three decades, as well as oratorios with soaring arias, dramatic recitatives, extraordinary fugues and double choruses that embody the splendor of the Baroque period.

Along with cantatas and passions, opera and oratorio belong in the category of dramatic musical work developed by Baroque composers. Opera, which presents theatrical drama with sung dialogue, heralded the triumph of homophonic style over polyphony. Invented in Italy, opera quickly caught on elsewhere. Jean-Baptiste Lully (1632–74) was the first major French composer of opera. His work influenced French musical style for decades; elsewhere, Bach and Handel would use Lully's French overture form extensively. The French style was also used in the keyboard works of Bach and Handel and is more widely known in that context (e.g. the *French Suites* of J. S. Bach). (See also "Introduction to Opera," pages 214–224.)

Italian composer Giacomo Carissimi (1605–74) played an important role in the early development of the oratorio and cantata. Oratorio is essentially unstaged opera on sacred themes, large-scale dramatic pieces performed in concert. The most famous example of oratorio, Handel's *Messiah* (1742), remains famous today. Oratorio also led to the form known as the passion, which is a kind of oratorio that dramatizes the death of Christ, for instance, Bach's *St. Matthew Passion* (1729). Smaller in scale, cantatas resemble oratorios but may have either secular or sacred subject matter. Bach wrote hundreds of cantatas; they became a standard part of Lutheran church services, weddings and secular ceremonies.

Of course, the contributions of the Baroque period did not stop with opera and oratorio. For the first time in history, instrumental music came to rival vocal music in its variety and complexity. This breakthrough led to a blossoming of instrumental forms, the development of new instruments and the emergence of virtuoso players. Composers explored the subtleties of various instruments for their own sake, not just as complements to vocal music. With the exception of lute and keyboard compositions, they no longer wrote pieces exclusively for voices or instruments; their works could be performed by either or both.

A fundamental aspect of the Baroque period was the art of counterpoint. Defining polyphony and counterpoint can be confusing, but it is helpful to remember that polyphony came first, followed by the theory of counterpoint, which developed gradually. Polyphony is basically the simultaneous sounding of two or more notes of different pitch. Counterpoint is the art of combining two simultaneous musical lines. The term derives from the Latin *contra-punctum,* "against note." It was first used in the 14th century, but in modern usage it is not distinct from polyphony (literally, "many sounding"). There is a tendency to apply *polyphony* to 16th- and 17th-century works and *counterpoint* to those of the early 18th century, the time of J. S. Bach—heir to the polyphonic art of the past. In general, polyphony is used to describe early music, while counterpoint refers to the further development of polyphony.

The chief form of contrapuntal music is the fugue. The early fugue of the 16th century evolved into the fully developed mature fugue form of the Bach period and later times. The name is derived from *fuga,* Latin for "flight." As a contrapuntal composition, a fugue features a theme or subject of firm character that permeates the entire structure, entering in one voice, and then in another. The subject is the source of unification. Fugues can be vocal or instrumental—written for solo instruments, such as the piano or violin, for a group of instruments, for several solo voices, or for full chorus.

In addition to Bach and Handel, major contributors to Baroque music include Italian violin virtuoso and composer Arcangelo Corelli (1653–1713), who specialized in chamber-music forms, such as the trio sonata and the orchestral concerto grosso. Henry Purcell, the most significant English composer of the period, created *Dido and Aeneas* (1689), the most notable masterpiece of English stage music until the 20th-century operas of Benjamin Britten. Dominant among the French were harpsichord masters François Couperin (1668–1733) and Jean-Philippe Rameau (1683–1764). They helped develop the suite, in which a solo instrument, such as the harpsichord or lute, performed a collection of stylized dances. Late in the period, Venetian violin virtuoso Antonio Vivaldi performed fervently; technically unique and exciting, his compositions for strings were of immeasurable importance in the development of instrumental music.

The Classical Period

Roughly paralleling the broader cultural period known as the Age of Enlightenment or Age of Reason, the Classical period (c. 1750–1825) of music built on and departed from Baroque precedents. It was preceded by a short artistic interim referred to as the Rococo period. Attracted to extravagance and aesthetic pleasure, Rococo composers replaced counterpoint or polyphonic texture, which they considered much too serious, with simple melodic structures. This so-called gallant style reached its height in Germany in the middle of the 18th century, promoted by Bach's four composer sons: Wilhelm Friedemann Bach (1710–84), Carl Philipp Emanuel Bach (1714–88), Johann Christoph Bach (1732–95) and Johann Christian Bach (1735–82). Rococo Italian composers included Giovanni Battista Sammartini (1701–75), Baldassare Galuppi (1706–85) and Giovanni Battista Pergolesi (1710–36).

The emergence of the Classical school allowed the symphony, the solo concerto, the instrumental sonata and the string quartet to flourish. The most important principle of musical structure from the Classical period to the 20th century was sonata form (also known as sonata-allegro form). It describes a single movement, most often part of a multimovement work, such as a sonata, symphony, concerto or string quartet; independent movements, such as an overture, may also be in sonata form. Typically, sonata form features three sections: exposition (the presentation of melodic material with specific key relationships); development (the working out of the exposition material in a variety of ways, moving through a number of keys); and recapitulation (the restatement of the original themes of the exposition, often modified). A coda (short section) is often included and serves to extend the movement, building tension and delaying the final cadence (close).

In the 17th century, the term *concerto* was applied to ensemble music (*concerti grossi,* for example, which could be played by three or four players or by an orchestra). By the 18th century, the term usually denoted a work in which a solo instrument (or group of instruments) contrasts with an orchestral ensemble, as in the Brandenburg Concertos of J. S. Bach. The Classical concerto that survived the Baroque period is best represented by the twenty-three piano concertos of Mozart. Although Beethoven's concertos (or concerti) are on a larger scale, they adhere to the principles of Classical design. The appeal of the concerto and sonata forms lay in their inherent flexibility.

The Classical symphony—an extended work for orchestra, usually in three or four movements—may be traced to the late 17th-century Italian overture (which had three movements in a fast-slow-fast pattern). The works of Haydn and Mozart represent the highest achievements in the Viennese Classical symphony. Beethoven's first two symphonies sound much like Haydn and Mozart, but his subsequent symphonies (Nos. 3–9) were unprecedented in grandeur and power. The more conservative Romantics—Mendelssohn, Schumann and Brahms—remained broadly faithful to the Classical conception of the symphony but made some far-reaching innovations that contributed to the developments in the Romantic period that followed.

Although the string quartet—a composition for four solo string instruments, usually two violins, a viola and a cello—was pioneered in various late Baroque compositions, it was not firmly established until the time of Haydn, with the creation of a four-movement scheme and texture (c. 1770). Haydn's only contemporary to reach his level in the medium was Mozart. Again, Beethoven's quartets are written largely within the established Classical framework, but with a new dramatic purpose, an expanded harmonic language, and scores with more richly sonorous and elaborated textures. These innovations, of course, were coupled with Beethoven's enormous imagination for compositional development.

The symphony, solo concerto, instrumental sonata and string quartet continued to develop within the Classical structure and remained a popular type of composition throughout the 19th century and up to the present day.

Composers also experimented with, and discovered the possibilities of, the major/minor tonal system, different kinds of chamber music and opera. As the Classical masters established the orchestra as it is known today (with the exception of some 19th- and 20th-century changes in the construction of certain instruments), the symphonic form grew rapidly in scale and significance.

Where the Baroque orchestra typically had twenty to twenty-five members, the Classical orchestra involved about forty members. But until late in the period, when the concert hall became popular, orchestras still performed in salons.

The Classical era was a golden age for chamber music, a kind of intimate ensemble music for two to eight instruments, one player to each part. Consisting of two violins, a viola and a cello, the standard string quartet dominated chamber music of the time. Other favored combinations included the duo combinations of piano and violin or piano and cello; the trio for piano, violin and cello; and the quintet, usually a combination of string or wind instruments or a string quartet with a solo instrument, such as the piano or clarinet.

As chamber music advanced, the Classical composers began to favor the piano over the clavichord and harpsichord as an instrument for the home. The piano's superior sonority and greater volume also made it popular in the concert hall, which was still a developing type of musical venue. With the development of the sonata-allegro form and new concepts in keyboard style, the piano sonata became a particularly challenging form of solo music. Also, the solo concerto, especially the piano concerto, gained in popularity.

The Classical period centers around the four Viennese masters—Joseph Haydn, Wolfgang Amadeus Mozart, Ludwig van Beethoven and Franz Schubert—and their contemporaries. Schubert, the last and latest of these, lived only thirty-one years and composed music that straddled the Classical and subsequent Romantic eras. Most importantly, he revolutionized the song form. By contrast, Haydn's long career spanned decades and made a wide-ranging impact on the symphonic form and the string quartet. He applied his genius to more than sixty string quartets that have since become an indispensable part of the Classical repertoire. Likewise, his more than one hundred symphonies constitute a unique contribution to the genre. Haydn was also a prolific composer of church music, songs, piano sonatas and the divertimento and solo concerto.

Starting his musical career as a child prodigy, Wolfgang Amadeus Mozart created a tremendous *oeuvre*. His mastery of everything musical allowed him to make complex technique appear effortless. He composed many of the period's finest examples of chamber music. One of the outstanding piano virtuosos of his time, Mozart wrote prodigiously for his favorite instrument. Of particular importance was his contribution of more than twenty concertos for piano and orchestra. Of his forty-one symphonies, those written in the last decade of his life had special significance, as they took the symphonic form to new heights in the world of classical music. Although Mozart wrote opera to earn money, he also had a passion for the form, as well as lyric gifts and an innate understanding of the human voice. He composed a number of brilliant operas, including *The Marriage of Figaro* (1786), *Don Giovanni* (1787), *Così fan tutte* (1790) and *The Magic Flute* (1791).

Ludwig van Beethoven transformed the sonata form of Haydn and Mozart by expanding its dimensions. His thirty-two piano sonatas have such significance that they are sometimes referred to as the pianist's "New Testament" (the

"Old" being Bach's *Well-Tempered Clavier,* 1722 and 1744). Conceived on a grand scale that made great demands on the orchestra, Beethoven's nine symphonies are masterpieces of form and dramatic intensity. His five piano concertos combine virtuosity with expanded symphonic architecture, and his one and only Concerto for Violin and Orchestra (1806) ranks as one of the gems of music. Notable for its concentration on the string quartet, his considerable chamber music catalog includes the supreme achievement of the five quartets composed in the last years of his life.

The Romantic Period

A revolution of expression, the Romantic period (c. 1825–1900) brought intellectual and emotional associations to the fore in music. Romantic music was inspired by meditations on destiny, God, nature, and political struggle, voicing each with maximum intensity. A powerful trend toward musical nationalism, primarily in Eastern Europe and Russia, also prompted composers to declare their passion for their homeland musically. Many wrote in their own language for the first time, adding a new linguistic variety to European vocal music. Emphasizing emotion and imagination over reason and formula, the Romantic composers cast aside the Classical rules governing the craft of composition and focused on the value of individual contributions. The period also saw a rising interest in the preservation of the music of the past for future generations. Now, instead of composing for the immediate gratification of a patron, composers wrote with an eye toward posterity.

The Romantics gradually elaborated on the genres, instrumental forms, and concise tonal structure inherited from the previous century. New instrumental genres, such as the waltz, mazurka, polonaise, impromptu and nocturne, reflected the Romantic temperament, in part by suggesting an air of improvisation. Art songs, known in Germany as *Lieder,* entered a period of heightened development, while program music—a kind of orchestral music with literary or pictorial associations—emerged. By the end of the 19th century, the old forms and tonality began to fade.

During the Romantic era, instrument makers instituted important improvements that expanded the technical capabilities of instruments. Musicians had better educational opportunities, and so composers found more and better-trained performers to play their work. At the same time, the public concert hall was firmly established. Orchestras naturally increased in size and proficiency, thereby bringing greater variety and new dynamics to symphonic expression. Orchestration—the technique of writing for orchestra—became an art form. In the tradition of Beethoven's nine masterpieces, symphonies grew twice as long as in the Classical period. Whereas Haydn wrote more than one hundred symphonies and Mozart forty-one, Schubert and the Romantic composers Anton Bruckner and Antonín Dvořák wrote nine, Peter Tchaikovsky six, and Robert Schumann and Johannes Brahms four.

Given the new complexities of the symphony, one of the most popular types of music to emerge in the Romantic period was the short, lyric piano piece. The 19th-century masters of the form included Schubert, Frédéric Chopin, Felix Mendelssohn, Schumann, Brahms and Franz Liszt. As never before, these composers exploited the technical and dramatic resources of the piano.

Blending the Classical and Romantic styles, Schubert wrote not only symphonies and piano pieces but also chamber music and more than six hundred lieder. Chopin's creative life centered around the piano, for his genius was wedded to the keyboard. His Nocturnes, Mazurkas, Etudes, Waltzes and Preludes for solo piano remain among the most popular with both audiences and pianists. Fastidious in his craftsmanship, Mendelssohn hoped to preserve the traditions of the Classical forms within the Romantic movement, an unpopular objective at the time. He was a prolific writer for the voice and also created violin concertos, chamber music and symphonies, in addition to short piano pieces. Schumann, meanwhile, represented the essence of German Romanticism as a piano composer and as a composer of Lieder, second only to Schubert.

Dedicated to the purity of Classical style, Brahms resolved to innovate within the tradition of the 18th-century masters. He proved his point with chamber music, orchestral works and concertos, drawing inspiration from Haydn and Bach. In terms of design, his four symphonies were without equal during the late Romantic period. Skillfully capturing the intimacy vital to chamber music, Brahms preserved 19th-century expressiveness and virtuosity in his piano works. His lieder naturally reflected the influences of Schubert and Schumann, but the Brahmsian style was most distinctive, reflecting an ever-increasing perfection of technique, concentration of emotion and melodic invention. Few song writers have maintained his consistent standard.

Composer, pianist, conductor and teacher Franz Liszt was one of the 19th century's major artistic figures. In pursuit of his primary goal, lyric expression, he created the symphonic poem, the most famous being *Les Préludes* (1848). Liszt also ranks alongside Chopin as one of the creators of modern piano technique, which allowed performers to discover the instrument's true potential. He himself enjoyed a notorious career as a piano virtuoso, during which he made a significant innovation in the staging of piano performances: Responding to the public's adoration of distinguished violin virtuoso Niccolo Paganini, Liszt decided to make himself more visible during piano performances. Instead of sitting with his back to the audience as was customary at the time, he turned the piano around to give listeners a full view of his profile and of his hands on the keyboard. This more-effective arrangement is still in use today.

Another important figure in Romantic music was Hector Berlioz, one of the daring innovators of the 19th century. Blessed with a completely original approach to music and a unique sense of sound, he opened up a new world of sonority through his genius as an orchestrator. Berlioz wrote works that embodied the literary influences of the period; his extraordinary *Symphonie fantastique* (1830), based on themes from his personal life, made him a Romantic indeed. Born a few years before the death of Berlioz, Richard Strauss inherited the

Romantic tradition. At the same time, he admired Classical composers and held Mozart in high esteem. His *oeuvre* is distinguished by several very popular operas, the most famous being *Der Rosenkavalier* (1909–10).

The expansion of the musical public and the growth of the music-publishing industry in the 19th century allowed choral music to flourish as well. Of the many choral masterpieces of the time, two stand out: Giuseppe Verdi's *Messa de Requiem* (1874) and Brahms's *A German Requiem* (1854–68). Major figures in the booming world of 19th-century opera include four Italians: Gioacchino Rossini, Vincenzo Bellini, Gaetano Donizetti and, of course, Verdi. France produced Georges Bizet and Germany Carl Maria von Weber (the founder of German Romantic opera), Strauss and Richard Wagner. In Russia, Tchaikovsky, Nicolai Rimsky-Korsakov and Modest Mussorgsky made great contributions to the form. (See also "Introduction to Opera," pages 214–224.)

The Twentieth Century

In essence, 20th-century classical music rejected the prevailing Austro-German style and forms of the previous century. Particularly in the United States, the popularity of German Romanticism began to decline early in the century. In its place arose not a single style but musical forms of great diversity, each with its own composers and audience. The various musical subdivisions of the 20th century include Expressionism, Primitivism, Neoclassicism, Serialism and, most recently, Minimalism. Entire styles came and went with relative frequency, sometimes within the music of a single composer. Composers expanded on elements present in earlier music and moved far beyond the old styles. Musical timbre, for instance, came to include every conceivable sound, even those not necessarily tuneful in the traditional sense.

The 20th century started with the post-Romantic era (c. 1890–1910), which produced a generation of composers who attempted to bridge the gap between the passing of Romanticism and the development of 20th-century styles. Gustav Mahler was a major force during this period. His nine completed symphonies made him the last in an illustrious line of symphonists consisting of Haydn, Mozart, Beethoven, Schubert, Bruckner and Brahms. Following in the footsteps of Schubert and Schumann, Mahler enriched the song cycle, most notable with *Das Lied von der Erde* ("The Song of the Earth," 1908), a cycle of six songs with orchestra.

The treatment of the orchestra during this period is especially significant. It was close to the turn of the century that the orchestra reached its largest size, as evidenced by such post-Romantic works as the symphonies of Bruckner and Mahler's Symphony No. 8 ("Symphony of a Thousand," 1906–07), scored for hundreds of singers and orchestra players. Around World War I, however, composers moved away from large orchestras and mammoth compositions and renewed their interest in smaller orchestral groups and chamber music.

The Impressionist movement (c. 1900–30) arose from the general feeling that composers had exhausted the possibilities of the traditional major/minor tonal system that had served classical music since the 17th century. In a conscious effort to break away from the dominant German music tradition, certain composers no longer considered dissonance a disturbance that needed resolution. They created work marked by a pronounced avoidance of tonal centers; this avoidance was crucial to their search for new harmonic possibilities. Among these composers was Maurice Ravel, who was repelled by the passion of 19th-century music, and Claude Debussy, who felt likewise. Debussy originated a distinctive new style of writing for the piano, from which emerged works essential to the modern repertoire. His best-known orchestral work, *Prélude à l'après-midi d'un faune* (1892–94), was inspired by a poem by Stephane Mallarme.

The trend toward increasing dissonance prompted some 20th-century composers, particularly Arnold Schönberg, to reject the conventional tonal system and attempt to replace it with atonality. In atonality, music has no tonal center or key; the idea is to work with harmony unrelated to a tonal system. But when they discarded tonal organization, these composers found they needed some systematic replacement. After an early atonal period in which he eliminated the distinction between consonance and dissonance, Schönberg slowly developed twelve-tone or tone row music, completing his final refinements about 1923. His system attached no special importance to any one note; because all notes have equal significance, twelve-tone music has no tonal center.

Like Schönberg, Igor Stravinsky belonged to the generation of modernists who came of age when the Romantic tradition was still alive. Stravinsky's major contributions include the early work *Le sacre du printemps* (1911–13); *Pulcinella* (1920), representative of his Neoclassical period; and, remarkably, a group of twelve-tone works written in his seventies. The music of Béla Bartók also reflected the trends of the time—polytonality, atonality, Expressionism, Neoclassicism and folk music—all intermingled with Classical and Romantic elements. Bartók's extraordinarily expressive string quartets are among the finest musical achievements of the 20th century. He is best known for his Concerto for Orchestra (1943) and the Music for Strings, Percussion and Celesta (1936). Both Stravinsky and Bartók stand as icons of 20th-century musical diversity. The generations who followed them inherited a legacy of revolution.

Early in the 20th century, classical music was still emerging. But American composer Charles Ives wrote "modern" and innovative music prior to World War I, although at the time he was virtually unknown. In fact, Ives worked with harmonies and rhythms that would not appear in Europe until World War I. Built on this foundation, American music soon flourished, producing the likes of Aaron Copland, George Gershwin, Samuel Barber, William Schuman, Elliott Carter, John Cage, Milton Babbitt and George Crumb. Minimalism appeared in the 1960s and developed as a reaction to the atonal, dissonant and technically difficult language of the contemporary avant-garde. The style is based on simple ideas repeated over a single pulse to mesmerizing effect. Late in the century, Minimalism reached its height in the works of Philip Glass and Steve Reich.

UNDERSTANDING CLASSICAL CATALOG LISTINGS

When written in a concert program or on an album cover, the titles of many compositions are followed by cryptic combinations of letters and numbers. These coded notations refer to catalog listings that serve as a standard means of organizing composers' works and establishing the chronology of their careers.

The most frequently used catalog notation is the opus number, abbreviated Op. (plural Opp.), as for instance in the title Concerto for Cello and Orchestra, Op. 104. A smaller opus number indicates an earlier work by the composer, a larger number a later work. A simple reference to number, the abbreviation No. (plural Nos.) places a work in chronological relation to other works of the same type by the composer, for example Rhapsody No. 12. When the two kinds of numbers are used in conjunction with each other (e.g., Symphony No. 5, Op. 67), they provide a fairly precise idea of when in the composer's career the piece was written.

Various capitalized letters appended to the titles of some composers' works generally stand for the names of the music historians who cataloged the *oeuvre* of those composers. The letters appear with a number that designates the work's position in the catalog. Among the most familiar of these notations are the "K" numbers assigned in 1862 (most recent revision, 1964) to Mozart's works by Ludwig Koechel, an Austrian botanist with an immense admiration for Mozart. Likewise, in 1978 Otto Deutsch assigned "D" numbers to Schubert's compositions. "BWV" numbers apply to Bach's works in the Bach Werke-Verzeichnis, a thematic index compiled in 1950 (with later revisions) by Wolfgang Schmieder; these replaced the "S" numbers originally used for Bach. Lettered notations appear as follows: Concerto No. 23 for Piano and Orchestra, K. 488; Symphony No. 5, D. 485; Mass in B Minor, BWV 232.

Unfortunately, historical information on compositions is not always accurate, so music historians cannot always date works with certainty. A higher opus number, for example, may be erroneously attached to an earlier piece. Nevertheless, opus and catalog numbers do help distinguish among classical compositions, which often have generic titles, such as Piano Concerto or Symphony No. 9.

STARTING A CLASSICAL MUSIC LIBRARY

Listeners interested in acquiring a well-rounded collection of classical music might start with the following major works. Restrictions of space do not allow for a representative listing of outstanding chamber music, or of solo instrumental or vocal compositions, but the compositions listed here represent the foundation of a solid classical library.

Baroque Period

JOHANN SEBASTIAN BACH: *Brandenburg Concertos* (1721), BWV 1046–1051; The Orchestral Suites (1724–31), BWV 1066–1069; Concerto for Two Violins and Orchestra in D Minor (1717–23), BWV 1043; *St. Matthew Passion* (c. 1736) BWV 244; Mass in B Minor (c. 1747–49), BWV 232

ARCANGELO CORELLI: Twelve Concerti Grossi, Op. 6 (c. 1739)

GEORGE FRIDERIC HANDEL: The Concerti Grossi, Opp. 3 (1734), 6 (1739); *Water Music* (1717); *Music for Royal Fireworks* (1749); *Messiah* (1742)

ANTONIO VIVALDI: *The Four Seasons*, Op. 8, Nos. 1–4 (c. 1725)

Classical Period

LUDWIG VAN BEETHOVEN: Symphony No. 3, Op. 55 ("Eroica," 1803); Symphony No. 5, Op. 67 (1807–08); Symphony No. 6, Op. 68 ("Pastoral," 1808); Symphony No. 7, Op. 92 (1811–12); Symphony No. 8, Op. 93 (1812); Symphony No. 9, Op. 125 (contains Schiller's "An die Freude" ["Ode to Joy"], 1822–24); Concerto No. 4, Op. 58 for Piano and Orchestra (1805–

06); Concerto No. 5, Op. 73 ("Emperor," 1809) for Piano and Orchestra; Concerto for Violin and Orchestra, Op. 61 (1806); *Leonore* Overture No. 3, Op. 72B (1805–06)

JOSEPH HAYDN: Symphony No. 45 ("Farewell," 1772); Symphony No. 88 (c. 1787); Symphony No. 94 ("Surprise," 1791); Symphony No. 101 ("Clock," 1793–94); Symphony No. 103 ("Drum Roll," 1795); Symphony No. 104 ("London," 1795); *Missa in tempore belli* ("Mass in the Time of War," 1796); *Lord Nelson Mass* (1798); *The Creation* (1796–98); *The Seasons* (1799–1801)

WOLFGANG AMADEUS MOZART: Symphony No. 29 in A major, K. 201 (1774); Symphony No. 36 in C major, K. 425 ("Linz," 1783); Symphony No. 38 in D major, K. 504 ("Prague," 1786); Symphony No. 39 in E-flat major, K. 543 (1788); Symphony No. 40 in G minor, K. 550 (1788); Symphony No. 41 in C major, K. 551 ("Jupiter," 1788); Concerto No. 23 in A major for Piano and Orchestra, K. 488 (1786); Concerto No. 24 in C minor for Piano and Orchestra, K. 491 (1786); Concerto No. 25 in C major for Piano and Orchestra, K. 503 (1786); Concerto No. 26 in D major for Piano and Orchestra, K. 537 ("Coronation," 1788); Concerto No. 27 in B-flat major for Piano and Orchestra, K. 595 (c. 1788–91); Concerto in B-flat major for Bassoon and Orchestra, K. 191 (1774); Concerto No. 1 in G major for Flute and Orchestra, K. 313 (1778); Concerto No. 2 in D major for Flute (or in C major for Oboe) and Orchestra, K. 314 (1778); Concerto No. 2 in E-flat major for French Horn and Orchestra, K. 417 (1783); Concerto No. 3 in E-flat major for French Horn and Orchestra, K. 447 (c. 1784–87); Concerto No. 4 in E-flat major for French Horn and Orchestra, K. 495 (1786); Concerto in A major for Clarinet and Orchestra, K. 622 (1791); *Sinfonia Concertante* for Violin, Viola and Orchestra, K. 364 (1779); *Eine kleine Nachtmusik* ("A Little Night Music," 1787), K. 525; Overture to *Le nozze di Figaro* ("The Marriage of Figaro," 1786), K. 492; Overture to *Don Giovanni*, K. 527 (1787); Overture to *Die Zauberflöte* ("The Magic Flute," 1791), K. 620; Requiem, K. 626 (1791)

FRANZ SCHUBERT: Symphony No. 4 ("Tragic," 1816), D. 417; Symphony No. 5, D. 485 (1816); Symphony No. 8 ("Unfinished," 1822), D. 759; Symphony No. 9 ("Great C Major," c. 1825–28), D. 944; *Rosamunde*, Overture and Incidental Music, Op. 26, D. 797 (1823); Mass No. 6 in E-flat major, D. 950 (c. 1828)

Romantic Period

HECTOR BERLIOZ: *Symphonie fantastique* (1830); *Harold in Italie* (1834); *Le carnaval romain* ("The Roman Carnival") Overture (1844)

GEORGES BIZET: *L'Arlesienne* Suite Nos. 1 and 2 (1872 and c. 1876)

JOHANNES BRAHMS: Symphony No. 1, Op. 68 (1855–76); Symphony No. 2, Op. 73 (1877); Symphony No. 3, Op. 90 (1883); Symphony No. 4, Op. 98 (1884–85); Concerto No. 2 for Piano and Orchestra, Op. 83 (1878–81); Concerto for Violin, Cello and Orchestra, Op. 102 (1887); *Academic Festival Overture*, Op. 80 (1880); Variations on a Theme of Joseph Haydn, Op. 56A (1873); *A German Requiem*, Op. 45 (1854–68)

ANTON BRUCKNER: Symphony No. 5 (1875–76); Symphony No. 7 (1881–83); Symphony No. 8 (1884–87); Symphony No. 9 (1891–96); *Te Deum* (1881–84)

ERNEST CHAUSSON (1855–99): *Poème* for Violin and Orchestra, Op. 25 (1896)

FRÉDÉRIC CHOPIN: Concerto No. 2 for Piano and Orchestra, Op. 21 (1829–30)

ANTONÍN DVOŘÁK: Symphony No. 8, Op. 88 (1889) and Symphony No. 9, Op. 95 ("From the New World," 1893); Concerto for Cello and Orchestra, Op. 104 (1894–95); *Slavonic Dances*, Opp. 46 (1878) and 72 (1886–87)

GABRIEL FAURÉ (1845–1924): *Pelléas et Mélisande* Suite, Op. 80 (1901); Requiem, Op. 48 (1887–90)

CÉSAR FRANCK (1822–90): Symphony in D Minor (1886–88); Symphonic Variations for Piano and Orchestra (1885)

MIKHAIL GLINKA (1804–57): Overture to *Ruslan and Ludmila* (1837–42)

EDVARD GRIEG (1843–1907): Concerto for Piano and Orchestra in A minor, Op. 16 (1868); *Peer Gynt* Suites No. 1 (1874–75) and No. 2 (1874–75)

FRANZ LISZT: Concerto No. 1 for Piano and Orchestra (1849); *Les Préludes* (1848); *A Faust Symphony* (1854–57)

GUSTAV MAHLER: Symphony No. 1 (c. 1884–88); Symphony No. 4 (1892); Symphony No. 5 (1901–02); Symphony No. 9 (1908–09); *Das Lied von der Erde* ("The Song of the Earth," 1908–09); *Songs of the Wayfarer* (1884); Songs from *Des Knaben Wunderhorn* (1892–98); *Kindertotenlieder* ("Songs on the Death of Children," 1901–04)

FELIX MENDELSSOHN: Symphony No. 3, Op. 56 ("Scottish," 1842); Symphony No. 4, Op. 90 ("Italian," 1833); Symphony No. 5, Op. 107 ("Reformation," c. 1830); Concerto for Violin and Orchestra, Op. 64 (1844); *The*

Hebrides or *Fingal's Cave*, Op. 26 (1830); Overture and Incidental Music for Shakespeare's *A Midsummer Night's Dream*, Opp. 21 (1826) and 61 (1843); *Elijah*, Op. 70 (1846–47)

MODEST MUSSORGSKY: *Pictures at an Exhibition*, orch. Maurice Ravel (1874, orch. 1922); *A Night on Bald Mountain* (1867)

NICCOLO PAGANINI: Concerto No. 1 for Violin and Orchestra, Op. 6 (c. 1817)

NICOLAI RIMSKY-KORSAKOV: *Capriccio espagnol*, Op. 34 (1887); *Scheherazade*, Op. 35 (1888); *Russian Easter Overture*, Op. 36 (1888)

GIOACCHINO ROSSINI: the opera overtures *La scala di seta* ("The Silken Ladder," 1812); *L'Italiana in Algeri* ("The Italian Girl in Algiers," 1813); *Il barbiere di Siviglia* ("The Barber of Seville," 1816); *La Cenerentola* ("Cinderella," 1817); *La gazza ladra* ("The Thieving Magpie," 1817); *Guillaume Tell* ("William Tell," 1829)

CAMILLE SAINT-SAËNS: Symphony No. 3, Op. 78 ("Organ Symphony," 1886); *Danse macabre*, Op. 40 (1874); *The Carnival of the Animals* (1886)

ROBERT SCHUMANN: Symphony No. 1, Op. 38 ("Spring," 1841); Symphony No. 3, Op. 97 ("Rhenish," 1850); Concerto for Piano and Orchestra, Op. 54 (1841–45); Concerto for Cello and Orchestra, Op. 129 (1850)

BEDŘICH SMETANA (1824–84): *The Moldau* ("Vltava"), from *Ma vlast* ("My Fatherland," 1872–79); Overture and Dances from *The Bartered Bride* (1863–70)

JOHANN STRAUSS, JR.: the waltzes *On the Beautiful Blue Danube*, Op. 314 (1867); *Tales from the Vienna Woods*, Op. 325 (1868); *Wine, Women, and Song*, Op. 333 (1869); *Emperor Waltzes*, Op. 437 (1889)

RICHARD STRAUSS: *Don Juan*, Op. 20 (1888–89); *Tod und Verklärung*, Op. 24 ("Death and Transfiguration," 1888–89); *Till Eulenspiegels lustige Streiche*, Op. 28 ("Till Eulenspiegel's Merry Pranks," 1894–95); *Also sprach Zarathustra*, Op. 30 ("Thus Spake Zarathustra," 1895–96); *Don Quixote*, Op. 35 (1896–97); *Ein Heldenleben*, Op. 40 ("A Hero's Life," 1897–98); waltzes from *Der Rosenkavalier* (1909–10); *Four Last Songs* (1948)

PETER TCHAIKOVSKY: Symphony No. 4, Op. 36 (1877–78); Symphony No. 5, Op. 64 (1888); Symphony No. 6, Op. 74 ("Pathétique," 1893); Concerto No. 1 for Piano and Orchestra, Op. 23 (1874–75); Concerto for Violin and Orchestra, Op. 35 (1878); *The Nutcracker Suite*, Op. 71a (1892); *1812 Overture*, Op. 49 (1880);

Overture to *Romeo and Juliet* (1869, 1870, 1880); Serenade for Strings, Op. 48 (1880); *Capriccio italien*, Op. 45 (1880)

GIUSEPPE VERDI: Requiem (1874)

RICHARD WAGNER: Prelude and "Liebestod" from *Tristan und Isolde* (1857–59); Prelude to Act III of *Lohengrin* (1846–48); *Siegfried-Idyll* (1870); Prelude to *Die Meistersinger von Nürnberg* (1862–67)

CARL MARIA VON WEBER: Concerto No. 1 for Clarinet and Orchestra, Op. 73 (1811); *Konzertstuck* for Piano and Orchestra, Op. 79 (1821); *Invitation to the Dance* (1819)

Twentieth Century

SAMUEL BARBER: Adagio for Strings (arranged from the String Quartet in B Minor, Movement II), Op. 11 (1936); Violin Concerto, Op. 14 (1939–40); *Knoxville: Summer of 1915* (1947; rev. 1950)

BÉLA BARTÓK: Concerto for Orchestra (1943); Concerto No. 1 for Violin and Orchestra (1905–07); Music for Strings, Percussion and Celesta (1936)

ALBAN BERG: Concerto for Violin and Orchestra (1935); Symphonic Pieces from *Lulu* ("Lulu Suite," 1934)

LEONARD BERNSTEIN: Overture to *Candide* (1956); Symphonic Dances from *West Side Story* (1961); *Chichester Psalms* (1965); Symphony No. 2: *The Age of Anxiety* (1949)

ERNEST BLOCH (1880–1959): *Schelomo* ("Solomon") for Cello and Orchestra (1915–16)

BENJAMIN BRITTEN: Four Sea Interludes from *Peter Grimes*, Op. 33A (1945); *The Young Person's Guide to the Orchestra*, Op. 34 (1946)

ELLIOTT CARTER: Variations for Orchestra (1954–55); Symphony No. 1 (1942); Concerto for Orchestra (1969)

AARON COPLAND: Ballet Suite from *Billy the Kid* (c. 1938); Four Dance Episodes from *Rodeo* (1942); *Appalachian Spring* (1943–44); *A Lincoln Portrait* (1942)

CLAUDE DEBUSSY: *Prélude à L'Après-midi d'un faune* (1892–94); *Nocturnes* (1897–99); *La Mer* (1903–05)

SIR EDWARD ELGAR (1857–1934): *Enigma* Variations, Op. 36 (1898–99); Cello Concerto (1919)

MANUEL DE FALLA: *Noches en los jardines de Espana* ("Nights in the Gardens of Spain," 1911–15); *El Amor brujo* ("Love, the Magician," 1915); *El Sombrero de tres picos* ("The Three-Cornered Hat," 1919)

GEORGE GERSHWIN: *Rhapsody in Blue* (1924); Concerto in F for Piano and Orchestra (1925); *An American in Paris* (1928)

ROY HARRIS (1898–1979): Symphony No. 3 (1938)

PAUL HINDEMITH: *Mathis der Maler* ("Matthias the Painter") Symphony (1934); *Symphonic Metamorphoses on Themes of Carl Maria von Weber* (1943)

GUSTAV HOLST (1874–1934): *The Planets*, Op. 32 (1914–16)

CHARLES IVES: *Three Places in New England* (1911–c. 1914); *The Unanswered Question and Central Park in the Dark* (1906); Symphony No. 4 (1910–16)

LEOŠ JANÁČEK (1854–1928): Sifonietta (1926); *Glagolitic Mass* (1926–29)

ZOLTÁN KODÁLY (1882–1967): Suite from *Háry János*, Op. 15 (1927); Te Deum (1936)

DARIUS MILHAUD (1892–1974): *La création du monde*, Op. 81 ("The Creation of the World," 1923); *Scaramouche* (1937)

KRZYSZTOF PENDERECKI (1933–——): *Threnody for the Victims of Hiroshima* (1960)

WALTER PISTON (1894–1976): Suite from *The Incredible Flutist* (1938); Symphony No. 4 (1950)

FRANCIS POULENC (1899–1963): Suite from *Les Biches* (1939–40); *Gloria* (1959)

SERGEI PROKOFIEV: Symphony No. 1, Op. 25 ("Classical," 1916–17); Symphony No. 5, Op. 100 (1931–32); Concerto No. 3 for Piano and Orchestra, Op. 26 (1917–21); *Peter and the Wolf*, Op. 67 (1936); Ballet Suites No. 1, Op. 64BIS and 2, Op. 64TER from *Romeo and Juliet* (1936); *Lieutenant Kije* Suite, Op. 60 (1934)

SERGEI RACHMANINOFF: Concerto No. 2 for Piano and Orchestra, Op. 18 (1900–01); Rhapsody on a Theme of Paganini for Piano and Orchestra, Op. 43 (1934)

MAURICE RAVEL: *Rhapsodie espagnole* (1907–08); *Ma mere l'oye* ("Mother Goose," 1911); *Daphnis et Chloe*, Suites No. 1 (1911) and 2 (1913); *La valse, poème choreographique* (1919–20); *Boléro* (1928); Concerto for the Left Hand for Piano and Orchestra (1929–30); Concerto for Piano and Orchestra in G major (1929–31)

OTTORINO RESPHIGI (1879–1936): *The Pines of Rome* (1923–24); *The Fountains of Rome* (1914–16)

ERIK SATIE: *Gymnopédies*, orch. Claude Debussy (1888, orch. 1896)

ARNOLD SCHÖNBERG: *Verklärte Nacht* ("Transfigured Night," 1917), Op. 4; Five Orchestra Pieces, Op. 16 (1909); Variations for Orchestra, Op. 31 (1926–28); *A Survivor from Warsaw*, Op. 46 (1947); Gurrelieder (1911)

ROGER SESSIONS (1896–1985): *When Lilacs Last in the Dooryard Bloom'd* (1970); Concerto for Orchestra (1972); *The Black Maskers* (1923)

DMITRI SHOSTAKOVICH: Symphony No. 1, Op. 10 (1924–25); Symphony No. 2, Op. 14 (1927); Symphony No. 3, Op. 20 ("The First of May," 1929); Symphony No. 4, Op. 43 (1936); Symphony No. 5, Op. 47 (1937); Symphony No. 6, Op. 54 (1939); Symphony No. 7, Op. 60 ("Leningrad," 1941); Symphony No. 8, Op. 65 (1943); Symphony No. 9, Op. 70 (1945); Symphony No. 10, Op. 93 (1953); Symphony No. 11, Op. 103 ("The Year of God," 1957); Symphony No. 12, Op. 112 ("The Year of 1917," 1960–61); Symphony No. 13, Op. 113 ("Babi Yar," 1962); Symphony No. 14, Op. 135 (1969); Symphony No. 15, Op. 141 (1971)

JEAN SIBELIUS: Symphony No. 2, Op. 43 (1901–02); Symphony No. 5, Op. 82 (1915); *The Swan of Tuonela*, Op. 22, No. 2 (1893); Finlandia, Op. 26 (1899–1900)

IGOR STRAVINSKY: *The Firebird* (1909–10); *Pétrouchka* (1910–11); *Le sacre du printemps* ("The Rite of Spring," 1911–13); Symphony in C (1939–40); *Symphony of Psalms* (1930); *Requiem Canticles* (1965–66); *Pulcinella:* Suite (1920)

MICHAEL TIPPETT (1905–——): *A Child of Our Time* (1939–41); Symphony No. 4 (1976–77)

EDGARD VARÈSE (1883–1965): *Arcana* (1925–27); *Ionisation* (1929–31)

RALPH VAUGHAN WILLIAMS: Fantasia on a Theme by Thomas Tallis (1910); Fantasia on *Greensleeves* (1934); Symphony No. 5 (1943)

ANTON WEBERN (1883–1945): Five Pieces for Orchestra, Op. 10 (1911–13); Symphony, Op. 21 (1928)

The Classical Orchestra and Its Conductor

When first established in the 18th century, the orchestra was an assemblage of instrumentalists rather than an organized ensemble. The early conductor focused on the mechanical aspects of coordinating a performance instead of the interpretation of compositions. As Western classical music and orchestra evolved over the centuries, so did the role of the conductor. The orchestra has now grown into an ensemble that may contain approximately eighty-five to more than one hundred players. This group is divided into four basic sections: strings, woodwinds, brass and percussion. Occasionally, the harp, piano or organ may be used, as well as a variety of other instruments that may be required by an eclectic repertoire. The number of players assigned to perform an individual piece of music may vary according to the composer's orchestration, the composition's style and the conductor's preference.

The *string section* consists of violins, generally arranged as follows

18 first violins
16 second violins
12 violas
12 cellos, also known as violoncellos
8–10 double basses, also known as contrabasses

The *woodwind section* is most often made up of

3 flutes
1 piccolo
3 oboes

1 English horn
3 clarinets
1 bass clarinet
3 bassoons
1 contrabassoon

The *brass section* most often includes

4 horns
4 trumpets
3 trombones
1 tuba

The *percussion section* consists of a variety of instruments that fall into two categories, those that can be tuned to a definite pitch and those of indefinite pitch. The *definite-pitch category* generally includes

    1 set of 2 or 3 timpani
    1 glockenspiel
    1 celesta
    1 xylophone
    1 set of chimes

The *indefinite-pitch category* of percussion most often consists of

    1 side or snare drum
    1 bass drum
    1 tambourine
    1 triangle
    1 set of cymbals

The string players usually share music stands, one stand for every two players, although occasionally each of the double basses will have its own. Each woodwind and brass player has his or her own music stand, while the distribution of music stands in the percussion section varies according to need.

The conductor's podium stands at center stage in front of the orchestra. Based on centuries of trial and error, the instruments are arranged to secure the best balance of tone. Although many orchestras follow a standard plan, with strings up front and brass and percussion in the back, conductors often alter this design to accommodate their personal desires, the requirements of the music or the specific acoustics of a concert hall.

Experienced listeners notice that the sound and performance style of an orchestra reflect the approach taken by the conductor standing on the podium. Beyond the basic skills and technical accomplishments required, the interpretative methods of the conductor are often intangible to untrained musicians. Few practicing conductors of the 20th century have been willing to write about their methods, but thanks to a number of notable composers of the 19th century, the conductor's craft has not gone completely unrecorded. Among those who have offered their opinions and insights on the problems of conducting were Weber, Berlioz, Liszt and Wagner, each of whom also possessed considerable literary gifts.

To bring a composer's score to life, the conductor must have an interpretative plan, for musical precision encompasses much more than playing the right notes together. The greater the composer's demands on the conductor, the greater the conductor's demands upon every orchestra member. In a successful performance, the players comprehend what the conductor is trying to accomplish. An orchestra cannot function if the ineptitude of its conductor allows a hundred

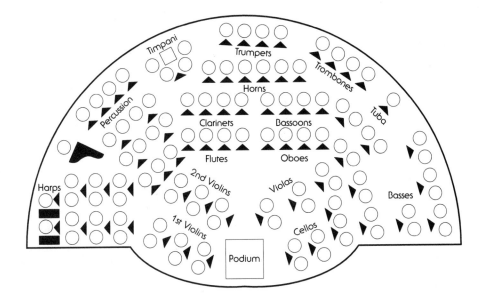

The Classical Orchestra

undirected players to ignore the composer's intentions and generate indiscriminate sound. Ideally, the conductor and the orchestra meld into a unified, indivisible entity.

In assessing the impact of an orchestra performance, the question becomes: precisely what part is the product of the conductor's craft, and what part comes from the skill of the orchestra? Obviously, an orchestra can produce sounds without the assistance of a conductor, just as a car can run without a driver. But without the guidance of a single musician, an orchestra's sounds will be undisciplined. Clearly, a conductor's success as a performer depends, to a certain extent, on the proficiency of the orchestra. Beyond that, the best conductors possess an innate conducting instinct, an interpretative gift, a strong technique and a high level of musicianship. Many conductors have one, two or possibly three of these traits, but few possess all four. It is the conjunction of all four gifts that distinguishes the truly great conductors throughout history.

Beyond technique and musicianship, the conductor relies on his or her personality to influence the orchestra. Hand and arm motions are of great importance, but they are not the only means of communication with the players. Leonard Bernstein, for instance, spoke of seducing musicians with his eyes to win them over to his way of doing things. The audience seldom witnesses such subtle moments of a conductor's performance. Instead, they respond to visible gestures that are integral to the orchestra's performance. Such gestures may either contribute to or detract from the audience's experience of the music.

Major Orchestras of the World

The many, many worthy orchestras throughout the world are too numerous to be listed here. Below is a representative sampling of some of the more famous bodies. Note that many conductors have maintained affiliations with more than one orchestra.

Academy of St. Martin-in-the-Fields: Established in 1958 by Neville Marriner, this ensemble takes its name from the church in London's Trafalgar Square where it first gave concerts. The orchestra, currently conducted by Iona Brown, records on the Philips label. Its repertoire focuses on the Baroque and Classical periods.

Amsterdam Concertgebouw Orchestra: This ensemble gave its first concerts in 1888, in its now famous hall. Willem Mengelberg, conductor from 1895 to 1945, led performances of Beethoven, Mahler, Strauss and Debussy that brought the orchestra to prominence. He was succeeded by Eduard van Beinum (1945–59); Bernard Haitink (1961–88—jointly with Eugen Jochum, 1961–64, and Kiril Kondrashin, 1979–81); and Riccardo Chailly (since 1989). The orchestra has recorded extensively for Philips Records.

Atlanta Symphony Orchestra: Emerging in 1947 as an offshoot of the Atlanta Youth Orchestra, this group became fully professional in 1966. Robert Shaw served as music director from 1967 to 1988; his successor since 1989 has been Yoel Levi.

Baltimore Symphony Orchestra: Established in 1914, this ensemble enjoys a close association with the Peabody Conservatory in Baltimore, where many of its players are faculty members. Under the Romanian conductor Sergiu Commissiona (1970–84), the orchestra rose to national prominence. Since 1985, David Zinman has maintained the organization's commitment to strong programming.

Berlin Philharmonic Orchestra: In its first hundred years of existence, starting in 1882, this orchestra had only four conductors: Hans von Bulow (1887–94), Arthur Nikisch (1895–1922), Wilhelm Furtwangler (1922–45, 1952–54; performances suspended immediately following World War II), and Herbert von Karajan (1955–89). The orchestra's original hall was destroyed during World War I. In 1963 the orchestra moved to its present home, the New Philharmonie by the Tiergarten. Claudio Abbado succeeded Karajan as conductor in 1990. The ensemble has made dozens of significant recordings on DGG, the Deutsche Grammophon Gesellschaft.

Boston Symphony Orchestra: Founded in 1881 by Henry Lee Higginson, this symphony commissioned many of the 20th century's significant orchestral compositions. Among its prominent conductors have been Arthur Nikisch (1889–93), Pierre Monteux (1919–24), Serge Koussevitzky (1924–49), Charles Munch (1949–62), Erich Leinsdorf (1962–69), William Steinberg (1969–72) and, since 1973, Seiji Ozawa. The orchestra performs in Symphony Hall, which opened in 1900 and is considered to have the most perfect acoustics in the United States. The orchestra's summer home is the Tanglewood Music Festival in Lenox, Massachusetts. Members of the orchestra also comprise the Boston Pops, founded in 1885. From early May to early July each year, the Pops performs light classical and popular music, including tunes from musical theater. Its most famous conductor was

Arthur Fiedler, who served from 1930 to 1979. His successor, John Williams, retired after the 1993 season; at press time a new conductor had not yet been named.

Chicago Symphony Orchestra: Founded in 1891, this ensemble occupies the elegant Orchestra Hall on the shores of Lake Michigan. The hall, opened in 1904, was built with proceeds from public subscriptions to the orchestra's performances. Among the group's prominent conductors have been Artur Rodzinski (1947–48), Rafael Kubelik (1950–53), Fritz Reiner (1953–63), and Georg Solti (1969–90). Solti's tenure was particularly brilliant in terms of the orchestra's repertoire, recordings, and numerous tours during those years. The era made the Chicago Symphony an important force in American musical life. Daniel Barenboim became music director in 1991.

Cincinnati Symphony Orchestra: Established originally in 1895, the ensemble performed until 1907, at which time a labor dispute forced it to disband. The group reorganized in 1909 under conductor Leopold Stokowski (1909–12). Subsequent conductors included Eugene Ysaÿe (1918–22), Fritz Reiner (1922–31), Thomas Schippers (1970–77), and Michael Gielen (1980–86). Jesús López-Cobos has served as music director since 1986. The orchestra performs in the Music Hall, built in 1878 and remodeled in 1971.

Cleveland Orchestra: Founded in 1918, the orchestra occupies Severance Hall, opened in 1931 as a memorial to the wife of a patron. Its early touring program helped spread serious orchestral music throughout the United States. Conductors have included Arthur Rodzinski (1933–43), Erich Leinsdorf (1943–44), and George Szell (1946–70), under whose direction the Cleveland became one of the finest American orchestras. Szell was succeeded by Lorin Maazel (1972–82) and Christoph von Dohnanyi (since 1982). The

orchestra gives summer concerts at the Blossom Music Center in Northampton Township and has made many recordings on the Columbia label, now Sony Classical.

Dresden Staatskapelle (Dresden State Orchestra): The oldest orchestra performing today, the Dresden traces its lineage to 1548, when it was organized to perform concerts at the Saxon Imperial Chapel. In the 20th century, the orchestra flourished under conductors Fritz Reiner (1914–21), Fritz Busch (1922–33), and Karl Böhm (1934–42). Among its post–World War II conductors have been Rudolf Kempe (1949–52), Kurt Sanderling (1964–67), Herbert Blomstedt (1975–85) and, since 1985, Hans Vonk. The orchestra records on the Philips and Angel labels.

Israel Philharmonic: Founded in 1936 as the Palestine Symphony, the Philharmonic is one of the world's most active touring ensembles, performing more than two hundred concerts a year away from Tel Aviv. The orchestra has collaborated with many great conductors, including Arturo Toscanini, Sir John Barbirolli, Leonard Bernstein, Serge Koussevitsky and Eugene Ormandy. In 1981, Zubin Mehta was elected music director for life, in recognition of his long and successful relationship with the group.

Leipzig Gewandhaus Orchestra: Dating from the mid–18th century, this group assumed its modern form around 1781, the year it occupied the Gewandhaus. In 1884 it moved into a larger building and now resides in a modern structure called The Gewandhaus. The orchestra's most influential conductor was Felix Mendelssohn (1825–43), who reintroduced the music of Bach and premiered the Schubert *Great C Major Symphony*. Among his successors have been Wilhelm Furtwängler (1922–29), Bruno Walter (1929–33) and, since 1970, Kurt Masur.

London Philharmonic Orchestra: When this ensemble was established in 1904, Hans Richter conducted its first concerts; he became its principal conductor from 1904 to 1911. Richter's successors have included frequent–guest conductor Arthur Nikisch, Josef Krips (1950–54), Pierre Monteux (1961–64), István Kertész (1965–68), André Previn (1968–79) and, since 1988, Michael Tilson Thomas. Its permanent home is the Barbican Arts Centre.

Los Angeles Philharmonic: Founded in 1919 by William Andrews Clarke, this orchestra was first conducted by Walter Henry Rothwell (1919–27). Subsequent conductors included Otto Klemperer (1933–39), Alfred Wallenstein (1943–56), Zubin Mehta (1962–78), Carlo Maria Giulini (1978–84), and André Previn (1986–89), who resigned after a dispute with the general manager. Finnish conductor Esa-Pekka Salonen was named music director in 1992. The orchestra occupies the Dorothy Chandler Pavilion in downtown Los Angeles and performs summer concerts at the Hollywood Bowl.

Minnesota Orchestra: Founded as the Minneapolis Orchestra in 1903, the orchestra changed its name in 1968 and began to offer a concert series in St. Paul as well. The orchestra's Minneapolis home is Orchestra Hall, designed by Cyril M. Harris; since 1985 its St. Paul home has been the Ordway Music Theater. Its conductors have included Bruno Walter (1922–23), Eugene Ormandy (1931–35), Jose Iturbi (1935–36), Dmitri Mitropoulos (1937–49), Antal Dorati (1949–60), Stanislaw Skrowaczewski (1960–79), Neville Marriner (1979–86) and, since 1986, Edo de Waart.

Montreal Symphony Orchestra/Orchestre Symphonique de Montréal: The symphony descended from two organizations—the Montreal Orchestra and the Orchestre des Concerts Symphoniques. Constituted in 1954, the present ensemble was led by conductors Igor Markevitch (1958–61), Zubin Mehta (1961–67), Franz-Paul Decker (1967–75), and Rafael Frühbeck de Burgos (1975–77).

Charles Dutoit became music director in 1977. The orchestra records on London Records.

New York Philharmonic: Tracing its ancestry to the founding of the Philharmonic-Symphony Society of New York in 1842, this orchestra is the oldest in the United States. During its first decades, the work of its principal conductors—including Leopold Damrosch (1832–85), Anton Seidl (1891–98), and Gustav Mahler (1909–11)—was supplemented by appearances by famous visiting conductors. Among these were Felix Weingartner, Richard Strauss, and Willem Mengelberg. In subsequent years the Society absorbed the New Symphony Orchestra, the National Symphony and, in 1928, the rival New York Symphony Society. Arturo Toscanini served as principal conductor of the combined group from 1930 to 1936. Subsequent conductors included John Barbirolli (1937–42), Arthur Rodzinski (1943–47), Bruno Walter (1947–49), and coconductors Leopold Stokowski and Dmitri Mitropoulos (1949–58). Leonard Bernstein (1958–69) became the orchestra's first American-born conductor. After tenures by Pierre Boulez (1971–77) and Zubin Mehta (1978–91), Kurt Masur became music director in 1991. The Philharmonic offers a regular series of Young People's Concerts. In 1962, it moved from Carnegie Hall to Philharmonic Hall (now Avery Fisher Hall), at Lincoln Center for the Performing Arts.

Orchestre de Paris: This ensemble dates from 1828, when it was founded as the Société des Concerts du Conservatoire. In 1967, during a period of civil and cultural unrest in France, the Conservatoire was disbanded and reconstituted as the Orchestre de Paris. Its conductors have included Charles Munch (1967–68), Serge Baudo (1969–71, with Herbert von Karajan as artistic adviser), Georg Solti (1972–75), Daniel Barenboim (1975–90) and, since

1990, Semyon Bychkov, who came to Paris from the Buffalo Philharmonic Orchestra.

Philadelphia Orchestra: In 1900, this orchestra formed under the sponsorship of the Symphony Society of Philadelphia and was conducted by Fritz Scheel, a student of the celebrated 19th-century conductor Hans von Bulow. A year later the group became the Philadelphia Orchestra Association. Leopold Stokowski conducted from 1912 to 1938, at which time his assistant, Eugene Ormandy, became music director. Ormandy's tenure of more than four decades (1938–80) ranks among the most brilliant in conducting history. He was succeeded by Riccardo Muti (1980–92) and, since 1992, Wolfgang Sawallisch. The orchestra performs at the Academy of Music. Their annual summer season begins in mid-June at the Mann Music Center in Philadelphia. They also appear for three weeks every August at the Saratoga Performing Arts Center in New York State.

Pittsburgh Symphony Orchestra: Established in 1895, this orchestra found the most notable conductor of its early years in American composer and cellist Victor Herbert (1904–10). Disbanding soon afterward, the ensemble reorganized in 1926 and again in 1937. Its later conductors have included Fritz Reiner (1938–48), William Steinberg (1952–76), André Previn (1976–84) and, since 1984, Lorin Maazel. The symphony's first home was the Syria Mosque, but since 1985 it has played in Heinz Hall for the Performing Arts.

St. Louis Symphony Orchestra: Tracing its roots to the founding of the St. Louis Choral Society in 1880, this group claims the rank of second oldest orchestra (after the New York Philharmonic) in the United States. It assumed its current configuration in 1900. Among its conductors have been Vladimir Golschmann (1931–58), Walter Susskind (1968–75) and, since 1979, Leonard Slatkin. The symphony moved from the Kiel Auditorium to the new Powell Symphony Hall in 1968. Since 1969 its summer residence has been the campus of Southern Illinois University, Edwardsville, where it performs as part of the Mississippi River Festival. The orchestra records exclusively for RCA Records/BMG Classics.

St. Paul Chamber Orchestra: Founded in 1959, this is one of the few professional chamber orchestras in the United States. Conductor Dennis Russell Davies (1972–79) fostered the orchestra's commitment to contemporary American repertoire. He was followed by Pinchas Zukerman (1980–85), who revived the classical tradition of conducting while playing the violin. The current music director is Christopher Hogwood, who conducts performances in the Ordway Music Theater.

San Francisco Symphony: Founded in 1911, this orchestra performed its first concerts under the direction of Henry Hadley. Among Hadley's successors have been Alfred Hertz (1915–30), Pierre Monteux (1935–52), Enrique Jorda (1954–63), Josef Krips (1963–70), Seiji Ozawa (1971–76), Edo de Waart (1977–85) and, since 1985, Herbert Blomstedt. Until 1980 the San Francisco Symphony also served as the orchestra of the renowned San Francisco Opera, and both operas and concerts were performed at the War Memorial Theater. The orchestra then split, with the opera orchestra remaining at the theater and the San Francisco Symphony moving into its new home next door, at Louise M. Davies Symphony Hall.

Vienna Philharmonic/Wiener Philharmoniker: This orchestra has offered subscription concerts without interruption since 1860; it was among the first societies to govern itself and elect its own conductor. Comprised of members of the Staatsoper Orchestra, the group has enjoyed the direction of a number of famous conductors, including Hans Richter (1875–98), Gustav Mahler (1898–1901),

Felix Weingartner (1908–27), Wilhelm Furt-wängler (1927–30, 1938–45), and Bruno Walter (1933–38). The Philharmonic's season originally consisted of a series of eight Sunday-morning concerts given in the hall of the Musikverein. There the Philharmonic made Beethoven's symphonies famous and presented the new works of Richard Wagner, Anton Bruckner, Johannes Brahms, Gustav Mahler, Richard Strauss, Maurice Ravel, Igor Stravinsky, and Paul Hindemith. Since 1925, it has been the principal orchestra of the famous summer Salzburg Festival, where it has appeared since 1879. The Vienna Philharmonic has not had a permanent conductor since World War II. Guest conductors have included Karl Böhm, Claudio Abbado, Leonard Bernstein, Lorin Maazel and James Levine.

Introduction to Opera

Opera—a form of theatrical drama that uses singing in place of spoken dialogue—inspires pleasure in some contemporary listeners and confusion in others. Many people unfamiliar with opera mistakenly consider it an inaccessible medium understandable only to the culturally sophisticated. To be sure, speakers of English encounter a language barrier in most operas, but they can nonetheless enjoy the form on a visceral level. Exciting plots unfold, involving murder, illicit love and other charged situations, intensified by music that adds its own emotional heat. The singing itself thrills audiences, as artists with athletic capacity project unamplified voices over an orchestra into the farthest reaches of an auditorium. Even while caught up in the drama of an opera, listeners admire the skillful execution of vocal feats: ringing high notes, rapid strings of notes (coloratura), floating pianissimos. Sometimes the simple loudness and stamina of a singer are enough to dazzle.

No matter how beautiful the music, an opera cannot succeed as opera unless it is based on an engaging, intelligible libretto. A libretto is simply the script of an opera, the document that describes the action and contains the words to be sung by the performers. Because it takes much longer to sing words than to speak them, librettos must be very compressed, matching a minimum of verbiage to a maximum of plot. Some librettos squeeze additional text into recitative passages that are half-spoken and half-sung, while certain types of opera allow spoken dialogue as well. Still, operas contain far fewer words than plays of comparable length; as a result many librettos, standing alone, suffer from sketchiness and literary crudity. Opera, however, has the advantage of evocative music that brings subtlety to plots and depth to characterizations.

A brief survey of opera must be confined to works that are actually performed with some frequency. While some of the less familiar early operas—those written before the time of Mozart—have recently been revived with great success, they remain relatively obscure. Among the important early opera composers were Jean-Baptiste Lully (1632–74) and George Frideric Handel, as well as Christoph Willibald Gluck, best remembered for *Orpheus and Euridice* (1762). Claudio Monteverde's *The Coronation of Poppea* (1642) proves how compelling and even contemporary an opera written centuries ago can remain.

OPERA TERMS

The world of opera has its own specific terminology. Consider the following:

The most familiar operatic terms delineate the vocal range of singers. In descending order of vocal range, the basic voice types for women are *soprano, mezzo-soprano* (literally, "half-soprano") and *contralto*. For men, the terms *tenor, baritone, bass-baritone* and *bass* designate the highest to lowest voices.

Certain words describe the "weight" of operatic voices. For instance, a *dramatic* voice has more power and amplitude than a *lyric* voice; a *spinto* voice lies between these two types. A *coloratura* is a light, high soprano capable of great agility, while a *Heldentenor* ("heroic tenor") has the volume to make himself heard over the huge orchestras used in Wagnerian opera. *Countertenors* are men who sing in a developed falsetto.

There are also terms for the various types of acting employed in opera. A *character tenor* specializes in humorous and/or sinister roles. A *buffo* is a bass who plays comedic parts, which often call for the delivery of rapid patter. A *trouser role* is one in which a female singer plays a boy or very young man, a convention requiring some willing suspension of disbelief on the part of the audience.

For humanitarian reasons, opera no longer uses *castrati,* men emasculated before their change of voice. Said to possess both the range of the female voice and the powerful lung capacity of the male, these legendary singers have no equivalent today. Their starring roles in Baroque opera must now be assigned to women or countertenors, or else shifted to a lower range than originally intended and sung by tenors and baritones.

Mozart and the Birth of Modern Opera

Although a number of composers successfully experimented with opera before he did, Wolfgang Amadeus Mozart ushered the form into the modern era. In many respects, his innovations determined the course that opera would take in the hands of subsequent composers. Familiarity with his works is therefore essential to an understanding of opera. In particular, *The Marriage of Figaro* (1786) and *Don Giovanni* (1787) embody the genius of this towering figure of the genre. While writing these two operas, as well as *Così fan tutte* (1790), Mozart worked with a talented and worthy collaborator, Lorenzo Da Ponte (1749–1838).

The Marriage of Figaro may be an *opera buffa* ("comic opera"), but its premise is deadly serious: Without ever openly opposing him, the servant Figaro must prevent his master, the Count, from stealing away his fiancée, Susanna, who is the Countess's maid. The opera celebrates the triumph of resourcefulness and wit over power and rank, while presenting charming and believable characters. Figaro transforms outrage into playfulness; Susanna expresses her deep love for Figaro by teasing him. The young page Cherubino, meanwhile, possesses a winning combination of boyishness and raging libido that amuses the ladies.

Although dispirited by her husband's straying, the Countess participates in the scheming of Figaro and Susanna. Each character retains his or her individuality even in the midst of complex interaction.

Centering around the legend of Don Juan, Mozart's *Don Giovanni* is a remarkable amalgam of comedy and tragedy. His collaborator Da Ponte, in fact, coined the term *dramma giocoso* (literally, "funny drama") to describe it. Endlessly and futilely throwing herself at the bored Don, who has already seduced and tired of her, Donna Elvira is at once ridiculous and pitiable. Similarly, the Don's final proud refusal to repent in the face of hellfire inspires both horror and admiration. Mozart supported the extravagance of his characters with a singularly dramatic score that had a profound influence on the composers of the Romantic period.

To the dismay of 19th-century audiences and the delight of their 20th-century counterparts, *Così fan tutte* ("All Women Behave Thus") takes a decidedly unromantic view of human relations. Courted by two supposed strangers (in reality, each other's fiancé in disguise) the opera's two antiheroines express exaggerated indignation that reflects poorly on the honesty of woman. Mozart paralleled the moral with music that broadly parodies serious opera.

Shortly before his untimely death, Mozart wrote a final *singspiel,* a kind of German opera with spoken dialogue. The libretto of *The Magic Flute* (1791) is a curious mixture of fairy tale, solemn Masonic ritual and broad clowning, which some audiences find baffling and others deeply moving. Equally diverse, Mozart's score contains a dizzying profusion of styles and forms. He created chatty ensembles for the wicked queen's henchwomen, naive folklike songs for the blithe bird-catcher, serious and exalted arias for the noble Sarastro, and even a fugal passage for the scene of the armored men. More than any other single work, *The Magic Flute* sums up and encapsulates Mozart's vast musical imagination.

OPERETTA

Like so many musical terms, *operetta* is loosely used and difficult to define. Presumably lighter than operas in subject matter, operettas are comedic, satirical and even sentimental—but never tragic. They are also lighter in form: Spoken dialogue alternates with songs and other musical numbers. Often colloquial, operetta may incorporate slang and local accents and allude to topical and regional issues.

Jacques Offenbach's saucy French operettas established the form. In such works as *Orpheus in the Underworld* (1858), he poked fun at serious opera. Delicately orchestrated and featuring skillfully conceived ensembles, the operettas of Johann Strauss, Jr., not only won popular success but also the esteem of composers such as Johannes Brahms and Gustav Mahler. The era of Strauss and Franz von Suppé (1819–95) is often deemed the "golden age" of Viennese operetta, while the "silver age" encompasses the more sentimental works of Franz Lehár (1870–1947) and the Hungarian-flavored works of Emmerich Kálmán (1882–1953).

Most familiar to English-speaking fans of operetta are the Victorian works of Gilbert and Sullivan, in which W. S. Gilbert's brilliant verse and quirky humor play as great a role as Arthur Sullivan's cultivated music. In America, Victor Herbert (1859–1924) produced a profusion of beautifully refined scores that were doomed by ineffective librettos. After the early hits of Sigmund Romberg (1887–1951) in the 1920s, American operetta was subsumed by the still more vernacular musical comedy presented in theaters. Since then, time has blurred the distinction between "high" and "popular" art, so that today's major opera companies frequently include certain operettas in their repertoire.

Italian Opera

The first generation of composers to elaborate on Mozart's legacy included many Italians, who no doubt gravitated to the genre because of their culture's enduring affection for vocal forms. A distinct style of opera emerged in Italy and was soon named *bel canto* (literally, "beautiful singing"). Although the term has also been applied to other kinds of opera and singing, it commonly designates the operatic style exemplified by the work of Gioacchino Rossini, Gaetano Donizetti, and Vincenzo Bellini (1801–31). In contrast to the heavier, more declamatory operas that came later, bel canto works emphasize the singing skills of performers through long, sustained vocal lines and the agile delivery of coloratura, rapid series of notes.

Rossini is best remembered for such comic operas as *The Barber of Seville* (1816) and *La Cenerentola* ("Cinderella," 1817). Some of his music expresses a delightfully malicious sense of humor, as in the quintet from *Barber,* in which four characters conspire to get rid of Don Basilio by persuading him that he is ill.

Several of Donizetti's numerous operas are still performed regularly. One of these, *Don Pasquale* (1843), is a miracle of economy in that every element advances the story of an infatuated old man's humiliation. In *The Elixir of Love* (1832), a warmer comedy, Adina reluctantly comes to realize that she loves the doting Nemorino, who is supposedly simpleminded. In the last act, "Una Furtiva Lagrima" ("One Secret Tear") is one of the most beloved arias for lyric tenor. Based on the novel by Sir Walter Scott (1771–1832), *Lucia di Lammermoor* (1835) contains such inspirations as the famous sextet in which the characters explore intense emotions in a moment of high conflict. Tradition has turned this opera's mad scene into a playground for added high notes and coloratura displays.

Bellini's name is forever linked with the phenomenon of melody, for he gloried in a generous gift for expressive vocal lines. The title role of *Norma* (1831), the opera for which he is best remembered, has acquired a special mystique among singers and fans. Vocally, the part of the Druid priestess demands a full, rich sound and exceptional agility; dramatically, it requires an imposing presence and expressiveness over a wide range of extreme emotions. When a great soprano decides to tackle this role, it becomes not simply a performance but an event.

Building on the foundations laid by the bel canto composers, Giuseppe Verdi composed his first opera in 1839 and his last in 1893. During this long and fruitful career, he constantly changed and refined his style, producing one of the greatest *oeuvres* in opera. Early efforts, such as the familiar aria "Ernani, involami" ("Ernani, let's run away") from *Ernani* (1844), display the new sweep and energy that Verdi brought to the bel canto style. But he did not stop there, instead moving on to bold experimentation almost immediately. In *Macbeth* (first version, 1847), a prime example of his early breakthroughs is Lady Macbeth's muted, eerie sleepwalking scene that forgoes conventional melody altogether.

Even the three famous operas of Verdi's middle period, composed one right after another, are impressively differentiated. *Rigoletto* (1851) focuses on a most unconventional title role: a hunchbacked and immoral jester whose only virtue is his love for his daughter. But the opera depicts this love with such conviction and detail that the audience feels deep sympathy for Rigoletto. *Il Trovatore* (1853) contains the kind of plot device for which opera has often been criticized. The story centers on an enraged gypsy who, seeking revenge on her enemy, plans to burn his infant son but mistakenly kills her own instead. Though the situation may strain credibility, audiences willing to suspend disbelief can enjoy an archetypically operatic display of raw emotion set to a particularly virile and robust score. In *La Traviata* (1853), Verdi presents an especially lurid subject. Basing the opera on a story by Alexandre Dumas, Jr. (1824–95), he graphically tells the tale of a courtesan who falls in love with a young, innocent provincial man, tries unsuccessfully to live down her past, and then dies of tuberculosis. This intimate opera includes a long, subtle and touching duet in which her lover's father slowly persuades the courtesan, Violetta, that it is her duty to relinquish his son.

Between "the big three" and *Aïda* (1871), Verdi wrote several operas that, over the years, have failed to attract as large a following, probably due to libretto problems. The script of *Don Carlo* (1867), for instance, contains a number of plot lines, none of them clearly central. While the web of intersecting relationships lends the opera a special richness, it also makes the story harder to follow than, say, that of *La Traviata* or *Aïda*. Despite its bombastic moments and the dominating presence of elephants in the triumphal scene, *Aïda* features a subtle score. As foreshadowed by its delicate, contrapuntal prelude, the opera's music sparkles with myriad evocative orchestral details. The tenor's "Celeste Aïda" ("Heavenly Aïda"), for example, has broad, catchy melody enhanced by the shimmering orchestral textures that surround it.

In his eighties, Verdi performed the inspiring feat of composing two remarkable operas that heralded a new phase in his development. *Otello* (1887) and *Falstaff* (1893) were based not on simplistic reductions of the plays by William Shakespeare (1564–1616), but on faithful adaptations by Arrigo Boito (1849–1919), himself a gifted composer. As much as these two works differ from each other, both showed a new degree of continuity in Verdi's music. The recitatives have so much melodic profile and the musical numbers so much flexibility that the distinction between the two is artfully blurred. In *Otello,* as in Shakespeare's play, Desdemona interrupts her willow song with spontaneous reflections, while in a stroke of musical irony, Iago's insidious murmuring at the close of his first big scene with Otello overlaps with the beginning of the joyful choral serenade that follows. In *Falstaff,* Alice's most memorable vocal lines appear not in an aria but in the midst of a gossipy ensemble of the merry wives. Despite the absence of easily hummable numbers, the overwhelming intensity of *Otello* and the bubbling musical inventiveness of *Falstaff* have won them popularity.

As Verdi's career drew to a close, younger Italian composers began to favor the notion of *verismo,* or operatic realism. In doing so, they took as their subjects believable, ordinary people instead of monarchs and mad gypsies. *Cavalleria Rusticana* (1890) by Pietro Mascagni (1863–1945) virtually defines the term. Fast-moving, hot-blooded and violent, its story seems thoroughly journalistic even today. Ruggiero Leoncavallo (1858–1919), in fact, based *I Pagliacci* (1892) on an actual murder case. Verismo, however, eventually became associated with the forceful, declamatory style of singing that these subjects demanded.

Virtually all Puccini's mature operas are produced today, and several rank among the most popular of all operas. But because he made few musical innovations, many musicians and critics begrudge him his large niche in the repertoire. Despite these criticisms, he was endowed with more than the gift of melody. Audiences may love his big, memorable numbers, but between them he crafted musical tissue of admirable sophistication and interest.

Puccini excelled in carefully building an act to a shattering climax. The youthful high spirits of the would-be artists in Puccini's *La Bohème* (1896) make Mimi's death at the opera's ending all the more poignant. *Tosca* (1900), on the other hand, revels in an especially extravagant theatricality: In just the second act, Tosca, a willful and capricious opera singer, is nearly raped, is forced to witness the torture of her lover, and is finally driven to stab her tormentor with a knife from his own dinner table. The Japanese setting of *Madame Butterfly* (1904) inspired Puccini to create a score of unusual delicacy and almost unbearable pathos. The audience can foresee the destruction of the vulnerable fifteen-year-old geisha even before she appears on stage.

Those who find most of Puccini's work overly sentimental still admire two of the three one-act pieces—*Il Tabarro* and *Gianni Schicchi*—that constitute *Il Trittico* (1918). *Gianni Schicchi* is a comedy about a money-grubbing family determined to circumvent the will of a rich relative. In *Turandot,* his last opera, Puccini leavens the story of Prince Calaf's courtship of icy, man-hating Turandot with gigantic choral scenes and with cynical clowning by the three sinister courtiers. The tenor aria "Nessum dorma" ("No one shall sleep") has become one of the most famous in all opera.

French Opera

Although the body of French opera cannot rival that of Italian opera for sheer volume, French composers have made important contributions to the genre. Giacomo Meyerbeer (1791–1864) was one of the great influences on 19th-century opera, but his works have long since fallen out of the standard repertoire.

Hector Berlioz's monumental and highly original *Les Troyens* (composed 1856–58) is acknowledged as one of the masterpieces of opera, but it is too expensive and insufficiently popular to be produced with any frequency. And while Charles Gounod's *Faust* (1859), once one of the most popular of operas, has a musically admirable score, its prettiness clashes disturbingly with its subject. By contrast, Gounod used his sweet, lyric gift to great advantage in *Roméo et Juliette* (1867).

But by whatever criteria one can judge opera—melody, orchestration, ensemble writing, characterization, dramatic pacing—George Bizet's *Carmen* (1875) is a masterpiece that still delights both sophisticated and less knowledgeable listeners. The heedlessness with which Carmen uses and discards lovers, and the boldness with which she scorns the slightest attempt to save her from her fate, make her not only one of the most gripping characters in opera but also a universal prototype. Those who have never seen *Carmen* know who she is. Bizet died shortly after composing *Carmen,* but with this one work he was transformed from a promising opera composer to a major one.

Jacques Offenbach's comedic gift, featured in his many operettas, also served his one serious opera. In *The Tales of Hoffmann,* he expertly captured the strange fantasies and quirky, morbid humor of German writer E. T. A. Hoffmann (1776–1822). Offenbach died in 1880, before he had committed the opera to its final form, and so performances and published editions contain significant variations.

Another French composer, Jules Massenet, wrote one of the few major French operas with French subject matter. *Manon* (1884) possesses a score notable for its urbane refinement and elegance as well as its passion.

Were it not for *Pelléas and Mélisande* (1902), audiences might never have imagined that Claude Debussy's soft-textured, elusive music could serve opera. He found the perfect subject for his unique style, however, in the ambiguous, symbolic Maurice Maeterlinck (1862–1949) play on which he based his opera of the same name. The scene in which Mélisande lets down her hair from a tower to envelop Pélleas below is as erotic as anything in music. Debussy heightened the sensuality of the opera by connecting its scenes with orchestral interludes that gave each act a flowing continuity. His opera is faithful to Maeterlinck in both spirit and text.

German Opera

Only Italian opera rivals German opera for scope, versatility and quantity. Between the careers of Mozart and Richard Wagner, German opera produced but two enduring works: Ludwig van Beethoven's *Fidelio* (1814) and Carl Maria von Weber's *Der Freischütz* (1821). Beethoven's only opera, in which the heroine manages to liberate her husband from unjust and illegal imprisonment just in time to save his life, exhibits the exalted mood found in many of his best-known instrumental works. Because Beethoven was notorious for writing technically difficult music, the singers who perform *Fidelio* are as heroic as the characters they play. *Der Freischütz* remains one of the seminal works of German Romanticism, filled with evocative elements, such as the spooky Wolf's Glen scene—in which a diabolical pact is sealed at midnight—and a folkish, irresistible hunting chorus. Wagner loved it, and his music owed much to its dark, rich orchestral and harmonic colors.

Although the creation of opera usually involves a good deal of collaboration, Wagner's operas expressed his idiosyncratic vision alone. Not only did he write his own librettos, he also directed the operas on stage and even designed the famous theater at Bayreuth specifically for their performance. In doing so, he revolutionized not only opera but classical music in general. By inventing a coherent syntax of chords that would previously have been considered unrelated, Wagner paved the way for the 20th-century weakening and subsequent rejection of tonality. In this respect, he influenced composers of utterly different sensibilities, such as Debussy and Schönberg.

Wagner's operas elevated the orchestra to unprecedented importance, not simply by allowing it to pour out such a grand flood of sound but by assigning it such a large share of the melodic interest. Unlike previous operas, his work does not consist strictly of vocal melody and orchestral accompaniment. Instead, the voices accompany the orchestra, in one sense. Logically, Wagner's innovation initiated a new approach to singing—one that was violently reviled by his detractors as unnatural and pushed. Undeterred, he pioneered even further, moving beyond style to form. The acts of his operas came to resemble vastly expanded symphonic movements that continuously developed a number of short motifs. This continuous structure is harder for listeners to assimilate than the older division into discrete arias and set pieces, but the sheer sonority and power of Wagner's music draws listeners to it.

Almost from the beginning, Wagner was drawn to large, symbolic themes. In each of his first two mature operas, *The Flying Dutchman* (1843) and *Tannhäuser* (1845), a man who has brought a curse upon himself is miraculously redeemed from the wrath of heaven by the innocent love of a self-sacrificing woman. The bold score of *Tannhäuser* explores emotional extremes, from Venus's sensual revels to Tannhäuser's anguished repentance. The title character of *Lohengrin* (1850), a knight of the Holy Grail come down to earth, makes perhaps the most famous entrance in all of opera: He appears on a skiff drawn by a swan. The bridal chorus in Act III is a tune known to all Americans as "Here Comes the Bride."

While most operas deal with love, the kind of all-consuming, obsessive love that can be consummated only in death is exemplified by Wagner's *Tristan und Isolde* (1865). From the first sighing phrase of the prelude to the last faint shudder of Isolde's "Liebestod" ("love-death" scene), the opera's score constructs an imposing monument to yearning. The pervasive chromaticism of the music represents a milestone in music history that announced the beginning of the dissolution of tonality. In fact, the term *Tristan chord* entered the language of music theory. The incomplete resolution of this chord made it a potent symbol of unfulfilled longing. Demonstrating the degree to which *Tristan und Isolde* shifted the musical emphasis from the stage to the orchestra pit, the "Liebestod" is frequently played as an orchestral piece without the voice part.

Wagner's one mature comedy, *Die Meistersinger von Nürnberg* (1868), illustrates his gift for adapting his musical style to the subject of each opera. With its preference for bright major keys and diatonic harmonies, this opera inhabits an entirely different world from that of *Tristan*.

One of the most ambitious works in all of Western art, Wagner's *The Ring of the Nibelung* (known as "The Ring Cycle") is a cycle of four full-length operas, written over several decades and first produced complete in 1874. Based on Norse legend, the cycle creates a mythical world of elemental power, which has been the subject of endless interpretation. The operas of the cycle display a profound disdain for practicality, challenging not only the skills of the performers but the theater's technical resources. For example, it begins with mermaids swimming in the Rhine and ends with the destruction of Valhalla, home of the gods, in a conflagration. If an audience cannot relate to the power struggles of gods, goddesses, giants and dwarfs portrayed in the introductory opera, *Das Rheingold,* they will no doubt be moved by the second, *Die Walküre.* The most popular and accessible of the Ring operas, it narrates the doomed, incestuous love of Siegmund and Sieglinde, and Brünnhilde's heroic protection of their child, Siegfried, in defiance of Wotan. *Siegfried* is a cheerful episode in the cycle; in it the impetuous young Siegfried frees himself from the exploitative Mime, ventures out into the world, and awakens Brünnhilde to love. In *Götterdämmerung* ("The Twilight of the Gods"), Siegfried and Brünnhilde are tricked into betraying one another, and Siegfried is treacherously slain, precipitating the collapse of the entire world of the Ring. This apocalyptic vision inspires a score full of tragic grandeur. Brünnhilde's immolation scene—the longest solo scene in the standard opera repertoire—gives some idea of the score's majesty.

Parsifal (1882), Wagner's last opera, returns to the knights of the Holy Grail, a subject touched upon in *Lohengrin.* In his second treatment of this subject, he was able to realize the mysterious, mythic atmosphere only hinted at in the earlier work, because of the expanded harmonic language developed in *Tristan.* The somber *Parsifal* has an extraordinarily slow, hypnotic pace; even those passages with fast tempos have a fluid, pulseless quality.

Wagner's operas continue to provoke impassioned partisanship and controversy. They are likely to leave a listener enthralled or repulsed, rather than indifferent. One other "Wagnerian" opera remains in the active repertoire: Engelbert Humperdinck's fairytale opera *Hänsel und Gretel* (1893) brings the gigantic machinery of Wagnerism to bear on a simple story. Children delight especially in the witch's poorly concealed malevolence.

Richard Strauss expanded on the technical innovations of Wagner to produce a highly individual body of work that contrasted with his predecessor's. In his sensationalistic *Salome* (1905), Strauss trumped the self-conscious decadence of the play by Oscar Wilde (1854–1900), culminating with the young Salome's obsessive, lascivious oration to the severed head of John the Baptist. The score's sudden shifts of key and excessive, hyperactive orchestration leave the listener dazed and exhausted. After the similarly disturbed and violent *Elektra* (1909), Strauss surprised his public with *Der Rosenkavalier* (1911). Set in 18th-century Vienna, the libretto, by Hugo von Hofmannsthal (1874–1929), is at once hilarious and profound, its characterization of the Marshallin setting a model for the graceful acceptance of aging. The liveliness, elegance and warmth of the score pay homage to Mozart, while the story's Viennese setting inspired Strauss to introduce the intentional anachronism of waltz strains recalling those of the (unrelated) Johann Strauss, Jr. Another well-known Strauss opera is *Ariadne auf Naxos* (final version, 1916), a comedy without chorus, scored for an energetic chamber orchestra and accessible to smaller opera houses.

Another 20th-century Austrian applied advanced musical techniques to opera with great success. Alban Berg's emotional warmth and dramatic flair made his work appealing to audiences, even as he experimented with challenging music. Despite its awesome musical complexity, *Wozzeck* (1925) caused an immediate international sensation when it appeared. Audiences who cannot begin to grasp the cerebral formal scheme of the music still respond to the opera's raw drama and to the composer's compassion for his tortured protagonist. Berg was not afraid to use whatever musical means would serve the moment, including frank, old-fashioned tonality. In his second opera, *Lulu* (1935), Berg resourcefully employs the twelve-tone system without altering his basic musical personality. The enigmatic, morally ambiguous libretto of *Lulu* makes it endlessly fascinating to some listeners and troubling to others.

Kurt Weill's best-known stage works are not opera per se; they are more often produced theatrically than by opera houses. But he created his own genre of musical drama, and at least one of his compositions, *The Rise and Fall of the City of Mahagonny* (1930, based on an earlier one-act treatment composed in 1928) demands the resources of the opera. This devastating critique of capitalism depicts an entire fictional city, complete with prize-fight ring and brothel. One number in particular, the famous "Alabama-song," is an unforgettable blend of squalid realism and romantic yearning.

Russian and Czech Opera

Although Russia boasts a rich operatic heritage that includes such composers as Michael Glinka (1804–57), Sergei Prokofiev and Dimitri Shostakovich, Western audiences have particular difficulty penetrating the Russian language barrier. Despite this impediment, Modest Mussorgsky's *Boris Godunov* (1874) has become a classic even in the West. Its title character dominates the opera whenever he appears, riveting audiences with his guilty hallucinations stimulated by the sound of a chiming clock. But the opera's carousing monks, lamenting village idiot, and realistic crowd scenes also offer a wonderfully panoramic experience. Debussy acknowledged Mussorgsky's boldly original work as an influence. Peter Tchaikovsky's *Evgeny Onegin* (1879) and *The Queen of Spades* (1890) are also performed internationally.

Language is likewise an impediment to the performance of Czech opera. Still, the charming folk comedy *The Bartered Bride* (1866) by Bedřich Smetana (1824–84) is well known, and Leoš Janáček (1854–1928) holds an increasingly important place in the 20th-century repertoire. Janáček's *Jenufa* (1904) illustrates his predilection for free, speechlike vocal lines and displays a realism that makes Italian verismo seem artificial by contrast. *The Cunning Little Vixen* (1923) treats its animal characters without condescension.

Operas in English

With the exception of Henry Purcell's *Dido and Aeneas* (1689), a work of dignity and charm, the English-language operas performed today come largely from the 20th century. Benjamin Britten's first and best-known opera, *Peter Grimes* (1945), sets its tragic story against the backdrop of a small English fishing village. Easily mounted without great expense, Britten's chamber operas, such as *The Rape of Lucretia* (1946) and *Albert Herring* (1947), are a boon to schools and smaller opera companies. Also set in England is the libretto for Igor Stravinsky's *The Rake's Progress* (1951) by poet W. H. Auden and Chester Kallman. A morality tale suggested by the rowdy engravings of William Hogarth (1697–1764), the work has a score that pays affectionate homage to 18th-century opera.

In the United States, George Gershwin's *Porgy and Bess* (1935), set in an African-American neighborhood in Charleston, S.C., has enjoyed enduring success. The early practice of replacing great quantities of Gershwin's music with spoken dialogue resulted in the false impression, long held, that *Porgy and Bess* was more a musical than an opera. In recent years, more faithful productions by major opera companies have proved the work to be grand and sweeping, very much in the operatic tradition. More recently, Philip Glass (*Satyagraha*) and John Adams (*Nixon in China*) have brought new audiences to the opera house. Their pageantlike operas, based on recent and distant history, incorporate dance and stylized movement.

OPERA COMPANIES AROUND THE WORLD

The history of opera is inextricably linked with the history of the world's famous opera houses. So closely identified are the glamour and heritage of the great opera companies with the splendor of the buildings they occupy that opera affi-cionados do not differentiate between these or-ganizations and their homes. For a resident ensemble with a long tradition of notable perfor-mances in a structure specially designed for op-era, the name of the company is most often the name of the venue. One need say no more than a single name to communicate both who is pro-ducing an opera and where it is being per-formed. Indeed, the notions of "opera company" and "opera house" have become indistinguish-able.

Among opera's best-known institutions are La Fenice in Venice and La Scala in Milan, both of which date from the 18th century and boast a direct role in the development of opera. La Fenice, for instance, premiered *Rigoletto* and La Scala premiered *Turandot*. Other internationally famous companies are the Wiener Saatsoper in Vienna, Covent Garden in London, the Metropolitan Opera in New York, the Chicago Lyric and the San Francisco Opera.

Because air travel has made it easy for big opera stars to perform all over the world, opera has lost some of its regional differences. Today, audiences in Vienna or Paris might hear essentially the same performances as those in New York or Chicago. Some companies have nevertheless preserved their individual character. For example, Bayreuth's covered orchestra pit allows for a unique balance of instrumental, vocal and dramatic elements in its Wagnerian productions. Glyndebourne, opera's summer home in England, is famous for the intimacy of its productions, while the outdoor opera at Italy's Baths of Caracalla is renowned for its expansiveness.

America has witnessed an enormous proliferation of regional opera, which has brought excellent productions to areas outside the largest cities. These less assuming companies may actually stage works that rely on ensemble acting (instead of sheer vocalism) more successfully than their grander counterparts do. Smaller cities without resident companies may also host touring productions sent out by companies such as the New York City Opera, the Houston Opera and the San Francisco Opera. Such opportunities allow opera fans across the country to experience opera as it was meant to be heard: in live performance.

Sacred Music

Music has always been inextricably linked to humanity's attempt to comprehend, explain and worship its deities. In almost every religion, music is thought to place the worshipper on a higher spiritual level, closer to God. Just as music has played a central role in religion and worship, religion has exerted, and continues to exert, a potent influence on musical composition and performance. An entire genre of music, in fact, devotes itself to the celebration of religious entities and values.

Sacred music has taken innumerable forms that employ a wide variety of compositional techniques and types of performers. Because it can draw the community into worship, choral music predominates in monasteries, synagogues, churches, theaters, concert halls and arenas. This is not to say that instrumental or solo vocal music is less important; indeed, some of Europe's most spiritually evocative music was written for the organ, as "sacred symphonies" for other instruments, or as devotional songs for the solo voice. But the powerful symbolism embodied by a chorus, as it gives voice to the soul of the entire community, has propelled choral music to the forefront of sacred composition.

During ancient times, all music—including sacred music—was transmitted to future generations via the oral tradition. Only gradually did a system of written notation develop. As a result, little of the music of ancient Egypt, Greece and Rome survives today. For similar reasons, it is equally difficult to determine the exact age of the ancient chants and instrumental music still used in Tibetan Buddhist monasteries and Orthodox Jewish synagogues, and in the Masses of the Eastern Orthodox and Roman Catholic churches, to name but a few. In all of these traditions, the most prevalent form of sacred musical expression was the chant. Chant describes a kind of rhythmically free-flowing, unharmonized, monophonic melody often intoned by the single voice of a cantor and then repeated by a larger group. In different religious traditions, these ancient tunes are still sung as they were thousands of years ago.

The evangelical fervor of the Christian Church, most specifically the Roman Catholic Church during the first centuries of the Christian era, accelerated the development of Christian music. Thus, in the West, a greater variety of sacred music forms developed over a shorter period than in other parts of the world, as the musical traditions of converted Jews, Greeks, Romans, Egyptians, Syrians and others were absorbed. Within a few hundred years, the Roman Church had attained such high levels of political and financial organization that it could exert a great deal of control over the development of music for liturgical purposes. The Church also fostered some experimentation with notation and encouraged the codification of a written form for the ancient chants.

Many chant traditions developed among early Christians, but in the Roman Church the one that would be perfected most quickly was Gregorian chant. The form was named after Gregory I, Pope from 590 to 604, who supposedly received the chants directly from the Holy Spirit. During his reign the chant melodies were standardized, and by the 8th century the chants were codified along with a theory explaining their modes (scales). The evolving form of the chants allowed for the development of polyphony (the combination of more than one voice part in counterpoint) and homophony (the use of several voice parts of a similar, rhythmically identical design).

The Church's patronage during the Middle Ages and Renaissance led to a gradual increase in the variety of European musical expression. Longer, more intricate compositions appeared, new instruments were invented and adapted to liturgical use, and musicians started to accompany multiple voices with instruments. High Renaissance sacred music reached its pinnacle in the perfectly balanced, conservative compositions of Giovanni Luigi da Palestrina (1525–94), who served as papal court composer in the latter part of the 16th century. Simultaneously, composers adapted less severe, more sensual, and lighter secular musical forms to church music. This trend continued for nearly five hundred years; even today, religious music is becoming more secularized, and popular music has been adapted for liturgical use.

Soon after the birth of opera in early 17th-century Italy, sacred music grew more passionate and dramatic; religious counterparts to opera developed soon thereafter, during the Baroque period. One of these, the oratorio, consisted basically of an opera without sets and costumes. Rather than the mythological subjects of most operas of the period, oratorios set Biblical stories to the splendid type of music developed in Baroque opera: Large-scale choruses, passionate recitatives, virtuosic arias and picturesque instrumental interludes became a part of church music.

By rejecting the philosophy and many of the practices of Roman Catholicism, the Protestant Reformation offered new avenues of expression to sacred composers. Thus, as the Roman Catholic Church continued to commission composers to write new motets, canticles, psalms, vespers and Masses, the Lutheran Church in Germany refined the cantata (which in Italy had most often been a secular work) for its specific religious purposes. Meanwhile, the Anglican Church created the verse anthem, and other denominations also pursued innovations.

By the 18th century, religious and secular musical styles became nearly interchangeable. Composers, such as Johann Sebastian Bach, George Frideric Handel and Wolfgang Amadeus Mozart, recast their own secular cantatas and operas as religious works, and took their sacred works into secular contexts. Mozart, for instance, was often taken to task by his patron and employer, the Prince-Archbishop of Salzburg, for what the prince considered to be Mozart's overly sensual, operatic Mass settings. Nevertheless, the cross-fertilization of sacred music with opera yielded some of the best-known masterpieces in all of sacred music: Handel's *Messiah* (1742), Bach's *St. Matthew Passion* (1727) and Mozart's unfinished *Requiem* (1791). During the 19th century, sweeping sacred works, such as Ludwig van Beethoven's massive *Missa Solemnis* (1819–23) and Hector Berlioz's *Requiem* (1837), to name only two examples, could no longer be performed at church services because of their length, symphonic tendencies and technical demands. Giuseppe Verdi's *Messa de Requiem* (1874) was so far removed from the liturgical context that it was dubbed his best opera.

During the 19th century, music of all descriptions continued to be written to meet the needs of specific churches at specific times. The grandeur of the old Roman Catholic traditions attracted composers of the Romantic period, who wrote concert music along sacred lines. Hundreds of Requiem Masses were written during this time such as Johannes Braham's *A German Requiem* (1854–68).

Starting in the late 19th century, religious music experienced an even more diverse flowering as the stylistic boundaries between religious and secular blurred even further. Applied to religious texts, folk melodies added an earthiness to the religious music of the United States, as exemplified by numerous popular hymns and African-American spirituals. Classical composers of the 20th century, such as Igor Stravinsky, Benjamin Britten and Leonard Bernstein, infused new life into the old forms of the Mass, motet, cantata and oratorio.

In the 20th century, the sacred music of the West picked up traces of the religious and musical practices of Asian, African, South American and Native American cultures. Popular music, jazz, blues, rock and folk styles showed up in the synagogues, churches and temples of an increasingly secularized society. Instead of spending a lifetime in only one religious tradition, sacred musicians could now explore many different forms. Christian rock bands perform at sports arenas, Christian folk songs fill Catholic churches and televangelist programs, Broadway-style tunes reverberate in synagogues, Gospel choirs sing the blues in recording studios, and Eastern Orthodox choirs perform in concert halls. New forms continue to develop, as do new outlooks on the role of sacred music in society.

International Ethnic Music

Since prehistory, ordinary people, no matter where or in what time they have lived, have expressed themselves through music. Whether that music consists of the simple percussion of rattles or complex ritual drumming, of energetic chanting or delicate vocal harmonizing, of meditative sitar improvisations or joyful panpipe tunes, it has fed the human heart and exalted the soul. Some ethnic music plays a role in worship, while some celebrates the culture that created it or simply entertains those who play and listen to it. In common with Western classical forms, eastern and western ethnic music claims ancient roots and time-honored traditions. But unlike formal orchestral music, folk forms transcend the concert hall to pervade everyday life; they are created, performed and enjoyed by people at all levels of society. This section outlines the major ethnic musical styles played around the world today.

Sub-Saharan Africa

Home to hundreds of peoples and languages, the continent of Africa extends over more than 11,000,000 square miles, making it the world's second-largest continent. It is no surprise, then, that this vast land mass produces a great diversity of music and musical styles. The music typically identified as African comes mostly from the southern two-thirds of the continent, which was long isolated from the rest of the world by the forbidding barrier of the Sahara desert. Via trade and slavery since the 16th century, however, this music has spread far beyond Africa to influence the cultures and music of other lands, in particular South and North America.

apala (Nigeria): Vocal and percussion music popularized by the late Haruna Ishola, apala offers a mixture of Muslim proverbs and traditional folklore that commands huge audiences among Nigeria's Yoruba people.

benga (Kenya): Greatly influenced by the rolling guitar lines and fast-paced rhythms of *soukous,* benga was created by the Luo people of western Kenya.

bikutsi (Cameroon): The music and dance of the Beti people, who reside in the western rain forest around the capital of Yaounde, bikutsi features riveting triple beats. The word itself means "beat the earth"; the music was originally used to enrage men before they went to war. Les Tête Brulées numbers among the best-known groups performing bikutsi.

chimurenga (Zimbabwe): Developed by the political singer-songwriter Thomas Mapfumo in the 1980s, this music is based on Shona *m'bira* playing. Its name means "liberation struggle music."

fuji (Nigeria): Descended from *apala,* this popular music celebrates the Islamic festival of Ramadan. It is acoustic music like *benga* or *chimurenga* that mixes different drums—talking, bata, bells and shekere. Alhaji Barrister and Ayinla Kollington rank as its best-known performers.

griots (Mali, Guinea, Senegal and Gambia): These are sacred storytellers or oral historians who sing songs recounting the history of their people, kings and ancestors. Their skills have been passed down from generation to generation, especially among the Wolof, Senafu, Peul, Toutcouleurs and Mandinke tribes, who were once part of the empire of Mali, which reached its peak in the 14th century.

highlife (Nigeria): A dance music from Ghana and eastern Nigeria, it became popular between the 1920s and the 1950s. Highlife had two distinctive genres: a dance-band form that blended European jazz-band instrumentation with local Akan and Ga rhythms, and a more relaxed acoustic version that used a clinking bottle for percussion. E. T. Menash stands as its most prominent performer.

juju (Nigeria): A Yoruba music that features the talking drum (an hourglass-shaped instrument) and electric guitar, juju has remained the most popular form of contemporary music played in Nigeria since the 1960s. Today it emphasizes large percussion sections, layered guitars, keyboard music and long jam (improvisational) sessions. King Sunny Ade, Babatunde Olatunji and Fela Anikulapo Kuti number among its best-known performers.

kwela (South Africa): This street pennywhistle music developed in the 1940s in the gospel choir tradition. It incorporates acoustic guitars and bass.

makossa (Cameroon): Developed around the port of Douala, this dance rhythm has antecedents that include earlier traditional percussion and guitar-based dance music. Manu Dibango and Sam Fan Thomas rank as its best-known performers.

marabi (South Africa): A mixture of Dixieland jazz and local South African pub music, marabi is one of the music styles that developed during the 1920s. Some researchers believe that it takes its name from Marabastad, a part of Pretoria. It features banjos, guitars and brass instruments.

mbaqanga (South Africa): Sometimes called "township jive," this is a rough, electric, bass-heavy sound that represents a hardened, electrified variation of the *kwela-marabi* sound. Mahlathini (Simon Mkabinde) and the Mahotella Queens are its most prominent performers.

m'bira (Zimbabwe): Named for the thumb-piano (called a sanza or kalimba in other cultures) on which it is played, this music was created by the Shona people. Traditionally performed by males and accompanied by the hosho rattle, m'bira music holds a considerable aura of mysticism as a way of communicating with spirits. Zimbabwe's modern musicians transposed m'bira lines onto the electric guitar to develop a contemporary interpretation of the music. Stella Rambisai Chiweshe stands as its best-known performer.

nyatiti (Kenya): The traditional lyre music played in western Kenya incorporates elements of Zairian *soukous* and features local musicians from urban areas singing in Swahili.

praise songs (Gambia): Sung mainly by *griots* to celebrate harvest, love and family values, praise songs come from Mandinkes who descend from Sunjata Keita, a founder of the empire of Mali (13th–15th centuries). The songs are usually accompanied by the kora, a twenty-one-string harplike instrument that is considered one of the most beautiful, both visually and aurally, in Africa. Youssou N'Dour, Baaba Maal, Salif Keita and Mansour Seck number among its best-known performers.

soukous (Zaire): Over the past half-century, this rumba-based dance music has become one of the most infectious, hip-swiveling styles of African music. Perfected during the 1970s, it highlights electric guitar passages based on transposed thumb-piano melodies, combined with sweet harmony choruses behind a lead voice. Franco, Pepe Kalle, Tabu Ley Rochereau and Kanda Bongo Man rank as its most prominent performers.

taraab (Tanzania): A classical Arabic music developed along the seaboard of East Africa, this is the music of the Swahili-speaking people of Zanzibar, a small island off the coast of Tanzania. Transported from the Middle East via merchant traders sailing the Indian Ocean during the Renaissance, taraab incorporates the concept of mystic trance and is often associated with weddings. Its name, in fact, derives from the Arabic verb *tariba,* meaning "to be moved or enchanted." Closely linked to Egyptian orchestrations of violins, ouds, tambourines, derbouka-style hand drums and the qanun Arabic zither, the music was performed in all-male social clubs until Zanzibar's revolution in 1964.

yodels (Central Africa): Considered among the earliest inhabitants of the world's longest-populated continent, the Pygmies occupy the central rain-forest region of Africa. They employ a call-and-response type of verse in which their vocal polyphonics, or yodels, are sung by both men and women. Vocals are accompanied by percussion instruments, such as sticks, drums, rattles and bells.

East Asia and Oceania

Asia, the largest continent and home to more than half the world's population, is also home to a wide variety of musical forms. Muslims, Hindus, Buddhists, Christians and followers of other religions have created many different styles of music for use in Asian worship. In Indonesia, for instance, large orchestras called gamelans play metal percussion instruments on ceremonial occasions and at temple festivals. Japanese Buddhist monks, meanwhile, are called to prayer by large gongs called kei; they chant accompanied by cymbals (hachi) and bells. At the ancient shrine of Kyoto, the music of bells echoes throughout the temple.

Other Asian music has a celebratory or cultural function. In Japan, traditional music is played on the koto, which was imported from China in the 7th century. The Chinese perform tone poems and other traditional music on a characteristic array of flutes and stringed instruments that are both bowed and plucked. On the islands of Tahiti, Hawaii and Caledonia, rhythmic chants and percussion provide musical enjoyment. Likewise, drumming and dancing are important features of life throughout French Polynesia. Because the Polynesians had no written language of their own, they long ago learned to use songs to preserve their heritage and chants to chronicle daily life. These aural records of their culture are passed down from generation to generation. Today, much of the ancient ritual music of Asia is still played; some of it has influenced the development of contemporary musical entertainment.

bhangra (originally India): This modern percussive dance-pop has roots in Punjabi ceremonial music that was originally played at harvest time and danced by men. Traditionally backed by big drums, today it incorporates modern instruments. Alaap and Premi are its best-known performers.

enka (Japan): A mixture of Buddhist chant and Kabuki narrative, this melodramatic song style is heard mainly in karaoke (sing-along) bars. Its name translates literally as "public speech."

gamelan (Indonesia): Originating as performers of court music, this orchestra type consists of five to forty players of carefully tuned gongs and other metal percussion instruments. The similar angklung from the north is an ensemble of metallophones (metal xylophones), gongs, flutes and drums.

gamelan salundring (Bali): Bali's most ancient form of musical ensemble plays haunting, beautiful music that is considered especially sacred. Five to seven musicians perform on metallophones made of iron rather than the more typical bronze.

genggong (Bali): Played on a Jew's harp, this is an essential part of the island's folk-music tradition.

ghazals (India): These deeply meaningful songs emphasize the poetry of the lyrics, which are light, semiclassical love couplets based on traditional Persian romantic poetry introduced during the Mogul Empire (1526–1857). Mehdi Hassan and Gulam Ali number among its most prominent performers.

kecak (Bali): In this trance ritual, a chorus of seventy-five to a hundred male Caks or Ceks (singers) chant to accompany the sanghyang, an ancient trance dance.

qawwali (Pakistan): Developed in Persia in the 11th century, this is the devotional music of North Indian Sufis, members of a mystical sect of Islam. Led by vocalists, qawwali features the tabla (small Indian hand drum) and harmoniums. The music is both inspirational and mystical, intended to lift the spirit of listener and singer closer to God. Nusrat Fateh Ali Khan and the Sabri Brothers rank as its best-known performers.

sanjo (Korea): This music was created by wandering minstrels of the 19th century, who presented dramatic stories and instrumental dances before village celebrations or noble festivals. It is played on the kayagum, a kind of zither.

suling (Bali): This is both the endblown flute and the music it makes.

Australia and New Zealand

The world's smallest, least-populous cultural area developed its music in relative isolation, yet that music is founded on the same basic instrumental and vocal principles used around the world. On the whole, the indigenous music of Australia and New Zealand consists of sacred music belonging to men's or women's secret societies. This ceremonial music is played at rites witnessed by everybody in the community. Chants have also been a part of their cultures for thousands of years.

aboriginal (Australia): Much of Australia's traditional music is played on the didjeridoo, the characteristic long, wooden trumpet. Today the instrument is incorporated into modern rock sung in the tribal languages of Pitjanjatjar, Warlpiri and Papunya.

wongga (Australia): This chant is usually performed by men, often while women dance. It makes use of the wooden didjeridoo trumpet, clap sticks and vocals by one or more song-men who set the rhythm. On ceremonial occasions, the dancers paint their bodies with traditional patterns and perform before an open fire.

The Caribbean and the Bahamas

Scattered from the Bahamas in the north to Trinidad in the south and from Barbados in the east to Cuba in the west, this multitude of islands has produced a plethora of musical styles. In the era of European conquest and plantation slavery (1500–1900), the original inhabitants of the islands were wiped out by disease and massacre, silencing their music forever. But the people displaced to the region on slave ships from West Africa brought their languages, religious rituals and musical traditions with them. Influenced by European culture, they developed *patois* or Creole languages and new forms of music, most notably Negro spirituals and hymns, the forerunners of modern-day Caribbean musical styles. In time, Jamaican *reggae* and Cuban music became the most influential forms of Caribbean music.

biguine (Martinique): This dance rhythm fuses 19th-century French ballroom dance steps with African rhythms.

bomba (Puerto Rico): Originating in coastal towns, bomba features call-and-response vocals between a lead singer and a chorus, accompanied by maracas, sticks and barrel-shaped drums.

calypso (Trinidad): Influenced by the music of nearby Venezuela, this music has distinctive African rhythms and melodies. The term *calypso* is a corruption of the Hausa word *kaiso*, meaning "bravo." Calypso is often heard at parties and in carnival tents. Gros Jean and Lord Kitchener number among its most prominent performers.

charangas (Cuba): In charangas bands, flute and strings carry the melody over a rhythm section and bass line, while timbales, conga drums, guiro and piano fill out a sound that supports two or three singers. Today, charangas is frequently played by Latin bands in New York, Miami, Los Angeles and other cities in the United States.

compas (Haiti): Sometimes called compas direct, this is Haitian *merengue* adapted to a Cuban–North American big-band instrumentation. It was developed by Nemours Jean-Baptiste in the 1950s. Tabou Combo is another of its best-known performers.

danzon (Cuba): This salon dance, originally played by wind bands and subsequently by *charangas* ensembles, is characterized by a distinctive rhythm. Modernized in the late 1930s by Arcano y sus Maravillas, danzon took its final version, called *mambo,* for harder dancing.

mambo (Cuba): In the 1950s the mambo portion of *danzon* dances inspired a separate music style also called mambo, which is related to *son.* Mambo groups consist of piano, bass, percussion, two violins and flute.

merengue (Dominican Republic): A fast, galloping, 2/4 dance rhythm that boomed in the 1980s, merengue features the reverberating tambora drum, which is played horizontally with a stick at one end and a hand at the other. Annual merengue festivals celebrate this Latin-Caribbean mix of African-slave and Spanish-colonial musics. Juan-Luis Guerra, Wilfrido Vargas and Francisco Ulloa rank as its best-known performers.

plena (Puerto Rico): This music originated among country people who played cuatro (a double-stringed guitar), bongos, guitar, scraper, congas and tambourine. Manuel Jimenez stands as its most prominent performer.

rara (Haiti): Based on voodoo rhythms and played on bamboo flutes and percussion, this folkloric Haitian carnival music is played very fast. It is associated with the roots-and-culture movement in Haiti. Boukman Eksperyans, Foula and Sanba Yo number among its best-known performers.

reggae (Jamaica): This bass-heavy music with a swaying rhythm emerged in the 1970s. Influenced by the teachings of Jamaican-born black nationalist Marcus Garvey (1887–1940) and the religion of Rastafarianism, the lyrics of reggae express the sentiments of oppressed people. Reggae has become immensely popular worldwide. Bob Marley, Jimmy Cliff and Peter Tosh rank as its best-known performers.

rumba (Cuba): This Afro-Cuban street-drum and vocal form is associated with a dance style originally popular in the cities of Havana and Matanzas. A solo vocalist and chorus are backed up by conga drums, metal shakers and a slit-tube percussion instrument. After the 1950s, the rumba evolved into an informal music style performed at local fiestas. Los Munequitos de Matanzas stand as its most prominent performers.

Santeria ceremony (Cuba): Members of the vodun (voodoo) cult of Santeria worship about twenty orichas, entities that combine Yoruba and Roman Catholic characteristics. During various rites and festivals, dancers perform roles in which individuals become possessed by spirits.

ska (Jamaica): This 1950s Kingston street music predates *reggae*; based on American rhythm-and-blues, ska is highlighted by syncopated beats, clipped guitar playing, piano chords and a small brass section.

soca (Trinidad): This modern pop music fuses soul and *calypso*. Mighty Sparrow ranks as its best-known performer.

son (Cuba, Puerto Rico): An Afro-Cuban music form, son first evolved in the rural eastern provinces of Cuba, combining African- and Spanish-derived elements such as Yoruba and flamenco musical traditions. It features a syncopated rhythm (clave) played on wooden sticks with improvised vocals or a chorus on top. Very popular in Cuba during the 1920s, son laid the foundation for much of that island's contemporary popular music. Celia Cruz and Lazaro number among its most prominent performers.

zouk (Guadeloupe, Martinique): This contemporary Antillean dance music takes its name from the Creole slang word for "party." Kassav and Zouk Machine stand as its best-known performers.

zouk-chouv (Martinique): A fusion of traditional chouval bois (a kind of fairground music) and zouk influence, this form employs electric instruments. Marce and Tumpak rank among its most prominent performers.

Europe and the Former Soviet States

Although most people think of European music in terms of classical orchestral music, a long folk-music tradition does exist there. In Bulgaria, for example, the State Female Vocal Choir preserves the lively culture and shimmering choral vibrations of the gypsies, while Hungarians still enjoy a traditional music that originated in the fields of farmers and shepherds. Greeks enjoy a richly diverse musical heritage that is still played on the violin, the Cretan lyra, the santouri, the outie and the bouzouki. Today, folkloric groups look to the aging folk musicians of the countryside for information on the performing styles and rich melodies of late medieval and early modern European music. Much of the music features archaic instruments, such as the hurdy-gurdy (a stringed instrument sounded by a rotating wooden disk), the hit gardon (a stringed instrument used for percussion), the shawm (an oboelike double-reed instrument), the three-stringed viola, the Jew's harp, the bagpipe and the zither.

Balkan wedding-band music (Albania, Bulgaria, Romania, the former Yugoslavia): Most often played at weddings, this fast-paced gypsy-jazz improvisational and dance music boomed in the late 1980s. Ivo Papasov is its best-known performer.

cabaret (Germany): This style of revue music is conventionally presented in small clubs, where dancers often perform colorful production numbers behind the musicians. It is most often associated with the bohemian community of Berlin during the 1930s. Kurt Weill stands as its most prominent composer.

chanson (France): Its name translating literally as "song," this musical style is central to French popular culture. Contemporary chanson music derives its power from the poetry and mood of the lyrics, as well as from their phrasing, i.e., the way the words occupy and shape the melody. Edith Piaf, Serge Gainsbourg and Françoise Hardy number among its best-known performers.

dance-house movement (Hungary): Modern folk groups play rural folk dances and original gypsy music using traditional instruments—the hurdy-gurdy, bagpipe, cymbalom, double bass, flutes and pipes. Muzsikas and Trio Bulgarka are its best-known performers.

fado (Portugal): A type of Portuguese folk song, fado has a distinctive rhythm and song style, usually melancholy, in a minor key suffused with emotional content. Amalia Rodrigues and Nuno Da Camara Pereira rank as its most prominent performers.

flamenco (Spain): This Andalusian song form with European and Moorish roots consists of various subtypes named for the districts of the region, such as malaguena, sevillana, etc. Best known as a kind of dance, flamenco combines gypsy, Indian, and Judeo-Arab music. Flamenco guitar playing is a suitably forceful style that differs markedly from the more delicate classical Spanish style. Modern flamenco is performed at private weddings and public fiestas. Manolo Caracol and Paco de Lucia number among its best-known performers.

jig (Celtic): This lively music features whistles, pipes and percussion such as the bodhran, and accompanies a ⁶⁄₈ dance step.

jojk (Finland, Norway): The Saami (Lapps) lay claim to one of the most ancient musical styles in Europe. Executed with a constricted throat and slightly open mouth, their traditional shrill-singing employs circular breathing techniques and shares some similarities with Eskimo songs.

klezmer (originally Eastern Europe): Featured at Jewish weddings, this energetic clarinet music was brought to North America and Israel by Eastern European Jews fleeing persecution before and during World War II.

open-throat music (Bulgaria): Based on a mixture of popular village songs and Byzantine liturgy, this polyphonic choral music has a Turkish-Oriental flavor. The Bulgarian Radio Choir and Trio Bulgarka are its best-known performers.

polka (Czech Republic): Originating in Bohemia, this type of energetic music in ²⁄₄ time accompanies the lively couple dance of the same name.

reel (Celtic): Formal intricately executed dance music for pairs or teams played in ²⁄₄ time. It was exported to North America by Scottish and Irish emigrants.

Middle East and North Africa

Islamic culture pervades the Middle East—the crossroads of the world—and strongly influences neighboring North Africa as well. During the Great Age of Islam from the 8th through 15th centuries, when Arabs dominated an area bound by Persia (Iran) in the East and Spain in the West, a classical Andalous style of music appeared across the Mediterranean region. This music survives in Morocco, while Berber folk music and the chanting and drumming of various Islamic sects and brotherhoods persist elsewhere in North Africa.

In the Middle East, music is played primarily on lutes, mandolins, violins and assorted percussion instruments, as well as on the oud (an Arab lute), the nay (an Arabic bamboo flute), the saz (a long-necked plucked stringed instrument), the qanun (a kind of zither), and the rabab (a single-string violin). Lyrics address both religious and secular subjects, and Western-style rock influences have begun to make a musical impact.

gnawa music (Morocco, Algeria, Tunisia): Notable among North African musical styles is that of the gnaoui, the descendants of Sudanese slaves who migrated north across the desert. These priests and healers are skilled musicians who produce trance-inducing music with a castanetlike iron cymbal called a qarqabe. Accompanied by the four-string sentir or guitar, the instrument makes a tiny, clanking sound that when repeated has a hypnotic effect.

jajouka (Morocco): The musicians who reside in the Rif mountain region near Tangiers are known for the feverish shrill of the double-reed horn instrument called the nay. They also use rapid drumming rhythms to create an ecstatic trance music.

malouf (Tunisia, Algeria): This music is a compound of the semiclassical Andalous style and local folk styles. Khmeyes Tarnan ranks as its most prominent performer.

rai (Algeria): This pop music voices rebellion against the restrictions of Islamic fundamentalism. Cheba Fadela and Cheb Haled stand as its best-known performers.

North America

Before Europeans arrived in North America during the 16th century, hundreds of indigenous cultures practiced a wide variety of distinctive religious, social and artistic customs. Each tribal group had its own musical style, which was inextricably bound to its religion. Music, a spiritual gift channeled through humans, linked the Indians to the supernatural world. Used primarily for worship and ceremony, songs celebrated major life events, accompanied rites of passage, bid welcome or farewell to visitors, summoned good luck and aided the healing of the sick.

Most Native American music was simple, monophonic vocal music that accompanied dancing. Some peoples cultivated harsh singing styles; others preferred high pitches and falsetto voices. Vocals were usually accompanied by percussion performed on such instruments as double-headed cylindrical rawhide drums; water drums; bells; vibrating sticks, boxes or poles; hand rattles made from gourds, coconut shells or turtle shells; and noisy mobiles on which were hung animal claws and bones, bird beaks and rattlesnake tails. Many peoples also used flutes of cane, clay or bark, often to mimic sounds heard in nature.

The music of North America evolved in response to contact with Europeans. Notable developments included the music of the Peyote Cult of the 18th century and the Ghost Dance movement of the late 19th century. Peyote Cult music integrated European language and musical styles, as well as certain aspects of Christian theology and symbolism. By contrast, Ghost Dance songs accompanied mystic rituals meant to hasten the return to power of the Indian and speed the destruction of the white invader. In the 20th century, Native American music has come to reflect the impact of the pan-Indian movement and its annual intertribal powwows. The powwows feature music prominently for its social and historical significance. Today, music provides Native Americans with a link to the past and to their cultural heritage.

South and Central America

Influenced by African, Caribbean, Spanish and European music, South and Central America have developed many musical styles. In Mexico, communities of descendants of the Maya and Aztec peoples enjoy heel-tap dancing to melodies produced on stringed instruments. Nicaragua nurtures several folk-music traditions integral to the preservation of its folklore, including the fiddle music of the far north, the Caribbean- and Creole-influenced forms of the East Coast, and the Miskito Indian and marimba styles of the northeast. Throughout the Andes Mountains, Quechua- and Aymara-speaking Indians play panpipes, flutes, bombo bass drums, rattles and guitars. Brazil, which occupies the largest part of the continent, has been particularly fertile. There, an especially strong African culture has produced distinctive Afro-Brazilian rhythms, such as samba, bloco and afoxe.

afoxe (Brazil): This is a combination of African rhythms and *reggae*.

bloco (Brazil): A kind of African-influenced drum-corps music performed at carnivals in eastern Brazil. The most famous bloco band is Olodum.

bossa nova (Brazil): A hybrid dance rhythm of *samba* and the local music of northeast Brazil, it was developed in the late 1950s in Rio de Janeiro. It has been described as samba with a jazz feeling. Joao Gilberto and Antonio Carlos Jobim are its best-known performers.

candomble (Brazil): This holy, black ritual dance gives reverence to Yoruba tribal gods and incorporates Bantu elements.

cumbia (Colombia): A rhythm of the Atlantic-Caribbean coast, it is commonly called *musica tropical*. This dance of black slave origins mixes elements of *soca* and *merengue*; it is played on traditional percussion and cane flutes. In the 1940s and 1950s, the tempo of cumbia was speeded up by modern bands, who adapted the rhythm for popular urban consumption. Joe Arroyo stands as its most prominent performer.

forro (Brazil): A hard-driving folk music that originated in the northeastern region of Brazil, forro is played on the accordion, the triangle and a shallow bass drum called a zabumba. It derives from European dance music and is popular in dance halls. Luis Gonzaga is its best-known performer.

lambada (Brazil): This fusion of *merengue* and salsa from the northeastern Bahia region of Brazil displays heavy Caribbean influence. It became popular in the mid-1980s in the dance halls of Brazil's northeast and gradually caught on in the cities. By the late 1980s this sexy, clinging dance with its hot rhythm caught the attention of Paris-based producers who capitalized on its sound. Kaoma is its best-known performer.

nueva cancion (Andes Mountains): Spurred by a rising awareness of Indian culture among students and intellectuals, this form of folk-protest song appeared in the 1950s. Violetta Parra of Chile is among its more prominent performers.

samba (Brazil): Developed in the early 1900s by blacks from the northeastern state of Bahia, samba is one of the basic rhythms of Brazilian popular music. It made its way to Rio de Janiero, where it came to be associated with carnival. Soon it dominated the country's popular music and became internationally popular. There are two main forms of samba: the drum-based samba played and chanted by the samba schools during Rio Carnival, and the samba-cancao ("sung samba") performed and sung at other times of the year. Caetano Veloso and Gilberto Gil number among its most prominent performers.

son (Mexico): Various versions of this kind of music are identified with specific regions. The son jalisense from the state of Jalisco produced the mariachi repertoire; the son jarocho from the Veracruz area is played on small guitars; the violin-heavy son Huasteca from the Huasteca region is played by small groups at bars and fiestas.

tango (Argentina): This Argentinean dance rhythm comes from the port cities of Buenos Aires and Montevideo. Supposedly imported by African slaves, it came into general use in ballroom dancing about the time of World War I. Early tango groups typically consisted of trios of violin, flute and guitar or harp. Later, when tango appeared in the cabarets, the instrumentation changed to include the piano, double bass and bandoneon (a small accordion). Carlos Gardel and Astor Piazzolla are its best-known performers.

FOLK INSTRUMENTS

balafon: This prominent instrument of West Africa, considered one of the most important components of African musical culture, is a wooden xylophone-like resonator.

bouzouki: This long-necked, teardrop-shaped Greek guitar is related to the Turkish saz and the Arab bouzouk.

bendir: This percussion instrument from North Africa consists of a large, circular wooden frame covered with a goatskin, inside of which one or several strings intensify the vibrations.

claves: A pair of resonating wooden percussion sticks.

didjeridoo: The Aborigines of Australia use circular breathing to play this long, single-note wind instrument.

duduk: This Armenian wooden oboe is made from apricot wood and delivers a warm, soft, slightly nasal sound.

guiro: A serrated gourd played by scraping a stick across the ridges. Originated in the Caribbean.

kanoun: A harplike Egyptian instrument dating from medieval times, the kanoun is found mainly in the Islamic regions of Asia, Africa and Europe.

kayagum: Similar to the Indian sitar or Japanese koto, this Korean twelve-string zither was invented more than 1,500 years ago. Its traditional repertoire is sanjo music.

kora: Usually associated with Mandingo culture, this twenty-one-stringed harplike lute is played in Mali, Gambia, Guinea and Senegal.

kulintang: This Muslim instrument is a set of small gongs with a penetrating sound.

likemble: The Zairean version of the mbira.

lute/oud: This guitarlike lute, whose Arabic form is called the oud, is known throughout the Middle East. It has a body shaped like half a pear, often decorated with a carved, circular rose inlaid with mother-of-pearl; its strings are plucked with a plectrum.

mbira: This Zimbabwean kalimba instrument consists of a tuned set of iron prongs on a half-gourd resonator. The prongs are plucked with the thumbs.

nay: This straight Moroccan flute made of reed is extremely difficult to play because the pipe is open at both ends and it has no mouthpiece.

nyatit: A seven-stringed lyre played in western Kenya.

sabar: A Senegalese drum played with a stick and one hand.

shakuhachi: Controlled by the partial covering of its five finger-holes, this Japanese flute produces a tone that ranges from a high shrill to a breathy middle range to a mellow low. Its melodies exploit the tension of shaded intervals, sliding away from true scale pitches.

surdo: An essential element in samba music, this Brazilian bass drum is very deep and loud.

tar: This hand-drum or tambourine from the Middle East has a wooden frame and is covered with goatskin.

timbales: Made with either a metal or a wood body, this pair of single-headed drums is played with sticks in Cuba.

valiha: Found in Madagascar, this bamboo tube instrument features strings stretched longitudinally around its circumference.

The Birth of American Popular Music

The evolution and development of popular music in the United States has mirrored the history and progress of the country. At first, American music was merely a collection of borrowed sounds, brought by immigrants from their old countries to their new land. In the young nation, however, the old musical styles gradually gave way to fresh ones that reflected the independent, individual character of Americans.

Music in the European Colonies

Most everyday music enjoyed by America's earliest white settlers was sacred in nature, generally consisting of psalms set to melodies. The texts of these songs were compiled in volumes called psalters, which were imported from Europe. In 1640, a group of dissatisfied New England ministers printed a new translation, commonly known as *The Bay Psalm Book*. The first book published in America, it eventually appeared in more than twenty-five editions. Its ninth edition, dating from 1698, included music as well as text, making it the first music book published in America. Another influential sacred collection was by the English minister and physician Isaac Watts (1674–1748) and was first published in America in 1729 by Benjamin Franklin. Watts's texts became staples of Protestant hymnody in the colonial era. The common method of singing psalms in church services was called "lining out"; a church elder would sing each line and pause while the congregation repeated it.

For the most part, early American secular music was also imported. The most common form of secular song was the ballad, a kind of narrative sung to common, familiar melodies. Typical ballad subject matter might be comic, violent, moral or supernatural, and ballads often described identifiable historical events. When European ballads reached American shores, they were often altered to reflect colonial circumstances. British songs, for instance, were frequently parodied during the Revolutionary War to ridicule the enemy. At the same time, British troops sang the derisive "Yankee Doodle," which American soldiers picked up and sang triumphantly.

Notable composers of the colonial era included Frances Hopkinson (1737–91) and William Billings (1746–1800). Born in Philadelphia, Hopkinson dedicated his *Seven Songs for the Harpsichord or Forte Piano* to George Washington, proudly claiming to be "the first Native of the United States who has produced a Musical Composition." In 1770, the Boston-born Billings published *The New England Psalm Singer,* the first collection composed entirely by an American, and in 1778 he published *The Singing Master's Assistant,* which included his song "Chester," one of the most popular patriotic songs of its time. A third composer of the era, Benjamin Carr (1768–1831), established the first music-publishing house in America, with branches in Philadelphia, New York and Baltimore. In 1814, the Carr firm published the first edition of "The Star-Spangled Banner."

The 19th Century

At the beginning of the 19th century, most common music in the new republic was still European in origin. Certain forms dominated, such as ballad opera, which combined spoken text and music, and popular songs whose melodies came with immigrants from Ireland, Scotland (e.g., "Auld Lang Syne," "Comin' Through the Rye") and Italy. Some of the period's successful composers were, in fact, English immigrants working in European styles but using distinctly American and, in general, patriotic subject matter.

In addition to public-spirited songs, the 19th century's most popular music was sentimental or topical, sometimes composed to mark historic occasions. Typical song subjects of the period included the completion of the Erie Canal, the first train run in New York State, and the arrival of horse-drawn streetcars in New York City. Two masters of the sentimental ballad were John Hill Hewitt (1801–90), the author of one of the era's best-loved songs, "The Minstrel's Return'd from the War" (1828), and Henry Russell (1812–1900), who gained fame performing his own compositions, notably "Woodman, Spare That Tree" (1837).

Yet a significant segment of America's population at the time was musically illiterate. In an effort to teach music to the uneducated, William Little and William Smith in 1801 published *The Easy Instructor,* a hymnal that pioneered the use of shape-notes. The head of each printed note was shaped to indicate its musical value: a triangle indicated *fa,* a circle *sol,* a square *la,* a diamond *mi,* etc. Hymnals using this method of notation began to appear throughout the country. Among the most popular shape-note collections were *The Southern Harmony and Music Companion* (1835) by William Walker and *The Sacred Harp* (1844) by Benjamin Franklin White, a version of which is still in use today. These collections included music drawn from a variety of sources, including New England psalms, secular and religious ballads, fuguing tunes, and folk hymns from the oral tradition.

The popularization of shape-note singing coincided with the pioneer migrations south and west. Shape-note hymnody reached a peak of acceptance and influence at camp meetings,—the intense, days-long, mass religious gatherings held in the frontier wilderness. The ecstatic fervor of these assemblies was most clearly manifested in the passionate singing of hymns. In the heated, boisterous atmosphere, the sacred songs were often altered; texts were transposed, and refrains and tag lines were added. Driven deep into the hearts of the pioneer singers, camp meeting spirituals, as they became known, were woven into American life and music.

Almost concurrently, a similar type of religious folk music originated among America's black population. West Africans brought to America as slaves carried with them their own time-honored set of musical values. In Africa, music figured prominently in daily life and was used for both work and religious purposes. It was polyrhythmic and antiphonal, often featuring call-and-response interactions of voices or instruments. Unlike much European music, it was spontaneous and improvised and structurally featured with short, repeated patterns of rhythm or melody.

These African musical influences were assimilated into the slaves' daily lives, giving rise to new and reshaped musical forms and song types. Most notable was the work song, performed during arduous or monotonous labor: A leader sang a line and the group sang a response, establishing a steady rhythm by which various plantation chores were performed. By contrast, the field holler was generally sung by a single person, although it was sometimes echoed by shouts from other workers. African rhythms were also preserved and transformed when slaves played the fiddle and the banjo, an instrument of African origin.

The development of black spirituals coincided with attempts to convert slaves to Christianity. Many slaves were eager to convert, not just because it conferred on them a degree of social standing but also because certain denominational aspects—the Baptist immersion ceremony, for instance—resembled African traditions. Some Christian music particularly appealed to converted slaves, who recognized the "lining out" of hymns as a call-and-response style similar to their own. At camp meetings—many of which were open to converted slaves, although the meetings themselves were often segregated—black and white musical traditions mixed and merged. But though many black spirituals had white counterparts, they evolved into a uniquely black form as they were adapted by slaves to their needs and circumstances. The songs varied in character and type: slow, sorrowful songs, such as "Sometimes I Feel Like a Motherless Child"; call-and-response hymns, such as "Michael, Row the Boat Ashore"; and highly rhythmic "jubilees," such as "All God's Chillun Got Wings."

The popularity and endurance of the spirituals were boosted by two events. In 1867, the first compilation of spirituals (or any black music) was published. *Slave Songs of the United States,* edited by William Francis Allen, Charles Pickard Ware and Lucy McKim Garrison, introduced the songs to a new, Northern audience. Four years later, the Fisk Jubilee Singers went on tour to raise money for that black Tennessee college. The nine young black singers, whose repertoire included spirituals, were enormously successful in the United States and abroad, particularly in England, where they sang for a delighted Queen Victoria. Before long, black spirituals became one of the most significant bodies of American folk music.

While sacred in nature, black and white spirituals would exert a marked influence on secular music forms. The two major avenues by which secular American popular music spread in the 19th century were minstrels and the brass and marching bands.

Minstrelsy was a unique type of American entertainment in which performers (largely white) appeared in blackface, performing comic skits and singing songs about plantation life. This kind of theater was vital to the circulation and popularization of certain kinds of American music with both black and white origins. It was an outgrowth of popular British theater and comic black songs popular in America during the late 1820s, tracing its birth to the career of Thomas Dartmouth "Daddy" Rice (1808–60). A blackface performer, Rice found international success performing his song "Jim Crow," which was inspired by a crippled black stablehand. Another successful minstrel performer was the composer Daniel Decatur Emmett (1815–1904), to whom the song "Dixie" is attributed. Emmett was a member of the first minstrel quartet, the Virginia Minstrels, who debuted in New York in February 1843. Numerous other minstrel companies soon formed and played to audiences across the country. In the musical portions of their shows, they played the banjo, violin, tambourine and bones (castanets).

The heyday of minstrelsy lasted roughly from the mid-1840s through 1870, although some troupes continued to perform for years afterward. Despite the fact that the shows perpetuated damaging racial stereotypes, they were noteworthy as a forum for the evolution and popularization of uniquely American music. Their repertoires were probably compiled from a variety of sources. Many Northern white minstrels performed popular ballads, British folk tunes or other European song types, along with caricatured and inaccurate imitations of black music. Still, some white minstrels familiar with black music may have presented accurate facsimiles of it to white audiences. When black performers themselves became minstrels after the Civil War, authentic black performance and music styles began to infiltrate the consciousness of white America.

In addition to Emmett, minstrelsy produced several noteworthy composers. James A. Bland (1854–1911), the author of "Oh, Dem Golden Slippers" (1879) and "Carry Me Back to Old Virginny" (1876), is generally considered the to be first African-American songwriter. Stephen Foster became the best-known and most significant composer of his time, writing more than two hundred songs, including "Oh! Susanna" (1848), "Camptown Races" (1850), "Old Folks at Home" (1851), "My Old Kentucky Home, Good Night" (1852), "Jeannie With the Light Brown Hair" (1854) and "Beautiful Dreamer" (1864). His fusion of Irish, Scottish, Italian and black influences into richly melodic songs marked him as a thoroughly American songwriter.

The second major means by which secular music was circulated in 19th-century America was the brass and marching band. Military and marching bands evolved in America during the colonial era, when concerts by British regimental bands inspired Americans to form bands of their own. When European manufacturers introduced brass instruments equipped with keys and capable of producing entire chromatic scales, the number of American bands mushroomed. By the Civil War, an estimated three thousand ensembles with more than sixty thousand members played in the United States. In the years that followed, brass bands in uniform became a staple of American life, performing regularly at ceremonies, parades and fairs. Local amateur bands were the pride of many small towns and cities. In New Orleans, brass bands appeared at all kinds of social functions, including funerals, and played a central role in the evolution of jazz.

Some Americans heard classical or orchestrated music for the first time as performed by brass bands, and in some far-flung western communities, local military bands provided the only available music. A typical 19th-century band program was eclectic, featuring overtures and selections from operas, patriotic songs, dance music, and other popular selections. Nevertheless, the rousing march tune became the signature style of band music.

Patrick S. Gilmore (1829–92), an Irish immigrant who composed "When Johnny Comes Marching Home" (1863), was a key figure in the popularization of bands in America. Leader of New York's 22nd Regiment Band, he established his group as one of the country's finest professional bands, a model for other ensembles across America. But the dominant figure in American brass-band history was John Philip Sousa (1854–1932), a violinist, composer for the musical stage, and conductor of the United States Marine Band. In 1892 he organized his own professional civilian band and went on to present lively and entertaining concerts regularly for forty years. He is best remembered as the composer of 136 stirring marches, including "The Stars and Stripes Forever" (1896), as well as numerous suites and operettas.

ONE NATION, MANY ANTHEMS

The subject of America has inspired many patriotic songs. Often originating from more than one source, many of these songs have acquired the status of anthems. These songs are familiar to most American citizens and stand as true examples of national music.

"The Star-Spangled Banner": The official national anthem of the United States was written during the War of 1812 by Francis Scott Key (1779–1843), a young Washington lawyer. An eyewitness to the British attack on Fort McHenry, which protected Baltimore, Key watched the battle unfold the night of September 13, 1814. The next morning, gripped by patriotic fervor, he hastily began writing the poem that became "The Star-Spangled Banner." Key's poem of four stanzas was set to music of "To Anacreon in Heaven," a well-known British drinking song. "The Star-Spangled Banner" was officially declared the American national anthem by Congress on March 3, 1931.

"America": Also know as "My Country 'Tis of Thee," this song has words written in 1832 by Samuel F. Smith (1808–95), set to the same melody as the national anthems of Austria ("Heil Dir im Siegerkranz") and Great Britain ("God Save the King" [or "Queen"]). Smith found the melody—whose precise European origins are unknown—in a songbook used for music instruction. Intrigued by the song, he wrote four verses of lyrics that conveyed a combination of patriotism and spiritual devotion. The song was first publicly sung in Boston on July 4, 1833, and was first published in 1837. It became popular during the Civil War and has remained so ever since.

"The Battle Hymn of the Republic": Julia Ward Howe (1819–1910) set the lyrics of this song to a melody that originated as a camp-meeting spiritual, "Say, Brothers, Will You Join Us?" Before Howe heard it, the spiritual had been secularized by Union Army soldiers into "John Brown's Body," a popular marching tune during the Civil War. When Howe overheard the song in 1861, she decided to write more dignified lyrics to the rousing tune and composed five new verses. First published in the *Atlantic Monthly* in February 1862, "The Battle Hymn of the Republic" captured the imagination of the country.

"America The Beautiful": Katharine Lee Bates (1859–1929), a professor of English literature at Wellesley College, wrote the lyrics to this song after traveling cross-country for the first time in 1893. In Colorado, after climbing Pike's Peak, she was inspired to write the four verses, which were first published two years later in a church magazine, *The Congregationalist*. By World War I, the poem had been published and set to music numerous times. The most durable version used the melody of a hymn, "Materna," which remains its tune today.

"God Bless America": The original music and lyrics of the most recent of America's well-known patriot ballads was composed by Irving Berlin. Written for his 1918 show *Yip, Yip, Yaphank,* it was not used until singer Kate Smith (1907–86) asked to sing it on an Armistice Day broadcast on November 11, 1938. Once Smith performed it on the radio, "God Bless America" became a huge national success. Berlin established a trust through which all royalties from the song would be donated to the Scouts of America. Many Americans feel it should be adopted as the official national anthem.

American Popular Music in the 20th Century

Founded on the musical traditions of Europe and Africa, American popular music did not truly come of age until the 20th century. Once it did, however, it produced numerous vital, distinctive and influential styles, which in turn spawned offshoots and hybrids that continue to recombine and evolve to this day. Some of American music's most spectacular successes—such as jazz, rock and soul—are those in which different historical influences fused and merged into something original and memorable. The types of music described here are recognized and enjoyed around the world as uniquely and unmistakably American. Because each shares common musical antecedents with the others, many of these American musical genres overlap.

The Blues

Irrefutably African-American, the blues are a folk music born out of the black experience and are distinguished by their vitality and directness of expression. The most common form of blues melody consists of twelve bars—three lines of four bars each. Blues lyrics typically occur in three-line stanzas, where the first and second lines repeat and the third changes to pull the narrative along. Most blues songs are about misfortune—infidelity, loneliness, death and other woes—but the blues can also be jubilant, comic or racy. Influenced by the work song and the field holler of slavery, the blues is about earthly rather than heavenly deliverance. Plantation music was also the likely source of the blue note, the microtonal flattening or bending of the third and seventh notes on the scale that is heard in blues and jazz.

While their origins are hazy, the blues most likely first appeared between the end of the Civil War and the turn of the 20th century. The Mississippi River Delta region, from which dozens of blues singers hailed, may have been their birthplace. The earliest form of blues was the country or rural blues, sung by itinerant singers who improvised songs, often accompanying themselves on guitar. Composer W. C. Handy (1873–1958) published the first blues songs in 1912 ("Memphis Blues") and 1914 ("St. Louis Blues").

Most Americans first heard the blues via early recordings, notably "Crazy Blues," recorded by Mamie Smith (1883–1946) in 1920. Smith's record was enormously popular, selling more than a million and a half copies in less than a year. Its success prompted a blues craze during which the classic blues singers— Gertrude "Ma" Rainey (1886–1939), Bessie Smith (1894–1937) and others— were recorded, often accompanied by jazz musicians. Record companies also sought out such country blues artists as Charley Patton (1887–1934), Bukka White (1906–77) and Blind Lemon Jefferson (1897–1929). Of all the country blues singers, Robert Johnson (c. 1912–38), whose haunting Delta sound and imagery was reinforced by a mysterious early death, remains one of the most influential.

In the 1930s, a tougher, more aggressive form called urban blues evolved, its style and content reflecting the great black migration into cities. Developed largely in Chicago and performed by such artists as Tampa Red (Hudson Whittaker, 1900?–1981) and William Lee "Big Bill" Broonzy (1893–1953), urban blues featured pianos, saxophones and other jazz instruments, while their lyrics addressed the harshness of city life. At the same time, a blues-based piano style called boogie-woogie arose, characterized by a driving left hand and a right hand playing fast, complex rhythm figures. Boogie-woogie was performed and recorded in Chicago by such masters as Meade Lux Lewis (1905–64), Albert Ammons (1907–49), Pete Johnson (1904–67) and Jimmy Yancey (1894–1951). In subsequent years, guitarists such as Muddy Waters (McKinley Morganfield, 1915–83) and Howlin' Wolf (Chester Arthur Burnett, 1910–76) arrived on the Chicago blues scene. These musicians, along with harmonica player Little Walter [Jacobs] (1930–68) and Mississippi guitarist B. B. King (born 1925), created electric blues using amplified instruments.

While the blues have a decidedly simple form, they allow for a great variety of expression, from the rough, folk sound of Leadbelly (Huddie Ledbetter, 1888–1949) to the forceful and elegant vocalizing of Joe Williams (born 1918). The twelve-bar structure of the blues has been used for composition and improvisation in jazz. Urban blues have also influenced such forms as rhythm-and-blues and rock 'n' roll, which in turn sustain the public's interest in blues. As a result, the blues continue to attract listeners today. Some performers, such as guitarist John Lee Hooker and singers Etta James and Taj Mahal, keep traditional blues alive, while others, such as guitarists Buddy Guy and Robert Cray, lend the form a contemporary rock edge.

Country and Western

Country and western music encompasses several subgenres that share characteristic instrumentation (including the steel guitar) and a slightly nasal vocal style. When it first emerged at the beginning of the 20th century, country music reflected the spirit of the rural South, a region somewhat removed from mainstream industrialized society. The early country repertory included folk songs as well as European and domestic ballads from the 19th century. String bands consisting of one or more violins, banjos and guitars and, later, mandolins, bass and steel guitars, made music in homes or for local gatherings.

In 1922, fiddlers Henry Gilliland (dates unavailable) and A. C. "Eck" Robertson (1887–1975) made the first authentic country recordings, "Sallie Gooden" and "The Arkansas Traveler," which were released the following year. Recorded in 1924 by Vernon Dalhart (dates unavailable), "The Prisoner's Song" was the breakthrough country record, selling more than four million copies. Record companies started promoting music expressly for the rural Southern market, and this so-called hillbilly music was played extensively by radio stations throughout the South. Barn Dance programs devoted exclusively to country music became a popular form of programming; the program first broadcast on WSM in Nashville in 1925 evolved into the Grand Ol' Opry.

Two key country acts had great success in the early 1930s: the Carter Family and Jimmie Rodgers. Hailing from Virginia, the Carters—Alvin Pleasant Carter (1891–1960), his wife Sara (1898–1979) and her sister Maybelle (1909–78)—sang in a traditional Appalachian-style three-part harmony, accented by Maybelle's unique guitar sound. The Carters recorded more than three hundred songs. Mississippi-born Rodgers (1897–1933) had a broad repertoire that included hobo, train and love songs as well as blues, punctuated by his signature vocal device, the yodel. After his early death from tuberculosis he was referred to as "the father of country music."

During World War II, country music spread across the nation. Its image improved, thanks to Hollywood films of the late 1930s that featured such singing cowboys as Gene Autry (born 1907), Tex Ritter (1907–74) and Roy Rogers (born 1912). Although these performers often sang songs from Tin Pan Alley rather than country tunes, their appearance linked the American West with country music in the public's mind. The term *hillbilly* music was replaced by the more dignified *country and western,* and western attire became an important part of the music's presentation.

New and distinct country styles flourished during and after the war. Building on the traditional, conservative music of the Southeast, southwestern performers assimilated popular music influences, notably big-band jazz, to produce western swing. Popularized by such groups as Bob Wills (1905–75) and his Texas Playboys, western swing added horns and black-style rhythms to the string group to create music for dancing. Western swing had its heyday in the 1940s, when one record by Wills's band, "New San Antonio Rose," sold three million copies.

By contrast, bluegrass relied exclusively on traditional instrumentation and musical styles. Rooted in the music of Bill Monroe (born 1911) and his Blue Grass Boys, a popular Grand Ol' Opry act of the late 1940s and early 1950s, the bluegrass instrumental style was forged by the banjo player Earl Scruggs (born 1924), a member of Monroe's group. Scrugg's style of right-handed, three-fingered banjo picking enabled him to play passages of great speed and complexity. Today, bluegrass bands typically include four to seven members playing only acoustic instruments (primarily violin, mandolin, guitar, string bass and five-string banjo), who trade solos just as jazz musicians do. The music is played and enjoyed by young musicians and audiences, often at annual bluegrass festivals held around the country.

Perhaps the most identifiable and durable style of country music is honky-tonk, which came to prominence in the late 1940s and early 1950s. Featuring a hard country sound, honky-tonk originated mostly at Texas saloons, or honky-tonks. Amplified instrumentation, a strong "sock" rhythm generated by guitar strings struck percussively, and dark lyrics marked a movement away from country's rural and pastoral origins toward a harsher, more industrialized outlook. Honky-tonk masters include Ernest Tubb (1914–84), who pioneered the use of the electric guitar in country music, Ray Price (born 1926), and George Jones (born 1931). The best-known and most influential honky-tonk performer was gospel- and blues-influenced Hank Williams, who composed "I'm So Lonesome I Could Cry," "Jambalaya," and many other standards.

More recently, country music has drawn influences from pop music. After Nashville became the world's country-music capital, a style of country-pop emerged that was called the Nashville Sound. Characterized by smooth rhythms and lush production, it was popularized by such crossover acts as Patsy Cline (1932–63) and Jim Reeves (1924–64). During the 1960s and 1970s, such country-style performers as Roger Miller (1936–92), Glen Campbell (born 1936), Johnny Cash and Willie Nelson drew inspiration and instrumentation from rock. New traditionalists, including Randy Travis (born 1959), Clint Black (born 1962) and Garth Brooks (born 1956), continue to incorporate rock elements into their performances.

Folk

The earliest figures of American folk music include Harvard professor Francis James Child (1825–96), who in the late 19th century documented the survival of Scottish and English ballads in the United States, and the Hutchinsons, a mid–19th-century family who performed a repertoire of popular tunes and political songs about abolition and temperance, among other causes. Similarly driven by both the traditions of the past and the politics of the present, modern American folk music traces its birth to the 1930s and 1940s.

At that time, such singers as John Jacob Niles (1892–1980) and Burl Ives (born 1909) performed contemporary versions of Anglo-American folk songs. Their peers included the Almanac Singers, made up of Pete Seeger (born 1919), Lee Hays (1914–81), Millard Lampbell (dates unavailable) and Woody Guthrie, who used folk songs to promote labor unionization. Composer of more than a thousand songs, Guthrie made numerous solo recordings, such as the 1940 collection *Dust Bowl Ballads* and American classics like "This Land Is Your Land" and "So Long, It's Been Good to Know You." When the Almanac Singers disbanded in 1942, Seeger and Hays joined with Ronnie Gilbert (born 1927) and Fred Hellerman (born 1927) to form The Weavers. The quartet found great success adapting folk music for a broad audience. Their 1950 recording of Leadbelly's "Goodnight, Irene" was the year's top-selling record. During and after his stint with The Weavers, Seeger authored or coauthored folk staples, such as "If I Had a Hammer" (1949), "Where Have All the Flowers Gone?" (1956) and "Turn Turn Turn" (1962).

By the late 1950s and early 1960s, various forms of folk music became extremely popular on American college campuses. Close harmony groups, such as The Kingston Trio and Peter, Paul and Mary, made folk music enjoyable and relevant for young people. At the same time, New York's Greenwich Village became the center of a growing folk scene, which included such singers as Joan Baez and Phil Ochs (1940–76). Bob Dylan, the key figure in contemporary folk, arrived there in 1961 and caused a sensation with his second album, *The Freewheelin' Bob Dylan* (1963). His work ranged from the tenderly romantic "Girl From the North Country" to the subtly yet powerfully political "Blowin' in the Wind." Although he worked in the folk idiom, his raspy voice and sensibility seemed contemporary, immediate and fresh. Dylan continued to compose and record unflinching protest songs that would inspire much of the politically charged rock that appeared during the decade. In 1965, he made the logical transition from folk to rock, where he continued to use popular music to express his own perspective and sensibility.

Gospel

Whether of white or African-American origins, contemporary American religious music falls into the gospel category. The development of these stylistically different forms reflected the urbanization of America, the influence of secular music styles, and the establishment of religious music as a self-supporting industry.

Dating from the urban revival movement of the late 19th century, white gospel music grew out of Sunday-school hymns intended to appeal to children—cheerful, rhythmic songs that were easily learned and remembered. Associated with revival meetings led in the 1870s by Dwight L. Moody (1837–99) and his chief singer-composer Ira D. Sankey (1840–1908), these compositions became known as gospel songs or hymns. Along with Phillip P. Bliss, Sankey compiled the six-volume *Gospel Hymns and Sacred Songs* over twenty years, starting in 1875. Its more than seven hundred hymns, including "Bringing in the Sheaves" and "What a Friend We Have in Jesus," became extremely popular. The best-known white gospel singers of the early 20th century were Charles McCallom Alexander (1867–1920) and Homer Alvan Rodeheaver (1880–1955), who performed with the evangelists J. Wilbur Chapman and Billy Sunday, respectively.

By the 1920s, white gospel had gained a secure foothold in the southern states. In that decade, James D. Vaughan (1864–1941) launched the first gospel radio station, in Tennessee, and hired several male gospel quartets to give free concerts to promote his gospel publications. Another gospel publisher, Stamps-Baxter of Dallas, published young gospel composers and staged all-night sings in the 1940s. These events helped establish white gospel in the world of secular entertainment, and it has remained a staple of contemporary Christian life in America.

Originating near the turn of the century, black gospel music emerged hand in hand with numerous African-American Christian sects. Services at these churches were often highly emotional and participatory and featured rhythmic singing and dancing. They began to include hymns by C. A. Tindley (c. 1851–1933), a Philadelphia preacher and composer whose work bridged the gap between the folk sentiments of black spirituals and the standardized texts of white hymns. Thomas A. Dorsey (1899–1993), a pianist and former bluesman, was inspired by Tindley to return to writing church music in the 1930s. Known as the father of gospel music, this composer of "Precious Lord, Take My Hand" and hundreds of other hymns helped establish gospel in African-American churches across the country.

Notable singers who popularized black gospel were Sallie Martin (1895–1988) and Mahalia Jackson, whose enormous voice and presence made her the most prominent gospel singer of all, black or white. Besides such female soloists, gospel has typically been sung by choirs and male quartets, who became like preachers working in four-part harmony. The popularity of gospel groups such as the Golden Gate Quartet, the Soul Stirrers and the Swan Silvertones (led by the distinct and memorable tenor of Claude Jeter [born 1919]) helped make black gospel a force in American culture. The form has served as the training ground for dozens of black singers, such as Aretha Franklin, who have brought the intensity of black gospel to secular music, particularly rhythm-and-blues and soul.

Jazz

Widely acknowledged as one of America's finest contributions to world music, jazz has roots in the blues, ragtime and brass-band music. Encompassing a long history and a wide range of styles, jazz is played by solo performers, small groups and large orchestras. Key elements of the form are the musical relationship between the soloist and the group, and the collective relationship of the individual instruments, known as the ensemble sound. Jazz is marked by musical deftness, a strong rhythmic sense and emotional expressiveness.

Appearing near the turn of the century, jazz has murky origins. It no doubt emerged in various places at about the same time, but New Orleans has traditionally been considered its birthplace. This Louisiana city was home to several of the earliest-known jazz musicians and was a hospitable environment for the merging of many musical styles. History had endowed New Orleans with a tolerance for African traditions, which were kept alive by the city's black residents. The mixed-blood Creole population learned both African- and European-style musicianship and passed their knowledge on to blacks and whites alike. Brass bands were extremely popular there and were featured at all sorts of social events. When these assorted elements collided with strains of blues and ragtime already in circulation, the result was jazz.

The next great strides in jazz development took place in the North, in Chicago and New York. The creators of jazz were probably exclusively black, but the movement northward allowed both black and white musicians to contribute to its evolution. In 1917, a white ensemble called the Original

Dixieland Jazz Band debuted at an upscale New York eatery, marking the introduction of jazz to polite white society. The group made the first jazz recordings for the Victor label that year, inspiring the formation of midwestern jazz groups, such as the Wolverines, with the legendary white trumpeter Leon Bismarck "Bix" Beiderbecke (1903–31), and Chicago's Austin High Gang. By the early 1920s, groups modeled after the Original Dixieland Jazz Band could be found throughout the United States.

In Chicago, several black musicians from New Orleans, such as pianist Ferdinand "Jelly Roll" Morton, made their mark. The Creole Jazz Band, led by Joe "King" Oliver (1885–1938), made some of the first substantial recordings by a black jazz band in 1923, featuring the talents of a young cornet and trumpet player named Louis Armstrong. In 1925, Armstrong began making the records commonly known as the "Hot Five" and "Hot Seven" sessions after the groups involved. Immediately recognized as jazz classics, the records established Armstrong as a pioneer creative force.

While Armstrong was defining the role of the jazz soloist, jazz ensemble style was also evolving. Classically trained musicians such as Ferde Grofe (1892–1972) and Paul Whiteman (1890–1967) experimented with large ensembles that played jazzlike dance music. In the process, certain principles of jazz arrangement were established, for instance, the use of a line of instruments to establish a song's melody and the use of instruments to play off each other in counterpoint. Closer to actual jazz were subsequent efforts by Fletcher Henderson, leader of a New York–based orchestra, and Don Redman (1900–64), his chief arranger. Together they worked out sample arrangements by which big bands of ten to fifteen instruments could make hot, driving dance music and individuals could solo without disrupting the flow of the group. Their blueprint was subsequently followed by most of the successful, big jazz bands.

In the 1920s, an era first called "The Jazz Age" by F. Scott Fitzgerald, jazz gained respectability and popularity, thanks to the booming recording and broadcasting industries. Newly popular forms of social dancing required plenty of lively music, and jazz fit the bill nicely. In the ensuing years the form continued to produce new styles, which in turn yielded others.

By the mid–1930s, the big-band sound dominated American popular music. Hundreds of bands, black and white, played dance music that ranged from sweet and romantic to genuine jazz. Whatever the style, in order to play jazz a band had to swing. Roughly speaking, *swing* is the lilt of a performance when all its rhythmic components fall into place. While not confined to the big-band style, the term came to define the music of the era.

Benny Goodman, a clarinetist known as the "King of Swing," is generally credited with popularizing the big-band sound about 1935. The popularity of his band inspired numerous other white musicians to form bands, including saxophonist Woody Herman, trombonist Glenn Miller and clarinetist Artie Shaw. Black bands also enjoyed success and accounted for most of the music's major stylistic developments. The dominant black orchestras were led by

Edward Kennedy "Duke" Ellington and William "Count" Basie. Ellington's popular hits included "Mood Indigo" (1931), "Sophisticated Lady" (1933) and "Solitude" (1933), as well as such extended works as the *Black, Brown and Beige* suite (1943). Basie and his band popularized a southwestern style of jazz, swinging hard and fast on such signature numbers as "One O'Clock Jump" (1937), "Swingin' the Blues" (1938) and "Jumpin' at the Woodside" (1938).

Despite its international success, the big-band era drew to a close after a decade as public tastes changed, the style stagnated, and World War II brought economic restrictions. Partly in response to the artistic and commercial restrictions of the big bands, the style of jazz called bebop began to emerge toward the end of the 1930s. Played primarily by small groups, often in the context of spontaneous and improvised jam sessions, bebop (also called bop) created ornate, elaborate melodies from the existing chords of songs, favoring a lighter rhythm, an accelerated tempo and sudden key shifts. In order to play it competently, a musician required impeccable technique.

The chief architects of bebop were alto saxophonist Charlie Parker and trumpeter John Birks "Dizzy" Gillespie. They often performed at Minton's, an after-hours club in Harlem, as did other bop greats, such as drummer Kenny Clarke (1914–85) and pianists Thelonious Monk and Bud Powell (1924–66). In 1945, Parker and Gillespie made the first of their series of classic bop recordings, including "Groovin' High" and "Salt Peanuts." Bop was soon showcased by small groups appearing in clubs on New York's famous 52nd Street. Although controversial, bop was quickly adopted by a younger generation of jazz fans and players. For the first time, jazz was played for its own sake, as a listening, rather than dancing, music.

Moving into the 1950s, a hard-swinging, simplified version of bebop called hard bop developed. A typical hard bop selection opened and closed with a melodic chorus played by the full band, with a number of alternating solos occurring in between. Commercially successful hard boppers, such as pianist Horace Silver (born 1928), bassist Charlie Mingus (1927–79) and drummer Art Blakey (1919–90), played moderate, funky tempos and blues-based compositions.

Emerging at nearly the same time as bop, cool jazz incorporated harmonic advances like bebop, but leaned toward studied and artistic methods of performance, sometimes featuring devices found in classical or symphonic music. Its sound was often dry or understated, in contrast to the more strongly rhythmic types of "hot" jazz. Proponents of the style included arranger Gil Evans (1912–88) and saxophonist Gerry Mulligan (born 1927), who with trumpeter Miles Davis recorded an influential series of sessions in 1950 called *Birth of the Cool*. On the West Coast, pianist Dave Brubeck (born 1920) experimented with meter, and trumpeter Chet Baker (1929–88) explored color and counterpoint. The Modern Jazz Quartet, a cool-jazz ensemble with pianist John Lewis (born 1920) and vibraphonist Milt Jackson (born 1923), included no wind instruments and seasoned its rhythmic textures with elements of Baroque and Renaissance classical music.

Two of the most influential jazzmen of the modern era were trumpeter Miles Davis and saxophonist John Coltrane. They made great stylistic advances working in a form loosely known as modal jazz, which featured improvisation based on modal harmonies, rather than chord progressions, and whose defining work was Davis's album *Kind of Blue* (1959), on which Coltrane also played. Coltrane's classic recordings were his own modal experiments *My Favorite Things* (1960) and *A Love Supreme* (1964).

By the early 1960s an avant-garde jazz movement arose that seemed to defy rules, granting total freedom to the improviser. Called free jazz after a 1960 recording by saxophonist Ornette Coleman, the discordant style substituted energy and intensity for harmony and restraint, leaving many jazz fans puzzled and uncomfortable. Free jazz spawned such noteworthy musicians as pianist Cecil Taylor (born 1933), who played percussively, and the saxophonists Albert Ayler (1936–1970) and Archie Shepp (born 1937). Coltrane also experimented with free jazz.

Today, jazz is a living music split into many styles. The commercially successful form known as fusion merges jazz-type musicianship with rock and funk rhythms. By contrast, a kind of neoclassical jazz has grown out of a revived interest in the traditional forms. This school has brought forth new players, such as the brothers Branford and Wynton Marsalis.

Pop

During the late 1950s and early 1960s, a form of music known as commercial pop emerged in the United States. Lighter-sounding but no less successful than rock 'n' roll, pop appealed mainly to young listeners and dancers. A coterie of New York–based songwriters, including composer-lyricist teams such as Carole King and Gerry Goffin (born 1939), Doc Pomus (1925–91) and Mort Shuman (born 1936), and Jerry Leiber (born 1933) and Mike Stoller (born 1933), treated youth-oriented music with a sense of craft and professionalism that recalled Tin Pan Alley. At the same time, songwriter, musician and record producer Phil Spector created a string of hit singles in the form of anthems to teen joy or angst, which were recorded by such groups as The Crystals and The Ronettes. Featuring a loud, dense "wall of sound," Spector's records were easily recognized. They helped establish the concept of brand-name pop made by a person or company with a reliable style, comparable to a certain make of car.

The hit factory that came to dominate American pop music during the 1960s was Motown Records in Detroit. Created by company founder Berry Gordy, Jr., the "Motown sound" popularized black music among a wide, mixed audience. Its potent combination of creative songwriting, production, and performance was exemplified by the work of Smokey Robinson and the Miracles, The Four Tops, The Temptations, Marvin Gaye, Stevie Wonder, and Martha and the Vandellas. Led by Diana Ross, The Supremes, Motown's flagship act, took twelve singles to the top of the pop sales charts, a feat surpassed only by The Beatles and Elvis Presley. For a time, Gordy's company was the most successful black-owned business in the United States.

Toward the end of the 1970s, a style of dance music called disco began dominating the pop and R&B charts. Starting primarily in urban ethnic and gay nightclubs, disco became an international phenomenon. Records full of repetitive, hypnotic rhythms and sexually suggestive lyrics were produced around the world. In the United States, the most distinctive and successful disco records were made in Philadelphia by veteran soul producers Kenny Gamble (born 1941) and Leon Huff (born 1942). They concocted a successful formula that paired urgent soul vocals with lush but driving arrangements, yielding a string of hits for such artists as The O'Jays, The Three Degrees, Teddy Pendergrass (born 1950), Lou Rawls (born 1936) and others.

In the 1980s, the primary innovation in pop was technological: the music video, a promotional device that allowed singers and bands to perform their latest releases on videotape or film, often in elaborate visual settings. Those who mastered the medium and created consistently memorable videos full of dazzle and effect became the key figures in American pop. Most notable among them were Michael Jackson and Madonna.

Ragtime

A lively, syncopated style of music that originated near the turn of the 20th century, ragtime was the first American popular music to be recognized and enjoyed internationally. Initially a piano music, it derived its name from the syncopated, or "ragged," rhythm played by the right hand to contrast with the marchlike bass rhythm played by the left. Ragtime was influenced by a rhythmic style of banjo playing in the plantation songs presented by minstrel shows, often as the accompaniment to the cakewalk, a complex dance.

Ragtime most likely began as an improvised music played by itinerant pianists in saloons or on riverboats in the Missouri and Kansas regions. While its rhythms were black in origin, ragtime's form, melody and harmony bore European influences. The first published piece of ragtime, "Mississippi Rag" (1897), was by white composer William H. Krell (1873–1933); the first piece by a black composer, "Harlem Rag" by Thomas Turpin (1873–1922), was published later that year. The major figure of ragtime remains Scott Joplin, whose "Maple Leaf Rag" (1899) sold more than a million copies. Joplin's compositions include more than three dozen rags, the ragtime opera *A Guest of Honor,* (the music for which has since been lost) and *Treemonisha* (self-published in 1911), an extended piece of musical theater.

The syncopated ragtime rhythm greatly influenced early examples of Tin Pan Alley songwriting and was often used to describe any strongly rhythmic song. For example, "Alexander's Ragtime Band" (1911) by Irving Berlin was not syncopated, despite the title. Originally played on piano, ragtime was later adapted for ensemble playing by several instruments. This form was certainly an ancestor of jazz. Another important link in the transition to jazz was a more elaborately rhythmic version of ragtime called "stride" piano, which featured a faster, looser, flashier use of the left hand, popularized by such Harlem pianists as James P. Johnson (1891–1955) and Thomas "Fats" Waller. Ultimately eclipsed by jazz, ragtime has been successfully revived several times, most notably in the 1940s and the 1970s.

Rap

The dominant style of American pop in the late 1980s and early 1990s has been rap music, also known as hip-hop. First heard in black neighborhoods of New York City during the late 1970s, rap features fast-talking rhymers called DJs. These characteristically outspoken and boastful vocalists speak over instrumental rhythm tracks. Once generated through "scratching"—the physical manipulation of records on turntables—rap's backing rhythms are now mostly assembled in the recording studio through "sampling"—the digital appropriation and rearrangement of sounds and rhythms from other records.

The first hit rap records, such as "Rapper's Delight" (1979) by the Sugarhill Gang and "The Breaks" (1980) by Kurtis Blow, launched a style that continued to evolve and flourish, primarily among black listeners. By the late 1980s, such rap artists as the strident high-concept group Public Enemy, or performers such as L.L. Cool J and Run-D.M.C. created songs about everything from urban protest to gangster fantasies. Gangsta rap expressed a point of view that was ferociously anti-establishment and aggressively sexual. Gaining a wide following among whites, rap overlapped with and influenced contemporary rock; in the early 1990s it included such acts as Ice T, NWA, Naughty by Nature and Arrested Development.

Rhythm-and-Blues

Introduced during the 1950s as a polite alternative to the term "race record," rhythm-and-blues was originally black music for black listeners. This type of African-American pop was typically performed by a small group, whose usually vocal-based, uptempo music featured a strong backbeat and favored roaring saxophones. Influenced in part by boogie-woogie piano rhythms and gospel-style singing, rhythm-and-blues arose at the end of the big-band era as a substitute dance music for urban African-Americans. R&B (as it became known) was fresh, lively and sexy, as exemplified by the playing of alto saxophonist Louis Jordan (1908–75) and the singing of Big Joe Turner (1911–85). Ballads were also a part of R&B, sung by gospel-influenced male groups, such as The Orioles, The Ravens, The Dominoes and The Drifters. Groups specializing in close harmony, often without musical backup, created a substyle of R&B called doo wop.

R&B came to prominence via small, independent, regional record labels that flourished in America from the late 1940s. The era of the independent label dates from the success of "I Wonder" (1945), a best-selling R&B ballad by Pvt. Cecil Gant. Nearly a decade later, the status of such labels was confirmed when the slow-dance number "Earth Angel" (1954) by The Penguins became the first R&B song on an independent label to appear on the pop charts. Both R&B and the independent labels were integral to the rise of rock 'n' roll, whose sound, market and audience would overlap considerably with R&B's during the mid-1950s.

Rock

In the 1950s, music intended primarily for a youthful audience grew from roots in rhythm-and-blues and country and western music. Raucous, irreverent and stylish, rock 'n' roll exploded to prominence as a combined result of the rise of independent record labels, the increase in the buying power of teenagers, and the blending of black and white musical styles. White teenagers began buying large quantities of R&B records in the early 1950s, searching for danceable beats that the Tin Pan Alley material of the time lacked. Radio disk jockeys, such as Cincinnati-based Alan Freed (1922–65, credited with popularizing the term *rock and roll*), picked up on this crossover trend and started playing R&B records. Many early examples of rock 'n' roll came from R&B performers such as The Coasters, The Drifters, Chuck Berry and Little Richard (born 1935). Similarly, records by certain rock 'n' rollers—Elvis Presley, for example— appeared on the rhythm-and-blues sales charts.

Rock 'n' roll scrambled together bits of blues, country, gospel and boogie-woogie and added a heavy backbeat. As it developed and spread, the form included a wide variety of styles and performers: the rolling New Orleans piano of Antoine "Fats" Domino; the frenzied, over-the-top look and sound of Little Richard; the twangy, country-influenced blues of Chuck Berry; the western-bop rock 'n' roll of Buddy Holly, and others. The western swing–influenced "Rock Around the Clock," by Bill Haley and the Comets, became the first rock 'n' roll record to top the pop charts, in May 1955.

Rockabilly, a style of rock 'n' roll heavily influenced by country music and instrumentation, but with an emphatic R&B backbeat, was the specialty of such performers as Gene Vincent (1935–71), Jerry Lee Lewis (born 1935) and Elvis Presley. Presley began his career in 1954 recording versions of "That's All Right," "Blue Moon of Kentucky," "Good Rockin' Tonight" and other songs. His absolutely original delivery transformed the different elements of these songs into something entirely new. Once audiences got a taste of the Presley style, rock 'n' roll exploded from an obscure musical hybrid into a cultural institution.

Beginning in the 1960s, rock 'n' roll faded while rock became a force around the world. Linked with the idealism and rebellion of the emerging youth movement, the music went through rapid shifts in style that emphasized creativity and experimentation. Directly influenced by American rock 'n' roll and blues forms, several British groups—most notably The Beatles, The Rolling Stones and The Who—established the new look and sound of rock music (long hair, electric guitars, etc.). Folk-singer Bob Dylan became a central figure in American rock in 1965. He released three classic albums in 1965 and 1966, *Bringing It All Back Home, Highway 61 Revisited* and *Blonde on Blonde.* His sophisticated poetic treatment of rock lyrics extended rock's expressive potential; his combined rock and folk sound inspired other folk-rock performers, such as The Byrds.

California served as the headquarters of American rock during the 1960s. In Los Angeles, home of The Byrds, The Doors created a dangerous and sexy sound, while Frank Zappa and the Mothers of Invention produced satiric, avant-garde art-rock. San Francisco spawned psychedelic rock, which was performed by such groups as Jefferson Airplane, The Grateful Dead, and Big Brother and the Holding Company.

In the 1970s, American rock was dominated by singer-songwriters of every stripe and by a type of loud, hard rock called heavy metal, inspired by such British bands as Led Zeppelin and transformed by such U.S. groups as Blue Öyster Cult and Kiss. Late in the decade, a stripped-down, experimental style of rock called new wave emerged. Inspired by groups including The New York Dolls and the Velvet Underground (the seminal 1960s art-rock band led by Lou Reed), some new-wave groups specialized in stylized music with a bohemian sensibility. Other new-wave musicians played an extremely loud, fast style of music called punk rock. Erupting simultaneously in New York and London, punk and new wave were marked by their simple energy and inspiration. American groups, such as The Ramones, Talking Heads, Blondie, the Patti Smith Group, Television, Devo and The B-52s, parlayed experimental playing styles and quirky lyrics into a genuine movement distinguished by its stylistic vitality and freshness.

By the 1980s, the surprises of new wave had been almost completely absorbed into mainstream rock. Music video came to dominate the rock scene, and heavy metal was revived and reinterpreted by such groups as Bon Jovi and Guns and Roses. At the same time, a new strand of alternative rock emerged, bringing success to such groups as R.E.M., Nirvana, Pearl Jam and the Red Hot Chili Peppers.

Soul

Late in the 1950s, a hard-edged style of African-American music became the music of black identity and struggle. The birth of soul is generally traced to the work of Ray Charles, who successfully combined the songs and performance styles of gospel with secular black music. Soul blossomed against the backdrop of the Civil Rights movement, performed by such artists as Solomon Burke (born 1936), Wilson Pickett (born 1941) and Joe Tex (1933–82). Otis Redding (1941–67), one of the most dynamic soul singers of the decade, composed such hits as "I've Been Loving You Too Long" (1965) and "(Sittin' On) The Dock of the Bay" (1968). Another architect of soul music was the fiery performer James Brown, known as the "Godfather of Soul." Between 1956 and 1971, nineteen of his records reached the two top slots on the R&B charts.

Soul music reached a crescendo of popularity with the arrival in 1967 of singer Aretha Franklin. Dubbed "Lady Soul" and "The Queen of Soul," Franklin brought the undiluted power of gospel singing to secular material, including such hits as "I Never Loved a Man (The Way I Love You)" (1967) and "Respect" (1967). Soul had a strong impact on both pop and rock.

Tin Pan Alley

By the beginning of the 20th century, 28th Street in New York City had become the center of America's music publishing industry. Nicknamed Tin Pan Alley for the cacophony of many pianos playing simultaneously in different publishers' offices, it lent that name to a particular type of songwriting that got its start there. The name also came to refer to the era when American popular music became both a big business and an art. The Tin Pan Alley era unofficially dates from the success of "After the Ball" (1892) by Charles K. Harris (1867–1930), a piece of sheet music estimated to have sold more than five million copies. A succession of American classics followed: "The Band Played On" (1895), "In the Good Old Summertime" (1902), "Give My Regards to Broadway" (1904), "Shine On, Harvest Moon" (1908), and dozens more.

Early Tin Pan Alley songs featured music that was simple and direct, often in waltz time; catchy, exotic influences from jazz and ragtime later crept in. Choruses grew in length and importance, for they made songs easy to remember. During the 1920s, several songwriters exemplified the Tin Pan Alley style, often writing for Broadway. They included Irving Berlin, whose "Always" (1925), "What'll I Do" (1924) and "Blue Skies" (1927) are typical of the simple beauty and economy of expression of his songs; Cole Porter, who delivered wit and sophistication in such songs as "Night and Day" (1932), "You're the Top" (1934) and "I Get a Kick Out of You" (1934); and George Gershwin, who wrote dozens of hit songs with his lyricist brother, Ira, including "Someone to Watch Over Me" (1926), "I Got Rhythm" (1930) and "Embraceable You" (1930).

Later Tin Pan Alley songwriters had the advantage of working in an era of developing technology. Radio broadcasting and records circulated their songs far more effectively than sheet music ever had, allowing for greater creativity and success. With the advent of sound film, songwriters had an entirely new market for which to compose.

Yet writing for the theater was still the way most of the classic Tin Pan

Alley songwriters established their reputations. From the 1930s through the 1950s, shows such as *Show Boat* (1927), *Oklahoma!* (1943), *Carousel* (1945), *South Pacific* (1949), *My Fair Lady* (1956), *Guys and Dolls* (1950) and *West Side Story* (1957) incorporated the best of Tin Pan Alley. Composers Jerome Kern (1885–1945), Richard Rodgers, Frederick Loewe, Leonard Bernstein, Frank Loesser and Stephen Sondheim worked with such lyricists as Oscar Hammerstein II and Alan Jay Lerner to perfect the art of telling a story through script and music. Many of their versatile, tightly crafted songs stood independent of the shows and became standards. Gems from the golden era of Tin Pan Alley are still performed by such singers as Frank Sinatra, Liza Minnelli, Barbra Streisand, Barry Manilow (born 1946) and Harry Connick, Jr. (born 1967).

FOREIGN ACCENTS

Many styles of ethnic music in the United States have resisted absorption into the musical mainstream. Each appeals to its own followers and has at times gained popularity among a broader audience.

Centered in Louisiana, Cajun music is made primarily by descendants of the Acadians, French colonists from the Canadian province of Acadia (now Nova Scotia) who emigrated to the Mississippi River Delta in the mid-1700s after being expelled by the British. The Cajuns have remained a distinct presence and community, with a distinct French dialect and an equally distinct music. Cajun music has always been highly rhythmic, used primarily for dancing at socials and house parties called *fais do-do* ("public dance" or "country dance"). By the beginning of the 20th century, a typical Cajun dance band included a fiddle, an accordion, a triangle and often a guitar. Throughout the years, Cajun music has absorbed influences from country and other popular styles and has used amplification. While it is recognized and enjoyed nationally, it also remains essentially regional, sung largely in French.

A separate style called zydeco arose concurrently with Cajun among blacks in Louisiana. Referring to a dance as well as to a style of music, zydeco is faster, more syncopated but less melodic than Cajun music. It reflects elements of rhythm-and-blues and usually features piano, ac-

cordion and washboard (*frittoir*), as well as saxophone, bass and drums. Among its best-known performers was the accordionist Clifton Chenier (1925–87).

By far the most consistently influential "foreign" styles in 20th-century American popular music have come from Latin countries, such as Argentina, Brazil, Cuba and Mexico. These styles have included the tango, which became a national fad in 1913; the rumba in the 1930s; the samba in the 1940s; the mambo, merengue and chachacha in the 1950s; and the bossa nova in the 1960s. Diverse entertainers, such as film star Carmen Miranda (1909–55), television personality Desi Arnaz (1917–86), bandleader Sergio Mendes (born 1941), rock guitarist Carlos Santana (born 1947) and pop singer Gloria Estefan (born 1958), have performed Latin-based music in a variety of media.

Latin music has exerted its strongest influence on jazz, almost from the birth of that genre. Latin rhythms were first widely circulated in the 1930s by the big bands led by Don Azpiazu (1893–1943), who scored a national hit in 1931 with "El Manicero" ("The Peanut Vendor"), and Xavier Cugat (1900–90). During the 1940s, the movement called Afro-Cuban jazz coalesced, chiefly through the efforts of Dizzy Gillespie. Cubop, as it was sometimes known, subsequently entered the repertoires of such jazz artists as Charlie Parker and bandleader Stan Kenton (1912–79). Collaborating with such Brazilian composer-performers as Joao Gilberto (born 1931) and Antonio Carlos Jobim (born 1927), jazzmen introduced the cool rhythms of bossa nova to all sorts of American pop in the 1960s.

Latin music made primarily by and for Hispanic-Americans has also flourished in cities with large Hispanic populations, such as Miami, Los Angeles and, most notably, New York. The best-known of these styles is salsa, which actually includes a variety of styles. Vibrant and uptempo, salsa combines brass and vocal *conjunto* instrumentation with flute and violin *charanqa* sounds, adding congas, timbales and other percussion. Salsa's many star musician-bandleaders include Eddie Palmieri (born 1936), Johnny Pacheco (born 1935) and Ruben Blades.

Near the border separating Texas from Mexico, a community of people known as Tejanos produce *Musica Tejana,* or "Tex-Mex" music. Combining French and German styles, such as the polka, with Spanish and Mexican ones, the form was first played by small dance bands in the 1940s and 1950s. Some bands began with solo accordionists and added guitars or *bajo sextos* (a kind of twelve-string bass). Others emulated the big swing bands by using brass and wind instruments and performing heavily arranged dance music. Today, Musica Tejana bands incorporate such modern styles as rock and soul, while still favoring polkas. The region is also home to the singing guitarist, or *guitarerro,* who specializes in romantic songs and ballads with political or protest content.

Music Festivals Around the World

Every year, thousands of music lovers attend hundreds of music festivals around the world. Whether they wish to hear classical, opera, folk, jazz or any kind of popular music, they can find it at a festival. Below are listed a selection of the most renowned music festivals held in North America and Europe. They cover almost the whole range of musical genres; some incorporate more than one type of music.

North America and the Caribbean

Anchorage Festival of Music
P.O. Box 103251
Anchorage, AK 99510
(907) 276-2465
Classical; June

Artpark
Artpark Box Office
Box 371
Lewiston, NY 14092
(716) 754-9001
Classical; Summer

Asheville Mountain Dance and Folk Festival
Asheville Chamber of Commerce
P.O. Box 1010
Asheville, NC 28802
(800) 257-1300/(800) 458-1300
Folk; August

Aspen Music Festival
P.O. Box AA
Aspen, CO 81612
(303) 925-3254
Classical; Summer

Banff Festival of the Arts
P.O. Box 1020
Banff, Alberta
Canada TOL OCO
(403) 762-6300
Classical; Summer

Bean Blossom Bluegrass Festival
Monroe Bluegrass Festival Headquarters
3819 Dickerson Road
Nashville, TN 37207
(615) 868-3333/(615) 824-3941
Bluegrass; Spring (held in Bean Blossom, IN)

Beethoven Festival of the San Francisco Symphony Orchestra
Symphony Box Office
Davies Symphony Hall
San Francisco, CA 94102
(415) 431-5400
Classical; June

Bermuda Festival
Bermuda Festivals, Ltd.
P.O. Box HM 297
Hamilton HM AX, Bermuda
(809) 295-1291/(800) 223-6106
Classical; January-February

Binghamton Summer Music Festival
c/o Anderson Center Box Office
SUNY
Binghamton, NY 13901
(607) 777-4777
Classical; Summer

Bix Beiderbecke Memorial Jazz Festival
The Bix Beiderbecke Memorial Society
2225 West 17th Street
Davenport, IA 52804
(319) 324-7170
Jazz; July

Blossom Music Center
Box 1000
Cuyahoga Falls, OH 44223
(216) 566-9330/(216) 920-1440
Classical; Summer

Boston Globe Jazz Festival
c/o The Boston Globe
Boston, MA 02107
(617) 929-2649
Jazz; June

Boston Pops
Symphony Hall Box Office
Symphony Hall
Boston, MA 02115
(617) 266-1492/(617) 266-1200
Pops; May-July

Bowdoin Summer Music Festival
Gibson Hall
Bowdoin College
Brunswick, ME 04011
(207) 725-3322/(914) 946-3450
Classical; Summer

Brevard Music Center
P.O. Box 592
Brevard, NC 28712
(704) 884-2011
Classical; Summer

Britt Festivals
P.O. Box 1124
Medford, OR 97501
(503) 773-6077/(800) 88-BRITT
Classical; Summer

Caramoor Music Festival
Box R
Katonah, NY 10536
(914) 232-5035
Classical; Summer

Central City Summer Festival
Central City Opera House Association
621 Seventeenth Street, Suite 1601
Denver, CO 80293
(303) 292-6700
Opera; Summer

Chautauqua Summer Music Program
Chautauqua Institution
P.O. Box 1095
Chautauqua, NY 14722
(716) 357-6200
Classical; Summer

Cincinnati Summer Opera Festival
Cincinnati Opera, Music Hall
1241 Elm Street
Cincinnati, OH 45210
(513) 241-2742
Opera; Summer

Colorado Music Festival
1035 Pearl Street, Suite 104
Boulder, CO 80302
(303) 449-1397
Classical; Summer

Connecticut Early Music Festival
P.O. Box 329
New London, CT 06320
(203) 444-2419
Classical; June

Cornell College Spring Music Festival
Cornell College
Mount Vernon, IA 52313
(319) 895-4000
Classical; Spring

Eastern Music Festival
P.O. Box 22026
Greensboro, NC 27420
(919) 852-0057
Classical; Summer

Festival Casals
P.O. Box 41227 Minillas Station
San Juan, PR 00940-1227
(809) 721-7727
Classical; June

Festival—Institute at Round Top, The
Post Office Drawer 89
Round Top, TX 78954
(409) 249-3129
Classical; May-July

Festival of American Folklife
Smithsonian Institution
Office of Folklife Programs
955 L'Enfant Plaza, S.W., Suite 2600
Washington, D.C. 20560
(202) 287-3424
Folk; Summer

Flagstaff Festival of the Arts
P.O. Box 1607
Flagstaff, AZ 86002
(602) 774-7750
Classical; July

Glimmerglass Opera
20 Chestnut Street
Cooperstown, NY 13326
(607) 547-2255
Opera; Summer

Grant's Annual Bluegrass and Old-Time Music Festival
Bill and Juarez Grant
Route 2, Box 74
Hugo, OK 74743
(405) 326-5598/(405) 326-6504
Bluegrass; August

Hollywood Bowl Summer Festival
c/o Los Angeles Philharmonic Association
135 North Grand Avenue
Los Angeles, CA 90012
(213) 972-7300/(213) 850-2000
Classical; Summer

International Country Music Fan Fair
Box 2804 Opryland Drive
Nashville, TN 37214
(615) 889-7503
Country; June

JVC Jazz Festival Newport
P.O. Box 605
Newport, RI 02840
(401) 847-3700
Jazz; August

Mann Music Center
1617 John F. Kennedy Boulevard
Philadelphia, PA 19103
(215) 567-0707
Classical; Summer

Marlboro Music Festival
135 South 18th Street
Philadelphia, PA 19103
(215) 569-4690
Marlboro, VT 05344
(802) 254-8163/(802) 254-2394
Classical; Summer

Meadow Brook Music Festival
Oakland University
P.O. Box 705
Rochester, MI 48309
(313) 377-2010
Classical; Summer

Mellon Jazz Festival
Academy of Music
Philadelphia, PA 19102
(215) 893-1930/(215) 561-5060
Jazz; June

Michigan Womyn's Music Festival
W.W.T.M.C.
Box 22
Walhalla, MI 49458
(616) 757-4766
Folk, Pop, Rock; August

Monterey Jazz Festival
P.O. Box Jazz
Monterey, CA 93942
(408) 373-3366
Jazz; September

Mostly Mozart Festival
Lincoln Center for the Performing Arts
New York, NY 10023
(212) 874-2424
Classical; Summer

Muny, The
Box Office, Forest Park
St. Louis, MO 63112
(314) 361-1900
Pops; Summer

Music at Gretna
P.O. Box 519
Mount Gretna, PA 17064
(717) 964-3836
Classical; Summer

Music Mountain
Music Mountain, Inc.
Box 671
Salisbury, CT 06068
(203) 496-1222
Classical; Summer

Musical Academy of the West Summer Festival
1070 Fairway Road
Santa Barbara, CA 93108
(805) 969-4726
Classical; Summer

National Music Camp
Interlochen School of the Arts
Interlochen, MI 49643
(616) 276-9221
Classical; Summer

New England Folk Festival
New England Folk Festival Association
1950 Massachusetts Avenue
Cambridge, MA 01241
(617) 354-1340
Folk; April

New Hampshire Music Festival
P.O. Box 147
Center Harbor, NH 03226
(603) 253-4331
Classical; Summer

New Orleans Jazz and Heritage Festival
New Orleans Jazz and Heritage
Foundation
P.O. Box 53407
New Orleans, LA 70153
(504) 522-4786
Jazz; April-May

New York Philharmonic Free Outdoor Park Concerts
132 West 65th Street
New York, NY 10011
(212) 580-8700
Classical; August

Newport Music Festival
P.O. Box 3300
Newport, RI 02840
(401) 846-1133/(401) 849-0700
Classical; July

Norfolk Chamber Music Festival
96 Wall Street
New Haven, CT 06520
(203) 432-1966/(203) 542-5537
Classical; Summer

Northwest Folklife Festival
Seattle Center
305 Harrison Street
Seattle, WA 98109
(206) 684-7300
Folk; May

Old Fiddler's Convention
P.O. Box 655
Galax, VA 24333
(703) 236-6355
Bluegrass; August

Ole Time Fiddler's and Bluegrass Festival
Fiddler's Grove, Inc.
P.O. Box 11
Union Grove, NC 28689
(704) 539-4417
Bluegrass; May

Orford International Music Festival
Centre d'Arts Orford
P.O. Box 280
Magog, Quebec
Canada JIX 3W8
(819) 843-3981
Classical; July-August

Ozark Folk Festival
P.O. Box 88
Eureka Springs, AR 72632
(501) 253-8737
Folk; November

Pacific Northwest Wagner Festival
Seattle Opera
P.O. Box 9248
Seattle, WA 98109
(206) 443-4711/(800) 426-1619
Opera; August

Paul Masson Summer Series
Paul Masson Vineyard
P.O. Box 1852
Saratoga, CA 95070
(408) 741-5181
Classical; Summer

Ravinia Festival
P.O. Box 896
Highland Park, IL 60035
(312) RAVINIA
Classical; Summer

Sacramento Dixieland Jazz Jubilee
2787 Del Monte Street
West Sacramento, CA 95691
(916) 372-5277
Jazz; May

San Francisco Symphony Pops
c/o Davies Symphony Hall
San Francisco, CA 94102-4575
(415) 431-5400
Pops; July

San Luis Obispo Mozart Festival
San Luis Obispo Mozart Festival Association
P.O. Box 311
San Luis Obispo, CA 93406
(805) 543-4580
Classical; July-August

Santa Fe Chamber Music Festival
P.O. Box 853
Santa Fe, NM 87504
(505) 983-2075/(800) 96-BRAVO
Classical; Summer

Santa Fe Opera Festival
Santa Fe Opera
P.O. Box 2408
Santa Fe, NM 87504-2408
(505) 982-3855
Opera; July-August

Saratoga Performing Arts Center
Saratoga Springs, NY 12866
(518) 587-3330
Classical; Summer

Spoleto Festival U.S.A.
P.O. Box 157
Charleston, SC 29402
(803) 722-2764/(803) 572-7863
Classical; May-June

Stratford Festival, The
P.O. Box 520
Stratford, Ontario
Canada N5A 6V2
(519) 271-4040
Classical; May-October

Tanglewood Music Festival
Festival Ticket Office
Symphony Hall
Boston, MA 02115
(617) 266-1492

Festival Ticket Office
Tanglewood
Lenox, MA 01240
(413) 637-1666
Classical; Summer

Telluride Jazz Festival
Box 505
Telluride, CO 81435
(303) 728-3171/(800) 525-3455
Jazz; August

Texas Folklife Festival
The Institute of Texan Culture
P.O. Box 1226
San Antonio, TX 78294
(512) 226-7651
Folk; August

Victoria International Festival
McPherson Playhouse Box Office
3 Centennial Square
Victoria, British Columbia
Canada V8W 1PS
(604) 386-6121/(604) 595-4522
Classical, July

Waterloo Summer Music Festival
Waterloo Village
Stanhope, NJ 07874
(201) 347-0900/(201) 347-4700
Classical; June-July

Wave Hill Performing Arts Series
675 West 252nd Street
Bronx, NY 10471
(212) 549-3200
Classical; September-May

Winnipeg Folk Festival
264 Taché Avenue
Winnipeg, Manitoba
Canada R2H IZ9
(204) 231-0096
Folk; July

Winterhawk Bluegrass Festival
P.O. Box 161
Tremont City, OH 45372
(513) 788-2526
Bluegrass; July (held in Hillsdale, NY)

**Wolf Trap Farm Park for the
Performing Arts**
1624 Trap Road
Vienna, VA 22182
(703) 255-1900
Classical; Summer

Worcester Music Festival
Worcester County Music Association
Memorial Auditorium
Worcester, MA 01608
(617) 754-3231
Classical; October-November

Europe

Aix-en-Provence Festival
Festival d'Aix
Palais de l'Ancien Archêveché
13100 Aix-en-Provence, France
42-23-11-20
Classical, Opera; July

Albi Festival of Music
Albi Festival de Musique
Office de Tourisme
Palais de la Berbie
81000 Albi, France
63-54-28-88
Classical, Opera; July-August

Aldeburgh Festival of Music and the Arts
Box Office, Aldeburgh Foundation
High Street, Aldeburgh
Suffolk IP15 5AX, England
0728/453543
Classical, Opera; June

Árhus Festival
Musikhuset
Thomas Jensen Allé
DK-8000 Árhus C, Denmark
86/12-12-33
Classical, Opera, Folk, Jazz; September

Athens Festival
Athens Festival Box Office
4, Stadiou Street
GR-10564 Athens, Greece
01/323-0049
Classical, Opera; Summer

Attergau Summer of Culture
Attergauer Kultursommer
St. Georgen Tourist Office
A-4880 St. Georgen im Attergau, Austria
07667/386
Classical; July-August

BBC Henry Wood Promenade Concerts
Royal Albert Hall
Kensington Gore
London SW7, England
071/589-8212
Classical; Summer

Belfast Festival at Queens
Festival Booking Office
25 College Gardens
Belfast BT9 6BS, Northern Ireland
0232/66-55-77
Classical, Opera; November

Bergen International Festival
Festspillene i Bergen
Box 183
N-5001 Bergen, Norway
05/32-04-00
Classical, Opera, Folk, Jazz; May-June

Berlin Festival Weeks
Berliner Festwochen
Budapester Strasse 50
D-1000 Berlin 30, Germany
030/2-54-840
Classical, Opera; September

Bratislava Music Festival
Musicfestspiele Bratislava
Michalská 10
CS-81536 Bratislava, Slovak Republic
011-42-7/334528
Classical, Opera, Folk; September-
October

Bregrenz Festival
Bregrenzer Festspeil
Postfach 311
A-6901 Bregrenz, Austria
05574/22-8110
Classical, Opera; July-August

Brighton International Festival
Festival Office, Marlborough Hall
54 Old Steine, Brighton
East Sussex BN1 1EQ, England
0273/28488
Classical, Opera; May

Bruges Early Music Festival
Collaert Mansionstraat 30
B-3000 Brugge, Belgium
050/33-22-83
Classical; July-August

Canterbury Festival
Canterbury Festival Box Office
59 Ivy Lane, Canterbury
Kent CT1 1TU, England
0227/455600
Classical, Opera; October

Carinthian Summer Festival
Carinthischer Sommer
A-9570 Ossiach, Austria
04243/510
Classical, Opera; July-August

Castel de Peralada International Music Festival
Festival Internacional de Musica de
Castell de Peralada
Peralada (Girona), Spain
972/53-81-25
Classical, Opera; June-July

Chorégies d'Orange
B.P. 180
84105 Orange Cedex, France
90-34-24-24
Classical, Opera; July-August

Days of Old Music
Tage Alter Musik
Forum Artium
Am Kasinopark 1
D-4504 Georgsmarienhütte, Germany
05401/34160
Classical; September (held in Osnabrück)

Dresden Music Festival
Besucherdienst der Dresdener
Musikfestspiele
Postfach 110
O-8012 Dresden, Germany
51/495-50-25
Classical, Opera; May-June

Dumfries and Galloway Arts Festival
Festival Office, Gracefield Arts Centre
28 Edinburgh Road
Dumfries DG1 1JQ, Scotland
0387/56479
Classical, Opera, Folk, Jazz; May-June

Edinburgh International Festival
21 Market Street
Edinburgh EH1 1BW, Scotland
031/226-4001
Classical, Opera; August-September

Europalia Festival
Palais des Beaux-Arts
Rue Ravenstein 23
B-1000 Brussels, Belgium
02/512-50-45
Classical, Opera; Fall

Festival of Sacred Music
Festival d'Art Sacré
4, rue Jules-Cousin
74004 Paris, France
161/42-33-43-00
Classical; Fall

Festival of Two Worlds
Associazione Festival dei due Mondi
Teatro Nuovo
Biglietteria Festival
06049 Spoleto, Italy
0743/44097
Classical, Opera; June-July

Festival of Wallonia
Rue Sur-les-Foulons 11
B-4000 Liège, Belgium
041/22-32-48
Classical, Opera; Summer

Flanders Festival
Algemeen Secretariat
Eugene Flageyplein 18
B-1050 Brussels, Belgium
02/649-20-80
Classical, Opera; September-October

Florence May Music Festival
Maggio Musicale Fiorentino
Biglietteria del Teatro Comunale
Corso Italia 16
50123 Firenze, Italy
055/2779236
Classical, Opera; April-July

Glyndebourne Festival
Lewes
East Sussex BN8 5UU, England
0273/541111
Opera; May-August

Handel in Oxford Festival
Music at Oxford
Cumnor Hill
Oxford OX2 9HA, England
0865/864056
Classical; July

Holland Festival, The
Netherlands Reservation Center
P.O. Box 404
2260 AK Leidschendam, The
Netherlands
070/320-25-00
Opera, Classical; June (held in
Amsterdam)

**Huddersfield Contemporary Music
Festival**
Box Office, Tourist Information Centre
Albion Street, Huddersfield
West Yorkshire HD1 2NW, England
0484/422288 ext. 2026/7
Classical, Opera; November-December

Interart Festival Center
P.O. Box 80
H-1366 Budapest, Hungary
011-36-1/1179910
Classical; several festivals throughout the
year

International Beethoven Festival
Internationales Beethovenfest
Mulheimer Platz 1
D-5300 Bonn, Germany
0228/774533
Classical; September-October

**International Festival of Music and
Dance**
Festival Internacional de Música y Danza
c/Gracia, 21, 4
18002 Granada, Spain
958/26-74-42
Classical, Opera; June-July

**International Festival of the Ancient
Organ of Valère**
Festival International de L'Orgue Ancien
Case Postale 2088
CH-1950 Sion 2, Switzerland
027/22-85-86
Classical; Summer

International Music Weeks
Settimane Musicali Internazionali
Riviera di Chiaia 200
Museo Pignatelli
80121 Napoli, Italy
081/761-28-57
Classical, Opera; June

Jyväskylä Arts Festival
Kramsunkatu 1
SF-40600 Jyväskylä, Finland
941/617-531
Classical; June

L'Ile-de-France Festival
4, rue de la Michodière
75002 Paris, France
161/42-65-07-22
Classical, Jazz; September-November

**Llangollen International Musical
Eisteddfod**
Eisteddfod Office
Llangollen, Clwyd
North Wales LL20 8NG
0978/860236
Classical; July

**London Festival Orchestra's Cathedral
Classics**
Festival Box Office
P.O. Box 1234
London SW2 2TG, England
081/671-7100
Classical; May-July

Lucerne International Music Festival
Luzern Internationale Musicfestwochen
Hirschmattstrasse 13
CH-6002 Luzern, Switzerland
041-23-52-72
Classical; August-September

Ludwigsburg Castle Festival
Ludwigsburger Schlossfestspeile
Postfach 1022
D-7140 Ludwigsburg, Germany
07141/28000
Classical, Opera, Jazz; Summer

Menton Festival of Music
Festival de Musique de Menton
Palais d L'Europe
Avenue Boyer, B.P. 111
06503 Menton Cedex, France
93-35-82-22
Classical, Opera; August

Montreux-Vevey Music Festival
Festival de Musique
Rue du Théâtre 5
Case Postale 162
CH-1820 Montreux 2, Switzerland
021/963-54-50
Classical; August-October

Mozart Week
Mozartwoche
International Stiftung Mozarteum
Postfach 34, Schwartzstrasse 26
A-5024 Salzburg, Austria
0662/73154
Classical, Opera; January-February

Munich Opera Festival
Münchner Opern-Festspiele
Maximillianstrasse 11
D-8000 Munich 2, Germany
089/22136
Opera; July

Music and Theater in Herrenhausen
Ernst-August Platz 8
D-3000 Hannover, Germany
0511/168-3903
Classical, Opera, Jazz; Summer

Musical Encounters
Rencontres Musicales d'Evian
47, rue de Ponthieu
75008 Paris, France
Fax: 42-25-60-66
Classical, Opera; May (held in Evian-Les-Bains)

Musical September
Septembre Musica
Vetrina per Torino
Assessorato Cultura
Piazza San Carlo, 161
10123 Torino, Italy
011/510-450
Classical; August-September

Musical Weeks of Ascona
Settimane Musicale di Ascona
Ente Turistico Ascona e Losone
CH-6612 Ascona, Switzerland
093/35-55-44
Classical; August-October

Paris Autumn Festival
Festival d'Automne à Paris
156, rue de Rivoli
75001 Paris, France
161/42-96-12-27
Classical, Opera; Fall

Patras International Festival
P.O. Box 1184
GR-26110 Patras, Greece
061/336-390
Classical, Jazz; Summer

Prague Spring International Music Festival
Bohemia Tickets International
P.O. Box 534
Prague 1-11121, Czech Republic
011-42-2/263747
Classical, Opera; May-June

Richard Wagner Festival (Bayreuth)
Richard Wagner Festspiele
Postbox 100262
D-8580 Bayreuth 1, Germany
0921/2-02-21
Opera; July-August

Salzburg Festival
Salzburger Festspiele
P.O. Box 140
A-5010 Salzburg, Austria
0662/84-25-41
Classical, Opera; July-August

San Sebastian Musical Weeks
Quincenza Musicial de San Sebastian
C/República Argentina
20003 San Sebastian, Spain
943/48-12-38
Classical, Opera; August-September

Santander International Festival
Festival Internacional Santander
Avda Calvo Sotelo, 15-5
39002 Santander, Spain
942/31-48-19
Classical, Opera; July-August

Savonlinna Opera Festival
Olavinkatu 35
SF-57130 Savonlinna, Finland
957/514-700
Classical, Opera; July-August

Schleswig-Holstein Music Festival
Postfach 38 40
D-2300 Keil 1, Germany
0431/56-70-80
Classical; June-August

Schwetzingen Festival
Schwetzinger Festspiele
Postfach 1941
D-6830 Schwetzingen, Germany
06202/4933
Classical, Opera; April-June

Stresa Music Weeks
Settimane Musicali
Palazzo dei Congressi
Via R. Bonghi 4
1-28049 Stresa, Italy
0323/31-095
Classical; August-September

Styrian Autumn
Steirischer Herbst
Sackstrasse 17/1
A-8010 Graz, Austria
0316/82-30-07
Classical; October

Swansea Festival of Music and the Arts
City Centre Booking Office
Singleton Street
Swansea SA1 3QG, Wales
0792/47-00-02
Classical, Opera; October

Taormina Arts
Taormina Arte
Via Pirandello 31
98039 Taormina, Italy
0942/21142
Classical, Opera; Summer

Utrecht Early Music Festival
Organisatie Oude Musiek
Postbus 734
3500 As Utrecht, The Netherlands
030/34-09-21
Classical, Opera; August-September

Verdi Festival
Fondazione Verdi Festival
Bigletteria Teatro Regio
Via Garibaldi 19
43100 Parma, Italy
0521/218678
Classical, Opera; September

Verona Arena
Arene di Verona
Information Office—Ente Arena
Piazza Bra, 28
37121 Verona, Italy
045/590109
Classical, Opera; July-August

Vienna Festival
Wiener Festwochen
Lehárgasse 11
A-1060 Vienna, Austria
0222/586-09-23
Classical, Opera, Jazz; May-June

Vienna's Musical Summer
Wiener Musik Sommer
Friedrich-Schmidt Platz 5
A-1082 Vienna, Austria
Classical, Opera, Jazz, Pops; Summer

Music Awards

Each year, the international music community bestows numerous awards upon its most accomplished members. Some of the honorees are selected by groups of their peers; others win recognition through competitions that showcase their talent. Included here is a representative sampling of the best-known awards and competitions.

The GRAMMY Awards

National Academy of Recording Arts and Sciences, Inc.
3402 Pico Boulevard
Santa Monica, CA 90405
(310) 392-3777

Awarded each year since 1958, the GRAMMYs recognize achievement in eighty artistic and technical categories, as well as outstanding lifetime contributions to the recording industry. Winners are chosen by the more than seven thousand voting members of the Academy. Listed here are each year's winners in the top five categories.

1993   Record of the Year: "I Will Always Love You," Whitney Houston
Album of the Year: *The Bodyguard Soundtrack,* Whitney Houston
Song of the Year: "A Whole New World," Alan Menken and Tim Rice (perf. by Celine Dion and Peabo Bryson)
Best Pop Vocal Performance, Female: "I Will Always Love You," Whitney Houston
Best Pop Vocal Performance, Male: "If I Ever Lose My Faith in You," Sting

1992   Record of the Year: "Tears in Heaven," Eric Clapton
Album of the Year: *Unplugged,* Eric Clapton
Song of the Year: "Tears in Heaven," Eric Clapton and Will Jennings (perf. by Eric Clapton)
Best Pop Vocal Performance, Female: *Constant Craving,* k.d. lang
Best Pop Vocal Performance, Male: "Tears in Heaven," Eric Clapton

1991   Record of the Year: "Unforgettable," Natalie Cole
Album of the Year: *Unforgettable,* Natalie Cole
Song of the Year: "Unforgettable," Irving Gordon (perf. by Natalie Cole)
Best Pop Vocal Performance, Female: "Something to Talk About," Bonnie Raitt

Best Pop Vocal Performance, Male: "When a Man Loves a Woman," Michael Bolton

1990   Record of the Year: "Another Day in Paradise," Phil Collins
Album of the Year: *Back on the Block,* Quincy Jones
Song of the Year: "From a Distance," Julie Gold (perf. by Bette Midler)
Best Pop Vocal Performance, Female: "Vision of Love," Mariah Carey
Best Pop Vocal Performance, Male: "Oh Pretty Woman," Roy Orbison

1989   Record of the Year: "Wind Beneath My Wings," Bette Midler
Album of the Year: *Nick of Time,* Bonnie Raitt
Song of the Year: "Wind Beneath My Wings," Larry Henley and Jeff Silbar (perf. by Bette Midler)
Best Pop Vocal Performance, Female: "Nick of Time," Bonnie Raitt
Best Pop Vocal Performance, Male: "How Am I Supposed to Live Without You," Michael Bolton

1988   Record of the Year: "Don't Worry Be Happy," Bobby McFerrin
Album of the Year: *Faith,* George Michael
Song of the Year: "Don't Worry Be Happy," Bobby McFerrin
Best Pop Vocal Performance, Female: "Fast Car," Tracy Chapman
Best Pop Vocal Performance, Male: "Don't Worry Be Happy," Bobby McFerrin

1987   Record of the Year: "Graceland," Paul Simon
Album of the Year: *Joshua Tree,* U2
Song of the Year: "Somewhere Out There," James Horner, Barry Mann and Cynthia Weil (perf. by Linda Ronstadt and James Ingram)
Best Pop Vocal Performance, Female: "I Wanna Dance with Somebody," Whitney Houston
Best Pop Vocal Performance, Male: *Bring on the Night,* Sting

1986   Record of the Year: "Higher Love," Steve Winwood
Album of the Year: *Graceland,* Paul Simon
Song of the Year: "That's What Friends Are For," Burt Bacharach and Carole Bayer Sager (perf. by Dionne & Friends)
Best Pop Vocal Performance, Female: *The Broadway Album,* Barbra Streisand
Best Pop Vocal Performance, Male: "Higher Love," Steve Winwood

1985   Record of the Year: "We Are the World," USA for Africa
Album of the Year: *No Jacket Required,* Phil Collins
Song of the Year: "We Are the World," Michael Jackson and Lionel Richie (perf. by USA for Africa)
Best Pop Vocal Performance, Female: "Saving All My Love for You," Whitney Houston
Best Pop Vocal Performance, Male: *No Jacket Required,* Phil Collins

1984   Record of the Year: "What's Love Got to Do with It," Tina Turner
Album of the Year: *Can't Slow Down,* Lionel Richie

Song of the Year: "What's Love Got to Do with It," Graham Lyle and Terry Britten (perf. by Tina Turner)

Best Pop Vocal Performance, Female: "What's Love Got to Do with It," Tina Turner

Best Pop Vocal Performance, Male: "Against All Odds," Phil Collins

1983   Record of the Year: "Beat It," Michael Jackson

Album of the Year: *Thriller,* Michael Jackson

Song of the Year: "Every Breath You Take," Sting

Best Pop Vocal Performance, Female: "Flashdance What a Feeling," Irene Cara

Best Pop Vocal Performance, Male: *Thriller,* Michael Jackson

1982   Record of the Year: "Rosanna," Toto

Album of the Year: *Toto IV,* Toto

Song of the Year: "Always on My Mind," Johnny Christopher, Mark James and Wayne Carson (perf. by Willie Nelson)

Best Pop Vocal Performance, Female: "You Should Hear How She Talks About You," Melissa Manchester

Best Pop Vocal Performance, Male: "Truly," Lionel Richie

1981   Record of the Year: "Bette Davis Eyes," Kim Carnes

Album of the Year: *Double Fantasy,* John Lennon and Yoko Ono

Song of the Year: "Bette Davis Eyes," Donna Weis and Jackie DeShannon (perf. by Kim Carnes)

Best Pop Vocal Performance, Female: *Lena Horne—The Lady and Her Music Live on Broadway,* Lena Horne

Best Pop Vocal Performance, Male: *Breakin' Away,* Al Jarreau

1980   Record of the Year: "Sailing," Christopher Cross

Album of the Year: *Christopher Cross,* Christopher Cross

Song of the Year: "Sailing," Christopher Cross

Best Pop Vocal Performance, Female: "The Rose," Bette Midler

Best Pop Vocal Performance, Male: "This Is It," Kenny Loggins

1979   Record of the Year: "What a Fool Believes," The Doobie Brothers

Album of the Year: *52nd Street,* Billy Joel

Song of the Year: "What a Fool Believes," Kenny Loggins and Michael McDonald (perf. by The Doobie Brothers)

Best Pop Vocal Performance, Female: "I'll Never Love This Way Again," Dionne Warwick

Best Pop Vocal Performance, Male: *52nd Street,* Billy Joel

1978   Record of the Year: "Just the Way You Are," Billy Joel

Album of the Year: *Saturday Night Fever,* Bee Gees and multiple artists

Song of the Year: "Just the Way You Are," Billy Joel

Best Pop Vocal Performance, Female: "You Needed Me," Anne Murray

Best Pop Vocal Performance, Male: "Copacabana," Barry Manilow

1977   Record of the Year: "Hotel California," Eagles

Album of the Year: *Rumours,* Fleetwood Mac
Song of the Year: "Love Theme from *A Star Is Born* (Evergreen),"
Barbra Streisand and Paul Williams (perf. by Barbra Streisand); tied
with "You Light Up My Life," Joe Brooks (perf. by Debby Boone)
Best Pop Vocal Performance, Female: "Love Theme from *A Star Is
Born* (Evergreen)," Barbra Streisand
Best Pop Vocal Performance, Male: "Handy Man," James Taylor

1976   Record of the Year: "This Masquerade," George Benson
Album of the Year: *Songs in the Key of Life,* Stevie Wonder
Song of the Year: "I Write the Songs," Bruce Johnston (perf. by Barry
Manilow)
Best Pop Vocal Performance, Female: *Hasten Down the Wind,* Linda
Ronstadt
Best Pop Vocal Performance, Male: *Songs in the Key of Life,* Stevie
Wonder

1975   Record of the Year: "Love Will Keep Us Together," Captain and
Tennille
Album of the Year: *Still Crazy After All These Years,* Paul Simon
Song of the Year: "Send in the Clowns," Stephen Sondheim (perf. by
Judy Collins)
Best Pop Vocal Performance, Female: "At Seventeen," Janis Ian
Best Pop Vocal Performance, Male: *Still Crazy After All These Years,*
Paul Simon

1974   Record of the Year: "I Honestly Love You," Olivia Newton-John
Album of the Year: *Fulfillingness' First Finale,* Stevie Wonder
Song of the Year: "The Way We Were," Marilyn and Alan Bergman
and Marvin Hamlisch (perf. by Barbra Streisand)
Best Pop Vocal Performance, Female: "I Honestly Love You," Olivia
Newton-John
Best Pop Vocal Performance, Male: *Fulfillingness' First Finale,* Stevie
Wonder

1973   Record of the Year: "Killing Me Softly With His Song," Roberta
Flack
Album of the Year: *Innervisions,* Stevie Wonder
Song of the Year: "Killing Me Softly With His Song," Norman
Gimbel, Charles Fox (perf. by Roberta Flack)
Best Pop Vocal Performance, Female: "Killing Me Softly With His
Song," Roberta Flack
Best Pop Vocal Performance, Male: "You Are the Sunshine of My
Life," Stevie Wonder

1972   Record of the Year: "The First Time Ever I Saw Your Face," Roberta
Flack
Album of the Year: *The Concert For Bangladesh,* multiple artists
Song of the Year: "The First Time Ever I Saw Your Face," Ewan
MacColl (perf. by Roberta Flack)

Best Pop Vocal Performance, Female: "I Am Woman," Helen Reddy

Best Pop Vocal Performance, Male: "Without You," Harry Nilsson

1971 Record of the Year: "It's Too Late," Carole King

Album of the Year: *Tapestry,* Carole King

Song of the Year: "You've Got a Friend," Carole King (perf. by James Taylor)

Best Pop Vocal Performance, Female: *Tapestry,* Carole King

Best Pop Vocal Performance, Male: "You've Got a Friend," James Taylor

1970 Record of the Year: "Bridge Over Troubled Water," Simon and Garfunkel

Album of the Year: *Bridge Over Troubled Water,* Simon and Garfunkel

Song of the Year: "Bridge Over Troubled Water," Paul Simon (perf. by Simon and Garfunkel)

Best Contemporary Vocal Performance, Female: *I'll Never Fall in Love Again,* Dionne Warwick

Best Contemporary Vocal Performance, Male: "Everything Is Beautiful," Ray Stevens

1969 Record of the Year: "Aquarius/Let the Sunshine In," 5th Dimension

Album of the Year: *Blood, Sweat & Tears,* Blood, Sweat & Tears

Song of the Year: "Games People Play," Joe South (perf. by King Curtis)

Best Contemporary Vocal Performance, Female: "Is That All There Is," Peggy Lee

Best Contemporary Vocal Performance, Male: "Everybody's Talkin'," Harry Nilsson

1968 Record of the Year: "Mrs. Robinson," Simon and Garfunkel

Album of the Year: *By the Time I Get to Phoenix,* Glen Campbell

Song of the Year: "Little Green Apples," Bobby Russell (perf. by B. J. Thomas)

Best Contemporary-Pop Vocal Performance, Female: "Do You Know the Way to San Jose," Dionne Warwick

Best Contemporary-Pop Vocal Performance, Male: "Light My Fire," Jose Feliciano

1967 Record of the Year: "Up, Up and Away," 5th Dimension

Album of the Year: *Sgt. Pepper's Lonely Hearts Club Band,* The Beatles

Song of the Year: "Up, Up and Away," Jim Webb (perf. by 5th Dimension)

Best Vocal Performance, Female: "Ode to Billie Joe," Bobbie Gentry

Best Vocal Performance, Male: "By the Time I Get to Phoenix," Glen Campbell

1966 Record of the Year: "Strangers in the Night," Frank Sinatra

Album of the Year: *Sinatra: A Man and His Music,* Frank Sinatra

Song of the Year: "Michele," John Lennon and Paul McCartney (perf. by The Beatles)

Best Vocal Performance, Female: "If He Walked Into My Life," Eydie Gorme

Best Vocal Performance, Male: "Strangers in the Night," Frank Sinatra

1965   Record of the Year: "A Taste of Honey," Herb Alpert and the Tijuana Brass

Album of the Year: *September of My Years,* Frank Sinatra

Song of the Year: "The Shadow of Your Smile," Paul Francis Webster and Johnny Mandel (perf. by Sergio Mendez)

Best Vocal Performance, Female: *My Name is Barbra,* Barbra Streisand

Best Vocal Performance, Male: "It Was a Very Good Year," Frank Sinatra

1964   Record of the Year: "The Girl from Ipanema," Stan Getz and Astrud Gilberto

Album of the Year: *Getz/Gilberto,* Stan Getz and Joao Gilberto

Song of the Year: "Hello, Dolly!" Jerry Herman (perf. by Louis Armstrong)

Best Vocal Performance, Female: "People," Barbra Streisand

Best Vocal Performance, Male: "Hello, Dolly!" Louis Armstrong

1963   Record of the Year: "The Days of Wine and Roses," Henry Mancini

Album of the Year: *The Barbra Streisand Album,* Barbra Streisand

Song of the Year: "The Days of Wine and Roses," Henry Mancini and Johnny Mercer (perf. by Henry Mancini)

Best Vocal Performance, Female: *The Barbra Streisand Album,* Barbra Streisand

Best Vocal Performance, Male: "Wives and Lovers," Jack Jones

1962   Record of the Year: "I Left My Heart in San Francisco," Tony Bennett

Album of the Year: *The First Family,* Vaughn Meader

Song of the Year: "What Kind of Fool Am I," Leslie Bricusse and Anthony Newley (perf. by Anthony Newley)

Best Solo Vocal Performance, Female: *Ella Swings Brightly with Nelson Riddle,* Ella Fitzgerald

Best Solo Vocal Performance, Male: "I Left My Heart in San Francisco," Tony Bennett

1961   Record of the Year: "Moon River," Henry Mancini

Album of the Year: *Judy at Carnegie Hall,* Judy Garland

Song of the Year: "Moon River," Henry Mancini and Johnny Mercer (perf. by Henry Mancini)

Best Solo Vocal Performance, Female: *Judy at Carnegie Hall,* Judy Garland

Best Solo Vocal Performance, Male: "Lollipops and Roses," Jack Jones

1960   Record of the Year: "Theme from a Summer Place," Percy Faith

Album of the Year: *Button Down Mind,* Bob Newhart

Song of the Year: "Theme From Exodus," Ernest Gold (perf. by Henry Mancini)

Best Vocal Performance Single Record or Track, Female: "Mack the Knife," Ella Fitzgerald

Best Vocal Performance Single Record or Track, Male: "Georgia on My Mind," Ray Charles

1959   Record of the Year: "Mack the Knife," Bobby Darin

Album of the Year: *Come Dance With Me,* Frank Sinatra

Song of the Year: "The Battle of New Orleans," Jimmy Driftwood (perf. by Johnny Horton)

Best Vocal Performance, Female: "But Not For Me," Ella Fitzgerald

Best Vocal Performance, Male: *Come Dance With Me,* Frank Sinatra

1958   Record of the Year: "Nel Blu Dipinto Di Blu (Volare)," Domenico Modugno

Album of the Year: *The Music From Peter Gunn,* Henry Mancini

Song of the Year: "Nel Blu Dipinto Di Blu (Volare)," Domenico Modugno

Best Vocal Performance, Female: *Ella Fitzgerald Sings the Irving Berlin Song Book,* Ella Fitzgerald

Best Vocal Performance, Male: "Catch a Falling Star," Perry Como

The Pulitzer Prize for Composing

Pulitzer Prize Office
702 Journalism
Columbia University
New York, NY 10027
(212) 854-3841

Although more familiar for its awards in journalism and letters, the Pulitzer organization also recognizes achievement in music composition. Since 1943, American composers have received the annual prize for major works first performed in the United States the previous year.

1993   Christopher Rouse, for *Trombone Concerto*
1992   Wayne Peterson, for *The Face of the Night*
1991   Shulamit Ran, for *Symphony*
1990   Mel Powell, for *Duplicates: A Concerto for Two Pianos and Orchestra*
1989   Roger Reynolds, for *Whispers Out of Time*
1988   William Bolcom, for *Twelve New Etudes for Piano*
1987   John Harrison, for *The Flight into Egypt*
1986   George Perle, for *Wind Quintet IV*
1985   Stephen Albert, for *Symphony, RiverRun*
        Special citation to William Schuman for his contributions to American music
1984   Bernard Rands, for *Canti del Sole for Tenor and Orchestra*
1983   Ellen Taaffe Zwilich, for *Symphony No. 1*

1982 Roger Sessions, for *Concerto for Orchestra*
Special citation to Milton Babbitt for his contributions to American music
1981 No award
1980 David Del Tredici, for *In Memory of a Summer Day*
1979 Joseph Schwantner, for *Aftertones of Infinity*
1978 Michael Colgrass, for *Deja Vu for Percussion Quartet and Orchestra*
1977 Richard Wernick, for *Visions of Terror and Wonder*
1976 Ned Rorem, for *Air Music*
Special posthumous citation to Scott Joplin for his contributions to American music
1975 Dominick Argento, for *From the Diary of Virginia Woolf*
1974 Donald Martino, for *Notturno*
Special citation to Roger Sessions for his contributions to American music
1973 Elliott Carter, for *String Quartet No. 3*
1972 Jacob Druckman, for *Windows*
1971 Mario Davidovsky, for *Synchronisms No. 6. for Piano and Electronic Sound, 1970*
1970 Charles Wuorinen, for *Time's Encomium*
1969 Karel Husa, for *String Quartet No. 3*
1968 George Crumb, for *Echoes of Time and the River*
1967 Leon Kirchner, for *Quartet No. 3*
1966 Leslie Bassett, for *Variations for Orchestra*
1965 No award
1964 No award
1963 Samuel Barber, for *Piano Concerto No. 1*
1962 Robert Ward, for *The Crucible*
1961 Walter Piston, for *Symphony No. 7*
1960 Elliott Carter, for *Second String Quartet*
1959 John LaMontaine, for *Concerto for Piano and Orchestra*
1958 Samuel Barber, for *Vanessa*
1957 Norman Dello Joio, for *Meditations on Ecclesiastes*
1956 Ernst Toch, for *Symphony No. 3*
1955 Gian-Carlo Menotti, for *The Saint of Bleecker Street*
1954 Quincy Porter, for *Concerto for Two Pianos and Orchestra*
1953 No award
1952 Gail Kubik, for *Symphony Concertante*
1951 Douglas S. Moore, for *Giants in the Earth*
1950 Gian-Carlo Menotti, for *The Consul*
1949 Virgil Thomson, for *Louisiana Story*
1948 Walter Piston, for *Symphony No. 3*
1947 Charles Ives, for *Symphony No. 3*
1946 Leo Sowerby, for *The Canticle of the Sun*
1945 Aaron Copland, for *Appalachian Spring*

1944   Howard Hanson, for *Symphony No. 4, Opus 34*
1943   William Schuman, for *Secular Cantata No. 2, A Free Song*

Van Cliburn International Piano Competition

Van Cliburn Foundation, Inc.
2525 Ridgmar Boulevard, Suite 307
Fort Worth, Texas 76116
(817) 738-6536

Held every four years since 1962, the competition brings together the world's most talented professional pianists ages eighteen to thirty. Gold medalists receive a cash award as well as the opportunity to perform at Carnegie Hall and to tour other major venues.

1993   Simone Pedroni, Italy
1989   Alexei Sultanov, U.S.S.R.
1985   José Feghali, Brazil
1981   André-Michel Schub, U.S.A.
1977   Steven De Groote, South Africa
1973   Vladimir Viardo, U.S.S.R.
1969   Cristina Ortiz, Brazil
1966   Radu Lupu, Romania
1962   Ralph Votapek, U.S.A.

Country Music Awards

Country Music Association
One Music Circle South
Nashville, TN 37203
(615) 244-2840

The members of the Country Music Association have honored the top country recording artists in a number of categories since 1967. Winners in two major categories are listed here.

1992   Entertainer of the Year: Garth Brooks
         Single of the Year: "Achy Breaky Heart," Billy Ray Cyrus
1991   Entertainer of the Year: Garth Brooks
         Single of the Year: "Friends in Low Places," Garth Brooks
1990   Entertainer of the Year: George Strait
         Single of the Year: "When I Call Your Name," Vince Gill

1989 Entertainer of the Year: George Strait
Single of the Year: "I'm No Stranger to the Rain," Keith Whitley
1988 Entertainer of the Year: Hank Williams, Jr.
Single of the Year: "Eighteen Wheels and a Dozen Roses," Kathy Mattea
1987 Entertainer of the Year: Hank Williams, Jr.
Single of the Year: "Forever and Ever, Amen," Randy Travis
1986 Entertainer of the Year: Reba McEntire
Single of the Year: "Bop," Dan Seals
1985 Entertainer of the Year: Ricky Scaggs
Single of the Year: "Why Not Me," The Judds
1984 Entertainer of the Year: Alabama
Single of the Year: "A Little Good News," Anne Murray
1983 Entertainer of the Year: Alabama
Single of the Year: "Swingin'," John Anderson
1982 Entertainer of the Year: Alabama
Single of the Year: "Always on My Mind," Willie Nelson
1981 Entertainer of the Year: Barbara Mandrell
Single of the Year: "Elvira," Oak Ridge Boys
1980 Entertainer of the Year: Barbara Mandrell
Single of the Year: "He Stopped Loving Her Today," George Jones
1979 Entertainer of the Year: Willie Nelson
Single of the Year: "The Devil Went Down to Georgia," Charlie Daniels Band
1978 Entertainer of the Year: Dolly Parton
Single of the Year: "Heaven's Just a Sin Away," The Kendalls
1977 Entertainer of the Year: Ronnie Milsap
Single of the Year: "Lucille," Kenny Rogers
1976 Entertainer of the Year: Mel Tillis
Single of the Year: "Good Hearted Woman," Waylon Jennings and Willie Nelson
1975 Entertainer of the Year: John Denver
Single of the Year: "Before the Next Teardrop Falls," Freddy Fender
1974 Entertainer of the Year: Charlie Rich
Single of the Year: "Country Bumpkin," Cal Smith
1973 Entertainer of the Year: Roy Clark
Single of the Year: "Behind Closed Doors," Charlie Rich
1972 Entertainer of the Year: Loretta Lynn
Single of the Year: "The Happiest Girl in the Whole U.S.A.," Donna Fargo
1971 Entertainer of the Year: Charley Pride
Single of the Year: "Help Me Make It Through the Night," Sammi Smith
1970 Entertainer of the Year: Merle Haggard
Single of the Year: "Okie from Muskogee," Merle Haggard

1969   Entertainer of the Year: Johnny Cash
       Single of the Year: "A Boy Named Sue," Johnny Cash
1968   Entertainer of the Year: Glen Campbell
       Single of the Year: "Harper Valley P.T.A.," Jeannie C. Riley
1967   Entertainer of the Year: Eddy Arnold
       Single of the Year: "There Goes My Everything," Jack Greene

Other Competitions and Awards

Andrew Wolf Chamber Music Award
Bay Chamber Concerts/All Newton
Music School
P.O. Box 91
Camden, ME 04843
(207) 236-2823

Arthur Rubinstein International Piano Master Competition
P.O. Box 6018
61060 Tel Aviv ISRAEL
3-523-9449

Baltimore Opera Vocal Competition for American Operatic Artists
527 North Charles Street
Baltimore, MD 21201
(301) 727-0592

Banff International String Quartet Competition
Banff Centre for the Arts
P.O. Box 1020
Banff, Alberta CANADA T0L 0C0
(403) 762-6180

Composers Guild Annual Composition Contest
40 North 100 W., Box 586
Farmington, UT 84025
(801) 451-2275

Concert Artists Guild New York Competition
850 7th Avenue, Suite 1205
New York, NY 10019
(212) 333-5200

Concorso Internazionale di Direzione d'Orchestra "Arturo Toscanini"
Piazzale Cesare Battisti 15
I-43100 Parma ITALY
521-27-10-33

Concorso Internazionale di Violino "Nicolò Paganini"
Palazzo Tursi
Via Garibaldi 9
I-16124 Genoa ITALY
10-20981

Concorso Internazionale "Vincente Bellini" per Pianisti e Cantanti Lirici
Viale Trieste 308
I-93100 Caltanissetta ITALY
934-59-20-25

Concours International de Chant de l'Opera de Paris
120 Rue de Lyon
F-75012 Paris FRANCE
1-40-01-19-75

Concours International de Flute Jean-Pierre Rampal
Concours International de Violin Yehudi Menuhin
5 Rue Bellart
F-75015 Paris FRANCE
1-47-83-33-58

Concours International d'Orgue "Grand Prix de Chartres"
75 Rue de Grenelle
F-75007 Paris FRANCE
1-45-48-31-74

Concurso Internacional de Piano Premio "Jaén"
Diputación Provincial
Instituto de Estudios Giennenses
23002 Jaén SPAIN
26-27-79

CPP/Belwin Student Composition Contest
Music Teachers National Association
12713 Summer Avenue NE
Albequerque, NM 87112
(505) 293-5666

Cravath Memorial Award
Musicians Emergency Fund, Inc.
820 Second Avenue, Suite 203
New York, NY 10017
(212) 986-8205

Folkestone Menuhin International Violin Competition
72 Leopold Rd.
London SW19 7JQ ENGLAND
81-944-5171

Gina Bachauer International Piano Competition
Bachauer International Piano Foundation
P.O. Box 11664
Salt Lake City, UT 84147
(801) 521-9200

Glenn Gould Prize
Canada Council/Glenn Gould
Foundation
99 Metcalf St., P.O. Box 1047
Ottawa, Ontario CANADA K1P 5V8
(613) 598-4310

Grawemeyer Award for Music Composition
University of Louisville School of Music
Louisville, KY 40292
(502) 588-6907

Hamamatsu International Piano Competition
Cultural Promotion, Hamamatsu City
103-2
Motoshiro-cho, Hamamatsu-shi
Shizuoka-ken 430 JAPAN
534-56-1106

Hannover International Violin Competition
Stiftung Niedersachsen
Ferdinandstrasse 4
W-3000 Hanover 1 GERMANY
511-31-50-83

International Competition for Female Composers
Elisabethstrasse 5
W-6800 Mannheim 1 GERMANY
621-41-46-16

International Jean Sibelius Violin Competition
Post Box 31
SF-00101 Helsinki 10 FINLAND
0-405-441

International Johann Sebastian Bach Competition
Thomaskirchhof 16, PSF 1349
0-7010 Leipzig GERMANY

International Mozart Competition of the Hochschule "Mozarteum"
Mirabellplatz 1
A-5020 Salzburg AUSTRIA
662-88908-200

International Tchaikovsky Competition
15 Neglinnaya St.
Moscow RUSSIA
925-96-49

Johann Sebastian Bach International Competitions
1211 Potomac St. NW
Washington, DC 20007
(202) 338-1111

Kathleen & Joseph M. Bryan Awards/North Carolina Symphony Young Artists Competition/Bryan International String Competition
North Carolina Symphony
P.O. Box 28026
Raleigh, NC 27611
(919) 733-2750

Leopold Stokowski Conducting Competition
American Symphony Orchestra
161 West 54th St., Suite 202
New York, NY 10019
(212) 581-1365

London International Piano Competition
28 Wallace Road
London N1 2PG ENGLAND
71-354-1087

London International String Quartet Competition
62 High Street
Fareham, Hants. PO16 7BG ENGLAND
329-283603

Loren L. Zachary Society National Vocal Competition for Young Opera Singers
2250 Gloaming Way
Beverly Hills, CA 90210
(213) 276-2731

Louis & Virginia Sudler International Windmusic Composition Contest
U.S. Marine Band
Eight & I Streets SE
Washington, DC 20390
(202) 433-4044

Louis Armstrong International Jazz Trumpet Competition
Thelonius Monk Institute of Jazz
5000 Klingle St. NW
Washington, DC 20016
(202) 895-1610

Ludwig van Beethoven International Piano Competition
Karlsplatz 2/2/9
A-1010 Vienna AUSTRIA
222-505-2061

Mae M. Whitaker Competition for Voice
Saint Louis Conservatory of Music
560 Trinity Avenue at Delmar
St. Louis, MO 63130
(314) 863-3033

Marguerite McCammon Voice Competition
The Opera Guild of Fort Worth
P.O. Box 100381
Fort Worth, TX 76185
(817) 731-0835

Marian Anderson Award
The Ives Center
P.O. Box 2957
Danbury, CT 06813
(203) 797-4002

Montreal International Music Competition
Place des Arts
1501 Jeanne-Mance St.
Montreal, Quebec CANADA H2X 1Z9
(514) 285-4380

National Competition for Orchestral Works
State University of New York
CT 118, SUNY New Paltz
New Paltz, NY 12561
(914) 257-3860

Oratorio Society of New York Solo Competition
Carnegie Hall, Suite 504
881 7th Avenue
New York, NY 10019
(212) 247-4199

Palm Beach Invitational International Piano Competition
Guild for International Piano Competitions
P.O. Box 3094
Palm Beach, FL 33480-3094
(407) 833-8817

Prague Spring International Music Competition
Hellichova 18
CS-118 00 Prague 1 CZECH REPUBLIC
533-192

Premio Internacional de Canto
Premio Internacional de Guitarra
Fundación Jacinto e Inocencio Guerrero
28013 Madrid SPAIN
1-247-6618

Pro Musicis Competition
Pro Musicis Foundation
140 West 79th St., Suite 9F
New York, NY 10024
(212) 787-0993

Rencontres Musicales d'Evian
International String Quartet Competition
6 Rue de Téhéran
F-75008 Paris FRANCE
1-44-35-26-90

Robert Casadesus International Piano
Competition
The Cleveland Institute of Music
11201 East Boulevard
Cleveland, OH 44106
(216) 791-5000

Rosa Ponselle International Vocal
Competition for Aspiring Young Artists
Rosa Ponselle Foundation
Windsor
Stevenson, MD 21153
(301) 486-4616

Santander International Piano
Competition
1000 Brickell Avenue
Miami, FL 33131
(305) 358-1502

Stravinsky Awards International Piano
Competition, The
1003 West Church St.
Champaign, IL 61821
(217) 352-0688

Sydney International Piano Competition
of Australia
P.O. Box 420, Double Bay
Sydney, N.S.W. 2028 AUSTRALIA
2-326-2405

Tokyo International Music Competition
Min-On Concert Association
1-32-12 Kita-Shinjuku
Shinjuku-ku Tokyo 169 JAPAN
3-5386-2887

University of Maryland International
Competitions
Office of Summer & Special Programs
University of Maryland
College Park, MD 20742
(301) 405-6544

Vienna International Competition for
Composers
Casinos Austria
Dr. Karl-Lueger Ring 14
A-1015 Vienna AUSTRIA

Walter W. Naumberg Foundation
International Viola Competition
144 West 66th St.
New York, NY 10023
(212) 874-1150

World Music Masters International Piano
Competition
Salle Gaveau
45 Rue La Boétie
F-75008 Paris FRANCE
1-45-62-69-71

Young Keyboard Artists Association
International Piano Competition
2276 Agave Bay, No. 6
Lake Havasu City, AZ 86403
(602) 453-9313

Music Funding Sources

Musicians can find financial support through numerous channels, including competitions, scholarships, fellowships and grants. Listed here is a selection of sources for music funding that covers a range of disciplines. Artists in search of other sources of financing should consult music conservatories, college and university music departments, and local and state government agencies, as well as foundation directories available in public libraries.

Affiliate Artists Inc.
37 West 65th Street
New York, NY 10023
(212) 580-2000

American Music Scholarship Association
1826 Carew Tower
Cincinnati, OH 45202
(513) 421-5342

ARTS—Arts Recognition and Talent Search
National Foundation for Advancement in the Arts
3915 Biscayne Boulevard, 4th floor
Miami, FL 33137
(305) 573-5502

ASCAP Foundation Grants to Young Composers
ASCAP Symphony and Concert Department
1 Lincoln Plaza
New York, NY 10023
(212) 870-7588

Avery Fisher Career Grants/Avery Fisher Artist Program
Lincoln Center for the Performing Arts
140 West 65th Street
New York, NY 10023
(212) 877-1800

Bagby Foundation for the Musical Arts
501 Fifth Avenue
New York, NY 10017
(212) 986-6094

BMI Foundation Grants/BMI Student Composers Awards/Lionel Newman Conducting Internships/Pete Carpenter Fellowhip
BMI Foundation
320 West 57th Street
New York, NY 10019
(212) 830-2520

British Columbia Art Scholarships Awards
British Columbia Cultural Services Branch
Parliament Buildings
Victoria, British Columbia CANADA
V8V 1X4
(604) 356-1718

Camargo Foundation Fellowships
P.O. Box 32
64 Main Street
East Haddam, CT 06423
(203) 873-3239

Canada Council/Conseil des Arts du Canada
P.O. Box 1047
99 Metcalfe Street
Ottawa, Ontario CANADA K1P 5V8
(613) 237-3400

Cintas Fellowships
Arts International, Institute of International Education
809 United Nations Plaza
New York, NY 10017
(212) 984-5370

Concerts Atlantique Foundation
54 West 21st Street, Suite 1206
New York, NY 10010
(212) 633-1128

Corporation of Yaddo
P.O. Box 385, Union Avenue
Saratoga Springs, NY 12866
(518) 584-0746

Edward F. Albee Foundation Residencies for Composers
14 Harrison Street
New York, NY 10013
(212) 226-2020

**Fromm Music Foundation at Harvard
University**
Harvard University Music Department
Cambridge, MA 02138
(617) 495-2791

**Fulbright Scholar Program for Faculty &
Professionals**
Council for International Exchange of
Scholars
3400 International Dr. NW, Suite M-500
Washington, DC 20008-3097
(202) 686-7866

Harold Shaw Award Fund
c/o Arts Presenters
1112 16th Street NW, Suite 620
Washington, DC 20036
(202) 833-2787

**Helene Wurlitzer Foundation of New
Mexico**
P.O. Box 545
Taos, NM 87571
(505) 758-2413

**International Summer Music Course
Awards**
Youth and Music of Germany
Markplatz 12
Weikersheim D-6992 GERMANY
07934-820

**Itzhak Perlman Award, Very Special
Arts**
John F. Kennedy Center for the
Performing Arts
Education Office
Washington, DC 20566
(202) 628-2800

**John Simon Guggenheim Memorial
Foundation**
90 Park Avenue
New York, NY 10016
(212) 687-4470

Kate Heal Kinley Memorial Fellowship
College of Fine and Applied Arts
University of Illinois at Urbana-
Champaign
608 East Lorado Taft Dr.
110 Architecture Building
Champaign, IL 61820
(217) 333-1661

**Kurt Weill Foundation for Music/Grants
Program**
7 East 20th Street, 3rd floor
New York, NY 10003
(212) 505-5240

**Liederkranz Foundation Scholarship
Awards**
6 East 87th Street
New York, NY 10128
(212) 534-0880

Little Emo Awards
Box 3155
Palos Verdes Estates, CA 90274
(213) 831-2256

MacDowell Colony Inc.
100 High Street
Peterborough, NH 03458
(603) 924-3886

Mendelssohn Composers Scholarships
Mendelssohn Scholarship Foundation
14 Bedford Square
London WC1B 3JG ENGLAND

**Metropolitan Opera National Council
Auditions Program**
Lincoln Center for the Performing Arts
New York, NY 10023
(212) 870-4515

**Music Assistance Fund Tuition
Scholarships/Orchestral Fellowships for
String Players**
New York Philharmonic at Avery Fisher
Hall
119 Lincoln Center Plaza
New York, NY 10023
(212) 875-5735

National Arts Club Music Scholarships
National Arts Club
15 Gramercy Park South
New York, NY 10003
(212) 475-3424

National Endowment for the Arts—Music Program
Nancy Hanks Center
1100 Pennsylvania Avenue NW
Washington, DC 20506
(202) 682-5445

Numerous grants available, including: American Jazz Masters Fellowship, Jazz Performance Fellowships, Music Fellowships, Music Professional Training Grants and Solo Recitalists Fellowships.

National Endowment for the Humanities
1100 Pennsylvania Avenue NW
Washington, DC 20506
(202) 786-0438

National Orchestra Institute Scholarships
Office of Summer & Special Programs
University of Maryland
College Park, MD 20742
(301) 405-6544

New Music Performance Studio Residencies
Yellow Springs Institute for Contemporary Studies & the Arts
1645 Art School Road
Chester Springs, PA 19425
(215) 827-9111

Olga Forral Foundation Inc.
Empire State Building, Suite 4510
350 Fifth Avenue
New York, NY 10118

Performing Arts Assistance Corp.
P.O. Box 1296 Ansonia Station
New York, NY 10023
(212) 874-2254

Presidential Scholarships
American Conservatory of Music
16 North Wabash, Suite 1850
Chicago, IL 60602
(312) 263-4161

Pro Musicis Sponsorship Award
Pro Musicis Foundation
140 West 79th Street, Suite 9F
New York, NY 10024
(212) 787-0993

Quest For Excellence Music Competition
WJR Radio
2100 Fisher Building
Detroit, MI 48202
(313) 873-9780

Richard Rodgers Production Award for the Musical Theater
American Academy & Institute of Arts & Letters
633 West 155th Street
New York, NY 10032
(212) 368-5900

Rome Prize Fellowships of the American Academy in Rome
41 East 65th Street
New York, NY 10021
(212) 517-4200

San Francisco Opera Center Auditions
San Francisco Opera
War Memorial Opera House
San Francisco, CA 94102
(415) 565-6491

Sinfonia Foundation
10600 Old State Road
Evansville, IN 47711
(812) 867-2433

Tanglewood Music Center Fellowhips
Boston Symphony Orchestra
Main House
Lennox, MA 01240
(617) 266-5241

Trebas Institute of Recording Arts Scholarships
6464 Sunset Boulevard, No. 1180
Hollywood, CA 90028
(213) 467-6800

Additional Sources of Information on Music

Books on Classical Music

Blume, Friedrich. *Renaissance and Baroque Music*. New York: Norton, 1967.

Bukofzer, Manfred F. *Music in the Baroque Era*. New York: Norton, 1947.

Copland, Aaron. *The New Music*. New York: Norton, 1968.

Einstein, Alfred. *Music in the Romantic Era*. New York: Norton, 1947.

Ewen, David, *Orchestral Music*. New York: Franklin Watts, 1973.

———. *The Complete Book of Classical Music*. Englewood Cliffs, N.J.: Prentice-Hall, 1965.

Gilman, Lawrence. *Orchestral Music*. New York: Oxford University Press, 1951.

Green, Elizabeth A. H. *The Modern Conductor*. 2nd edition. Englewood Cliffs, N.J.: Prentice-Hall, 1969.

Griffiths, Paul. *Modern Music*. New York: Braziller, 1981.

Holoman, D. Kern. *Evenings with the Orchestra*. New York: Norton, 1992.

Swafford, Jan. *The Vintage Guide to Classical Music*. New York: Vintage/Random House, 1992.

Books on Music in General

Apel, W. *Harvard Dictionary of Music*. Cambridge, MA: Harvard University Press, 1974.

Blom, Eric, revised by David Cummings. *The New Everyman Dictionary of Music*. London: Weidenfeld & Nicholson, 1981.

Bohle, Bruce, ed. *The International Cyclopedia of Music and Musicians*. 11th edition. New York: Dodd, Mead, & Co., 1985.

Clarke, Donald. *The Penguin Encyclopedia of Popular Music*. London: Penguin Books, 1989.

Harvard Brief Dictionary of Music. New York: Simon & Schuster, 1961.

Hitchcock, H. Wiley, and Stanley Sadie, eds. *The New Grove Dictionary of American Music*. New York: Grove Dictionaries, Inc., 1986.

Hurd, Michael. *The Oxford Junior Companion to Music*. London: Oxford University Press, 1979.

Jacobs, Arthur. *The Penguin Dictionary of Music*. 5th edition. London: Penguin Books, 1991.

Kennedy, Michael. *The Oxford Dictionary of Music*. New York: Oxford University Press, 1985.

Machlis, Joseph. *The Enjoyment of Music*. 5th edition. New York: Norton, 1984.

Morehead, Philip D., and Anne Macneil, eds. *The New American Dictionary of Music*. New York: Dutton, 1991.

Performing Arts Libraries and Museums of the World. Paris: Editions du Centre Nationale de la Recherche Scientifique, 1992.

Randel, Don Michael, ed. *The New Harvard Dictionary of Music*. Cambridge, MA: The Belknap Press of Harvard University Press, 1986.

Sadie, Stanley, ed. *Grove Dictionary of Music and Musicians*. 7th edition. London: Macmillan Publishers, 1980.

Sadie, Stanley, ed., with Alison Latham. *The Norton/Grove Encyclopedia of Music*. New York: Norton, 1988.

Salzman, Eric. *Twentieth-Century Music: An Introduction*. Englewood Cliffs, N.J.: Prentice-Hall, 1967.

Scholes, Percy A., revised, reset and edited by John Owen Ward. *The Oxford Companion to Music*. 10th edition. London: Oxford University Press, 1974.

Stern's Performing Arts Directory. New York: DM, Inc. (annual).

The Musical America Directory of the Performing Arts, 1993 Edition. New York: Musical America Publishing, 1992.

Books on Music History

Abraham, Gerald. *The Concise Oxford History of Music.* London: Oxford University Press, 1985.

Crocker, Richard L. *A History of Musical Style.* New York: McGraw-Hill, 1966.

Ewen, David. *All the Years of American Popular Music.* Englewood Cliffs, NJ: Prentice-Hall, 1977.

Ferand, Ernst T. *Improvisation in Nine Centuries of Western Music.* New York: Arno Volk Verlag, 1961.

Grout, Donald Jay. *A History of Western Music.* Revised edition. New York: W. W. Norton & Co., 1973.

Hamm, Charles. *Yesterdays: Popular Song in America.* New York: Norton, 1979.

Howard, John Tasker, and George Kent Bellows. *A Short History of Music in America.* New York: Thomas Y. Crowell Co., 1967.

Miller, Hugh M., and Dale Cockrell. *HarperCollins College Outline—History of Western Music.* 5th edition. New York: HarperPerennial, 1991.

Ulrich, Homer, and Paul A. Pisk. *The History of Music and Musical Style.* New York: Harcourt Brace Jovanovich, 1963.

Books on International Ethnic Music

Afropop Worldwide: 1992 & 1993 Guide. Brooklyn, NY: Worldwide Music Productions, 1992.

Bebey, Francis. *African Music: A People's Art.* Westport, CT: Lawrence Hill Co., 1969.

Chernoff, John Miller. *African Rhythm and African Sensibility.* Chicago, IL: University of Chicago Press, 1979.

Graham, Ronnie. *The Da Capo Guide to Contemporary African Music.* New York: Da Capo Press, 1988.

Stapleton, Chris and May. *African All Stars.* London: Paladin, 1987.

Sweeney, Philip. *The Virgin Directory of World Music.* New York: Owl Books, 1992.

Books on Jazz and the Blues

Baraka, Imamu Amiri. *Blues People.* Westport, CT: Greenwood Press, 1980 (reprint).

Claghorn, Charles Eugene. *Biographical Dictionary of Jazz.* Englewood Cliffs, NJ: Prentice Hall, 1982.

Kernfield, Barry, ed. *The New Grove Dictionary of Jazz.* London: Macmillan, 1988.

Oliver, Paul, Max Harrison and William Bolcom. *The New Grove Dictionary of Gospel, Blues and Jazz.* New York: W. W. Norton and Company, 1986.

Schuller, Gunter. *The History of Jazz.* New York: Oxford University Press, 1968.

Books on Musical Instruments

Buchner, Alexander. *Folk Music Instruments.* New York: Crown Books, 1972.

Diagram Visual Info. Ltd. *Musical Instruments of the World: An Illustrated Encyclopedia.* New York: Facts on File, 1976.

Marcuse, Sibyl. *A Survey of Musical Instruments.* New York: Harper & Row, 1975.

Sachs, Curt. *The History of Musical Instruments.* New York: W. W. Norton & Co., 1940.

Books on Opera

Budden, Julian. *The Operas of Verdi*. Volumes 1-3. London: Oxford University Press, 1981.

Earl of Harewood, The, ed. *The New Kobbe's Complete Opera Guide*. New York: G. P. Putnam's Sons, 1987.

English National Opera Guides. London: Riverrun Press, various dates.

Gammond, Peter. *The Illustrated Encyclopedia of Opera*. New York: Crescent Books, 1979.

Grout, Donald J. *A Short History of Opera*. 3rd edition. New York: Columbia University, 1988.

Hughes, Spike. *Great Opera Houses*. London: Weidenfield and Nicolson, 1956.

Mayer, Martin. *The Met*. New York: Simon and Schuster, 1983.

Pleasants, Henry. *The Great Singers*. New York: Simon and Schuster, 1966.

Rasponi, Lanfranco. *The Last Prima Donnas*. New York: Knopf, 1982.

Rudel, Anthony. *Tales from the Opera*. New York: Simon and Schuster, 1985.

Sadie, Stanley. *The New Grove Dictionary of Opera*. London: Macmillan Press, Ltd., 1992.

Smith, Patrick J. *The Tenth Muse*. New York: Knopf, 1970.

Traubner, Richard. *Operetta*. New York: Oxford University Press, 1983.

Books on People in Music

Baker, Theodore, revised by Nicolas Slonimsky. *Baker's Biographical Dictionary of Musicians*. 8th edition. New York: Schirmer, 1992.

Cummings, David M., and Dennis K. McIntire, eds. *International Who's Who in Music and Musician's Directory*. 12th edition. Cambridge, England: Melrose Press, Ltd., 1990.

Ewen, David, ed. *Musicians Since 1900: Performers in Concert and Opera*. New York: H. W. Wilson, 1978.

Kutsch, K. J., and Leo Riemens. *A Concise Biographical Dictionary of Singers*. Philadelphia: Chilton Book Co., 1969.

Morton, Brian, and Pamela Collins, eds. *Contemporary Composers*. Chicago and London: St. James Press, 1992.

Osborne, Charles, ed. *The Dictionary of Composers*. New York: Taplinger Publishing Company, 1977.

Southern, Eileen. *Biographical Dictionary of Afro-American and African Musicians*. Westport, CT: Greenwood Press, 1982.

Books on Popular Music

Bindas, Kenneth J., ed. *America's Musical Pulse*. Westport, CT: Greenwood Press, 1992.

Browne, C. A., revised by Willard A. Heaps. *The Story of Our National Ballads*. New York: Thomas Y. Crowell Co., 1960.

Chase, Gilbert. *America's Music*. 2nd edition. New York: McGraw-Hill, 1966.

Crampton, Luke. *Rock Movers and Shakers*. London: Branson Marketing, 1991.

Hamm, Charles. *Music in the New World*. New York: Norton, 1983.

Hardy, Phil, and Dave Laing. *Encyclopedia of Rock*. London and Sydney: MacDonald and Co., 1987.

———. *The Faber Companion to 20th-Century Popular Music*. London: Faber and Faber, 1990.

Kingman, Daniel. *American Music: A Panorama*. 2nd edition. New York: Schirmer Books, 1990.

Kingsbury, Paul, and Alan Axelrod. *Country: The Music and the Musicians*. New York: Abbeville, 1988.

Malone, Bill C. *Country Music USA*. Austin, TX: University of Texas Press, 1968.

Nettle, Bruno, revised and expanded by Helen Myers.

Folk Music in the United States: An Introduction. 3rd edition. Detroit: Wayne State University Press, 1976.

Nye, Russel. *The Unembarrassed Muse*. New York: Dial Press, 1970.

Roberts, John Storm. *The Latin Tinge*. New York: Original Music, 1985.

Sanjek, Russell. *American Popular Music and Its Business*. Volumes 1-3. New York: Oxford University Press, 1988.

Shaw, Arnold. *Black Popular Music in America*. New York: Schirmer Books, 1986.

Stambler, Irwin. *Encyclopedia of Rock, Pop, and Soul*. New York: St. Martin's Press, 1977.

Tobler, John, ed. *Who's Who in Rock & Roll*. New York: Reed International Books, 1991.

Ward, Ed, Geoffrey Stokes and Ken Tucker. *Rock of Ages: The Rolling Stone History of Rock and Roll*. New York: Rolling Stone Press/Summit Books, 1986.

Wilder, Alec. *American Popular Song: The Great Innovators, 1900–1950*. New York: Oxford University Press, 1972.

Books on Sacred Music

Ewen, D. *Hebrew Music: A Study and an Interpretation*. New York: Bloch Publishing, 1931.

Jacobs, A. *Choral Music*. London: Penguin Books, 1963.

Mees, A. *Choirs and Choral Music*. New York: Greenwood Press, 1969.

Robertson, A. *Sacred Music*. New York: Chanticleer Press, 1950.

Ulrich, H. *A Survey of Choral Music*. Santa Barbara, Calif.: Harcourt Brace Jovanovich, 1973.

Books on Theory and Technique

Bach, C. P. E., translated and edited by William J. Mitchell. *Essay on the True Art of Playing Keyboard Instruments*. New York: Norton, 1949.

Bailey, Derek. *Musical Improvisation: A Complete Guide*. Englewood Cliffs, NJ: Prentice-Hall, 1980.

Chase, Mildred Portnoy. *Improvisation: Music from the Inside Out*. Berkeley: Creative Arts Books, 1988.

Coker, Jerry. *Improvising Jazz*. Englewood Cliffs, NJ: Prentice-Hall, 1964.

Dart, Thurston. *The Interpretation of Music*. New York: Harper & Row, 1963.

Kruger, Karl. *The Way of the Conductor: His Origins, Purpose and Procedures*. New York: Scribner's, 1958.

Murphy, Howard Ansley, and Edwin John Stringham.

Creative Harmony and Musicianship: An Introduction to the Structure of Music. Englewood Cliffs, NJ: Prentice-Hall, 1951.

Piston, Walter. *Harmony*. 3rd edition. New York: Norton, 1962.

Rudolf, Max. *The Grammar of Conducting*. New York: Schirmer, 1950.

Saminsky, Lazare. *Essentials of Conducting*. London: Dobson, 1958.

Sessions, Roger. *The Musical Experience of Composer, Performer, Listener*. Princeton, NJ: Princeton University Press, 1950.

Stone, Kurt. *Music Notation in the Twentieth Century*. New York: Norton, 1980.

Periodicals

Acoustic Guitar
Strings
P.O. Box 767
San Anselmo, CA 94979
(415) 485-6946

Billboard
1515 Broadway
New York, NY 10036
(212) 536-5031

Cadence: The American Review of Jazz & Blues
Cadence Building
Redwood, NY 13679
(315) 287-2852

Chamber Music Magazine
Chamber Music America
545 8th Avenue, 9th floor
New York, NY 10018
(212) 244-2776

Chorus!
2131 Pleasant Hill Road, Suite 151-121
Duluth, GA 30136
(404) 497-1902

Classical Guitar
Ashley Mark Publishing Co.
Olsover House
43 Sackville Road
Newcastle Upon Tyne NE65TA
ENGLAND
091-276-0448

Contemporary Music Review
Harwood Academic Publishers
P.O. Box 90
Reading, Berkshire RG1 8JL
ENGLAND
0734-560080

Down Beat
180 West Park Avenue
Elmhurst, IL 60126
(708) 941-2030

Ear: Magazine of New Music
131 Varick Street
New York, NY 10013
(212) 807-7944

Guitar Player
Keyboard Magazine
20085 Stevens Creek Boulevard
Cupertino, CA 95014
(408) 446-1105

International Musician
1501 Broadway
New York, NY 10036
(212) 869-1330

Jazz Journal International
1/5 Clerkenwell Road
London EC1M 5PA ENGLAND
071-608-1348

Jazz Times
7961 Eastern Avenue, Suite 303
Silver Spring, MD 20910-4898
(301) 588-4114

Keyboard Classics
223 Katonah Avenue
Katonah, NY 10536
(914) 232-8108

Musician
33 Commercial Street
Gloucester, MA 01930
(508) 281-3110

Opera Monthly
P.O. Box 816
Madison Square Station
New York, NY 10159
(212) 627-2120

Opera News
70 Lincoln Center Plaza
New York, NY 10023
(212) 769-7000

Performance Magazine
1203 Lake Street, Suite 200
Fort Worth, TX 76102-4504
(817) 338-9444

Rolling Stone
1290 Avenue of the Americas
New York, NY 10104
(212) 484-1616

Spin
6 West 18th Street
New York, NY 10011
(212) 633-8200

Stereo Review
1633 Broadway
New York, NY 10019
(212) 767-6000

Symphony Magazine
777 14th Street NW, Suite 500
Washington, DC 20005
(202) 628-0099

Libraries and Museums

Listed here are a number of museums and libraries that specialize in music. In addition, many colleges, universities, conservatories and large public libraries have extensive music-related archives.

Academy of Music Library and Archives
Broad and Locust Streets
Philadelphia, PA 19102
(215) 875-7658

Alabama Music Hall of Fame
Highway 72 W
Tuscumbia, AL 35674
(205) 381-4417

American Antiquarian Society
185 Salisbury Street
Worcester, MA 01609
(508) 755-5221

A.M.L.I. Central Library For Music and Dance
26 Bialik Street, P.O. Box 4882
65241 Tel Aviv ISRAEL
03-658106

Andrea dell Corte Public Library of Music
Villa Tresoriera
Corso Francia 192
I-10145 Torino ITALY
011-746072

Archive of Folk Culture
Library of Congress
Washington, DC 20540
(202) 707-6590

Australia Music Centre
P.O. Box 9, Grosvenor Street
Sydney N.S.W. AUSTRALIA
02-27-1001

Australian Opera Company Library
AMP Centre
50 Bridge Street
Sydney N.S.W. 2000 AUSTRALIA
231-2300

Central Music Library
10 Buckingham Palace Road
London SWIW 90D ENGLAND
071-798-2192

Company of Fifers & Drummers Library & Museum
Ivorytown, CT 06442
(203) 767-2237

Country Music Hall of Fame & Museum
Country Music Foundation Library & Media Center
4 Music Square East
Nashville, TN 37203
(615) 256-1639

Delta Blues Museum
114 Delta Avenue
Clarksdale, MS 38614
(601) 624-4461

E. Azalia Hackley Collection of Negro Music, Dance & Drama
Department of Music and Performing Arts
Detroit Public Library
5201 Woodward Avenue
Detroit, MI 48202
(313) 833-1488

Elmer Belt Library of Vinciana
Dickson Art Center
405 Hilgard Avenue
Los Angeles, CA 90024
(213) 743-6362

George E. Case Collection
University of South Carolina at Spartansburg Library
800 University Way
Spartansburg, SC 29303
(803) 599-2619

Godspeed Opera House Library of the American Musical Theatre
East Haddam, CT 06423
(203) 873-9664

Graceland
3764 Elvis Presley Boulevard
Memphis, TN 38116
(901) 332-3322

Harriet M. Spaulding Library
New England Conservatory of Music
33 Gainsborough Street
Boston, MA 02115
(617) 262-1120

Historic New Orleans Collection
533 Royal Street
New Orleans, LA 70130
(504) 523-4662

Hungarian State Opera Archives and Museum
Budapest VI Népköztársaság u.22
HUNGARY
312-550

Institute of the American Musical
121 North Detroit Street
Los Angeles, CA 90036

International Foundation Mozarteum
Mozart Archive and Mozart Museum
Schwartzstrasse 26 und Getridestrasse 9
Salzburg AUSTRIA
882263

Joan Baillie Archives of the Canadian Opera Company
227 Front Street East
Toronto, Ontario M5A 1E8 CANADA
(416) 363-6671

La Scala Theatre Museum
Livia Simone Theatre Library
Filodramatici 2
Milano ITALY
02-805-3418

Lee Conklin Antique Organ Museum
105 Fairview
P.O. Box 256
Hanover, MI 49241
(517) 563-8328

Liberace Museum
1775 East Tropicana
Las Vegas, NV 89119
(702) 798-5595

Library of the Royal Conservatory of Music
Rue de la Régence 30
1000 Bruxelles BELGIUM
512-2369

Miles Musical Museum
Highway 62 W
Eureka Springs, AR 72632
(501) 253-8961

Moravian Music Foundation
Peter Memorial Library
20 Cascade Avenue
Winston-Salem, NC 27107
(910) 725-0651

Museum of the American Piano
211 West 58th Street
New York, NY 10019
(212) 246-4646

Music Center Operating Company Archives, The
The Music Center of Los Angeles
135 North Grand Avenue
Los Angeles, CA 90012
(213) 972-7200

Music House, The
7377 U.S. 31 N
Acme, MI 49610
(616) 938-9300

Musical Museum and Library, The
Route 12-B
Deansboro, NY 13328
(315) 841-8774

Musical Wonder House
18 High Street
Wiscasset, ME 04578
(207) 882-7163

National Library—Division of Music
2 rue Vivienne
75084 Paris Cedex 02 FRANCE
1-4703-8850

National Library—Museum of the Opera
Place Charles Garnier
75009 Paris FRANCE
073-9093

National Theatre Archive
1321 Pennsylvania Avenue NW
Washington, DC 20004
(202) 347-0365

New York Public Library at Lincoln Center—Music Division
111 Amsterdam Avenue
New York, NY 10020
(212) 870-1646

Newberry Library
60 West Walton Street
Chicago, IL 60610
(312) 943-9090

Peabody Conservatory Library
21 East Mount Vernon Place
Baltimore, MD 21202
(410) 659-8255/(410) 659-8179

Pierpont Morgan Library
29 East 36th Street
New York, NY 10016
(212) 685-0610

Polish Arts & Culture Foundation
1290 Sutter Street
San Francisco, CA 94109
(415) 474-7070

Radio City Music Hall Production Archives
1260 Avenue of the Americas
New York, NY 10020
(212) 637-4000

RCA's Original Studio B
Roy Acuff Place & Music Square West
Nashville, TN 37203
(615) 242-9414

Rebel State Commemorative Area
State Highway 1221
Marthaville, LA 71450
(318) 472-6255

Richard Wagner Museum & Archive
Haus Wahnfreid
Wahnfreidstrasse 1
8580 Bayreuth GERMANY
0921-25351

Rock Hall of Fame & Museum
50 Public Square, Suite 545
Cleveland, OH 44113
(216) 781-7625

San Francisco Performing Arts Library & Museum
399 Grove Street
San Francisco, CA 94102
(415) 255-4800

Shrine to Music Museum, The
Clark & Yale Streets
Vermillion, SD 57069
(605) 677-5306

Stearns Collection of Musical Instruments
University of Michigan School of Music
Ann Arbor, MI 48109
(313) 763-4389

Weill-Lenya Research Center
Kurt Weill Foundation for Music
7 East 20th Street
New York, NY 10003
(212) 505-5240

Yale University Collection of Musical Instruments
15 Hillhouse Avenue
New Haven, CT 06520
(203) 432-0822

Yesteryear Museum
Regina Place & Harriet Drive
Whippany, NJ 07981
(201) 386-1920

Organizations and Unions

In addition to the musicians' organizations and unions listed here, scores of more specific associations serve particular groups of artists. General performing-arts alliances also provide many services of value to musicians.

American Composers Alliance
170 West 74th Street
New York, NY 10023
(212) 362-8900

American Federation of Musicians
1501 Broadway, Suite 600
New York, NY 10036
(212) 869-1330

American Guild of Musical Artists
1727 Broadway
New York, NY 10019-5284
(212) 265-3687

American Music Center, Inc.
30 West 26th Street, Suite 1001
New York, NY 10010-2011
(212) 366-5260

American Musicological Society
201 South 34th Street
Philadelphia, PA 19104
(215) 898-8698

American Symphony Orchestra League
777 14th Street NW, Suite 500
Washington, DC 20005
(202) 628-0099

ASCAP (American Society of Composers Authors and Publishers)
1 Lincoln Plaza
New York, NY 10023
(212) 595-3050

BMI (Broadcast Music Inc.)
320 West 57th Street
New York, NY 10019
(212) 586-2000

Canadian Music Centre
20 St. Joseph Street
Toronto, Ontario M4Y 1J9 CANADA
(416) 961-6601

Chamber Music America
545 8th Avenue
New York, NY 10018
(212) 244-2772

Conductors' Guild Inc.
P.O. Box 3361
West Chester, PA 19381
(215) 430-6010

Country Music Association Inc.
One Music Circle South
Nashville, TN 37203
(615) 244-2840

Gospel Music Association
P.O. Box 23201
Nashville, TN 37202
(615) 242-0303

International League of Women Composers
Southshore Road, Box 670
Point Peninsula
Three Mile Bay, NY 13693
(315) 649-5086

Mu Phi Epsilon
2212 Mary Hills Drive
Minneapolis, MN 55422-4252
(612) 588-2212

Music Critics Association Inc.
7 Pine Court
Westfield, NJ 07090
(908) BEETHOVEN

National Academy of Popular Music and Songwriters Hall of Fame
875 3rd Avenue, 18th floor
New York, NY 10022
(212) 319-1444

**National Academy of Recording Arts
and Sciences, Inc.**
3402 Pico Boulevard
Santa Monica, CA 90405
(310) 392-3777

National Jazz Service Organization
P.O. Box 50152
Washington, DC 20091-0152
(202) 347-2604

National Music Council
Box 5551
Englewood, NJ 07631-5551
(201) 871-9088

National Oratorio Society
6686 Brook Way
Paradise, CA 95969
(916) 877-8360

New Music Alliance
508 Woodland Terrace
Philadelphia, PA 19104
(215) 382-2521

OPERA America
777 14th Street NW, Suite 520
Washington, DC 20005-3287
(202) 347-9262

**Recording Industry Association of
America**
1020 19th Street NW, Suite 200
Washington, DC 20036
(202) 775-0101

Songwriters Guild of America
276 Fifth Avenue, No. 306
New York, NY 10001
(212) 686-6820

Part III
DANCE

Glossary of Dance Terms

abstract ballet: A ballet composition in which pure movement takes precedence over story. The choreography is its own reason for being. Michel Fokine's *Les Sylphides* exemplifies this style of ballet; the dance is governed by music, not plot. Another example would be *Symphonic Variations* by Sir Frederick Ashton.

abstract dance: Any composition of dance movements performed without literal or implied meaning beyond the movements themselves. Also, a type of experimental dance that originated in Germany in the early 1920s.

adagio: In ballet, a movement performed slowly (in contrast to allegro). Frequently used in training to increase balance and control and to develop line. It is also the first part of a standard pas de deux.

alegrias: A flamenco rhythm form. Also, a flamenco woman's solo dance in which the performer twists the train of her long skirt with one foot while she spins around.

allegro: A quick tempo. In dancing, allegro contrasts with adagio. The term also describes a regular feature of ballet classes, following the adagio, that is devoted to turns and leaps.

animal dance: A form of social dance in which the participants imitate the movements or other characteristics of a specific type of animal.

arabesque: A ballet position in which the dancer stretches a raised leg to the rear and holds the torso erect while extending one or both arms.

assemblé: A ballet jump taken on one foot, with the opposite leg raised, landing on two feet in fifth position.

attitude: In ballet, a pose in which the dancer creates an elegant line by bending one raised leg at an angle of forty-five to ninety degrees.

ballerina: A principal female dancer in a ballet company. The term is also used more loosely to identify a female ballet dancer who, though not a principal, is highly skilled.

ballet: A theatrical form of dance first developed in 16th-century French and Italian royal courts and performed to music. Although ballets of the modern era are not always set to classical scores, ballet steps and poses still employ five classic foot positions, and legs are rotated outward from the hip, or "turned out."

ballet d'action: The earliest form of ballet that told a single story over the course of a long performance. Developed in 18th-century France.

balletomane: An admirer of ballet. The term was coined by Arnold Haskell to describe the extreme enthusiasm of Russian ballet fanciers of the 19th century.

ballon: In ballet, the springy quality of jumps considered essential for lightness and lift.

ballroom dances: Social dances set to music that were originally created for the aristocracy in the early Renaissance. The most popular ballroom dances have included the minuet, waltz, foxtrot, rumba and tango.

barre: A wooden rail affixed horizontally to the wall of a dance studio and grasped to help maintain balance during opening exercises of dance classes.

bas: A ballet term meaning "low," which refers to the position of the arms when they are placed down, near the body.

basse danse: A Renaissance social dance type performed by upper- and middle-class couples in the Low Countries, France and England. It consists of simple steps, rises and bows in prescribed patterns. The Italian *bassa danza* contained similar movements, with more varied patterns.

battement: From the French word for "beating," a ballet movement in which the bottom of the foot brushes firmly against the floor as it moves from one position to another.

batterie: In ballet, a beating movement in which the dancer strikes the legs together or swiftly crosses and uncrosses them during a jump.

belly dancing: A traditional dance of the Near and Middle East performed by dancers who sway from side to side while undulating their lower torsos.

bharata natyam: A type of South Indian classical dance, widely regarded as the most musically complex and elegant, performed solo by women. It is characterized by quick, emphatic steps, sophisticated rhythms, intricately coordinated movements of the head and arms, and elaborate gesturing of the hands and face. Bharata natyam was originally performed by temple dancers. Though now largely a concert art, it remains devotional in tone. It can involve narrative or consist of pure movement without plot. In its sophistication, some consider bharata natyam a counterpart to Western ballet.

bolero: A traditional dance of Spanish origin, performed in ¾ time with castanets, guitar and song as accompaniment.

bourrées, à pas de bourrée: In ballet, linked, small steps en pointe, taken with the feet kept close together.

buck-and-wing: A solo tap dance of African-American origin that employs leaps and kicks.

bugaku: Court dances introduced to Japan from Korea in the 12th century, performed by groups of four, six or eight male dancers.

cabriole: A ballet movement in which the dancer, during a leap with both legs extended, beats the lower leg against the upper leg, and then lands on the lower.

cachucha: A Spanish dance performed with castanets in ¾ time.

cakewalk: An African-American dance of energetic, free-form steps that became a mainstay of vaudeville and minstrel shows at the end of the 19th century. According to tradition, the dancer who performed the most difficult steps was rewarded with a piece of cake.

caller: In square dances, the person who calls out the steps to be performed.

cancan: Originated in the dance halls of Paris at the end of the 19th century, the cancan captured the exuberance of the *fin de siècle* in its trademark high kicks. The painter Henri de Toulouse-Lautrec helped make the dance famous in his many renderings of the cancan dancers of the Moulin Rouge.

character dance: Any dance not part of the classical dance tradition, such as folk dance.

chassé: The French word for "chased" refers to a sliding ballet step in which one foot "chases" the other while gliding across the floor.

choreography: The art of designing dance movement. Also, the collection of steps, movements and gestures that comprise the grammar and syntax of ballet.

ciseaux: A ballet jump in which the legs open wide to second position, resembling scissors.

classical ballet: The steps and gestures of ballet technique, which are characterized by an elegant line, rapid leg work and pinpoint balance. Refined over centuries, it is a distinct style of ballet that contrasts with other styles, such as romantic ballet.

closed positions: In ballet, positions in which the feet touch. The first, third and fifth positions are closed positions (see also *open positions*).

conga: A popular ballroom dance of Afro-Cuban origin performed in ¼ time with a step-step-step-kick rhythm. The conga originated as a line dance in Latin countries during carnival season.

contraction: A dance technique, originated by Martha Graham, in which dancers contract and relax pelvic muscles during the intake and exhalation of breath, thereby changing the curve of the torso. It provides the basis for the taut and dramatic movements of the Graham style.

contredanse: Any of a number of traditional country dances of European origin.

contretemps: A ballet step taken off the beat, in countertime.

corps de ballet: Literally, the "body of ballet," the members of the company who perform ensemble rather than solo and who represent the lowest rung in the company hierarchy.

csardas: A Hungarian courtship dance characterized by spinning movements and syncopated rhythms.

dégagé: A slide of the foot outward from one of the five classic ballet positions of the feet. The dégagé allows dancers to make a graceful transition between positions or movements.

demi: A term meaning "half," used for ballet positions or poses intentionally performed at less than full range of movement or intensity. For example, a demi-plié calls for half-bent knees.

detourné: In ballet, a backward turn in the direction of the back foot, reversing the position of the feet.

disco: A Latin-influenced style of social dance that originated in discotheques during the 1970s and is characterized by gyrating movements performed to music with a pulsating beat. Disco represented a return to synchronized dancing in couples after two decades during which young social dancers preferred improvised rhythms.

eccentric dancing: A type of American specialty dancing, to jazz rhythms, in which performers favor individual style over conventional dance movements. Eccentric dancers include such forms as tap dancing and contortionism in their acts.

échappé: A jump taken from fifth position and landing in second or fourth. In the most common échappé, the dancer begins in the fifth position and springs into second.

elevation: A ballet dancer's ability to spring high into the air in leaps.

en l'air: French for "in the air," a ballet step executed with one or both legs off the ground. The opposite is par terre ("on the ground").

en pointe: In ballet, a technique of dancing on the tips of the toes.

entrechat: A rapid crossing of the legs at the thigh and lower calf while the dancer is in midair.

entrée: The entrance onstage of one dancer or a group of dancers.

extension: In ballet, the extraordinary flexibility of dancers, such as their ability to extend the legs in any direction with ease.

fandango: A Spanish dance in ¾ or ⅝ time for two people, accompanied by some combination of guitar, castanets and song.

fifth position: In ballet, a stance in which one foot is placed directly in front of the other and parallel to it, with the heel of each foot aligned with the toe of the other.

first position: In ballet, a posture in which the heels of the feet touch and the feet form a straight line with the toes pointed outward.

five positions: The five positions of the feet that are the basis for all movement in ballet (see also *first position, second position,* etc., and diagram on page 302).

flamenco: A Spanish dance of gypsy origin, characterized by intricate heel tapping, castanet flourishes and guitar accompaniment.

flower drum dance: A Chinese dance performed to intricate drumbeats.

Five basic postiions of the feet for ballet

1st   2nd   3rd

4th
open

4th
crossed

5th

folk dance: A dance originally created by a people for celebration, ritual or recreation, rather than for professional performance. Having evolved over generations, folk dances can be found in all cultures. Professional folk-dancing troupes are increasingly popular today.

fourth position: In ballet, a stance in which one foot is placed in front of the other and parallel to it, with the feet separated by the length of about one step. The heel of the front foot is positioned before the instep of the rear.

fox-trot: An American ballroom dance in ¼ time with many variations.

gavotte: Initially a French peasant dance in ¼ time, the gavotte was refined and danced by aristocrats at the courts of Louis XIV and XV.

glissade: A gliding ballet step enabling the dancer to move easily in any direction. Frequently used as a preparation for a leap or intermingled with other steps.

grand: A French word meaning "big," used in combination with other ballet vocabulary to indicate an increase in the size of a movement. For example, a grand jeté.

habanera: For couples, a dance from Havana with a tangolike rhythm in a leisurely ⅔ time.

hornpipe: A dance from Great Britain performed in duple time and thought to have been named for a musical instrument.

hula: A dance native to Hawaii, originally a part of religious worship.

impresario: A financier and organizer of public performances of any theatrical group for profit, especially ballet and opera companies.

Indian dance: Incorporating both classic and folk forms, the dance of India originated in ancient times and was closely tied to mythology and religion. Some types of Indian dance are: *bharata natyam* (see entry); *kathakali* (see entry); kathak, or nautch dancing, from North India, which developed as a temple and court dance but at times declined to brothel entertainment; kuchipudi, a dance-drama form; and the sinuous orissi dance from the state of Orissa.

jarabe: A Mexican courtship dance that features prancing and clicking steps.

jazz dance: A 20th-century dance style inspired by the syncopated rhythms of jazz music. Notable examples include the Charleston, the blackbottom and the jitterbug. Later in the century, jazz dancing developed into a form of theatrical dance.

jeté: From the French for "thrown," a ballet jump in which the dancer pushes off one leg, sails through the air and lands on the other leg.

jig: A lively British Isles folk dance in ⅝ or ¹²⁄₈ time, the jig was a staple of 16th- and 17th-century theatrical performances.

jitterbug: A jazz dance of the 1930s that evolved from the lindy hop. Accompanied by swing music, the jitterbug was danced at a frenzied pace and featured both regular floor steps and acrobatic "air steps."

Kabuki dance: A style of Japanese theatrical dance, three hundred years old, Kabuki represents a synthesis of traditional Japanese folk, court and holy dances. Integrating music, movement and language, all-male casts enact tales of conflict and revenge.

kathakali: A classical men's dance-drama genre from Malabar and surrounding regions of southern India, known for its elaborate costumes and makeup.

khon: A classic Thai dance in which male performers depict historic tales.

khorovod: A category of circle dance native to the former Soviet states.

krakowiak: A lively Polish dance from Krakow, traditionally danced by either a couple or a group in ⅔ time. Now a staple of Polish dance troupes.

legong: A traditional Balinese dance performed at feasts by young girls wearing silk sheaths and elaborate headdresses. The dance depicts the story of a king going to war and leaving the woman he loves.

leotard: A one-piece exercise garment designed to reveal the body's form and line, often worn by dancers for practice or class. Invented by French acrobat Jules Léotard.

lift: In ballet, the lifting of the female dancer by the male—a move requiring strength and careful timing.

limbo: A dance of the West Indies in which a participant leans over backward and repeatedly maneuvers under a horizontal stick, which is placed closer to the ground for each pass.

lindy hop: A precursor of the jitterbug named in honor of Charles Lindbergh's 1927 flight across the Atlantic.

mambo: A ballroom dance in rapid ¼ time, introduced to the United States from Cuba after World War II.

macumba: An exotic Brazilian dance that evokes ancestral spirits.

mazurka: A Polish dance of peasant origin performed in ¾ time by four or eight couples to the accompaniment of national songs. It is characterized by stamping of feet and clicking of heels.

minuet: An 18th-century French court dance in ¾ time. The minuet epitomized stately elegance and was a mainstay of the opera stage as well as the ballroom.

modern dance: An American and European dance style that arose in the early 20th century in opposition to the rigid formalism of ballet. Modern dance encompasses many forms, from the balletic to the experimental, and continues to evolve.

morris dances: Fifteenth-century English folk dance with intricate steps, generally performed in ¾ time. Dancers wore bells tied to their legs and some wore costumes, such as The Fool or Queen of the May.

notation: A written record of dance movements created in order to preserve and remember them. Choreographers have used different notation methods throughout dance history, such as Labanotation (invented by Rudolf von Laban) and Benesh Dance Notation (developed by Rudolf and Joan Benesh).

open positions: Ballet positions in which the feet do not touch, i.e., the second and fourth positions (see also *closed positions*).

opera-ballet: A blending of Italian opera and French court ballet into an elaborate theatrical production that featured singing, dancing and lavish scenery. The form enjoyed great popularity from the late 1600s to about 1750.

par terre: French for "on the ground," the opposite of en l'air, "in the air."

pas: From the French, a ballet "step."

pas de chat: A ballet step resembling a cat's leap, that starts from a fifth-position plié. The knees lift and bend in succession in the air.

pas de deux: In ballet, a dance for a ballerina and her male partner.

pericon: The national dance of Argentina, performed in cowboy boots and spurs.

pirouette: A rotation of the body done once or several times on one leg, with the toe of the working leg touching the knee of the supporting leg. This movement can also be executed in second position, in arabesque, or in attitude.

plié: A ballet movement in which the hips, legs and feet turn outward while the knees bend. Pliés are a classic barre warm-up exercise.

pointe: The very tip of the toe, where female ballet dancers appear to rest their weight while standing and dancing "en pointe." Pointe work is one of the foundations of classical ballet.

polka: A Bohemian dance in ²/₄ time using the half step. The polka gained great popularity throughout Europe and the United States in the 19th century.

polonaise: The Polish national dance, performed in ³/₄ time. It originated as a court processional in the 17th century and gained favor as a social dance throughout Europe about two hundred years later.

port de bras: Five positions of the arms that correspond to ballet's five classic positions of the feet. Also, a general term for the carriage of the arms. (See diagram page 306.)

prima ballerina: The leading female dancer in a ballet company.

principal dancer: A member of a ballet company who performs the principal, or starring, roles.

promenade: In ballet, a stately turn of the body held in an unchanging position or, in a pas de deux, a turn in which a ballerina is guided slowly by her partner.

quadrille: A square dance for four couples that was very popular in France under Napoléon I. After traveling across the Atlantic, it served as a prototype for American square dances.

reel: A Scottish dance performed in ⁴/₄ time on the tips of the toes.

relevé: A ballet move in which the dancer rises from a flat foot to half pointe or full pointe.

révérence: The formal bow ballet dancers make at the end of a class or as part of a curtain call.

rock 'n' roll: A generic term encompassing all dances performed to rock music, generally executed by two people dancing to their own improvised rhythms.

romantic ballet: Ballet of the Romantic period in the Western arts of the 19th century, emphasizing themes of tragic love and epitomized in such works as *Giselle*. This was a technically significant period for its widespread use of pointe work and for the ascen-dancy of the tutu as the preferred stage costume of the ballerina (see also *classical ballet*).

rond de jambe: French for "circle of the leg," a ballet leg movement in which a large circle is traced with the foot on the floor. In ronds de jambe en l'air, the raised foot and leg trace a circle in the air.

rumba: A Cuban ballroom dance with African roots, executed in ²/₄ or ⁴/₄ time. Celebrated for its rhythmic eroticism, the rumba reached U.S. shores in the late 1920s.

samba: A Brazilian ballroom dance in ²/₄ or ⁴/₄ time, introduced to the United States in the 1930s.

sauté: In ballet, a jump taken by both feet and landing in the same position.

second position: In ballet, a posture in which the feet, separated by about the length of a foot, form a straight line with the toes pointed outward.

soft shoe: A type of tap dance performed in shoes with leather soles but without metal taps.

soloist: In a ballet company, a dancer ranked between the corps de ballet and the principals. Soloists perform supporting roles.

square dance: An American folk dance performed by couples moving to the direction of a caller and accompanied by a small band, generally with a fiddler. The dance derives its name from the square formation in which couples stand for some of the dances. Other traditional formations include a circle (a "dance in the round") and two parallel lines (a "line dance").

tango: A ballroom dance from Argentina performed in ²/₄ time. The tango swept Europe and the United States in the early 1900s and became a perennial social dance favorite.

tap dancing: An American jazz dance featuring complex, syncopated heel-and-toe tapping in shoes bearing special metal cleats.

Port de bras

1st

2nd

2nd
demi-seconde
(half-second)

3rd

4th
en haut
(above)

4th
en avant
(in front)

5th
en hour
(above)

5th
en avant
(in front)

5th
en bas
(low)

tarantella: A dance of southern Italy performed in rapid ⅝ time, created in the city of Taranto.

third position: In ballet, a stance in which one foot is placed directly in front of the other and parallel to it, with the heel of the front foot positioned next to the instep of the rear.

turnout: A basic technical foundation of ballet, requiring the legs to be rotated outward from the hips at a ninety-degree angle.

tutu: A traditional ballet skirt worn either hip-length or between the knee and ankle.

variation: In ballet, a solo dance.

Virginia reel: A line-dance version of square dancing, in which couples assemble in two sets of parallel lines and take turns dancing between them with intricate steps.

volé: French for "flown." A ballet term indicating a movement performed in the air.

waltz: A whirling German-Austrian dance in ¾ time, the waltz became a ballroom craze in 19th-century Europe and was frequently accompanied by the music of Austrian composer Johann Strauss.

The Basics of Dance

Dance is one of the most elemental and universal of arts. For thousands of years, human beings have created compositions out of movement, gesture and rhythm—the raw materials of dance. In Egypt, a limestone fragment from approximately 1000 B.C. depicts a woman performing an acrobatic somersault as part of a ritual dance at Thebes. An image from an ancient temple wall at Tanjavur in India reveals a female adorned in bracelets, swaying energetically in a predecessor to the bharata natyam, a classical dance of India. In Mexico, a clay figure from the Aztec period shows a man dancing at a religious festival. Sometimes regarded as the most democratic of all arts, dancing requires only the human body as an instrument of expression and, therefore, it is common to every culture. Its simplicity makes dance one of the most basic art forms.

History of Dance

Most historians divide dance into three general categories: ritual, folk (or social) and artistic. The oldest dance forms—ritual dances—strove to link humans with natural and divine forces. In effect, they served as sacrificial rites or prayers. Ritual dances invoked deities to protect crops, stave off illness, and make nature bountiful, especially in its supply of animals to be hunted. Used in an effort to make contact with past and future generations, these dances helped form and preserve the cultural traditions of the people who created them.

Folk dance—the next link in the chain of dance evolution—brought clans, communities, and villages together to mark important occasions, such as birth, death and marriage. Peasant dances gave people an opportunity to watch potential mates display such physical skills as balance and coordination, and show off strength and vigor. In the Basque sword dance, for example, men cross their swords to create a platform on which they lift another male dancer above their heads in a display of manly power; in the Ukraine, male dancers in a gopak leap high and touch their toes with speed and agility.

An aristocratic version of the folk dance, the court dance mirrored the steps of peasants in a style more intricate and less purely physical. The differences between court and peasant dancing reflected the development of refined etiquette among the upper classes. Pictures from the period show gentlefolk dancing prettily with their hands clasped and peasants cavorting energetically. The minuet, the courante, the gavotte, basse danse: All were popular court dances that expressed dignity and grace befitting the nobility. Indeed, some considered the volta, a court dance involving quick steps and leaps, unseemly for those of a certain rank. Court dances and their peasant counterparts form the two foundations of modern social dance.

From the spectacle of court dance arose dancing as an art form. During the early Renaissance, for the first time, rules dictating the proper way to dance were formulated and written down. In addition to canons on dance and musical accompaniment, the Renaissance spawned a different style of dance, considerably more expressive and individualistic than what had been the norm during the Middle Ages. Dancing masters not only instructed students but also choreographed original works, introducing greater artistry and inventiveness into dance steps. The new emphasis on codification and creativity laid the groundwork for the birth of the ballet.

Physical Dance Elements

Whether ritual, social or creative, all dance forms share common elements that identify them as "movement made significant"—choreographer Martha Graham's definition of dance. The components of "significant movement" include gesture, dynamics, spatial design, steps and, most crucial of all, rhythm. Complementing dance movement and enhancing its significance are music, costume and decor.

Rhythm turns accented and unaccented movements into a coherent pattern. The *one*-two-three of a waltz or the distinctive pulse of a rumba exemplify rhythmic movement organized in different sequences. Rhythm originates in the body's natural movements, such as breathing or walking, and, more specifically, in the alternating contraction and relaxation of muscles. Emile Jaques-Dalcroze, the inventor of eurythmics, a school of rhythmic body movement, tried to encourage dancers' muscles to greater grace by exploiting their natural rhythms.

Most dance historians view musical rhythm as an offspring of rhythm in dance. The stamping foot, not music, was the original rhythm marker of dance; the second was provided by ornaments the dancers tied to their bodies. People later learned to supplement natural rhythm with more advanced noise makers:

musical instruments. In time, dancers learned to play off musical rhythm with counterpoint and syncopation—the stressing of an "off" beat. The great tap dancers, for example, could create infinitely varied counterpoints of standard time with their feet.

Rhythm predominates in many dance traditions. African dance, accompanied by drums and other percussion instruments, depends on precise skill in maintaining complex rhythms. In the Akbia women's funeral dance of the southern Sudan, for instance, drummers beat a single rhythmic pattern for days. Dancers of the Watutsi tribe from Rwanda, East Africa, use anklet bells to mark the rhythm of the dance as they perform gigantic steps in perfect unison. In the West, Spain boasts the most elaborate dance rhythms: Using heel taps called taconeo, as well as castanets and hand claps, dancers move in traditional rhythms to the staccato strumming of a guitar accompanist. Flamenco rhythms, a gypsy tradition, are so well defined that each bears a different name: alegrias, bulerias, farruca, seguiriyas, soleares, tango and zambra.

Rhythm orders dance steps—the leaps, hops and jumps that create a pattern of movement, sometimes called a "floor pattern." Rudolf von Laban, an early dance theorist, identified five basic types of steps as the sources of all others: gesture, stepping, locomotion, jumping and turning. In ballet, for example, a pirouette is an elaborate turn on one foot, while a grand jeté calls for a leap from one leg to another, with an arabesque landing. A step may also be defined as the transfer of weight from one bodily support to another, from the left leg to the right, for example. This shifting of weight, according to Laban, serves as the basis of all steps—and of all dance.

Just as steps produce floor patterns, vertical movement between planes creates the spatial designs of a dance. When a ballet dancer rises en pointe, leaps, pliés or flings herself on the floor, she travels between spatial planes, creating what Martha Graham called "an animate composition in space." Most dance forms contain myriad levels of movement and usually display either an upward or downward orientation. In general, low movement, with its emphasis on gravity, implies earthiness and a closeness to the ground. A middle level of space is frequently used for movement from one part of the floor to another. Neither partaking of the earth nor towering above it, the middle level is often one of transition between high and low. Higher planes require elevation—either jumping, leaping or pointe work—actions that defy gravity and resemble flight. A dancer poised above the earth projects lightness and effortless soaring, an image epitomized by ballet's ethereal reach toward the heavens. In any type of dance, the juxtaposition of high and low creates visual excitement.

Diversity in movement is achieved not only in travel across planes but also by means of dynamics—the measure of force and emphasis with which a motion is executed. Dynamics can change the sweep of a stately leg lift into the flash of a chorus-line kick. Comparable to hue in painting or timbre in music, dynamics affects the surface texture of dance. Fast movements suggest aggressiveness, force or strength, while slow motions imply calm and lyricism. A good choreographer blends these effects, interspersing vigorous and soothing dynamics. In some dance forms, several dynamics can emerge at once, as with flamenco, which combines frenetic heel tapping with smooth, flowing arm movements.

Dance acquires greater expressiveness through gesture. Gestures of the face and body range from the grotesque to the barely discernible: A furious grimace, a wringing of hands, a shadow of sorrow crossing a ballerina's brow all qualify as gesture. Some cultures choreograph gestures into dance as purposefully as they compose steps. Bharata natyam, a form of Indian classical dance, prescribes thirteen head gestures, thirty-six specific glances, seven movements of the eyeballs, nine of the eyelids, six each for nose, cheeks and lower lip, seven for the chin, nine for the neck and sixty-seven hand gestures—all in the service of clarifying the drama in the dance.

Gesture has always belonged to the world of theatrical dance. The first theory of gesture is recorded in *The Code of Terpsichore,* a treatise on dance written in 1828 by Carlo Blasis, a dancer at England's King's Theater and director of La Scala's academy of dance in Milan. Blasis divided gesture into natural and artificial categories, defining natural gesture as physical manifestations of emotion and artificial gesture as symbols of social or worldly phenomena. His preference for "natural" gesture presaged the tastes of ballet masters a century later.

In Western classical dance, pure movement and gesture converged during the 17th century in Italy's commedia dell' arte. The Italians infused ballet with greater spirit and vitality—and incorporated it into pantomime. Within two hundred years, French ballet schools were teaching mime as part of classical training, although classical stage tradition was still calling for only the subtlest gesturing. Pantomime and gesture found a place in ballet, most notably in such 19th-century works as *Coppelia* and *Swan Lake,* but these elements are not of great consequence in contemporary dance.

Music and Costume

While not a physical component of movement, music plays a primary role in the history and creation of dance. Music and dance are inseparable partners because both are organized around patterns of rhythm. Sometimes the music inspires the steps; at other times choreography dictates the style and length of the musical composition. In some cases, though, music and dance are composed separately and then brought together. Whatever their source, music and dance can produce masterworks when combined, such as Igor Stravinsky's ballet *The Firebird* and Aaron Copland's *Appalachian Spring*. In social dance, too, music and movement cross-fertilize, producing such dual sensations as Strauss's waltzes; the jazz-inspired Charleston, blackbottom and jitterbug; and rock 'n' roll's twist. But the synergy between motion and melody took thousands of years to develop fully; in its earliest days, dance dominated the pairing.

Ancient dances needed simple accompaniment, which dancers themselves provided with clapping, stomping and chanting. In hunting dances, for example, vocalizations imitated the howls and calls of prey. In time, simple instruments ornamented the natural rhythms of dance: A drum sounded percussion beats; a flute trilled a melody. This tradition of self-accompaniment still exists in non-Western dance, such as that of India, where classical performers tie bells around their ankles to keep time to their own movements. Although primitive, early music-making met the most important requirement for successful accompaniment by sharing a rhythm structure with the dance. Notes and steps began, ended, sped up and slowed down in tandem.

Unity between music and movement forms the basis of most classical dance traditions, and no more so than in ballet. This oneness of movement and melody arose because ballet music was tailor-made to the dance. Like the costume mistress or the scenery designer, the ballet composer worked from the specifications of the choreographer. This approach to music-making generally produced unimpressive scores, but sometimes the confines of ballet composition inspired masterpieces, such as Peter Tchaikovsky's *The Nutcracker, Swan Lake* and *Sleeping Beauty.*

Beginning in the early 20th century, ballet choreographers discovered a wellspring of beautiful music in an unexpected source: the concert hall. Michel Fokine choreographed *Les Sylphides* to Chopin's piano pieces in 1907, and in 1912 Russian ballet idol Vaslav Nijinsky choreographed a work to Claude Debussy's impressionistic *L'Après midi d'un faune* ("Afternoon of a Faun"), a gem of the repertory. Although critical and popular disappointments at the time, these daring experiments opened a frontier in ballet. Other choreographers would soon follow with great success, inventing steps to works by Bach, Mozart and Schönberg and to other pieces never intended for the dance.

According to dance legend, Nijinsky also broke new ground in another area of dance, that of costume. In a 1910 production of *Giselle,* he wore a daring jerkin (a short, close-fitting jacket) that is said to have offended many ladies in the audience. The incident added titillation to the annals of dance-costume history.

Dance costume encompasses a broad spectrum of design, from the spare tunics favored by the ancient Greeks to the elaborate lacquered masks of Japan's gigaku dance plays. Whether they appear in folk, social, ritual or theatrical dances, costumes are always made with the same requirements in mind. The weight of wigs and masks, the bulk of cloth, the fit and style of shoes all affect a dancer's range of movement. For example, both 17th-century ballerinas and the Bambera dancers of Mali suffered under burdensome costumes—the ballerina in a horsehair wig, high boots, gloves and molded leather corsets; the Bambera dancer in a wooden mask that engulfed the entire head.

Technical virtuosity demands lightweight costumes that liberate a dancer's body, allowing a full range of movement. The Egungun Eleve of the West African Yoruba—who incorporate acrobatics into their dances—prefer plain cloth garments for performance. In ballet, meanwhile, the tutu has grown shorter since the turn of the century when ballerinas mastered pointe work, pirouettes and other virtuosic feats.

Non-Western costume characteristically envelops dancers in ornamental robes, masks, headdresses or hand-held properties (props)—all of which are inseparable from the dance itself. In India's classical kathakali dance, the lead dancers undergo a four-hour makeup application, each color of makeup symbolizing a different human quality, such as evil. In Nigeria, the Efe dance costume radically transforms the dancer with an enormous wooden face worn over the head and shoulders.

The embellishment of costume in African and Asian dance finds its Western counterpart in theatrical dance. Ballet vacillated between the extravagant and the spare before the advent of the tutu in the 1830s. Earliest ballet dress reflected the fashions of the 1600s: wigs, masks and heavy materials. Coming from this tradition, French ballerina Marie Sallé caused a scandal when she appeared in a 1734 staging of *Pygmalion* wearing a simple tunic. But the style took hold, and the neoclassic era of the early 1800s embraced a simpler aesthetic, with plain white dresses that resembled ancient Greek vestments. During the Romantic era, the tutu reigned supreme in its earliest form: a floating skirt of white gauze that fell to midcalf. Not until the early 1900s did the skirt rise to hip length to reveal the exquisite movements of the dancers' legs.

Choreographer Fokine stripped ballet of its costume excesses early in the 20th century. Determined to reduce some of the dance form's artifice, he began using authentic folk dress. Liberated from yards of drapery, ballerinas still endured the pinch of corsets until Isadora Duncan discarded both corset and shoes at the turn of the century. Duncan, a modern dancer, abhorred ballet and rebelled against it, but in doing so she made a mark on that discipline. Her flowing garments epitomized the simplicity of early modern dance and also reflected a new ethic of female dress. Street fashions of the time soon reflected her uncorseted influence.

Duncan, however, represents only one tradition in modern dance costume; the other legacy sees costume design as an opportunity for artistic expression. In 1922, Bauhaus School painter Oscar Schlemmer revised notions of dance costume with the *Triadic Ballet,* an abstract work inspired by Cubist painting. Dancers appeared as geometrical figures wearing costumes of padded cloth, coated with metallic or brilliantly colored paint. Audiences marveled as the performers careened around the stage like a collective moving canvas.

Martha Graham also used costume creatively, wrapping herself and her female dancers in dresses and skirts consisting of yards of cloth that swirled around the body. In *Lamentation,* for example, Graham enveloped herself in a dress of jersey material, which she pulled and stretched to emphasize the lines of her body. Although she chose materials carefully, Graham espoused an almost spartan taste toward costume, rejecting anything ornamental or excessive. Her preference for simplicity was adopted by generations of modern dancers who, to this day, emphasize the physical rather than the decorative aspect of the dance.

Choreography and Dance Notation

Choreography is the art of designing dance movement. It includes the arrangement and organization of steps and motions into a cogent pattern. In its power as an art, choreography is the equal of music, architecture, painting, sculpture and poetry—disciplines to which it is often compared. Within the dance world, choreography belongs in the province of theatrical dance, where creativity and invention have traditionally been most prized. Older dance forms, such as ritual or folk dance, have developed over generations, created and modified by countless groups and individuals. They represent a process of slow evolution rather than choreographic design.

The choreographic process is unlike the creative process of any other art. Because the raw material of choreography is the human body in motion, the choreographer must work directly with dancers, trying out ideas and improvising steps until the dance slowly emerges. Unlike the poet or the painter, who creates in solitude, the choreographer almost never composes a piece in private with pen and paper. Choreographers sometimes describe their work as improvisational, emerging from a process of trial, error, inspiration and observation.

Many influences work within a choreographer, the most common being music. But choreographers have also acknowledged other inspirations, including literature, nature and the fine arts. In *Letter to the World,* for example, Martha Graham drew on the life and poetry of Emily Dickinson to create a dance. Isadora Duncan composed dances in response to the freedom and beauty of the wild, finding ideas in the movement of trees, waves and weather. And in *Minutiae,* Merce Cunningham brought the fine arts onto the stage in the form of a multimedia sculpture by artist Robert Rauschenberg.

The Building Blocks of Choreography

Choreographers may proceed from small concerns to large ones when creating a new dance. Beginning with single steps, they will invent whole phrases of movement, much as a writer joins individual words to form sentences. Along with phrases of steps, choreographers invent patterns in space, known as the design of the dance. Finally, the choreographer grapples with the large-scale concerns of the dance: Will it have one act or two? Will a solo be followed by a group dance or by a couple? In assigning an overall structure to the dance, the choreographer completes the process of creating a new work.

Before beginning a new project, some choreographers decide on a definite theme or purpose. That purpose might be to deliver a message or create a beautiful design. An intent may run the gamut from silly to serious: to challenge the eye with unexpected shapes, to provoke emotion, to rebel against traditional forms, or to communicate the joy of movement. The dance troupe Pilobilus, for example, specializes in complex, illusionistic formations of dancers that tease the audience's perceptions. In a more serious vein, choreographer Anna Sokolow has indicted the concentration camps of Nazi Germany in *Dreams,* a dance that explores themes of persecution and bravery. As these works demonstrate, choreographers can present both lighthearted and serious themes with equal success, so long as the gist of the dance remains clear.

After resolving the question of purpose, a choreographer may choose to tackle the dance's technical aspects: phrasing and design. Choreographers group movements together in phrases. In a well-constructed phrase, the movements cohere with a clear beginning, middle and end, or by another logic unique to the dance. The foundation of the phrase may be design—the motif of movements in space—or rhythm—a pattern of accented and unaccented beats. In either case, the phrase must have a recognizable shape. After creating a phrase, a choreographer can repeat it, add new phrases, experiment with variations on the phrase and then return to the original. Like a phrase in music, a phrase in dance can yield many variations.

Phrases tend to revolve around a single organizing principle known as the high point. The high point is the focus of the phrase, the moment of greatest intensity. It can be marked by an increase in tempo, an extreme change in motion or even a sudden cessation of movement. High points fall either at the beginning, the middle or the end of a phrase, each placement lending the phrase a different shape. High points at the beginning produce a movement that begins very fast and gradually dies out; placed in the middle of a phrase, the high point manifests as movement that starts out less intensely, builds and recedes; and a high point located at the end of the phrase extends movement in a final climax. Just as they change high points in phrasing, choreographers vary the lengths of phrases to create more visually exciting works.

Phrasing's partner in choreography is design—the patterns a dance creates in space—which give individual movements a larger, encompassing shape or context. A design may be symmetrical or asymmetrical, straight or angular, three-dimensional or two-dimensional, low to the ground or elevated in the air. Design incorporates geometric form into dance. The arabesque, for example, appears as a triangle to the eye, while a standing body presents a cylindrical shape. In designing a dance, a choreographer uses shape as a painter might, balancing and juxtaposing geometric figures to create a dynamic canvas.

Choreographers begin their arrangement of shape with line. Curved or circular, symmetrical or asymmetrical, lines in dance form the blueprint of the choreographic design and may imply something more than a choreographer's aesthetic judgment. Symmetrical lines, for example, may evoke a feeling of calm and stability, whereas asymmetrical lines may suggest unresolved energy, change, growth or wildness. Some choreographers strive for asymmetry in their works because they believe it suggests action and vibrancy. A body tilted at the waist or holding one arm up and the other down, or a dancer standing with one leg turned in and the other out are examples of asymmetrical positions that suggest movement even when the performer is at a standstill.

After completing the phrasing and design of a dance, a choreographer advances to the final stage: creating an overall structure or form. For the most part, music has proven to be the greatest influence on recent dance form. A musical score frequently determines the length, number of sections and tempo of a dance. In fact, many customary musical structures have been adopted as dance structures, including binary, ternary, rondo, theme-and-variation, and fugue arrangements (see *Glossary of Musical Terms,* Part II, page 121).

In the ternary form, for example, the dance proceeds in an ABA pattern, starting and ending with the same series of movements. In the theme-and-variation construct—popular because of the inventiveness it allows choreographers—an initial "statement" of movement undergoes a series of developments called variations. And the fugue form creates a complex composition of movement in which one or two themes are elaborated by a succession of dancers.

The narrative form of dance has its roots in stories rather than in music. To convey the progress of a plot, a dance progresses in clear, linear sequences (sometimes marked by choreographers as ABCDEFG, etc.), each presenting a piece of the story. A good choreographer links these sequences seamlessly, so that each seems to flow inevitably into the next. Complex narratives have long dominated Eastern dance traditions, such as Bali's legong, in which dancers depict the story of a king going to war and leaving the woman he loves. In the West, ballet has thrilled audiences with dramatic narratives, beginning in the 18th century with the ballet d'action.

Other concerns addressed by choreographers include the proportion of one part of a dance to another, the transition between sections of the dance, the logical development of the principal theme or story, and the unity of the dance—the stage at which all the elements come together, creating a more or less coherent whole. But it is important to realize that, no matter how coherent a dance may seem, the process of its creation may not have been coherent at all. Every artist works differently, according to the needs of the moment and the chaos of the moment, and no work is wholly logical in gestation or structure.

Choreographic Notation

In order to record a dance on paper, choreographers may use their own shorthand or one of several systems of dance notation. Over a period of approximately five hundred years, a variety of dance notations have developed, in part due to cultural changes but also because of the ephemeral nature of dance and its dependence on oral tradition. For centuries many dances were lost, although others were preserved. The movements of a body swirling through space and time are difficult to pinpoint and have been recorded with varying success. It was not until the 20th century that choreographers finally hit upon systems that could accurately set the entire body's movements down on paper. The story of their labors begins in ancient Egypt.

The earliest attempts at recording individual dances probably began with the invention of hieroglyphic writing in Egypt thousands of years ago. With more certainty, scholars point to mid–15th-century Spain as the birthplace of modern dance notation. In the municipal archives at Cervera, Spain, lay two manuscripts with written symbols denoting combinations of steps, one using vertical and horizontal pen marks and the other employing letters as abbreviations for dance steps, for example, an "R" for *reverencia* ("bow").

Abbreviations for steps also informed the notation system of Margaret of Austria. Her *Livre des basses danses* ("Book of Basse Dances"), published about 1460, and *Art d'instruction de bien dancer* ("The Art of Teaching Good Dancing"), which followed a decade later, both illustrate this early form of notation. But a century would pass before step abbreviations were more fully integrated into musical scores in Thoinot Arbeau's *Orchésographie,* published in 1588. *Orchésographie* helped to establish regular forms of the most popular dances by providing a manual for their step pattern. The system succeeded as long as dance maintained the same style, but when a wider variety of steps became popular, the system was outmoded. A new form of notation was needed.

In 1700, the Frenchman Raoul Auger Feuillet published the notation method invented by Pierre Beauchamps as *Chorégraphie, ou l'art de décrire la danse* ("Choreography, or the Art of Describing Dance"). The system, based on "track drawings," indicated the dancer's relation to the room and featured symbols representing steps. Feuillet placed the symbols along a floor pattern to show in which direction and how a dancer should move. His exact renditions of floor patterns enabled others to reconstruct the dances of his day centuries later. Europeans took notice of the new type of notation and quickly put it to use. Publishers in England, Germany, Spain and Italy adapted Feuillet's invention to their own nations' dances.

During Feuillet's lifetime the art of ballet began to emerge from the court dancing he notated. His system served the nascent art by reconstructing on paper the steps across the floor. Unfortunately, Feuillet was unable to depict body position, arm movements and other essential aspects of ballet. This challenge was first met by Arthur Saint-Léon, who placed stick figures on a musical staff: Those steps performed on the ground were placed on the bottom lines and steps performed in the air were moved up to the third line of the staff. A similar system was published in Germany by Albert Zorn in 1887; *Grammatik der Tanzkunst* ("Grammar of the Art of Dancing") grew popular at European dancing academies but shared many of the same limitations as Saint-Léon's innovation: its complexity, its failure to record accurately the timing or musical coordination of movements; and its assumption of the choreographer's drawing ability.

Subsequent innovators tried to use musical notation to indicate dance steps, but none succeeded until Vladimir Stepanov. A dancer at the Imperial Ballet in St. Petersburg, he devised a notation system that detailed both the placement of the body and the length of time a movement should be performed. Stepanov's method was taught at the Imperial Ballet Academy in St. Petersburg and published in Paris in 1892 under the title *Alphabet des mouvements des corps humain*. The system became the most widely used in theaters of the 19th century, and with it he recorded the entire repertory of the Imperial Ballet. After the Russian Revolution Stepanov left his homeland, carrying notebooks filled with dance notation. With these priceless documents, he introduced the finest Russian ballet repertory to the West.

As modern dance developed, choreographers needed a system capable of notating an array of movement outside the ballet vocabulary. This desire for a more "scientific" and less balletic dance notation led Rudolf von Laban, a Hungarian dancer, teacher and choreographer, to develop a system that could depict a full range of human movement. He devised a new set of symbols and a method for arranging them, so that the left, center and right sides of the body could all be shown. Laban could record not only the positions of the body and hundreds of steps but also whether a movement should be executed gently or forcefully. In Germany, he first published the system as *Choreographie* in 1926, but English speakers know his system as Labanotation.

Without competition for approximately twenty years, Labanotation lost some favor in the mid-1950s with the invention of Choreology, widely known as Benesh Dance Notation, a British system devised by Joan and Rudolf Benesh. The Benesh Notation is written on a five-line stave, with the dancer shown from behind. The top line indicates the position of the top of the head, the second line does the same for the shoulders, the third addresses the waist, the fourth the knees and the fifth the feet. Other symbols show the dynamics, rhythm and phrasing of the movement.

Benesh Dance Notation and Labanotation now dominate the field of dance notation. The introduction of videotaped rehearsals and performances, however, has taken the place traditionally held by notation. Many companies now create abundant documentation of their dances on film and tape, hoping that this will help to preserve their dances for posterity. Nevertheless, when reviving a dance that has slipped from the repertory, ballet masters and mistresses will always rely, if possible, on the memories of dancers who formerly appeared in it.

Biographies of Notable Choreographers, Dancers and Impresarios

Adams, Carolyn (1943–——): Dancer. An outstanding American member of the Paul Taylor Dance Company, Adams joined the group in 1965 after studying dance in New York and Paris and remained for seventeen years. Taylor choreographed roles for her in *Post Merid-* *ian* (1966), *Orbs* (1966), *Public Domain* (1968), *Esplanade* (1975) and other pieces. He described her as "unmannered and wondrous" and praised her remarkable lightness.

Ailey, Alvin (1931–89): Dancer and choreographer. Ailey, a notable African-American dancer, was also the celebrated choreographer of *Blues Suite* (1958), *Revelations* (1960), *Cry* (1971) and other works that present a dynamic amalgam of ballet, modern, jazz and African-American dancing. Originally inspired by the work of Katherine Dunham, he was a disciple of Lester Horton before studying in New York with Martha Graham, Doris Humphrey and others. He made his first New York appearance in 1957; as a performer in musical theater and ballet he absorbed the streetwise, the vernacular and the urban into his sensibility. Soon after he arrived in New York, he founded a dance company (later known as the Alvin Ailey American Dance Theater) and an affiliated school. As a choreographer, he often took the black experience as his subject matter to create narrative as well as abstract dances. He set his work to a wide range of music, from traditional spirituals to Duke Ellington, from Janis Joplin to Pink Floyd, and from Benjamin Britten to Eric Satie. In assembling a multiracial company that reached a large international audience, Ailey significantly expanded the bounds of dance. The company continues to perform a broad repertory, including Ailey's own work.

Alonso, Alicia (1921–——): Dancer. A Cuban ballerina renowned not only for her dancing but also for her strength of spirit, she made her name in New York after studying at the School of American Ballet. She danced in Broadway musicals before joining American Ballet Theatre, where she earned a reputation both for her classical artistry in such ballets as *Giselle* and for her interpretation of modern ballets, including Anthony Tudor's *Undertow* (1945). In 1948 Alonso returned to Cuba and founded her own company, Ballet Alicia Alonso (later renamed Ballet Nacional de Cuba), and opened a ballet school in Havana. She allied herself with the Castro regime and considered herself a revolutionary, but she continued to appear abroad as well; her partnership with Russian dancer Igor Youskevitch became legendary. As her eyesight began to fail in her unusually long career, Alonso danced at peril but with triumph. She brought warmth and passion to the typically cool persona of the ballerina.

Ashton, Sir Frederick (1906–88): Choreographer and dancer. This progenitor and mainstay of British ballet first took an interest in dancing when, as a boy, he saw Anna Pavlova perform in Peru. He trained with Leonide Massine and Marie Rambert, danced with Rambert and Ida Rubenstein, and choreographed for various English companies over a long career. His last affiliation was with the Royal Ballet, where he worked closely with Ninette de Valois and where he served as associate director (1952–63) and director (1963–70). Ashton's choreography is well known for the pas de deux and for a lyricism considered typically English in its restraint, delicacy and musicality. Primarily interested in pure dance for dance's sake, he yet worked effectively within different theatrical traditions, for instance restaging the Russian classics. Among others, Margot Fonteyn credited Ashton as a significant formative influence. His dances include *Les Rendezvous* (1933), *A Wedding Bouquet* (1937), *Illuminations* (1950), *La fille mal gardée* (1960), *Monotones* (1966) and *Enigma Variations* (1968).

Astaire, Fred (1899–1987): Dancer and choreographer. An accomplished American musician and songwriter as well as a formidable dancer, Astaire began performing professionally at age seven. For many years he toured in vaudeville with his older sister Adele before winning larger fame as a dancer and choreographer in the movies and elsewhere. Various dancing partnerships characterized his career, starting with Adele and peaking with Ginger Rogers, the most famous among a string of female stars. He was also associated with the dancer-choreographer Hermes Pan in Hollywood and worked closely with composers Irving Berlin, Jerome Kern and Cole Porter on films featuring dances set to their music. An impeccably well-mannered virtuoso of tap and ballroom dancing, he elevated a popular genre to the status of art form without robbing it of its vitality. This ingenious perfectionist invented dances of baroque complexity (as when he danced on a golf course in the 1938 movie *Carefree*) and tossed off performances with amazing nonchalance. His many film credits include *Flying Down to Rio* (1933), *The Gay Divorcée* (1934), *Top Hat* (1935), *Follow the Fleet* (1936), *Swing Time* (1936), *Shall We Dance* (1937) and *Funny Face* (1956).

Baker, Josephine (1906–75): Dancer and entertainer. This dancer and singer, famed for appearing at the Folies-Bergère in Paris wearing nothing but a skirt of bananas, was born out of wedlock to an African-American mother in the slums of St. Louis, Missouri. She first performed at age thirteen with a local jazz act; after leaving home to seek her fortune in musical theater, she danced in the choruses of touring revues. Baker's style was sinuous, fluid and seductive, shocking to more conservative people of the time. She made her name only after reaching Paris, where she won a loyal following among less inhibited audiences. For many years, this glamorous and outrageous performer toured the world. She married a series of men and even kept a pet cheetah. During World War II she joined the French Resistance and later became a French citizen. She adopted a multiracial array of children and spent her money so lavishly that she lost some of her property. She died after making numerous, much-publicized farewell appearances.

Balanchine, George (1904–83): Choreographer. Balanchine, who valued ballet for its own sake, inherited a theatrical ballet tradition that he recast and purified according to his own vision. Born in St. Petersburg, Russia (his father was the composer Meliton Balanchivadze), he studied at the Petrograd Conservatory of Music and at the Imperial Ballet School, graduating from the latter in 1921. His early efforts at choreography offended Soviet audiences, but when he joined Serge Diaghilev's Ballets Russes in 1924 he met with a better response. Before he left that troupe in 1929 he met the composer Igor Stravinsky, who became a valued collaborator. Balanchine's ballets from that period include *Apollon Musagete* (1928) and *The Prodigal Son* (1929). He came to the United States shortly thereafter and founded the New York City Ballet and the School of American Ballet in 1933 with Lincoln Kirstein and Edward M. M. Warburg. Gathering talented dancers about him, Balanchine started to create an enormous body of work. His neoclassicism, descended from that of Marius Petipa, revealed itself in manifold ways; he also departed from the classical medium. Critics noted his emphasis on large and powerful ballet movements and his paring down of soft, refined gestures, which allowed young American dancers to perform his version of classical ballet easily and naturally. Through his work, Balanchine altered the look and the dynamic capabilities of ballet dancers. He tended to use slim, long-limbed performers capable of athletic, quick and exact maneuvers. He expected dancers to move musically across great expanses of space and to impose no extraneous personal or theatrical mannerisms on the dance. Among the innumerable standouts he cultivated were Patricia McBride, Arthur Mitchell, Diana Adams, Tannaquil LeClerc, Maria Tallchief, Suzanne Farrell, Jacques d'Amboise, Kyra Nichols and Peter Martins. Balanchine's ballets include *Serenade* (1935), *Theme and Variations* (1946), *The Firebird* (1949), *The Nutcracker*

(1954), *A Midsummer Night's Dream* (1962), *Don Quixote* (1965), *Slaughter on Tenth Avenue* (1968) and many others. Working on Broadway, in Hollywood, on television and in opera, he choreographed such musicals as *On Your Toes* (1936) and produced several festival seasons for the New York City Ballet.

Balasaraswati [Tanjore Balasaraswati] (1920–84): Dancer. She was considered her generation's best exponent of bharata natyam, a highly refined South Indian solo dance genre performed exclusively by women. Born in Madras, India, she studied primarily under Kandappa Nattuvanar. Balasaraswati started her studies at age four, made her debut at seven and went on to perform extensively in India and elsewhere in the world. She also taught at the Music Academy in Madras. Her power as a mime and an actress was the equal of her gift as a dancer.

Baryshnikov, Mikhail (1948–——): Dancer. This Latvian-born dancer has been hailed for his technical brilliance, precision, elegance, coolness and daring. He trained at the Riga Choreographic School and the Vaganova School in Leningrad, joining the Soviet Union's Kirov Ballet in 1967. Although he enjoyed great success in his native country, he defected to the West in 1974. Baryshnikov developed a prodigious classical technique even while seeking out new theatrical experiences. He tried his hand at the modern dances of Martha Graham, Twyla Tharp and Mark Morris, appeared in several movies and acted on Broadway. But classical ballet remained his focus, first as a member of at the American Ballet Theatre and then as a guest of many companies around the world. In 1978, Baryshnikov left ABT and joined the New York City Ballet in order to work with the aging George Balanchine. Within a year he danced in more than twenty new ballets, but he found it physically taxing to adjust to the demands of the Balanchine technique at a

relatively late age. In 1980 he became artistic director of ABT, a role that put him at the center of more than one financial and artistic controversy. Before resigning that post, Baryshnikov managed to make some difficult and much-needed changes at the company. His recent activities have included involvement with the White Oak Dance Project, marketing a line of dancewear and bottling his own signature fragrance.

Bausch, Pina (1940–——): Dancer and choreographer. This German ballet dancer, known primarily for her concert ballets, studied with such major dance figures as Kurt Jooss, Antony Tudor, José Limon and Paul Taylor. Soon after she was appointed ballet master of the Wuppertal State Opera Dance Theater in 1973, she began inventing concert ballets performed to the music of Igor Stravinsky and Kurt Weill.

Beauchamp, Pierre (1636–1705): French nobleman, dancer, choreographer and ballet master who served as superintendent of the ballets of the King of France. Many name him as creator of the five classic positions of ballet.

Bejart, Maurice (1928–——): Dancer and choreographer. This Frenchman has choreographed highly theatrical dances that merge classical, modern and jazz idioms in a Dionysian manner. Sometimes considered a sensationalist as well as a neoexpressionist, he has demonstrated the power to move mass audiences in unusually large spaces. The sweeping emotional scale of his dances well suits amphitheaters and stadiums. Bejart studied at the Marseille Opera Ballet School and danced with its parent company, as well as with Ballets de Roland Petit and the Royal Swedish Ballet. Over the years he has formed several companies, the best known being the Ballet of the 20th Century, founded in 1960. Bejart's ballets include *Le sacre du printemps* (1959),

The Damnation of Faust (1964) and *Nijinsky, Clown of God* (1971).

Berkeley, Busby (1895–1976): Choreographer. The name of this American stage and screen director and choreographer is synonymous with the extravagantly patterned dances he created for large numbers of dancers. A military academy graduate, he served as a lieutenant in the U.S. Army in 1917; his experience overseeing parade drills later helped him organize the intricately coordinated, large-scale dances that made him famous. Berkeley worked as an actor before discovering his metier as a Broadway and Hollywood director. He created musical numbers in which the individuality of the dancers took second place to panoramic design. To show the facets of his dances to best advantage, he set the camera in unusual positions, often directly above the dancers. His use of point-of-view changed the way dance was subsequently filmed.

Bournonville, August (1805–79): Dancer, choreographer and teacher. This Danish dancer created an independent style and distinct approach for the Royal Danish Ballet that has prevailed to this day. He first studied dancing with his French-born father and then with Auguste Vestris in Copenhagen and Paris. Bournonville developed a technique known for its lightness and precision in the air and for its detailed, delicate, yet natural-looking virtuosity. Stylistically, he was a synthesist, combining many influences. A dedicated partisan of dance, he worked for decades to dignify the discipline in his native country. Before he quit dancing to teach, choreograph and direct the Royal Danish Ballet, he earned renown as the great Maria Taglioni's partner. He taught Lucile Grahn and choreographed roles for her in *Valdemar* (1835) and in his version of *La Sylphide* (1836). His more than fifty ballets also include *Napoli* (1842) and *La Ventana* (1856).

Brown, Carolyn (1927–——): Dancer and choreographer. A founding member of the Merce Cunningham Company, this American influenced Cunningham both as a technically brilliant performer and as a collaborator from 1952 through 1972. Brown studied Denishawn technique with her mother and then at the Juilliard School in New York before joining the Cunningham troupe. There, Cunningham choreographed almost all the roles she danced expressly for her; many of his extant works include these roles. Brown has also taught and written on dance.

Brown, Trisha (1936–——): Dancer and choreographer. A former member of the Judson Dance Theater, she grew up in Washington State and studied ballet, tap and jazz there as a child. She then moved on to modern dance with Merce Cunningham, Louis Horst and José Limon. After graduating from Mills College as a dance major, she participated in a workshop with Ann Halprin, Yvonne Rainer, Simone Forti and others in San Francisco. She then organized the dance department at Reed College in 1958. One of the paybacks of her workshop experience was her encounter with improvisational technique, which allowed her a certain freedom. Brown moved to New York and studied with Robert Dunn, who introduced her to the Judson Memorial Church as a performance space. Under Dunn's tutelage she developed a dance creed before forming a company of her own. Her early work included solos for herself and group pieces performed largely by non-dancers. Her pieces include *Rulegame 5* (1964), *Planes* (1968), *Accumulation* (1971) and *Locus* (1975).

Bruhn, Erik (1928–86): Dancer and choreographer. His cool dignity, courtliness, clarity and elegance personified a male ideal in classical ballet. Born in Copenhagen, he studied at the Royal Danish Ballet School and danced first with its parent company. He went on to perform frequently as a guest artist with such companies as American Ballet Theatre, the New York City Ballet and the National Ballet of Canada. While he also worked as a choreographer, Bruhn was better known for his stagings of such classic dances as *Swan Lake* and *Romeo and Juliet* than for his original ballets. His administrative roles included stints as associate director of the National Ballet of Canada and director of the Royal Swedish Ballet.

Camargo, Marie [Marie-Anne de Cupis] (1710–70): Dancer. This French ballet dancer was known for her technical brilliance and great energy in executing feats more often expected of male performers. She was also the recognized rival of Marie Sallé, a very different and distinguished dancer of the same era. Camargo shortened the skirts of her costumes to show off her skillful footwork and was celebrated for the technique thus revealed.

Childs, Lucinda (1940–——): Dancer and choreographer. This American postmodern choreographer was an important member of the Judson Dance Theater in New York, where collaboration and innovation met in the 1960s and changed the course of modern dance. Childs did not want to do the representational work typified by the achievements of Martha Graham and others. Instead, she gravitated toward the relative abstract purity of Merce Cunningham, her teacher at Sarah Lawrence College, who had repudiated the literary, dramatic, psychological, musical and expressionistic aims of early modern dance in favor of abstract yet individual pieces. But, like other Judsonites, Childs opened up the palette of dance even further than had Cunningham. In Judson performances, non-dancers danced, sometimes to nonmusic or in unconventional spaces; their movements incorporated everyday actions, gestures and objects that had previously been considered off the dance map. For example, in the early dance *Carnation* (1964), Childs manipulated curlers, a colander, sponges and a plastic bag. In her *Street Dance* (1964), two dancers mingled with people on a Manhattan street while the audience watched from the window of a nearby artist's loft and a tape recording offered commentary on what was taking place below. Her earliest work consisted mainly of solos; later, her dances involved groups of dancers. Childs's work became both more theatrical and more minimalist in the years after her involvement with Judson. Her choreography for the lavishly staged opera *Einstein on the Beach* (1976), by Robert Wilson and Philip Glass, is one example of her evolving theatrical sensibility. Her most recent dances have revealed a minimalistic purity, a resistance to overt virtuosity and a lyric composure.

Culberg, Birgit (1908–——): Dancer and choreographer. This Swedish ballet dancer was trained in the 1930s by Kurt Jooss in England and in the mid-1940s by Lillian Karina in Stockholm. In 1945 she created the Svenka-dansteater, a company for which she choreographed her best-known work, *Miss Julie* (1950). From 1957 to 1967 she served as a guest choreographer for world-class ballet companies, including the New York City Ballet and the American Ballet Theatre. In 1967 she settled again in Stockholm and formed her own company, The Birgit Culberg Ballet.

Cunningham, Merce (1922–——): Dancer and choreographer. As a choreographer, Cunningham makes highly formal dances, often using "chance" techniques that go against the grain of ballet and much modern dance. His dances owe their power to both forms as well as to his own original vision. Born in Centralia, Washington, he studied ballroom, tap and folk dancing as a child before performing in vaudeville. He continued his dance training at Bennington College in 1939, after which Martha Graham invited him to join her company. Cunningham danced there as a soloist for five years, during which Graham created leading roles for him in such dances as *Letter to the World* (1940) and *Appalachian Spring* (1944). He began choreographing in 1943 and formed his own company in 1952. Since the 1940s his steady musical collaborator has been John Cage; other experimental composers with whom he has worked include Morton Feldman and Christian Wolff. He has also worked with such visual artists as Robert Rauschenberg and Jasper Johns. Cunningham's dances tend to forgo the central focus of most dances, according to which the most important action takes place in the middle of the stage, with secondary action arrayed around it in a basically hierarchic fashion. Instead, his dancers move in patterns that seem spontaneous and unconstrained by spatial convention, even though the dancing is demanding on its own terms, requiring a balletic precision and speed. The effect of a Cunningham dance is like that of a scene from nature: Things happen according to a logic that, while powerful, is partly submerged. Among the hallmarks of his work has been the independent development of a dance and its musical score; since Cunningham does not choreograph "to" music in the usual sense, the score does not illustrate the dance and the dance does not illustrate the score. Devoted to movement for its own sake and liberated from the requirements of storytelling, emotional formulas and stage artifice, his dancers express their unique physical selves in the moments and with the movements given to them. Cunningham's use of chance techniques, though celebrated, is only part of his contribution to dance, since his use of chance in many dances is limited. Still, chance has had an impact on his aesthetic, creating a version of order in the absence of obvious structure—a sense of order in constant change. Cunningham's

many dances include *Summerspace* (1958), *Rune* (1959), *Channels/Inserts* (1981) and *Loosestrife* (1991).

d'Amboise, Jacques (1934–———): Dancer and teacher. One of the earliest and most distinguished male interpreters of the George Balanchine style, this American joined the New York City Ballet in 1950 after studying at the School of American Ballet. Balanchine created roles for him in *Raymonda Variations* (1961), *Episodes* (1959) and other ballets; his frequent partners included Diana Adams and Suzanne Farrell. An exceptional dancer, d'Amboise had a typically American breadth, brio, musicality and energy ideally suited to the exacting decorum of ballet as Balanchine remodeled it. He choreographed a number of dances himself, including *The Chase* (1963) and *Irish Fantasy* (1964). When his performing career ended, he established the National Dance Institute, which teaches children in New York and other cities and has produced extravagant annual performances.

Dean, Laura (1945–———): Choreographer and dancer. A composer as well as a choreographer, this American was educated at New York City's High School for Performing Arts and at the School of American Ballet. She danced with Paul Taylor, Meredith Monk, Kenneth King and others before forming her own company, Laura Dean Dancers and Musicians, in 1976. Her creations there include *Spiral* (1977) and *Music* (1979). Dean's experience in both classical and modern dance has served her well, although she is best known for her work in modern. Her choreographic signature—a kind of ritual spinning performed by an ensemble—came to Dean only when she set out to free herself from the sum total of her previous dance training. Another aspect of her inventiveness was her desire to make sense, intuitively, of worldwide political changes in the late 1960s; a new era seemed to demand a new kind of dancing. Dean's modern work, often set to minimalist scores by Steve Reich and others, has frequently been compared to Middle Eastern dervish dancing because of its spinning motif, its devotion to simple forms and patterns, and the dancers' mystical abandon to motion. A similar preoccupation with the geometrical infuses her ballets, which are marked, like her modern pieces, by a rhythmic intensity that borders on obsession. Her ballets include *Night* and *Fire,* commissioned in 1982 by Robert Joffrey for the Joffrey Ballet. Dean has also created ice dances at the invitation of the skater John Curry. By her own admission, regardless of the genre she works in, Dean uses order to find freedom.

de Jong, Bettie (1933–——): Dancer and teacher. Although she danced in the companies of Martha Graham, Pearl Lang and others, she became most closely associated with the Paul Taylor Dance Company, which she joined in 1962. Born in Sumatra of Dutch parents, de Jong possessed a physical exoticism that inspired the many roles Taylor created for her. The choreographer especially admired her ability to capture the absurd with her body. She became ballet mistress of Taylor's company in 1973 and has since taught his master classes, as well as teaching at various other schools of dance in the United States and England.

de Mille, Agnes (1905–93): Dancer and choreographer. Born into a distinguished American theatrical family (which included Cecil B. de Mille), she had to go against the grain of society to launch a career as a woman in dance. Physically, de Mille was not naturally suited to ballet and met with general discouragement in her early years as a solo concert artist and choreographer. This attitude changed with the premiere of *Rodeo* (1942) in a production mounted by the Ballet Russe de Monte Carlo. Like many of her dances, *Rodeo* drew on American culture as a bona fide

subject in a way few dances in the classical genre had done before, combining a balletic vocabulary with the verve of popular and vernacular forms. De Mille's accomplishments as a choreographer extended to many Broadway musicals, such as *Oklahoma!* (1943), *Brigadoon* (1947) and *Paint Your Wagon* (1951), and to some movies. She was also associated for decades with the American Ballet Theatre, and was much admired for her memoirs and writings on dance and the American theater.

de Valois, Ninette (1898–——): Dancer, choreographer and teacher. Like Marie Rambert, she helped to chart the course of British ballet in the 20th century. De Valois was born in Ireland and studied dance in London with Cecchetti. She first worked in pantomime and at the Royal Opera, then joined Serge Diaghilev's Ballets Russes in 1923 for a few years. She established two schools of ballet in London, the first in 1926 and the second in 1931, encouraging her students to dance in productions at theaters in and around the city. Meanwhile, de Valois began staging and choreographing ballets of her own, beginning with *Les Petits Riens* (1928); others included *La Creation du Monde* (1931), *The Rake's Progress* (1935) and *Checkmate* (1937). Eventually, her evolving troupe of dancers became known as the Vic-Wells Ballet, then as Sadler's Wells. In its current incarnation as the Royal Ballet, it is Britain's most prominent classical company, supported as an institution by the Royal Ballet School. The repertory of the Royal Ballet is infused with de Valois's enthusiasm for 19th-century classic ballets, complemented by the dramatic content of some of her own work. As an administrator, creator and teacher, de Valois shaped the lives and careers of countless English dancers.

Diaghilev, Serge (1872–1929): Impresario. Founder of the Ballets Russes, he invigorated dance by introducing revolutionary talent to Europe at a time of ennui and decadence, as he guided this art from an old century to a new one. Born in Perm, Russia, Diaghilev wanted to become a composer, but he was discouraged from that endeavor and instead studied law in St. Petersburg. Along with such friends as the painters Leon Bakst and Alexandre Benois, he published a noted magazine, *The World of Art*, from 1899 to 1904. He worked briefly for the Imperial Theatres in St. Petersburg, then left to organize art exhibitions there and in Paris. After successfully producing the opera *Boris Godunov* in Paris, he presented a troupe of dancers to that city in 1909. His troupe, which included Anna Pavlova, Ida Rubenstein, Tamara Karsavina and Michel Fokine, received an enthusiastic response. The following year, Diaghilev presented many of those dancers in a repertory that included *Scheherezade*, *The Firebird* and *Giselle*. Vaslav Nijinsky became his star dancer and choreographer, as well as his lover; when Nijinsky married, the older man suddenly renounced him. Although Diaghilev did not dance, choreograph, compose, paint or design, in his roles as manager and cultural provocateur he vitally influenced the work of those who did. He incited the imaginations of his collaborators and promoted avant-garde work in various media, at the same time building an audience for it. Important contributors to the Ballets Russes included Pablo Picasso, Jean Cocteau, Igor Stravinsky, Eric Satie, Leonide Massine and George Balanchine. Diaghilev continued to produce dance seasons around the world until his death.

Draper, Paul (1909–——): Dancer. This American was a great success at tap dancing, both unaccompanied and set to classical and other music, before he was blacklisted during the McCarthy era. Largely self-taught, Draper began as a ballroom dancer and teacher, worked in vaudeville for a time and lived, off and on, in Europe before developing a distinguished solo act. He was not interested in the customary rhythms laid down by tap dancers; they struck him as noisy and unkempt. So, in the 1940s and 1950s, he sought out classical music as a background and inspiration to tap, augmented it with his knowledge of ballet, and made it a concert art. He danced successfully at the Plaza Hotel in New York, at nightclubs and in many theaters and opera houses across the country, establishing a partnership with classical harmonica player Larry Adler. Draper also appeared in such films as *Colleen* (1936) and *The Time of Your Life* (1948). After he was blacklisted as a communist by the House Un-American Activities Committee, he continued to work as a teacher at Carnegie-Mellon University and elsewhere.

Duncan, Isadora (1877–1927): Dancer and teacher. A native of San Francisco, she was not appreciated by most of her American contemporaries; the liberties she took in art, politics and life made her unpopular. However, in her various revolts—especially her dismissal of ballet and theatrical tradition—Duncan found an enthusiastic response in Europe and influenced the work of many modern dancers and choreographers there. She also received an enthusiastic welcome from European artists in general, to whom she remained an example of untrammeled artistic instinct, heroic for her pursuit of freedom in art at all costs. Duncan studied ballet as a child, but not for long, and as a teenager she taught social dancing. She was largely self-educated, although her mother, a music teacher, divorcée, atheist and devotee of the arts, nurtured her freethinking ways and her love of classical music. Duncan's career began when she left San Francisco in 1895 and joined a touring theatrical company. It didn't suit her and she next became a frequent solo performer in ladies' salons in New York and other cities before departing for Europe with her family in 1899. There, she worked to reinvent dance using nature and classical Greek art as models. She danced barefoot to musical masterworks, by preference in lofty spaces; her dancing seemed rapturously improvisational, calling on the simplest movements and sculptural poses with lyric dignity. None of her dances were notated and few were photographed, so the details of their composition are cloudy. Revered in Europe, Duncan opened the first of several dance schools in Berlin in 1904. She first toured Russia in 1905 and, considered a Bolshevik sympathizer, became especially beloved there. She made the acquaintance of Michel Fokine, who acknowledged her impact in his ballet *Eunice* (1908), in which classical dancers appeared barefoot, wearing Greek tunics. Duncan did not win respect during her occasional trips home to America. Her controversial personal and political life offended those who misunderstood her impulsive abandon. She died when her long scarf got caught in a wheel of her car and strangled her.

Dunham, Katherine (1909–——): Dancer, choreographer and teacher. An African-American anthropologist and social reformer as well as a leader in dance, Dunham earned an M.A. from the University of Chicago before formulating a dance technique and assembling a company. As a dancer, Dunham was praised for her showmanship and timing, as a choreographer for her vibrantly theatrical revues and concert pieces. Her approach to movement relies on African tradition and on the fieldwork she conducted as an ethnologist in Haiti. Her work appeals to broad audiences, and she and her company broke color barriers while touring the American South and beyond. At the suggestion of impresario Sol Hurok in the 1940s, Dunham embarked on more commercial work, such as *Cabin in*

the Sky (1940), which she cochoreographed with George Balanchine for Broadway; she also worked in film on such productions as *Stormy Weather* (1943). Dunham's pedagogical energy is also impressive: She has established schools in New York City, Haiti and the slums of East St. Louis. In 1987 the Alvin Ailey American Dance Company restaged fourteen of her dances in a tribute to African-American dance greats.

Elssler, Fanny (1810–84): Dancer. This Austrian rival to Italian dancer Marie Taglioni won acclaim for her triumphantly earthy performances as a ballerina: Though she danced in the Romantic mode, her personal style was dramatic, voluptuous and passionate. The daughter of composer Franz Joseph Haydn's valet, she was sent at Haydn's direction to study ballet in Vienna as a child. She made her debut at the Vienna Hoftheater in 1822. In addition to advancing the popularity of the Romantic ballerina, Elssler made character dancing—theatrical dances based on various ethnic traditions, notably Russian and Spanish—more familiar throughout Europe, Russia and America. By the conclusion of her career at the age of forty-one, she had reportedly earned more than a million dollars, an enormous fortune at the time.

Farrell, Suzanne (1945–——): Dancer. A principal dancer with the New York City Ballet, Farrell served as an important instrument and inspiration to choreographer George Balanchine. Although he created dances for many ballerinas, she is usually considered his particular muse. Born in Cincinnati, Farrell won a Ford Foundation scholarship to study at the School of American Ballet in 1960 and joined the NYCB a year later. Critics noted her mastery of balance and her ability to achieve difficult movements with little support or visible effort. She left an unmistakable mark on the company's repertory; even since her retirement, the troupe's dancers still emulate her. Roles created for her by Balanchine included those in *Meditation* (1964), the "Diamonds" section of *Jewels* (1967), *Tzigane* (1975), *Don Quixote* (1965), in which the choreographer occasionally played the title character opposite Farrell's Dulcinea, and *Slaughter on Tenth Avenue* (1968). Farrell left the NYCB in 1969 after marrying another company member, Paul Meijia. However, she returned to New York and Balanchine in 1975 after dancing with Maurice Bejart's Ballet of the 20th Century in Brussels. Hip trouble precipitated her retirement in 1989.

Feld, Eliot (1943–———): Choreographer and teacher. The works of this American choreographer of ballets is noted for merging classical, modern, folk and jazz idioms in a musically acute way. His visual sense is inventive and, in its forms and impact, avidly sculptural. He began his career as a dancer with American Ballet Theatre in 1963 after studying at the School of American Ballet and elsewhere; he also performed with modern dance troupes and in the movie *West Side Story* (1961). The success of *Harbinger* (1967), Feld's first dance, allowed him to pursue choreography single-mindedly. He has founded and directed several ballet companies since leaving ABT, most recently Feld Ballets/NY, which performs his work; he also established an affiliated school, the New Ballet School, in 1978. Feld's ballets include *At Midnight* (1967), *Intermezzo No. 1* (1969), *Danzon Cubano* (1978), *The Jig Is Up* (1983), *Aurora I* and *Aurora II* (both 1985), *Contra Pose* (1990) and *Endsong* (1991).

Fokine, Michel (1880–1942): Dancer and choreographer. A gifted dancer and influential teacher, Fokine brought lasting innovation to modern ballet as a choreographer. Beginning in 1909 and living mostly in France, this Russian-born artist worked in association with Serge Diaghilev to give the Ballets Russes such dances as *Les Sylphides* (1909),

Firebird (1910), *Le Spectre de la rose* (1911) and *Petrushka* (1911). His work gave new dignity to ballet; what had once seemed a frivolous genre, born of sentimental music, improbable stories and stagy effects, found recognition as an art with complex standards, capable of moving audiences and sustaining bold aesthetic experiments. In their experimental aspects, his ballets impressed his colleagues in fine arts, music and the theater with their imaginative power and relevance. Fokine, like the Ballets Russes in general, collaborated with outstanding artists of the day—composer Igor Stravinsky, for one—and in this respect summoned the best of contemporary art-making to the ballet. His choreographic creed included a wish to minimalize the conventional language of gesture in ballet, to revivify the role of ensembles, to let dance engage the entire body, to seek drama, when possible, instead of customary and banal scenarios, and to aim for a new or newly modified classical language in each new dance. Fokine left Diaghilev when the impresario focused on cultivating the dancer Vaslav Nijinsky as a choreographer. He then worked free-lance in Europe and the United States, settling in New York in 1923. Over the course of his career he staged more than sixty ballets.

Fonteyn, Margot [Margaret Hookham] (1919–91): Dancer. For many years Fonteyn was the reigning ballerina of Great Britain. Her matchless lyricism and good manners endeared her to balletomanes around the world and significantly raised the standard of English dancing. She grew up in Shanghai and London, studied with Vera Volkova and at the Sadler's Wells Ballet School, and first performed with the school's affiliated company, which was later named the Royal Ballet. In the course of her long career, she was associated closely with choreographer Frederick Ashton: He created roles for her in *Symphonic*

Variations (1946), *Cinderella* (1948), *Sylvia* (1952), *Marguerite and Armand* (1958), *Ondine* (1958) and other ballets. Fonteyn was an exceptional Princess Aurora in *The Sleeping Beauty* and distinguished herself in other 19th-century classics; in these, her vernal delicacy and strong technique served each other exceptionally well. In addition to her longtime alliance with the Royal Ballet, Fonteyn danced as a guest artist with many companies in and out of Europe. She developed, late in life, a challenging and acclaimed professional partnership with the flamboyant Rudolph Nureyev. Her artistic resilience prolonged and preserved her life as a dancer beyond the point at which most ballerinas must retire.

Forsythe, William (1949–——): Dancer and choreographer. This American danced with the Joffrey Ballet from 1971 to 1973. In 1976 he choreographed his first ballet, *Urlicht,* set to the music of Gustav Mahler, for the Stuttgart Ballet. His other works include *Flore sub-simplici* (1977), *Orpheus* (1979), and *Whisper Moon* (1981). During the 1984–85 season he assumed the directorship of the Frankfurt Ballet.

Fracci, Carla (1936–——): Dancer. This Italian ballet dancer was legendary for her interpretation of Giselle. Beginning in 1958, she performed at Milan's La Scala, dancing in such varied works as Anton Dolin's *Pas de Quatre,* Antony Tudor's *Jardin aux lilas,* José Limon's *The Moor's Pavanne,* and Bournonville's *Flower Festival in Genzano.* Fracci also danced principal roles in such classic ballets as *Coppelia* and *La Sylphide,* many restaged especially for her. She is the great-grandniece of opera composer Giuseppi Verdi.

Fuller, Loie (1862–1928): Dancer. Though not a dancer in the strict sense, she staged solo theater pieces of opulent, transitory and seductive beauty that significantly influenced dancers of her time and thereafter. She was born in Illinois, studied only scantily, performed in

vaudeville and burlesque acts, and debuted with her own work at the Folies-Bergère in Paris in 1892. Intent on creating radiant theatrical illusions, Fuller experimented with the mechanical means at her disposal, especially lighting and costumes. She was extremely popular in Europe, where she toured widely. She started a vogue with such pieces as *The Serpentine Dance* (c. 1905), which evoked a sunrise and inspired onlookers with its lavish yet lyrical effects. Fuller remained mistress of the genre in her lifetime.

Gades, Antonio (1936–——): Choreographer and dancer. This Spaniard became an international sensation while performing a modernized version of the flamenco at the 1964 World's Fair in New York. At age thirteen he performed at Spain's Circo Price, then went on to join Ballet Espagnol in 1952. After nine years with the company, he worked in Italy in the early 1960s and made his London debut in 1970. He has appeared in films, and in 1983 collaborated with director Carlos Saura on a film version of *Carmen.*

Gordon, David (1936–——): Dance constructor. A leading American experimentalist, he prefers not to be described as a choreographer. Instead of making dances, he assembles "constructions" that combine elements of unconventional theater, dance, vernacular movement, verbal play, and the real world, utilizing what some observers consider an ironic show-business mentality as intent on subversion as it is on entertainment. Though often called a postmodernist, Gordon rejects the label. A native New Yorker who studied with Merce Cunningham, he danced with Yvonne Rainer and James Waring during the 1960s and was active as a performance artist with the Judson Dance Theater before performing with the Grand Union in the 1970s. Gordon has also worked with his own group of dancers, the David Gordon Pick Up Co., on a project basis. Company members come and go, and, as its name suggests, the troupe itself is deliberately provisional; the process of Gordon's work and its presentation are more changeable than those of most choreographers. Still, he has allowed larger companies, such as American Ballet Theatre, the Dance Theater of Harlem and the Paris Opera, to perform his dances in hopes of challenging their dancers and broadening their repertories. Gordon's constructions include *Random Breakfast* (1963), *Not Necessarily Recognizable Objectives* (1978), *Framework* (1983) and *Field, Chair and Mountain* (1984).

Graham, Martha (1893–1991): An originator of modern dance and one of the 20th century's seminal artists. Raised in Pittsburgh and California, she studied with Ruth St. Denis and Ted Shawn at their Los Angeles school and danced with the Denishawn Company before striking out on her own. She pursued a vision and an evolving technique drastically different from those of her contemporaries and forebears, and assembled a company of dancers to express these. Highly theatrical, the Graham style invested great drama in a dance language of starkness and formal contrasts, which was capable of invoking conflict, violence, wit and lyricism. Critics responded to the burning intelligence and control evident in her dances. Some of her works explore Greek myth, Native American legend, the lives and work of writers Emily Dickinson and the Brontë sisters, and aspects of the American past in a searchingly psychological manner. Other Graham dances, though, are abstract in nature. Her technique was based on the rhythms of breathing and on the contraction and expulsion of muscular tension, relying on emotion to provide form. Graham taught or otherwise influenced many dancers and choreographers, some of whom (e.g., Merce Cunningham and Erick Hawkins, who was her husband) went beyond it in order to follow paths of their own. She collab-

orated with or commissioned work from leading composers and artists, including Aaron Copland, Paul Hindemith and Isamu Noguchi. Among her more than one hundred dances are *Primitive Mysteries* (1931), *American Document* (1938), *El Penitente* (1940), *Letter to the World* (1940), *Deaths and Entrances* (1943), *Appalachian Spring* (1944), *Dark Meadow* (1946) and *Errand into the Maze* (1947). Graham danced and choreographed over an unusually long and rich career; she also founded and directed a school in New York.

Grisi, Carlotta (1819–99): Dancer. A leading Italian Romantic ballerina, Grisi premiered the title role in *Giselle* (1841), a significant work of the Romantic period and a classic in ballet's continuing canon. She first danced in the corps of La Scala. At the age of fourteen she met the French choreographer and ballet master Jules Perrot, who became her mentor, her lover and finally her husband. Perrot took her to France, but Grisi also danced in many other European countries, won the amorous attention of critic Theophile Gautier, and eventually left her husband for another dancer.

Hawkins, Erick (1909–———): Dancer and choreographer. This American choreographer began his career as a dancer after an education in classics at Harvard. He studied at the School of American Ballet and danced with classical troupes before joining Martha Graham's company, where he danced from 1938 to 1951. Hawkins was an important dancer to Graham, virile and leonine; she created many roles with him in mind, including those in *Letter to the World* (1940), *Deaths and Entrances* (1943), *Appalachian Spring* (1944), *Dark Meadow* (1945) and *Diversion of Angels* (1948). They also married, but neither the personal nor the professional partnership lasted. Hawkins left Graham's entourage to form his own company, in collaboration with the composer Lucia Dlugoszewski and the sculptor Ralph Dorazio. Unlike Graham's, his approach to dancing concentrates on natural ease and avoids the appearance of strain; the movements look youthful, unfettered, sensuous and lyrical. Ritual preoccupies him, as do Asian sensibilities, poetry and nature.

Holm, Hanya (1898–1992): Choreographer and teacher. A German-born modern-dance choreographer, Holm enjoyed a career that spanned nearly the whole range of her chosen art form. Once a convent-school pupil, she studied at the Dalcroze Institute in Frankfurt-am-Main and with the German choreographer Mary Wigman, whose company she joined in 1921. At her mentor's suggestion, she founded the Mary Wigman School in New York in 1931, and five years later launched a company of her own. During the 1930s, Holm also became associated with the Bennington College School of the Dance, and in 1941 she established the Center of the Dance in the West in Colorado Springs. In addition to her work in modern dance, Holm worked as a choreographer and director of numerous highly regarded Broadway musicals, including *Kiss Me, Kate* (1948), *Reuben, Reuben* (1955), *My Fair Lady* (1956) and *Camelot* (1960). In frequent demand as a teacher at American colleges and universities, she nonetheless believed that dancers must teach themselves. Her own students included Glen Tetley and Alwin Nikolais.

Horton, Lester (1906–53): Dancer and choreographer. This modern dancer formed a technique of his own and made his influence felt as a teacher to Alvin Ailey, Joyce Trisler, Carmen de Lavallade and others. Born in Indianapolis, he became an expert on Native American Indian dances. His work and view of dance were also marked by Japanese theatrical traditions. In 1934 Horton formed his own company, the Lester Horton Dancers, and opened his own theater in Los Angeles in 1948.

Humphrey, Doris (1895–1958): Dancer, choreographer and teacher. Born and first trained in and around Chicago, Humphrey studied and danced with the Denishawn Company in California from 1917 to 1928 while pursuing work on her own choreography. She is considered one of the leading lights of early modern dance. Like the other moderns, she learned from her mentors in order to go her own way. For her, dance was a continuum between fall and recovery, gravity and balance, and she was more interested in this underlying principle than in the guidance offered by music or by previously established forms. She hoped that the unadorned profundity of her belief and the depth of her engagement in dance would make her dances meaningful to many people. With Charles Weidman, another former Denishawn dancer, she established her own company. Some of her early dances were *Color Harmony* (1928), *Water Study* (1928) and *Air for the G String* (1928). At the same time, she also worked on Broadway, a very different milieu. In her noncommercial work she involved herself increasingly with gestural motion and the dramatic element in dance. Forced to stop dancing in 1945 as the result of trouble with her hip, she ended her association with Weidman at the same time, but continued to work as artistic director of the José Limon Company. Humphrey was also a noted teacher. Her many dances include *The Shakers* (1931), the trilogy *Theater Piece, With My Red Fires* and *New Dance* (1936), *Passacaglia in C Minor* (1938), *El Salón Mexico* (1943) and *Lament for Ignacio Sanchez Mejias* (1946).

Jones, Bill T. (1951–——): Choreographer and dancer. This American postmodern choreographer is known for his confrontational and challenging work. Theatrical, physically risky and highly charged politically, much of it was done in collaboration with his partner, Arnie Zane, who died of AIDS-related lymphoma in 1988. Jones met Zane, an African-American photographer, when both were students at the State University of New York at Binghamton. Before forming Bill T. Jones/Arnie Zane & Company in 1982, Jones studied ballet, African dance, various modern techniques and contact improvisation, which proved especially liberating to his work in partnered dance. Together the two men choreographed numerous dances, including the trilogy *Monkey Run Road*, *Blauvelt Mountain* and *Valley Cottage* (1979–81). Jones's dances include *Last Supper at Uncle Tom's Cabin/The Promised Land* (1991), *Last Night on Earth* (1992) and *Fete* (1992).

Jooss, Kurt (1901–79): Choreographer. Working in the Expressionist mode, this German was among the first, as a choreographer, to bring together ballet and modern dance. He studied and danced with Rudolf von Laban before establishing the Neue Tanzbuhne (New Dance Stage), for which he choreographed new works. Jooss later began the Folkwangschule für Musik, Tanz, und Sprechen (1927) and the Folkwangbuhne and Dance Theatre Studio (1928); in 1929 he assumed the leadership of the Dance Group of the Essen Opera House. His signature work is *The Green Table* (1932), a satirical antiwar manifesto.

Keeler, Ruby (1910–93): Dancer. The first tap dancer to become a bona fide screen star, this American showed off a style of buck-and-wing dancing on Broadway and in movies that came to symbolize the headiness of the 1920s. She began dancing professionally in New York, appearing when she was thirteen in *The Rise of Rose O'Reilly* (1923), a George M. Cohan show. Keeler went on to great success in other Broadway productions, in the Ziegfeld shows and in New York nightclubs. In 1928 she went to Los Angeles to make a movie for 20th Century Fox. When she stepped off the train, she happened to catch Al Jolson's eye and was introduced to him; they married shortly thereafter. Keeler's career in films burgeoned: She won fame in *42nd Street* (1933) and then appeared in *Gold Diggers of 1933* (1933), *Footlight Parade* (1933) and others. In many of her movies she worked with Busby Berkeley. Keeler made a celebrated comeback, at the age of sixty, in a revival of *No, No, Nanette* (1970) on Broadway.

Kelly, Gene (1912–——): Dancer and choreographer. This American movie star was a gifted dancer in stage and screen musicals of the 1940s and 1950s and made a pioneering contribution as a choreographer. Until 1937 he worked as a Pittsburgh dance teacher, having graduated from his mother's dance academy. His big break came with his performance in the lead of *Pal Joey* on Broadway (1941). From there, Kelly went to Hollywood, where he choreographed and directed *Singin' in the Rain* (1952) and in which he danced with his signature swashbuckling elan. He also affixed his signature to *For Me and My Gal* (1942), *On the Town* (1949), *An American in Paris* (1951) and many other productions. Additional achievements include his television special *Dancing Is a Man's Game* (1958) and a ballet, *Pas de Dieux* (1960), choreographed at the invitation of the Paris Opera Ballet, for which Kelly was the first American choreographer to complete a commission. He was named a Chevalier of the Legion of Honor of France in 1960.

King, Kenneth (1944–——): Dancer and choreographer. A former member of the Judson Dance Theater movement, he began to perform in New York in 1964 while a student at Antioch College. Like others in the Judson movement, King liked to combine many media—film, narrative, objects, text, speech and wordplay, unconventional decor, costume, vernacular movement, computer technology—with an analytic form of improvisation. He was also known to portray various existing characters in his dances, such as Patrick Duncan, the son of Isadora Duncan. King did much work inspired or influenced by philosophers, including Nietzsche in *Metagexis* (1973) and Husserl in *Praxiomatics (The Practice Room)* (1974); some critics have considered him a mystic. His pieces include *cup/saucer/two dancers/radio* (1964), *Blow-Out* (1966), *Print-Out* (1967–68), *Battery* (1975–76) and *RAdeoA.C.tiv(ID)ty* (1976).

Kirkland, Gelsey (1953——): Dancer. A much-admired American dancer with the New York City Ballet and American Ballet Theatre, Kirkland became as well known for her startling memoir *Dancing on My Grave* (1986) as for her stage performances. Trained at the School of American Ballet, she joined NYCB in 1968 and left for ABT in 1974. She danced leading roles in *The Firebird, Coppelia, Giselle, Don Quixote* and many other works, most memorably in partnership with Mikhail Baryshnikov. Critics remarked on her elegance, precision and musicality as well as her confidence, imagination and daring. But in her book, Kirkland described the drug abuse, physical injuries and emotional distress that she experienced, and which she believed to be common in the lives of dancers. Since her virtual retirement from dancing, she has taught and coached dancers in New York City.

Kylian, Jiri (1947——): Dancer and choreographer. This Czech choreographer is known for his abstract dances. Trained in ballet at the Polish Conservatory and the English Royal Ballet School, he joined the Netherlands Dance Theater in 1975, becoming its artistic director three years later. His works, created almost exclusively for his company, include *Torso* (1975), *Eligia* (1976), *November Steps* (1977), *Symphony in Psalms* (1978) and *Intimate Letters* (1979).

La Argentina [Antonia Mercé] (1890–1936): Dancer. Praised as the most remarkable Spanish dancer of any era, she brought nobility and elegance back to a traditional dance form that had declined. Born to two Spanish dancers in Buenos Aires, she studied ballet and was made premiere danseuse of the Madrid Opera at age eleven. A few years later, she gave up ballet to study indigenous Spanish dance under the tutelage of her mother. Especially interested in refining the use and sound of castanets, La Argentina started touring as a traditional dancer at age eighteen and became very popular as well as critically acclaimed. In one year, she gave thirty-eight sold-out concerts in New York alone. One day while dancing for friends, she died of a heart attack.

Laban, Rudolf von (1879–1958): Pioneer of modern dance and choreographic dance notation. Known primarily as a teacher and choreographer, this Slovakian inspired and influenced the modern dance movement in Germany from the 1910s through the 1930s. In 1925 he established the Institute of Choreography in Würzburg, then moved to Berlin in 1930 to direct the Berlin State Opera. His innovative system of dance notation (Labanotation) specified not only the shape and direction of each dance movement, but its purpose and level of energy.

La Meri [Russell Meriwether Hughes] (1898–1988): Dancer, teacher and writer. La Meri brought ethnic dances of many nationalities and traditions to American audiences and was an authority who did not hesitate to cross academic boundaries when it suited her to do so. Born in Louisville, Kentucky, she studied ballet, modern dance and the indigenous dancing of Mexico, Spain, Hawaii, South America, Africa, India, Ceylon, the Philippines and Japan, among others, traveling the world to perform as well as to study. From 1942 to 1956, she ran the Ethnologic Dance Center in New York, offering training to such dancers as Matteo and Juana; she also taught at many dance festivals, colleges and universities. La Meri wrote various books on dance, as well as several collections of poetry. Her choreography includes a South Indian bharata natyam version of the classic ballet *Swan Lake* (1941).

Lifar, Serge (1905–86): Dancer and choreographer. Born in Kiev, Russia, Lifar joined Serge Diaghilev's Ballets Russes in 1923, creating such important works as *Apollon Musagete* (1928) and *The Prodigal Son* (1929). In 1929 he moved to France to direct the Paris Opera Ballet, where he choreographed and appeared as a principal dancer. He also directed the company for twenty-nine years. His most successful creations included *Bacchus and Ariadne* (1931), *Icare* (1935), *Alexandre le Grand* (1937), *Les Mirages* (1944), *Phaedre* (1950) and *Romeo et Juliette* (1955). In 1945 he was forced out of the Paris Opera Ballet as punishment for collaboration with the Nazis in occupied Paris, but he returned in 1947.

Limon, José (1908–72): Choreographer, dancer and teacher. Limon was a Mexican-American modern dance choreographer who placed passion above formalism in his work. After studying at their school, Limon danced in the company of Doris Humphrey and Charles Weidman from 1930 to 1940. He founded the José Limon American Dance Company in 1947. Influenced technically by Humphrey, Limon also brought a social conscience to bear on his dances, along with a gift for narrative and a preoccupation with Mexican mythology and culture. *The Moor's Pavane* (1949), inspired by Shakespeare's Othello, was his first important piece and is still considered his greatest; others include *Emperor Jones* (1956), *Missa Brevis* (1958) and *I, Odysseus* (1962). In addition to choreographing and dancing, Limon taught at the Juilliard School in New York, Connecticut College and many other institutions.

Louis XIV (1638–1715): As king of France from 1643 to 1715, he helped to make dance popular in courtly circles. A dedicated dancer himself, Louis earned his sobriquet "The Sun King" from his role in *La ballet de la nuit*, a dance he performed in 1653. In it, he positioned himself at the center of a group of courtiers who circled him like planets. Some historians believe the king used dance as a political tool to keep order among quarrelsome courtiers. Regardless of the motive, his dancing master, Pierre Beauchamps, laid down rules of ballet that persist to this day.

MacMillan, Sir Kenneth (1929–92): Dancer and choreographer. This Scotsman attended England's Sadler's Wells Ballet School and afterward joined the company. As a choreographer he was known for his full-length revivals of such classic ballets as *Swan Lake* and *The Sleeping Beauty*. MacMillan's other ballets include *Romeo and Juliet* (1965), *Anastasia* (1971), *Manon* (1974), *Valses nobles et sentimentales* (1966) and *The Four Seasons* (1975). Ballet companies around the world have adopted his works. Knighted in 1983, he served as principal choreographer for the Royal Ballet from 1977 to 1992.

Makarova, Natalia (1940–——): Dancer. Born in Leningrad, she trained at the Vaganova School and joined the Kirov Ballet after graduating in 1959. In pursuit of greater artistic freedom, she defected to the West in 1970 while the Kirov was performing in London. In ensuing years, she danced with American Ballet Theatre, the Royal Ballet in England and other companies, and staged such ballets as *La Bayadère* (1980). One of the foremost dancers of her generation before her retirement, Makarova is thought to have set new standards, in particular, for Romantic roles in classic dances, such as *Giselle*. She was versatile, too, dancing roles in modern ballets by Antony Tudor and other choreographers.

Markova, Alicia [Lilian Alicia Marks] (1910–——): Dancer. An English-born dancer renowned for her delicacy and lightness, she began her career as a member of Serge Diaghilev's Ballets Russes in 1925 after studying ballet in London. She was a ballerina with the Camargo Society in 1931 and with Ballet Rambert and the Vic-Wells Ballet, among her many later affiliations. She appeared in early English productions of classic ballets and worked closely with Frederick Ashton, who created roles for her in *La Peri* (1931), *Les Rendezvous* (1933) and other works.

Martins, Peter (1946–——): Dancer and choreographer. Successor to George Balanchine as ballet master in chief of the New York City Ballet, Martins was born in Copenhagen and studied at the Royal Danish Ballet School with Erik Bruhn, Stanley Williams and others in the tradition of August Bournonville. After joining the Royal Danish Ballet in 1965, he performed periodically as a guest artist with the NYCB and became a principal dancer there in 1970. At NYCB Martins earned respect for his pure and noble virility as well as for his virtuosic strength, and was noted for his skill in partnering ballerinas, especially Suzanne Farrell. Under Balanchine he learned new ways to dance, and during the late 1960s he became closely associated with the title role in the master's *Apollo* (1967). Balanchine created roles for him in *Duo Concertant* (1972) and other ballets; Jerome Robbins did so as well in *In the Night* (1970) and *The Goldberg Variations* (1971). Martins ended his performing career in 1983. His first choreographic effort, *Calcium Light Night,* debuted with the company in 1977 and many others have followed, including *Lille Suite* (1980), a suite from *Histoire du soldat* (1981) and *Ecstatic Orange* (1987). He became co–ballet master in chief of NYCB with Jerome Robbins following Balanchine's death in 1983; after the departure of Robbins, Martins has continued alone.

Massine, Leonide (1895–1979): Dancer and choreographer. A product of the Moscow Bolshoi School and the Bolshoi Ballet, this Russian danced with Diaghilev's Ballets Russes beginning in 1914. Diaghilev encouraged Massine's choreographic efforts, which culminated in such ballets as *Parade* (1917), *The Three-Cornered Hat* (1919), *Pulcinella* (1920), *Le Beau Danube* (1924) and *Gaité Parisienne* (1938). Massine the dancer was best known for his comic and character roles. As a choreographer he was witty, worldly and theatrical; under Diaghilev's aegis, he collaborated with outstanding painters of the day, such as Picasso, who designed the costumes for *Parade*. He was artistic director of the Ballet Russe de Monte Carlo from 1932 to 1941, and in 1946 performed in the film *The Red Shoes*.

Mitchell, Arthur (1934–——): Dancer, choreographer and teacher. Born in Harlem in New York City, he became an important dancer with the New York City Ballet, one of only a few African-Americans ever to join the company. He was trained at the High School of Performing Arts and at the School of American Ballet and also studied at the Katherine Dunham School of Dance. After joining NYCB in 1955, he performed with great distinction despite the racism of some outside the company who objected to a black man dancing with a white woman. George Balanchine created roles for him in *A Midsummer Night's Dream* (1962) and *Agon* (1957). Mitchell danced abroad with various companies and worked to help establish others, but returned home to found his own company, the Dance Theatre of Harlem, in 1968 after the assassination of Dr. Martin Luther King, Jr. The purpose of DTH and its affiliated school is to further the careers of black dancers; though the school is integrated, the company remains black. DTH's repertory includes dances by Balanchine and Mitchell and such classics as

Swan Lake and *Giselle* (1984), the latter a Creole version by Mitchell.

Moiseyev, Igor Alexandrovich (1906–——): Impresario. Trained as a ballet dancer at Moscow's Bolshoi School, this Russian also worked in ballet as a choreographer, creating such works as *Salammbo* (1932) and *Spartacus* (1958). But he made his name primarily as an impresario, director and choreographer of Russian folk dance. Founded in 1937, his first troupe of largely amateur dancers—later known as the Moiseyev Folk Dance Ensemble—toured the world in 1955. On that original trip and on subsequent international tours the company had great impact, inspiring the growth of folk dances of various traditions in many nations. The company's ranks are now filled with professionals who perform a repertory of hundreds of dances, Russian and non-Russian.

Monk, Meredith (1943–——): Dancer and choreographer. This American dancer is known in part for resisting the role's usual limits. She studied dance at Sarah Lawrence College and with Martha Graham and was also influenced by Merce Cunningham, especially in her choice and use of theatrical space. An experimentalist, Monk became part of the Judson Dance Theater generation in New York City, sharing their preoccupation with mixed media (in her case, film, lighting, sound and text) and novel performance locales and techniques. For instance, she often made use of venues without proceniums and performed for audiences who would sometimes move from setting to setting with the dancers, even participating in the work itself. Though Monk's training in dance was solidly physical, her attitude to the making and staging of dances is theatrical, musical, restless and intellectual. She is as well known for her musical composition as for her movements and has sought out a wider audience of theatergoers, not just dance fans. To a great ex-

tent, Monk lets her work grow out of its place of origin, as she is often averse to restaging pieces in places other than where they were first produced. Her works include *Blueprint* (1967), *Juice* (1969), *Overload* (1969), *Tour: Dedicated to Dinosaurs* (1969), *Education of the Girl Child* (1973), *Quarry* (1976) and *Turtle Dreams* (1983).

Morris, Mark (1956–——): Dancer and choreographer. Born in Seattle, he studied dance there and then performed with Laura Dean Dancers & Musicians, the Eliot Feld Ballet, the Lar Lubovitch Dance Company, the Hannah Kahn Dance Company and the Koleda Balkin Dance Ensemble. He formed the Mark Morris Dance Group in New York in 1980 and was widely received as the most promising modern-dance choreographer of his generation. Praised for his musicality, eclecticism and wit, Morris was viewed by critics as a solid hope for the future at a time when modern dance in general seemed to be diminishing in its scope. Although Morris's work is often compared with that of the early moderns, it is generally considered to be his own invention, despite his talent for assimilating influences. He mingles ethnic, classical, modern and popular genres with both seriousness and a sense of mischief. The resulting dances range from a send-up of *The Nutcracker,* called *The Hard Nut* (1991), to *O Rangasayee* (1984), a solo by and for Morris in the style of bharata natyam, a classical form of South Indian dance. As a performer, he moves from luxuriant abandon to devout parody to pictorial delicacy and beyond. Outspokenly gay, he seems to choreograph primarily for a company of androgynous friends. Morris has also contributed to the White Oak Dance Project. His dances include *Gloria* (1984), *Lovey* (1985), *Championship Wrestling After Roland Barthes* (1986), *Striptease* (1986) and *Drink*

Only to Me with Thine Eyes (1988), created for the American Ballet Theatre.

Neumeier, John (1942–——): Choreographer. This American ballet choreographer is best known for his reinterpretations of the classics. He worked at London's Royal Ballet School in the early 1960s and joined the Stuttgart Ballet in 1963. In 1969 he moved to the Frankfurt Ballet, then on to the Hamburg State Ballet in 1973. His works include *The Nutcracker* (1971), *Swan Lake* (1976), *Hamlet Connotations* (1976) and *The Sleeping Beauty* (1978).

Nicholas, Fayard (1918–——) and **Harold** (1924–——): Known professionally as the Nicholas Brothers, they began dancing in 1930 when Fayard was eleven and Harold seven. The two African-American boys soon made their names in acts that played at Harlem's Cotton Club in New York City. They were just children, but they danced like professionals and with acrobatic panache, not only uptown but on Broadway, in movies and abroad. They subsequently appeared in more than fifty films, including *Tin Pan Alley* (1940) and *Stormy Weather* (1943). In the 1980s, Harold appeared in the movie *Tap* (1989), while Fayard contributed choreography to *Black and Blue* (1989) on Broadway.

Nijinska, Bronislava (1891–1972): Choreographer, dancer and teacher. The sister of Russian dancer Vaslav Nijinsky, she became better known for her choreography than for her dancing. Like her brother, Nijinska was associated with Serge Diaghilev's Ballets Russes, after first studying at the St. Petersburg Imperial Ballet School and dancing at the Maryinsky Theater. Her most enduring work includes *Les Noces* (1923) and *Les Biches* (1924). Set to music by Stravinsky, *Les Noces* takes a traditional Russian peasant wedding as its subject but is wholly modern in its treatment, while *Les Biches,* set to music by Poulenc, is a satire about sexual ambiguity

and social mores in the 1920s. In addition to the Ballets Russes, Nijinska was associated with such companies as the Paris Opera, the Ballet Russe de Monte Carlo and the Grand Ballet du Marquis de Cuevas. She was also an influential teacher and established a school of her own in Los Angeles in 1938.

Nijinsky, Vaslav (1890–1950): Dancer and choreographer. Arguably the 20th century's most brilliant male dancer and the creator of a handful of ground-breaking ballets, this Russian dramatically altered the possibilities and prospects of dance. Nijinsky's impact is felt even by those who never saw him perform; his legend takes up where his life left off. He trained at the St. Petersburg Imperial School of Ballet and joined the Ballets Russes when the company was founded by impresario Serge Diaghilev. As part of that troupe, Nijinsky won an immediate following in roles choreographed by Michel Fokine and others. Among his strengths were an astonishing leap, dazzling small footwork in the air, virile power coupled with a provocatively androgynous allure, and technical mastery joined with imaginative license. His ballets, which included *The Afternoon of a Faun* (1911) and *Le sacre du printemps* (1913), were perhaps more controversial than he was, offering a primal abandon and modernist innovations that scandalized even sophisticated audiences. Nijinsky's career was cut short by his marriage and debilitating mental illness; Diaghilev, his former lover, expelled him from the company and never forgave him for marrying.

Nikolais, Alwin (1912–93): Choreographer. This American created dances that are events of theater in contrast to works of movement; his multidisciplinary approach to modern dance was unique and ran counter to trends favoring psychology and narrative. He did not begin to study dance until he was twenty-three. Before then he worked as a piano accompanist at silent movies, in a marionette theater and as a lighting designer. His interest in staging and producing allied arts helped draw him to dance, where his work was enriched by his previous experience and continuing preoccupations. Nikolais studied modern dance at Bennington College and with Hanya Holm, Martha Graham, Doris Humphrey, Charles Weidman and Louis Horst. During the 1930s, he choreographed works for the Federal Theater Project in Hartford, Connecticut, where he began to devise a dance notation system. In 1948 he was made director of the Henry Street Playhouse, an experimental theater in New York City. He formed his own company at the playhouse and established a school there to support the company. For company members, who included Murray Louis and Phyllis Lamhut, he choreographed such dances as *Lobster Quadrille* (1949). Nikolais began producing his most characteristic work in 1953 when he made *Masks, Props and Mobiles*. His dances, many of them full-evening-length works, are typically pure dances composed for groups of dancers. They don't tell stories or fulfill logical scenarios but convey energy abstractly in its many forms: visual, musical and kinetic. Nikolais is known in part for his inventive use of props, costumes, decor and lighting to create or highlight detailed, large-scale imagery; he also experimented early with sound-recording technology and electronic music in constructing his own scores. Partly because of these ingenuities, he was invited to do work for television. His dances include *Kaleidoscope* (1956), *Prism* (1956), *Cantos* (1957), *Imago* (1963) and *Triptych* (1967).

Noverre, Jean-Georges (1727–1810): Dancer, choreographer, teacher and dance theorist. Parisian-born Noverre is known for the aesthetic and technical foundation he laid for ballet in his book *Lettres sur la danse et sur les ballets* (1760). He is thought to have invented and advanced the ballet d'action, a type of ballet in which story and dramatic development are more important than pure dance. Disinclined to use the elaborate courtly costumes, props and accessories then popular in Paris, he tried working elsewhere, though an early foray in England was not a success. Working in partnership with the composer Christoph Gluck in Vienna from 1767 to 1774, he contributed to a production of *Iphigenie en Tauris* (1774). Two years later, he was named ballet master of the Paris Opera at the behest of his former pupil, Marie Antoinette. He choreographed more than 150 ballets.

Nureyev, Rudolph (1938–93): Dancer. One of the outstanding male dancers of the 20th century, he was as intent on fashioning a legend of his life as of his art. By his own example, he also influenced and encouraged boys to consider classical dance as a career. Born on a train in the Bashkir Republic of the U.S.S.R., Nureyev was raised in a family of Tatar peasants. He first trained in dance locally, then continued his studies at the Leningrad Ballet School in 1955, where his chief teacher was Alexander Pushkin. Several years later, he joined the Kirov Ballet and toured with that company in Europe. While dancing in Paris in 1961, Nureyev decided he wanted more freedom than the Kirov would permit and so defected to the West. Though he did not join any company as a permanent dancer, he performed in leading roles in Europe, Canada and the United States and was a frequent guest artist with the Royal Ballet in London. Compromised technically by his relatively late start as a dancer, Nureyev nevertheless possessed a typically Russian power and a dramatic, even rapacious, stage persona that seized the imagination of audiences around the world. He became especially well known for his partnership with Margot Fonteyn of the Royal Ballet (she was eighteen years his senior); the scale and passion of his dancing complemented the lyric delicacy of hers. Among other choreographers, Frederick Ashton created a role for him in the ballet *Marguerite and Armand* (1963), Maurice Bejart in *Songs of a Wayfarer* (1971) and Martha Graham in *Lucifer* (1975). In addition to dancing, Nureyev staged ballets, choreographed and tried his hand at conducting. For several years he was director of the Paris Opera Ballet. Nureyev died of AIDS.

Pavlova, Anna (1881–1931): Dancer. Pavlova was a "ballerina's ballerina" who may have done more than any other to awaken public interest in the art of dance. She was born to a peasant and a laundress in St. Petersburg and entered the St. Petersburg Imperial Ballet Academy at the age of ten, where her soft, ethereal style attracted attention. After graduation she joined the Maryinsky Theater, and later appeared with Serge Diaghilev's Ballets Russes. Unlike most leading dancers of the day, she also performed around the world for many years in concerts that she produced herself. Also unlike most ballerinas of her era, she formed her own touring company and traveled tirelessly, covering 300,000 miles in fifteen years, to bring classical dancing to thousands of people. Pavlova was closely associated with the work and aesthetic of Michel Fokine, who danced with and created ballets for her. But while Fokine was considered revolutionary, Pavlova's taste in ballet, as revealed in the dances mounted by her company, was conservative, sentimental and trivial. That taste, however, did not restrain her power as a performer. To audiences, she seemed to represent a living ideal; her impact was profound. She was also known for cultivating personal as well as professional glamour. Pavlova's repertory ranged from her most famous role in Fokine's *The Dying Swan* (1907) to solos of debatable merit, invented and staged by herself. She died of pneumonia, as she was asking a nurse to fetch her swan costume.

Petipa, Marius (1819–1910): Dancer, choreographer and teacher. During fifty years at the Russian Imperial Ballet, Petipa helped set the future course of classical dancing. A seminal figure, he is still influential today, not only because of the enduringly popular ballets he created or staged but also because he revived an art that might otherwise have faded. He was born in Marseilles to a French dancer and teacher, Jean Petipa, with whom he first studied; Auguste Vestris was also his teacher. Petipa later became known as a partner of Fanny Elssler at the Paris Opera; he also danced elsewhere in France and Spain before arriving in St. Petersburg, Russia, in 1847. An impressive performer, he was hailed by Russian audiences for performances in *Giselle, Le Corsaire* and other ballets. While working as an assistant to Jules Perrot he began to choreograph. His first ballet to stir attention was *The Daughter of Pharaoh* (1862), produced the year he was made ballet master and chief choreographer of the Russian Imperial Ballet. His other works included *Don Quixote* (1869), *La Bayadère* (1877), *The Sleeping Beauty* (1890), *Swan Lake* (with Ivanov, 1895) and *Rayiponda* (1898). Petipa's greatest achievement is generally thought to be *The Sleeping Beauty,* set to a score he commissioned from Peter Tchaikovsky. Both in terms of music and of dance, that work raised the standards of ballet, at once paying tribute to the form's origins as a French and Italian court spectacle while ushering it forward. Petipa married twice and retired in 1903.

Petit, Roland (1924–———): Dancer and choreographer. After training in ballet at the school of the Paris Opera, this Frenchman joined the company in 1940. From 1945 to 1948 he worked in the Ballets des Champs-Elysées, choreographing his own works, such as *Les Forains* (1945) and *Les Amours de Jupiter* (1946). He left to form his own company, Les Ballets de Paris de Roland Petit. During the 1950s he worked successfully in film, creating dances for Leslie Caron in *Daddy Long Legs* and *The Glass Slipper,* among other projects. In 1972 he was appointed artistic director of the Ballets de Marseilles. Later works include *Nana* (1976) and *Marcel Proust Remembered* (1980).

Plisetskaya, Maya (1925–——): Dancer. This Russian ballerina exemplified the style of the Bolshoi Ballet. She trained at the Bolshoi's school, later joining the company and performing to ecstatic reviews in Grigorovich's *The Stone Flower* (1954) and *Swan Lake* (1972), Moiseyev's *Spartacus* (1958), Alberto Alonso's *Carmen Suite* (1967) and her own creation, *Anna Karenina* (1972).

Rainer, Yvonne (1934–——): Dancer and choreographer. A San Franciscan, Rainer moved to New York in 1956 and began studying ballet and modern dance relatively late. She worked with Martha Graham, Robert Dunn, James Waring (with whom she danced from 1961 to 1965), Ann Halprin and others, and also took to heart the influence of Merce Cunningham, John Cage and Erick Hawkins. She was a cofounder of the Judson Dance Theater based at the Judson Memorial Church in New York City in the early 1960s. Like other Judson collaborators, she wanted to free modern dance from the theatrical conventions of her predecessors. She hoped to reveal an uncompromised physicality displayed in ordinary gestures, motions and even some seemingly clumsy "found" movements. Utilizing compositional techniques that included games and chance methods, she rejected the designed, symmetrical dance entity. Theatrical venue has also played an important part in the presentation of her work: She has often chosen huge spaces (gyms, factories, etc.) to show her dances at their best. In the aftermath of Judson, Rainer began to create dances for large casts of mixed professionals and nondancers and became a force behind the formation of the Grand Union.

She ceased choreographing in 1973 in order to make films. Her dances include *Continuous Project—Altered Daily* (1962), *Ordinary Dances* (1962), *We Shall Run* (1963) and *Trio A* (1966).

Rambert, Marie (1888–1982): Teacher and company director. Polish-born Rambert helped give Great Britain a contemporary tradition in ballet. Before becoming a pupil of Emile Jaques-Dalcroze in 1910, she studied medicine in Paris. She was recruited by Serge Diaghilev to help Vaslav Nijinsky come to terms with the complicated Stravinsky score for the dancer's ballet-in-progress, *Le sacre du printemps* (1913). Rambert later went to London and opened a ballet school there in 1920. With her own students serving as dancers and choreographers, she formed a ballet company initially named Marie Rambert Dancers; it became known as the Ballet Club in 1930, and was retitled Ballet Rambert in 1935. In addition, she contributed to activities of the Camargo Society, established in 1930 to further the growth of English ballet. Though Rambert did not choreograph original work, she collected and presented the talents of others to great effect, notably the choreographers Frederick Ashton and Antony Tudor and the dancers Celia Franca (founder of the National Ballet of Canada) and Peggy van Praagh (later artistic director of the Australian Ballet).

Robbins, Jerome (1918–——): Choreographer. In aesthetic temperament both a classicist and a showstopper, Robbins is a choreographer who has managed to combine ballet with Broadway. His work is distinguished by an enthusiasm for mixed genres, variation in tone from abstract to frankly theatrical, and, when rehearsed in accordance with his vision, precise nuance in execution. Born in New York, he has worked there throughout his career, incorporating into some of his dances a reckless metropolitan vitality and a sensibility that reflects the city's hardships and vices.

Robbins studied classical, modern and ethnic dance, as well as acting and music, with Eugene Loring, Antony Tudor and others before beginning work as an actor at the Yiddish Art Theater when he was nineteen. In 1940 he became a member of American Ballet Theatre, where his first dance, *Fancy Free,* premiered in 1944. Extremely popular, the ballet was turned into a Broadway musical, *On the Town* (1944), by its composer, Leonard Bernstein. While continuing to choreograph in ballet and musical theater, Robbins was named associate artistic director of the New York City Ballet in 1949. At NYCB he created *Afternoon of a Faun* (1953), *The Cage* (1951) and *The Concert* (1956). In 1957 he created, choreographed and directed the stage musical *West Side Story*. An enormous success, the show toured widely and was made into a movie for which Robbins received two Oscars, for direction and choreography. In 1958, he formed his own company, Ballets: USA, and toured Europe. Named ballet master of NYCB in 1969, he became co-ballet master in chief with Peter Martins after the death of George Balanchine, but he later left the company. Some of his best-known musicals and ballets are *The King and I* (1951), *Gypsy* (1959), *Funny Girl* (1964), *Fiddler on the Roof* (1964), *Dances at a Gathering* (1969), *The Goldberg Variations* (1971) and *Watermill* (1972).

Robinson, Bill "Bojangles" (1878–1949): Dancer. Legend has it that this supremely gifted tap dancer danced for pennies as a child on the streets of Richmond, Virginia. In 1898 he left the South for New York and worked steadily in vaudeville, but was not discovered by a broader audience until he appeared in the all-black Broadway revue *Blackbirds* in 1928. After working in partnership with such dancers as George Cooper, Robinson became the first African-American solo entertainer accepted by white audiences. Though he did not

invent the stair dance, he perfected and popularized it, tapping his way up and down a flight of steps and producing a virtuosic range of sounds. He appeared in such nightclubs as Harlem's famed Cotton Club and in restaurants and shows, as well as in films, including *Stormy Weather* (1943). He became famous as Shirley Temple's co-star in *Rebecca of Sunnybrook Farm* (1938) and several other movies. Robinson was eventually criticized for his perceived deference to whites and lack of racial pride, but some who knew him well denied that either charge had merit.

Rubenstein, Ida (1885–1960): Dancer and company director. This Russian ballerina was a member of Serge Diaghilev's Ballets Russes from 1909 to 1915. An actress as well as a dancer, she studied privately with Michel Fokine, the company's choreographer, who saw in her an exoticism well suited to the Ballets Russes. He choreographed *Salome* (1913) for her, but the dance was banned because it bared too much flesh. Fokine created other noted roles for Rubenstein in *Cleopatra* (1909) and *Scheherazade* (1910). She later formed a troupe of her own, some say to challenge Diaghilev's supremacy. As director of a company that included such luminaries as Leonide Massine and Bronislava Nijinska, Rubenstein was much appreciated.

Sallé, Marie (1707–56): Dancer. One of the most famous ballerinas of her day, she had ideas of her own about new directions ballet might take. Born in France, Sallé performed in London and Paris and was a well-known rival of Marie Camargo. She rejected the elaborate costumes usually worn by ballerinas of that period; in her version of *Pygmalion* (1734), she danced in a simple tunic. For this and other radical views, she became a favorite of Jean-Georges Noverre. She preferred an unadorned classical style over the vaunted virtuosity of a dancer like Camargo.

Sarry, Christine (1947–——): Dancer and

teacher. Sarry brought an arrestingly quick and avid imagination to leading roles in such ballets as Agnes de Mille's *Rodeo* (1942) and Eliot Feld's *Harbinger* (1967) and *At Midnight* (1967). Born in Long Beach, California, she studied with Richard Thomas, Carmelita Maracci and others before joining the Joffrey Ballet in 1963. She became a member of American Ballet Theatre in 1964 and was named a principal dancer in 1973. A year later, she joined Feld's American Ballet Company, where she performed until retiring from the stage. Since then, Sarry has taught at The New Ballet School in New York.

Shankar, Uday (1900–77): Dancer and teacher. This Indian dancer and sometime collaborator of Anna Pavlova formed his own company, school and dance center in the 1930s. By touring the West, he brought Indian dancing to audiences who had known nothing of it. In his prime, Shankar was an impressive dancer, but his lasting contribution is considered to be his effort to reclaim Indian traditional dancing. He also explored the possibilities of fusing Western and modern genres and sensibilities with ancient Indian forms.

Shawn, Ted (1891–1972): Choreographer, dancer and teacher. This American spurred the growth of the modern genre in America, particularly in collaboration with Ruth St. Denis, his wife and frequent dance partner. Shawn was also that rare male who had a formative influence on early modern dance: He cultivated other male dancers and began the work of battling the American stigma on men who dance. A midwesterner, he first performed in Denver in 1911. He met St. Denis while touring with his own small company in 1914, and they subsequently set up their own business partnership, the Denishawn Company. After their marriage and partnership concluded in 1932, he organized the All-Male Dancers Group in 1933 and set out on the first of many successful tours. Shawn's legacy includes a farm, Jacob's Pillow, in Massachusetts. There he established a dance studio that gradually evolved into an important annual dance festival that continues today.

Sokolow, Anna (1912–——): Choreographer and dancer. This American choreographer saw dance as an opportunity for intense drama and social criticism. She studied at the School of American Ballet and with Martha Graham and other modern dancers before performing with Graham's company from 1930 to 1939. Best known for her choreographic achievement, she began presenting her own dances in 1934. She challenged audiences with such works as *Dreams* (1961), in which her subject was Nazi Germany and concentration camps. An adamant individualist, Sokolow believed that modern dancers in her lifetime were not sufficiently independent, not willing to risk rejection in artistic experiment. Throughout her career, she maintained an interest in the arts in Mexico and created some of her work there, as well as training Mexican dancers and founding the first Mexican modern dance troupe in 1939. She also choreographed for Broadway productions and for the Joffrey Ballet. Her dances include *Lyric Suite* (1953), *Session for 6* (1958), *Metamorphosis* (1957) and *Rooms* (1959).

St. Denis, Ruth (1877–1968): Dancer, choreographer and teacher. With Isadora Duncan, Loie Fuller and Martha Graham, this American helped to lay the foundations of modern dance. According to the lore of the moderns, St. Denis was a rampant individualist first. Her early résumé ranged off the beaten track: She rode in bicycle races, danced en pointe for the public although she had almost no ballet training, and dabbled in modeling and acting. Her interest in dance sprang from a whimsical source: One day while in Buffalo, New York, she glimpsed a cigarette advertisement depicting the goddess Isis and decided she wanted to become something like Isis—a goddess of the dance. Her first piece, *Radha* (1906), evoking Hindu spirituality, had a victorious debut in New York City. On the strength of that success, the fledgling choreographer toured Europe, dancing there in solos of her own design for three years. In her pursuit of spiritual enlightenment, St. Denis repeatedly looked to the East for inspiration, but even as a devotee she needed her freedom. A shift in her work occurred when she met and married the dancer Ted Shawn in 1914. Together, in a partnership known as the Denishawn Company, they not only created and staged numerous dances but also did their best to build an institution. They cultivated an aesthetic, a technique, a fund-raising operation and affiliated schools (the Denishawn Dance School, begun in Los Angeles in 1915, was the first). When the marriage ended in 1932, the institution faltered, too, but St. Denis continued to choreograph, perform and record performances on film into her old age. She launched the New York School of Natya with La Meri in 1940 and influenced scores of dancers, more enduringly than either Duncan or Fuller. Her dances include *Spirit of the Sea* (1915), *Kuan Yin* (1919), *White Jade* (1926) and *Ishtar of the Seven Gates* (1923).

Taglioni, Marie (1804–84): Dancer. Celebrated for technical achievement and an ethereal stage persona, this Italian defined the Romantic ballerina. The daughter of Filippo Taglioni, a dancer and choreographer, she was her father's student and his muse. Together, they made ballet a less material, more spiritual affair than it had been; more than one observer characterized her as an angel. One of the Taglionis' contributions to ballet was the refinement (some claim the invention) of the pointe shoe, by means of which she rose mysteriously to the tips of her toes. Another innovation was her favored costume, which fitted her torso tightly, bared her arms and shoulders, and featured a skirt shorter than

was customary. The trappings of the old 18th-century stage and wardrobe were not for her; she preferred a theatrical domain of fairies, spirits and transcendent possibilities. Both Taglionis were best known for his ballet *La Sylphide* (1832).

Tallchief, Maria (1925–——): Dancer and teacher. At the height of her career with the New York City Ballet, Tallchief exemplified the artistic ideals of George Balanchine, the company's founder and for six years her husband. She and her sister Marjorie, who was also a dancer, trace their ancestry to the Osage Indians of North America. Her speed, strength and musical attack were considered peculiarly American—and exceptionally fine—in roles ranging from the Firebird, in Balanchine's ballet of that name (1949), to the Sugar Plum Fairy in his *Nutcracker* (1954). Tallchief also appeared to acclaim in *Allegro Brillante* (1956), *Divertimento* (1947), *Swan Lake* (1951) and other ballets. After leaving NYCB in 1965, she settled in Chicago, where she established a ballet company and school.

Taylor, Paul (1930–——): Choreographer and dancer. An American choreographer of modern dance, Taylor is known in part for his independence from fashion and for his eclectical body of work. In creating dances, he has often broken rules and defied expectations. Initially an athlete and painter, he studied dance with Martha Graham, Antony Tudor and others. He danced in the companies of Graham—where he appeared in leading roles, premiering some of them—and Merce Cunningham before forming his own troupe in 1954. His work includes abstract, theatrical, narrative and lyric dances that typically fuse aspects of ballet with modern. Also characteristic of Taylor's work is a dark moral view; some of his dances suggest a profound belief in the baseness of nature, human and otherwise. At times, however, he seems to regard the base with irony or visceral humor, a distinctive sense of the comic rather unusual in dance. He also creates pieces that exalt classicism while adapting it—*Aureole* (1962) is one—and others that cross into popular idioms. *Company B* (1991), for instance, is set to songs by the Andrews Sisters. Representative works in his large repertory are *Arden Court* (1981), *Last Look* (1985), *Syzygy* (1987) and *Speaking in Tongues* (1989). Dancers in Taylor's company have included Bettie de Jong, Carolyn Brown, David Parsons and Twyla Tharp.

Tharp, Twyla (1941–——): Dancer and choreographer. Her name is synonymous with earnestly playful, virtuosic dances that fuse a modern-dance sensibility with pop and classical elements. An experimentalist, she represents the 1960s dance generation like no one else. Partly because her work won great popularity, she played an important role in bringing dance to a large American audience in the dance "boom" of the 1960s and 1970s. Born in rural Indiana, Tharp was given a name by her mother that would stand out on a marquee if she went to work in the theater. By her own account, her mother encouraged her early on to make a success of herself in dance. While still a child, she moved to California, where her parents ran a drive-in movie theater. She studied dance of many genres as well as music and baton twirling, then attended Pomona and Barnard colleges while also pursuing dance training with Martha Graham, Merce Cunningham and others. After graduating from Barnard in 1963, she joined the Paul Taylor Company. Tharp left Taylor in 1965 to pursue choreography; her early dances included the solo *Tank Dive* (1965) and *Re-Moves* (1966). Like the members of the Judson Dance Theater movement, she enjoyed using nontraditional spaces (e.g., gyms and meadows) for her dances, and she choreographed pieces adaptable to performance in very different places. By comparison with prevailing Judson standards, however, her work was more physically demanding and theatrically expressive. From the beginning her dances have stressed design, although some look tossed-off, casual and impetuously free. Tharp is known for mixing classical, modern and popular genres; the pop influence—as well as her very American penchant for athleticism—gives some of her work a misleadingly simple look. In 1976 she won great acclaim for her stylistic innovations in *Push Comes to Shove*, which was performed by Mikhail Baryshnikov. Her other dances include *Deuce Coupe* (1973), *Eight Jelly Rolls* (1971), *Nine Sinatra Songs* (1976) and *Baker's Dozen* (1979), the last cochoreographed with Jerome Robbins. She has worked on Broadway (*Singin' in the Rain,* 1985) and in film (*Amadeus,* 1984) as well. Her later work has increasingly involved balletic elements. Although her company has been disbanded, she continues to choreograph and perform for and with various dance companies.

Tudor, Antony (1909–87): Choreographer and teacher. A latecomer to ballet who credited his interest in the form to George Balanchine, Tudor made an important contribution to dance. A working-class Londoner, he studied with Nicholas Legat, Marie Rambert and Margaret Craske. He became associated with the Ballet Club, later the Ballet Rambert, for which he choreographed his earliest pieces, *Jardin aux Lilas* (1936) and *Dark Elegies* (1937). Psychological realism found a unique place in Tudor's ballets: With narrative delicacy and power, his profoundly evocative gestural and physical language expressed volatile feelings and social relationships. He established the London Ballet after leaving Ballet Rambert in 1938, and in the 1940s he began a long-lasting professional relationship with American Ballet Theatre. He became director of the Metropolitan Opera Ballet School in 1950 and taught at New York's Juilliard School for many years while continuing to choreograph a diminishing number of dances generally considered minor. Tudor ignited the careers of dancers of various eras, including Nora Kaye, Hugh Laing, Sallie Wilson and Gelsey Kirkland. He was as well known for his adversarial, acerbic coaching as for the ballets he created and restaged.

Ulanova, Galina (1910–——): Dancer. This Russian was most closely associated with the Bolshoi Ballet for the duration of her career. She studied at the Petrograd State Ballet School before joining the State Academic Theater for Opera and Ballet (formerly the Maryinsky Theater) in 1928, later joining the Bolshoi. As a dancer, she was beloved for her warmth, her physical accomplishment and her musicality. She was a powerful actress who did not seem to act and a dancer whose strength seemed natural, not technical. Renowned for her performances in such classic ballets as *Romeo and Juliet, Giselle* and *Swan Lake*, she first performed in the West in 1945. Roles were created for her in *Red Poppy* (1949) and *Stone Flower* (1954), among other productions. She retired from dancing in 1962 and continued to work for the Bolshoi as a ballet mistress.

Weaver, John (1673–1760): Dancer, choreographer and teacher. This Englishman was also a dance theorist and writer, as well as the founder of English pantomime. He was a leader of English ballet from 1700 to 1736, working as a ballet master and featured dancer in comic and character parts. He produced many ballets and became known for his gift with pantomime. Weaver is best regarded for his dance *The Loves of Mars and Venus* (1716–17) at Drury Lane.

Weidman, Charles (1901–75): Dancer, choreographer and teacher. Gifted in mime and satire, Weidman worked closely with Doris Humphrey for seventeen years, beginning in 1928. They were both midwesterners and met while dancing with the Denishawn Company. Together, they formed a company and school, making their mark on modern dance in partnership and alone. Weidman succeeded with such dances as *And Daddy Was a Fireman* (1936), *Fables of Our Time* (1948) and *The War Between Men and Women* (1954). After the company with Humphrey dissolved, he formed a troupe of his own and became a highly regarded teacher whose students included Sybil Shearer, Eleanor King, Jack Cole and José Limon.

Wigman, Mary (1886–1973): Dancer and choreographer. A leader of German Expressionism, Wigman favored large choruses of dancers and repetition of movement in her work. She was a student of Emile Jaques-Dalcroze and Rudolf von Laban, making her professional dance debut in 1914 and her choreographic debut in 1919. She opened her own school in Dresden; it was closed by Germany's Nazi-controlled government in the 1930s. Nevertheless, her students toured Europe, Great Britain, and the United States during the same decade, performing in such Wigman creations as *Choric Movement* (1926), *Two Monotonies: Restrained and Turning* (1926), *Vision IV: Witch Dance* (1926) and *Totenmal* (1930).

Youskevitch, Igor (1912–——): Dancer and teacher. This Russian danseur noble performed on many continents with Bronislava Nijinska's Ballets de Paris, the Ballet Russe de Monte Carlo, American Ballet Theatre and other companies. Elegant, long-limbed, with a princely deportment both modest and grand, he was sought after by ballerinas, dancing to particular acclaim with Alicia Alonso. George Balanchine created the leading male role in *Theme and Variations* (1946) for him. Following his retirement from the stage, Youskevitch began a career as a teacher at the University of Texas and at his own school on Long Island, New York.

History of Ballet

As implied by the word—which comes from the Italian *ballare,* "to dance"—*ballet* appears to have originated in Italy. Established as a courtly art during the Renaissance, ballet was first intended as an amusement for royalty and their noble attendants. Large casts of courtiers danced in glittering spectacles, as did some members of royal families. These performances were often devised to glorify a monarch and place members of the court in appropriate relation to the ruler. Early ballets frequently assumed mythological themes that linked contemporary political sovereignty with the divinely ordained monarchs of the past. But in many respects, early ballet differed greatly from its current form. In setting, casting, technique, audience, music, story and other accoutrements, early ballet was apparently much less extensive and less fluid in its range of movement, and more literary in its composition, structure and content.

Ballet to the 19th Century

Early ballet teachers like Domenico of Piacenza (died c. 1462), with his disciples Antonio Cornazano (1431–c. 1500) and Guglielmo Ebreo (born c. 1440), first went to work in Italy in the 1400s. They often accepted commissions to create and stage pieces for official and formal occasions that might combine the presentation of a performance with a festive, luxurious meal for the powers-that-be. Along with dancing, these productions included a variety of features, such as recitations, songs, instrumental music and elaborate theatrical props. Some even seem to have involved audience participation.

This sort of entertainment reached its height at the Parisian court, fostered by the enthusiasm of Catherine de Medici, mother of Henri III, who brought Italian fashion, including dance fashion, with her to France. One of Catherine's attendants, a fellow Italian who took the name of Balthasar de Beaujoyeulx (died c. 1587), was instrumental in the development of the choreography and staging of 16th-century ballet. Working at the behest of Catherine, he created the *Ballet comique de la reine* to celebrate the marriage of Marguerite de Lorraine to the Duc de Joyeuse. The choreographer described this early ballet as "the geometrical groupings of people dancing together, accompanied by the varied harmony of several instruments." He turned to poetry for a plot and added sets and costumes to create one of the first examples of classical ballet as it is known today. De Beaujoyeulx's ballet was filled with gods and goddesses, a castle, a garden, a vault, much dialogue, three mermaids, twelve dancing naiads, four dryads, a stag, a dog, an elephant, a lion, a tiger, a hog and a serpent.

The *Ballet comique de la reine* did not include several elements considered standard in modern ballet. It was not performed on a proscenium stage but in a large room at floor level, with the audience occupying raised seats around it. It also lacked many of the steps used by modern ballet dancers, as well as today's athletic approach to movement. Compared to ballet of today, the dancing of de Beaujoyeulx's era was stilted, relying on gesture and on fairly static floor patterns. The complicated costumes, meanwhile, distorted the outline of the dancers' figures, substituting ornament for natural form. Nonetheless, the ballet represented a genuine advance in classical dance.

De Beaujoyeulx's audience was limited to the upper echelon of society, too. When they watched ballet, this audience of powerful, worldly people looked for reflections of their social stature. Ballet's innate aristocracy was thus born in royal circles, and to some extent it has endured, although later choreographers amended it. Ballet dancers still carry themselves with dignity, aspire to physical nobility, and seem to serve a purpose above the mundane, whether musical, personal, choreographic or idiosyncratic.

The dance continued as a courtly art in France throughout the 1600s, though with some modifications. One was the recruitment of professional dancers and performers for ballets that grew in sophistication and required a correspondingly higher level of technical ability. Another development of the period was the gradual adoption of proscenium stages for ballets, beginning in France under Italian auspices. Successive French monarchs continued to support the art and to use it for political purposes. Under their patronage, choreographers framed ballets as thinly disguised tributes to their rulers and as extended allegories about their achievements.

Louis XIV, popularly known as "The Sun King," ruled France—and ballet—from 1643 to 1715. The ballets he commissioned and promoted directly reflected a desire to maintain and regulate his might. Perhaps as a natural result, these works focused largely upon gods, and gave them the charm and cunning of royal personages. The Sun King himself studied dancing under Pierre Beauchamps, a relative of the playwright Molière. In addition to teaching the king, Beauchamps was apparently the first teacher to codify the five foot positions that underlie ballet technique to this day. The positions are significant because they determine the body's stance both on the ground and in the air, and because they produce the characteristic "turn-out" in the hips and legs of ballet dancers. Originally borrowed from the sport of fencing, turn-out creates a position of openness and readiness. From this starting point, a ballet dancer can engage in movements that extend the line of the body with grace and power.

Though he may have had mixed motives in his pursuit of balletic excellence, Louis XIV also sought to institutionalize ballet so that it would endure beyond the span of his own life and reign. By establishing the Académie Royale de Danse in 1661, he gave official recognition to dance instruction; when he formed the Académie Royale de Musique in 1669, he laid the groundwork for the eventual emergence of the Paris Opera and its attendant ballet company. The oldest ballet troupe still at work today, the Paris Opera Ballet thus owes its existence to the sponsorship of The Sun King.

Eighteenth-century opera-ballet continued in the tradition of the lavish royal displays of previous centuries, combining elements of music, dance and theater in productions of gemlike vividness and high style. A number of French dancers also developed a virtuosity bordering on wizardry, including Gaestan Vestris (1728–1808) and his son Auguste (1760–1842), as well as Marie Sallé and Marie Camargo. These two rivals brought such different qualities to ballet that they were, in a sense, incomparable. While Sallé was a dramatic purist, Camargo was an exuberant technician, so strong that she was known to step in for unavailable male dancers. With the emergence of stars on the dance stage came a growth in the sophistication and demands of audiences, which was only abetted by an influx of brilliant Italian dancers.

The 18th century gave birth to more than one form of classical dancing. In contrast to the opera-ballet, which unfolded in a series of vignettes, the ballet d'action followed a single dramatic line over the course of a long performance.

THE AUDITION

What happens at a ballet audition? Simply put, would-be dancers who have trained for many years enter a bare studio and perform before a daunting audience of ballet masters and mistresses. They try to dance instead of practice, to impress prospective bosses or teachers and win places for themselves in the ranks of professional dance companies or their affiliated schools. At an audition, sweat and talent join in a striking partnership with youth.

At a midwestern audition held in the 1980s by the American Ballet Theatre School, eighty-two aspirants showed up to try out for a very few coveted places in the school. Headquartered in New York City, the dance capital of America, the school is one of the country's most prestigious, serving as a training ground for future members of the American Ballet Theatre and also for ABT II, the junior company. Competition at the school is formidable and enrollment quite selective.

These high stakes engendered tension and excitement in the auditioners. Most were girls between the ages of fourteen and eighteen who had already been ballet students for many years. They wore uniforms of black leotards and pink tights. Each had already acquired the combination of self-discipline and suppleness that gives a dance performance the feeling of beauty held in balance. At the audition, the hard-won physical control of each dancer was scrutinized closely.

At many auditions, individual entrants are unceremoniously eliminated at any point the evaluator may desire. If they are too heavy or too old or can't point their feet properly, they are simply told to leave the floor, one by one, after the first or second combination has been danced. Other audition masters prefer to take a more humane approach, allowing everyone to persevere together until nearly the end, when most are dismissed as a group.

Several ballet mistresses supervised the ABT audition, while others looked on. It was difficult to keep track of the eighty-two entrants, since they all danced at once according to identical instructions. First they warmed up at the barre, and then they moved to the center of the room and danced unsupported, where their weaknesses could be revealed. The exercises were similar to those they had danced in their classes: frappés, attitudes, pliés and the like.

From the midwestern group, four national semifinalists were chosen. The ABT would select others at auditions in Denver, San Francisco, Los Angeles and half a dozen other cities around the country. After further evaluation, more weeding out and boiling down, a handful of new ABT students would be named from among the semifinalists. The chosen few would then travel to Manhattan to pursue their dream.

Emphasizing the potential of dance as a form of drama, the ballet d'action was advanced through the choreographic work of Jean-Georges Noverre (1727–1810) and Gaspero Angiolini (1731–1803). Noverre was also a dance theorist and the author of *Lettres sur la danse et sur les ballets* (1760), which advocated the development of ballet as a dramatic entity rather than as a forum for the exhibition of physical feats. In much the same line of reasoning, Noverre urged the elimination of disfiguring costumes and shoes that got in the way of dancers' movement.

During the era of the French Revolution (1789–99), some ballets strayed from the standard mythological subjects to consider, at some distance, the lives of ordinary people and even peasants. Meanwhile, such choreographers as Salvatore Viganò (1769–1821) began making ballets that presaged the dawn of the Romantic period in dance. Viganò gradually incorporated gestural movement—long a mainstay of ballet—into the dancing itself in order to enhance dramatic unity and impact.

The Romantic Period

During the Romantic period in ballet (roughly 1830 to 1850, with some Romantic works postdating that decade) the object of the dance was to go beyond material facts, leaving behind the rational, physical, workaday world. Romanticism implied a yearning for ideal experience; under its sway ballet strove to symbolize that experience in emblems, such as fairies and sylphs. Romantic ballets relied increasingly on the use of pointe technique to create the impression of ethereal transcendence.

An art of steadfast illusionism, Romantic ballet found its fulfillment in the choreography of Filippo Taglioni (1777–1871), August Bournonville (1805–79), Jules Perrot (1810–92) and Arthur Saint-Léon (1821–70); in the teaching of Carlo Blasis (1797–1878); and in the dancing of Carlotta Grisi (1819–99), Marie Taglioni (1804–84), Fanny Cerrito (1817–1909), Lucile Grahn (1819–1907) and Fanny Elssler (1810–84).

As this list of dancers suggests, the ballerina was essential to the creation of balletic illusion during the Romantic period. Strong male dancers had tantalized earlier audiences with their brio, polish and bravado, but women held sway on the Romantic ballet stage. With the help of coaches and choreographers, they made technical strides that served to enhance their aura of chaste otherworldliness. Where Charles Didelot (1767–1837)—the French choreographer who first proposed that female dancers wear tights—had hoisted ballerinas on wires in *Flore et Zephyre* (1796) to suggest aerial flight and heavenly existence, ballerinas in the next century learned to create the *illusion* of floating with their own bodies and with toe shoes.

Encouraged by her choreographer father, Marie Taglioni attained the look of a sylph partly by dancing on the tips of her toes. To dance en pointe as she did, though, required more than a wish to do so. Ballerinas who sought to master the technique needed muscular strength, plenty of practice and powerful concentration.

The perfect vehicle for Taglioni's remarkable talent came from her father, who choreographed *La Sylphide* (1832) to music by Jean Madeleine Schneitzhoeffer (1785–1852). A story of romantic love and spiritual ardor, the ballet paid its respects to the world of folklore, fairies and magic. Cast as a sprite, Taglioni completely embodied a sylph in her performance and was a study in the beauty of elusiveness, according to most observers. The costume given her by her father emphasized her diaphanous quality, its long, full, gauzy skirt seeming to clothe her in layers of mystery.

August Bournonville, the Danish choreographer, dancer and teacher, made a version of *La Sylphide* that has enjoyed a longer theatrical lifespan than Taglioni's; many European and American companies include this piece in their current repertories. The son of the Royal Danish Ballet's director, Bournonville trained in Denmark and Paris and performed in Paris before inheriting his father's job and shaping Scandinavian ballet. His technique, artistic point of view and ambition in ballet were singularly his own, but they have influenced dancers around the world. Precision and delicacy on the ground and in the air, combined with a lightness, subtlety and buoyancy of musical attack, were and are some of the hallmarks of Bournonville-schooled dancers. The Royal Danish Ballet continues to cultivate this style and preserve the Bournonville repertory, which, in addition to *La Sylphide*, includes such works as *Napoli, The Kermesse in Bruges* and *Konservatoriet*.

Giselle (1841) is usually considered a prototypical Romantic work. The combined product of composer Adolphe Adam (1803–56), poets Heinrich Heine (1797–1856) and Théophile Gautier (1811–72), and choreographers Jean Coralli (1779–1854) and Jules Perrot (1810–92), among others, the ballet concerns a doomed love affair between a peasant girl and a nobleman. In two parallel realms, the worldly and the supernatural, human folly and hopes unfold as characters are enticed by love and tormented by evil spells. Designed to show off Carlotta Grisi to best advantage, *Giselle* did that and more: The ballet has survived as a dramatically vital work of art.

Other stalwarts of the Romantic repertoire include Perrot's *Le pas de quatre* (1845) and *Coppelia* (1870) by Saint-Léon. Originally choreographed to showcase the rich talents of Grisi, Taglioni, Grahn and Cerrito, *Le pas de quatre* has been reconstructed by 20th-century choreographers in England and the United States. *Coppelia,* based on a story by German writer E. T. A. Hoffmann (1776–1822), is a Romantic work with a comic twist that tells the story of ideal love disguised. It, too, is represented in the repertories of many present-day ballet companies, enjoyed as much for its clever plot as for its aesthetic qualities.

Despite the achievements of Romantic choreographers and dancers, ballet-making seemed to wane toward the latter years of the 19th century. Virtuosos continued to dance, whetting the insatiable appetites of European fans, but both Europe and America experienced an end-of-the-century choreographic gap.

The United States had as yet no national ballet company, and Americans wishing to see ballet had to wait for foreign stars to visit on tour. In need of fresh ideas and new talents, ballet found both in Russia.

Russian Ballet

Though long isolated from Europe, Russia, in fact, absorbed and adapted a great deal of Western culture, especially under the guiding hand of enlightened monarchs like Catherine II. Russian ballet originated in theatrical productions of the 17th century that combined dancing, music and drama. Nonetheless, the art did not blossom until much later, when foreign teachers and talents arrived. Then Frenchman Jean-Baptiste Landé established the St. Petersburg Ballet School in 1738 and Italian Filippo Beccari began a school of the dance in Moscow in 1764. Both schools were the predecessors of the great Russian ballet companies yet to emerge. Didelot, Blasis, Perrot and Saint-Léon also worked in Russia, in the 1800s. But the single most important European influence on Russian dance was French-born Marius Petipa, who not only remade ballet in his adopted country but also changed its forms and meanings for most of the world in the 20th century.

Petipa came to St. Petersburg as a dancer in 1847 and stayed there for more than sixty years, instructing Russian dancers, performing on Russian stages, choreographing ballets and teaching ballet composition. Ballet burgeoned during Petipa's time with the support of Russian rulers and state patronage. During his tenure at the St. Petersburg Imperial Theatre, Petipa choreographed more than sixty full-length ballets and many shorter pieces. He also sought out Russian composers—Peter Ilich Tchaikovsky, Alois Louis Minkus (1826–1917) and Aleksandr Glazunov (1865–1936)—to create music to his specifications for new ballets. While Petipa did not always strive for especially high standards and churned out some amusements for sentimentalists, a number of his ballets set the terms for classical dancing in the generations to follow. These include *La Bayadère* (1877), *The Sleeping Beauty* (1890), *Swan Lake* (1895) and *Raymonda* (1898). He choreographed *Swan Lake* with his assistant, Lev Ivanov (1834–1901), who choreographed *The Nutcracker* (1892) when Petipa was indisposed by poor health.

In addition to providing Russian dancers with a new canon of ballets, Petipa reformed their training. He invited Russian and European teachers to help him in St. Petersburg, including Enrico Cecchetti (1850–1928), Pavel Gerdt (1844–1917) and Christian Johansson (1817–1903). By combining Danish, French, Italian and native Russian traditions into one technique, Petipa helped Russian dancers achieve enormous breadth, flexibility and strength, and expanded their imaginative vision. Eventually, it was a Russian who challenged the French immigrant who for so long had challenged the Russian ballet.

Michel Fokine, a young Russian dancer and choreographer with the Maryinsky Theatre, grew tired of some aspects of the Petipa style and its outlook on classical dancing. Along with his peers in music and art circles, this graduate of the Imperial School of Ballet wanted ballets to unite dancing, music and visual elements with more cohesiveness. Fokine believed that the classical language could respond with more specificity, originality and sensitivity to the particular requirements of any ballet, whether musical, dramatic, or otherwise. Because Petipa's reforms of dancing had been academic by nature, Fokine saw them as a bulwark against progress and artistic experiment, which tends to be free, not formal. The Russian valued expression over tradition, as is evident in such disparate works as *Les Sylphides* (1909), *Petrouchka* (1911), *Firebird* (1910) and *Scheherazade* (1910).

Fokine did not, of course, do his work in isolation. In fact, artistic collaboration was an important element of his career. Much of this collaboration arose from his relationship with a Russian impresario and patron of the arts, Serge Diaghilev. A nobleman and one-time law student, Diaghilev had wanted to become a composer but gave it up and gravitated toward a community of painters and musicians who represented the fledgling avant-garde in turn-of-the-century St. Petersburg. After founding an influential art magazine that published this coterie's views, Diaghilev organized a performance of Russian opera in Paris in 1908, then expanded his entrepreneurial purview to include ballet in 1909. The touring dance company he assembled included Fokine, as well as Anna Pavlova (1881–1931), Tamara Karsavina (1885–1978), Vaslav Nijinsky (1889–1950) and other dancers of remarkable talent who, until then, had achieved little more than local renown. When the Ballets Russes opened in Paris, it was met by a storm of astonished acclaim. Expecting little from the previously unheralded Russians, Western audiences were dazzled by an exotic production of passionately vivid technique.

The Ballets Russes continued to work with a constantly changing cast of performers and artistic collaborators under Diaghilev's direction until his death in 1929. Many experts believe that this company's impact—not only on ballet, but on related arts—remains unrivaled to this day. Previous classical companies had, of course, used contributions from stage designers, costumers, composers, scenarists and other artists, but these collaborators usually followed the specific instructions of the choreographer or the producer. The effect was entirely different in a Ballets Russes production such as *Parade* (1917), for which painter Pablo Picasso (1881–1973) provided the set and costumes, composer Erik Satie the music, writer Jean Cocteau (1889–1963) the book, and choreographer Leonide Massine the choreography. Not only was each collaborator uniquely gifted, but each created independently. Although they ultimately answered to Diaghilev, who wanted to shape world taste by shocking it, his artists enjoyed great license.

But Diaghilev was a driven, intemperate man. He fired Nijinsky, his protegé, after the dancer decided to marry. Nijinsky had smitten audiences across the globe with his dancing and had choreographed a handful of fine ballets with Diaghilev's encouragement, including *Afternoon of a Faun* (1912), *The Rite of Spring* (1913) and *Jeux* (1913). Diaghilev, however, could not stand rejection by the object of his affections. The impresario frequently appeared fickle in his search for fresh talent for fresh trends, and Nijinsky was but one casualty. Still, scores of artists sought to work with him, including the composers Claude Debussy, Igor Stravinsky, Sergei Prokofiev, Maurice Ravel, Francis Poulenc (1899–1963) and Darius Milhaud (1892–1974); the painters Georges Braque (1882–1963), Maurice Utrillo (1883–1955), Joan Miró (1893–1983), Giorgio de Chirico (1888–1978), Henri Matisse (1869–1954) and Picasso; and such dancers and choreographers as Bronislava Nijinska (1891–1972), Alicia Markova (born 1910), Anton Dolin (1904–83), Lydia Sokolova (1896–1974) and George Balanchine (1904–83). The artists, dancers and choreographers who worked with Diaghilev reconfigured the appearance and purpose of their respective arts, most notably ballet.

Although a member of the Ballets Russes for only a relatively short time, Balanchine gained notice for his choreographic originality while there. This Russian-born dancer and musician trained in St. Petersburg, and in four years with Diaghilev choreographed many works, including *Barabau* (1925), *Jack in the Box* (1926), *The Triumph of Neptune* (1926), *La Chatte* (1927), *Apollon Musagete* (1928), *The Prodigal Son* (1929) and *Le Bal* (1929). The Ballets Russes folded after Diaghilev's death, and Balanchine joined the Ballets Russes de Monte Carlo along with many other former Ballets Russes members. Founded in 1932 by René Blum and Colonel W. de Basil, the company enjoyed Balanchine's choreographic direction only briefly, until he left it to form a company of his own, Les Ballets, in New York in 1933.

TOE SHOES

Ballet may be a sublime amusement, but the main tools of ballerinas—their toe shoes—are decidedly unromantic. While toe shoes have allowed countless sylphs, sprites, princesses and femmes fatales to cast spells from the ballet stage, they have also caused many a blister among ballerinas. Usually invisible to audiences, the hardships of dancing en pointe are considerable and chronic because even veteran dancers suffer from sore and battered feet.

In an attempt to make toe shoes more comfortable and reliable, toe-shoe makers have developed a specialized and expensive craft. Ballerinas spend a great deal of time taking care of their toe shoes, in part because they go through so many pairs. Each dancer in the New York City Ballet, for instance, wears out a minimum of twelve pairs of toe shoes during an ordinary week, at a cost of several hundred dollars. NYCB dancers typically order their shoes from England, where they are hand-sewn. Each dancer's shoes are always made by the same artisan, identified by a mark on each shoe.

When they get a new pair of toe shoes, ballerinas prepare them for use in various ways. They may soak the toes in water or alcohol to soften them or flatten toes that are too round. They may cut the satin from the toe or roughen the leather soles to make them less slippery. They may remove the insole, bend the shoe if it is too straight, bang it against a hard surface to make it less noisy, or sew on decorations. After all this, toe shoes often last for only a single performance.

Ballet in the United States

In London during the 1930s, a young American historian, poet and arts patron named Lincoln Kirstein (born 1907) saw Balanchine's work and became convinced that the choreographer could make a tremendous impact in the United States, which at that time had little ballet of its own. Kirstein invited Balanchine to form a ballet company with private backing in the United States, and Balanchine agreed, provided he could first establish a ballet school. He opened the School of American Ballet in New York City in January of 1934; in six months the fledgling student company gave its first performance, consisting of Balanchine's *Serenade* (1935) and other ballets.

Balanchine fulfilled his vision of American ballet over the next fifty years. In his adopted home, he drew on distinctly American reserves of energy, athleticism and naïveté to reinterpret the tradition he had inherited. When taken together, his many technical and musical renovations of that tradition created a balletic neoclassicism, a purification of past style to fit the present. At the New York City Ballet, the last of his companies, all dancers—from apprentices to principals—served the demands of music, speed and precision in movement.

In Ballanchine's ballets, the dancers served not as literary characters but as delicately fashioned, highly individual musical forces who responded to music by dancing musically. Whether or not the ballets took on a distinctive American cast, they were filled with American colloquialisms of all kinds. For example, dancers' bodies and their rhythms were sometimes jazzy, impetuous, asymmetrical or fantastic. Balanchine's work was modern because it acknowledged the art of the past while breaking new artistic ground.

From the start, the New York City Ballet was mainly a repository of Balanchine's own immense body of work. But it also performed work by other choreographers, both before and after Balanchine's death in 1983. At that time, principal dancer Peter Martins became co–ballet master in chief with choreographer Jerome Robbins (Robbins later stepped down from the position, leaving Martins sole director). While seeking to preserve Balanchine's ballets, Martins commissioned new work from a range of other choreographers and contributed many ballets of his own to the company's repertory.

Although NYCB, headquartered at Lincoln Center for the Performing Arts in New York City, has been called a company without stars, it has a hierarchy much like any other ballet company. The rank of principal dancer is the most prominent, followed by that of soloists and the corps de ballet. Corps members dance as an ensemble, while soloists and principals perform by themselves, with a partner or in small groups. Some dancers begin in the corps or as company apprentices shortly after graduating from the School of American Ballet, which remains the main source of new company members. These performers gradually work their way up in rank, hoping to catch the attention of a choreographer or ballet master or mistress before too many years have passed. Others, especially if they come from another company, may start at a higher level. Many dancers remain in the corps for the balance of their careers; at NYCB, corps dancers are often considered equal in skill and musical acuity to soloists dancing elsewhere.

Even beyond the New York City Ballet, American ballet will probably continue to show the influence of Balanchine for a long time to come, as his former dancers teach and assume artistic direction of companies and schools around the country. Balanchine, in fact, helped launch the careers of some of America's most brilliant dancers, including Maria Tallchief (born 1925), Diana Adams (born 1926), Suzanne Farrell (born 1945), Edward Villella (born 1936), Jacques d'Amboise (born 1934), Gelsey Kirkland (born 1953), Arthur Mitchell (born 1934), Kyra Nichols (born 1958), Darci Kistler (born 1964), Merrill Ashley (born 1950), Allegra Kent (born 1938), Tanaquil LeClerc (born 1929) and Patricia McBride (born 1942). His impact has also been international, as companies around the world continue to stage his work with the assistance of the Balanchine Trust.

Other ballet traditions thrive in the United States, too. American Ballet Theatre, founded in 1940, performs an eclectic repertory of full-length, 19th-century story ballets, plus classics by choreographer Agnes de Mille, a panoply of modern pieces by the likes of Twyla Tharp, Paul Taylor and David Gordon, and 20th-century European works by Antony Tudor, Kenneth MacMillan and many more. Unlike the New York City Ballet, ABT built an audience by showcasing stars. The ABT repertory has been solidly theatrical in its orientation, although not exclusively so, and at its best it has demanded a high level of theatrical and balletic performance. The company has also invited such choreographers as Robbins, de Mille, Tharp and Eliot Feld to create new ballets for its repertory. Drawn from around the world, such dancers as Fernando Bujones (born 1955), Rudolph Nureyev (1938–93), Carla Fracci (born 1936), Cynthia Gregory (born 1946), Erik Bruhn (1928–86), Anthony Dowell (born 1943), Marcia Haydée (born 1937), Natalia Makarova (born 1940), Patrick Bissell (born 1957), Gelsey Kirkland and Mikhail Baryshnikov have danced with the ABT. Baryshnikov, a Russian expatriate, headed the company for ten years after dancing there and with the New York City Ballet. Kevin McKenzie, a distinguished ABT dancer, is now the company's artistic director.

The Joffrey Ballet, the Dance Theatre of Harlem, the Alvin Ailey American Dance Theater, the San Francisco Ballet and Feld Ballets/NY each offer a distinctive view of what ballet can be and become. Adept at addressing the preoccupations of successive American generations through ballet, the Joffrey has also restaged lost works from the 20th-century ballet canon with particular success (e.g., Massine's *Parade*), and has brought the work of English choreographer Sir Frederick Ashton to the American public. The Dance Theatre of Harlem, founded by former New York City Ballet principal Arthur Mitchell, has presented gifted African-American dancers in ballets old and new, standard and revisionary. Pointing up the increasingly close affinity between classical and nonclassical dance forms, the Alvin Ailey American Dance Theater fuses jazz, modern, ballet and the African-American idiom in works by Ailey and other choreographers. The San Francisco Ballet has increasingly assumed the Balanchine mantle under the leadership of Helgi Thomasson (born 1942), while Feld Ballets/NY presents only the work of Eliot Feld, striking a note of uncompromising individualism.

In recent years, European dance companies have grown more accessible to Americans, and American companies have toured the world extensively. England's Royal Ballet, representing the British academic tradition, visits the United States every few years, as do the Kirov and Bolshoi Ballets from Russia and the Paris Opera Ballet. Outstanding new dancers are brightening the familiar repertories of these companies; several of them, including Manuel Legris of the Paris Opera Ballet and Viviana Durante of the Royal Ballet, have put in guest appearances with American companies, too.

BALLET SCHOOL

Dance education should take place early in life so that immature talents can be properly molded. Dance study can take many forms. For generations, children have pored over Noel Streatfeild's novels, such as *Ballet Shoes* and *Theater Shoes*, drawn in by her tales of the lives and work of dancers. Legions of parents have taken their children to see *The Nutcracker*. Some children learn to dance in gym class or see lectures and demonstrations by professional dance companies in their school auditorium, or attend a local ballet class.

A few, however, choose to study dance formally, with an eye toward a career in the field. Most professional dance schools are competitive, expensive, intensive and enriching. Because the physical demands of a dance career make it such a short one, schools try to train dancers quickly, early and safely to enter companies while still in their teens.

Children can bring great avidity to ballet. They are curious and eager to learn something new and complex. The best teachers try to give shape and sense to children's energy without undoing the desire to dance. They do not allow the spontaneity and freedom of ballet to disappear under the weight of the genre's formalism. After years of study under skilled teachers, young dancers can become competent. But the real source of their ability as ballet dancers is innate talent.

Unfortunately, many talented children never have the opportunity to study ballet seriously. Despite the existence of a number of scholarships, most professional dancing schools are beyond the reach of all but the well-to-do and, by extension, of many minority hopefuls. Although talent does not observe class distinctions, opportunity can.

Some dance professionals have recently tried to create new opportunities for economically disadvantaged students. For instance, the New Ballet School in New York City, founded by choreographer Eliot Feld in 1978, seeks out dance talent in traditionally excluded populations, auditioning thousands of public-school children each year in all the city's boroughs. The few who are admitted to study at the school attend totally free of charge; transportation and dance clothes are also provided. These students not only study dance but they also mingle with professional dancers. Similarly, Jacques d'Amboise's National Dance Institute and the Dance Theatre of Harlem reach into communities to inspire and aid young dance talents. Qualified candidates can continue ballet study at the Professional Performing Arts School, which also offers a full academic curriculum.

Introduction to Modern Dance

The term *modern dance* identifies a kind of dancing that emerged as early as 1890, when certain choreographers and dancers rebelled against the academic ballet tradition. As the form has continued to grow and change, it has come to encompass abundantly different ways of moving, philosophies of performance and approaches to theatrical collaboration. More than any other sort of dance, modern has outgrown successive definitions, for the depth of individualism represented in the dances and the dancing is always seeking to redefine itself.

Despite a tendency toward diversity and divergence, however, modern dances have certain common bonds, especially when placed in contrast to ballet. For one, modern dances are not duty-bound to be attractive or harmonious in their design. Asymmetry can be an asset; so can chaos. Composition is certainly a prime concern in modern dance, and technique is often central to its performance, but modern has traditionally been more willing than ballet to address worldly ideas and concrete realities directly. Where ballet was originally the amusement of kings, modern has been more democratic in its origins, interests and scope. Modern choreographers may base their dances on the Holocaust, AIDS, feminism or Frank Sinatra. They follow their own individual tendencies, whether literary, comic, primitive, imagistic, gymnastic or anything else.

Similarly, modern accepts gravity as an accomplice instead of an antagonist. Modern dancers, who often dance barefoot, prize contact with the ground and use their bodily weight as a positive force. Unlike ballet dancers, who aim to create an illusion of lightness and floating, modern dancers usually don't disguise their mass. They present themselves with a more straightforward physicality than ballet dancers do, without straining to idealize the body or turn it into a symbol. They are not obliged to seem ethereal.

The roles of male and female are also defined more indefinitely than in classical dance. Though the degree of freedom varies from dance to dance, the individual is generally more important than his or her gender. As a result, modern dancers seem more like real people onstage than ballet dancers do. They assay a range of physical challenges, but they do more than serve as athletic bodies. Since their faces are not entirely masked by makeup, they may express their feelings facially or through their bodies. Much of the excitement of modern dance has to do with the impression it gives of a strikingly human kind of spontaneous urgency or casual freedom. Formality and constructed drama also have their place in the genre, as do complex stage effects, costumes, decor and diverse sorts of music, but modern expresses itself through the individual dancer.

Thus, modern dance can be defined in relation to ballet. Rather than preserving a repertoire and an array of formal techniques, it explores the outer limits of what dance can mean in modern times. As a reaction to what has come before, it reflects the shifting relations between alternative and dominant cultures. One sign of modernity in dance is a willingness to comment on or cross the line traditionally separating the established and the experimental. Indeed, classical ballet has recently taken a cue from modern and begun to examine that boundary as well. Modern dance's challenge to longstanding aesthetic and moral assumptions was central to its genesis and remains a force today.

The Birth of Modern Dance

Today, modern dancers live and work all over the world, including, notably, in Japan, Germany and France. And two Europeans, François Delsarte (1811–71) and Emile Jaques-Dalcroze (1865–1950), were certainly forebears of modern. But the story of modern dance is largely the story of Americans, for it was a change of attitude that made modern dance possible in the first place. This inventiveness may have come from the lack of a long theatrical and classical dance tradition in the United States. Nonetheless, modern has enjoyed less widespread public acceptance in the United States than has ballet, even though the ballet tradition is of European origin.

Along with Mary Wigman (1886–1973) and the German expressionists, Isadora Duncan, Loie Fuller and Ruth St. Denis created the form now known as modern dance. Duncan, who favored dancing to large-scale pieces of symphonic classical music (such as the work of Ludwig van Beethoven), looked to ancient Greece for moral and aesthetic inspiration. She danced barefoot in a loose tunic, giving the impression that her apparently simple movements—walks, skips and grandly evocative poses—were improvised in a burst of elation on the spur of the moment. Unlike the most distinguished ballerinas of her day (none of whom were American), Duncan didn't strive to win the admiration of ladies and gentlemen by displaying feats of technique. Instead, she hoped to rouse audiences to the more fundamental power of dance, a power she considered spiritual. Duncan based her dances on a principle of unity in nature and believed dancers should follow the inherent flow of a piece. For her, dancing was not entertainment but self-expression.

Duncan's conviction must have been quite impressive, for though few records survive of her methods or her works, she had an enormous impact in her day and became a legend in dance. She imposed a personal, musical, and dramatic standard on dance that still elevates the form. Dancing, in her view, was not just something to do but something to *feel*. Although dance before Duncan often had the image of frivolity, she showed that it could also be a creed as sustaining and serious as any religion. Connoisseurship had little to do with her art; compassion mattered more. This attitude made the dance more democratic; anyone, given the inclination, might enjoy it or be moved by it.

Loie Fuller's contribution to early modern dance was perhaps more technical than spiritual. Her experiments with lighting and costume design caused a sensation at the Folies-Bergère in fin-de-siècle Paris. To evoke a kind of sensuous bliss, she called on allied arts for dances that celebrated the play color in streams of silk and beams of light, as well as with motion and music. Fuller, like Duncan, wanted to awaken audiences to the power of perception.

Fuller's richly visual approach was a far cry from the stage effects of classical dancing, which seemed literary and stilted by comparison. Ballet in late 19th-century America seemed to summon only minor imaginative efforts that repeated endlessly what had already been done. At its worst, classical dancing of the time offered a highbrow sideshow for audiences who liked looking at the flash of well-formed legs.

Ruth St. Denis began her career in a commercial milieu not unlike Fuller's, dancing without much previous training in the touring Broadway shows of David Belasco (1853–1931). Even after her conversion to modern dance, St. Denis remained a theatrical showwoman, although, like Duncan and Fuller, she believed in serving a higher purpose when dancing. Her taste was both glamorous and pure. St. Denis's mystical bent, supple body and frequently Asian overtones expanded the purview of dance both technically and imaginatively, refreshing its innate theatricality with new vision and energy.

Working with her partner and husband Ted Shawn, St. Denis infused her works with many different styles of dancing: classical, Native American, East Indian, ballroom, Spanish and others. With the assistance of Shawn's business instincts, she also made a good start at institution-building. This was a rare achievement among the early moderns, who tended to perform as soloists unaffiliated with schools or entourages. Not only did she establish herself as a leading figure in modern dance and create a body of work independent of her own abilities as a performer, but she also cultivated many talented young dancers. This second generation of moderns would claim and then abandon her, driven to make dances of their own.

The Quintessential Moderns

The work of the second generation of American modern dancers was, by most standards, startling and individual. In the hands of such choreographers as Doris Humphrey, Charles Weidman and Martha Graham, modern continued to be a means of and medium for independent expression.

Humphrey, who danced for eleven years with Shawn and St. Denis, left their company in 1928 to form her own company with Weidman. Her technique involved a principle that she termed "fall and recovery." As she worked, she focused on the dynamics of balance that are evoked as a dancer's body responds to and collaborates with gravity. Her dances addressed psychological schisms and contradictions, whether experienced by a family (*Day on Earth*, 1947) or by larger communities (*The Shakers*, 1931). Her most important piece was probably the trilogy *New Dance* (1935–36). She was also an important influence on the career of José Limon.

During his partnership with Humphrey, Weidman often choreographed with wit. His *Is Sex Necessary?* (1947), for example, was inspired by James

Thurber's work of the same name. On other occasions, he brought a social conscience not found in the canon of classical ballet, to such dances as *Lynchtown* (1936).

Because of her imaginative and moral scope as well as her specific innovations, Graham had a profound influence, not only in the dance world but among artists in many disciplines. Although she studied at the Denishawn School, she departed drastically from the aesthetic preferences of St. Denis and Shawn once she set out on her own. Unlike St. Denis, who was known for the sinuous reveries of her dances, Graham preferred a percussive and explosive kind of movement. Her pioneering style was striking for its starkness, angularity, and depth of expression. Both physically and dramatically challenging, her technique was based on the intake and outflow of breath, on a contraction and release that created strong contrasts and a rhythm of disjunction.

Beyond the marked influence of her technique, however, Graham made an impact with her subject matter. She addressed a wide range of ideas in her repertory, including the mythological and psychological, the narrative and abstract, and the American and classic Greek. In doing so she opened new areas of reflection to other dancers and theater people, to both her peers and her inheritors. Graham also focused intensely on women's experiences and put women at the center of many pieces as dramatic and moral witnesses. Her preference for commissioning original scores, sets and costumes for her works was also a departure that established a new standard. Powerfully original collaborators, such as sculptor Isamu Noguchi and photographer Louis Horst, made contributions to her productions. The breadth of Graham's vision radiated outward, calling forth a response of similar magnitude from surrounding artists.

During her long career—she died in 1991 at the age of 97—Graham also built a highly regarded company and school. The strength of these institutions permitted her to perfect her technique and develop a marvelous repertory. Critics and audiences have yet to see what will become of Graham's company and school without her guidance. But whatever happens, her descendants in dance have already made unique contributions to the genre. They include Erick Hawkins (who was once Graham's husband), Anna Sokolow, Merce Cunningham and Paul Taylor. All were influenced by her, and all created work that was very much their own.

Like Graham, Hawkins has worked with many collaborators, including composer Lucia Dlugozewski and sculptor Ralph Dorazio, to create and stage his dances. And as with Graham, his use of props and costumes, including masks, has contributed vividly to the power of his work. But Hawkins favors a harmoniously fluid style of movement, eschews overt conflict, and seems to demonstrate an aesthetic far removed from hers. He established his own company in 1957.

The intensely dark dances of Sokolow, who danced with Graham's company until 1939, are striking and fierce in their imagery, like Graham's. But her dances often take urban, Jewish, or Mexican themes as their subjects and jazz as their music. The dances include *Lyric Suite* (1954), *Rooms* (1955), *Session for Six* (1958) and *Dreams* (1961).

Cunningham, who has been another enduring and original force in modern dance over a long period, danced with the Graham company for five years in the 1940s. When he launched his own company in 1953, he made a more distinct break from Graham than the others. Yet, if any single figure links archmodernist Graham with the postmodern generation of the 1960s, it is probably Cunningham.

Cunningham's work is well known for several unusual strategies. One is his use of chance in composing dances. For example, he may toss a coin to decide the order in which groups of movements take place. He has also given collaborative work a different twist. When he works with composers and designers (including John Cage and Robert Rauschenberg), each collaborator creates independently, without reference to the others. Until a score is complete, Cunningham rehearses his dances without music, according to time cues. A designer may paint a backdrop without seeing any part of the dance and without hearing the music.

Similarly, Cunningham does not assign a hierarchy of significance to various elements of the stage or of the dance itself. Instead, his dances feature many movements taking place simultaneously in different areas of the stage. As a result, they do not seem to have a readily explicable linear, forward movement. Even though Cunningham's vocabulary derives partly from modern, partly from ballet, partly from natural imagery and impulses, and partly from his imagination, his assembled works seem displaced from any sources.

Cunningham forces the audience's attention away from sets, costumes and the like and toward dance itself as the thing that matters most. His method of collaborating underscores the effect, for each element remains pure and independent of the others. And in using chance to choreograph, he both seeks order and abandons it. Instead of imposing an idea on a dance, he allows it to be shaped by forces beyond his sphere of influence.

Nevertheless, Cunningham dances look exact and specific, carefully enunciated in the dancers' extended legs and articulated feet. His dancers have a striking ability to perform contradictory movements in close sequence without seeming to prepare for them. Aspects of his techniques are quite balletic, from a certain erectness of stance to a fineness of balance and precision of the feet. But the Cunningham dancer's torso and arms are not moved in classical ways; the dynamic range of their bodies is loose, broad, wild and certainly not decorous. In a Cunningham work, gravity seems admired rather than balletically denied. All of his innovations have helped to redefine and liberate dance.

Paul Taylor, one of the outstanding male dancers of his generation, trained in both ballet and modern. His notably virtuosic, gutsy, uninhibited style as a dancer and choreographer have also owed something to his experience as an athlete. This cross-pollination has allowed him to generate an *oeuvre* that is both individual and diverse. Having started out in the companies of Graham and Cunningham, he later became one of the rare outsiders to be invited to perform, on occasion, with George Balanchine's New York City Ballet. He founded his company, the Paul Taylor Dance Company, in 1954.

Taylor and his dances are often said to offer two contradictory aspects. One, his lyrical and affirmative side, is springy, playful, euphoric and rather classically inclined in terms of fluidity, clarity, uplift and line. This aspect shines through in dances like *Aureole* (1962), in which the forthrightly muscular and barefoot dancers dart and glide and traipse with extraordinary fleetness and energy. By contrast, Taylor's "dark" dances show the other aspect of his work. They seem to assume the worst about human motives and behavior and depict the play of base instincts with an uncanny, mordant accuracy. In either kind of dance, point of view matters greatly. Taylor's physical style—highly energetic, distortional, yet classic—thus accompanies an equally distinctive imagination and judgment.

Taylor was also known as an experimentalist in the early part of his career. For instance, in his perhaps ironically titled solo piece *Epic* (1957), a man in a suit takes to the stage and assumes a series of positions. Most of his movements require only slight incremental and gestural adjustments, and are made in a sequence determined rhythmically by a sound recording of a telephone operator's repeated message. Works like *Epic*, which were indeed called dances and were performed for the most part by dancers, did not, however, strike everyone who saw them as dances. This piece, for instance, was greeted at first with a measure of critical derision, but Taylor was not to be the last choreographer to create such challenging and subversive works.

The Judson Movement

In the 1960s, a loosely affiliated group of choreographers and other artists came to be associated with the Judson Memorial Church in New York City's Greenwich Village. Individually, they began to create dances that challenged the modern sensibility as it had developed to that point. The dances did not all fit into one type, and it would not be accurate to say that Judson began as a movement; instead, it began as some dancers and dances. But the experimentation at Judson arose as an answer to, and a rejection of, the modern tradition, so the works performed there did have a common motivation. The kind of dance that originated at Judson came to be known as postmodern.

Postmodern dance, like modern, has meant many things and is a relative term. Most fundamentally, it suggests a chronological turning point, the moment at which modern dance was seen by some artists to cease serving the needs of the moment. As time went on, postmodernism became more specific in its meanings. Postmodern choreographers sought a kind of dance that was less narrow in its theatrical motivation, less exclusively formal in its concerns, and less dedicated to serving the self and self-expression alone.

The Judson group got its start in a dance-composition workshop given by composer Robert Dunn at the suggestion of John Cage. Held at the Merce

Cunningham studio and elsewhere, the workshop began in 1960. It attracted dancers and choreographers, many with ties to Cunningham, who felt the need to strive in new directions, beyond what most classes and performance opportunities would then permit. In 1962, Dunn and a few others approached the Rev. Alvin Carmines of Judson Memorial Church for permission to give a dance concert there. The church was already serving as a site for concerts and happenings, and also as a center for the politically oriented residents of the neighborhood. Carmines agreed, and so in July 1962, the Judson became a public gathering place for dancers as well.

Among the Judson movement's hallmarks was the collective spirit of the choreographers, performers and other artists working together. Whatever their individual styles, each shared a desire to fuse different artistic impulses into something new. The ideal at Judson was to move beyond established modern dance, which some found unwelcoming to newcomers and aesthetically set in its ways, a stronghold for those who already held the reins. The Judson group would remain open to new dance ideas. Beyond this, the collective was defined broadly. It encompassed dancers, choreographers, painters, musicians, composers and others, but in larger terms, it also included the audience and the surrounding community. Judson dance concerts were not intended solely for connoisseurs or the usual art fans, and in fact, they attracted a very mixed audience.

One of the ways in which postmodern dancers took modern dance off its pedestal at Judson was to change the nature of the space they performed in. They considered the venue not a stage but a performance space. Rather than setting up lights and backdrops, they used the space in its natural state. Depending on their needs and tastes, the performers used various parts of the church at various times, from the sanctuary to the gym to a gallery to a choir loft. Judsonites like Trisha Brown, Lucinda Childs and Meredith Monk also became well known for their willingness to venture beyond the walls of the church. For example, Monk's *Juice* (1969), danced by a cast of seventy-five in three distinct parts, was performed on the Guggenheim Museum's huge spiral ramp, at a Barnard College theater, and in a downtown loft. In *Street Dance* (1964), Childs positioned her audience at the window of Rauschenberg's Manhattan loft, while two dancers blended in with the everyday activities on the street below and an audiotape explained the event to the audience.

Judson dances incorporated styles of physical movement not normally associated with theatrical dance, thereby reexamining what dancing was and could be. Where previous genres of dance shaped the body in a set variety of patterns and styles, according to various tempos and theatrical exigencies, Judson dance let the body go, encouraging it to be itself while in performance. Forgoing inherited artifice to focus instead on the body's everyday reality and energy, the Judsonites composed dances largely of movements that almost any ambulatory person could perform.

In the 1970s, this purified palette of movement became even cleaner and clearer as postmodern dance advanced into physical minimalism, analogous to minimalism in music and fine art. Minimalist choreographers hoped to draw attention to bare geometric structure, which was exposed in the repetition of simple phrases and in accumulating patterns. As embodied in the cool and abstract work of Lucinda Childs, this dance could look pristine, clarifying and ascetic. Or, as in dances by Laura Dean, it might seem warmed by repeated phrases and swelling patterns that have an enchanting, ecstatic and intrinsically communal feel.

The 1980s and 1990s

In the 1980s, a new theatricality seized some of the postmodernists, as well as certain dancers and choreographers new to the scene. While collaborative efforts between artists and composers continued, former Judsonites, including Brown and Childs, began to perform in proscenium theaters for more conventional audiences. These dancers organized themselves into companies that developed repertories and embarked on national and foreign tours, much as ballet companies had done for years. Where many Judsonites had dismissed virtuosity as an onerous legacy, choreographers in the 1980s adopted more exacting technical standards. Trained dancers came into greater demand; Laura Dean even began choreographing pieces for ballet dancers working en pointe. Narrative reentered dances, sometimes in the guise of confession or autobiography, reviving interest in dance as a means of self-expression. Experimentation continued, too, so that in the 1980s and early 1990s, modern dance seemed to become increasingly eclectic.

This trend toward the eclectic had begun earlier, in the work of Twyla Tharp and her successive companies. Tharp studied ballet, modern and popular forms of dance before performing with Taylor's company for a couple of years in the early 1960s. Although never a member of the Judson group, she worked in an experimental vein not unlike Judson's own during the Judson era. She wanted to remove some previous guiding assumptions from dance and consider what new things dance might do. But from the start, Tharp took eclecticism to an extreme that usually impressed viewers as quite theatrical, in contrast to the reduction inherent in the Judson manner. She was never really a minimalist, nor did she choreograph for nondancers. Instead, she preferred to regard performance as a special event set apart from, and more intensely prepared for than, most moments in everyday life.

Tharp enjoyed some recognition from the beginning of her choreographic career, but she made a leap into the public eye in the 1970s. For the Joffrey Ballet she choreographed *Deuce Coupe* (1973), to be danced to the music of the Beach Boys before a commissioned graffiti backdrop. The work displayed Tharp's signature—a witty, fast-paced amalgam of popular, classical and modern movements, along with the aggressively intense, exuberant attack of her dancers. Later works built on this style, even those choreographed in a classical mode, including *Push Comes to Shove* (1976) and *Nine Sinatra Songs* (1976).

Like Tharp, Alvin Ailey thrived on eclecticism. His distinctive version fused jazz, modern and African-American dance and music into a theatrical experience that never stinted on emotion and always spoke for African-American cultures as well as the modern-dance art form. In dances like *Revelations* (1960) and *Cry* (1971), Ailey pulled experience from his own life and made it universally understandable. Even after his death, the Alvin Ailey American Dance Theater remains vital. It performs lyric, narrative and more abstract pieces by Ailey and other choreographers, such as Ulysses Dove and Bill T. Jones.

Altogether different from both Tharp and Ailey, the Pilobolus collective was and is uniquely eclectic. Founded on a whim in 1970 at Dartmouth College, the group originally consisted of mostly untrained students and their teacher, Alison Chase. The group attacked dance with athletic vigor and virtuosity, fashioning works that looked like gymnastic fantasies done purely for the exhilaration of the experience. Although the cast of dancers has changed over the years, Pilobolus's aesthetic has remained fairly constant. The company blends dance with physical feats and is best known for building sculptural constructions of human bodies. Because the members of the company work collaboratively on most dances and rely to a great extent on improvisation as a mainstay compositional technique, Pilobolus is reminiscent of Judson.

Mark Morris studied and performed modern, folk and ballet before organizing his own company to present his dances in the 1980s. Like his contemporaries, he combines diverse elements and tendencies in his work, from the Baroque to the Balkan and from the East Indian to the Duncanesque. His parodic version of the ballet *The Nutcracker*, called *The Hard Nut* (1991), includes pointe work in some portions and shows how a revisionary sensibility can borrow selectively from past dance traditions and even mock them while moving ahead into the future.

Many other choreographers, dancers and companies have helped define and develop modern, postmodern and contemporary dance. Partly as a result of the American dance "boom" of the late 1960s and 1970s, partly as a result of the growth of pop culture, contemporary dance experienced a growth spurt at the end of the 20th century. With the aid of public and private funding, television exposure, and the confluence of allied arts on the stage at dance concerts, modern dance has remained a distinctly American art form.

CONTACT IMPROVISATION

A technique and philosophy of movement with social and political implications, contact improvisation emerged from the work of postmodern choreographer Steve Paxton in the 1970s. Others later adopted the method, which has changed the way dance is created and how it feels. The point of contact is to risk and sustain a direct physical relation with the ground and with other people.

As a compositional method, contact snubs the usual goals of choreography; as a way of dancing, it neglects the usual goals of performance.

Instead, contact is governed by a communal principle and by an interest in inventiveness without prescription. Dancing that employs the technique is shared among the members of a small ensemble according to the give-and-take of touch and the shifting of weight. Although contact is based on partnerships, the dancing extends beyond them, creating a kind of community in action.

At the dance studio, contacters, as they are sometimes called, begin with a warm-up. Unlike other dancers, they do it in an oddly supine fashion, for they rely on gravity as a positive physical collaborator. One dancer might lie on her back while her partner lifts her arm gently from the floor and carefully, rhythmically, turns it to and fro in the air. Another might walk on all fours, with her legs more or less straight, her face close to the floor. Some dancers pair up and rest their backs together, while others roll around slowly.

After warming up, contact dancers practice falls, a hallmark element of contact style. Because the method demands that dancers give in graciously to the benign forces of gravity and momentum, they must learn how to let their weight meet the ground without fear of injury.

They also learn how to share weight with one another. In a duet, the basic unit of contact dancing, the couple does not conceal or hold back their true weight. Rather, partners let their weight rest fully on each other, no matter how small or large each may be.

A dancer who does a handstand may seem virtuosic in contact's terms, but the movement's climactic moment comes when his feet touch the ground at the end. Two dancers who lie on top of each other, back to back, the lower raised up on his arms and legs and the upper completely relaxed, probe the limits of physical trust and intimacy. In faster-paced episodes of improvisation, dancers may utter odd sounds as they make discoveries or follow whims that take them by surprise. Floppy, skipping movements may metamorphose without warning into lifts or falls. Two partners may bring their torsos together before launching into a series of hops.

Devoted contacters reject choreography, an art of premeditation. As they follow spontaneous inspiration, they seek access to a source of energy larger than themselves—a goal shared by many other forms of dance.

Dance on Stage and Screen

Dancing has always been part of American mass entertainment. Rooted largely in social dance styles rather than formal arts, such as classical ballet and modern dance, the dancing seen on stage and screen in the United States constitutes a performing art in its own right. Humble and familiar in origin, and accessible to a much larger audience than the elite forms, this kind of dance has an honored place among the distinctly American popular arts.

Of the numerous influences that blended into stage and screen dancing, one of the most important came from the southern states in the 19th century. There, in plantation slave quarters, various American art forms got their start: Jazz, tap dancing, minstrelsy and vaudeville all trace their lineage back to the rough-hewn communal amusements created by slaves for their own enjoyment from the wealth of knowledge they had brought from Africa on slave ships. Whites did eventually play a role as audiences, performers, impresarios, promoters and, frequently, exploiters, but these popular forms remained the inventions of African-Americans.

Some of their dances served religious or ritual purposes, others celebratory and recreational purposes. On the plantations, African forms evolved to meet the needs and realities of a harsh and restricted life. Slaves mixed African, Caribbean and certain European styles they were exposed to for the first time to create entirely new dances and techniques. These included such imitative "animal dances" as the pigeon wing, the buck dance and the buck and wing (a synthesis of the clog dance and the jig), as well as different versions of European social dancing and, significantly, the cakewalk.

At first, slaves danced among themselves at their leisure, but their skill and imagination gradually attracted enthusiastic white audiences (the families of plantation owners), who invited slaves into their homes to perform. Slave-holders sometimes pitted their own slaves against each other or against those of other masters in dance competitions. Often, the object was to select the couple with the best cakewalk.

Minstrel-Show Dancing

Plantation dance contests and performances eventually inspired white performers to imitate black dancing in minstrel shows. Before that, African-American performance styles had rarely been seen in American theaters, although an acting troupe called The African Company had appeared at a theater in New York City from 1821 to 1823. The official birth of minstrelsy dates from 1828, when Thomas Dartmouth "Daddy" Rice (1808–60) debuted as "Jim Crow" in a song-and-dance act. As legend has it, Rice, a white man, admired the informal performances of an unnamed elderly black man and copied him in his own act. Rice danced to the song "Jump Jim Crow" in what has been called a cross between a jig and a shuffle—a sort of loose-limbed comic caper.

Whatever the particulars of his show, Rice helped establish a hugely popular theatrical form that thrived for the next fifty years—white men lampooning black men before paying white audiences—although these performances in blackface no doubt bore little resemblance to authentic black dancing. Along with William Henry Lane (1825–52), a black performer who danced as "Master Juba," Rice served as a model for the many minstrel troupes that began to make a name for themselves in the 1840s, such as the Virginia Minstrels. Black performers entered minstrelsy only after emancipation in the 1860s. By then, the character of the form—physical grotesqueries, slavish docility and genial pratfalls—was already firmly established. The first minstrel company run by blacks was the Plantation Minstrel Company; Primrose and West's Forty Whites and Thirty Blacks, founded in 1893, was an integrated troupe.

In minstrel shows, an emcee introduced a series of acts involving comedy, singing and dancing by a chorus and soloists. A dance known as the walk-around—a sort of full-company buck-and-wing—was a regular feature, as was the breakdown, known sometimes as the hoedown. Also frequently performed were the essence dance, the chicken flutter, the burlesque African polka and others.

Vaudeville and Tap Dancing

As minstrelsy faded in popularity, other forms began to take its place, including circuses, carnivals, theater and vaudeville. When it opened in 1852, the stage version of Harriet Beecher Stowe's (1811–96) novel *Uncle Tom's Cabin* gave black entertainers one of their first opportunities to act in a mainstream play. Vaudeville began to take off after its 1881 debut at Tony Pastor's New Fourteenth Street Theatre in New York. In 1889, *The Creole Show,* a minstrellike show produced by African-Americans, hit New York and introduced Dora Dean (1872–1950) and Charles Johnson (1871–1950) to a wide public. Johnson and Dean later launched their own popular and enduring vaudeville act. Conceived and performed solely by African-Americans, the musical *A Trip to Coontown* (1898) made the first significant departure from the minstrel format. Not long after, in 1913, *Darktown Follies* premiered in Harlem, with momentous consequences.

Follies differed from minstrel shows in that it was more narrative and romantic and less of a madcap mélange. Of all its elements, the show's dancing had the strongest impact, especially a dance called "Ballin' the Jack," which soon started a craze. *Darktown Follies* helped establish Harlem as a center for black cultural life, where people from far and wide could come to take in a show, to dance at the Savoy Ballroom and listen to music in various nightclubs.

For the most part, vaudeville acts traveled the country via circuits of theaters, such as the Orpheum, the Pantages and the Loews circuits. Most vaudeville circuits were all-white, but the Theater Owners Booking Association (T.O.B.A.) represented black artists. Performers nicknamed the T.O.B.A. "Tough on Black Asses" because they had to weather racial intolerance almost anywhere they performed. The most celebrated single vaudeville house was probably New York's Palace Theatre, but practically every major city boasted a handful of vaudeville theaters. Even most smaller towns had at least one vaudeville venue. By the late 1910s, American vaudeville theaters numbered in the thousands. They presented a motley assortment of acts that could include trained animals, slapstick, female impersonators, novelty musicians, a capella vocalists, magicians and, of course, tap dancers. Via the circuit, vaudeville brought dance entertainment to large numbers of Americans throughout the country.

In 1921, at the start of the Harlem Renaissance, an outstanding piece of musical theater capitalized on the earlier successes of African-American artists. *Shuffle Along* was an all-black, full-scale orchestral entertainment with a chorus line including the as-yet-undiscovered Josephine Baker), glamorous stars and impressive tap dancing. Many other African-American musicals followed in its wake. The Apollo Theatre in Harlem presented scores of great acts, offering stage shows, movies and newsreels from morning till night. *Runnin' Wild* (1923) brought the Charleston dance style to a broad audience, while *Blackbirds of 1928* won fame for tap-dancer Bill "Bojangles" Robinson. Much later, Robinson would go on to appear with Shirley Temple (born 1928) as an actor and dancer in the movies.

Robinson, considered tap's leading man, danced in good company, for many superlative black tap dancers took to the vaudeville stage. Although tap was danced by whites as well, African-Americans invented it, refined it and interpreted its many rhythms from the 1800s to the present. Tap entered its heyday at the turn of the century and enjoyed a swell of popularity for about thirty years. As popular music evolved from ragtime to jazz to swing to bebop, tap developed on a parallel course. Tap may also have been a response to the mechanistic clatter and fast pace of life in the industrial age, but it drew on an amalgam of ancient African, English and Irish traditions. It seemed somehow to express the mood of Americans, for it was performed on a mass scale in musicals, revues and burlesque acts, at speakeasies and on street corners.

Tappers ranged from the very young to the very old and from superior soloists to bevies of glamorous competents. Willie Covan (1897–1988), for example, started his career as what was called a "pick" (short for *pickaninny,* a derogatory term for a black child) at age five in Chicago. Picks, a staple in show business, danced, sang, acted, joked and carried on in choruses as backup for a star, usually female. Covan graduated from vaudeville to movie musicals during the 1930s and had a pronounced influence on other dancers as chief dance teacher at MGM studios.

While many tappers were black men, some women—white and black—drew a great deal of attention to the dance form. Most female tappers worked as chorines, hoofers assembled in large groups that executed perfectly synchronized dancing. A few, however, stood out. Although considered rather less than a whiz at buck dancing, her specialty, Ruby Keeler won by charm what others did purely by mastery. Already dancing at thirteen in a George M. Cohan production, *The Rise of Rosie O'Reilly* (1923), she worked on Broadway and in nightclubs. Late in the 1920s, while working in Los Angeles, she met and married singer-actor Al Jolson. Keeler somewhat reluctantly appeared in movies, most notably *42nd Street* (1933), *Footlight Parade* (1933), *Dames* (1934) and *Gold Diggers of 1933* (1933). She capped her career in 1970 with the Broadway revival of *No, No, Nanette.*

Tappers were a potent presence on the national vaudeville circuits, but they also appeared in nightclubs, which were local by nature. Harlem's Cotton Club, one of the most famous, opened in 1923 to present all-black revues to white-only audiences. With acts such as singer Lena Horne (born 1917), dancers Bill Robinson and the Nicholas Brothers, jazz musician Cab Calloway (born 1907), and various comedians, the Club was a huge success until it closed in 1939. Another Harlem venue, the Hoofer's Club, also made New York a center of tap talent that drew dancers from all over to test their mettle in the best of company.

Dance in the Movies

In the 1930s, vaudeville waned and tap moved into the movie theater, both in films and as live acts before or after screenings. Enormously talented dancers and choreographers, such as Gene Kelly (born 1912), Fred Astaire (1899–1987), Hermes Pan (1911–90), Busby Berkeley (1895–1976), Shirley Temple, Ann Miller (born 1923) and Eleanor Powell (1912–82) brought tap to audiences on an unprecedented scale.

Astaire and Kelly shone particularly brightly as stars of the genre, not only on screen but behind the scenes as planners, masterminds and imaginative thinkers. In order to bring dance to the new medium of film in a way that would serve both well, producers, directors and cinematographers had to learn how to present it. Dance directors, as they were called, engineered the fit between dance and drama and so assumed an important role in the movies. Included among their number were Pan, Nick Castle (1910–68) and Charles Walters (1911–82). Preparing both dancers and nondancing actors and actresses for their work on the silver screen were dance coaches, such as Louis DaPron (born 1913), as well as a few ballet teachers, such as the English-born Ernest Belcher (1882–1973).

Various cinematic innovations allowed filmmakers to translate dance to the movies. Working closely with Pan as well as with composer George Gershwin, Astaire advised cameramen to minimize the use of cutaway shots, because they kept the camera from shooting the dancer's whole figure, focusing instead on less important details of feet, scenery, chorus or other distractions. This technique tended to interrupt the flow of the dance for the viewer so that it could not be observed from start to finish, as on the stage. As the movie musical developed, so too did new camera angles that enabled dance to be presented as an artful, live spectacle. Even dances that did not really entail much movement, such as some of Busby Berkeley's lavish production numbers, were craftily filmed to suggest motion.

Of course, Astaire also worked in front of the camera. He became especially famous for his dancing with partners (especially Ginger Rogers [born 1911]) in such films as *The Gay Divorcé* (1934), *Top Hat* (1935) and *Shall We Dance* (1937). Likewise, Kelly won acclaim for his innovations in film dancing. He made most of his contributions in front of the camera, drawing on a range of sources— ballet, modern, vaudeville hoofing and sheer athletic bravado—and merging them fluently. He took great pains to perfect his dancing in extended rehearsal periods and, when possible, insisted that dance scenes be shot on location. *An American in Paris* (1951), *On the Town* (1949) and *Singin' in the Rain* (1952) survive as examples of the way in which Kelly's high style combined with his boyish, knockabout vigor. The injection of street realism into later movie musicals, such as *West Side Story* (1961), might never have come about without his influence.

Although ballet itself—with a few exceptions, including *The Red Shoes* (1948) and *The Turning Point* (1977)—never made much of a mark on the movies, one ballet choreographer did. George Balanchine, the Russian-born founder of the New York City Ballet, eagerly met the challenge of creating dance for the movies, a medium he believed possessed great potential for this art form. He worked on *The Goldwyn Follies of 1937, I Was an Adventuress* (1940) and *On Your Toes* (1936).

The tap sequences of movie musicals ran the gamut from the ornately elaborate crowd scenes favored by Berkeley to the supremely elegant partnership between a man and a woman favored by Astaire. The styles of individual dancers varied as much as did their dances. Charles "Honi" Coles (1918–93), for instance, personified the lyric intricacy of rhythm tap. A onetime vaudevillian best known for his performance as the Scarecrow in *The Wizard of Oz* (1939), Ray Bolger (1904–87) was a prime exponent of legomania, a kind of comic, complex, seemingly awkward and fantastically double-jointed tap. The Four Step Brothers incorporated splits, flips and other gymnastics in their acts, while Jimmy Slyde (born 1930) gained fame for his technique of sliding and tapping. Inspired by classical music, Paul Draper (born 1909) originated ballet-tap; Brenda Bufalino (born 1950) later found similar inspiration in bebop. As tap specialties developed, many dancers chose to specialize, although some remained versatile. One such generalist was Peg Leg Bates (born 1908), a one-legged dancer who seemed capable of any kind of tap.

Musical Theater and Beyond

In the 1940s, tap began to slip in popularity; by the 1950s, movie musicals had also lost much of their audience. Some popular dancers found a new forum on television variety shows, like Ed Sullivan's, but more turned to musical theater. Starting in the 1940s, that medium underwent a transformation that opened new doors for professional hoofers.

In 1943 Rodgers and Hammerstein's *Oklahoma!* forever changed American musical theater. The play tackled weighty subjects, liberating musicals from their role as mere light entertainment to one for expressing serious concerns. In addition, *Oklahoma!* benefited from the genius of choreographer Agnes de Mille, who developed a unique style of dance for the production by blending American folk dance with ballet. The combined innovations in music and dance earned *Oklahoma!* a five-year run on Broadway and a permanent place in the annals of American musical theater.

Fourteen years after *Oklahoma!,* dance innovation in musical theater continued with *West Side Story* (1957). This modern retelling of *Romeo and Juliet* was choreographed and directed by dancer Jerome Robbins, with music by Leonard Bernstein. If de Mille captured the spirit of American folk dance in her work, Robbins appropriated the gestures of street-hardened youths in his. Robbins's startling choreography marked the ascendancy of the choreographer as director in American musical theater.

Choreographers continued their reign in the 1960s, with the energetic and sensual work of Bob Fosse, director of *Pippin* (1972), *Chicago* (1975) and *Dancin'* (1978). Director Michael Bennett (1934–87) brought musical-theater choreography to new heights when he created a musical about dancing in musicals, *A Chorus Line* (1975). His later shows included *Ballroom* (1978), *Dreamgirls* (1981), *My One and Only* (1983) and *Grand Hotel* (1989).

The newest medium for dance as entertainment is the rock video, on which performers execute intricately choreographed fantasies. Among the major lights of this form are Michael Jackson, Janet Jackson and Madonna. They have brought professional dancing to a new pitch by interpreting the latest social dance forms and communicating the results to an audience of millions.

JANE GOLDBERG

Tap's roots are mostly male and black, but Jane Goldberg (born 1948)—white, female and Jewish—has made a career of the genre. She possesses few of the usual attributes of tappers except the most basic: dedication and talent. Born long after tap's heyday, she trained first as a modern dancer and then worked as a journalist. Her life changed when, in 1972, she saw *Carefree* (1938), her first Fred Astaire–Ginger Rogers movie.

Astaire's performance inspired Goldberg to take up tap. But whereas Astaire regarded tap dancing as simple entertainment, Goldberg doesn't. She is a historian of tap whose seminars, articles and archives have almost as much significance for the form as her dancing does. Her Changing Times Tap Dancing Company is dedicated to the preservation of tap, but Goldberg also wants to secure a future for the art by exploring and expanding its conventions. Because she considers tap not only a kind of dancing but also a form of percussion music, her experiments follow a different logic from that of many contemporary tappers.

In order to study tap when it was at a low ebb,

Goldberg had to track down once-celebrated hoofers who had slipped into obscurity. She managed to locate John Bubbles (1902–87), Charles "Honi" Coles (1917–93) and others. Sneaking into the exclusive Copasetics Ball in Harlem, she watched dancers in action and danced with them. She interviewed the tappers and set about taping their oral histories.

Her efforts, however, have not ended with study. Goldberg has organized "By Word of Foot" festivals, where rarely seen tap masters talk about tap and dance for aspiring tappers. When she organized her company, she began presenting the best of the senior generation of tappers in performance with enthusiastic young dancers like herself. Changing Times has toured the United States and Europe, winning praise for programs that include authentic, old-fashioned hoofing, as well as Goldberg's innovations. For example, Goldberg choreographs what she calls topical tap dances, in which she raps about politics, sex and feminism while she taps. Although she is not the only youthful tapper around, Goldberg is considered one of tap's most vocal, offbeat and effective advocates.

International Folk Dance

In nearly all cultures, people dance. Indeed, it seems more exceptional not to dance than to do so, and only a few communities—including, apparently, certain Sumatran and Indonesian peoples—have refrained. The purpose of dancing varies among cultures, according to their history and circumstances. Dance can serve as court entertainment for rulers, as a mode of worship, or as a rite meant to ensure good hunting or abundant crops. It may extol a monarch, propitiate a god or imitate a river; it may be seen in the highly wrought gestural language of South India, or in the intimate companion to song in Chinese opera. Throughout the world, dance is ancient, essential and highly diverse.

Africa

The African dance tradition incorporates diverse styles from hundreds of cultures across the continent. From the Ivory Coast to the Sudan, dance plays a central role in traditional African spiritual and social life. Each important community event—a birth, death or even the coronation of a new leader—includes the traditional dances. In Mali's Dogon Territory, for example, mourning ceremonies feature a dance to help the souls of the dead depart from earth. Villagers commonly employ dance for healing and for the exorcism of demons as well.

Most African dances take one of two patterns: the circle or the line. Common to warrior cultures, line dances include the yake, a Nigerian men's dance enacted with axe-sticks and spears. Yake dancers stand shoulder to shoulder as they walk and stamp with deeply bent knees, throwing their axes into the air as they leave the line. Touches of individuality appear more often in group circle dances, which may combine solo performances as part of the overall design. For example, the Olu Kanaanwa dance for unmarried girls gives each an opportunity to shine in a brief solo performance. Whatever their basic form, African dances usually separate men and women, or allow one sex to join the other's dance only at a predetermined moment.

As African dancers move, they generally maintain a low center of gravity, close to the earth. In one common posture, dancers lean over with their torso almost parallel to the ground. In another, they arch their spines backward while pushing the hips forward. Rhythm drives each step and movement of African dance; participants maintain rhythms of great intricacy, dancing to the accompaniment of percussion instruments, song or both.

Also integral to many African dances are masks. Masked dancers perform chiefly in religious rites, representing animals, nature spirits, ancestors, gods and other elements of African belief. Masks come in many sizes, designs and shapes. Many recall antelopes, hares, lions, monkeys and other animals. Still others represent typical village characters, such as a young girl, a thief or a farmer. Masks can be abstract as well as representational. For example, the Awa of the Sangha region wear the sirige mask, essentially a rectangular "face" with a fifteen-foot blade attached to the front. Dancers touch the tip of the blade to the ground while bending backward and forward, marking the boundaries of the horizon. Instead of masks, some dancers may use colored face paint.

Asia

China: In Quinghai Province, archaeologists found a neolithic earthenware bowl etched with dancers, demonstrating the art's antiquity in China. Most ancient dances depicted daily work. Dance entered a golden age during the T'ang dynasty (618–907), when the royal court enjoyed lavish masked dances as well as simpler Buddhist promenades, brought to China from Japan and Korea. During this era, rulers collected the traditional songs and dances of the Han, a Chinese ethnic group residing in the north. Han dances were compiled into a book called *Arts of Wen Kang,* which is essentially a description of Han dances, especially masked ones, and a dervish-style whirling dance.

About 1000 B.C., China entered an era of expanded foreign trade and commerce that stimulated cultural growth. Folk dance gained in popularity, as did acrobatics, wrestling, and poetic dramas set to music. One dance in particular, the flower drum dance, became a mainstay. Performed to intricate drumbeats, this dance required dancers to assume poses that echoed the beats. Many variations of the dance developed, such as the Fengyang flower drum, which included a gong as well as a drum.

Over hundreds of years, Chinese classic dance evolved into a sophisticated, theatrical art form, culminating in the golden age of the Peking Opera at the end of the 18th century. The opera wove music, movement, song and story into spectacular dramas. Popular Peking Opera works included a dramatization of Lo Kuan-chung's 14th-century novel *The Romance of Three Kingdoms.*

India: This ancient culture engages in several traditional dance forms, some of which date back two thousand years or more. Indeed, according to Hindu teaching, Nataraja (a manifestation of the god Shiva) set the universe in motion by dancing. In India, then, dance is a means of worship as well as a form of entertainment.

Bharata natyam is India's primary classical dance form. Attributed to the god Brahma, who created it as a religious rite for his followers, it was for centuries performed devotionally in temples. A solo dance for females, bharata natyam is highly formalized, intricate and wildly rhythmic. Dancers use their hands and face to perform detailed gestures while stamping out a complicated beat. Each movement has a precise narrative, mythological and emotional meaning.

Orissi dance resembles bharata natyam, but its movements are smoother and its dynamics less staccato. It has a more languorous, seductive quality. Kathak, another form, also involves complex beating footwork. It originated as a religious dance in the northern regions of India.

The state of Kerala produced kathakali, a colorful, theatrical dance form designed for mythic storytelling on a lavish scale. Elaborately costumed performers act as well as dance tales from Indian mythology, especially those recounted in the epics *Ramayana* and *Mahabharata.*

Indonesia: In Java and Bali, gamelan music sets the rhythm of the dance. Gamelan requires percussion, woodwind and strings and is performed in a range of five to seven notes. Dancers move with slow, controlled motions, easing from one position to the next with smooth transitions. They depict myths and legends drawn largely from Indian lore. In Java, classic dances include the bedoyo and the serimpi, performed by men. Bali's most famous dance is the legong, a women's dance that tells of a king going to war and leaving his queen and the maiden he loves.

As in India, dancers from Java and Bali draw from a catalog of stylized gestures of the hand, head and eye. Both traditions call for dancers to be adorned with beautiful textiles, either printed by batik or otherwise brilliantly colored. Men and women, for example, wear a *kain,* a cotton cloth folded about the waist. In addition, Javanese and Balinese styles call for headdresses and a wide assortment of masks.

Japan: From the 6th to 16th centuries, Japan benefited from a cultural influx from China and Korea, which included a style of dance now known as gigaku. Simple and elegant, gigaku became integral to Buddhist rites and to the entertainment at royal courts. While enacting stately, ritualized gestures, gigaku dancers wore dazzling costumes and carved, lacquered wood masks. During this era, court dances, called bugaku, provided another form of entertainment for Japanese aristocrats. A synthesis of ancient Chinese, Indian and Korean music and dance, bugaku presented male dancers to the music of drums, bells, flute and panpipe.

Another form of Japanese dance, Nō, gained favor among Samurais in the 14th to 16th centuries. A dance drama, Nō draws on history and legend for its stories about gods, demons, warriors and others, presenting them in three "acts." With exquisitely slow motions, dancers in beautiful masks move to drums, flutes and Buddhist chants. Performers enact Nō dramas only in specially designed theaters, with scrubbed pine boards serving as a backdrop. Nō's repertory includes the classics *The Well-Curb* and *Lady Aoi* by master 15th-century writer Zeami Motokiyo.

Japan's most exalted classic dance is the Kabuki, a theatrical dance dating from the early 17th century. Male dancers weave music, movement and language in their depictions of tragedy and revenge. Playing both men and women, they draw on the traditions of Nō dance and of the puppet play (ningo-shibai), from which Kabuki borrowed its splendid style of scenery. As Kabuki dance-dramas gained popularity, special theaters arose to accommodate them.

While Buddhism inspired many classic dance forms, Shinto beliefs inform the folk dances of Japan, which were first performed during traditional feasts, such as the Festival of the Dead. Dances to Shinto spirits were believed to encourage a plentiful harvest, rain and good fortune. Most included masks representing such animals as boars, herons, horses or deer—or mythic beasts, such as dragons. The lion-mask dance, brought to Japan via China and Korea, became so popular it was adopted by Kabuki.

Korea: In medieval Korea, court dances and masked dances developed into a national art form that blended folk and classical traditions. In particular, the tradition of masked dances and dance plays continued into the modern era. In their most primitive form, masked dances evoke deities and natural spirits, combining religion and folk magic. During the Great Silla era (668–935), dance included acrobatics, pantomime, juggling and swordplay. By the 17th century, the masked folk play, or sandae togam kuk, gained popularity as a widespread form of entertainment. And by the mid-1800s, Koreans delighted in the gu gug, dramatic songs danced to gesture and simple group movements.

Thailand: Thai dance-dramas combine theater, literature, poetry and history. The distinctive style of Thai dance features deeply flexed knees, with fingers and toes curved backward. Transitions from one pose to another are dynamic and sudden. Khon, the most classic form of Thai dance, depicts historic tales. Male dancers not only flex their knees

but also open their legs widely to the equivalent of western ballet's second position. In the traditional Thai female dance, lakhon, dancers bend their knees but keep them together. Dance costumes for both sexes are topped by a *tchedah,* an elaborate headdress of gilded buffalo hide bejeweled with tiny mirrors. The dance of Cambodia mirrors that of neighboring Thailand in all ways but one: Cambodian dance employs only male dancers.

NATYAKALALAYAM

Located in suburban Chicago, the Natyakalalayam school is directed by Hema Rajagopalan, an Indian-born bharata natyam dancer. Her students, mostly the young daughters of Indian immigrants, follow a course of study that combines the demands of an ancient classical Asian dance tradition with Hindu cosmology, Indian history, and informal spiritual counsel. They learn bharata natyam, a South Indian form of dance that looks every bit as old as it is.

At Natyakalalayam, students practice a bent-legged, plié-like stance, from which they stamp, twist and flex their bare feet. With their arms, they articulate a stylized, elaborate series of gestures; their heads, necks and faces express an intricate range of emotions, from the diabolical to the sweetly flirtatious. They may jump from time to time, but they never leave their strictly erect orientation for long. With propriety and exuberance, they dance much as the devadasiyan (temple dancers) did centuries ago.

The many minutely codified poses and movements of the dance include seven nose movements, thirteen poses of the head, thirty-six kinds of glances, twenty-four single-hand positions, thirteen double-hand positions and 108 karanaon, arm movements coordinated with leg movements. Each gesture has a specific meaning that varies with the context and story suggested by particular dances. In addition, bharata natyam dancers need strong acting skills to convey the nine standard emotions to their audiences.

Besides dramatizing spiritual contact between gods or godheads and worshipers, bharata natyam is also a much-admired medium of pure dance. Due partly to the efforts of such disparate dancers and choreographers as Uday Shankar, Anna Pavlova, Ruth St. Denis and Ted Shawn, the bharata natyam tradition has won prestige as perhaps the world's most venerable and easily one of the most intricate dance genres.

Europe

The Balkans: For Balkan people, folk dancing has often provided a statement of cultural pride during periods of foreign domination. The group dance remained popular in the

Balkans long after its decline in the rest of Europe because the Balkans—isolated for centuries under the Ottoman Empire—took longer to learn about the new style, couple dancing. Circle and line dances prevailed for years. Known as kolo, or "wheel," circle dances might be open or closed; similarly, line dances could vary between the straight and the S-shaped. Perhaps the best-known dance to come from the Balkans is the hora, now most closely associated with Israel.

Group dances sometimes highlighted individual performances, such as the calusari from Bulgaria, the rusalije from Bulgaria and the barbunci from Transylvania. In Croatia, villagers preferred the drmesi, in which people formed a basket by reaching around their nearest neighbor and holding the hand of the next dancer. When couple dancing appeared in the Balkans after the end of Ottoman domination, it rarely included physical contact. Bulgaria's rucenica, Serbia's katanka and Romania's geamparalele were all dances in which couples didn't touch.

Eastern Europe: Traditions of the West temper those of the East when it comes to the dances of Eastern European countries. For example, Viennese influences brought the polka to old Bohemia, making it a national dance of the Czech Republic. Like the polka, most Czech dances feature quick turning and lively footwork. In the furiant, another Czech favorite, couples cross the floor in ¾ rhythm, stepping swiftly and furiously. The Slovak Republic's many regional dances include the markovy tance, or poppy dance, which depicts the cultivation of the poppy by farmers.

In Hungary, military themes inspire many of the traditional dances. Strong, staccato movements, heel clicking, and the rattle of spurs all evoke a culture constantly under siege from foreign invaders. The verbunk dance, for example, dates back to an era when a sergeant and his young soldiers would dance in villages to attract recruits. Women's dances include several performed with beautifully embroidered pillows, a traditional gift to brides from their bridesmaids. Women

also dance with men in the csardas, a syncopated courtship dance in which women spin away from, then toward, men with building speed. Often the women use handkerchiefs to link themselves with their partners.

Poland has spawned folk dances of international reputation and popularity, such as the mazurka and the krakowiak. Poland's national dance, the mazurka, includes complex floor patterns and variations, all shouted out by a caller. Originating in Masovia, a region of central Poland, the mazurka's ¾ or ³⁄₂ rhythm was adopted by many other dances. The krakowiak also includes varied floor patterns, many of which dancers improvise. A product of Kraków, the krakowiak requires liveliness and speed with its ²⁄₄ rhythm. Both of these celebrated national dances changed as dancing masters added dramatic flourishes for use in the theater or the ballrooms of European royalty. Similarly, the chodzony—a Polish parade dance of humble origin—gained majesty as the polonaise, a standard processional for the opening of a ball in the early 19th century.

Former Soviet States: In a region as vast as the former Soviet empire, thousands of dances comprise a rich folk tradition. Regional styles create tremendous variety in the dance, yet folk dances throughout the area share many similarities. Most traditions employ the circle dance or khorovod, perhaps the oldest form of dance in the republics. Originally sung by dancers while they moved, the khorovod celebrated nature, harvests, weather and the tilling of the land. In some khorovods, dancers improvised solos in the center of the circle—a contest highlighting strength or beauty. Regional adaptations of the dance include the Ukrainian metelitza and the Russian pourgaviyouga, which send dancers into a flurry of motion, imitating a snowstorm.

Several traditions stand out among the former Soviet republics. Ukrainian dances are distinguished in the celebration of athletic ability; quick and light movements highlight agility and endurance. Taken from the Cossack tradition, male dances include the gopak, in which a dancer demonstrates his dexterity and strength with soaring and complex leaps and steps. In Byelorussia, dances blend Ukrainian and Russian styles, celebrating the earth while soaring above it. The most famous Byelorussian dance, the krizachok, contains calculated missteps designed to provoke laughter. In Georgia, styles for male and female dances differ dramatically. Women emphasize gliding steps and graceful carriage, while men celebrate daring horsemanship and fierceness. One male dance, the khorumi, dramatizes a battle in the mountains, imitating the galloping and leaping of horses.

France: Linked with the traditions of Catalonia in Spain, the troubadours of medieval France were for the most part traveling Provençal entertainers who sang songs intended as accompaniment to dancing. As they wandered the countryside, their music encouraged the growth of new dance forms. Later, the French imported country dances from England; these remain popular today. In the 16th century, French nobles began to systematize and refine dancing. A monk named Thoinot Arbeau wrote *Orchésographie* (1588), a guide for dancers that outlined the social and technical goals of the dance. The book was influential in courtly circles in France and Spain.

In the 17th century, Louis XIV, a patron of dance and a dancer himself, took the art to a new level, staging elaborate masques, theatrical spectacles and balls at Versailles. The Sun King helped lay some of the foundations of ballet, both in France and indirectly in Russia, as French style traveled to Russia in the time of Peter the Great. However, French influence on ballet began to decline in the 18th century.

Germany and Austria: Roving German Minnesingers ("love singers") made music for dancers in the 12th and 13th centuries. At that time, the Germans favored group dances over those for couples. For example, the Reigen, a chain dance, showed up on many occasions, from nuptials to harvests. Germans had their own versions of the maypole and sword dances popular in Britain, though other dances seem to have been peculiarly German. One dance, for instance, imitated death throes and was performed during the era of the Black Death. German artisans contrived their own guild dances and some villages also invented their own unique forms.

Dances that still prevail in Germany are of relatively recent vintage, with few more than 150 years old. Contredanses (country dances) are popular in the northern part of the country, while couple dances dominate the central section. A kind of step dance, the Schwarzwälder Bauerntanz, reconciles opposing assemblies of women and men. And in the Schuhplattler, men light into exuberant displays of clapping, kicking and jumping to win female approval. The Ländler, originally from Austria, is an early version of the waltz, in which a woman, held closely by her partner, is turned rhythmically and occasionally kissed.

Greece: Greek celebrations, large or small, call for dancing. Born out of the traditions of the country's shepherds, fishermen and farmers, Greek dances contain rudimentary combinations of steps and floor patterns that are repeated in varying combinations. Moving to the sound of music, dancers step to the side and close their feet, or walk toe-to-heel. As the dance gains momentum, participants may turn, whirl, jump and hop, but these flourishes are not integral to the dance.

While stepping, dancers flow in and out of circles, sometimes creating long chains by holding each other's hands, wrists or shoulders. Sometimes they grasp the ends of hand-kerchiefs across the circle. Traditionally led by men, the circles can form around a solo dancer who performs feats of athleticism. Women and men once danced separately, but now join together in such dances as the tesh-koto.

Italy: Dancing has been an important part of Italian cultural life since the Renaissance, when dancing teachers became established and helped define professional, courtly and peasant dance forms. In the courtly realm, dance teachers were highly respected and in-fluential, serving as dance coaches and some-times as dance classifiers. Italian dance teachers codified the distinction between danze, couple dances appropriate for anyone, and balli, dances with pantomime meant for aristocrats. In balli, nobles often acted out the political and social intrigues of their lives.

Italian dances that have survived to the present include sword and maypole variants and a descendant of the old saltarello, a court-ship dance for a couple or a larger group. The quick-paced and dramatic tarantella from Apulia, originally danced to help expel the tarantula's poison from the body, is now mainly a dance of courtship. Rather like the tarantella is the furlana, a passionate and un-bridled wooing dance for one or several couples.

Spain and Portugal: Spain boasts an excep-tionally rich ethnic dance tradition. Appar-ently older than most other European forms, Spanish dance has roots in Mediterranean genres dating from 1600 B.C. Also unique to Spanish dance was the pronounced Moorish influence from the 8th to the 15th centuries. Folk dances vary in different regions of Spain and include the sevillanas from Andalusia and the ball de cascabels from Catalonia. The jota, one type of which hails from Aragon and another from Valencia, is a couple dance per-formed to a background of castanets. It is

distinguished by the virtuosity of the male partner in executing quick footwork and pre-cise leaps.

A number of forms, however, are practiced on a wide enough scale that they have the character of national dances. Like the jota, the fandango (originally Andalusian) is spir-ited and highly rhythmic. Performed by a soloist or by a couple, it follows triple time and can be accompanied by castanets, tam-bourines and/or violins. Bolero, another type of Spanish dance, was originally a popular form, but Italian ballet teachers transformed it into a more balletic style. It is now known as a dance of delicate, light and precise style that evokes the daintiness of ballet with its footwork and airiness.

Spanish flamenco dancing is renowned for its passion and technical challenges, as well as for its accompanying music, provided by guitars, singing, castanets and hand clap-ping. Brought to Spain by gypsies in the mid–15th century, the dance may be of Egyptian or Indian origin. It reflects Asian dance traditions in elegant, narrowly cir-cumscribed arm movements and a highly stylized stance. Moreover, the fierce rhyth-mic stamping for which flamenco is also known bears some resemblance to types of Indian dancing. An improvisational form, it is danced by women and men, often but not always in duets, while musicians play and serve as a kind of participatory audience. The dance often represents erotic combat leading to symbolic possession.

United Kingdom and Ireland: Dancing dates far back in English history. For instance, scholars have identified a danced fertility rite of the Anglo-Saxon era, which was meant to mark the occasion of Easter. During medieval times, roving entertainers brought news, leg-endary tales and frisky, sportsmanlike physi-cal dancing from village to village. The carol, which melded dance with song, arose early in the English tradition. Whereas carols were rural dances accompanied only by singing, the branle required instrumental accompaniment and was danced at court. Other dances well known in England included the saraband (a favorite of Charles II), the slow-moving measure (a form of the French basse danse), the hey (descended from the farandole), the courante, the galliard (a virtuosic solo for a man attended by a female partner), and la volta. Elizabeth I was particularly fond of the last two.

Organized as line dances and as rounds, country dances were performed by an assemblage of couples. One type of country dance, the jig, was meant for a solitary man, but occasionally was danced by a couple. The jig was the progenitor of the galliard and the gigue. Country dances originated in England, traveled to France where they were called contredanses, and also crossed the Atlantic, transformed into American and Canadian square dances.

The morris dance is thought to have predated the Christian age. Its source may have been indigenous, it may have come from a Moorish dance of 16th-century Spain, or it may have derived from later Moorish dances. Whatever its origins, it developed into many different versions over the centuries. Traditionally danced in blackface, the morris required an all-male cast wearing bells on their legs.

Maypole dances are another form traditional to and popular in England. Performed on May 1st to mark the return of the growing season, these dances center around a symbolic tree with ribbons attached. The dances are not exclusively British, however; they are commonly found in other parts of Europe, as well as India and the United States.

The sword dance is believed to have entered England via Danish invaders in the 6th century. Like the morris dance, it called for blackface. Performed in winter, it served as a communal rite of death and rebirth. Nowadays, the sword dance is executed by half a dozen men in a ring, each wielding a sword.

Hailing from Scotland, another type of sword dance demands extremely quick and precise footwork around two crossed swords. Other Scottish dances also remain distinct from English forms. In the 16th century, for instance, the Scots devised their own form of the branle. Scottish reels, flings and morris dances all took on their own particular flavor as well. Danced on the tips of the toes with bagpipe or vocal accompaniment or no music at all, reels are danced in $\frac{1}{4}$ time by two or more couples. Highland flings express triumph with kicking steps executed in $\frac{1}{4}$ time.

The well-known Irish jig is not exclusively Irish in its origins; the form is reminiscent of Scottish reels. Step dancing, another celebrated Irish genre, is highly rhythmic and springy from the waist down but strikingly still from the waist up. Rather like ice skaters, step dancers clasp their hands behind their backs and take off to a delicate yet powerful stream of pulsing sound. They seem to sprint in place, taking vertical flights in tiny increments.

MAZOWSZE

In 1948, Tadeusz Sygietyński and Mira Ziminská established the Polish folk dance troupe Mazowsze at Karolin, an estate twenty miles from Warsaw. Sygietyński was a composer and folklore scholar who wrote many of Mazowsze's folk tunes and lyrics himself. Ziminská, his wife, was one of Poland's leading actresses, who made her name in the play *Soldier of Madagascar*.

When they set to work, Polish dances were for the most part performed by peasants in provincial living rooms and village watering places during religious holidays and winter doldrums. Opera houses and their audiences scorned folk dance. Sygietyński and Ziminská started a school at Karolin and recruited children to study a demanding curriculum of ballet, music and folk dance. They also traveled far and wide, searching for the roots of Polish dance. Most Polish folk dances date from the 18th century, some as early as the 14th, but older generations had kept them alive. The school at Karolin closed in 1956, a few years after the company began intensive touring. Since then, company dancers have been chosen by audition. Successful candidates are ballet-trained, musical, exuberant and robust.

Now a 120-member ensemble of dancers, singers and musicians, Mazowsze has thirty-nine dances gathered from twenty regions of Poland in its repertory. Every dance has been edited down to its essence for the theater. True to tradition, the dancers perform opulently shod, sashed and beribboned; one costume alone can weigh as much as twenty-seven pounds. Mazowsze takes ninety-eight wardrobe trunks on tour to accommodate more than one thousand costume changes in each concert. The many-colored wools, velvets, laces, hand-embroidery and floral headdresses worn in performance are strictly authentic. Some costumes have been recon-structed from fabric originally used in rural dances many years ago. Others are made by peasants expressly for Mazowsze.

A typical Mazowsze program includes such old favorites as the sprightly polka and courtly polonaise, plus wedding dances, tatras and other mountain dances, and numbers performed by dancers dressed as storks and frogs. The twenty or so dances featured in a concert are performed full tilt and without pause, requiring great stamina. Songs, brisk steps, striped and whirling skirts, and such props as whips, sticks and hatchets turn a Mazowsze performance into an exciting and exhausting marathon.

One dance, the krakowiak, is named in memory of Krak, a legendary Polish hero who killed a dragon and then founded Kraków, Poland's capital until 1596. Like most Polish folk dances, the krakowiak originated as a peasant dance, but it was later borrowed and refined by Polish aristocrats. It is danced by couples moving in a circle to a ¾ rhythm. Metal rings worn on the belts of the male dancers rattle and jangle as the men jump. While dancing, the couples sing about the Vistula River, which flows by Kraków, "As long as the river will flow, so long will Poland live—forever."

Since the death of Sygientyński, Ziminská has served as Mazowsze's sole director, assisted by vice director Jerzy Wojcik. The team has continued to invite Polish septuagenarians with tapping feet to re-create the dances of their youth and remember the lavish costumes they wore.

Middle East

Some of civilization's oldest dances have roots in the Middle East. In ancient Egypt, the annual flooding of the Nile inspired festivals and pageants full of dancing. Adorned with masks and head ornaments, groups of dancers happily greeted the river goddess, Isis. Astronomers, regarded as high priests, ordered a special dance of the stars, in which participants moved from east to west, mirroring the path of the sun. The Egyptians' imitation of the movements of the stars has often been cited as the first circle dance, the format of most Middle Eastern dances. In ancient Persia, practitioners of Zoroastrianism danced and chanted the gatha, a sacrificial rite using fire.

Middle Easterners of many religions incorporate dance into their rituals. Persian Sufi dancers whirl in ecstasy in the zuleyka and the yusuf. In the secular realm, young men, called *khawal,* partake in the Egyptian tradition of impersonating women in dance. Applying henna and kohl to their faces, they dance in groups of three or four, usually in celebration of a birth or marriage.

In the Jewish state of Israel, weddings and other celebrations are often accompanied by the hora, a circle dance of Romanian origin. Participants place their hands on their neighbors' shoulders and, in ¾ time, take a sliding step to the right followed by a step-hop to the left. Sometimes the circle breaks into two concentric rings that move in opposite directions.

SUFI DANCING

Some religions prohibit dancing as a profane activity, but in others, the dance is a means or a proof of faith. Among the Sufis, a mystic Islamic fellowship whose philosophy has ancient roots in the Middle East, dancing has traditionally been considered a holy thing, closely associated with spiritual matters. Characterized by ritual spinning, Sufi or dervish dancing is practiced both by high-ranking members within the faith and by the rank and file. The point is to partake in the dance rather than to watch it. Because the dance is a form of worship, it is meant for the many, not the few.

Different associations of Sufis observe somewhat different practices. The dancing might be characterized as meditation in movement or as a grounded experience in ecstasy. Both a devotional rite and a down-to-earth folk dance, Sufi dancing does not necessarily require special costumes or mastery of difficult steps, although some practitioners may prefer them. In its simplest form, it calls for little or no music and relies instead on relatively straightforward chants and prayers. The most refined forms of dervish dancing, however, can become quite complex.

Sufi dancers dance in a circle, often holding hands. Most dances involve repetitious circular movement, singing the praises of Allah, and making spiritual contact with the other dancers. As the dancers move round and round, they might hum, bow, stamp, take breaths and clasp hands. The circular dances seem to have no beginning or end.

North America and the Caribbean

Canada: Before Europeans laid claim to the northern portion of North America, the region's first inhabitants—Eskimos and various other Native American groups—performed ancient dances of their own devising. The newcomers brought dances with them and gradually fashioned Canadian dance traditions from these raw materials.

The truly indigenous dances of Canada evolved to meet the demands of life's fundamental occasions: birth, death, puberty, war and celebration. The prairie chicken dance of the Blackfeet and other tribes, for example, was inspired by the circular courtship dances of grouse and turkey. It required men to display grace and prowess while wearing flamboyant costumes, for the amusement of women. During the dance, the strutting men passed through successive concentric circles. The green corn dance, meanwhile, expressed thanks for good harvests through a ritual of symbolic destruction and renewal. And the scalp dance of the Algonquins of southern Canada marked the slaughter of members of a rival tribe. It involved not only the warriors themselves but their wives, daughters and other tribe members.

Dances brought to Canada from other continents include Scottish reels, French contredanses, and favorites of the Slavs, the Irish, the English and the Germans. French precursors yielded the Canadian square dance, while French and Irish fiddle music enriched many French Canadian dances. A dance heralding the northern lights is peculiar to New Brunswick.

The Caribbean: The dance of the Caribbean melds African and European traditions. Slaves preserved the congo, the juba, the coromanti and a score of other African dances from Yoruba, Dahomey, and many points on Africa's western coast, bringing them to Jamaica, Trinidad, Haiti and other Caribbean islands. After they encountered Europe's quadrille and minuet, the slaves combined two very different dance traditions into their own language of movement. For example, the Scotische—a Caribbean dance derived from Scottish, French, Irish and English traditions with a dose of Afro-Caribbean rhythm—revolutionized the reel and the jig.

In Jamaica's camp style quadrille, dancers' bodies remain low to the ground and feet flat on the floor, two characteristics of Afro-Caribbean dancing. African movement is also centered around the pelvis, as in such Jamaican dances as the dinkie minie and kumina. All Caribbean dance incorporates African polyrhythms—different rhythms played on a variety of percussion instruments simultaneously. Limbs, hands and feet often move in isolation, responding here to a bongo and there to a bass drum.

As prized as coordination is a dancer's agility, tested nowhere as in Trinidad's limbo. Two men hold a stick horizontally while a third slinks under it, face toward the stick. As the stick moves closer to the ground, the dancer must bend lower and lower as he passes beneath the stick without touching it. Limbo requires a very flexible torso and back, both a part of Caribbean dance movement.

Mexico: In Mexico, the mingling of Spanish and Native American cultures has produced music and dance both Spanish and Indian in character. The violin, flute, bongo, guitar, cymbals, gourds and rattles create a lively accompaniment to Mexico's favorite dances, the jarabe and the huapango. The jarabe, among the oldest of Mexican dances, arose in the state of Jalisco. The steps of the dance imitate the movements of prancing horses and the clicking of hooves. A dance of courtship, the jarabe features brilliantly embroidered costumes and serapes. Also popular is the huapango, a dance of field workers in which couples move around a raised platform. At the dance's start, young men block the path of women with whom they want to dance and, without speaking, take up their partner. At the dance's end, movement often yields to song, especially tunes about jilted lovers.

United States: Dancing among the Native American peoples of the region now occupied by the forty-eight contiguous United States was both ceremonial and social. Accompanied by voices, drums or rattles that set a constant beat, the dances varied in style and purpose. Among the Iroquois in the eastern United States, dance was sacred. Men and women together performed the coon, pigeon, robin and fish dances, imitating animals' movements to help ensure a plentiful supply of meat. They also performed ceremonial dances indoors in a longhouse during the yearly Green Corn Festival. The Iroquois created more than thirty formal dances, in most of which the dancers stamped and shuffled their feet as they moved counterclockwise in a circle.

Across the continent from the Iroquois, the

southwestern-based Zuni enacted many cere-monial dances, several of them masked. At the summer solstice, they performed the dance of the kianakwe or "ghost people." During the winter, masked dancers imper-sonated the kachinas, or "kind spirits." At a yearly shakalo festival, Zunis alternated ka-china dances with dancing clowns.

On the Great Plains, Cheyenne warriors danced the arrow renewal ceremony, the sun dance and the animal dance. A ceremony common to most Plains Indians, the sun dance was believed to aid world renewal and bring new life to the tribe. Like many Native American dances, those of the Plains Indians generally required three or four days to com-plete and combined dance with spiritual rites and celebration.

(For information on the folk and social dance of Americans of European and African de-scent, see "Social Dance in the United States," page 384.)

THE NORTH AMERICAN INVITATIONAL BAGPIPE, DRUM AND DANCE COMPETITION

Ethnic dance traditions can sometimes travel great distances without much loss of authenticity. Scottish dance enthusiasts in North America, for instance, constitute a large "clan" that preserves the dance and musical heritage of their fore-bears. Once a year, the North American Invita-tional Bagpipe, Drum and Dance Competition brings together men and women from Canada and the United States to perform Highland flings, arcane sports and boisterous music. About two hundred similar affairs take place each year in various Celtic outposts of non-Celtic countries.

Almost all the participants lay claim to Scottish ancestry. Clan descendants trace their lineage to the Highlands of northern Scotland. There, clan gatherings were traditionally held to keep war-riors and civilians fit and loyal. Bagpipers per-formed a paramilitary function, playing before battles in order to intimidate the enemy with their wailing. Tartans were used like flags to distinguish friend from foe.

At a typical North American Invitational, dancers and players perform and mingle, recall-ing and celebrating their ancestral past. Hun-dreds of men, women and children sport kilts and other Scottish garb and participate in various con-tests and processions. Dancers compete all day, accompanied by a solitary piper and evaluated by several judges. Categorized by age and by level of proficiency, the dancers execute intricate footwork and airborne leaps. At the end of the festival, the winners go home with cash, but ev-eryone goes home with a renewed sense of pride in their ethnic dance heritage.

South and Central America

Latin American or *mestizo* dance is firmly rooted in the folk traditions of Central and South America. This enormous region reflects the diverse influ-ences of indigenous peoples, Spanish and Portuguese conquerors and African slaves. From Europe arrived the waltz, mazurka and polka, all mainstays of the colonial ballroom. On the other end of the dance spectrum lay the earthy lrhythms of Brazil's modinha and other traditional dance forms. The latter style colored the aristocratic dances of the ballroom, creating the sensual hybrid of Latin American dance.

The most popular dances of South America include the el gato, an Argentinian couple dance accompanied by song and performed in a legato rhythm. During a pause in the music, dance partners recite verses to each other. Hailing from both Argentina and Uruguay is the pericon, meaning "large fan." A spirited round dance in ⅜ time, the pericon—a dance of cowboys—is performed in boots with spurs to the songs of wandering musicians. It is the national dance of Argentina. The macumba typifies the exoticism of Brazilian dance. Part dance, part ritual, the macumba evokes ancestral spirits in movement and song. It has inspired other Brazilian dances, such as the chiba and the cururu.

Social Dance in the United States

Social dance brings people together to mark an occasion, to celebrate a happy event, or to foster friendship and fun. Some social dance forms, such as the waltz, join pairs of people as couples; others, such as the twist, call for solo dancing; still others, such as the square dance, require the coordination of a large ensemble. Unlike ballet and modern dance, social dancing is mostly a participatory art. Instead of sitting and watching professional dancers perform people take part in some action of their own, often without special training. Although the degree of technical facility demanded of the dancers will vary according to the dance, the social dance floor is open to anyone. Some devotees dance for pleasure at home or in nightclubs, while others dance competitively for cash prizes.

The Roots of American Social Dance

American social and folk dances grew out of European and African antecedents, both rustic and courtly. The waltz, for example, was probably derived from a type of galliard, called la volta, favored by Elizabeth I of England. When English settlers arrived on North American soil, they brought it with them. Likewise, American contra dances (the name comes from the French contredanse and the English country dance) had their origins in rural England and were then refined in the ballrooms of such monarchs as Charles II. Since the 18th century, they have been popular in the United States, and especially in New England. Once introduced to America, dances from other continents became thoroughly American, altered to suit the tastes of a new home.

Pioneers in the Appalachian mountains translated European dance traditions into a form of their own, known as the Appalachian mountain dance. One descendant of the Appalachian mountain dance is clogging, which resembles tap dancing but has a rougher rhythm. Clogging originated in northern England, where it is still danced in wooden shoes, but American dancers prefer lighter-weight variants with metal pieces attached to the soles. Cloggers produce a characteristic patter with their feet that is usually simpler and more forthright than tap patterns, although they are capable of extraordinarily spirited, rhythmic outbursts.

In the early 19th century, Americans combined elements of the Appalachian mountain dance with aspects of certain contra dances to create the square dance, a quintessentially American folk form with many spin-offs. In square dancing, groups of couples dance in a square formation, responding to a caller who tells them what figures to perform. The caller is rather like an impromptu choreographer, dictating the progress of the dances on the spur of the moment. The western square dance, a later version of the standard form, was more energetic and demanding in pace, although it included much the same type of figures. Especially in the West, the square dance served an important social function, assembling far-flung homesteaders for communal entertainment.

Like square dances, barn dances brought neighbors together. To celebrate the construction of a new barn, they practiced a very American dance genre that also owed much to European forebears. In turn, the barn dance became popular in Europe in the 19th century with the rise of democracy and the growth of public dance halls. The form combined aspects of the pas de quatre, the schottische, the galop and the mazurka in the typical slide, hop and walk— with variations—of two partners.

One dance that originated in this country was the two-step, inspired by John Philip Sousa's composition *Washington Post March* (1891). A brisk dance, the two-step was performed by a couple in ⁶/₈ tempo with quick, springy steps and skips. The two-step, which adapted easily to various venues and musical accompaniments, eventually spawned the fox-trot. American-made, it traveled abroad with great success.

PLANTATION DANCING

In the 17th through 19th centuries, slaves brought distinctive forms of music and dancing to America from Africa. Serving both religious and secular purposes, African music was based on emphatic and sometimes complex rhythms that were piped, drummed, strummed, clapped, stamped, shouted and sung. Likewise, some dances appeared in rituals, others in celebrations; many incorporated masks.

Once they were sold into slavery, bound in shackles and sent to America, Africans danced less often of their own free will. Sometimes their captors forced them to dance, often with whips, while aboard the slave ships. The "exercise" kept slaves fit on their way to market and provided amusement for the slavers. Right from the start, slave dances reflected the clash of cultures.

In the West Indies, black slaves mixed African forms with European influences to produce new dances that were frequently used in voodoo rites and other spiritual practices. Some of these forms filtered into the United States, where slaves were also developing their own kinds of dance. A major event in the evolution of plantation dancing came in the 19th century, when most slave owners prohibited the use of drums. Slaves substituted washtubs, hand-clapping and foot-stamping to provide rhythms for their singing and dancing. One result was the transformation of the human body into an instrument of percussion, which had a direct impact on dance.

Accompanied by bones, tambourines, banjos, fiddles, pots and pans, individual slaves danced not only on the ground but on raised wooden surfaces, such as tables. Hard surfaces provided the right kind of sounding board for the footwork of the buck dance, the pigeon wing and the buck-and-wing. In another dance, the juba, the arms and feet became percussion instruments that beat against the ground and the body.

Ring dances allowed large numbers of slaves to dance together. This configuration generated various popular animal dances, such as the buzzard lope. Water dances, meanwhile, entailed dancing while carrying vessels of water on the head. Slaves also devised their own versions of reels, quadrilles and other forms danced by their masters. Occasions for dancing included harvests, holidays and quilting sessions. In New Orleans, levee dancing, quadroon balls and voodoo-inspired shindigs comprised a tradition all their own.

For slaves and free African-Americans alike, dancing retained some of the religious significance it had had in Africa. In Baptist and several other Protestant denominations that discouraged music and dancing, congregations partook of the shout ceremony in their place. Over time, the melodic marching and processionals of the shout grew increasingly complex and choreographic. The ensemble rhythms knit congregations together in a physical demonstration of moral unity.

Ballroom Dancing

From the beginning, social dancing in America also proceeded along more formal lines in a sort of equivalent of Old World court dancing. George Washington and Thomas Jefferson were both fond of dancing, although New England Puritans regarded dance as a devilish sport. From the early days of the republic, the *beau monde* attended balls, and foreign-born dancing masters in Boston, Philadelphia and New York taught the minuet and other French dances to genteel folk. American dancing teacher Allen Dodworth (1848–99) presided over the Dodworth Dancing Academy in New York, and published a book, *Dancing and Its Relation to Education and Social Life,* in 1885. Dodworth and his colleagues considered themselves moral arbiters and the protectors of propriety.

Among the ballroom dances popular in 19th-century America were the quadrille, the mazurka, the schottische, the polka, the polonaise and the waltz. A contredanse of French origin, the quadrille came to the United States via England. It was a dance for four couples in five parts, each set in a distinct rhythm, the last of which was called the galop. The mazurka, a Polish folk dance, made its way to upper-crust Russia and England before reaching America. Mazurkas were usually danced by four or eight couples in ¾ time; the stamp or tap of the heel on the second beat gave it an earthy zest not generally seen in ballrooms. A German round dance named for the Scots (though it had little to do with them), the schottische resembled the waltz but was danced to polka music. The Czech folk roots of the polka, danced in ¾ time, gave it quick, vigorous snap and intimacy between partners that provoked some stern moralizing. Unlike the folksy polka, the polonaise was courtly in mood and in source, devised in Poland as a military processional to celebrate wartime victory.

But of all types of ballroom dancing, the waltz was probably the most prevalent and long-lasting in the United States. Set in ¾ time, the waltz had its beginnings in the German folk dance called the ländler. It was romantic, requiring partners to dance closely, and exciting, involving a heady yet delicate series of whirling turns. The Viennese version circled in a single direction, while the Boston variant, an American invention, turned in several, though more slowly. Both elegant and sexy, the waltz worried certain straitlaced Americans, but the dance outlived its opposition as Americans, like Europeans, fell for it.

Dancing to Popular Music

Starting late in the 19th century, the explosion of American popular music spawned a whole new category of dances. Altogether different from folk and ballroom dancing but equally seductive, these dances responded to new musical and social imperatives. The dances set in motion by American ragtime music, such as the turkey-trot, the bunny-hug and other "animal dances," were much wilder than most dances seen to date. Like the syncopated rhythms of ragtime, they originated in the dance forms practiced by African-Americans, first as slaves on southern plantations and then as performers in minstrel shows. The frenetic pace of ragtime dancing and its boisterously uninhibited character were more plainly physical than other forms of social dance. Indeed, some dance halls banned them, as well as other provocative dances of African-American origin, such as the funky butt, the itch and the mooche.

Perhaps the best-known example of ragtime's lasting dance legacy was the cakewalk. Usually presented as the closing feature in minstrel shows, this dance was a competitive affair for couples, who tried to outdo each other with style and daring in a flamboyant promenade. Appearing in the American South during the 1880s, the cakewalk originated with African-Americans, who supposedly learned it from Native Americans. Although first danced by amateurs, it became a favorite stage offering overseas, as well as at home.

Requiring energy, athleticism and an adventurous attitude, ragtime dances appealed particularly to the young. For the first time in America, social dancing came to be identified with youthfulness, an association that would continue into the 20th century. Subsequent dances and dance trends served as musical and physical expressions of the hopes and feelings of young Americans.

At the same time, some professionals strove to formalize the new, "hot" dances and to teach them, much as ballroom dancing had been taught. They hoped to make the dances respectable, thereby winning them a wider audience. Two such popular dance promoters were Vernon Castle (1887–1918) and his wife Irene (1893–1969). Although considered libertine by some standards (she wore no corsets), they attracted a large following of socialites who wanted to learn how to dance in new ways. The Castles set up shop in New York, at the Castle House for the Teaching of Correct Dancing. They appropriated and toned down such dances as the tango, a raw, erotic dance that had come to America from Argentina by way of Cuba and Haiti. The Castles also created and popularized the Castle walk, danced on the balls of the feet with the legs held stiff.

The Castles' success inspired a whole new generation of social dance teachers, epitomized by Arthur Murray (1895–1991). These teachers showed America how to dance the rumba, the Charleston, the foxtrot, the jitterbug (also known as the lindy hop), the shimmy, the samba, the mambo and the cha-cha. The rumba, a kind of erotic combat, arrived in the United States via Havana, Cuba, where Americans went to drink and dance during Prohibition. The Charleston, however, was all-American, the perfect expression of the Jazz Age. High kicks and swiveling knees characterized its giddy, hectic attack. Named for the city in South Carolina where the dance originated among African-American shipyard workers, the Charleston burst on the scene at the Ziegfeld Follies in 1923.

Without the Ziegfeld Follies, there might never have been a fox-trot. Dreamed up by a music-hall artist named Harry Fox (1897–1962), it was a skittish, step-filled, almost nervous dance. Danced in ¼ time, the fox-trot was similar to the two-step, but depended on a broken rhythm. The British calmed it down into something called the saunter. In the 1930s, the jitterbug became the rage. Renamed the lindy hop after Charles Lindbergh's historic transatlantic flight in 1927, it came of age only with the rise of swing music. The lindy included flashy "air steps" done off the ground, virtuosic male solos and exhilarating body tosses of the woman by her partner.

It is no surprise, then, that dance halls, high school gyms, basements and backyards saw much dancing in the first decades of the 20th century. In the years leading up to the Great Depression, dance marathons captured the American imagination as a new outlet for expression. At marathons, amateur contestants paid for the opportunity to dance for hours on end in the hope of coming away with a cash prize. These grueling competitions, endured by dancers desperate for escape or cash, remain an icon of the Great Depression.

The next big change in American social dancing came with the advent of rock 'n' roll in the 1950s. The sights and sounds of Elvis Presley and other performers inspired young people to ditch old wildness for new. Combining rhythm-and-blues with country and western influences in a rowdy, sexy style, Presley danced with his hips while he sang.

Most famous of the early rock dances was the twist, introduced by Chubby Checker (born 1941) in 1960 on the television show *American Bandstand*. It soon appeared in New York nightspots and around the country. Like many dances made popular in the 1950s and 1960s, such as the frug, the pony, the mashed potato, and the swim, the twist required no real skill, just a display of enthusiasm and energy from a person dancing alone in a large group. Social dances of the 1960s were oriented toward a group, rather than a couple, and emphasized mobile hips, jerking motions, wiggling, and spasmodic weight shifts.

In the 1970s, disco dancing revived some of the self-conscious strutting and seduction of earlier social dancing. Danced by couples, disco incorporated precision turns and stylized moves. Never subtle, always pumping, the dance was both exhibitionistic and highly wrought. In the movie *Saturday Night Fever* (1977), John Travolta (born 1954) defined the disco aesthetic.

The 1970s and 1980s also saw the introduction of reggae music from Jamaica, whose sinuous rhythms required an altogether different style of dancing. American pop produced its own form of smooth, synthetic dance music in the 1980s, typified by such performers as Michael Jackson and Madonna. Rejecting this manufactured style were the African-American hip-hop and rap artists who invented break-dancing. A product of the streets, this highly stylized, gymnastic form was most often performed there. It has evolved into new club forms that survive alongside less-challenging freestyle dancing.

Dance Festivals Around the World

North America and the Caribbean

American College Dance Festival Association
Point Park College
201 Wood Street
Pittsburgh, PA 15222
(412) 392-3477/3496

American Dance Festival
P.O. Box 6097, College Station
Durham, NC 27708
(919) 684-6402

American Dance Festival West
Salt Lake City, UT
(801) 355-ARTS

Ann Arbor Summer Festival
Ann Arbor, MI
(313) 747-2278, 764-2538

Banff Festival of the Arts, The
Banff Centre for the Arts
P.O. Box 1020
Banff, Alberta
T0L 0C0 Canada
(403) 762-6157

Bay Area Dance Series
Oakland, CA
(510) 762-BASS

Chautauqua Festival
Box 1098, Department 6
Chautauqua, NY 14722
(716) 357-6234

Colorado Dance Festival
Box 356
Boulder, CO 80306
(303) 442-7666

Columbia Festival of the Arts
Columbia, MD
(410) 715-3044

DanceAspen Summer Festival
P. O. Box 8745
Aspen, CO 81612
(303) 925-7718

**Dancing on the Edge Festival of
Contemporary Dance**
Firehall Arts Center
Vancouver, B.C. Canada
(604) 689-0691

Dance Portland
Portland Performing Arts Center
Portland, ME
(207) 761-0591

Downtown Dance Festival
Battery Dance Company
380 Broadway, 5th floor
New York, NY 10013
(212) 219-3910

**Festival Internationale de Nouvelle
Danse**
4060 Boulevard Saint-Laurent,
Bureau 204
Montreal, Quebec
H2W 1Y9 Canada
(514) 287-1423

Florida Dance Festival
Tampa, FL
Contact: Florida Dance Association
MDCC/Wolfson Campus
300 N.E. Second Avenue, Suite 1412
Miami, FL 33132
(305) 237-3413

Havana International Ballet Festival
Ballet Nacional de Cuba
Calzada No. 510
Habana 4, Cuba
Phone n/a

Huntington Summer Arts Festival
Huntington Arts Council
213 Main Street
Huntington, NY 11743
(516) 271-8442

**Interlochen Arts Festival of the
Interlochen Center for the Arts**
Interlochen Arts Academy
P.O. Box 199
Interlochen, MI 49643-0199
(616) 276-9221

Jacob's Pillow Dance Festival
P.O. Box 287
Lee, MA 01238
(413) 243-0745

Lincoln Center Out-of-Doors
Lincoln Center Plaza/Damrosch Park
70 Lincoln Center Plaza
New York, NY 10023
(212) 875-5150

Los Angeles Festival
P.O. Box 5210
Los Angeles, CA 90055-0219
(213) 689-8800

National Dance Week
c/o Capezio Ballet Makers
1 Campus Road
Totowa, NJ 07512
(201) 595-9000

Next Wave Festival
Brooklyn Academy of Music
30 Lafayette Avenue
Brooklyn, NY 11217
(718) 636-4100

Ohio Ballet Summer Festival
Ohio Ballet
354 East Market Street
Akron, OH 44325
(216) 375-7900

Pacific Northwest Festival
Seattle Opera
P.O. Box 9248
Seattle, WA 98109
(206) 443-4700

Ravinia Festival
1575 Oakwood Avenue, P.O. Box 896
Highland Park, IL 60035
(312) 728-4642

San Francisco Ethnic Dance Festival
San Francisco, CA
Contact: City Celebration
(415) 474-3914

Saratoga Performing Arts Center
Saratoga State Park
Saratoga Springs, NY 12866
(518) 587-3330

Serious Fun
Alice Tully Hall
Lincoln Center for the Performing Arts
New York, NY 10023
(212) 875-5050

Spoleto Festival U.S.A.
P.O. Box 157
Charleston, SC 29402
(803) 722-2764

Three Rivers Arts Festival
207 Sweetbriar Street
Pittsburgh, PA 15211
(412) 481-7040

Utah Arts Festival
168 W. 500 N.
Salt Lake City, UT 84103
(801) 322-2428

Victoria International Festival
103-3737 Oak Street
Vancouver, B.C.
V6H 2M4 Canada
(604) 736-2119

White Mountain Summer Dance Festival
Laura Glenn Dance
162 West 21st Street
New York, NY 10011
(212) 929-5733

Wolf Trap Farm Park for the Performing Arts
1624 Trap Road
Vienna, VA 22182
(703) 255-1900

Europe and Asia

Aberdeen International Youth Festival
Aberdeen, Scotland
Contact: AIYF
3 Nutborn House, Clifton Rd.
London SW19 4QT
England
0044-81-946-2995

Athens Festival
Contact: Dimos Vratsanos
1 Voukourestiou St.
10564 Athens, Greece
322-1459

Avignon Festival
Contact: Alain Crombecque
8 bis Rue de Mons
F-8400 Avignon, France
90-82-67-08

Berlin Festival
Budapester Strasse 50
D-1000 Berlin 30, Germany
30-25489/0

Berner Tanztage
Contact: Association Berner Tanztage
Box 440CH-3000
Bern 5, Switzerland
41-3126-48

Bolzano Danza
Bolzano, Italy
0039-471-970660

Chateauvallon Festival de Danse
Chateauvallon, France
94-22-14-06

Dansa Valencia
Avda Campanar 32, 46015
Valencia, Spain
96-386-32-90

Dark Music Days
Laufasvegur
101 Reykjavik, Iceland
1-24972

Dresden Music Festival
Contact: Direktion Dresdener
Musikfestspiele
Postfach 6
Günzstrasse 31
0-8019 Dresden, Germany
0351-459-4040

Edinburgh International Festival
21 Market Street
Edinburgh EH1 1BW
Scotland
31-226-4001

Festival D'Avignon
Contact: Bureau du Festival
BP 492
84073 Avignon Cedex, France

Festival de Danca de Campos do Jourdao
Claudio Santoro Auditorium
Sao Paulo, Brazil
55-011-61-3806

Festival Internacional de Musica y Danza de Granada
c/o Gracia 21, 4th floor
18002 Granada, Spain
58-26-74-47

Festival International Danse à Aix
Aix-en-Provence, France
Reservations: 42-26-20-93
Workshop information: 42-41-24-54.

Festival International Montpelier Danse
7 Boulevard Henri IV
34000 Montpelier, France
67-61-11-20

Festival of Two Worlds, Spoleto
Contact: Festival die Due Mondi
Teatro Nuovo
06049 Spoleto, Italy

Holland Dance Festival Den Haag
Kleine-Gartmanplantsoen 21
1017 RP Amsterdam, The Netherlands
020-27-65-66

Holland Festival
Netherlands Reservations Center
P.O. Box 404
NL-2260 AK Leidschendam,
The Netherlands

International Dance-Theatre Festival
Contact: Fred Traguth, Director
TTW Bonn e.V.
Postbox 2467
D-5300 Bonn 1, Germany
0228-2830-75

International Folkloric Dance Festival
General Secretary
Kasteeldreef 61
2120 Schoten, Belgium
03-6585512

Internationale Tanzwerkstatt Bonn
Postbox 24 67
D-5300 Bonn 1, Germany
63-23-26

Istanbul International Festival
Yildiz Kultur ve Sanat Merkezi
Yidiz-Besiktas 80700
Istanbul, Turkey

Kuopio Festival
Tulliportinkatu 27
70100 Kuopio, Finland
358-71-282-1541

Lyon Biennale de la Danse
Lyons, France
33-72-41-00-00

Munich Summerstage
Munich, Germany
Contact: Joint Adventures
089-7242515

Osaka International Festival
Osaka International Festival Society
6-7 Ginza 6-chome
Chuo Ku, Tokyo, 104 Japan
03-571-1136

Singapore Festival of the Arts
MCD Building 15th Story
512 Thomson Road
Singapore 1129
2589595

Springdance Festival
C/o G. Brugmans
Keistraat 2
3512 HV Utrect, The Netherlands
30-319-364

Tivoli
Vesterbrogade 3
DK-1620 Copenhagen V, Denmark

Vienna Festival
Lehargasse 11
A 1060 Vienna, Austria
02225861676

Dance Awards and Competitions

Each year, the international dance community gives scores of awards to dancers, choreographers, producers, companies and students. Here are a few of the most significant awards, followed by a selection of dance competitions.

Dance Awards

Capezio Dance Award
Capezio Foundation
1 Campuz Road
Totowa, NJ 07512
(201) 595-9120

Since 1952, a committee of dance critics and educators has selected one person annually for recognition as a major contributor to the art form. The Capezio Foundation grants the honoree a cash award to assist him or her in future work.

1994	Urban Bush Women
1993	Dance/USA
1992	Frederic Franklin
1991	John Curry, Katherine Dunham, Darci Kistler, Igor Youskevitch
1990	Jacques D'Amboise
1989	Edward Villella
1988	Charles "Honi" Coles
1987	Fred Astaire, Bob Fosse, Rudolph Nureyev, Jac Vanza
1986	Antony Tudor
1985	Doris Hering
1984	William Christensen, Harold Christensen, Lew Christensen
1983	Harvey Lichtenstein

1982   Alwin Nikolais
1981   Dorothy Alexander
1980   Walter Terry
1979   Alvin Ailey
1978   Hanya Holm
1977   Merce Cunningham
1976   Jerome Robbins
1975   Robert Irving
1974   Robert Joffrey
1973   Isadora Bennett
1972   La Meri, Reginald and Gladys Laubin
1971   Arthur Mitchell
1970   William Kolodney
1969   John Martin
1968   Lucia Chase
1967   Paul Taylor
1966   Agnes de Mille
1965   Maria Tallchief
1964   José Limón
1963   Donald McKayle
1962   Barbara Karinska
1961   Ruth St. Denis
1960   Martha Graham
1959   Sol Hurok
1958   Alexandra Danilova
1957   Ted Shawn
1956   Genevieve Oswald
1955   Louis Horst
1954   Doris Humphrey
1953   Lincoln Kirstein
1952   Zachary Solov

Dance Magazine Awards
Dance Magazine
33 West 60th Street, 10th floor
New York, NY 10023
(212) 245-9050

Awarded annually since 1954, the Dance Magazine Awards honor dancers, choreographers, designers, administrators, historians, musicians and others whose achievements in dance deserve special attention in the opinion of the editors. Recipients may be newcomers or veterans and may come from any dance discipline, from ballet to Broadway.

1993   Pierre Dulaine and Yvonne Marceau, Bill T. Jones, Beatriz Rodriguez

1992   Darci Kistler, Meredith Monk, Helgi Thomasson

1991   Virginia Johnson, Mark Morris, Jennifer Tipton

1990   Garth Fagan, Eliot Feld, Danya Holm

1989   No awards

1988   "Dancing for Life," Moscelyne Larkin and Roman Jasinski, P. W. Manchester, Kyra Nichols

1987   Merrill Ashley, Trisha Brown, Liz Thompson, David White, Doris Hering

1986   No awards

1985   Charles "Honi" Coles, Richard Cragon, Frederic Franklin, Heather Watts, Walter Sorell

1984   Alexandra Danilova, Robert Irving, Donald Sadler, Tommy Tune, Dance Masters of America

1983   Jeannot Cerrone, John Neumeier, Michael Smuin, Martine van Hamel

1982   Fernando Bujones, Laura Dean, Arnold Spohr, Lee Theodore

1981   Selma Jean Cohen, Sir Anton Dolin, Twyla Tharp, Stanley Williams

1980   Patricia McBride, Ruth Page, Paul Taylor, Herbert Ross and Nora Kaye

1979   Aaron Copland, Jorge Donn, Erick Hawkins, Jean Babilée

1978   Mikhail Baryshnikov, Raoul Gelabert, Bella Lewitzky

1977   Murray Louis, Natalia Makarova, Peter Martins

1976   Michael Bennett, Suzanne Farrell, E. Virginia Williams

1975   Alvin Ailey, Cynthia Gregory, Arthur Mitchell

1974   Gerald Arpino, Maurice Béjart, Anthony Tudor

1973   The Christensen Brothers, Rudolf Nureyev

1972   Anthony Dowell, Judith Jamison

1971   No awards

1970   No awards

1969   Sir Frederick Ashton, Carolyn Brown, Ted Shawn

1968   Erik Bruhn, Katherine Dunham, Carla Fracci

1967   Eugene Loring, Alwin Nikolais, Violette Verdy

1966   Carmen de Lavallade, Sol Hurok, Wesleyan University Press

1965   Edwin Denby, Margaret H'Doubler, Maya Plisetskaya

1964   John Butler, Peter Gennaro, Edward Villella

1963   Gower Champion, Pauline Koner, Robert Joffrey

1962   Isadora Bennett, Margot Fonteyn, Bob Fosse

1961   Melissa Hayden, Anna Sokolow, Gwen Verdon

1960   Merce Cunningham, Igor Moiseyev, Maria Tallchief

1959   Dorothy Alexander, Fred Astaire, George Balanchine

1958   Alicia Alonso, Doris Humphrey, Gene Kelly, Igor Youskevitch

1957   Lucia Chase, José Limón, Alicia Markova, Jerome Robbins

1956   Agnes de Mille, Martha Graham
1955   Jack Cole, Gene Nelson, Moira Shearer
1954   Dance on TV: *Adventure* (CBS), Tony Charmoli (NBC), Max Liebman (NBC), *Omnibus* (CBS)

Dance Competitions

American Ballet Competition
P.O. Box 328
Philadelphia, PA 19105
(800) 523-0961

(Contact for information on the Maya/St. Petersburg [Russia] and Varna [Bulgaria] international competitions.)

American Dance Spectrum
312 North Street
Randolph, MA 02368
(617) 767-GOLD

British Columbia Jazz Dance Competition
P.O. Box 670
Prince Rupert, B.C.
V8J 3S1, Canada
(604) 627-7982

Capezio Dance Award
1 Campuz Road
Totowa, NJ 07512
(201) 595-9120

Concours International de Danse de Paris
36 rue de Laborde
75008 Paris, France
1-45.22.28.74
attention: Cyril La Faurie

Dance Educators of America
Box 509
Oceanside, NY 11572-0509
(516) 766-6615

National Dream Convention and Competition
Dance Makers, Inc.
310 Sweetbrier Rd.
Greenville, SC 29615
(803) 244-4959
attention: Marjorie Perry

Dance Olympus/Dance America Competitions
Dept. DM, 1795 Express Drive North
Smithtown, NY 11787
1-800-44DANCE

Grand Prix International Video Danse
1 avenue Gabriel
F-75008 Paris, France
331-42-66-9144

ITT International Ballet Competition
Teatterikulma, Meritulinkatu 33
SF-00170 Helsinki, Finland
(0) 135761
attention: Ms. Rittaola

National Choreography Competition for New Works in Contemporary Dance and Ballet
Sala Olimpia
Plaza de Lavapies
Madrid, Spain
527-46-22

Presidential Scholars in the Arts
400 Maryland Avenue S.W.
Washington, D.C. 20202
(202) 401-1365

Tokyo International Choreography Competition
1-32-13 Kita-Shinjuku
Shinjuku-Ku
Tokyo 189, Japan
(3) 5386-2887

Tremaine Dance Competition
14531 Hamlin Street #104
Van Nuys, CA 91411
(818) 988-8008

USA International Ballet Competition
Contact: Sue Lobrano
P.O. Box 55791
Jackson, MS 39296-5791
(601) 355-9853

Dance Funding Sources

Most grants and other funding for dance artists come from state and federal agencies, rather than private sources. The following is a selected list of providers, as well as several sources of information on dance-grant opportunities. Note that many state and local institutions fund only residents of their area.

Alabama State Council on the Arts and Humanities
Division of Cultural Affairs
One Dexter Avenue
Montgomery, AL 36130
(205) 242-4076

Alaska State Council on the Arts and Humanities
411 West Fourth Avenue, #1E
Anchorage, AK 99501-2343
(907) 279-1558

Allied Arts Council of Southern Nevada
3750 South Maryland Parkway
Las Vegas, NV 89119
(702) 731-5419

Arie and Ida Crown Memorial
222 N. LaSalle St., Suite 2000
Chicago, IL 60601

Arizona Commission on the Arts
417 West Roosevelt
Phoenix, AZ 85003
(602) 255-5884/(602) 255-5882

Arkansas Arts Council
The Heritage Center, Suite 200
255 East Markham Street
Little Rock, AR 72201
(501) 324-9337

Artists Foundation
8 Park Plaza
Boston, MA 02116
(617) 227-2787

Arts Council of Florida
Division of Cultural Affairs
Department of State, The Capitol
Tallahassee, FL 32399-0250
(904) 487-2980

Arts Council of New Orleans
821 Gravier Street, Suite 600
New Orleans, LA 70112
(504) 523-1465

Asian Cultural Council
280 Madison Avenue
New York, NY 10016
(212) 684-5450

Associated Grantmakers of Massachusetts
294 Washington Street, Suite 840
Boston, MA 02108
(617) 426-2606

AT&T Foundation
550 Madison Avenue
New York, NY 10022-3297
(212) 605-6734

Bloomington Area Arts Council
202 East Sixth Street
Bloomington, IN 47408
(812) 334-3100

Boston Arts Commission
Boston City Hall, Room 608
Boston, MA 02201
(617) 725-3245

Bronx Council on the Arts
1738 Hone Avenue
Bronx, NY 10461
(212) 931-9500

California Arts Council
2411 Alhambra Blvd.
Sacramento, CA 95817
(916) 739-3186

**California Community Foundation
Funding Information Center**
606 South Olive Street, Suite 2400
Los Angeles, CA 90014-1526
(213) 413-4042

Cecil B. de Mille Trust
223 W. Alameda, Suite 101
Burbank, CA 91052
(818) 263-6300

**City of Los Angeles Cultural Affairs
Department**
433 South Spring Street, 10th floor
Los Angeles, CA 90013
(213) 485-2433

**Colorado Council on the Arts and
Humanities**
Grant-Humphreys Mansion
750 Pennsylvania Street
Denver, CO 80203
(303) 894-2617

**Commonwealth of Pennsylvania Council
on the Arts**
Finance Building, Room 216
Harrisburg, PA 17120
(717) 787-6883

Connecticut Commission on the Arts
227 Lawrence Street
Hartford, CT 06106
(203) 566-4770

**Council for International Exchange of
Scholars**
3007 Tilden Street, N.W., Suite 5M,
Box GPOS
Washington, D.C. 20008-3009
(202) 362-3442

Cultural Arts Council of Houston
1964 West Gray, Suite 224
Houston, TX 77019-4808
(713) 527-9330

Dallas Dance Council
P.O. Box 740511
Dallas, TX 75374-0511
(214) 348-4116

Dance Council of Central Pennsylvania
821 Farmingdale Road
Lancaster, PA 17601
(717) 393-7395

Delaware State Arts Council
State Office Building
820 North French Street
Wilmington, DE 19801
(302) 577-3540

**District of Columbia Commission on the
Arts and Humanities**
410 Eighth Street, N.W., 2nd floor,
Suite 500
Washington, D.C. 20004
(202) 724-5613

Donors Forum
55 West Jackson Blvd.
Chicago, IL 60604
(312) 431-0260

Durham Arts Council, Inc.
120 Morris Street
Durham, NC 27701
(919) 560-2716

**Federal Council on the Arts &
Humanities**
1 McPherson Square
Washington, D.C. 20005
(202) 456-6200

Federation of State Humanities Councils
1012 14th Street, N.W., #1007
Washington, D.C. 20005
(202) 393-5400

**First National Bank of Chicago
Foundation**
One First National Plaza
Chicago, IL 60670
(312) 732-6948

Foundation Center
79 Fifth Avenue, 8th floor
New York, NY 10003-3050
(212) 620-4230

Foundation Center
312 Sutter Street, Room 312
San Francisco, CA 94108
(415) 397-0903

Foundation Center
1001 Connecticut Avenue, N.W.,
Suite 934
Washington, D.C. 20036
(202) 331-1401

Gap Foundation, The
One Harrison Street
San Francisco, CA 94105
(415) 291-2757

**Georgia Council for the Arts and
Humanities**
2082 East Exchange Place, Suite 100
Tucker, GA 30084
(404) 493-5780

Grants Information Service
Dallas Public Library
1515 Young Street
Dallas, TX 75201
(214) 670-1468

Greater Columbus Arts Council
55 East State Street
Columbus, OH 43215
(614) 224-2606

Greater Louisville Fund for the Arts
623 West Main Street
Louisville, KY 40202
(502) 582-0100

**Guam Council on the Arts and
Humanities**
Office of the Governor
P.O. Box 2950
Agana, Guam 96910
001-671-477-7413

Harkness Foundations for Dance
145 E. 48 Street, Suite 26-C
New York, NY 10017
(212) 755-5540

**Hawaii State Foundation on Culture and
the Arts**
335 Merchant Street, Room 202
Honolulu, HI 96813
(808) 548-4145

Idaho Commission on the Arts
304 West State Street
c/o Statehouse Mall
Boise, ID 83720
(208) 334-2119

Illinois Arts Council
State of Illinois Center
100 West Randolph Street, Suite 10-5000
Chicago, IL 60601
(312) 814-6750

Indiana Arts Commission
402 West Washington Street, Room 702
Indianapolis, IN 46204
(317) 232-1268

Institute of International Education
809 United Nations Plaza
New York, NY 10017-3580
(212) 984-5328

Iowa State Arts Council
State Capitol Complex
1223 East Court Avenue
Des Moines, IA 50319
(515) 281-4451

Kansas Arts Commission
Jayhawk Towers, Suite 1004
700 Jackson
Topeka, KS 66603
(913) 296-3335

Kentucky Arts Council
31 Fountain Place
Frankfort, KY 40601
(502) 564-3757

Louisiana Department of Culture, Recreation, and Tourism
Division of the Arts
P.O. Box 44247
Baton Rouge, LA 70804
(504) 342-8180

Lower Manhattan Cultural Council
42 Broadway, Room 1749
New York, NY 10004
(212) 432-0900

Maine Arts Commission
55 Capitol Street
State House Station 25
Augusta, ME 04333
(207) 289-2724

Maryland State Arts Council
15 West Mulberry Street
Baltimore, MD 21201
(301) 333-8232

Mayor's Council on the Arts
City Hall
Burlington, VT 05401
(802) 658-9300

Maytag Corporation Foundation, The
c/o Maytag Corp.
403 W. 4th Street North
Newton, IA 50208
(515) 791-8905

Meyer and Morris Kaplan Family Foundation
191 Waukegan Road
Northfield, IL 60093
(708) 441-6630

Michel Fokine Fund
New York Community Trust
2 Park Avenue, 24th floor
New York, NY 10016
(212) 686-1000

Michigan Council for the Arts, Cultural Affairs
1200 Sixth Street
Detroit, MI 48226
(313) 256-3731

Milwaukee Artist Foundation
820 E. Knapp Street
Milwaukee, WI 53202
(414) 276-9273

Minneapolis Arts Commission
City Hall, Room 200
Minneapolis, MN 55415
(612) 673-3006

Minnesota State Arts Board
432 Summit Avenue
St. Paul, MN 55102
(612) 297-2603

Mississippi Arts Commission
239 North Lamar Street, Suite 207
Jackson, MS 39201
(601) 359-6036

Missouri Arts Council
Wainwright Office Complex
111 North Seventh Street, Suite 105
St. Louis, MO 63101
(314) 340-6845

Montana Arts Council
48 North Last Chance Gulch
Helena, MT 59620
(406) 444-6430

National Endowment for the Arts,
Nancy Hanks Center
1100 Pennsylvania Avenue, N.W.
Washington, D.C. 20506
(202) 682-5400

Nebraska Arts Council
1313 Farnam-on-the-Mall
Omaha, NE 68102
(402) 595-2122

Nevada State Council on the Arts
329 Flint Street
Reno, NV 89501
(702) 688-1225

New England Foundation for the Arts
678 Massachusetts Avenue
Cambridge, MA 02139
(617) 492-2914

New Hampshire State Council on the
Arts
Phoenix Hall
40 North Main Street
Concord, NH 03301
(603) 271-2789

New Jersey State Council on the Arts
4 North Broad Street, CN306
Trenton, NJ 08625
(609) 292-6130

New Mexico Arts Division
228 E. Palace Avenue
Santa Fe, NM 87501
(505) 827-6490

New York Foundation for the Arts
155 Avenue of the Americas, 14th floor
New York, NY 10013
(212) 366-6900

New York State Council on the Arts
915 Broadway
New York, NY 10010
(212) 387-7000

North Carolina Arts Council
Department of Cultural Resources
Raleigh, NC 27601-2807
(919) 733-2821

North Dakota Council on the Arts
Black Building, Suite 606
Fargo, ND 58102
(701) 239-7150

Ohio Arts Council
727 East Main Street
Columbus, OH 43205
(614) 466-2613

Oregon Arts Commission
835 Summer Street, N.E.
Salem, OR 97301
(503) 378-3625

Performing Arts Assistance Corp.
P.O. Box 1296, Ansonia Station
New York, NY 10023
(212) 874-2254

Pittsburgh Dance Council, Inc.
719 Liberty Avenue
Pittsburgh, PA 15222
(412) 355-0330

Rhode Island State Council on the Arts
95 Cedar Street, Suite 103
Providence, RI 02903-4494
(401) 277-3880

San Francisco Arts Commission
25 Venice, Room 240
San Francisco, CA 94102
(415) 554-9671

Santa Fe Council on the Arts
806 Falda de la Sierra
Santa Fe, NM 87501
(505) 988-1878

Schubert Foundation, The
234 W. 44th St.
New York, NY 10036
(212) 944-3777

Selz Foundation, Inc., The
230 Park Avenue
New York, NY 10169
(212) 309-8240

South Carolina Arts Commission
1800 Gervais Street
Columbia, SC 29201
(803) 734-8696

South Dakota Arts Council
108 West 11th Street
Sioux Falls, SD 57102
(605) 339-6646

State Arts Council of Oklahoma
Jim Thorpe Building, Room 640
2101 North Lincoln Blvd.
Oklahoma City, OK 73105
(405) 521-2931

Tacoma Arts Commission
747 Market Street, Suite 134
Tacoma, WA 98402
(206) 591-5191

Tennessee Arts Commission
320 Sixth Avenue North, Suite 100
Nashville, TN 37243-0780
(615) 741-1701

Texas Arts Council
3939 Bee Caves Road, Suite 1A
Austin, TX 78746
(512) 934-8400

Texas Commission on the Arts
P.O. Box 13406, Capitol Station
Austin, TX 78711
(512) 463-5535

Theatre Development Fund
1501 Broadway
New York, NY 10036
(212) 221-0885

U.S. Department of Education
400 Maryland Avenue, S.W.
Washington, D.C. 20202
(202) 245-3192

Utah Arts Council
617 East South Temple Street
Salt Lake City, UT 84102
(801) 533-5895

Vermont Council on the Arts, Inc.
133 State Street
Montpelier, VT 05633-6001
(802) 828-3291

Virginia Commission for the Arts
223 Governor Street
Richmond, VA 23219-2010
(804) 225-3132

Washington State Arts Commission
9th and Columbia Building
Room 110, Mail Stop GH11
Olympia, WA 98504
(206) 753-3860

Western States Arts Foundation
236 Montezuma Street, Suite 200
Santa Fe, NM 87501
(505) 988-1166

Wisconsin Arts Board
131 West Wilson Street, Suite 301
Madison, WI 53703
(608) 266-0190

Wisconsin Dance Council
610 Langdon Street
722 Lowell Hall
Madison, WI 53703
(608) 263-8927

Wyoming Council on the Arts
2320 Capitol Avenue
Cheyenne, WY 82002
(307) 777-7742

Additional Sources of Information on Dance

Books on Ballet

Anderson, Jack. *Ballet and Modern Dance*. 2nd ed. Princeton, N.J.: Princeton Book Company, 1992.

————. *Choreography Observed*. Iowa City: University of Iowa Press, 1987.

Au, Susan. *Ballet and Modern Dance*. London: Thames and Hudson, 1988.

Ballanchine, George, and Francis Mason. *Ballanchine's Festival of Ballet: Scene-by-Scene Stories of 404 Classical and Contemporary Ballets*. London: W. H. Allen, 1984.

Clarke, Mary, and Clement Crisp. *Ballerina*. Princeton, N.J.: Princeton Book Company, 1987.

————. *Ballet: An illustrated History*. Rev. ed. London: H. Hamilton, 1992.

Dunning, Jennifer. *But First a School: The First Fifty Years of the School of American Ballet*. New York: Viking, 1985.

Garafola, Lynn. *Diaghilev's Ballets Russes*. Oxford, England: Oxford University Press, 1989.

Garcia-Marquez, Vicente. *The Ballets Russes*. New York: Knopf, 1990.

Guest, Ivor. *The Romantic Ballet in Paris*. 2nd rev. ed. London: Dance Books, 1980.

Kirstein, Lincoln. *Movement and Metaphor: Four Centuries of Ballet*. London: Pitman Publishing, 1971.

Koegler, Horst. *The Concise Oxford Dictionary of Ballet*. 2nd ed. Oxford, England: Oxford University Press, 1987.

Lieven, Peter. *The Birth of the Ballets Russes*. New York: Dover, 1973.

Searle, Humphrey. *Ballet Music*. New York: Dover, 1973.

Volkov, Solomon. *Balanchine's Tchaikovsky*. New York: Anchor, 1985.

Wiley, Roland John. *Tchaikovsky's Ballets*. Oxford, England: Oxford University Press, 1985.

Books on Choreography

Blom, Lynne Anne, and L. Tarin. Chaplin. *The Intimate Act of Choreography*. Pittsburgh: The University of Pittsburgh Press, 1982.

Humphrey, Doris. *The Art of Making Dances*. New York: Holt, Rinehart, and Winston, 1959.

Smith, Jacqueline M. *Dance Composition: A Practical Guide for Teachers*. Surrey, England: Lepus Books, 1976.

Thuesen, B. W. *The Choreographer*. Virginia: Tidewater Dance Guild, 1972.

Books of Dance Criticism and Theory

Cohen, Selma Jeanne. *Dance as a Theatre Art: Source Readings in Dance History from 1581 to the Present*. New York: Dodd Mead, 1974.

Copeland, Roger, and Marshall Cohen. *What Is Dance?: Readings in Theory and Criticism*. Oxford, England: Oxford University Press, 1983.

Croce, Arlene. *Afterimages*. New York: Knopf, 1977.

————. *Going to the Dance*. New York: Knopf, 1982.

Denby, Edwin. *Dance Writings*. New York: Knopf, 1986.

Greenfield, Louis, and William Ewing. *Breaking Bounds*. San Francisco: Chronicle Books, 1992.

Jowitt, Deborah. *The Dance in Mind: Profiles and Reviews 1976–83*. New York: Godine, 1985.

Kirstein, Lincoln. *Lincoln Kirstein: A First Bibliography*. Philadelphia: Eakins Press, 1978.

————. *By With To & From: A Lincoln Kirstein Reader*. New York: Farrar, Straus & Giroux, 1991.

Levinson, André. *André Levinson on Dance*. Shelburne, VT: University Press of New England, 1991.

Martin, John Joseph. *The Modern Dance*. Princeton, N.J.: Princeton Book Co., 1989.

Sorell, Walter. *Dance in its Time*. New York: Columbia University Press, 1986.

Terry, Walter. *I Was There: Selected Dance Reviews and Articles, 1936–1976*. New York: Audience Arts, 1978.

Books on Dance in General

Buckman, Peter. *Let's Dance: Social, Ballroom and Folk Dancing*. New York and London: Paddington Press, 1978.

Chujoy, Anatole, and P. W. Manchester. *The Dance Encyclopedia*. New York: Simon & Schuster, 1967.

de Mille, Agnes. *The Book of the Dance*. Phoenix: Golden Press, 1963.

————. *To a Young Dancer*. New York: Little, Brown, 1962.

Jonas, Gerald. *Dancing*. New York: Abrams, 1992.

Poor Dancers' Almanac. New ed. Durham: Duke University Press, 1993.

Raffle, W. G. *The Dictionary of the Dance*. New York: A. S. Barnes and Company, 1975.

Reynolds, Nancy, and Susan Reimer-Torn. *Dance Classics*. Chicago: A Cappella 1991.

Sorell, Walter. *The Dance Has Many Faces*. New York: Columbia University Press, 1966.

Thomas, Tony. *That's Dancing!* New York: Abrams, 1984.

Books on the History of Dance

Clarke, Mary, and Clement Crisp. *The History of Dance*. New York: Crown Publishers, 1980.

Emery, Lynne Fauley. *Black Dance from 1619 to Today*. 2nd rev. ed. Princeton, N.J.: Princeton Book Company, 1988.

Haskins, James. *Black Dance in America*. New York: Harper Collins, 1989.

Harper Collins, 1989.

La Meri. *Dance as an Art Form: Its History and Development*. New York: A. S. Barnes and Company, 1933.

Long, Richard A. *The Black Tradition in American Dance*. New York: Rizzoli International Publications, 1989.

Sachs, Curt. *World History of the Dance*. New York: W. W. Norton and Company, 1937.

Sorell, Walter. *The Dance Through the Ages*. New York: Grosset & Dunlap, 1987.

Books on Modern Dance

Anderson, Jack. *Ballet and Modern Dance*. Princeton, N.J.: Princeton Book Company, 1986.

Brown, Jean. *The Vision of Modern Dance*. Princeton, N.J.: Princeton Book Company, 1979.

Cohen, Selma Jeanne. *The Modern Dance*. Middletown, Conn.: Wesleyan University Press, 1966.

McDonagh, Don. *The Rise and Fall of Modern Dance*. Chicago: A Cappella Books, 1990.

Morgan, Barbara. *Martha Graham: Sixteen Dances in Photographs*. New York: Morgan & Morgan, 1941.

Stearns, Marshall and Jean. *Jazz Dance: The Story of American Vernacular Dance*. New York: Macmillan Company, 1971.

Books on People in Dance

Ashley, Merrill. *Dancing for Balanchine*. New York: Dutton, 1984.

Bentley, Toni. *Winter Season: A Dancer's Journal*. New York: Random House, 1982.

Blair, Frederika. *Isadora*. New York: Quill, 1986.

Bournonville, August. *My Theatre Life*. Trans. and annotated by Patricia N. McAndrew. Middletown, Conn.: Wesleyan University Press, 1979.

Buckle, Richard, ed. *Dancing for Diaghilev: the Memoirs of Lydia Sokolova*. San Francisco: Mercury House, 1989.

Buckle, Richard. *Diaghilev*. New York: Atheneum, 1979.

———. *Nijinsky*. London: Weidenfeld and Nicolson, 1971.

Cohen, Selma Jeanne. *Doris Humphrey: An Artist First*. Middletown, Conn.: Wesleyan University Press, 1972.

de Mille, Agnes. *Martha: The Life and Work of Martha Graham*. New York: Random House, 1991.

———. *Portrait Gallery*. New York: Houghton Mifflin, 1990.

Duncan, Irma. *Duncan Dancer: An Autobiography*. Middletown, Conn.: Wesleyan University Press, 1966.

Farrell, Suzanne. *Holding on to the Air*. New York: Summit Books, 1991.

Fokine, Michel. *Fokine: Memoirs of a Ballet Master*. Boston: Little, Brown, 1961.

Fonteyn, Margot. *Autobiography*. New York: Knopf, 1976.

Gherman, Beverly. *Agnes de Mille*. New York: Atheneum, 1990.

Gordon, Suzanne. *Off Balance*. New York: Pantheon, 1983.

Graham, Martha. *Blood Memory: An Autobiography*. New York: Doubleday, 1991.

Guest, Ivor. *Fanny Elssler*. London: Adam and Charles Black, 1970.

Hammond, Bryan, and Patrick O'Connor. *Josephine Baker*. Boston: Bulfinch Press, 1991.

Hirschhorn, Clive. *Gene Kelly, a Biography*. Rev. ed. New York: St. Martin's Press, 1984.

Karsavina, Tamara. *Theatre Street*. New York: Dutton, 1961.

Kendall, Elizabeth. *Where She Danced*. New York: Knopf, 1979.

Kirkland, Gelsey. *Dancing on My Grave*. New York: Doubleday, 1986.

Koner, Pauline. *Solitary Song*. Durham, N.C.: Duke University Press, 1989.

Kostelanetz, Richard, ed. *Merce Cunningham: Dancing in Time and Space*. Chicago: A Capella, 1993.

Magriel, Paul, ed. *Nijinsky, Pavlova, Duncan: Three Lives in Dance*. New York: Da Capo, 1976.

McDonagh, Don. *George Balanchine*. New York: Twayne, 1983.

Money, Keith. *Anna Pavlova: Her Life and Art*. New York: Knopf, 1980.

Mueller, John. *Astaire Dancing*. New York: Knopf, 1985.

Nijinska, Bronislava. *Early Memoirs*. Trans. and ed. by Irina Nijinska and Jean Rawlinson. New York: Holt, 1981.

Nijinsky, Romola, ed. *The Diary of Vaslav Nijinsky*. Berkeley, Calif.: University of California Press, 1936.

Nijinsky, Romola. *Nijinsky, and The Last Years of Nijinsky*. New York: Simon and Schuster, 1980.

Ostwald, Peter. *Nijinsky: A Leap into Madness*. New York: Lyle Stuart, 1990.

Percival, John. *Nureyev: Aspects of the Dancer*. New York: G. P. Putnam, 1975.

Perlmutter, Donna. *Shadowplay: Antony Tudor's Life in Dance*. New York: Viking, 1991.

Rose, Phyllis. *Jazz Cleopatra: Josephine Baker in Her Time*. New York: Doubleday, 1989.

Shelton, Suzanne. *Divine Dancer: A Biography of Ruth St. Denis*. New York: Doubleday, 1981.

Sherman, Jane. *Soaring*. Middletown, Conn.: Wesleyan University Press, 1976.

Siegel, Marcia. *Watching the Dance Go By*. Boston: Houghton Mifflin, 1977.

Sorell, Walter. *Looking Back in Wonder: Diary of a Dance Critic*. New York: Columbia University Press, 1986.

Taper, Bernard. *Balanchine*. New York: Collier, 1974.

Taylor, Paul. *Private Domain*. New York: Knopf, 1987.

Terry, Walter. *Ted Shawn, the Father of American Dance*. New York: Dial Press, 1976.

Tharp, Twyla. *Push Comes to Shove: An Autobiography*. New York: Bantam Books, 1992.

Vaughan, David. *Frederick Ashton and His Ballet*. New York: Knopf, 1977.

Libraries and Museums

African American Museum of Fine Arts
3025 Fir Street, Suite 27
San Diego, CA 92102
(619) 696-7799

Arts Resource Consortium Library
1285 Avenue of the Americas, 3rd floor
New York, NY 10019
(212) 245-4510

Artswire, c/o New York Foundation for the Arts
5 Beekman, #600
New York, NY 10038
(212) 233-3900

Asia Society
725 Park Avenue
New York, NY 10021
(212) 288-6400

Boston Conservatory of Music
Albert Alphin Music Library
8 The Fenway
Boston, MA 02215
(617) 536-6340

Boston Public Library
Boylston Street
Boston, MA 02116
(617) 536-5400

Chicago Public Library
Fine Arts Division—Art Section
78 East Washington Street
Chicago, IL 60602
(312) 269-2858

Cleveland Public Library
325 Superior Avenue N.E.
Cleveland, OH 44114
(216) 623-2800

Composers and Choreographers Theatre, Inc.
Master Tape Library
25 West 19th Street
New York, NY 10010
(212) 989-2230

Costume Collection
601 West 26th Street
New York, NY 10001
(212) 989-5855

Costume Institute of the Metropolitan Museum of Art
1000 Fifth Avenue and 82nd Street
New York, NY 10028
(212) 879-5500

Dance Films Association, Inc.
250 West 57th Street
New York, NY 10019
(212) 586-2142

Dansmuseet
Laboratoriegatan 10
115 27 Stockholm, Sweden
08-667-9512

Free Library of Philadelphia
Music Department
Logan Square
Philadelphia, PA 19103
(215) 686-5322

Getz, Leslie (Private Archive)
239 El Camino Real
Menlo Park, CA 94025
Open by appointment; phone n/a

Harvard University Theatre Collection
Wadsworth House
Cambridge, MA 02138
(617) 495-3650

Hoblitzelle Theatre Arts Library
University of Texas
Austin, TX 78712
(512) 471-3811

Japan Society, Inc.
333 East 47th Street
New York, NY 10017
(212) 832-1155

Library of Congress
Independence Avenue at First Street, S.E.
Washington, D.C. 20540
(202) 707-5000

Los Angeles Public Library
630 West 15 Street
Los Angeles, CA 90015
(213) 626-7461

Museo del Barrio, El
1230 Fifth Avenue
New York, NY 10029
(212) 831-7272

Museum of Contemporary Art
250 South Grand Avenue
Los Angeles, CA 90012
(213) 621-2766

Museum of the City of New York
5th Avenue and 103rd Street
New York, NY
(212) 534-1672

**New York Public Library for the
Performing Arts at Lincoln Center**
111 Amsterdam Avenue
New York, NY 10023
(212) 870-1657

**Peabody Institute of the Johns Hopkins
University**
Peabody Conservatory Library
21 East Mt. Vernon Place
Baltimore, MD 21202
(301) 837-0600

**San Francisco Performing Arts Library
and Museum**
399 Grove Street
San Francisco, CA 94110
(415) 255-4800

Smith College
Werner Josten Library for the
Performing Arts
Mendenhall Center
Northhampton, MA 01060
(413) 584-2700

**Smithsonian Institution, Performing Arts
Program**
Museum of American History, Room 310
Washington, D.C. 20560
(202) 357-4173

Sterling Memorial Library
Crawford Collection on the Modern
Drama
Yale University
New Haven, CT 06510
(203) 432-4771

**University of Cincinnati, College
Conservatory of Music**
Gomo Memorial Music Library
101 Emery Hall
Cincinnati, OH 45221
(513) 475-4471

University of North Carolina
Dance Collection, Walter Clinton
Jackson Library
Greensboro, NC 27412
(919) 379-5246

Wadsworth Atheneum
600 Main Street
Hartford, CT 06103
(203) 278-2670

Walker Art Center
Vineland Place
Minneapolis, MN 55403
(612) 375-7624

Schools and Studios

Below is a list of selected dance schools and studios. Almost every city has dance education opportunities for the interested student, and most major universities have dance departments. Check dance periodicals, local telephone directories and university catalogues for more information.

Alvin Ailey American Dance Center, The
211 West 61st Street
New York, NY 10023
(212) 767-0940

Balasaraswati School of Music and Dance
P.O. Box 227, Prince Street Station
New York, NY 10012
(212) 627-1076

Ballet Arts Minnesota
528 Hennepin Ave., #305
Minneapolis, MN 55403
(612) 340-1071

Ballet Hispanico of New York School of Dance
167 West 89th Street
New York, NY 10024
(212) 362-6710

Ballet West
50 West 200 South
Salt Lake City, UT 84101
(801) 524-8300

Benesh Institute of Choreology
12 Lisson Grove
London NW1 6TS, England
Phone n/a

Berkeley Ballet Theater
2640 College Avenue
Berkeley, CA 97404
(510) 843-4687

Boston Ballet School
19 Clarendon Street
Boston, MA 02116
(617) 695-6950

California Institute of the Arts
24700 McBean Pkwy.
Valencia, CA 91335
(805) 255-1050

Cecchetti Society, Inc., USA
818 Bell Air Dr.
Sacramento, CA 95822
(916) 422-2117

Centre de Danse International
Le Gallia
27 Boulevard Montfleury
06400 Cannes, France
93-99-04-04

Colorado Ballet School
1278 Lincoln
Denver, CO 80203
(303) 756-6899

Connecticut Nutmeg Ballet Company
21 Water Street
Torrington, CT 06790
(203) 482-4413

Dance—June Lewis and Company
48 West 21st Street, 7th floor
New York, NY 10010
(212) 741-3044

Dance Theatre of Harlem's Professional Training Program
466 West 152nd St.
New York, NY 10031
(212) 690-2800

David Howard Dance Center, The
211 West 61st Street
New York, NY 10023
(212) 757-9877

Erick Hawkins School of Dance
38 East 19th Street
New York, NY 10003
(212) 777-7355

Fort Worth School of Ballet
6841 B Green Oaks Rd.
Fort Worth, TX 76116
(817) 731-2779

Garden State Ballet School
6 South Street
Morristown, NJ 07960
(201) 623-1033

Gus Giordano Dance Studio
614 Davis Street
Evanston, IL 60201
(708) 866-9442

Harid Conservatory
2285 Potomac Rd.
Boca Raton, FL 33431
(407) 997-2677

Houston Ballet Academy
1921 West Bell
Houston, TX 77019
(713) 523-6300

Interlochen Arts Academy
P.O. Box 199
Interlochen, MI 49643
(616) 276-7472

Isadora Duncan Dance Foundation
141 West 26th Street, 3rd floor
New York, NY 10001
(212) 691-5040

Joel Hall Dance Studios
1225 W. School Street
Chicago, IL 60657
(312) 880-1002

Joffrey Ballet School (American Ballet Center)
434 Avenue of the Americas
New York, NY 10011
(212) 254-8520

Juilliard School, The
60 Lincoln Center Plaza
New York, NY 10023-6577
(212) 799-5000, ext. 255

Laban/Bartenieff Institute of Movement Studies
11 East 4th Street
New York, NY 10003
(212) 689-0740

Laban Centre for Movement and Dance
Laurie Grove, New Cross
London SE14 6NH, England
071-692-4070

Limón Institute
622 Broadway, 5th floor
New York, NY 10012
(212) 777-3353

London Contemporary Dance School
The Place, 17 Duke's Road
London WC1H 9AB, England
071-387-0152

Lou Conte Dance Studio
218 S. Wabash, 3rd floor
Chicago, IL 60604
(312) 461-0892

Martha Graham School of Contemporary Dance
316 East 63rd St.
New York, NY 10021
(212) 838-5886

Merce Cunningham Studio
55 Bethune Street
New York, NY 10014
(212) 691-9751

Meredith Baylis American Dance Institute
12745 Ventura Blvd.
Studio City, CA 91604
(818) 760-2167

Nancy Hauser Dance Co./School
1940 Hennepin Avenue
Minneapolis, MN 55403
(612) 871-9077

New Ballet School, The
890 Broadway, 8th floor
New York, NY 10003
(212) 777-7710

Nikolais and Louis Dance Lab
375 West Broadway, 5th floor
New York, NY 10012
(212) 226-7700

92nd Street Y—Dance Center
1395 Lexington Avenue
New York, NY 10128
(212) 415-5552

North Carolina School of the Arts
200 Waughtown Street
P.O. Box 12189
Winston-Salem, NC 27117-2189
(919) 770-3291

Pacific Northwest Ballet School
301 Mercer Street
Seattle, WA 98109
(206) 441-9411

Paris Opera School of Dance
8, rue Scribe
75009 Paris, France
40-17-33-33

Paul Taylor School
552 Broadway
New York, NY 10012
(212) 431-5562

Pennsylvania Ballet School
1101 South Broad Street
Philadelphia, PA 19147
(215) 551-7000

Pittsburgh Ballet Theatre School
2900 Liberty Avenue
Pittsburgh, PA 15201
(412) 281-6727

Royal Ballet School, The
155 Talgarth Road
London W14 9DE, England
071-748-5243

Royal Danish Ballet School
Royal Theatre
P.O. Box 2185
1017 Copenhagen K, Denmark
33-322020

Ruth Page Foundation School of Dance
1016 N. Dearborn Pkwy.
Chicago, IL 60610
(312) 337-6543

San Diego School of Ballet
5304 Metro St.
San Diego, CA 92110
(619) 294-7374

San Francisco Ballet School
455 Franklin Street.
San Francisco, CA 94102
(415) 861-5600

School of American Ballet
144 West 66th Street
New York, NY 10023
(212) 877-0600

School of Chicago Ballet
5650 S. Woodlawn Avenue
Chicago, IL 60637
(312) 667-5934

School of Cleveland Ballet
1375 Euclid Avenue, #110
Cleveland, OH 44115
(216) 621-3633

School of the Atlanta Ballet, The
P.O. Box 11549
Atlanta, GA 30355
(404) 874-8695

School of the Hartford Ballet
224 Farmington Ave.
Hartford, CT
(203) 525-9396

Trisha Brown Company School
225 Lafayette St., Suite 807
New York, NY 10012
(212) 334-9374

Tulsa School of Ballet
3315 East 33rd Street
Tulsa, OK 74135
(918) 742-5425

Universal Ballet Academy
4301 Harewood Road, N.E.
Washington, D.C. 20017
(202) 832-1087

Washington School of Ballet
3515 Wisconsin Ave., N.W.
Washington, D.C. 20016
(202) 362-1683

Woodpeckers Tap Dance Center
170 Mercer Street
New York, NY 10012
(212) 219-8284

Theaters and Concert Halls

Few theaters present dance exclusively, but almost every university auditorium and performing-arts center around the country features dance from time to time. Below is a list of venues that specialize in dance. Check local arts listings for dance performances in other settings.

Auditorium Theater, The
50 East Congress Parkway
Chicago, IL 60605
(312) 922-2110

City Center Theater
131 West 55th Street
New York, NY
(212) 581-7907

Civic Opera House, The
20 North Wacker Dr.
Chicago, IL 60606
(312) 346-0270

Cooper Square Theater
50 East 7th Street
New York, NY 10003
(212) 228-0811

Dance Center of Columbia College
4730 North Sheridan Road
Chicago, Illinois 60640
(312) 271-7804

Dance Place
3225 8th Street, N.E.
Washington, D.C. 20017
(202) 269-1600

Dance Theatre Workshop
219 West 19th Street
New York, NY 10011-4079
(212) 691-6500

Dance Umbrella Boston, Inc.
380 Green Street
Cambridge, MA 02139
(617) 492-7578

Dance Umbrella (U.K.)
c/o Riverside Studios
Crisp Road
London W6 9RL, England
81-741-4040

Danspace Project
St. Mark's Church-in-the-Bowery
131 East Tenth Street
New York, NY 10003
(212) 674-8112

Dixon Place
258 Bowery
New York, NY 10012
(212) 219-3088

Emanu-El Midtown YW-YMHA
344 East 14th Street
New York, NY 10003
(212) 674-7200

Evolving Arts Dancespace
622 Broadway
New York, NY 10012
(212) 777-8067

Gowanus Arts Exchange
295 Douglass Street
Brooklyn, NY 11217
(718) 596-5250

**John F. Kennedy Center for the
Performing Arts**
Washington, D.C. 20566
(202) 416-8800

Joyce Theater
175 Eighth Avenue
New York, NY 10011
(212) 691-9740

Kitchen, The
512 West 19th Street
New York, NY 10011
(212) 255-5793

Knitting Factory, The
47 East Houston Street
New York, NY 10012
(212) 219-3006

La Mama
74A East 4th Street
New York, NY 10001
(212) 254-6468

Metropolitan Opera House
70 Lincoln Center Plaza
New York, NY 10023
(212) 362-6000

Mulberry Street Theatre
179 Varick Street
New York, NY 10014
(212) 691-5788

National Performance Network
C/o Dance Theater Workshop
219 West 19th Street
New York, NY 10011-4079
(212) 645-6200

New York State Theater
Lincoln Center Plaza
New York, NY 10023
(212) 870-5570

Pace Downtown Theater
One Pace Plaza
New York, NY 10038
(212) 346-1398

Performance Space 122 (P.S. 122)
150 First Avenue
New York, NY 10009
(212) 477-5288

Symphony Space
2537 Broadway
New York, NY 10025
(212) 864-1414

Triplex Performing Arts Center
Borough of Manhattan Community
College
199 Chambers Street
New York, NY 10007
(212) 618-6642

Wexner Center for the Arts
North High Street at 15th Avenue
Columbus, OH 43210
(614) 292-5785

Organizations and Unions

American Dance Guild
33 West 21st Street
New York, NY 10010
(212) 627-3790

American Guild of Variety Artists
184 Fifth Avenue
New York, NY 10010
(212) 675-1003

Career Transition for Dancers
1727 Broadway, 2nd floor
New York, NY 10019
(212) 581-7043

Congress on Research in Dance
Department of Dance
State University of New York
Brockport, NY 14420-2939
(716) 395-2211

An organization of dance scholars and researchers with an interdisciplinary interest, CORD publishes a journal and holds annual conferences and occasional symposia.

Dance Critics Association
P.O. Box 1882, Old Chelsea Station
New York, NY 10011
Phone n/a

The DCA is an international association of dance critics whose activities include education, an annual conference, periodic symposia, and publication of a newsletter and other materials.

Dance Notation Bureau
31 West 21st Street, 3rd floor
New York, NY 10010
(212) 807-7899

Dance/USA
777 14th Street, N.W., #540
Washington, D.C. 20009
(202) 628-0144

Dancing in the Streets
131 Varick Street, Room 901
New York, NY 10013
(212) 989-6830

Harkness Center for Dance Injuries
301 East 17th Street
New York, NY 10003
(212) 598-6022/6146

Laban Institute of Movement Studies
31 West 27th Street, 4th floor
New York, NY 10001
(212) 689-0740

Metropolitan Dance Association
4201 16th Street, N.W.
Washington, D.C. 20011
(202) 829-3300

National Artists Equity Association
P.O. Box 28068, Central Station
Washington, D.C. 20038
(202) 628-9633

Society of Stage Directors and Choreographers
1501 Broadway, 31st floor
New York, NY 10036
(212) 391-1070

Space for Dance: Partners for Livable Places
Livability Clearing House
1429 21st Street, N.W.
Washington, D.C. 20036
(202) 887-5990

Volunteer Lawyers for the Arts/Lawyers Committee for the Arts
918 16th Street., N.W.
Washington, D.C. 20006
(202) 429-0229

Index

415